Replacement copy May 2016

The Cathedrals of England

SOUTHERN ENGLAND

BY NIKOLAUS PEVSNER AND PRISCILLA METCALF

WITH CONTRIBUTIONS BY VARIOUS HANDS

VIKING

VIKING

Penguin Books Ltd, Harmondsworth, Middlesex, England
Viking Penguin Inc., 40 West 23rd Street, New York, New York 10010, U.S.A.
Penguin Books Australia Ltd, Ringwood, Victoria, Australia
Penguin Books Canada Ltd, 2801 John Street, Markham, Ontario, Canada L3R 1B4
Penguin Books (N.Z.) Ltd, 182–190 Wairau Road, Auckland 10, New Zealand

First published 1985

Designed by Gerald Cinamon

Type set in 9/11 Aldus
by Rowland Phototypesetting Ltd, Bury St Edmunds, Suffolk, England
Printed in Great Britain by
Balding & Mansell Ltd, Wisbech, Cambs, England

Frontispiece: Exeter Cathedral

British Library Cataloguing in Publication Data

Pevsner, Nikolaus
   The cathedrals of England: Southern England
   I. Title   II. Metcalf, Priscilla
   726'.6'09422   NA5461

ISBN 0-670-80124-0

Library of Congress Catalog Card Number
   84-51886

Dedicated by the compiler
to
Nikolaus Pevsner
1902–83

LECTOR
SI MONUMENTUM REQUIRIS
CIRCUMSPICE

Newcastle-upon-Tyne

Carlisle

Durham

Middlesbrough

Ripon York

Lancaster

Bradford Leeds

Blackburn Wakefield

Salford Manchester

Liverpool Sheffield

Chester Lincoln

Southwell

Derby Nottingham

Shrewsbury Lichfield Leicester Norwich

Peterborough

Birmingham Coventry Ely

Worcester Northampton Bury St Edmunds

Hereford

Gloucester St Albans Chelmsford

Oxford Brentwood

Bristol London Rochester

Wells Guildford Canterbury

Salisbury Winchester

Chichester Arundel

Exeter Portsmouth

Truro Plymouth

0   50   100 miles

0   50   100   150 km

Contents

Foreword

'Pevsner's cathedral descriptions' are among the most brilliant parts of his *Buildings of England* series – not only the big set-pieces on Ely Octagon, the spatial experiments at Bristol and Wells, the Lincoln 'crazy vaults', but the whole sustained disciplined coverage of these for the most part marvellous buildings. Many people have wished that his descriptions could be brought together, revised where required by increase in knowledge since they were first published in that series between 1951 and 1974. When Sir Nikolaus asked me to do this, he thought the book should be more than a gathering of updated B of E texts: dealing as it does with only one building-type, it could be moulded a little by the compiler. Much is just as it was, but wherever seemed useful I have altered wording, rearranged paragraphs, woven in new matter and removed obsolete matter, inserted cross-references, improved sign-posting and placed buildings and furnishings more specifically in their settings, rewritten texts originally written before the series got into its stride (e.g. Exeter, Southwark Anglican), edited contributions from other scholars and offered a few small thoughts of my own: e.g. on Chichester crossing tower, Durham kitchen vault, the Ely Octagon restorations, Liverpool nave bridge, St Paul's dome, Worcester nave pavement, attitudes to monuments in Westminster Abbey, the Victorian naves at Bristol and Southwark, and, here and there, on historicism in the Middle Ages. (Sir Nikolaus's views on historicism or revivalism, as I have pointed out in the General Introduction, were far from monolithic.) In smaller matters, the Glossary looks askance at one or two accepted terms used in the text (spherical triangle, syncopated arcading). But it has all been to the one end of making this the architectural description of the species English Cathedral that Sir Nikolaus had in mind. It is a pleasure to present it in this new context and demonstrate again how there was always the appreciative eye and word for quality, how even amid the austerest prose such phrases as 'that irresistible *excelsior*' (as at Worcester) arose. Whether I have done too little or too much is for readers to judge: young ones may think the former, elders the latter. The revision of well-known texts, like the restoration of well-loved cathedrals, invites infinite fuss.

Part of the fascination of such buildings lies in the fact that each one is different. Yet they can be roughly grouped as follows (fuller definitions are given in the General Introduction): medieval cathedral churches, former abbey churches, and former collegiate churches; enlarged parish churches, medieval and later; the one C 17 cathedral church built as such; Victorian buildings of the revived Roman Catholic Church; and new buildings of the past hundred years. At present England has sixty-one cathedrals, nineteen Catholic and forty-two Anglican. (For the following cathedrals, see the B of E *London* volumes: Russian Orthodox, Paddington; Ukrainian-in-exile, Westminster; Greek Orthodox, Camberwell (by Oldrid Scott, Waterhouse and Belcher respectively). For Welsh, Scottish and Irish cathedrals, see the B of W, B of S, and B of I series.) To the sixty-one English cathedrals we add Westminster Abbey: in its special role as coronation church, sometime royal burial church, and independent 'Royal Peculiar', it has had much architectural, sculptural and decorative influence on some of the medieval cathedrals. We leave out Bath Abbey, which since the C 12 has been only nominally part of a bishop's title (see Wells), and also great churches like Beverley and Selby that are not seats of diocesan bishops: church-administrative history, not church-architectural history, dictates our subject. One might have made this book 'Pevsner's Great Churches' and omitted the so-called parish-church cathedrals, thus inviting problems of how many ruined abbey churches to include and evading the architectural problems of the working diocesan church. At first Sir Nikolaus himself wondered whether our inclusion of Westminster Abbey might be inconsistent, but subsequently he agreed with an early version of this foreword. One can but observe that a country tolerant of Royal Peculiars may not mind inconsistency too much. And the entirely consistent architectural historian may not exist. So we can display the virtuosity of his description of Westminster Abbey among its peers, making the number of our entries sixty-two. And a mixed lot they are.

As they would have made too huge a single volume, the book is in two volumes, divided geographically by an imaginary line from the mouth of the River Severn to the mouth of the River Blackwater – that is, keeping Oxford, St Albans and the small cathedrals of Essex south of it and the Three Choirs cathedrals of Gloucester, Hereford and Worcester and the cathedrals of East Anglia north of it. Each entry concentrates on the main vessel, with cloister, chapter house, library and closely attached buildings only. Details of precinct or close, and of detached deaneries and bishops' palaces, are omitted except in summaries of surroundings. Important as such related buildings often are – e.g. the Castle at Durham – their inclusion would have meant a less concentrated and unbearably bulky text. Like the rest of the cathedral town, these can be found in the relevant B of E volume. Gold and silver plate, with a very few exceptions, joins the list of mobile items excluded, though new treasuries for displaying diocesan plate are mentioned. With the exception of a few large tapestries, textiles are omitted (banners, frontals, vestments, kneelers). Also omitted are bells, books (and candles), but important chandeliers are in. Chests, tables and chairs are out save for a few very old and interesting ones.

Sir Nikolaus's prescription for the B of E volumes was this: after library research by an assistant for printed sources to fortify his own knowledgeable observation, he made his own notes on the spot and wrote his description at the end of the same day, later checking details against photographs or local knowledge. Sometimes he added brief contributions from other scholars' research, but without undertaking deeper research himself. The aim was to attend mostly to features one can see (e.g. referring only occasionally to timber roofs hidden by vaults), and on the whole to be selective – the most significant and justifiable departure from that rule here being David O'Connor's survey of all the York glass.

It should be added that the Leverhulme Trust funded initial research for a number of B of E volumes.

Authors of the original texts, where not Pevsner, are named at the head of the entry. As time and the county series went on, Sir Nikolaus called in younger scholars to take on part of the load, some of whom produced cathedral descriptions that now appear here. John Newman (Canterbury and Rochester), the late David Verey (Gloucester) and Alexandra Wedgwood (Birmingham St Chad's) have revised their own texts, with suggestions and additions from me. John Hutchinson, who had a hand in the original text on York Minster, revised it in accord with the latest restoration work there, and he also revised Ripon with some additions from me. I have revised the late Ian Nairn's texts on Chichester, Guildford and Arundel, with help from specialists. Anthony Quiney rewrote Truro, George McHardy rewrote Brentwood, and Philip M. Draper of Bristol contributed the new entry on Clifton, all with insertions by me. I have been able to use and slightly revise David Lloyd's entries on Portsmouth and Elizabeth Williamson's recent revisions of Durham, Southwell, Derby, Leicester and Nottingham, and am grateful to them. Bridget Cherry's advice and moral support from the Buildings of England office have been indispensable throughout. She and John Newman have both kindly read and commented on the General Introduction. Most of all I thank the copy editor Judith Wardman, the picture editor Susan Rose-Smith and especially Catriona Luckhurst for their help on this unusually complicated book.

Many scholars have helped. One most useful was George McHardy, who went round nineteen major cathedrals as well as many smaller ones for us, checking the old text 'on site' with a diligent eye. Michael Swanton sent much useful matter on Exeter, and I am grateful to Michael Laithwaite for checking monuments there. From historians of art and architecture we had Sir John Summerson's comments on St Paul's and the two Liverpool texts, John

Maddison's on Lichfield and Chester, Eric Fernie's on Norwich, and Peter Draper's on Lincoln; also from Thomas Cocke on C 17 and C 18 restorations, Jane Geddes on medieval ironwork, Michael Gillingham on organ cases, J. Mordaunt Crook on the Victorian decoration of St Paul's and the restoration of Salisbury chapter house, Julian Munby on Chichester and Oxford, Jeffrey West on Chichester, and on stained glass Martin Harrison and David O'Connor most liberally, on Catholic furnishings Roderick O'Donnell most lavishly, and miscellaneous observations on a number of cathedrals from Peter Howell, John Martin Robinson, Christopher Wilson, Andor Gomme and David Palliser. Members of the staff of the Victoria and Albert Museum patiently answered questions. This book is a splendid example of the scholarly community's willingness to help; for any mistakes in my use of it, of course, they are not to blame. Indeed the British Archaeological Association's recent conference publications on the English cathedrals (see Recent Literature) show a resurgence of the keenest interest in medieval art and architecture among young scholars since the C 19 – now with an added sense of the C 19.

We particularly thank the Deans of Chichester, Ely, St Paul's and Salisbury for answering questions; Monsignor Canon Bartlett for reading the text on Westminster Cathedral; and Dean Emeritus Holderness of Lichfield and Canon Lowther Clarke of Chichester for writing to us earlier with information. We are much indebted to reports on the furnishings of Chester and York published by the late Canon Addleshaw; and Canon Ingram Hill has been most helpful to me about Canterbury. Among cathedral archivists and librarians, L. S. Colchester at Wells has been wonderfully informative and helpful, and Mrs Audrey Erskine at Exeter most kindly went over my text, as did N. H. MacMichael our text on Westminster Abbey, where too the late librarian Howard Nixon so kindly answered questions.

Peter Burman, Secretary to the Cathedrals Advisory Commission for England, kindly informed the cathedral architects about this book. I am especially anxious to mention the cathedral architects or, as sometimes entitled, surveyors of the fabrics of these great and often awkward buildings, especially those who, when they heard of the book, immediately volunteered help and subsequently put up with many questions: Stephen Dykes Bower, a thesaurus of lore on many fabrics, particularly at Westminster Abbey, as well as Peter Foster, his successor there; Bernard Ashwell on Worcester and Gloucester; Alan Rome on Peterborough, Salisbury and others; John Phillips on Westminster Cathedral and Truro; and on Derby and Portsmouth Anthony New of Seely & Paget, who also shared much information he was about to publish in a cathedrals book of his own; also Mrs Corinne Bennett most minutely on Winchester; Ian Curry most fully on Durham restorations; and subsequently Peter Miller on Ely, Peter Gundry on Exeter, Charles Brown on Lichfield and Coventry, Ronald Sims on Chester, Southwark, Southwell and Newcastle, Keith Darby of Feilden & Mawson on Norwich – and from there particularly, for information sent over many years, Arthur B. Whittingham, the former cathedral architect, now its archaeological consultant. For the historian, a word with the learned architect to dean and chapter can be so rewarding; present restorations become more comprehensible the more one understands the nature of the site, the stone, the client, the craftsmen – and the restorations done before. Gerald Cobb's recent book on the 'forgotten centuries' since the Reformation shows, for one group of cathedrals, what a complex matter is that intermittently continuous performance, restoration.

Among the archaeologists, Warwick Rodwell has most generously summarized the excavations at Wells, so has Derek Phillips with John Hutchinson for York, and Tim Tatton-Brown has most fully answered many questions on Canterbury. For Winchester, although Martin Biddle unfortunately had no time to revise his own brief report of 1966 in B of E *Hampshire* for us, the Biddles' detailed reports will be found in the relevant periodicals and in their own final publication, and no doubt this will be the case with their excavation at St Albans. Cathedral archaeology really needs a book to itself, as well as continual progress reports, and we cannot do it full justice here. On the whole, let me say most emphatically, the willingness of so many people – historians, librarians, architects, archaeologists – to help us is a recognition of Sir Nikolaus's national influence in urging official help to the causes they are engaged in. Many have told me how much they owe to him.

It would have been tempting to add more items of literary interest, and a few could not be resisted, e.g. the epitaphs of Jane Austen at Winchester and Richard Jefferies at Salisbury. For an obscure reference naming the designer of Charlotte Yonge's memorial at Winchester we are indebted to the County Archivist Miss Margaret Cash and the Winchester Archivist Mr A. P. Whitaker. And, in time to correct old notions about Donne's monument in St Paul's, Professor Emeritus Kathleen Tillotson directed me to Dame Helen Gardner's conclusions on the matter. Architectural historians need friends in other disciplines; some of them are aware that they need us. Tempting too to extend our musical references, but organs or at any rate their cases are more our business than organists, save those known also as composers who received memorable memorials. One can never forget that the performance of cathedral music is one of the greatest arts of England.

Old hands among B of E readers will recall that the sequence of description is seldom that of the visitor starting at the west door. We begin more often though not invariably with the earliest surviving part of the building, often though not always the east end. Exteriors usually though not always precede interiors, and those are followed in varying sequence by cloisters etc. and furnishings; the place of the chapter house in the text sequence is especially variable. So the framework is flexible and sign-posted by headings, and individual lists of contents indicating chronology have been supplied for the more complex cathedrals. 'Furnishings' include fixtures and fittings, sometimes with monuments and/or stained glass separately. While the glass is treated as furnishing, window tracery is usually described as part of the architectural exterior. Architectural sculpture, including bosses and capitals *in situ*, is described with the architecture, but movable statues are with furnishings. It may be found that since we went to press even quite big fittings have mysteriously moved about in keeping with new liturgical ways. Visitors will understand that not every corner of a cathedral described here is always open to the public, though a quiet word to a verger may help. These are busy working buildings that must occasionally be closed to sightseers, in part and for short periods.

It is good to be allowed so many illustrations. A few have been chosen from antiquarian motives, to show features since altered or no longer in place, e.g. the screens at Hereford and Birmingham, and pre-war views of St Paul's. Some of our antiquarian views were engraved in the early c 19 for John Britton's *Cathedral Antiquities* volumes, with their pre-Victorian flavour. For medieval cathedral plans we have been able to use the fine set published in the *Builder* during 1891–3, from an unbound set in the library of the Society of Antiquaries. Both our Glossary and Recent Literature sections have short introductions added for the use of those seeking more help on terminology and bibliography than we have space for.

May I add appreciation for British Rail, by which comfortable day trips to all the English cathedrals are and always should be possible. The writing of the B of E series had to depend for county coverage on a motor car. For the more single-minded journeys in aid of this book, only trains would do. And for the modern pilgrim, an unpackaged tour on foot from the station to each great focal building should be a ritual part of the visit. In the larger cathedrals in the 1980s bookshops, plumbing, even sometimes feeding (in season) for visitors have arrived since I first went round in the 1950s. One has heard from Sir Nikolaus's old students about the rigorous all-day cathedral tours he led them on. With this book we can sample the splendid rigours of his descriptions, and compare one cathedral with another, at our own speed. For me it has been rather like restoring a cathedral.

Westminster, 1983   Priscilla Metcalf

General Introduction

The begetter of this book began his *Outline of European Architecture* in the 1940s, when so much European architecture was under stress, by discriminating: 'A bicycle shed is a building; Lincoln Cathedral is a piece of architecture.' A cathedral is more indeed than 'a building'. More too than a work of art, very much more than a museum of works of art. Churchmen quickly remind us of its purpose as centre of worship and generator of prayer for a widespread diocese. Such a fabric is more than a setting for ritual observance and religious experience, more than a seat of administration, more than a teaching place, more than a concert hall. Ministered to by centuries of clergy and craftsmen, the medieval fabrics are mosaics of communal memory, memorials to English men and women's own pasts. These fabrics can be dated, as if by tree-rings or geological strata, by their layers of architectural styles. Pioneering structurally they were, often it seems blindly bold, rearing high vaults on huge piers over shallow foundations before pumps able to remove deeper ground-water were invented. Crypts and undercrofts, we shall find, were only partly if at all underground. In the engineering sense, most cathedrals were more complex than most castles. We try to know what all the functions performed in cathedrals were, so that we may understand all that the masons and carpenters were up to. More bequests endowing altars and chantries meant more east-end expansion, more elaborate processions needed wider ambulatories, new shrines meant practical arrangements for channelling pilgrims in and out, the monks' choir must be separated from the laymen's nave, and there seem to have been at various periods special uses for galleries and porches and cloisters. A medieval cathedral can be seen as an arena for the continuous performance, centuries deep, of functions formed and re-formed for the glory of God and of the Church by human hopes and skills and energies, an arena cherished with stubborn devotion, however vandalized by time and wars and good intentions. Sometimes a shell, sometimes a dynamo, decaying and reviving, decaying and reviving, a cathedral is a record of human aspirations. Its layers of architecture are part of the record, supplementing the often fragmentary written record.

Just before the Reformation, England had – besides many great non-diocesan churches – seventeen cathedral churches. That is, it had two archbishops and fifteen bishops under Rome. Nine of the cathedrals had been run from the start by secular canons under statutes that went on after the Reformation – the so-called Old Foundations: Chichester, Exeter, Hereford, Lichfield, Lincoln, London St

Paul's, Salisbury, Wells, York. And there were eight monastic cathedrals, reconstituted at the Reformation with secular canons under new statutes – the New Foundations: Canterbury, Carlisle, Durham, Ely, Norwich, Rochester, Winchester, Worcester. (The fuller history of these dioceses' shifting seats and boundaries, of course, is not so tidy.)

To these cathedrals Henry VIII added six old abbey churches: Bristol, Chester, Gloucester, Oxford, Peterborough and, as cathedral of Middlesex, Westminster. Westminster's cathedral status proved to be temporary, so then there were twenty-two Anglican cathedrals. Much later, two more pre-Reformation monastic churches were made cathedrals, St Albans in 1877 and St Saviour's (former priory church of St Mary Overie) Southwark in 1905, both after post-Reformation use as parish churches. Three medieval collegiate churches (big parish churches served by colleges of canons and so having large eastern arms), Ripon, Manchester and Southwell, became cathedrals in 1836, 1847 and 1884 respectively. (Ripon in the c 7, like Coventry in the c 12, had been briefly the seat of a bishop.) Manchester, less cathedral-like than the other two, is sometimes listed with the Anglican 'parish-church cathedrals' – Birmingham, Blackburn, Bradford, Bury St Edmunds, Chelmsford, Coventry, Derby, Leicester, Newcastle, Portsmouth, Sheffield, Wakefield – large town churches consecrated as cathedrals between 1882 and 1927. Entirely new Anglican cathedral churches have been built during the past century at Truro, Liverpool and Guildford, and at Coventry to replace the bombed medieval church there. Which in all comes to forty-two Anglican cathedrals in England today, including the seats of the two archbishops at Canterbury and York. Our forty-third Anglican entry is Westminster Abbey, with its considerable influence on the architecture of some of the others and its peculiar status as, in a way, a national cathedral (see also the Foreword above, and p. 162).

Of Roman Catholic cathedrals today in England there are nineteen, with some changes since thirteen were authorized in 1850. Besides the two metropolitan cathedrals at Westminster and Liverpool, these are at Arundel, Birmingham, Brentwood, Bristol (Clifton), Lancaster, Leeds, London (Southwark), Middlesbrough, Newcastle, Northampton, Norwich, Nottingham, Plymouth, Portsmouth, Salford, Sheffield and Shrewsbury. A number of them were envisaged as, necessarily modest, cathedrals even before 1850, the initial architectural impetus coming from *Pugin*. Two of the architecturally most exciting departures of the past century in cathedral design have been the two metropolitan cathedrals. The irony will of course strike the thoughtful reader, that every medieval church was built under Rome. The post-Fire St Paul's in the City of London was the first Anglican cathedral built as such. All the present-day Catholic cathedrals are 'R.C. new series'.

To summarize the sixty-two structures in a different way, we now have twenty-six mainly medieval large complicated buildings, *Wren's* large c 17 building, two mainly c 18 buildings of parish-church size (Birmingham, Derby), ten parish-size mixtures of many periods c 12–20, fourteen equally modest buildings of the early c 19 to early c 20, and finally nine of more distinct cathedral character built during the past century that form a striking series, proceeding from extreme revived medievalism through degrees of dilution to extreme modernism: Arundel (R.C.), Norwich (R.C.), Truro (Angl.), Westminster (R.C.), Liverpool (Angl.), Guildford (Angl.), Coventry (Angl.), Liverpool (R.C.) and Clifton (R.C.). The long course of cathedral time in this country runs from 602, when St Augustine consecrated his cathedral at Canterbury, on to 1973, when Clifton Cathedral was consecrated at Bristol: almost fourteen centuries so far.

Before the Christian era, a number of present-day cathedral sites were under Roman occupation of one sort or another. Part of a Roman fortress has been found under the crossing at York. A well-shaft under Southwark (Angl.) Cathedral has yielded Roman sculpture, not necessarily *in situ*. At Chichester the mosaic floor of a Roman house can be seen below the south choir aisle. A Roman villa lies under Southwell. At Chester, Exeter, Gloucester, Lincoln and others, remains of the Roman town have been found round about. But pre-Christian religious use of these sites is harder to prove. Wren's workmen digging the foundations of St Paul's turned up evidence of pottery kilns and a cemetery, but no legendary temple to Diana. But Augustine in 602, according to Bede, was rehallowing a church built for Roman Christians, and recent excavation south of the crypt at Canterbury found remains of what may have been a pre-Christian Roman temple there. At St Albans there are strong traditions of a Roman Christian shrine to St Alban, England's first Christian martyr, on the site of his martyrdom in Verulamium's extramural cemetery on the hill – somewhere under the present cathedral. And a similar cemetery outside the town walls is thought to lie under Bristol Cathedral. Excavating under a working cathedral is obviously difficult, especially when money is needed to keep it standing. Only dire need for major work on the tower foundations at York presented that great opportunity.

So to the architecture and appurtenances of Christianity. First, SAXON remains. Little is left of the cathedrals' pre-Conquest predecessors. An evocative and very early survival is Wilfrid's crypt at Ripon of *c.* 670, a little earlier than his crypt at Hexham. Such a crypt with its narrow vaulted gangways reflected the Early Christian catacombs at Rome. From the other end of the pre-Conquest period, four centuries after Wilfrid, dark monastic passages survive at Westminster Abbey (south-east of the main cloisters, especially the east–west passage to the Little Cloister) that still give a sense of the very early Middle Ages. Of excavated remains requiring more trained imaginations to decipher, considerable traces of Saxon churches have recently been found near their successors at Winchester, Exeter and Wells (and may be present at e.g. Rochester and Worcester), with axial siting of separate churches as is known to have been the case at Canterbury. At Peterborough outlines of a Saxon church can be seen under the south transept, and at Southwell a possibly Saxon pavement is under the north transept. At St Albans in the Norman transept Saxon material was re-used (triforium colonnettes), as Roman bricks were re-used in the tower. Inevitably there survive from this period, followed by so much rebuilding, more mobile carvings than static buildings. Some remarkably sophisticated c 7 sculpture from Reculver in Kent is in the crypt at Canterbury. At Norwich the Bishop's Throne, three times moved about East Anglia, is now recognized as of the c 7. (The c 13 throne at Canterbury, perhaps also a fragmentary c 13 stone seat at Ely, must have been modelled on more ancient seats.) There is a late c 7 cross shaft and base at Ely. The so-called Hedda Stone at Peterborough, thought to be a shrine-cover, is of *c.* 800, and the battered font at Wells is now believed to be of similar date. A carved roundel of Christ at Gloucester of *c.* 950 is, like the Reculver carvings, of European importance. Durham has carvings of the early or mid-c 11, found under the chapter house. Bristol has a magnificent relief of *c.* 1050, a Harrowing of Hell scene, probably from a cemetery chapel on the abbey site. A lesser survival is a small relief of an angel at Manchester, thought to come from an earlier church on the site.

It is of psychological interest that, after the Norman Conquest, special reverence was shown for the remains of pre-Conquest saints upon their reburial in new Norman churches – as it were striking retrospective Anglo-Saxon attitudes out of anxiety to root the English Church in St Augustine's mission from Rome rather than in a transplant from Normandy. Examples of the translation of saints' bones to new shrines were at Ely (St Etheldreda) and Winchester (St Swithun), and of bishops at Wells (retrospective effigies *c.* 1200, now recumbent but possibly made to stand in the main reredos), at Hereford (the rigidly uniform ready-made series of posthumous effigies lining the early c 14 pilgrim route), at Ely (retrospective painted portraits, now vanished, on former screen-walls behind the choir stalls when at the crossing) and at Winchester (bone-chests on the presbytery screens). Such warmed-over memorials conferred credibility on their successors.

In the first thirty years after the NORMAN Conquest, i.e. before 1100, major building or rebuilding was energetically begun at (chronologically) Canterbury, Lincoln, Old Sarum (see under Salisbury), Rochester, St Albans, Winchester, York, Ely, Worcester, London St Paul's, Gloucester, Chichester, Chester, Durham and Norwich; and during the next half-century at Hereford, Southwell, Peterborough, Carlisle and Oxford. Today the most telling Norman remains are the gigantic choir and nave at Durham, the crypts of Worcester, Gloucester and Canterbury, the transepts of Winchester (north), Ely, St Albans, Hereford (south), Chester (north) and Peterborough, and the naves of Rochester, St Albans (north-east), Ely, Gloucester, Chichester, Southwell and Oxford, all with changes to windows which by enlarging the light-source altered the overall effect. Also there are the chapter-house entrance remains at Winchester and the lower walls of Worcester chapter house; the central towers of St Albans and Norwich (the latter with later spire), and the mighty side towers at Exeter (two) and Rochester (one). A type of 'westwork' consisting of a single narthex-tower flanked by west transepts, a Germanic formation, is represented in this country by Ely, and in a sense even earlier at Lincoln; Hereford had one until 1786. At Wells the initial layout of c. 1190 may at first have intended such a formation instead of the screen as built with the eventual pair of towers. The first of the Norman screen fronts with, originally, five stepped arched recesses, was that of Lincoln, later imitated at Bury St Edmunds Abbey; on the origins of the single recess at Tewkesbury, see Lincoln, and on the C13 development of three niches, see Peterborough. No Norman east end survived later rebuilding in any English cathedral. At Peterborough and Winchester the curve of the central apse can be detected, and the presumed plan of side apses is marked in the floor; see also the former Norman work marked on our plans of Ely, Lichfield, St Albans, and the excavations at York. At Canterbury, Norwich and Gloucester surviving north-east and south-east chapels (see also *Chapels* below) reflect the radiating-chapel type of east end, apparently first built in England at Battle Abbey. A feature of Norman monastic planning was the choir run through the crossing, as can still be seen at e.g. Gloucester, Winchester, Norwich and St Albans – as if chanting below and bellringing above ought to soar together up the central tower as up a chimney. Structural design was empirical: Winchester's new tower promptly fell in 1107; Durham's pioneering rib-vaults over the choir had to be rebuilt in the C13 (but the original aisle vaults remain); Worcester's early C12 chapter house had to be partly reshaped in the C14; flying buttresses had to be added to Southwark's C13 choir in the C14. Meanwhile, certain formations such as

the alternating octagonal and circular piers probably already present in the early Norman choir at Canterbury appeared at Peterborough (presbytery and transepts) and Oxford (nave), and then in the new choir (begun 1175) at Canterbury, from which their use spread to Lincoln and Southwark. In the half-century after 1150 tentative transitional work, between Romanesque and Gothic, was appearing at Bristol (chapter-house vestibule), in work of the 1170s at Ripon, and in west bays at Worcester after damage in 1175. But by 1200 great Gothic works were already in full swing at Canterbury, Wells and Lincoln.

Norman architectural carvings include, pre-eminently, the tympanum over the Prior's Door at Ely of c. 1135, and the C12 reliefs on Lincoln west front. As for more mobile work, furnishings (so aptly in French *les mobiliers*) in their several categories are summarized later in this introduction, but even a quick survey of Norman architecture should sample the flavour of such fittings as these: the pair of stone reliefs from a screen of c. 1125–30 at Chichester, both majestic and poignant; the grand black marble fonts of c. 1140–50 at Winchester and Lincoln; the marble effigies of C12 abbots and bishops at Peterborough, Salisbury and Exeter; and the turned-wood throne-like chair of c. 1200 at Hereford and the door-knocker or sanctuary ring at Durham – the former one of the most important pieces of medieval furniture in Britain, the latter one of the great examples of European metalwork. In a sense, Norman art in England culminated in the monumental stained-glass ancestor figures at Canterbury: although presiding over an early Gothic rebuilding, they are Romanesque in spirit – and, as Sir Nikolaus said of Durham, spirit is what counts.

The Gothic style arrived in England from France c. 1175 at Canterbury in the idiom of the C12 Île de France, while Cistercian Gothic arrived in the northern abbeys (see Ripon). From Canterbury it went to Wells mixed with West Country influences shared with, e.g., Worcester's west nave bays. At Wells this assimilated style is still visible in the transepts and nave, begun before 1200. Meanwhile Gothic also went from Canterbury to Lincoln, from c. 1190, in the hands of one superlative individual artist, in the east transepts and as continued from c. 1200 in St Hugh's Choir, though the strangely planned east end does not survive. Late in the C12 also came Portsmouth chancel, and the Chichester retrochoir was begun. So by 1200 England, long before Germany and Spain, had begun to make out of French Gothic its own native style.

The fully assimilated style called EARLY ENGLISH was in force by the first decade of the C13. Soon after 1200 Winchester retrochoir was begun, subsequently influencing Southwark retrochoir, begun after 1212, and the Salisbury east end, started in 1220. There began a series of rectangular east ends, opening out the darker Norman apsed formation, and some, as apparently at Winchester, intended to house saints' shrines. New work at Rochester was vaulted by 1214, at Worcester begun in 1224, at Southwell and Ely by 1234, and from 1242 Durham's great Chapel of the Nine Altars was added to the old east end like the crossing of a T, as was then being done at Fountains Abbey. Yet in 1220 a polygonal-apsed Lady Chapel was added to the Norman church at Westminster Abbey; this chapel (probably heightened) survived the ambitious re-building of the church from 1245 until finally it was replaced by the Henry VII Chapel in the C 16. The plan of that C 13 chapel may well have influenced Gloucester's C 13 Lady Chapel (rebuilt) and very likely the plan of Lichfield's Lady Chapel a century later. (Further on eastward ex-tension, and on the east end as feretory, see *Chapels* below.)

The purest Early English work is to be found at Salis-bury, with its entirely rectangular plan, its lancet windows, its cool dark accents of Purbeck marble, as already used at Canterbury and Lincoln. On the Englishness of such black or grey minor shafting – a draughtsman's linear emphasis little used in France – see Canterbury (William of Sens's choir), Lincoln (St Hugh's interior) and Salisbury (in-terior); and, for pre-Canterbury examples, Rochester chapter house. But Salisbury's east-transept formation – i.e. with a second set east of the main transept producing what might be called a cross-of-Lorraine plan – stemmed ultimately from the third church at Cluny. This plan, adding elbow-room and light at the high altar, first appeared in England in the Canterbury choir of *c.* 1100 and subsequently in Roger's choir of *c.* 1160 at York, but more emphatically in the Canterbury rebuilding begun in 1175 and then at Lincoln from 1192 (also in the 1190s intended at Hereford, only realized there *c.* 1300), and in the 1220s at Salisbury, Worcester and Rochester. These of the fifty years after 1175 all made full-height east crossings. (Side bays that look like east transepts on plan, but lower than the main vessel and not producing a proper crossing, occur later at Exeter and Wells, not really east transepts except on plan; quite the reverse was to happen at York in the 1390s with the heightening of a pair of aisle bays that project like east transepts in elevation but not on plan.)

A characteristic element of Early English work was the disciplined vitality of the so-called stiff-leaf decoration of capitals and mouldings that had developed out of Norman crocketed work, until more naturalistic foliage ornament began to replace it in the 1270s. Surviving stained glass most typically Early English, sub-fusc in tone and filling lancets free of tracery, is the grisaille glass at Salisbury and in the north transept at York; on reasons for introducing grisaille glass, i.e. more light at less expense and the possible influence from Cistercian monks' austere chur-ches, see the introduction to York glass. The glowing colour of the late C 12/early C 13 glass at Canterbury made a church darker, gloriously so. A stain that would produce bright yellow came into use, probably from the Arab world, only in the C 14.

Tracery had already appeared at the heads of openings, both of windows and of gallery arches, by the mid-C 13. At first it was of the transitional, pierced-solid kind called plate tracery. Early examples of that are in Winchester retro-choir, and there was blank plate tracery in the Great Hall at Winchester by 1236. Plate tracery appeared in the Salisbury transepts, on the chapter-house staircase at Wells and in the north transept gallery at York. But it was soon superseded by the lighter openwork of bar tracery introduced from France, first used at Reims *c.* 1210–20, and in England especially at Westminster Abbey. There, with the most whole-hearted use of French C 13 cathedral forms in England, rebuilding was begun in 1245, and the eastern arm, transepts and chapter house were complete by 1255. Its openwork tracery of foiled circles, also known as geometrical tracery, gave the name often used for that developed C 13 style called Geometrical in England. A few great circular windows had already been begun in this country: in the late C 12 east transepts at Canterbury, in the Lincoln transepts by 1220 (north, Dean's Eye; the flowing tracery of the Bishop's Eye on the south is early C 14); in the York south transept the rose of 1220–55; and the rose-windows in both Westminster transepts were originally part of the 1245–55 programme. In fact, as Sir Nikolaus pointed out, the original north rose at Westmin-ster (later much renewed) was apparently so close to the roses of the Paris transepts, begun only in 1258, that a common pattern, now missing, must be deduced. But unlike certain French cathedrals, no medieval English cathedral was given a west rose-window. Old St Paul's extension of 1256–80 had a great east rose, but how soon Durham's east-end (Nine Altars) rose existed, before *Wyatt*, is not clear. (The east round window at Oxford is of course C 19.)

As windows were enlarged and vaults heightened, more supports were needed: there are modest flying buttresses on the Trinity Chapel extension of *c.* 1180 at Canterbury, but the first spectacular tiers of them appeared at West-minster Abbey, supporting the tallest vessel in England (eastern arm; those of the nave of course date from its C 14–16 completion; prominent flying buttresses for the C 13 chapter house there were added in the C 14). Internal diagonal buttresses at Gloucester were inserted to reinforce the central tower. Meanwhile, as at St Paul's, when new east ends were built, they were given great east windows: under the rose at St Paul's were seven lights, the rose as it were forming their upper tracery (as e.g. in Notre Dame south transept). In the north of England came the eight-light window at Lincoln (Angel Choir), *c.* 1275, and at Ripon seven lights, *c.* 1290, and the great six-light north window of the late 1280s in Durham's Nine Altars Chapel, followed in the early c 14 by the nine-light east window at Carlisle. Exeter's great east window of the 1290s was partly rebuilt in 1389–90 with nine lights; its great west window of the 1340s (much renewed) has nine. Deftly handled development can be seen in Exeter's other window traceries from the 1290s on, in the same vein as court work in London (below).

By the mid-c 13 the rib-vault type initiated c. 1100 at Durham had received a new member, the tierceron rib, one pair to each half-bay in Lincoln nave, presumably soon after 1233, and in Ely presbytery between 1234 and 1252, in both places allied with a transverse ridge rib taken only partway across. The next step, at Westminster c. 1253 in the first nave bays past the crossing (i.e. part of the original building programme to buttress the central tower), took the ridge rib all the way across, as was done thereafter in the rest of that nave. Further playing with the tierceron idea ensued at Exeter late in the c 13, first in the Lady Chapel with two pairs of tierceron ribs to each half-bay, and then three pairs each in the presbytery and so right through the cathedral, producing a forest of branches with the vaulting-shafts that supported all these new ribs. An apotheosis of tiercerons formed part of the timber lantern of the Octagon at Ely. The next and smaller element was the lierne rib, from which networks of ribs could be built up (see further below).

At west ends the c 13 continued the English fashion for screen fronts. The Norman stepped niches of Lincoln and Bury St Edmunds Abbey became three huge equal niches at Peterborough, while at Wells and Salisbury ranks of sculpture provided showcases of biblical figures (see *Architectural sculpture* below). Inside, some of the best c 13 sculpture in England remains *in situ* in the Westminster south transept, censing angels in spandrels below the rose-window; and in the Angel Choir at Lincoln, angels in spandrels again; winged creatures suiting such triangular fields just as flying victories had fitted those of Roman triumphal arches. Late in the century came the superb foliage carvings in Southwell chapter house, and some lovely, similar, but simpler foliage in the Lincoln cloisters. Fine c 13 sculpture no longer in place includes the figure now in Winchester retrochoir, without attributes but thought to represent the Church or the Synagogue; the damaged Christ in Majesty re-used in Worcester refectory; and the seated Christ now at Swynnerton but probably made for Lichfield's west gable. c 13 decorative painting miraculously survives on the nave ceiling at Peterborough. c 13 architectural painting is best represented by the series of Crucifixion scenes on the northeast nave piers at St Albans, also by various elongated figures at Westminster, e.g. in the south transept. c 13 panel painting of high quality is represented by retable

panels of European importance now in the ambulatory at Westminster.

Sir Nikolaus's readers know that he constantly spoke from a European point of view that embraced England. 'The architecture of England between 1250 and 1350 was, although the English do not know it, the most forward, the most important, and the most inspired in Europe', he said in his *Outline*; since he first wrote that, they have learnt to know it. The century 1250–1350 produced, first, the growing assurance of c 13 English work we have just seen, followed by a new handling of architectural space, at Bristol and Wells and Ely, which Sir Nikolaus especially enjoyed describing and was the first to celebrate for English readers as it deserved, and, third, the work at London and Gloucester that announced a vigorously native English style that was to persist to the end of the Middle Ages. That is, the period 1250–1350 contained these major developments: the matured stage of Early English style sometimes called Geometrical, the excitement of the Decorated style, and the first stage of the Perpendicular.

The so-called DECORATED style was more than a matter of decoration. The introduction to B of E *North Somerset and Bristol* (1958) put it thus: 'Architecture is the art of shaping space for utilitarian as well as emotional purposes. No style has ever existed in architecture that was not primarily concerned with space. And in space also 1300 was the moment of a great change in England, a change of international importance. c 13 space had possessed the same clarity as c 13 decoration. Now space began to flow, unexpected interpenetrations were sought, and thus effects obtained which must have been as disquieting to some and as thrilling to others as were the spatial innovations of c 20 architecture when first they were seen.' In fact, 'designers turned away from . . . harmoniousness and regularity in pursuit of a new ideal of complexity, intricacy, perhaps even perversity. It was an attitude familiar to those who have experienced the revulsion from Impressionism to Post-Impressionism, an attitude comparable also to that of the Mannerists about 1520 towards the High Renaissance. No more calm perfection; let us have imperfection provided it is not calm.' Goodbye Salisbury, welcome Bristol and Wells. Immediately after 1300, the new east ends of Wells and Bristol were 'leading for England and for Europe . . . the composition of Lady Chapel and retrochoir at Wells and of chancel, chancel aisles, and Lady Chapel at Bristol and also the sensational strainer arches at Wells, all this is conceived in terms of open spaces merging with each other and of surprising and not easily understood vistas, diagonally through space. The arrangement of the piers in the Wells retrochoir seems at first as arbitrary as the arrangement of the bridges and transverse little vaults of the chancel aisles at Bristol. The very fact that both Wells and Bristol here worked in terms of the "hall", the room with nave and aisles of equal height [as had indeed been done in Winchester and Salisbury retrochoirs in a simpler way], is telling enough. For this became the *leitmotif* of the most creative Late Gothic style on the Continent, the German *Sondergotik*. English *Sondergotik*, already with all the characteristics of an anti-classic style, is 150 years older.' The next tremendous step, in the 1320s, was the making of diagonal vistas with the Octagon at Ely.

Already in the 1290s the vocabulary of the just-emerging Decorated style had been enriched by the new pageantry and power of the court of Edward I, and from *c.* 1290 there was a recognizable court style, notably in the series of Eleanor Crosses set up along the route of his queen's funeral journey from Lincolnshire to London, and also in certain tombs. The wide-arch-flanked-by-narrow-arches of the Crouchback tomb at Westminster († 1296) and the tomb at Ely of Bishop William of Louth (latinized as Luda; † 1299) soon appeared at Bristol (Berkeley Chapel entrance, Lady Chapel reredos). A little flying-ribs motif that appeared first, so far as we now know, at Lincoln (Easter Sepulchre, pulpitum passage vault), on a slightly larger scale at Bristol and then in Southwell pulpitum may reflect some vanished spirited work on one of the Eleanor Crosses, of which only three now remain. Some fifty years after the flying ribs at Lincoln and Bristol, the motif appeared at Prague Cathedral (sacristy and porch): proof of the impact of English design abroad in the c 14. The immensely popular motif of the ogee arch, composed of two S-curves meeting at an acute angle, first appeared in the decoration of the Eleanor Crosses and on Crouchback's tomb, and then gradually, sinuously spread about the country, to the Norwich cloisters, to the window tracery of Wells chapter house, to the Exeter throne canopy, and traceries and canopies all over England. For canopies, ogee arches developed three-dimensionally to become 'nodding ogees'. The most inventive handling of the ogee now surviving is that burst of elegant playful fantasy, the sedilia canopy at Exeter of *c.* 1320. We can only guess what was lost of such work in England to the vandals of the 1540s and 1640s, and indeed later times. A small element already mentioned is the lierne or short linking rib (first used in St Stephen's Lower Chapel, Westminster Palace). With it net-like vaults could be built up that were medieval equivalents of small domes: Wells Lady Chapel has a most fascinating example, the range of its ambiguities suggesting comparison to the earlier Southwell chapter-house vault and even to the later Durham monks' kitchen vault. These were only a few of the elements exploited by the Decorated style's space-handlers. The most glorious enclosure and exposure of space in the early c 14 was of course the pyrotechnical Ely Octagon, perhaps the most marvellous example of co-operation between mason and carpenter of the entire Middle Ages.

The royal palace at Westminster contained seeds of both Dec and Perp. St Stephen's Lower Chapel and part of the shell of the Upper Chapel were built 1292–7; the Upper Chapel was completed in 1320–6 and 1331–48, served as the House of Commons from 1547, and was burnt in 1834. St Stephen's Chapel and the chapter house and cloisters added in 1332 to the old St Paul's Cathedral, burnt in 1666, are the most important offstage characters in the story of English Gothic. If it were not for Hollar's c 17 engravings of St Paul's before the Great Fire, and for drawings made by various early c 19 artists of the ruins of the Houses of Parliament immediately after the fire of 1834, London's rightful place in the history of the PERPENDICULAR style would not be known. The Lower Chapel of St Stephen's with its lierne vaults still exists. But the vanished Upper Chapel with its descending mullions (vertical mouldings taken down the wall below an opening) was the key monument. How much did that continue the style of York nave, begun in 1291? The interior of York nave, reflecting the style the French call Rayonnant, used descending mullions to unify clerestory with triforium (as had been done at St-Denis and Clermont-Ferrand), and in that insistence upon verticals York nave must be called proto-Perp. In the chapter house and cloisters of St Paul's as recorded by Hollar, mullions were carried down over the wall-face and the window tracery was rectilinear: inevitable human response in the 1330s to bursts of curvaceous fancy in the 1320s. The West Country was the next receptacle of these new ideas after London, not only in the great east window of Wells presbytery, glazed before 1339, with its 'verticals standing hard on arches or pushing up against arches' (B of E *North Somerset*), but more especially in the south transept at Gloucester, begun in 1331, with its four-centred arches, its panelling and, in its great south window, mullions running straight up to the arch.

The subsequent encasing of the Norman eastern arm at Gloucester was intended to honour the burial there of Edward II. Much of the grandest cathedral work in the Perp style encased or rebuilt Norman work. The uncompromising verticality of the one reinforced that of the other. The eastern arms at Gloucester (1337–67) and Norwich (1362–9, 1472–99) and the naves of Winchester (*c.* 1345–66, *c.* 1394–1404) and Norwich (1464–72) all show their Norman bones through the new framework. At Canterbury demolition of Lanfranc's nave left the old pier and wall foundations, so the c 11 plan still dictated the c 14/15 plan, though not of course the tremendous elevation reared upon it.

The completion or rebuilding of great naves raises the matter of HISTORICISM, or revivalism, in the Middle Ages, i.e. the question of style-consistency in big complex buildings not finished all at one go but carried on or reconstructed by later generations. First, as to the matter of the long sides of an internal space such as a nave: to make the north side of Chester nave of *c.* 1490 match (but for a few details) the south side begun *c.* 1360 can be called 'self-conscious conservatism . . . typically English' (B of E *Cheshire*), and to leave the north side of St Albans nave in its Norman state opposite the early C 14 south side (omitting for the moment the matter of the C 13 west bays) can mean 'conflict' and 'no peace for the eye' (B of E *Hertfordshire*). But consider: (1) the St Albans south arcade fell down and had to be replaced, and rebuilding *à la normande* in the C 14 was very much less likely than Chester's rebuilding *à la* 1360 in 1490; and (2) the alternative, a C 14 rebuilding of the Norman north piers *à la* C 14, would have meant the loss of their precious paintings and of a unique sense of the original building embedded there: that consideration should mitigate our sense of 'conflict' between the opposing elevations as they stand. In long buildings such as these, the style of spaces added east or west is a different matter, whether we call it historicism or conservatism, affection for the past, or 'keeping in keeping', or tact. For a new age to continue the same style farther east or west in such buildings, the case may be that of *Ramsey's* regard in Lichfield presbytery for the parts east and west of it so that he unified the whole building (a point which our new text stresses more than B of E *Staffordshire*). Deliberate continuity of design at York from the nave rebuilding, begun 1291, to the rebuilding of the eastern arm, begun 1361, is called unusual for the Middle Ages (B of E *Yorkshire: York and the East Riding*), though of course style-consistency westwards was a feature of Westminster Abbey because of the ceremonial and iconographical character peculiar to that church. The whole matter of expecting the styles of successive stages of a complex building to evolve in an organic way, of being surprised if consistency with earlier stages was preferred to development, reflects the outlook of architectural historians trained to believe in Progress as a biological growth – the organic view of history. In the end, rising above this, Pevsner concludes that the homogeneity of Westminster Abbey is admirable.

The issue of historicism diverted us from the progress of the Perp style. One Perp invention was the FAN-VAULT, first developed on a minor scale in the West Country in the 1350s, at Hereford (chapter house, ruined) and at Gloucester (east cloister walk). Both can be attributed to one man (called *Thomas of Cambridge*, after a hamlet near Gloucester), though exact dates and sequence are unclear. The single 360° cone formerly in Hereford chapter house seems clearly derived from the cluster of ribs in Wells chapter house of half a century before. The Gloucester half-cones were, perhaps, immediately adapted from the Hereford cone. Yet the series of rib-clusters vaulting Exeter Cathedral from end to end could have suggested Gloucester's half-cones first – and this man *Thomas*, known to have

worked at both Hereford and Gloucester, is thought to have been familiar with Exeter as well. It was only in the middle of the next century that the fan-vault developed on a larger scale, as at Sherborne Abbey and, in eastern England, in Canterbury Lady Chapel, completed after 1468. (Construction of the little fan-vaulted Stanbury Chapel at Hereford of *c.* 1480 was, incidentally, overseen by a brother of Archbishop Morton of Canterbury.) At King's College Chapel, Cambridge, preparations for fan-vaulting, only carried out in 1512–15, were in hand by the 1480s. At the end of the C 15 (between 1496 and 1508) the fan-vaulted retrochoir or New Building went up at Peterborough. By then many fan-vaults had been made in England. A final metamorphosis came in the Henry VII Chapel at Westminster during 1503–9, though only after intermediate experiments had taken place at Oxford, at the Divinity School by 1483 and in the present cathedral by 1503, and on a lesser scale at Winchester in the south-east (Langton) chapel between 1493 and 1500; and mildly reflected in Prince Arthur's Chantry at Worcester from 1504.

Next TOWERS, the first visible feature of an English medieval great church, some spired and some not. A crossing tower usually reflects an initially Norman plan; surviving Norman towers are at Norwich and St Albans. The earliest surviving spire is Oxford's of the C 13 (Rochester's being of 1904). The tallest spire in England now is Salisbury's at 404 ft (begun 1334), outdone for two centuries by that of Old St Paul's at 489 ft (1315) until it was hit by lightning in 1561. Of other ambitious early C 14 spires, the one on Lincoln's central tower was blown down in 1548; the west towers there were spired from the C 15 until 1807. Lichfield's three towers were spired in the 1320s and, though the central tower fell in the Civil War and there has been much rebuilding since, three spires still stand, the only triple set until *Pearson* emulated Lincoln's medieval skyline at Truro. In the C 15 the present spire at Norwich was built to replace one hit by lightning in 1463. Chichester's C 15 spire collapsed in 1861 and was rebuilt. The spire, the most poignantly symbolic part of a cathedral, is also its most vulnerable member. Of unspired towers, the tallest was Canterbury's Bell Harry (1490s) at 250 ft until *Sir Giles Scott's* tower at Liverpool reached 330 ft. One of the mightiest is at Durham, rebuilt in the C 15; the C 12–13 west towers there once had C 14 spires. Three noble central towers are those at Hereford (early C 14), Wells (1315–22 and 1440) and, perhaps the noblest, Worcester (1357–74); and one of the most elegant is at Gloucester (*c.* 1450) with its open coronet. Ely's great C 14 timber lantern is unique anywhere; the C 15 stone lantern or crown at Newcastle (Angl.) is one of a series with Continental connections. York's great keep-like central tower and beautiful west towers were finished in the 1470s.

Among the parish churches made cathedrals in the past century are three dramatically tall early c 15 spires, the one surviving beside the new Coventry Cathedral and those on Wakefield and Sheffield cathedrals. Spires were to be revived in the c 19 by the Catholic architects *Pugin* and *Hansom* (see below).

An important auxiliary to great churches is the CHAPTER HOUSE, often, though not always, east of the east cloister walk, and in England often, though not always, of centralized polygonal form. The Continent had centralized churches, baptisteries, treasuries, but not, for some reason, centralized chapter houses. One of the oldest English examples is the very early c 12 chapter house at Worcester, originally circular, with central pier and ten vaulting-compartments; it became structurally necessary to make it ten-sided in the c 14. (Hereford's former c 14 chapter house was ten-sided, and one wonders what shape its c 12 predecessor had.) Lincoln's chapter house, begun c. 1220, is ten-sided; the one built soon after at Beverley was eight-sided, now gone. Lichfield's elongated octagon, which dates from c. 1240, is said to have been so designed for its larger chapter when allied with Coventry. The first with the structural assurance to fill each side almost entirely with window was at Westminster (octagonal), laid out by 1249 and in use by 1257; the big flying buttresses had to be added in the c 14. The octagon at Wells was laid out by c. 1250, when the undercroft was built (main chapter room completed c. 1306). Salisbury's (octagonal) was being built from c. 1279. All these had the central pier. Then, before c. 1290, two octagonal chapter houses were contrived without central piers: York's with its timber ceiling and Southwell's stone-vaulted on a smaller scale; and subsequently, in the early c 14, at London St Paul's. There were also rectangular chapter houses (some with apsed east wall) at Bristol, Canterbury, Chester, Durham, Gloucester and Oxford. One would like to know more about the acoustics of these talking-houses, especially at Westminster, where the first House of Commons sat for a while. Those with the more considerable vestibules (e.g. York, Lichfield, Chester, Salisbury, Westminster) will have had more privacy for their discussions than those opening directly off the cloisters (Oxford, Worcester). A room with related functions but separate from the chapter house, at least in the later Middle Ages, was the CONSISTORY COURT. At Lincoln this was held in the south-west nave chapel, at Wells in a chapel off the east cloister. At Norwich the originally Norman Bauchun Chapel was refitted for the purpose c. 1500 with vault-bosses illustrating Chaucer's *Man of Law's Tale*. (Chester retains in its south-west nave chapel a unique early c 17 set of consistory-court furniture: one wonders what the medieval precedents were.)

It was by no means only the great monastic churches that had the quadrangle of covered passages called CLOIS-TERS. These were generally though not always fitted into the angle between nave and transept, more often on the south, sometimes on the north. Sometimes there was no fourth walk next to the nave (but at Wells it is now known that one was originally intended, with open space between it and the nave wall, as imitated at Salisbury). Chichester's irregular layout embracing the transept was unique. In general, the east walk, as most essential for circulation, was built first (e.g. at Westminster and Norwich). At the monastic churches, the monks were usually housed and fed in ranges alongside and over the cloister walks (but see Worcester). When fully glazed the walks themselves may have served for studying and teaching (e.g. carrels at Gloucester and Worcester); now when we see the walks without their glass we think of them as out-of-doors. The main surviving medieval cloisters (many replacing Norman ones) are, with later interferences and additions, at: Lincoln, c 13 (and c 17); Westminster, c 13–14; Salisbury, c 13; Norwich, c 13–15; Gloucester, c 14; Canterbury, c 14–15; Worcester, c 14–15; Chichester, c. 1400; Hereford, early c 15; Wells, c 15–16; Durham, c 15; Chester, early c 16; and there are more partial remains at Bristol, Ely and Oxford. The prior's, abbot's or bishop's doorway from the cloister to the nave aisle, often but not invariably from the east walk, was given architectural and sculptural importance.

Upstairs the east cloister range of a monastic cathedral generally contained the monks' dormitory, but from the c 15 at Wells (full length of the range) and Salisbury (half the length) that space contained the cathedral LIBRARY; only after the Reformation did the corresponding space at Westminster become the library (when Camden was librarian and writing his *Britannia* there). At Gloucester (north side) and at Winchester (south side) the library is over the slype or east–west passage against the transept. At Hereford the famous chained library is now in a former sacristy over the north transept east aisle, and at Lichfield it is over the chapter house (but the library over the chapter house at Ripon was originally the Lady Chapel). Cathedral and abbey libraries were centres of medieval learning, as well as repositories of archives that help us to read medieval architecture.

Surviving monastic quarters, e.g. dormitories and refectories, are only briefly summarized in the text, e.g. for Canterbury, Durham, Gloucester, Chester, Westminster and Worcester. But we must single out one fascinating structure, another centralized space, at Durham: the octagonal c 14 KITCHEN with its possibly Islamic-influenced stone vault, also possibly influenced by the circle-enclosing ribs of the c 13 Nine Altars vault nearby. (The probably c 14 stone kitchen at Glastonbury, with its truncated-pyramid roof, is described in B of E *South and West Somerset*.) On the other hand, the timber roof of the late c 13 bishop's kitchen at Chichester (its central lantern-opening now closed) rests on the earliest known hammer-beams. So, by c. 1290, cathedral builders' techniques were such that comparatively small octagonal spaces could be roofed without a central pier, as proved in York and Southwell chapter houses, and an open central lantern could rest upon either stone vaults or wooden hammer-beams: the way towards conception of the Ely Octagon in the 1320s was ready.

To return to the main vessel of a cathedral, it has many CHAPELS. As we have seen, these could be not only little auxiliary spaces but extensions of the main vessel. Those extending the basic plan eastwards include the Trinity Chapel at Canterbury and the very different Nine Altars Chapel at Durham, as well as numerous mostly square-ended Lady Chapels, as at Bristol, Chester, Chichester, Exeter, Gloucester, Hereford, Salisbury, Wells and Winchester, and the polygonal-apsed chapel at Lichfield; and east of the northern arm at Bristol (Elder Lady Chapel), Canterbury, Ely and Peterborough (now gone) – the last two probably influenced in that position by a former north-east chapel at Lincoln. North-east and south-east apsidal chapels of oddly imperfect orientation (ENE and ESE respectively) had been part of the early Norman work at Canterbury and Norwich (also at Gloucester, but NE and SE respectively there); a pair of slightly later counterparts in that regard are at Sens. Indeed, Westminster Abbey's four mid c 13 apsidal chapels also have no unambiguously eastern walls for altars. Between those two pairs at Westminster, and pre-dating them, was the early c 13 polygonally apsed Lady Chapel replaced in the early c 16 by Henry VII's bigger chapel intended as both Lady Chapel and burial chapel for himself. In that dual role, on the brink of the Reformation, it was the culmination of English cathedral chapels. The chapel as saint's-shrine-container had been elaborated long before, primarily at Canterbury for Becket's shrine and at Westminster for St Edward the Confessor's shrine, the latter both saintly and royal (see Shrines below). Henry VII intended his own burial chapel to have similar importance, but it was a more secular sort of importance (as emphasized by the mercantile air of the figures carved upon the walls). Although initially he had intended it to be a burial chapel for the saintly Henry VI, the age of pilgrimage to shrines was over.

Side chapels visible as such externally include the Berkeley Chapel at Bristol, part of the late c 13/early c 14 reconstruction of the east end, and interesting for its vestibule vault (see flying ribs, above) and for the first of those, apparently Islamic-influenced, concave-framed niche openings. The Zouche Chapel at York was probably part of the c 14–15 rebuilding of the eastern arm and contains rare contemporary cupboards. Rectangular spaces at the east end of the aisles were often annexed by bishops

for their own burial chapels, as at Ely at the end of the c 15. Winchester has the outstanding series of bishops' chantries (i.e. enclosures within larger open spaces for the chanting of memorial masses): six from 1366 to 1555, from nearly the beginning to beyond the end of the Perp style. Prince Arthur's Chantry at Worcester, begun shortly after Henry VII's Chapel at Westminster, was in a sense a try-out for the latter's sculptural decoration. Indeed, Henry VII meant his own tomb-enclosure to stand like a chantry in the centre of his chapel at Westminster, not at its east end as decided by his successor. St Anselm's Chapel at Chester is an interesting example of a Norman abbot's chapel altered in the early c 17. And finally, two-storey chapels at Westminster are those of Henry V and Abbot Islip, with the tomb downstairs and a chantry chapel for celebration of masses upstairs. The most ancient two-storey chapel in England was the bishop's chapel at Hereford, begun 1095, but little of it is left. (Bishops' chapels, e.g. at Ely, Wells and Durham, are only summarily mentioned in our text, as parts of their palaces, for which see the relevant B of E volume.) The most important English two-storey chapel no longer exists as such, St Stephen's in the Palace of Westminster, already described, influenced in this respect by the Sainte Chapelle in Paris.

Here we should mention the accompanying parish church that often stood near, attached to or even separately inside a great monastic church – to keep the neighbours out of the monks' way. Of those alongside, St Margaret's Westminster and St Nicholas Rochester still stand. St Augustine the Less at Bristol and St Michael at Worcester are gone, as is St Mary Major at Exeter, where an early predecessor may have been the original Saxon cathedral. The present cathedral at Bury St Edmunds was once the parish church nearest the great abbey. Until the early c 19 at Southwark a c 14–15 church of St Mary Magdalene stood attached to the south-east choir transept angle, demolished but recorded by Gwilt and so by Dollman (see London, Southwark, Angl.). At Chester it was only from the 1530s (until 1881) that the south transept itself served as a screened-off parish church; and there have been other such arrangements. The Lady Chapel at Ely owes its survival to such post-Reformation use, and the Lady Chapel at St Albans owes its life to use as a grammar school.

ARCHITECTURAL SCULPTURE. The display of sculpture on the c 13 west front at Wells, despite centuries of wear and tear, becomes with the latest conservation work much more rewarding to study than it was. So Sir Nikolaus's judgements of 1958 can be tempered a little. The quality of the figures on Exeter's c 14–15 west front is also becoming clearer. The c 14 motif of cross-legged kings there also appears on Lincoln and Lichfield west fronts, the latter inevitably much restored owing to the nature of the stone.

Sculpture on porches, e.g. Lincoln's Judgement Porch, has also suffered wear and tear, as have other outdoor figures of quality, such as one on the south side of the choir at Lichfield. We have mentioned various figures now *ex situ*, such as the late C13 Christ at Swynnerton, probably from Lichfield's west front. Of interior figures surviving *ex situ*, the loveliest is the half-length Virgin and Child of *c.* 1500 at Winchester (now presbytery), one supposes made for the Lady Chapel altered in the late C15. (Distinctions between architectural sculpture and furnishing sculpture inside a medieval cathedral alive with carved walls and fittings need not be too rigorous.) More strictly architectural sculpture inside and *in situ* remains at Westminster Abbey, almost three centuries apart: of the C13 in the ambulatory chapels (fragmentary), on the south transept south wall, and in the chapter house; while for early C16 sculpture the Henry VII Chapel is the *locus classicus* in England. And there is the C13 work at Lincoln (St Hugh's Choir, Angel Choir) and, considerably restored, at Worcester (east transepts, choir triforium). Lincoln also has gorgeous decorative carving on the gateways to the choir aisles. Every medieval cathedral has its carved bosses – of stone or wood depending on the vaulting material – fastened like brooches at the joins of the vaulting-ribs, and often much larger than they appear from the floor. The nave vault at Norwich, for example, has a lavish display of them. In positions near enough to be closely inspected, bosses were elaborately carved, e.g. in Norwich cloisters, one under the pulpitum at York, and the central boss of the Wells Lady Chapel vault. A set of C15 wooden bosses displayed at Southwark show how they 'plugged in' to the vaulting system. Much of both decorative and figure sculpture in great medieval churches was concentrated on prominent fixtures such as pulpitum and reredos, and this brings us to furnishings.

MEDIEVAL FURNISHINGS. Of these only a precious residue has survived. (A few have been briefly referred to above with the architecture.) Cathedral furnishings add immeasurably to, much more often than they detract from, cathedral architecture. The longer the period when layers of fittings were being deposited, the more evocative the resulting mixture, especially where post-Reformation fittings of quality have accrued since. Within a few square yards at Chichester, for example, are a Roman mosaic floor, powerful Romanesque reliefs, C14 misericords, C18 brass chandeliers, windows by the C19 *Kempe* and the C20 *Chagall*, and a C20 tapestry by *Piper*. The more fortunate parish churches contain such multiple textures on a lesser scale. The nearest secular comparison, of shorter time-span, is of course with the English country house that has kept its contents.

The PULPITUM (originally meaning 'raised platform', from the same word-source as 'pulpit') was the prominent partition between nave and choir. Unlike the wooden rood screen of a parish church (e.g. Manchester Cathedral's handsome one of *c.* 1500) this barrier in the bigger churches was usually of stone, one bay deep and roofed, with a little east–west vaulted passage through the centre, and sometimes enclosing a staircase. Since at least the C14, organs have often been put on top. Medieval pulpitums, with later alterations, exist at a number of cathedrals. Rochester's has C13 remains amid the *Scott* and *Pearson* work. Of the early C14: Lincoln, the most elaborately and beautifully carved of all; also Southwell, nearly as much so; Exeter, partly opened up in the C19; and, of the C14 much restored, Wells and St Albans. Of the C15: Canterbury and York, both with statues of kings, Norwich, Ripon and Chichester, this last three-arched like Exeter's but now lacking the veranda and rear-enclosure dimension. On trends towards transparency in later screens, see *Victorian furnishings* below.

In the case of the medieval REREDOS, it is easy to single out the most precious survival, the Neville Screen at Durham. London work of the 1370s, it has been attributed to *Henry Yevele*. The slim verticals of its canopy supports can be seen as development, probably from Exeter's now-vanished reredos of the 1320s, for which the accompanying sedilia are evidence (see below). The multiple tabernacles of Durham's screen, still semi-transparent, became a century later the tall solid wall of niches of the Winchester reredos and St Albans reredos, both of the 1480s (today with Victorian figures). In the C14 an ensemble of such pieces as the Neville Screen included one or more sets of priests' seats or SEDILIA (in Saxon times combined with the bishop's throne when that stood east of the high altar; see below). The glorious set of three seats at Exeter, along with a surviving canopy fragment in a north chapel there, suggest the quality of excitement that the Exeter reredos must have had. To compare such heaped-up fantastic canopies with the austere unambiguous character of the Aquablanca tomb at Hereford, of fifty years before, is to see the difference between the C13 and the early C14.

The next most prominent fixture to the high altar was the bishop's THRONE. As demonstrated at Norwich, this anciently stood at the east of the apse behind and above the altar. A curved wooden bench at Winchester may have been part of the priests' seating beside the throne in the Norman apse there. When east ends became rectangular, and perhaps also for acoustical reasons, the throne was placed nearer the choir, on the south side. Post-Conquest religious ceremonial seats surviving in England represent more than one type, all with Continental connections: the C13 marble throne at Canterbury is in the Saxon tradition of those at Hexham and Norwich (and its own predecessor 'formed out of a single stone'); the turned-wood chair of *c.* 1200 at Hereford is a Romanesque royal or episcopal seat; and the originally painted wood-panelled coronation chair enclosing its symbolic stone at Westminster is a Gothic royal seat. Early in the c 14 improved woodcarving techniques produced the matchless Exeter throne canopy, unique in Europe – elaboration of the canopy taking over from that of the seat itself. Hereford's must have come soon after. Later in the c 14, not content with the possibilities of canopies, the bishop of Durham placed his seat on top of his own tomb, at the side of the presbytery but emulating the old altitude of Saxon bishops and so looking down his nose upon both high altar and choir.

Some two centuries of glorious woodcarving are represented in the sets of medieval CHOIR STALLS surviving in English cathedrals, with their canopies supported on slender shafts and their bench-end figures and misericords under the seats (see below). Chronologically the stalls range mainly between early c 14 and early c 16, with later interferences, at: (c 14) Winchester, Hereford, Chichester, Wells, Ely, Gloucester, Lincoln, Worcester, Chester; (c 15) Carlisle, Norwich, Ripon; (early c 16) Manchester, Westminster (Henry VII), Bristol, Oxford. Rochester has remains of c 13 stalls, without misericords. Exeter has the earliest complete set of MISERICORDS, of the c 13 but long since departed from their original stalls. After them come the misericords at Salisbury. The Ely stalls are thought to be by the master of the Octagon lantern, *William Hurley*. The stalls of Chester, Lincoln (altered) and York (burnt) may have been from the workshop of the later c 14 master carpenter *Hugh Herland*. The stalls dating either side of 1500 at Ripon and Manchester, and also Beverley, are attributed to *William Brownfleet* of Ripon. The misericord, by the way, was a little shelf on the underside of the upturned seat, against which the occupier could lean while standing during long services (some London bus-shelters have similar mercies). The subject-matter of those little carvings – far from authority's eye, like the loftier vault-bosses – could be delightfully irreverent and undidactic, often inspired by folklore, and more often secular than biblical. Also, a unique piece of woodcarving must be mentioned, the c 14 pyx canopy at Wells.

Medieval FONTS, some also with elaborate canopies (e.g. at Bradford and Newcastle), usually stood in the nave near the north or west entrance door, baptism being the believer's way in, though fonts, like lecterns and pulpits, have long since become the most mobile of furnishings. The tub-shaped stone font at Wells may be much older than the present cathedral; much of its decoration has been chiselled off. That shape, with arcaded saints round it, was continued e.g. in the c 12 font at Hereford. Such tubs may originally have stood directly on the floor for adult baptism. A large ribbed tub of the c 12 is at Ripon. A c 12 font made of lead is now in Gloucester Cathedral, with arcaded saints and scrolls from the same mould as others in that region. The black Tournai marble fonts at Lincoln and Winchester, of the mid-c 12, are of international quality and grandeur. Peterborough's font-bowl, possibly of local marble, with undulating rim, is of the c 13. As for Perp fonts, Norwich has a sumptuous though time-worn 'Seven Sacraments' one, octagonal with attached figures; c 15 octagonal fonts at Newcastle and Ripon have concave sides with shields.

Medieval LECTERNS and PULPITS. Three fine brass eagle lecterns of East Anglian provenance and dating from around 1500 are at Newcastle (Angl.), Peterborough and Southwell, and there is a similar one at Exeter. The presence of near-relations not only in many parishes but also as far off as Italy (Urbino Cathedral, St Mark's Venice) suggests an active export trade from East Anglia. But the handsome brass pelican lectern in Norwich Cathedral, of the late c 15 except for lower figures added in the early c 19, is thought to be Flemish. A magnificent late c 15 Flemish brass lectern, now in New York and previously at Oscott College, was for a while in St Chad's Cathedral at Birmingham, where the Flemish c 16 carved wood pulpit given with it survives without canopy. (We can also mention here the rare c 15 brass chandelier, possibly Flemish, in the Berkeley Chapel of Bristol Cathedral. On memorial brasses, see *Monuments* below.) A few stone reading desks survive. A built-in stone lectern is part of the c 14 screen between north transept and eastern aisle at Gloucester, apparently for taking attendance as monks filed past into the choir. And a refectory pulpit – for edifying readings during meals – is part of the c 13 wall structure within the north range of the cloister at Chester. A small canopied stone relief of the New Jerusalem, now on a windowsill at Worcester, may come from a c 14 or c 15 pulpit: it was incorporated in a pulpit made in 1642 to replace one broken up by soldiers. Four carved wooden pulpits survive in cathedrals from the years around and after 1500, the earliest probably that in Winchester choir, followed by one made for the Henry VII Chapel and now in the nave at Westminster; and two Flemish pulpits, one already mentioned in St Chad's Birmingham and one at Carlisle acquired in the c 20. Wells has a monumental c 16 nave pulpit of stone, given in the 1540s and surprisingly Renaissance in character.

Much screenwork of stone or wood survives in the cathedrals, and much more must have existed. Some of the handsomest and oldest screens are of IRONWORK, one of the earliest crafts. For c 13 ironwork see Chichester (some of it now in the Victoria and Albert Museum), also work of the 1290s at Westminster, Lincoln and Winchester, perhaps all of it by *Thomas of Leighton*. The c 14 west choir gates at Canterbury in an Islamic pattern were emulated in smoother c 19 work in the north and south gates there. At Wells the sturdy Bekynton Chantry screen is a rarity of the c 15. Henry V's Chantry gates at Westminster show early use of iron tracery, by *Roger Johnson*. The iron screen of Duke Humphrey's c 15 tomb at St Albans, sometimes called c 13, may be contemporary with the tomb. In a number of cathedrals, early ironwork remains as scrollwork on medieval wooden doors, e.g. on the west doors at Lichfield.

One of the most glorious of English medieval arts was that of STAINED GLASS, and a surprising amount has survived the slings and arrows of centuries. York Minster has the most complete collection from all periods since the c 12; our description has its own introduction after the other York furnishings. Canterbury is especially important for glass of the c 12–13; indeed, for the grandeur of the c 12 ancestor figures originally enthroned around the eastern clerestories, it is unparalleled. Some precious c 13 medallions remain in Hereford Lady Chapel; there is fine c 13 glass in the Dean's Eye (north transept) at Lincoln, and some late c 13 glass remaining on Wells chapter-house staircase and at Exeter. Early c 14 glass of high quality, dating both before and after the coming of silver-stain for making yellow, survives at Wells; precious fragments from Ely Lady Chapel are similar to work at York, and there is fine tracery glass in Oxford's St Lucy Chapel. Iconoclasts often missed the glass in the upper traceries. The largest spread of c 14 glass fills the great east window at Gloucester, where the canted-in side panels of glass fit into the canted-out spurs of the presbytery side-walls as if set by a jeweller – a lovely piece of precision engineering to combat wind pressure. The mason-in-charge is thought to have been that same *Thomas of Cambridge* who apparently designed the first fan-vaults: if so, one of the most fertile minds of that fertile time.

Medieval WALL PAINTING and PANEL PAINTING. Inner surfaces between and above the windows were also rich with colour. Only a little survives in proportion to what was. Important c 12 wall paintings survive in two chapels at Canterbury, walled off until the c 19. Norwich nave vault has faded remains of late c 12 painting, and there is c 13–14 work in the ambulatory. On the west wall of Rochester nave are some late c 12 sketches for a programme of decoration, and there is c 13 painting as well. At Winchester, work of great quality in the little Holy Sepulchre Chapel of *c.* 1200, north of the crossing, has scenes, found under later work, that are still fresh in colour and related in style to the c 12 Winchester Bible. Also at Winchester there are mid-c 13 vault paintings in the north-east chapel and early c 16 paintings in the Lady Chapel similar to work in Eton College Chapel. St Albans has an unusual amount of surviving c 13–16 wall decoration and, pre-eminently, the c 13 Crucifixion scenes on the north-eastern nave piers. Westminster has a striking series of elongated figures of the late c 13/early c 14, the earlier ones on the south wall of the south transept and in

St Faith's Chapel behind it, the later ones on the sedilia facing both sanctuary and ambulatory. Lichfield has recently revealed work of *c.* 1400 in the south choir aisle, also a small c 14 Crucifixion in a niche. And Exeter has early c 16 wall paintings in north transept and retrochoir. Two especially fine painted timber ceilings remain: on a large scale, the Peterborough c 13 nave ceiling, one of the most important medieval painted ceilings in Europe, and, on a smaller scale, that of the early c 16 prior's room at Carlisle. There are traces of early c 16 decoration on the vaults at Chichester (Lady Chapel) by *Lambert Bernard*, which must originally have been more delightful than his panels (transepts) with portrait medallions of bishops and kings, rightly compared by Ian Nairn to cigarette cards. Of valuable panel painting, retable panels now in the ambulatory at Westminster are, as already said, among the finest of the c 13 in Europe; and at Norwich in St Saviour's and St Luke's Chapels, panels of the late c 14/early c 15 are of high quality and interest. A rare late c 14 royal portrait hangs on a nave pier at Westminster, representing Richard II, and apparently his votive gift to St Edward's shrine.

Medieval PAVEMENTS. The finest spreads of c 13 floor tiles in England are in Winchester retrochoir and in Westminster chapter house. Many related tile designs can be seen in the British Museum. Also of the c 13, and far more rare and sumptuous, are the inlaid pavements, one formerly surrounding the shrine of St Thomas à Becket in Trinity Chapel at Canterbury, and at Westminster the sanctuary pavement with remains of the shrine pavement east of it. The Westminster pavements are known to have been made by Roman craftsmen, the *Cosmati*, brought here for the purpose. Less is known of the origins of the Canterbury workmen, though a pink marble used is thought to be Mediterranean. The most-used floors and steps in such buildings will have been repaved many times for safety's sake; there is fine c 18 paving at York, and some of the handsomest pavements now are Victorian (see below).

Which brings us to the SHRINES, miracle-working saints' tombs that brought pilgrims and revenue to many cathedrals. The tomb itself, in every case, survives only in fragments or not at all. Their gold and jewelled ornaments invited pillage, not only after the Reformation but before. The c 15 watching lofts at St Albans and Oxford were pieces of furniture installed to ensure security. At Canterbury in the c 12 and c 13 watching chambers were contrived in the building itself to overlook Becket's tomb both before and after it was moved from temporary accommodation in the crypt to the Trinity Chapel built for it. The shrine itself, by *Walter of Colchester*, is gone; marks in the elaborate pavement show where it stood. The architectural form of east ends could be dictated by prudent entrepreneurial placing of shrines, as was possibly the case with the c 13 retrochoir at Winchester (St Swithun) and Old St

Paul's (St Erkenwald). The acquisition of a miracle-making martyr at Rochester provided funds for c 13 rebuilding of the east end and may have dictated the size of the east transepts there. At Hereford, when Bishop Cantilupe was canonized in the early c 14, his tomb, now in the north transept, was moved to the Lady Chapel and the choir aisles were embellished as pilgrim routes in and out. The holiest spot for a shrine was behind the main altar in the space called the feretory, e.g. St Edward the Confessor's at Westminster at the heart of Henry III's new east end: here only the c 13 base is original. At St Albans what remains is the very early c 14 base, reconstructed from two thousand fragments in the c 19; and St Frideswide's shrine at Oxford and St Werburgh's at Chester were also reconstructed in the c 19. There also survive little portable shrines, one of the c 13 of Limoges enamel being now kept in the library at Hereford. (Late c 13 enamelling on copper plates sheathing an effigy in St Edmund's Chapel at Westminster is thought to have been done at Limoges, a more unusual import than a tiny portable shrine.)

Medieval MONUMENTS. Royal tombs were also worth having. At Westminster, still with their effigies, are those of (feretory) Henry III, Eleanor of Castile, Edward III, Richard II and his queen, the figures of gilt bronze, also Philippa's of marble, and Henry V (restored); and (Henry VII Chapel) the effigies of Henry VII and his queen, of gilt bronze, and those of Elizabeth I and Mary of Scots, of marble, as well as some chests without effigies and the tombs of numerous relations. The sculptors included the late c 13 *William Torel*, the early c 16 *Torrigiani*, and the early c 17 *Maximilian Colt*. (Here, for the sake of mentioning the royal effigies at Westminster together, we have trespassed on our post-medieval summary.) At Winchester the supposed tomb of William II, a plain low gabled chest, may be that of Henry of Blois. William's uncle, Duke Robert of Normandy, is buried at Gloucester, with a c 12 wooden effigy of great interest. King John's c 13 marble effigy at Worcester is of high quality. One of the first and most beautiful effigies of alabaster is Edward II's, of the early c 14, at Gloucester. At Canterbury the stiff copper-gilt effigy of the Black Prince contrasts with the elaborate alabaster figures of Henry IV and his queen. A study of tomb sculpture is essential to the history of dress, ecclesiastical, secular and military. For details of armour, note e.g. Duke Robert's at Gloucester, probably mid-c 12, and William Longespée's of the early or mid-c 13 at Salisbury, also the mid- or late c 15 armour of Robert Lord Hungerford there. And details of c 13 armour have been revealed on Wells west front. Canterbury and York have their series of archbishops' tombs, as other medieval cathedrals have their tombs of bishops, rewarding not only as records of episcopal dress but, like the tombs of all the well-buried, for their architectural and sculptural features.

One marvellous tomb is that of Bishop Bridport († 1262) at Salisbury, with its shrine-like canopy and its bar tracery following the new Westminster style. Two tombs commemorating deaths of the 1530s, yet without a hint of the Renaissance detail which had started to creep into English decorative carving in the 1520s, Bishop Sherbourne's at Chichester and Archbishop Warham's at Canterbury, show how a death-date is no indicator of the date of an artist's commission; the latter tomb is known to have been made in 1507, long before Warham died in 1532. Caution is also wise in case of over-eager c 19 restorations of tombs, e.g. of the Fitzalan tomb in Chichester nave and the Courtenay tomb in Exeter south transept; pre-Victorian engravings of tomb sculpture can be helpful. Another warning: medieval tombs have endured a deal of moving about from one part of a cathedral to another, with separations of chests from canopies etc., ever since the Reformation.

In a special category was the flat memorial BRASS, either a cut-out figure indented in a stone slab or an engraved sheet, the latter an imported Continental type. Many were lost, robbed for the material; others were turned over and re-used. At Hereford by 1717 there remained 170 indents of lost brasses, though a few fine brasses still remain there, the best being that of Bishop Trillek, mid-c 14. At Canterbury there are now no brasses at all, only indents. Exeter has two fine brasses, both c 15, of special interest for Canon Langton's vestments and Sir Peter Courtenay's armour. The epitome of the successful merchant's memorial is the great Thornton double brass of the early c 15, now in Newcastle (Angl.) Cathedral, of the incised sheet type, probably Flemish. One of the biggest and most interesting brasses in England is that of Bishop Wyvil or Wyville at Salisbury, adapting a theme from tales of chivalry to the celebration of a triumphant lawsuit and unique in showing the weapons peculiar to trial by combat (north-east transept, with facsimile in the nave for brass rubbers).

Medieval master CRAFTSMEN designed furnishings as well as architecture. *Henry Yevele*, to whom many buildings are attributed, produced tomb chests for Westminster Abbey, *William Hurley* apparently designed both the great timber lantern at Ely and the stalls below; and *Hugh Herland*, whose celebrated timber roof at Westminster Hall rested on Yevele's walls, is thought to have supplied choir stalls to three northern cathedrals. One marvels at the travels of some of these men, who also had to visit quarries and forests to select their materials. Perhaps master painters and sculptors travelled less when cathedral and monastic libraries were so rich in illustrated manuscripts to copy. Yet models as portable as illuminated manuscripts, embroidered vestments and imported woven silks, and small metalwork such as miniature shrines, carried patterns along clerical and commercial routes inside and outside the country. And craftsmen themselves going from one job to another carried ideas in their heads and their sketchbooks. There is no room in such a rapid survey as this introduction to characterize the known medieval craftsmen-designers of architecture and furnishings referred to in the text, for whom see the index under: Alexander, Attegrene, Bertie, Beverley, Brownfleet, Cambridge, Canterbury, Clyve, Colchester, Everard, Farleigh, Gloucester, Hedon, Herland, Hoo, Hoton, Hurley, Joy, Lesyngham, Lewyn, Lock, Luve, Mapilton, Montacute, Noiers, Norreys, Orchard, Patrington, Ramsey, Reyns, Roger, Sens, Smythe, Sponlee, Wastell, William, Witney, Wodehirst, Woodruff, Wynford, Yevele; and of course Mr Harvey's biographical dictionary. Next we proceed to the domain of Mr Colvin (for both, see Recent Literature) and after.

Cathedrals after the Reformation

Except for the rebuilding of Old St Paul's after the Great Fire (and one new parish church later to become a cathedral, *Archer*'s St Philip's Birmingham), no new cathedral was built in England after the Reformation until *Pugin*'s c 19 Catholic cathedrals. Apart from St Paul's, the architectural works of deans and chapters between c 16 and c 19 consisted of rebuilding, repairing and adorning the medieval fabrics, especially after the two periods of vandalism in the 1540s and 1640s. Of the twenty-two cathedral structures of Elizabeth's reign all but Salisbury (1220) had been begun between the 1070s and the 1180s. So looking after them was no new exercise, although some generations were readier to ignore the need than others, and both the spiritual and the social incentives had altered. Political, religious, art-historical and social changes had coincided in the Reformation with the end of the Gothic style and the rise of Renaissance classicism and the gradual change from craftsmen-designers to architects. Shifts in architectural attitudes to cathedrals in the four centuries since the Reformation are best illustrated by noting what succeeding architects did with them.

If inevitably at first no cathedrals were built, a great burst of sumptuous house-building for the new men of the day was inevitably followed by sumptuous tomb-making for the same clients. Between the 1530s and the 1630s the principal additions inside English cathedrals were the monuments of Elizabethan and Jacobean peers, politicians and merchants, in lavish but limited variation on a few newly learned classical themes (see the preface to Westminster Abbey furnishings), followed in the early c 17 by the more truly classical sculpture of *Nicholas Stone* and *Hubert Le Sueur*, both at Westminster, and the former also

at St Paul's, Southwark and Portsmouth, the latter at Winchester. Meanwhile, the battered and partly emptied cathedrals themselves increasingly needed attention. In the 1630s it was part of Archbishop Laud's policy to urge restoration and adornment, particularly at St Paul's and Winchester, where the work was encouraged by Charles I and designed by the King's Surveyor, *Inigo Jones*. Both for Jones's new pulpitum at Winchester and for his new west portico at St Paul's, there was no question of reviving medieval style: both must be utterly classical. Yet at Winchester the new ceiling inserted in the crossing tower in 1635, with the king's portrait on the main boss above Jones's pulpitum, was a neo-medieval wooden fan-vault; and his encasing of the Norman parts of St Paul's was tactfully, minimally Tuscan, nearest classical mode to Romanesque: seeds of Anglo-Gothic attitudes for the next hundred years. Reverence for medieval forms was not dead. Furnishings of the 1630s also survive at Oxford (pulpit with ogee-ribbed open canopy, glass by the *Van Linge* family) and at Chester (consistory-court furniture, redecoration of St Anselm's Chapel).

Even in the second hiatus, during Civil War and Commonwealth, when more battering and emptying of cathedrals took place, there was recording of cathedrals, e.g. in the engravings of Hollar and the writings of Dugdale and others. After the restoration of the monarchy and the established Church, the shoring-up and renovating of old churches began again. And then one of the landmarks of English architecture, its first Protestant-built cathedral, was in effect brought about by the destruction of its predecessor in the Great Fire of London in 1666. With all of the new St Paul's classical elements, its dome and its orders, *Christopher Wren* fused Gothic elements, such as the long-naved cruciform plan, in an Anglican synthesis. In details of plan there is likeness to Lincoln (placing of nave chapels) and Ely (enlarged crossing). At both Lincoln and Ely, Wren acted as consultant for rebuilding works, of north cloister and library at the former, of the north transept's north-west corner at the latter: for both, a Tuscan round-arched simplicity was thought to be the right note in the context, though a doorway at Ely was French in inspiration *via* a design of his own for St Mary-le-Bow. At Salisbury Wren supervised strengthening of the tower. At Westminster, where London smoke was already damaging stonework, he was in charge of restoration, assisted by *William Dickinson*; their work on the north transept was later redone by *Scott* and *Pearson*. Wren gave his views on Gothic, at Salisbury in 1668 praising its proportions and freedom from over-ornamentation and making only structural criticisms; at Westminster in 1713 reporting in a similarly businesslike and objective way: Gothic was an interesting practical problem.

In the early c 18, after Wren's death, *Nicholas Hawks-moor* designed Westminster's west towers, which Abbot Islip had not managed to complete. Hawksmoor had been in charge of repairing original medieval work at Beverley, but was also interested in recreating Gothic skylines as he had done at All Souls College, Oxford. His church tower for St George-in-the-East (initially designed for St Alphege Greenwich) seems to have been inspired by the Ely Octagon lantern (pre-*Essex*; see below). In silhouette his Westminster towers are spirited approximations of medieval towers. Yet he cared about the preservation of Gothic buildings 'Martyr'd by Neglect' (see St Albans).

Even before the Great Fire created new opportunities for craftsmen, the Restoration stimulated church arts: great brass lecterns made in London in the early 1660s by *William Burroughs* are at Canterbury, Lincoln, Wells and Queen's College Chapel at Oxford. But in the late c 17/ early c 18 the furnishing of St Paul's and the City churches stimulated the decorative crafts more than at any time since the high Middle Ages. Sculptors such as *Grinling Gibbons*, *Edward Pierce* and *Jonathan Maine* worked both in stone and in wood: St Paul's is a *locus classicus* for their work, as only a few City churches still are. *Jean Tijou*'s masterly ironwork, of European quality, at St Paul's and Hampton Court is echoed at Derby and Birmingham by that of *Robert Bakewell*. A majestic Corinthian throne canopy at Canterbury was designed probably by *Hawksmoor* in his most superbly classical manner. But he rebuilt the medieval pulpitum at Westminster in his own Gothic (rebuilt in the 1830s by *Blore* in *his* Gothic, still with inner-passage vault in *Henry Keene*'s late c 18 Gothic). The nave face of this pulpitum holds two niches where the medieval side altars will have been, which, after Hawksmoor's work, were immediately filled by *William Kent*'s Newton and Stanhope monuments (executed by *Rysbrack*), not at all Gothic. But Kent designed a pulpitum himself for Gloucester Cathedral that was a variation on Exeter's c 14 pulpitum in his own furniture-designer's Gothic, later replaced. York Minster in the 1730s was entirely repaved in black and white marble (the black, or some of it, was really deep blue) in a bold classical key design by *Lord Burlington* in association with Kent; this paving remains in the nave. In this period *James Gibbs* (architect of St Martin-in-the-Fields in London and of the main body of the present cathedral at Derby) tactfully used the round arch at Lincoln in interior screen walls under the Norman west towers; that is, approximating a Norman arch as Jones and Wren had done. Gibbs, incidentally, also designed memorial sculpture: his Craggs monument at Westminster precedes Kent's Shakespeare figure there in adopting the artificial bent-knee pose from the antique (but the elaborately negligent knee had already appeared in England in the paintings of Hilliard and Oliver). As for

c 17–18 stained-glass design, it became more and more like contemporary painting (as tapestry design was also doing): see the Nineveh window of the 1630s by *Van Linge* at Oxford, and much c 18 work by *William Peckitt* of York, especially at York.

In the mid-c 18 architects began to take Gothic more seriously and cathedrals began to be recognized as sources of styles to be used elsewhere, while to a few deans their restoration became intellectually interesting. Both Ely and Lincoln owe much to intelligent restoration by the architect *James Essex*. Even so, in restoring the exterior of the Octagon lantern at Ely, he seems to have misread existing remains of its appearance and turned it into a not very exciting work of masonry rather than the triumph of carpentry suggested in early c 18 engraved views, which *Scott* later had the good sense to follow in his own restoration. At Carlisle in 1765 the bishop, happening to be President of the Society of Antiquaries and keenly interested in medieval architecture, had his nephew *Thomas Pitt* design new choir furnishings, of which only fragments survived Victorian disapproval. In the late 1780s began the cathedral restorations of *James Wyatt*. Quantitatively these pale beside *Scott*'s (below): Wyatt worked on or was consulted at Lichfield, Salisbury, Hereford, Durham, Ely and also Westminster Abbey. He is worst remembered for his tidying of the nave and destruction of glass at Salisbury and for his proposal to demolish the galilee at Durham. But he has been unjustly maligned for his work on Hereford nave after the west tower fell: there he was self effacing. His Gothic fantasizing on cathedral themes was done for country houses.

By the second quarter of the c 19 designs for renovation of cathedrals by men like *Salvin* and *Ferrey* and *Blore* were serious antiquarian exercises. As late as the 1820s the ages-old tradition of a cathedral's master mason designing his own work had been maintained at Exeter by *John Kendall*, but by then that was unusual. Increasingly in the c 19 the relative responsibilities of master masons, clerks of the works, architects or surveyors to deans and chapters, and consultant architects from London or from other cathedrals varied from one cathedral to another (see e.g. *Durham* and *Worcester*).

Which brings us to the cathedral restorations of *George Gilbert Scott* (knighted in 1872) at Chester, Chichester, Durham, Ely, Exeter, Gloucester, Hereford, Lichfield, Oxford, Ripon, Rochester, St Albans, Salisbury, Winchester, Worcester and also Westminster Abbey (not counting all his other ecclesiastical work). There are two reasons why Scott's church restorations are better regarded than they were, apart from the usual pendulum-swing in such matters: recent research has found evidence for the previous existence of some of his more daring conceits, e.g. Chester's south-east chapel roof (though hardly as high as he made it); and a sober realism about weathering stonework and the results of neglect accepts that much now stands that, but for him, would have fallen. It is also right, in all cases of amendment to fabric or lack of same, to consider what the client – deans and chapters, and sometimes lay committees – wanted done or not done, and could afford.

Another endlessly debatable consideration is the old matter of tact in adding new work to existing fabric, illustrated by the naves of *Street* at Bristol and *Blomfield* at Southwark. Quite apart from the superior quality of both new and old at Bristol, the problem was the same: how to design a modern introduction to old work of great interest without upstaging it. Both men, it may be thought, achieved this successfully. The other principal Victorian figure in cathedral works was *John Loughborough Pearson*, the architect of Truro and restoring architect at Peterborough, Westminster Abbey and Lincoln. Controversies during the two stages of his work at Peterborough illustrated the gathering forces of lay opinion anxious to defend historic buildings from change and even destruction. The founding of the Society for the Preservation of Ancient Buildings by William Morris in 1877 was set off in opposition to Scott's doings at Tewkesbury. The ageing of physical structures coincided with all the other stresses and strains affecting the Victorian Church. One angry voice, for example, was that of the Rev. J. C. Cox, LL.D., F.S.A., addressing the Royal Archaeological Institute's summer meeting at Dorchester in 1897 on 'The Treatment of Our Cathedral Churches in the Victorian Age', and 'an attack it is intended to be', admitting that the fabrics were in better repair than in 1837 or even 1867, but mourning 'irreparable destruction of much that is ancient'. Perhaps he was thinking of Scott's brand-new east end at Oxford, though there we now know that the previously Perp window had already been redone in 1853. Dr Cox deplored 'the playing at parish church with the whole of the cathedral . . . and hence endeavouring to obliterate the proper division between quire and nave' (i.e. presumably he disliked the transparency of Scott's screens), and he objected to the 'undue giving way to the rage for gigantic organ effects' and 'the pervading influence of sound', perhaps referring to the immense organ of which the case remains in Worcester south transept.

There is now more appreciation for VICTORIAN CATHEDRAL FURNISHINGS than there was, one barometer being regard for *Scott's* choir screens. Instead of the solid walls of medieval pulpitums or their c 18 or early c 19 replacements, a new semi-transparency between choir and nave was indeed wanted by Victorian chapters. So Scott seems to have worked up his designs from medieval wooden rood screens and iron chantry screens. His first cathedral screen is at Ely (1851), and he followed its type in designs for Lichfield, Hereford, Worcester and, with simpler elements, Salisbury. (In the mid-c 20 those for Hereford and Salisbury were dispensed with.) At Winchester and Chester in the 1870s he took as his point of departure the carved-wood canopies of the return stalls against the screen. But Durham posed difficulties for a screen-designer in the extreme majesty of its architecture and in the, to him unsympathetic, c 17 Gothic of its choir stalls, and the screen there has less character than most of Scott's furnishings. Other Victorian work of great quality appears in splendid pavements designed by Scott (Durham, Worcester, Gloucester, Oxford) and *Pearson* (Bristol, Peterborough, Truro). The bold key pattern at Worcester, although Scott claimed he was inspired by the marble floor at Amiens, is much closer to the Burlington–Kent paving at York, an c 18 source that a high Victorian might not rush to claim. Scott at Durham and Pearson were obviously influenced by the c 13 Cosmati pavements at Westminster.

Three Victorian furnishings of unusual quality were shown in the 1862 Exhibition in London: Scott's Hereford screen, made by the Coventry metalworker *Skidmore*; Scott's great rood cross formerly at Chester (q.v.); and Gloucester's most spirited of eagle lecterns, designed by the young *J. F. Bentley*. Victorian stained glass is particularly well represented at Lincoln and Ely. Bradford and Peterborough have very early examples of glass made by Morris & Co., early enough to include designs by *Rossetti* as well as by *Webb* and *Morris*. At Oxford there is even an early *Burne-Jones* window designed before he worked for Morris & Co., but the Burne-Jones windows Oxford is best known for were for Morris's firm in the 1870s. These have a lyrical quality. In the 1880s Burne-Jones and Morris produced exciting windows for St Philip's Birmingham (not then a cathedral): windows more like brass bands in their splendour, perhaps not entirely suited to Archer's cool c 18 interior. A later, twilit Burne-Jones window is at Norwich (north transept).

When in the 1870s it was proposed to have a whole new cathedral built at Truro in Cornwall, many voices within the Anglican Church protested that 'another cathedral from an English architect' was impossible (Dean Goodwin of Ely, quoted by Owen Chadwick). But Truro and three more Anglican cathedrals by English architects were indeed to be built by the 1960s, charting the final stages of Gothic tradition in England: complete absorption at Truro culminating in Gothic apotheosis at Liverpool, followed by dilution at Guildford and rethinking at Coventry. The progress of Roman Catholic handling of the Gothic tradition in c 19–20 England, to provide the new cathedrals needed, went a little differently.

Although the Catholic Emancipation Act was passed by Parliament in 1829, there were officially no Catholic cathedrals until the hierarchy was restored in 1850. But the young *A. W. N. Pugin* had cathedrals in mind when he designed St George Southwark in 1838–9, St Chad Birmingham in 1839, and St Barnabas Nottingham in 1841; and in 1850, when they became cathedrals, his somewhat smaller St Mary Newcastle, also designed in 1841, was made the fourth of his cathedrals in England. They are much less complex than the old medieval fabrics, more on a scale with the Anglican 'parish-church cathedrals' (see below). Nevertheless, Pugin was intensely conscious that he was designing the first new English cathedrals in the Gothic style since the Reformation. (For Truro, after St Paul's, was to be only the second Anglican cathedral in England built new.) In spite of the needs of large congregations, and the resources of a very few rich patrons, Pugin was never able to build on the scale his Church was later able to afford for Bentley at Westminster. Nor are most of the beautiful fittings Pugin designed still in place. But the 'R.C. new series' cathedrals started worthily with him, and the Catholic Gothic tradition was continued by his son and by architects such as *Hadfield* and the *Hansom* family. At Norwich the grand church (only recently made a cathedral but designed on a modest-cathedral scale) by the sons of Sir Gilbert Scott actually owes more to Scott's last achievement in St Mary's Cathedral at Edinburgh.

The Roman Catholic break with English Gothic tradition was made in 1894 at Westminster. It was felt that Gothic should not be used so near Westminster Abbey, and *John Francis Bentley* made masterly use of Byzantine and Italian inspiration instead. Westminster Cathedral is rich in fittings and in handsome marbles; only the mosaic wall-coverings are weak. The next time a Catholic metropolitan cathedral was to be built, in the 1930s at Liverpool, the Church went architecturally to the opposite extreme, commissioning *Lutyens*'s vast classical design that was meant to outdo St Paul's if not St Peter's. But it was too vast, and only the crypt was built. Now *Gibberd*'s bold centralized design has been built upon that crypt, in fine contrast to *Sir Giles Scott*'s Anglican cathedral. And a quite different, equally non-traditional, smaller cathedral has been built at Clifton, Bristol. The Catholic hierarchy abandoned the Gothic tradition sooner than the Anglican hierarchy did.

Meanwhile, with the growth of urban populations between the 1880s and the 1960s, deans and architects pursued various stratagems for turning certain large parish churches into small cathedrals by extension of existing spaces. Medieval cathedrals of course had incessant additions but to fabrics already elaborate, especially east of the crossing. Extension of parish-church cathedrals has had to be mainly eastward, where the site has allowed it, for bigger choirs and new ambulatories and vestries (as variously at Chelmsford, Derby and Wakefield), some-times also creating transepts and crossing where none were before (Blackburn, Bury). Portsmouth was extended westward, but dramatic plans for still more extension were abandoned. Sometimes the site was so cramped by other buildings, as at Leicester and Newcastle, that rearrangements and elaborate refitting were concentrated within existing chancels. Some Roman Catholic cathedrals have cleared space by rejecting fine original fittings, as at Birmingham and Sheffield. Bold action at Brentwood switched orientation of the whole church through 90°, as was for a time intended at Sheffield's Anglican cathedral, and Northampton has twice had its orientation switched through 180°. The greatness of great churches built from the start as such is a matter of scale and eludes these scaled-up churches. But the interest of their histories can be respected where the evidences have not been lost in the enlarging process.

A seasoned medieval master mason, presumably consulting other specialists such as the water-carpenter or the roof-carpenter, during his lifetime might himself design bridges and towers and halls and cathedrals or parts thereof. So in the c 20, the architect who acted as consultant for the external design of Battersea Power Station and collaborated on the design of Waterloo Bridge designed the Anglican cathedral at Liverpool. And the architect of the Catholic cathedral there also designed passenger terminals for Heathrow Airport and planned Harlow New Town. Some techniques and some materials and many secular building-types have changed or evolved since the Middle Ages, along with human (or inhuman) ideas about scale. The cathedral is an old building-type, despite new ideas about the performance of its functions. And cathedrals are still patrons of the decorative arts. Certain cathedrals are especially distinguished for their c 20 furnishings, in new cathedrals especially Coventry and Liverpool R.C., in old cathedrals especially Chichester, also Salisbury and Manchester.

It is right that we should mention the restorative crafts of conservation work now being employed in the never-ending care of ageing fabrics. During the war of 1939–45 Coventry, Exeter, Manchester and, in London, St Paul's and Southwark R.C. cathedrals and Westminster Abbey suffered direct hits, as did the precincts of Canterbury and Norwich, and there was lesser damage to the Anglican cathedrals at Liverpool and Birmingham. New enemies are traffic vibration and oil-burning pollution of the air. An old enemy is lack of money for conservation. It is usual to reflect that cathedrals remind us of the transience of human life and the durability of human institutions. May the fabrics we celebrate endure.

PRISCILLA METCALF

The Cathedrals of England

SOUTHERN ENGLAND

Arundel

(Based on B of E *Sussex*, 1965, by Ian Nairn, and Steer 1973, and information from George McHardy, Roderick O'Donnell and John Martin Robinson.)

Cathedral since 1965, until 1973 dedicated to St Philip Neri. Built 1870–3 for the fifteenth Duke of Norfolk to designs of 1869 by *Joseph Aloysius Hansom* (who in early life had produced Birmingham Town Hall, the hansom cab and the *Builder* journal). Hansom's design here was not far, either geographically or in style and spirit, from R. H. Carpenter's Lancing College chapel, begun 1868, the latter more vigorous but neither building as convincing in close view as Pearson's work in that style (see *Truro* below). Nevertheless, Arundel Cathedral is dramatic on the ridge of the town as counterpoise to the Castle, and together they form one of England's great mock-medieval views, visible for miles across West Sussex.

Lofty nave, transepts and apsed chancel in French Gothic style and on a cathedral scale, but without the N W tower and prominent E Lady Chapel originally intended. Vaulted throughout. Tall narrow aisles and ambulatory, these proportions seeming to increase the internal dimensions (length 185 ft, height 72 ft internally). Eight-shafted piers as at Bourges. Hansom's details are a mixture of English and French – part of the mid-century attempt to create a new style out of such mixtures. But Hansom's Gothic has the scenic values relished by an architect who began his career as a pre-Victorian. (Yet his assistant who made the working drawings, *Herbert Gribble*, was to design the Brompton Oratory.) Compare Arundel with the Late Victorian Gothic of the Scott sons for the same donor (*Norwich R.C. Cathedral*; see companion volume).

All the stone CARVINGS, including the medallions in the apsidal arcade spandrels above the sanctuary, by *Farmer & Brindley*. – Good STAINED GLASS, vigorous in design and colour, much of it designed by Hansom and made by *John Hardman Powell*. The lower apse windows by *Hardman* and some of the stone statues come from the chapel at Derwent Hall, Derbyshire (submerged in a reservoir 1935). – On the Lady altar, ormolu rococo TABERNACLE made in London by *J. F. Kandler* in 1735 for the eighth Duke's private chapel at Arundel Castle. – SHRINE in N transept, by *Malcolm Lawson-Paul*, 1971, to the C16 St Philip Howard, one of the English martyrs sanctified in 1970 and an ancestor of the Duke of Norfolk. But the rest of the Fitzalan-Howard family are buried in the private mortuary chapel adjoining the Anglican church near by.

On parish church, castle and town, see the latest edition of B and E *Sussex*.

Brentwood

(Contribution by George McHardy, slightly revised, with information from Anthony New.)

Cathedral since 1917. The first church, opened in 1837, now minus its pinnacles and with a low modern addition across its front (and with adjoining priests' house of 1836), can still be seen to the S of the present building. By *Flower*, architect of Romford (R. O'Donnell), it is of yellow brick with stone dressings, in a minimal Gothic and very domestic-looking, despite its battlements, turret and two-light transomed windows. By 1858 it had become too small. Plans were drawn up by Wardell to enlarge it, but they were abandoned in favour of making the building into a school and erecting beside it a new church on a grander scale by *Gilbert Blount*. This was completed in 1861 and remained substantially the same until alteration and enlargement in the 1970s. It consisted of aisled nave with N porch, chancel with flanking chapels and a N E sacristy. All of ragstone, with polygonal S W turret, and of that assertive character of much church work of the 1860s. Though the modern additions are in harmonizing ragstone, the mid-Victorian part has been re-roofed in concrete tiles to match the new work.

Moreover, the architect for these alterations and additions of 1972–3, *A. J. Newton* of Burles Newton & Partners, found an ingenious if highly controversial solution to keeping part of the old fabric while enlarging for parish needs and for cathedral services. The axis of the old cathedral has been turned through 90°. The whole N arcade and N wall were removed and the building extended N to create an approximately square space, with the congregation sitting in an arc before the altar, which is set against the old S arcade, now filled in. N and W of the main seating area are spaces (hall and meeting room) which can be added to it or shut off. The old chancel is now the Blessed Sacrament Chapel.

Among the old fittings kept are the remaining (internal) roofs, the font and the STAINED GLASS. That from the windows in the demolished N wall is now in the N wall of the hall. The rest includes a S E window by *Mayer & Co.*, Munich, and a N E window by *O'Connor*, London, 1862. New furnishings include the tabernacle by *Michael Clark* and stained glass by *Goddard & Gibbs*. Above the entrance, bronze sculpture of St Helen by *Ferdinand Stuflesser*.

On the surrounding town, see the latest edition of B of E *Essex*.

1. ARUNDEL Designed 1869 by Joseph Aloysius Hansom. The nave

33

Bristol

CATHEDRAL CHURCH
OF THE HOLY AND UNDIVIDED TRINITY
(formerly of ST AUGUSTINE) *Anglican*

(Based on B of E *North Somerset and Bristol*, 1958, considerably revised, with information from Bridget Cherry, Thomas Cocke, Eric Franklin, Michael Gillingham and Alan Rome.)

Plan, Fig. 2, from the *Builder*, 1891, by Roland Paul, showing *Street*'s nave (but reporting the vaulting incorrectly; see our text). The eastern arm is shown before *Pearson* restored the medieval position of the high altar, moved the choir westward, and replaced a crossing screen of 1860 (the C 16–19 pulpitum having been two bays E of the crossing).

Some references (see Recent Literature): Bock 1965; Bony 1979; Cobb 1980; Dickinson 1976; Gomme 1979; Harrison 1980; Harvey 1978; Little 1979; Quiney 1979; Remnant 1969; Smith 1977.

INTRODUCTION

The one-time abbey church lies alongside College Green, its former churchyard, outside the old town and up a short steep hill from the harbour, where sea-going ships used to penetrate the heart of the town. The curtilage of the abbey's land ran down to the water's edge, and the abbey

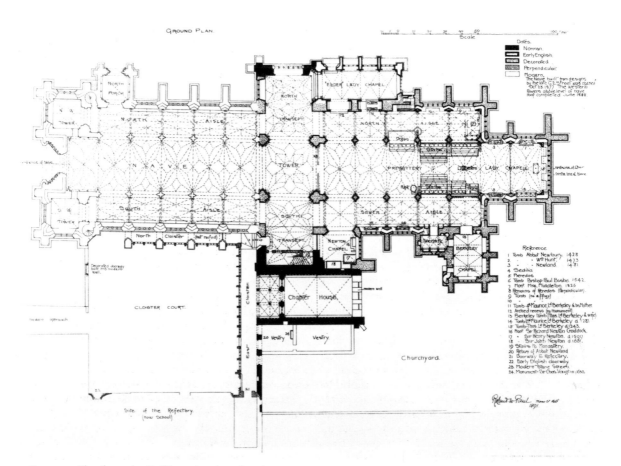

2. BRISTOL Plan from the *Builder*, 1891 (see above)

3. BRISTOL The north-east side from College Green

overlooked the bustle of wharves and cranes that made Bristol. A maritime air still seems to season the stonework of the cathedral's eastern arm, where bold frames for tomb niches almost suggest the powerful form of a ship's wheel, and vaults formed like flaring trusses and flying ribs smack of sails and rigging – or of shipwrights' timberwork. Despite the presence of great churches in other ports, and of ships' bells and flags in many other great churches, Bristol's cathedral has the saltiest history of any in England. Even the altar silver savours of *Robinson Crusoe* and perhaps *The Ancient Mariner*: in 1711 two Bristol ships under Captain Woodes Rogers returned safely and richly from a three-year round-the-world privateering voyage, and the ship-owner John Rumsey thereupon gave to the cathedral two candlesticks (by *Gabriel Sleath*, 1712) as thank-offerings for the loot; on the way Rogers had res-cued Alexander Selkirk, the original of Defoe's Crusoe, from his desert island, and an albatross shot on this voyage may have surfaced in seamen's tales Coleridge heard at Bristol.

In the C 12 this ground on the hill outside the town is thought to have been a holy place in long memory of a visit in 603, long before there was a town, by St Augustine, the apostle to the English, whose name lingered here for over five centuries – a theory based on nice consideration of documents that cry out for further evidence from excavation within these precincts (Dickinson 1976). It has been tentatively suggested that the C 11 Harrowing of Hell relief now in the S transept originally surmounted the doorway to a cemetery chapel on the site (Smith 1977). An abbey of Augustinian canons was founded here c. 1140, probably at first on the nearby site of St Augustine the Less (a parish church much rebuilt in the C 19 and lately demolished) nearer the E slope of the hill. But the position of the surviving chapter house, in the style of 1150–70, shows that the placing of the monastery church on the present cathedral site was part of the original intention. This church was dedicated c. 1170. The founder c. 1140, assisted in the 1150s by gifts from Henry II, was Robert Fitz-harding, who became Lord Berkeley and died a canon of his foundation. This was of the reformed kind influenced by St-Victor in Paris.

Little remains of the Late Norman buildings, and a representation of the church on a C 12 seal is hard to decipher (Little 1979). What does remain is of considerable interest, especially the chapter house, a most ornate example of what animated effects could be obtained with purely abstract motifs, orgies of zigzag, also two motifs that herald a later Bristolian and West Country style: arcades in which supports and arches have one continuous moulding and arcades with intersected arches. And in the chapter-house vestibule the presence of pointed arches between the 'aisles' suggests that the church had Tran-sitional features too. The early C 13 added to the church a Lady Chapel E of the N transept; this remains as the Elder Lady Chapel, showing signs of influence from Wells.

What gives Bristol its unique importance is the work begun by Abbot Knowle (treasurer from 1298, abbot from 1306) and carried out by the time Knowle was buried before the rood altar in 1332. This was a new eastern arm with aisles and eastern Lady Chapel, and a low chapel with antechapel, or vestibule, S of the S choir aisle. That chapel, later called the Berkeley Chapel, was begun at the same time as the main vessel, or a little sooner if building began outside the walls of a narrower Norman E end. A burial took place in the arch between aisle and chapel in 1309. So by then the chapel was probably complete and the main vessel's walls were up. The extraordinary aisle vaults will have preceded the main vault, but an exact date for vaulting is unknown. The arms of Humphrey de Bohun (buried, however, at Exeter) in the glass of the great E window limit this glazing to the period 1313–22. And that would seem to mean vaulting as well as roofing already completed before 1322, unless one can agree with Harvey (1978, p. 225) that vaulting could safely be done close to newly glazed windows. The main vault, quite different from the aisle vaults, has liernes. The first liernes appeared in St Stephen's Crypt vault at Westminster (where work was suspended between 1298 and 1320), and then in the probably Westminster-inspired vault at Pershore. Possibly the Bristol main vault was contemporary with that of the Wells Lady Chapel, thought to have been complete by 1319, but there the liernes were quite differently handled. At any rate, the Bristol spatial experiments were taking place in the first three, principally perhaps the first two, decades of the C 14.

From the point of view of spatial imagination – which is after all the architectural point of view *par excellence* – Bristol's eastern arm is superior to anything else built in England or indeed in Europe at the same time. It proves incontrovertibly that English design surpassed that of all other countries in the first third of the C 14. And since the management of space for emotional purposes is so entirely what matters at Bristol, the interior shall here, exceptionally in this book, be described and analysed at once and the exterior only subsidiarily. But first, while still in introduction, to summarize the master whom Knowle employed.

The workshop for this rebuilding programme, by 1306 (when Knowle became abbot) if not before, came under the direction of a mason of great and singular genius who inspired a new outlook in those working under him and later moving elsewhere. (Exciting work in Bristol was also being done at St Mary Redcliffe, probably by members of the abbey workshop.) The Bristol master must have known what was going on in London, especially at St Stephen's Chapel in the Palace of Westminster and in tomb design at Westminster Abbey. He seems to have known France also, St-Urbain at Troyes, which he may have liked better than any other building, and the Sainte Chapelle in Paris. Bony (1979) suggests a royal mason who had worked in the English provinces of France. It will have been one who also observed the new roof timberwork in the more palatial English domestic halls. And he must have been in touch with the workshop at Wells, not far away. He was a man of supreme inventiveness in matters of decoration as well as of space. He was also a man of wilful character, capricious and some may say perverse. In decoration he shunned current motifs; even the ogee arch, quite a recent creation that became at once very popular elsewhere, interested him less. Nor did the current motifs of flowing tracery: they were too easy. Instead he experimented with certain subtly applied discordances, with sudden straight lines and right angles in the middle of Gothic curves, and with curves that are concave where one would expect them convex, and with arches standing on their heads. But such decorative in-novations alone would not necessarily be proof of genius. The Bristol master's handling of space is. No one then alive, or at any rate then building, could compete with his choir aisles in the superb synthesis of structural ingenious-ness with spatial thrills, unexpected diagonal views in all directions. And to develop (from a small-scale original at Lincoln?) a whole vault of flying ribs only, entirely unfilled with cells, was his *tour de force* in the Berkeley antechapel: it may sound merely playful, in fact it is aesthetically of the greatest charm. An unusual feature at Bristol is its 'one-storey' elevation throughout, as of a college chapel, or St Stephen's Upper Chapel at Westminster but with aisles, resulting in the hall-form discussed below. The transoms dividing Bristol's windows horizontally had been introduced in the grander domestic halls, e.g. the late c 13 Bishop's Palace at Wells.

Work on the abbey church came to an end about the middle of the c 14, when the Newton Chapel had been added and a new s transept begun. Then there was a long break. Only during c. 1470–1515 were the s transept completed and the crossing tower and N transept rebuilt.

Chapel, N transept, central tower, N cloister walk, abbey gateway, and rearrangement of choir and sanctuary with new fittings, including the fine pavement and his son's choir screen.

Medieval freestone work here is mainly of the fine Dundry limestone of which much of the city is built, from a quarry south of Bristol.

4. BRISTOL South-east view before the riots of 1831

Abbot Newland before he died in 1515 also began to rebuild the Norman nave (still standing until then), but his work only reached the sill-height of the aisle windows – or did his demolition just take the Norman walls down to that level, as at Exeter? The ground lay open, except for some houses, for more than three centuries. After Bristol was given cathedral rank in 1542, the post-Reformation see was poorly endowed (Cocke). During 1836–97, while continuing as a cathedral with its dean, Bristol shared a bishop with Gloucester. Finally during 1868–88 a new nave and w towers were built to designs by *George Edmund Street*; after his death in 1881 the towers were completed 1887–8 by *John Loughborough Pearson*. Also by Pearson: restoration 1890–1900 (completed by his son) of the main Lady

INTERIOR AND EXTERIOR

A century before Knowle's building work, the ELDER LADY CHAPEL was added to the Norman church by Abbot David c. 1210–20 (Little (1979) suggests nearer 1230). The chapel is placed, not in the usual position at the E end, but to the N of the old church (cf. Ely). It is four bays long, vaulted, and slender in its proportions. The ground stage on the N side has blank arcading with pointed trefoiled arches on shafts of Purbeck marble. The capitals have stiff-leaf. It is known that the Abbot asked the Dean of Wells for the loan of a carver (or a designer; see Colchester and Harvey (1974) on Wells). There is indeed a close connection with the w parts of Wells nave. Foliage appears on the stops for the hoodmoulds as well, and in most of the spandrels. In others there are little genre-scenes such as a monkey playing the pipe, a goat carrying a rabbit, a fox and a goose, but also St Michael and the Dragon. At the sill of the tall windows of the upper stage runs a roll-moulded course, interrupted for every bay and terminated by a small head sucking the round bar of the roll moulding (cf. N porch Wells). The bays are divided by tall Purbeck shafts. The N windows are groups of three closely placed stepped single lancets. Externally the groups are separated by buttresses. The parapet and pinnacles above, however, are clearly Perp. Inside the windows are shafted, the shafts being entirely detached and again of Purbeck marble. Their capitals are moulded and of Purbeck marble also. The E window is of five lights with seven small circles, containing quatrefoils, trefoils and a cinquefoil. That must be of the later C13, say c. 1270–80 (cf. Wells chapter-house staircase), and the mouldings inside show indeed the difference from the N windows. On the S wall including the sedilia and piscina, the same composition is applied as on the N wall, except that the windows are blank and that two big later arches towards the chancel aisle have been inserted. The arch towards the transept (the Norman transept of course at the time) has orders of Purbeck colonnettes, three to the W, one to the E. The circular moulded capitals are again of Purbeck marble. The arch mouldings have several rolls. The vault must be later, and may date from the time of the E window. It is quadripartite, with a longitudinal ridge rib (cf. the passage to the undercroft, Wells chapter house) and the transverse arches not broader than the ribs. The ribs consist of three rolls and deep hollows. The middle roll carries a fillet.

The two arches towards the chancel aisle are Perp. They have pointed tunnel-vaults with two bands of quatrefoil panelling. Their E and W walls are hollowed out a little into recesses, and there is pretty ribbed coving to lead up to the tunnel-vault.

The CHANCEL (choir and presbytery) with its aisles is the great surprise of Bristol. The high vault is broad rather than high – only 50 ft to the apex of the vault – and four bays long (or five including the ambulatory behind the altar, which is in no way structurally separate, as we shall see when we enter the Lady Chapel E of it). The piers again are rather broad. The main motif of their section is two broad wave mouldings. The most remarkable thing about the piers (if they were designed soon after 1298) is that they have capitals only to the thin triple shafts facing the nave. All the rest runs into the arches in continuous mouldings, a challenge to E.E. clarity, though indeed on the authority of much minor C12 and C13 work in the West Country (e.g. the triforium of Wells nave).

The vault has liernes in addition to tiercerons. It is, side by side with the Wells Lady Chapel, the earliest lierne vault in the West Country (and depending on the dating of Pershore), but not the place where the lierne vault was invented. The source is the undercroft of St Stephen's Chapel at Westminster, which was completed by the beginning of the C14. The sense of innovation was acute, however, in the Bristol designer of this vault; for only thus can it be explained that he emphasized the parts bounded by the liernes by means of cusping. The cusping of ribs seems to have originated here. It was soon taken up at the Wells choir, the Tewkesbury choir, and at St Mary Redcliffe. The way of setting out the vault can perhaps best be explained by saying that the master first designed a normal vault with transverse arches, diagonal ribs, ridge ribs, and one pair of tiercerons each way. Then, however, he studiously avoided the meeting of the tiercerons and the ridge ribs by splitting the ridge ribs so that instead there result kite-like lozenges. These kites are the area of the liernes. (Both St Stephen's crypt and Pershore choir, on the other hand, keep their ridge ribs.) The cusping incidentally stops above the altar. The ambulatory bay and the Lady Chapel are without it. They were probably the first to be built. There are big bosses at all major junctions of the vault.

But the chancel can at no moment be seen without taking in the aisles as well. Those who have tried to follow this analysis on the spot will have noticed that. For Bristol is a hall-church, that is a church in which the aisles are of the same height as the nave, a type of design which was to become the *Leitmotif* of Late Gothic architecture in Germany, but appears here, perhaps for the first time in Europe, with its spatial potentialities fully realized. (St-Nazaire at Carcassonne is the other church that may compete for the title.) The source has been variously considered. Poitou had gone in for hall-churches ever since the C12, but with very different proportions. St-Serge at Angers of c. 1200 is more comparable (and Bony (1979) sees influence from Angevin vaults at Bristol). But it is perhaps more likely that the Bristol master was influenced by such English retrochoirs as those of Winchester and Salisbury, and the Temple choir in London. Their source in its turn may well be aisled secular or monastic halls, a type that flowered in C13 bishops' palaces.

So much for sources. But they matter little in the case of Bristol; for what the master has made of them is wholly original and far more ingenious than any predecessor's work. The chancel aisles at Bristol have large four-light windows. They have transoms with a full assignment of tracery below as well as in the head. There are to the N and S two alternating designs. Below the transoms they alternate between twice two-light arches with Y-tracery and arches with reversed arches on top, or if one looks at it another way, intersected ogee arches. The wilfulness of this motif and its ambiguity are a first introduction to the personal character of the Bristol master. Only the E windows differ.

5. BRISTOL Choir and presbytery, early C14

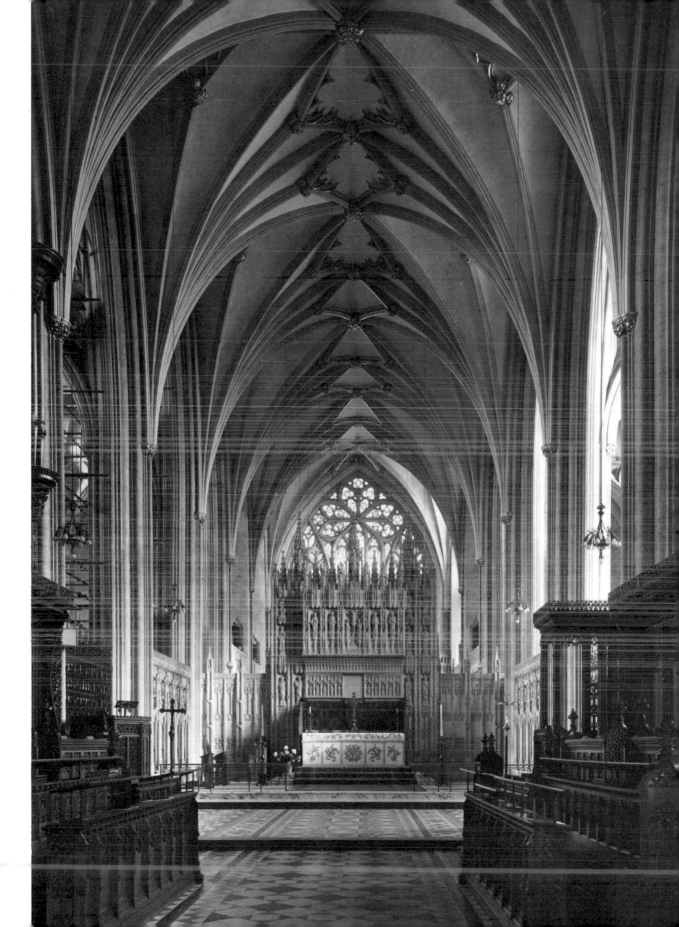

They are of three lights with six unencircled diagonally placed quatrefoils in the head, backed from the sides by two mouchettes. Battlements and pinnacles outside, not as a continuation of the buttresses. A pierced parapet was begun but not completed, with triangles filled by cusped lozenge patterns, similar to E end parapets at Wells. (*Street* designed Bristol's nave parapet in this manner, perceptively, long before fragments of the eastern arm's medieval one came to light.) At the sill level of the windows inside runs a wall-passage. It cuts through the piers between the windows, which are really an inner extension of the buttresses. The passage openings have arches of two convex (not concave) curves, addorsed as it were – a typical Bristol conceit, less pronounced in the Lady Chapel. Excellent small heads within the gables so formed. The passage's parapet is probably *Pearson's*.

The weight of the chancel vault is conveyed to the outer aisle walls by a device which more than anything makes the Bristol interior unforgettable. There are, one might say, flying buttresses thrown across the aisles at the level of the springing of the vaults, but they are given the form of bridges from arcade pier to outer wall. Each bridge can be compared with – and might indeed be inspired by – a tie-beam on arched braces in a timber roof. (And, hall-church though it be, there is the further ambiguity that the arched braces imply lower aisle-height.) Big mouchette-shaped spandrels, big enough to look through them into neighbouring aisle vaults with ease. The aisle vaults again are something of consummate ingenuity. They can essentially be defined as transverse tunnel-vaults, an effective method of buttressing (in England cf. Fountains Abbey). But they consist here of two bays of rib-vaulting with longitudinal (that is transverse) ridge ribs. The flash of genius in the arrangement is that in each little vault the cell resting on the bridge is simply left out. That makes the transverse arch and ribs on the middle of the bridge stand as it were on tip-toes, a tight-rope feat right up there (and, again the timberwork analogy, like a crown-post truss, i.e. the post with four-way struts). It also allows us to look yet more freely from vault to vault. The hall-elevation as such makes for diagonal vistas across a whole room at eye-level, to an extent impossible and indeed undesirable to the C 13. Now this hankering after spatial surprise is extended to the vaulting zone, that is vistas are opened up not only diagonally across but also diagonally up.

This spirit of ingenuity and surprise pervades all the master's work. Attached to the S aisle on the S side is the Berkeley Chapel with its antechapel. The chapel apparently became the Berkeley Chapel only thanks to a chantry foundation made after the death of a Lady Berkeley in 1337, but since Lady Joan, wife of Thomas Lord Berkeley, was buried between the chancel aisle and the chapel in 1309, the architecture of the chapel belongs to the early

6. BRISTOL Choir aisle vaults, after 1298

years of the C 14. The ANTECHAPEL or vestibule is entered by a doorway with cusped and sub-cusped arch and ogee gable. Side arches blank with steep gable – a composition like that used for tomb canopies by the court school of London about 1300 (and invoked in the Lady Chapel reredos, below), though here restored beyond redemption. But the inner arch towards the antechapel is genuine and full of interest. For it is made up simply of big roll mouldings dying into the jambs. The antechapel itself affords final proof that my explanation of the spatial intention of the master is not too subtle or too latter-day. For in this little room the master has placed under a flat stone ceiling and in support of it a whole system of flying arches and ribs in three bays. It is like a text-book demonstration *in nuce* of the Gothic system of vaulting. Transverse arches, cross ribs, flat ridge ribs. They are all there, and big bosses at the junctions. But there are no cells. (The first flying ribs, apparently of the 1290s, seem to be those of Lincoln's Easter Sepulchre, on a miniature scale; others

7. BRISTOL Berkeley antechapel, c. 1300. Flying-rib vault

similar in type and scale to Bristol's appeared in the pulpitum passages at Lincoln and Southwell, the former perhaps contemporary with Bristol's, the latter c. 1320–40.) The corbels of the vault incidentally still have naturalistic foliage, another sign of an early date. In the s wall are three deep recesses with ogee arches and much leafwork. One of them has a flue leading to an outlet in a pinnacle. It was presumably a place for baking communion wafers. In the N E corner a niche set diagonally, also a characteristic touch. Big head above (cf. Marchia tomb, † 1302, Wells).

Now down the steps (this is a sloping site) into the BERKELEY CHAPEL itself, a much quieter room of two bays with a simple cross-ribbed vault with ridge ribs. The windows are of three lights, the lights lancet-shaped and the middle one lower than the others to make room for a dagger and two elongated pointed trefoils in the spandrels. In the w wall, high up, a window in the form of a spheric triangle. In the s wall three niches of a very curious design, again the first introduction to a motif which, for its very

perversity, this cunning master loved dearly. The niches are pointed-trefoiled and in the spandrels are placed little heads under straight gables, or rather straight bars set gable-wise. This delight in the discord between curved and straight we shall meet more than once.

The arch between the chapel and the aisle was kept open to receive the monument to Lord Berkeley. The effigy exists no longer *in situ* (but see below) and so it is advisable to treat the arch as part of the architecture. (For the frieze under it, see *Furnishings*, Chancel, Whitefriars screen, below.) The form of the RECESS is the *nec plus ultra* of the master's cavalier treatment of Gothic precedent. He seems to be set on avoiding at all costs the normal pointed arch and even the already too normal ogee arch. Instead there is again the sharply spiced meeting of straight and curved. The inner frame of the recess consists partly of five straight lines, arranged as a half-octagon, as it were, and enclosing an arch made up of three semicircles on two quarter-circles. But the dominant outer frame is made up of four bold semicircles on two quarter-circles, all set concavely, resulting in what might be described as a Chinese shape were it not more appropriate to see Arabic origin: this hollow-sided form was then entering English ornament, e.g. in manuscripts and window tracery, apparently by way of Islamic ornament on imported luxury goods arriving, e.g., in the port of Bristol. The arches and the points between them are given the familiar crocket and finials in all innocence. Splendid heads and busts as stops of the outer quarter-circles. There are three such recesses in the s aisle, but only this one pierces the wall. The lower, ogee-gabled niche at the E end of the s aisle, sometimes called a Victorian remodelling, was already there in Britton's view of 1830.

Then we enter the LADY CHAPEL. It may well be that in the usual way building operations began here, but there seems no development of style in these early parts and so the work of 1298–c. 1330 can be treated as one. The Lady Chapel again, on the strict spatial principle of the hall-church, is of the same height as nave and aisles, and as the ambulatory behind the high altar. The chapel is two bays long. Its E window, that is the E window of the whole church, is of nine lights and of a perversity of design which is in this case not counterbalanced by any of the delights available to the master as soon as he dealt with space. The tracery of the window is in three parts. The three-light l. and r. parts have very steep arches with reticulation. The middle part has first, halfway up, a transom band of three diagonally-placed quatrefoils and then three bold stepped lights looking like Tablets of the Law, and above them a big and nastily spreading trefoil, subdivided by minor tracery. It is a most disconcerting end to the vista, although Bony sees the strong central motif as a typical Dec triumphal finish to the church's long axis. It would be more

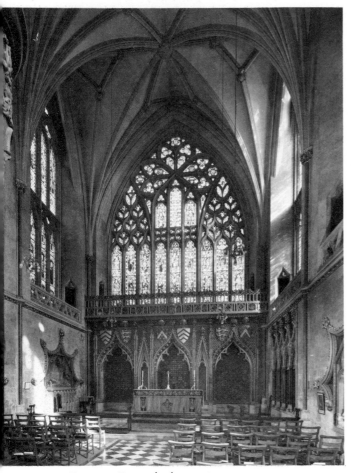

8. BRISTOL East end, after 1298,
east window glazed by 1322

royal interest here. In the mouldings ballflower ornament appears, another hallmark of the early C14. Frieze of big heads (again cf. Marchia monument, Wells) and big fleurons. The elaborately transparent crested parapet of the wall-passage above is by the initials W.B. proved to be an addition of Abbot Burton (1526–39). The SEDILIA, like the reredos and the N and S wall-recesses, are part of the architectural design of the Lady Chapel. They are now C19 work but apparently accurate reconstruction from sufficient old parts, presumably by *Pearson* (the originals having been partly hidden behind a C17 tomb: Cobb 1980, Fig. 3). The motif of the arches is one already met in the window tracery, four quite harmless pointed arches, but on them concave-sided crocketed gables with finials, or rather pointed arches the wrong way up. The whole can, as has been pointed out before, be read as intersected ogee arches. But the crocketing is against that most reasonable interpretation. Reredos, sedilia and other parts are gaily coloured, the work of Professor *Tristram*, based on minute bits of colour found in many places. In the walls of the Lady Chapel are three tomb recesses of the same design as in the S aisle.

About 1330–40 the NEWTON CHAPEL was added in the angle between the Norman S transept and chapter house and the new chancel aisle, a much taller and opener chapel than that of the Berkeleys. One bay only, with a quadripartite vault and windows of less interesting details too. Evidently the great master had died or left. Tracery with three circles containing three unencircled trefoils each, or with one large unencircled quatrefoil. The bay of the aisle incidentally on which the chapel borders also differs from the others and may well be the last completed. It has a straightforward octopartite vault (i.e. with diagonal and ridge ribs only). Above the chapel a small chamber, perhaps a treasury.

The TRANSEPTS and the CROSSING, it will be remembered, are in their walling Norman, but in nearly all that is visible of the late C15 to early C16. Norman only one small window above the arch into the Newton Chapel (an arch incidentally which is quadruple-chamfered and dies into the imposts), and one block-capital in the SW corner now helping to support the S transept vault. There is also a Norman staircase in the thickness of the wall in the SE corner, and another hidden in the N chancel aisle. The S transept was probably vaulted under Abbot Hunt (1473–81), the crossing later, and the N transept later still. The S transept S window is Perp and of no great interest. It is high up, because the monastic buildings adjoin here. The staircase to the former Dormitory survives, with a small vault. The N transept N side has a window by *Pearson*. The E window is Perp, but the W windows of both transepts correspond to the chancel windows. The vaults of crossing and transepts are designed on the lines of the chancel,

dominating without *Pearson*'s high altar reredos, with which, however, he restored the position of the medieval one, though its height is unknown. (The Lady Chapel altar was the high altar only from 1542; *see* valuable series of views in Cobb.) The N and S windows of the Lady Chapel are similar to those of the chancel aisle, but the western ones are only of three lights and have transom bands of reticulation units. The wall treatment and the vault treatment are as in the chancel, but without cusping of liernes.

The E wall below the window is taken by the stone REREDOS, part of the architectural design. It consists of three ogee arches with narrow steeply-gabled niches between, that composition initiated by royal masons. The arches are cusped, and one cusp on each side again has the signature of the master, straight sides. The back of the arched fields is closely diapered, as the early C14 liked it, and bears shields, some with royal leopards – suggesting though they differ considerably from one another. That of the s transept is the simplest, that of the N transept is heavy with liernes and bosses. In the crossing it is interesting to observe that the idea of splitting the ridge ribs to obtain liernes is no longer fully understood. There are pairs of additional liernes without that meaning. The cusping of the lierne lozenges is maintained. The crossing piers have much sturdier shafts than the master of the chancel allowed himself. In the s transept a handsome if confusing design is adopted by which diagonal ribs cross each of the two bays singly as well as both jointly. There is no ridge rib here.

The CENTRAL TOWER is not visible from inside. Outside it rises vigorously to two tall storeys with five transomed (and partly blocked) two-light windows to each face on each storey. Paired buttresses at each corner join partway up to become a diagonal buttress, more elaborately combined at the stair-turret corner. Parapet with blank arcading and unassertive corner pinnacles. This tower, of c. 1466–71 according to Harvey (1978), had to be strengthened and partly rebuilt by *Pearson* in 1893. Its character is cubic, not aspiring.

Street began the NAVE in 1868, the year when he was appointed architect of the Law Courts in London, and was soon to start his churches of St Mary Magdalene Paddington and St John the Divine Lambeth. With his taste for noble muscular c 13 work, how could he continue the work of so individual a genius, whose style must have seemed to him flippant (in the fluently playful, not necessarily irreverent sense)? What Street told his building committee in 1867 was this: 'The object should be in fact to make the character of the work so distinct as to enable anyone hereafter at all versed in the matter to pronounce from the internal evidence of the work itself that it was not executed by the same men who built the choir' – i.e. that the nave was built in the c 19, not the c 14 – though he hoped to produce the effect of 'similarity at a distance'. So we must not underestimate Street. The nave – what most worshippers and visitors see first – was to be the vestibule to a work of genius, which he did not feel it his business to upstage, rather to prepare the way to (cf. Blomfield's problems at Southwark). What he did was to accept the fundamentals from his predecessor and normalize the details. The aisles are as high as the nave and the windows are transomed. Their tracery is Geometrical, that is, preparatory. The w towers have forms of the late c 13 rather than the early c 14. Inside, the differences are even more illuminating. The nave has normal tierceron vaults with prominent ridge ribs and no liernes; it was finished thus by Street (the *Builder* plan of 1891 quite wrongly shows nave vaulting like the chancel's, which is odd, as Paul knew the cathedral so well). The piers are sensibly designed with proper capitals, big naturalistic ones, and Purbeck shafts to emphasize the principle of the pier. The aisles have their

9. BRISTOL Nave by G. E. Street, begun 1868. Screen by F. L. Pearson, 1904

bridges, but Street, instead of leaving out cells, constructs the little transverse vaults differently so that what he leaves out are vertical planes, the pointed tympana or wall-arches. (This takes some seeing.) Finally, the recesses along the aisle walls are normalized. Below the w rose window, the c 20 has filled the former w doorway with plain plate glass and unexpected daylight.

Pearson finished Street's towers, wisely, without the little hipped pyramidal roofs of Street's original design (its one touch of the 1860s, almost suggesting Victorian château roofs and so likely to date badly). The long view from College Green does not really suffer from Street's idea of his proper relation to the c 14 work. His western arm is exactly as long as the medieval eastern arm, a balance that might seem too simple here, were it not that Street in a survey in 1866 had discovered foundations for a N nave wall indicating six bays. He thought it Knowle's

C14 rebuilding: either it was Newland's start in the early C16, or it was Norman remains left by Newland. Again the relation in height of w towers to crossing tower may be a little too reasonable. In general, after the thrills of the chancel interiors, one could be impatient with the respectable performance of a sensible architect – but it may be more perceptive to take it as the performance of a sensitive architect who knew when to hold back. It is hard to see what else could have been done short of being as frankly individual again. For points of view and for accounts of rearrangements before Street took over, see Cobb 1980; Gomme 1979.

FURNISHINGS, E TO W

Lady Chapel For reredos, sedilia and niches *see* architectural description above. STAINED GLASS. Of the Jesse Window at the E, little original work remains, notably the seated Virgin. But far too much was done by *Joseph Bell*, the restorer of 1847 (yet the N and S windows of 1847 are seen by Harrison as admirable work with glowing colour). The heraldry of the E window, including arms of Humphrey de Bohun, makes a date *c.* 1320 probable. – MONUMENTS. Later abbots recumbent in the early C14 recesses: Abbots Newbery † 1473, Hunt † 1481, and Newland † 1515. At Newland's feet two angels, such as are usual at the head, holding a shield. In one of the niches of the Newbery tomb-chest a headless statuette still stands. – Small ORGAN incorporating part of 1786 *chaire* case from the main organ (Gillingham).

Chancel REREDOS by *Pearson*, 1899. Incorporated with stone side SCREENS that were previously part of the C16 pulpitum dividing the choir when there was no nave for the laity. Worked into these screens a rood screen from spoils of Bristol's Whitefriars Church, given to the new cathedral in 1542 by Thomas White (fragments on S aisle side of the sanctuary with White's initials and arms of Edward Prince of Wales; see also *Berkeley Chapel*, frieze, below). – The CHOIR STALLS were erected in 1520 by Abbot Robert Elyot, whose initials are on them (Remnant 1969). Much flamboyant tracery. After restoration in the 1860s they were more carefully dealt with by *Pearson* in the 1890s. They have a valuable set of twenty-eight original MISERICORDS with subjects including Adam and Eve, Samson and the lion, a mermaid, Reynard the Fox, the bear caught in the cleft oak, dancing bears, the killing of a pig, and husband and wife tilting with brooms, the spinster leading apes in hell, a woman taking corn to a windmill, and so on. – Pair of ORGAN CASES, 1682–5, with rich carving, formerly the organ's E and W faces when it was on the pulpitum (Gillingham). Handsome PAVEMENT by *Pearson*: his elegant paving designs (cf. also at Peterborough) have been much underestimated.

North chancel aisle REREDOS. Against the E wall remains of a Perp stone reredos. – STAINED GLASS, E window. Late C17, said to be the gift of Nell Gwyn. – TILES. C15, at the E end. – MONUMENTS. East wall. Bishop Bush † 1558, Bristol's first bishop, deposed by Queen Mary as a married man. Cadaver under a low six-poster with tent top, short fluted Ionic columns and chaste Roman lettering round the cornice, but Gothic inscription on tomb below. – John Campbell † 1817. By *Tyley*. Urn on a square base, with a seated woman in front of it. – Robert Codrington † 1618. Two of the usual kneelers facing each other; but to the l. and r. standing angels pull up curtains hanging from a big semicircular canopy. Open segmental pediment with achievement. – North wall. Mrs Mason † 1767, wife of William Mason the poet. By *John Bacon* to a design of *James Stuart*. On the sarcophagus a medallion showing husband and wife. – Robert Southey † 1843, Poet Laureate 1813–43. Bust by

10. BRISTOL Bust of Robert Southey † 1843, by E. H. Baily

Baily. – Coffin lid with a foliated cross and inscription to 'VILLAM LE [?]EOMETER': William the Geometer, apparently a C13 surveyor (designer of the Elder Lady Chapel?), not *in situ*. – William Powell † 1769. By *J. Paine Jr*. Obelisk with inscription above. Below, big remarkably classical base and in front of it a seated genius with portrait medallion, equally classical. – Maurice ninth Lord Berkeley † 1368 and his mother. Under the E arch between aisle and Elder Lady Chapel, two recumbent effigies, both slender figures, originally finely carved. Tomb-chest with ogee niches, and good C19 ironwork. – The E window of the Elder Lady Chapel has GLASS by *Hardman*.

Berkeley Chapel CHANDELIER. A great rarity, from the Temple Church at Bristol: brass, late C15, possibly Flemish. Square leaves decorate the arms. Central figures, the Virgin above St George. – FRIEZE inserted in the N wall under the open recess: part of the Whitefriars screen given in 1542, with Islamic-looking ornament (see *Chancel*).

South chancel aisle STAINED GLASS. On the E, Holy Spirit window by *Keith New*, 1962. – MONUMENTS. The tomb to the Lord Berkeley who died in 1321 has already been mentioned. It has no figures. – But in two more of the wall recesses are the effigies of two Knights, probably Berkeleys, and the appearance of the later, slim with crossed legs, would fit a date *c*. 1320–5. The earlier may be Maurice II † 1281. – Mrs Middleton † 1826 (N wall). With a big kneeling female figure. Signed by *E. H. Baily*. – Mary Brame Elwyn † 1818. Woman seated on a Grecian chair in front of an altar. – William Brame Elwyn † 1841. Relief of him sinking back and surrounded by mourning relatives. By *Baily* (both S wall). – Flanking the Berkeley antechapel doorway, a pair of consoles that once supported the C17 organ on the pulpitum.

Newton Chapel SCREEN to the W. Timber, of simple design, probably C15. – MONUMENTS. Against the E wall short tomb-chest with lozenges. – Also a Late Perp canopy

11. BRISTOL Berkeley Chapel. Early C14 niche. Late C15 chandelier

with panelled projecting sides against which stand spiral-fluted columns. Instead of an arch a horizontal top with cresting. Quatrefoil-panelled coving inside. – Sir Henry Newton † 1599. Big tomb-chest with recumbent effigies. The kneeling children small against the tomb-chest. The back architecture uninteresting. – Sir John Newton † 1661. Still with recumbent effigy. But the composition is made Baroque by two detached twisted columns. Top with open pediment, the sides ending in scrolls. – Elizabeth Charlotte Stanhope † 1816. By *Westmacott*. A Flaxman conception. The young woman is seen standing up and being received by an angel behind her. – Memorial to Bishop Trelawny, bronze plaque with two angels, by *Alfred Drury*.

Crossing Screen with tall, wide open four-centred arches. By the younger *Pearson*, 1904. – PULPIT. Its panels with Flamboyant tracery from the pulpit given, it is said, by Abbot Elyot in 1525.

North transept STAINED GLASS. E window, early-c14 fragments and more c15 fragments. In Pearson's N window, glass by *Powell* in memory of Edward Colston, 1890. – MONUMENTS. Abbot David, resigned 1234, † 1253. Coffin lid with no longer recognizable effigy in shallow relief. The slab comes from the Elder Lady Chapel, whose initiator Abbot David was. – Major W. Gore † 1814. By *Tyley*. Two standing figures of soldiers l. and r. of a base for an urn. Portrait medallion on the base. Rather big and rather silly, in the theatrical gestures of the soldiers. – Mary Carpenter † 1877. Circular medallion with portrait. By *J. Havard Thomas*, 1878.

South transept SCULPTURE. Large slab with relief of the Harrowing of Hell (Christ harrying Hell for the redeemed, the figures on the r., while Satan writhes below). Earlier than the abbey, possibly from a cemetery chapel on the site (Smith 1977). Late Anglo-Saxon rather than Early Norman, say *c.* 1050: note the very disorderly and excited arrangement of the folds of the mantle, and the profile of Satan. – The slab stands on a pair of NORMAN COLONNETTES with decorated multi-scalloped capitals. Probably from the cloister. – MONUMENTS. Emma Craufurd. By *Chantrey*, 1823. Grecian altar with double-portrait in profile. – Bishop Gray † 1834, by *Baily*. Portrait on the pedestal of an urn. Two standing angels l. and r.

Nave and aisles PULPIT. 1903. – FONT. Small, c16? – MONUMENTS. Dame Joan Young † 1603 and Sir John Young. Only her effigy, recumbent. Tomb-chest with kneeling children. But the lid is carried by two small winged genii at the corners. Black columns and simple top. The sculptor is known, *Samuel Baldwin* of Stroud. – Sir Charles Vaughan † 1630. Semi-reclining figure. Two columns, and outside two remarkably quiet, classical allegorical figures. The top architecture also remarkably classical. Open segmental pediment with two reclining figures and thick garlands below the ends of the segmental sides of

12. BRISTOL Sculpture, *c.* 1050. The Harrowing of Hell

the pediment. – Dean Elliot † 1891. Recumbent effigy by *Forsyth*, 1895. – Dean Pigou † 1916. Recumbent effigy by *N. A. Trent*.

CLOISTER, CHAPTER HOUSE, GATEHOUSE

CLOISTER. Of the Norman cloister no more exists than the two colonnettes in the S transept referred to above. (The entrance to the chapter house is dealt with below.) The entrance to the cloister down several steps from the transept is c19 work, but at the S end of the E walk, the only walk surviving, there is a doorway with a depressed ogee gable and crockets climbing up the outside of the jambs as well as the gable. This seems to belong to the early c14.

13. BRISTOL Chapter house, interior, *c.* 1150–70

The present w wall of the E walk cuts into it. This has three-light openings with four-centred heads and cannot be earlier than the late C 15. Against the N pier, where the beginning of the N walk also remains, are two niches. The roof corbels with heads are original. – STAINED GLASS. Precious fragments of C 14 and C 15 glass in the openings. – MONUMENTS. Thomas Daniel † 1802. White and brown marble. Big standing putto. – Elizabeth Draper, Sterne's Eliza, a typical and very good work by *John Bacon*, 1780, with two amply draped standing allegorical figures. – Elizabeth Cookson † 1852. In the most exuberant Rococo taste. The forms are exactly those one would use for a fireplace. The inscription is in the place of the hearth opening. – A. A. Henderson † 1807, with the figure of a kneeling young Roman.

EAST RANGE. This is in its masonry still Norman. On the upper floor was the Dormitory. Below, the principal room is the CHAPTER HOUSE, completely Late Norman, i.e. of c. 1150–70, with its vestibule. The VESTIBULE is low, and three bays wide by two bays deep, to cover the depth of the dormitory above and allow the chapter house greater height. The three openings from the cloister are round-arched with columns with many-scalloped capitals. But the arches between the 'aisles' of the vestibule are pointed, as the bays are not square: early for pointed arches, but cf. Malmesbury and St John Devizes. The six bays are rib-vaulted; the ribs are rolls with beaded sides. Small bosses. Blank arches on shallow niches along the N and S sides with segmental heads and a continuous roll moulding. – The chapter house itself is entered by a doorway flanked by twin-arched windows with a middle colonnette of Purbeck marble, possibly original, and if so an early use of the material. The chapter house is again rib-vaulted, in two high and large bays. The transverse arches are flat with rolls l. and r. The flat top has two zigzags affronted, as it were, to form a frieze of lozenges. The cross-ribs have bold zigzags. The decoration of the N and S walls is indeed a striking example of what animated effects the Late Norman style can achieve with nothing but abstract material. Lowest tier with the same blank arches or shallow niches as in the vestibule. Upper tier with a blank arcade of intersected arches, the shafts alternatingly plain and spiral-fluted with beading, the arches all spiral-fluted with beading and a little nailhead. Then the large lunettes, patterned in such a way that again the effect is that of enriched zigzag work. Yet only one of the four lunettes has an actual un-intermittent band of vertical zigzag. The others are rather like diagonally interwoven strands. The w wall is different (with a lunette filled by arcading with intersected arches which rise absurdly to the apex and then fall again). The E wall was rebuilt after the riots of 1831, and again in mid-C 20 with much clear glass engraved with lists of deans etc., bringing in more light than a Norman

space is used to. – The rest of the cloister area is closed to visitors. To the E of the S range, the Abbot's Lodging became the Bishop's Palace, ruined in the riots of 1831; the last of the ruins were cleared away in 1963.

w of the C 19 nave, the GREAT GATEHOUSE. This has its Late Norman gateways, one for carriages and one for pedestrians. Again (as in the chapter house) spiral-shafted and beaded columns and capitals, here with leaf-decoration. Arches with zigzag, zigzag placed at an angle to the surface, and more such motifs. The interior rib-vaulted, again with zigzag and beading on transverse arches and ribs, and with ribs and interlaced blank arcades on the E and w walls. In one of the arch mouldings on the S, i.e. the Abbey, side, a roll moulding running through medallions. The upper parts were rebuilt c. 1500 (arms of Abbot Newland), but drastically restored in the C 19.

Further on monastic remains, College Green, the harbour and the city of Bristol, see the latest edition of B of E *North Somerset and Bristol.*

Bristol: Clifton

CATHEDRAL CHURCH OF ST PETER
AND ST PAUL *Roman Catholic*

(Contribution by Philip M. Draper, slightly revised.)

Bristol (at Clifton to avoid the same title as an Anglican bishop) was one of the thirteen Catholic sees established in England in 1850. The present arresting structure on Pembroke Road is the newest of the C 20 English cathedrals. It replaces the C 19 Cathedral of the Apostles on Park Place (see B of E *North Somerset and Bristol*, 1958), now left disgracefully to rot: it incorporated in a remarkable neo-classical shell, begun by *Henry Goodridge* 1834, *Charles Francis Hansom's* neo-Romanesque interior of 1848 and façade of 1878 (comments by Peter Howell and Roderick O'Donnell, 1982).

The new cathedral, designed 1965 by *F. S. Jennett, R. Weeks* and *A. Poremba* of Percy Thomas & Partners, was begun in 1970 and consecrated in 1973. In plan it is an irregular hexagon, the main part of the cathedral being pentagonal with attached entrance narthex, baptistery, and chapel l. of the sanctuary. The chief exterior feature is a dominant lantern with tripartite flèche rising over the sanctuary. Two main entrances are the portal of St Paul from Clifton Road and the portal of St Peter from Pembroke Road, the latter raised over the entry to the car-park, which, with a social centre, is sited under the cathedral, as the ground is sloping. The interior is impressive, the nave fairly low, with complicated roof design, and the sanctuary seemingly flooded with light and reaching ever higher (the

14 and 15. BRISTOL: CLIFTON
Architects Jennett, Weeks and Poremba of Percy Thomas
& Partners. Designed 1965, built 1970–3

illusion failing, however, under the lantern space). This is not, as Liverpool is, a theatre in the round. In the N W corner to the r. of St Paul's door, the Lady Chapel, and to the E the baptistery and Blessed Sacrament Chapel, and on the l. the narthex with its upper galleries.

None of the FURNISHINGS is from the old cathedral. FONT by *Simon Verity*. The Portland stone base is hexagonal, with fishes and doves, and the Purbeck bowl is circular, with carved inscription. – Portal DOORS by *William Mitchell*, given by the City and County of Bristol. They are of fibreglass and metallic filler, and show the arms of the City and the Bishop of Clifton. – STAINED GLASS in the narthex by *Henry Haig*, the larger depicting the Pentecost, the smaller Jubilation. The windows are made of over 8,000 pieces of glass set in epoxy resin. – Stations of the Cross, low-relief CARVINGS in concrete by *Mitchell*. – SCREEN to Blessed Sacrament Chapel and votive candle STAND by *Brother Patrick* of Prinknash Abbey. – STATUE of the Madonna in the Lady Chapel by *T. Jones*.

For the local setting of Clifton, see the latest edition of B of E *North Somerset and Bristol*.

Canterbury

CATHEDRAL CHURCH OF CHRIST *Anglican*

(Based on B of E *North East and East Kent*, 1983, by John Newman, further revised, with information from Canon Ingram Hill, Jane Geddes, Frank Jenkins, Tim Tatton-Brown and John Newman.)

Plan, Fig. 16, from Britton's *Cathedral Antiquities*, 1821–3.

Some references (see Recent Literature): Caviness 1977, 1981; Cherry 1978; Harvey 1978; McLees 1973; Woodman 1981.

INTRODUCTION

The silvery grey mass of the cathedral as it appears in the distance, say from Harbledown Hill or St Thomas's Hill to the W, or from the medieval city wall, rising above the jumbled red roofs of the city, seems almost conventionally perfect, with its lofty central tower and its pair of W towers, vigorously pinnacled but quite low. Indeed only in the view dead E from, say, Rheims Way is the shortness of the W towers, here seen as a broad plinth for Bell Harry, really overcome. But in the close view it is Wastell's tower that draws everything together, slender but strong, and tall

enough to stand against the long extended body of the building, from the W towers to the turrets and battlements of the strangely castle-like E end. Inside, the classic grandeur and poise of the C14 nave, and the leggy, experimental C12 choir stay visually separate. As for the unique series of floor-levels rising eastward from the nave, neither camera nor pen can convey the actual mounting experience, the *O altitudo!* for pilgrims streaming up to Becket's shrine.

Throughout the history of the Christian Church in England, since St Augustine's mission from Rome in 597 to reconvert the country, Canterbury Cathedral has stood at its heart, the seat of the Archbishop, Primate of all Eng-

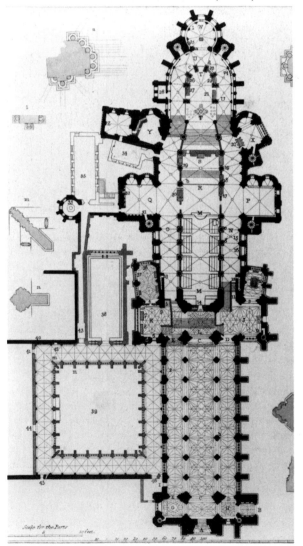

16. CANTERBURY Plan from Britton, 1822 (see left)

17. CANTERBURY Air view from the south-east in 1935

land. The Saxon cathedral remains only in the words of Edmer, who knew it before 1070. During 1070–7 the first Norman archbishop, Lanfranc, rebuilt the cathedral church much larger. That too has virtually disappeared, though the present nave and main transepts stand on Lanfranc's foundations. (The scene of Becket's murder in 1170 was Lanfranc's N transept.) Today the shell of the choir and E transepts remains as the work of Lanfranc's successor Anselm, work consecrated in 1130: a shell only, because the choir was gutted by fire in 1174. The interior of the choir was rebuilt in 1175–9 under a French master mason, *William of Sens*, and extended eastwards under his successor *William the Englishman* in 1179–84 to house the shrine of the new archbishop saint, Thomas à Becket. The successors of Lanfranc's nave and transepts are Perp; the decision to rebuild was taken in 1378, and work went on for almost a century after that, all to a consistent design. The building of the great central tower during the 1490s, it has recently been discovered, took place in two separate phases with a distinct change of intention partway. Lanfranc's N W tower lasted until the early C 19, when, sad to say, it gave way to a replica by *George Austin* of the early C 15 S W tower. So there is no irregular, Frenchily picturesque W front. Austin, the cathedral surveyor, carried out the first major restoration *c.* 1820–48; *W. D. Caröe* carried out the second, renewing pinnacles and tracery, in the 1920s, and there was some work on the S E side of the choir by *J. L. Pearson* in 1888–90.

The total internal length is 515 ft, that of the E transepts 155 ft 8 in., of the W transepts 125 ft. The choir vault is 69 ft high, the nave vault 80 ft high. The W towers are almost 157 ft in height, the central tower, including the

18. CANTERBURY View from the south-west

pinnacles, is a few inches short of 250 ft. The cathedral is largely built of Caen stone, but Quarr stone is also used in the Lanfranc and Anselm work (that is, French limestone was supplemented by southern English limestone), and Kentish rag in some of the later medieval work, e.g. the nave buttresses; all other stones present (e.g. Doulting, Portland, Bath etc. and today Lepine from France) came with restoration work. In the c 15 brickwork, for its greater lightness, was used faced with stone, c. 1470 in the NW gable and in the 1490s for the central tower. Inside, as well as the Purbeck marble shafts introduced by William of Sens in work begun 1175, additional stones include a rare pink marble, probably Mediterranean, used in the Trinity Chapel work of the 1180s around Becket's shrine; fragments of it also survive from the shrine itself. Marble used in the c 13 shrine of Edward the Confessor at Westminster may be comparable to it. (Our new information on materials comes from Mr Tatton-Brown.)

Documentation for the building is far fuller than for any other English medieval cathedral. Bede recounts the foundation of the cathedral by Augustine. Edmer, a monk of Canterbury, early in the c 12 tells in a long but puzzling description what it looked like before fire destroyed it in 1067, as well as much about the rebuildings under Lanfranc and Anselm. Most precious of all is Gervase's eye-witness account of the building before the fire of 1174 and of the progress year by year in rebuilding the choir in the 1170s and 80s. Finally, in 1845, Professor Robert Willis published his architectural history of the cathedral, in most respects the last word on the subject. Part of his translation of Gervase is reprinted in Salzman 1967.

ROMAN REMAINS

In 1975 part of a masonry building was excavated in the angle between the nave and s w transept of the present cathedral, apparently well below the bottom of the Norman cathedral's foundation trenches (Jenkins). Farther to the E, in 1979–80 a large Roman mosaic was found, partly cut through by St Gabriel's Chapel of the crypt (s side). Associated finds suggest that the building containing the mosaic may have been a Roman temple (Tatton-Brown).

THE SAXON CATHEDRAL

Bede says that Augustine in 602 rehallowed a church that had been built for Roman Christians, and consecrated it as Christ Church. In the mid-c 8 Cuthbert built a second church, dedicated to St John, E of Christ Church and almost touching it, i.e. in an axial layout familiar from St Augustine's Abbey nearby (and cf. the Saxon layout at Wells) The second church was for baptisms, certain judicial trials and burials. What the first church was like we do not know. Archbishop Odo c. 950 heightened the walls, but it was completely pulled down by Lanfranc. Edmer, a schoolboy at the time, made a detailed description of it in his *De Reliquiis S. Audoeni, etc.* It was arranged, he says, in some respects like St Peter's at Rome; i.e. there was an E apse, raised above a crypt. The church also had a w altar, probably in an apse, so that the plan was like the abbey church at Abingdon of 675, to give an English parallel, and like the Early Christian plan of e.g. Orléansville in North Africa, and the early c 9 plan of Fulda. Edmer speaks also of aisles, and two towers, about the middle of the church, outside or above the aisles. If by 'super' Edmer meant outside, then he will have been describing towers of the sort familiar from Ottonian examples (cf. Exeter). The s tower had an altar in it.

ARCHBISHOP LANFRANC'S CATHEDRAL

Lanfranc, abbot of Bec, was in 1066 nominated by Duke William as first abbot of St-Étienne at Caen. When William captured the throne of England, Lanfranc did not have long to wait for further promotion; in 1070 he was called over to become the first Norman Archbishop of Canterbury. At once he set about rebuilding the cathedral, and,

says Edmer, practically completed it in seven years. That was extraordinarily fast work. The E end, where building began, has gone, leaving no trace. The ends of the transepts, however, are marked; the s transept by a chunk of the s wall, and by c. 20 ft of the SE quoin, with pilaster buttresses set back from the angle, and a string-course of almost square profile taken round them; the N transept by much masonry of the w wall, and the NW quoin, with two nicks in the angle, not one. (Part too of the NE quoin remains, masked by the chapter house.) So the transepts were one bay deep, two bays E–W. Gervase tells us that each had an E apse. There is evidence that Lanfranc's transept chapels were slightly longer than the c 15 E chapels of the present NW and SW transepts: on the N, above the Lady Chapel fan-vault, are remains of the s part of a stilted apse (Tatton-Brown), while outdoors on the s, the foot of Langton's c 13 tomb can be seen sticking through the E wall of St Michael's Chapel.

There was a crossing tower. The nave, with aisles, coincided in dimensions with the present nave, eight bays plus a ninth over which stood the two w towers. The NW tower, recorded by Buckler's measured drawings, was extremely severe, with a pronounced taper, clasping buttresses, cut back several times at the angles, and eight stages in all, marked by string-courses. Simple arcading on the top three stages. Parts of Lanfranc's towers are still visible inside, though not to the public eye: e.g. a cushion capital etc. of the E face of the NW tower, now above the N aisle vault; and fragments of the base of his central tower in the roofs below Bell Harry tower (Tatton-Brown). Lanfranc's church also had a crypt (see below). Even these scanty remains are enough to show that Lanfranc's cathedral was nothing but a transplantation from Normandy. indeed, to be more precise, own brother to the abbeys at Caen, St-Étienne and Ste-Trinité, begun in the 1060s. As Willis was the first to note, not only the plans but the dimensions of transepts and nave are the same at Canterbury and St Étienne to within a foot: the nave 187 ft long and 72 ft wide, the transept 127 ft across. The w front was, in the massing, close to Ste-Trinité, the towers more firmly expressed than at St-Étienne.

ARCHBISHOP ANSELM'S CHOIR

Lanfranc's choir was short-lived. Under his successor Anselm a new choir took its place, stupendously increased in size, with a second pair of transepts and three E chapels, all raised upon a crypt. The new choir exceeded even Lanfranc's nave in length and width; the total area of the cathedral was practically doubled. No reason is given to explain this vast enlargement; but the result was to provide seven new altars, and we know that many of the early, beatified archbishops were reburied with great solemnity in the Norman cathedral. Perhaps then, as Willis says, 'shrine-room' was needed. At any rate, the new building was not only large, it was sumptuously decorated. William of Malmesbury laid great emphasis on the splendour of the decoration – stained glass, marble pavement, wall paintings ('adeo splendide erexit, ut nihil tale possit in Anglia videri, in vitrearum fenestrarum luce, in marmorei pavimenti nitore, in diversicoloribus picturis . . .'). Prior Ernulf (1096–1107) began the work. Anselm financed it for the first seven years, from 1096. The choir was completed under Ernulf's successor, Conrad, and consecrated in 1130.

EXTERIOR. The fire of 1174 gutted the choir but left the outer walls standing. Externally they were heightened by William of Sens, but very little modified. Only the Trinity Chapel at the E end was demolished, to make way for William the Englishman's very much larger Trinity Chapel. The plan of Ernulf's choir is strangely complicated. The choir aisles run from the crossing for five bays, before a second pair of transepts opens out, deeper than the w transepts, so that each has two E apses, not one. Projecting w stair-towers. The third church at Cluny was being built at this very moment, c. 1095–1100, with two pairs of transepts. The choir aisles continue E of the transepts for one more bay, and then the curvature of the apse begins. As it does so, a square chapel with an E apse and a w stair-turret projects, masking the curve. The N chapel is dedicated to St Andrew, the s to St Anselm. The turrets, aligned with the aisle walls, stand askew to the chapels, which hug the curve. The chapels are apsed. This plan, which looks so odd outside, enables the chapels within, in spite of their position, to have altars facing due E. In France radiating chapels were not obliged to be aligned to the E, but in England for some reason that obligation was felt. Hence the contorted chapel plans at Canterbury, and also at Norwich, Lincoln (St Hugh's Choir), Leominster and Muchelney. All these excrescences tend to mask the great length of the choir, but we could deduce that it was nine bays long, with an apse and ambulatory, even if Gervase had not told us that. The E chapel, as has already been said, was removed in 1180.

Examination of the exterior may as well begin on the SE with ST ANSELM'S CHAPEL. The elevation has two storeys, the lower being the crypt. Above each comes a deep band of blind arcading, except that the apse is stopped below the upper band. Broad pilaster buttresses, with cut-back angles, clasp the corners of the chapel, and a slimmer one marks the s wall off into two bays. String-courses are continued round the buttresses at all levels, the lower two plain, the top three with billet moulding. The windows are large, those that light the crypt plain, the main windows, best seen in the apse, lofty, shafted, with a double roll round the head. The two s windows were replaced in 1336 by a grand Dec five-lighter, with in the

head a circle full of ogee-lobed trefoils, and big subcusped trefoils l. and r., the main cusps split back like swallow-tails. Such an idiom had been developed at Canterbury more than thirty years before, e.g. on Prior Eastry's screen (see Furnishings, Choir, below), and before that in the chancel at Chartham.

The SOUTH-EAST TRANSEPT gives a fuller idea of Ernulf's architecture. The system is exactly the same as before, except that the upper band of arcading is eliminated and all the string-courses are plain. The third level of windows represents Ernulf's clerestory (but only represents it, because the undercut string-course and the leaves on the shaft capitals show that this is late C 12, not early C 12, workmanship). The clerestory over the aisles was of course replaced by the work of the 1170s. So it is in the transepts alone that we have the full Ernulfian elevation. William of Sens heightened the transept with a second, pointed, set of clerestory windows and, a memorable feature, a rose-window in the s wall at this level. The gable was either renewed by Austin early in the C 19 or, more likely, replaced in 1930 (Tatton-Brown). The staircase-tower, projecting to the w, rises free for two whole stages above eaves level. It must, as we shall see in a moment, have been heightened in the mid-C 12. So the transept rises prodigiously lofty, and to appreciate the early C 12 building properly, one has to reduce it in the mind's eye to its original, stockier proportions. The impression then is of spacious orderliness, with large areas of plain walling organized by the buttresses and string-courses. Above the main window heads, and at the same level on the windowless tower, spring shallow relieving arches, spanning the space from buttress to buttress. The windows do not all sit centrally under the arches, which seem not merely functional, strengthening the wall, but a further attempt to articulate the dumb wall surface. The low band of arcading gains maximum emphasis, by contrast, a prestissimo rhythm of colonnettes, spanned by tiny arches, and a second sequence of intersecting, billet-moulded arches. The colonnettes, almost all renewed, alternate round and octagonal, some with zigzag or a scale pattern on them; the block capitals are, some of them, richly carved with interlace, leaves or even figure scenes. Crumbled as the carving is, one can appreciate the style well enough. It is a style to be met again in the crypt. The staircase-tower is obviously alien to the rest, with its crust of surface carving that leaves hardly a square inch of smooth wall. Yet the lowest of the four rows of arcading has the intersecting, billet-moulded arches just as has been described. That then is the top of Anselm's work, meant as a lacy fringe, like the arcading on St Anselm's Chapel. The top three stages of the tower on the other hand break out into a riot of zigzag, the shafts are composite, set against tiny diapered piers, and there are no intersecting arches.

19. CANTERBURY The west end in 1822

Scallop, not block, capitals. The timber spirelet on top has 'secret' notched-lap joints in it, therefore dating to the late C 12 or early C 13 – certainly post-1174 fire – and perhaps some of the earliest structural timberwork in Kent, certainly in the cathedral (Hewett and Tatton-Brown, *Archaeologia Cantiana*, 92, 1976).

The AISLE windows fill the full width of three bays, in a narrow–wide–narrow rhythm. Here in particular one realizes how exceptionally large these windows are for the early C 12. Willis supposed that they were heightened in 1175 and the old arches, with chip-carved patterns on the voussoirs, reset; but the voussoirs will fit only at their present height. William of Malmesbury mentions the 'light from the glass windows' as the first of the memorable features of Anselm's choir. In 1130 it must indeed have seemed astonishing.

On to what these great windows threw light we hardly know now. We do know that this choir had alternating round and octagonal piers, as they were rebuilt in that form after the fire and Gervase said the new pillars were like the old in form (see below on the late C 12 interior). This early C 12 alternation would seem to have been influential elsewhere, e.g. *c.* 1120 at Peterborough (Cherry 1978). The only internal features of Ernulf's work to survive the fire and the subsequent remodelling are wall-shafts and part of the wall-arcading along the aisle walls. In position and size the arcading corresponds with the external arcading, but it is left plain. Probably then it was painted, and maybe one should imagine the interior blazing with colour, illuminated by an ample flow of light. Certainly there was no high vault, but a wooden ceiling, which Gervase says was well painted.

Externally the N side of Ernulf's choir matches the S side. But the Treasury, a square building (now a vestry), was put up *c.* 1150 on an open arcaded ground storey on the N side of the NE Chapel of St Andrew, and was heightened in the late C 13. That it was an addition is apparent, not only because it cuts across the external arcading of St Andrew's Chapel, but also because the arcading on the Treasury is of the more advanced kind, found on the tops of the staircase-towers, with compound shafts to support the intersecting arches. The Treasury is ashlar-faced, divided by pilaster buttresses into two bays each way. Entrance arches with outward-pointing zigzag and interlocking noughts and crosses. The ground-storey vault corresponds, two bays by two, on a central compound pier, its round responds taking the transverse arches, but making no provision for the ribs of the quadripartite bay vaults. Scalloped respond capitals enlivened in places with beading and foliage across the mouths of the scallops. Although the Treasury shares a wall with the Infirmary beyond (see B of E *North East and East Kent* under *Monastic buildings*), its interior can only be reached from St Andrew's Chapel. The memorable

thing about it is that the whole area, almost a square (23 ft by 22 ft 9 in.), is covered by an octopartite rib-vault. Nothing like it survives in England. John Bilson compared it closely with the vault of the crossing at Montivilliers in Normandy, which does without the Canterbury wall ribs. The experimental nature of the Treasury vaulting comes out in the way the ribs are brought down, some on wall-shafts (one with heads like those on the central boss), while others die into the wall. W of the Treasury the ruined substructure of the passage which linked it to the choir aisle. The NE transept stair-tower was heightened just like its fellow on the S side. High up in the wall of the NE transept a recess with four squints, belonging to the C 15 Prior's Chapel, linked to the Prior's lodging, and giving a view of four altars in the cathedral.

CRYPT. First some notes on the old Norman (Lanfranc's) crypt, contributed by Mr Tatton-Brown. The W wall of the present W crypt incorporates the W wall of Lanfranc's crypt, the earliest Norman crypt in England. Unlike Anselm's this crypt had three equal bays N–S. The scar from its vaults (lower than Anselm's) is still visible on the W wall, and the two corner columns, capitals (early cushions and abaci) and bases are certainly Lanfranc. The central two capitals and bases are Lanfranc's moved (see Tatton-Brown 1979), and the Lanfranc walling is clear as only rubble work (sandstone, flints, re-used Roman etc.), while Anselm's work is Caen and Quarr-stone ashlar.

Anselm's new Norman choir was in its entirety raised upon a crypt, a crypt more lofty and spacious than any previously built in England, standing so far above ground that it is full of light; the type, that is to say, of the crypts of St Maria im Capitol, Cologne, and of Speyer, both mid-C 11. The choir is thus many steps higher than Lanfranc's nave. Steps lead down to N and S of the crossing, the walls of the N flight diapered with an incised pattern, each grooved, formed of two strands, as it were, one passing over, one under at every intersection. Stones set lozenge-wise in the S flight. The fire of 1174 did not touch the crypt; nor did William of Sens, except for putting in three stout piers, their capitals re-used from Ernulf's choir, to support new choir piers that did not sit squarely on pre-existing ones in the crypt. So the crypt is remarkably perfectly preserved (although partly enclosed as a museum at present). Nave and aisles, divided by piers; the nave subdivided into a further nave and aisles by two rows of columns, twenty-two in all. They support groin-vaults with broad, unmoulded transverse ribs, resting on semicircular responds against the piers. The system continues into the transepts, with one free-standing column and two E apses, equipped with PISCINAS and AUMBRIES, and into the chapels, St Gabriel's (S) and Holy Innocents' (N), which each have an apse, with plain PISCINA and AUMBRY, and two free-standing columns to take the vault.

20. CANTERBURY Prior Ernulf's crypt (begun 1096) in 1822

21. CANTERBURY Capital, before 1130, in Ernulf's crypt

The glory of the crypt is the carved capitals of the columns. (For the C7 carvings from Reculver, see *Furnishings* below.) The plain block shape is left untouched on the responds but the columns not only have shafts fluted spirally or in zigzags, or carved with a scale pattern, but carving on the undersides and the faces, the four semicircular fields that the block capital offers. This is the most ambitious, most finely conceived and, equally important, the best preserved Early Romanesque sculpture in the country. Some capitals have bold interlacing beaded strands, others, e.g. the two in Holy Innocents' Chapel, splendidly luxuriant leaves. But the most ambitious are carved with figure subjects, almost all of creatures fighting, their antagonism giving the linear patterns into which the designs naturally fall a lithe vigour that is tremendously exciting. The N column of the central pair in the nave has perhaps the most brilliant design of all, a wyvern fighting a dog. Another face of this capital is carved with jugglers. A similar comical subject, animals playing musical instru-

ments, is in St Gabriel's Chapel. The s capital in the bay furthest w seems different in feeling from the rest, more tender and truer to nature. The subjects are a man on horseback, a doe, and a man struggling with a beast. The evidence that the carving was done after the capitals were in place is one other of the s capitals, which has only one face finished; on yet another the design (of interlacing strands) is merely blocked out. The octagonal column in the N transept of the crypt, with crockets on the capital snapped off, is evidently a substitution of 1175. (But a simplified Corinthian capital at the w end of the s aisle, though it cries out that it is an intruder, may be contemporary with the rest; one like it occurs once in the Infirmary Chapel.)

The two E bays of the crypt nave are swallowed up in the deliciously filigree stone screens of the CHAPEL OF OUR LADY OF THE UNDERCROFT. These screens are cut into by the canopy of the monument of Lady Mohun, who died in 1404, and had in 1396 founded a chantry in the crypt. Masses were, however, said for her in the 1370s, in early 1371–2 Lady de Maun is recorded as donor of £66 13s. 4d. and an iron grille at the w end was paid for in 1378–80, so construction of the chapel must date from the 1370s (Woodman 1981).

The s transept of the crypt was relined in 1363 as the BLACK PRINCE'S CHANTRY (now used as the Huguenots' church), founded in return for a dispensation that allowed the Prince to marry a kinswoman, Joan, Countess of Kent. Piers were formed round the Norman ones, with slender clustered shafts. Lierne vaults with some fine carved bosses, low enough to be well seen: the pelican in her piety, on a nest in an oak tree; Samson and the lion. Two carved faces of immured Norman capitals have been exposed.

For the E crypt, see *Trinity Chapel crypt* below.

THE LATE C12 REBUILDING AND EASTWARD EXTENSION

In 1170 Archbishop Thomas à Becket was murdered in the N W transept of the cathedral. The political consequences of the murder were serious enough for Henry II, but it was also an act the most sacrilegious imaginable; so it is hardly surprising that miracles soon began to be worked at the tomb of the martyred archbishop. A second calamity came hard on the heels of the first. In 1174 fire gutted the choir, destroying the glass and the wall paintings, and left the arcades a tottering wreck. Gervase tells us that the monks at first wanted to patch them up. They summoned a number of masons, from France as well as from England, and asked their opinions. The one who impressed them, by 'his lively genius and good reputation', was *William of Sens*, so the rest were dismissed, and William was left to come to the conclusion that the Norman arcades and

clerestory must be demolished. That meant that the width, but not the height, of the new work was fixed; William of Sens was able to design an interior elevation virtually unrestricted by what already stood.

Before we embark on a description, Gervase's chronicle of the building must be briefly repeated. It allows us to follow the construction year by year, a unique experience as far as English medieval architecture is concerned. Work began at the w end of the choir, and during 1175 two piers each side were erected. In 1176 came a third pier each side and the arches of these first three bays, together with the aisle vaults to support them. In 1177 two further bays were completed, and the triforium, clerestory and high vault for all five bays. During 1178 William of Sens supervised the construction of the sixth bay of the choir, and the transepts, and at the beginning of 1179 was preparing to turn the high vault over the high altar when he fell from the scaffolding so severely that, recovering only slowly, he had to return to France, leaving the work to a successor, *William the Englishman*. Thus it was English William's task to build the Trinity Chapel and Corona. He completed the new crypt by 1181, and set up the outer walls of the Trinity Chapel. In 1182 the piers went up, and the walls of the Corona. By the end of 1184 all was vaulted and structurally complete. They must have worked at a prodigious speed – no wonder, as donations must have poured in. So for the second time the cathedral grew a great eastward extension. The new Trinity Chapel was to be a chapel in honour of St Thomas, because, says Gervase, it was in the old one that Thomas had said his first mass, and under which he had been buried. After the rebuilding Thomas's tomb was replaced in the crypt, for the shrine was not set up until 1220. The original purpose of the Corona is not altogether clear. Gervase calls it 'turris'. (The Archbishop's Throne only stood in it c. 1800–1977.)

Lanfranc had introduced a new kind of cathedral architecture to England, and now, a century later, William of Sens initiated a second revolution, by importing the Early Gothic style of the Île de France. Gervase puts his finger on the essential differences between the new choir and the old: the piers were increased in height but not in girth, i.e. made of slenderer proportions, so that the new choir is higher by the height of the whole clerestory; there is a vault not a flat roof, plenty of marble shafting is used, and the capitals are carved, not plain. That is to say, there is a dramatic increase in height, but none in the other dimensions, and the supporting shafts are stressed rather than the supporting wall. The arcade arches are pointed, but by no means all the subsidiary ones, and of course the vaults are all rib-vaults. All these features can be found elsewhere in England, combined to form truly Gothic structures, even a little before 1175, at Ripon and at Roche Abbey, Yorkshire, c. 1170, the culmination of a Cistercian tradition. By c.

1180 Wells was begun, and Gothic was firmly established in the North and West. Canterbury, to say it again, is not an indigenous growth like these; but it was the over-whelming prestige of Canterbury that ensured the swift spread of the new style throughout the country.

Detailed description naturally starts inside, with the w half of the choir. The w respond each side is Ernulf's, heightened 12 ft to match the new piers; see the shallow base moulding, compared to the boldly moulded new pier bases with their undercurling spurs. The piers alternate round and octagonal, a plan also Ernulf's, as we have already deduced from Gervase. The foliage capitals, of noble acanthus fronds, are so close to contemporary French capitals that they must have been carved by a Frenchman. No two are alike, but all are designed with a classic restraint that equals any on the Continent. A development in style is discernible. The fronds on the 1175–6 capitals are carved as units. The fronds of the next year's capitals on the other hand, the w piers to the transepts and the pier w of each, tend to break up into separate indented lobes, like oak leaves. This busier handling is exploited further in the pier capitals of the next year, in the E half of the choir. The fronds clothe a circular or octagonal funnel, and develop into crockets at the diagonals to support a square abacus, chamfered at the corners. Pointed arches with two moulded orders, and an inconspicuous row of nailhead. At the next level come the gallery openings, two pairs per bay, with pointed arches and semicircular superarches over each pair. Shafts for each member of the arches, with crocket, not acanthus, capitals and square abaci. Clerestory, with a passage, and a single, shafted light, pointed. The vaults are sexpartite, pointed in section, the ribs with a billet between the three rounded mouldings, intersecting at big bosses of foliage. The carved foliage and the sexpartite vaults are part of the common stock of French church architecture in the 1170s. But the elevation, considered more closely, is derived specifically from Sens. There too the columns are inordinately lofty, the arches that span them relatively narrow, and in particular the gallery is pushed high up out of the way, and has the same paired openings. In two vital respects William departed from his model. First, his sex-partite vaults were not given alternately major and minor supports, for the variation round–octagonal does not affect the spatial rhythm. So whereas the space strides majestically down the nave of Sens, double-bay by double-bay, the flow at Canterbury is smooth and uninterrupted, in spite of the fact that the sexpartite vaults draw the bays into pairs. The second departure is more serious. At Sens the piers are coupled, here they are single. This stresses their height, and the disparity between the high arcades and the low gallery and clerestory above is undeniably disturbing.

So far nothing has been said of the most striking decorative element introduced by William of Sens, the use of black polished Purbeck marble. It is used for all the minor verticals, i.e. the gallery and clerestory shafts, and the wall-shafts that stand on the abaci of the arcade capitals to take the vault ribs, set in trios or singly according to the number of ribs there are to carry. The horizontals that are picked out in black marble are the upper member of all abaci, and a thin billet-moulded string-course, at gallery sill-level, carried round the shafts as a shaft-ring. This play of dark on light is worked out with admirable logic and consistency. Dark shafts were to become all the rage in England (e.g. at Salisbury in the early C13). In France, however, they were barely known. Professor Jean Bony points only to Notre Dame la Grande, Valenciennes, of 1171, and remarks that detached marble shafts had occurred in England even earlier at Iffley, and in the crypt of York Minster; to which he might have added the chapter-house doorway at Rochester, and the mid-C12 nave piers at Dover Priory.

To complete our survey of the first three years' work, we must look at the CHOIR AISLES. The outer walls retain much that is early C12 undamaged. Below the windows, as has been noted above, runs blank shafted arcading, with plain block capitals. Several shafts and capitals were replaced in the 1170s, so that one can compare the axe-cut mouldings of c. 1100 with the chisel-carved ones of 1175. Ernulf's wall-shafts were also retained, and adapted by making them higher (see the change from several blocks per course to one block) and by removing the subsidiary shafts, which were not needed when a rib-vault replaced Ernulf's groin-vault (as one supposes it to have been, surely not a tunnel-vault as Willis thought). The ribs are trimmed with tiny rows of dogtooth, except the transverse ribs, which are not only semicircular, not pointed, but have powerful zigzag overlapping the roll mouldings. This is an extremely early appearance of dogtooth; and such under-cut zigzag would also be hard to parallel at a date as early as this.

So to the EAST TRANSEPTS. They are identical, except as noted below; so the description describes both. William of Sens emphasized the entrance arches by clothing these four piers in detached marble shafts, one against each of the eight faces, with their own small capitals, masking the main capital, as e.g. at Laon. There is a second tier of shafts to take the many vault ribs that converge here. Shaft-rings. The transepts, unlike the aisles, were carefully remodelled to obscure the fact that the walls are Ernulf's up to the sill of the second clerestory. This makes a four-storey elevation. The main windows and the blank arcading below keep to the Norman proportions, but the mouldings and shafting are brought up to date, the former chiselled into a slim roll or a double roll sown with dogtooth, the latter given Purbeck shafts and crocket capitals. One or two early C12 bases remain, and the chip-

23. CANTERBURY South choir aisle,
looking up to Trinity Chapel

carved voussoirs of the blank W window. The SE transept keeps the round-headed arches of the arcading, but in the NE transept the arches are just pointed. At gallery level comes a second band of blank arcading, the arches acutely pointed; at clerestory level, the wall-passage is screened with arches on shafts, five per bay, a wide, round-headed one flanked by pairs of pinched pointed ones. In the second clerestory the windows are pointed and distinctly taller; in front of the wall-passage trios of pointed arches are set, on skinny Purbeck shafts and crazily elongated. The centre-piece of the end wall is a big rose window, quite plain, without the spoke-like radiating colonnettes one would expect. Moulded string-courses, two with billet, mark the stages. Sexpartite vault, on slender wall-shafts taken down to the ground. The E apses have rib-vaults too, their entrance arches made pointed and given especially complex, undercut mouldings, on crocket capitals and Purbeck

shafts. Note the felicitous design of the bases here. More significant is the fact that the abaci of these shafts are round, not square, an important inflection of the French vocabulary.

E of the transepts there are four more bays of the CHOIR (the presbytery, strictly speaking). William of Sens completed these, according to Gervase, except for the high vaults. A change is at once apparent. The simple alternation of round and octagonal piers is given up in favour of a series of greater variety: first a round pier each side; then an octagonal one with four attached shafts of Purbeck marble and bases for four more shafts, i.e. like the piers flanking the transept openings; then a pair formed of a couple of round shafts with two marble shafts in the angles; and finally an octagonal pier, turning to round a third of the way up. The choir aisles pursue the same system as before, but this is made difficult by the curve that Ernulf's walls take in these three bays, preparing for the apsidal ambulatory. All the wall-shafts here are William's, but Ernulf's wall-arcading survives, and so do the interiors of ST ANDREW's and ST ANSELM's CHAPELS. Both have rib-vaults. That would be a notable fact if the vaults really belonged to the building of c. 1100. But the fact that there is an incomplete series of angle shafts, and the way the vault cuts slightly into the window voussoirs (e.g. in the W wall of St Andrew's Chapel), make it more likely that they are a later adaptation, done before the fire. In St Anselm's Chapel, the shaft capitals are, some of them, carved with stylized flowers and beaded interlace; e.g. one in the apse with more uncompleted carving. In 1178 the entrance arch was reinforced with two more mouldings and shafts with crocket capitals, to mask the thickened walls where the new, wider Trinity Chapel starts away. (In 1889, when J. L. Pearson strengthened the walls of St Anselm's Chapel and removed a late C12 buttress wall built across the chapel apse to support the choir roof, a well-preserved early C12 fresco was revealed, see Furnishings below.)

With that we have reached the point where William the Englishman took over. The fact that William of Sens had carried the choir past the chapels, narrowing the two E bays of the central vessel (and the three E bays of the aisles), shows that the decision had already been taken to enlarge the Trinity Chapel to take arcades, or rather to give room for the shrine of the martyred archbishop, and an ambulatory round it. It is at once clear, however, that English William departed from his predecessor's design from the start. The last piers erected in 1178 begin octagonal and turn to round a third of the way up. Apparently then the last bay was left incomplete by William of Sens. More important than this is the change in floor level. The Trinity Chapel stands sixteen steps higher than the choir, but the steps were not prepared for, since they cut across the base and shaft of the last choir piers.

The conclusion is that it was William the Englishman's idea to build the new crypt (for the new Trinity Chapel needed a wholly new crypt to stand on) decisively higher than Ernulf's crypt. To follow the building year by year one must descend now into the TRINITY CHAPEL CRYPT.

24. CANTERBURY Trinity Chapel crypt, 1179–81

Height is achieved by the vault, which is sharply pointed, yet spans wider distances than Ernulf's bays; for William divides his central space by a single arcade, not two. The vault has ribs, those in the main part of the crypt with a fillet on the central, raised moulding, a form that was to recur constantly in England all through the C 13. Bosses at the intersections, carved as stylized flowers. The main supports are thick, short round piers in couples, with round bases and round, simply moulded capitals, all of Caen stone, except the abaci, which are of Purbeck marble. No square forms, one notes. Semicircular transverse arches, with a slight chamfer, except in the apse, where the piers come closer together and the arches have to be pointed and stilted to reach the same height. The central arcade stands on piers that are of Purbeck marble, very slender round

shafts, with round bases and capitals, the latter deep and with many mouldings. At the E end the crypt chapel (Jesus Chapel) under the Corona also has a rib-vault, with a splendid boss of acanthus leaves. The boss emphasizes by contrast the most forcible impression of the crypt as a whole: its lack of carved decoration. Smooth, moulded forms prevail. Admittedly, in the crypt a simpler treatment is understandable; though Ernulf's crypt is proof enough that not all crypts were treated simply. One dwells on the point because in England, but not on the Continent, by the early C 13, these moulded, unenriched forms, enlivened by the contrast of colour and texture that Purbeck marble gave, were favoured even in the main parts of cathedrals, above ground. Salisbury, begun in 1220, is of course the *locus classicus* of this.

The WATCHING CHAMBER, built above the ambulatory of Ernulf's crypt, where the steps rising to the Trinity Chapel create a pocket of space, was for watching over the safety of Becket's tomb when that was in the new crypt. The space is only about 10 ft high, but an exceedingly depressed quadripartite vault is managed, two bays with moulded ribs, the ribs of the N bay given dogtooth. Bosses never carved. (The watching chamber for the shrine in the Trinity Chapel above was contrived over the E end of the S choir aisle.)

Reascending to the Trinity Chapel, up the sixteen steps, one is aware of a change from the choir, in proportions rather than in idiom. Although the floor level is so much higher, the roof ridge runs on from the choir at exactly the previous level: that is to say, the total height of the elevation is reduced. Yet gallery and clerestory continue at the same level. Only the arcades are reduced in height, or to be more precise, the pier shafts are shortened. William the Englishman's purpose was to unify choir and Trinity Chapel in the distant vista from the W. Seen thus, the apse of the Trinity Chapel was the back drop to the shrine, and the canted E bays of the choir focused attention on it, like the wings of a stage set. If the two were to be read as part of the same set, they had necessarily to share unbroken horizontals. But the proportions of the Trinity Chapel elevation are decisively altered, and, one must say, improved. No longer is the arcade so lofty that the gallery shrinks to an inconspicuous band. Here arcade, gallery and clerestory are balanced evenly against one another. But what crucially strengthens the elevation is the coupling of the arcade piers in depth. Did William the Englishman know from personal experience that that was how the piers in Sens Cathedral were coupled, or had his predecessor left designs in the lodge? And the piers here are made of three types of stone (Purbeck marble, the rare pink marble previously noted and a white pelletal limestone) that make them visually yet stronger. The pink marble is also used for alternate bases, shaft-rings and capitals in the ambulatory (the unworn ones, Purbeck being softer) as well as for lozenges etc. in the pavement around the shrine (Tatton-Brown). Otherwise Purbeck marble is employed as before. The w pier each side has a crocket capital, of Purbeck marble; the rest revert to being of freestone, carved with

25. CANTERBURY Trinity Chapel in 1822

acanthus fronds, with a bunch of leaves projecting to take the soffit moulding. Here the dissolution of the fronds, already noted, into individual lobed leaves springing from a thick central vein is even more noticeable. Arch mouldings, however, exactly as in the choir. Billet and small dogtooth among the crisp angle mouldings. Altogether the vocabulary of the two Williams is almost identical; it is what they are saying that is different. English William still does not exclude the round-headed arch, e.g. from the widest bays of the main arcade. The gallery openings, four per bay, and two in the apse (a real triforium here), are as before, except that the fours are no longer subdivided, two and two. Finally, at the highest level, the clerestory windows are coupled, and screened inside by arches on a slender central shaft. Wall-passage. Rib-vaults, a quadripartite bay plus

the apse, with splendid leaf bosses, bigger than those in the choir vault.

Spacious aisles, vaulted as the choir aisles, with saw-toothed zigzag round the transverse arches. The aisles are full of light from the generous windows. The vaults spring from marble wall-shafts set against projecting piers. The skeleton structure of the Trinity Chapel is here most forcibly felt.

The CORONA, only 27ft in diameter, re-echoes the elevation of the Trinity Chapel. No arcades, of course, but windows that occupy the full width of each bay, repeating the proportions of the apse arcades. Zigzag round the arches. No piers, but Purbeck wall-shafts brought down to the ground. Shaft-rings. Triforium, with single, not grouped, shafts. Nine-sided vault, the tenth rib omitted over the entrance arch. Doorways (with, quite likely, the original wooden doors of the 1180s) l. and r. of the entrance arch, to staircases up to the triforium wall-passage and on to the roof.

CHOIR AND TRINITY CHAPEL EXTERIOR. As we have seen, William of Sens needed to do little to the exterior of the choir, except heighten the aisle walls and raise a new clerestory. Shafted, pointed clerestory windows, and similar ones, on the s side only, to light the gallery. The heightened aisles got additional light from broad trefoil-headed windows, with a scale pattern overlapping the outer moulding, a peculiar motif not used elsewhere in the post-fire work. Structurally the most important feature outside is the flying buttresses that slip inconspicuously down over the aisle roofs. They transmit some of the thrust of the choir vault to the outer walls, and need to, for, as we have seen, the clerestory walls are hollowed out with a wall-passage. They are the earliest exposed flying buttresses in England, although it had of course long been normal to buttress high vaults secretly by transverse arches within the galleries. The heightening of the E transepts has already been described.

The Trinity Chapel and Corona, as has been pointed out, William the Englishman new-built from the ground up. The contrast with the Norman building is decisive. That, for all its large windows, and its bands of arcading, is a structure of load-bearing walls punctured here and there by openings, and reinforced at the angles by shallow buttresses. The Trinity Chapel on the other hand is a frame, of deeply projecting buttresses, and walls which are reduced to little more than vertical and horizontal members by the great windows that occupy space from buttress to buttress. Even by French standards of c. 1180, Canterbury is notably thoroughgoing in the extent that supporting walls are done away with. The great projection of the buttresses is structurally needed, not chosen for visual effect; that one can be sure of by looking at the Corona staircase-towers, which, since the walls are solid, keep

shallow, clasping buttresses. The flying buttresses fall into place as part of this bracing system, though they start so low down, at the level of the sills of the clerestory windows, and are so puny, that they are of relatively little use. Wall buttresses carried up above eaves-level as counterweights. In France, e.g. at St-Remi, Reims, c. 1170–5, far vaster and more adventurous flying buttresses were already in use. In the external decoration there is no such break with the Norman past. Mouldings may have changed, become bolder, less elaborate, and undercut; but they are used in the same ways as before. Horizontal string-courses mask the levels of sill, window head and the springing of the window arches. As for verticals, there are window shafts, with shaft-rings and crocket capitals, and similar shafts in the cut-back angles of the buttresses. Arcading only at clerestory-level on the Corona staircase-towers. The Corona battlements and buttress tops date from 1748–9, largely renewed in artificial stone. Until the mid-c 18 the Corona walls were unfinished.

MAIN TRANSEPTS, NAVE AND TOWERS

The rebuilding of Lanfranc's nave and transepts was first proposed before 1370, by Prior Hathbrand, who opened a subscription list. Work began in 1378, under Archbishop Sudbury (†1381), who paid for the demolition of the old nave (presumably keeping the piers as cores; see *Interior* below) and 'duas alas in parte posteriori ecclesie . . . erexit'. Arthur Oswald (*Burlington Magazine*, 1939) interpreted 'alas' as aisle walls. Certainly, the nave was the first part to be built up again. But then there was a second pause, until 1391, when Prior Chillenden was elected. Leland called him 'the greatest Builder of a Prior that ever was in Christes Church'. Under him the nave was carried on, vaulted c. 1400, and finished by 1405.

Henry Yevele is thought to have been master mason here. His name appears among the highest class of those receiving Christmas livery of the Prior of Canterbury in 1398, the first relevant year for which the lists are preserved. Yevele was at the time King's Master Mason. The shaft-rings on the nave piers are the strongest internal evidence that he designed the nave, for reasons to be given. Yet the attribution has been strongly challenged, on the basis that the documentation, such as it is, may not suggest that Yevele played a leading role, and that a more natural interpretation would be that Thomas Hoo was master mason, an analysis that also minimizes Yevele's role at Westminster Abbey (McLees 1973). But there seems to have been a large payment to Yevele in 1379–80, and his foremost champion, Mr John Harvey, remains in no doubt about the matter (e.g. in Harvey 1978 and *Canterbury Cathedral Chronicle*, 1982). Further on the question, see *Interior* below.

To continue this introductory summary of the Perp work. The s transept was vaulted after 1414, the N transept built from 1448 to after 1468, both following the nave design in practically all respects. The latter, the place where Becket had been murdered, was deeply hallowed. So it seems that hesitation was felt about touching the Norman fabric of it. Eventually, when such scruples were overcome, the original floor level was left unraised. Contemporaneously the Lady Chapel was thrown out E of it. St Michael's Chapel that answers it, E of the s transept, was built c. 1420–8. Meanwhile at the w end, the sw tower was rebuilt in 1424–34, *Thomas Mapilton* being master mason. Its fellow had to wait until 1832 before *George Austin* made it match. The crossing tower had been prepared for under Prior Chillenden, but the tower itself rose only a century later, designed by *John Wastell* and built from c. 1490. The vault bears the arms of Archbishop Warham, who was installed in 1503.

With this outline of events before us, an approach can be made to the w half of the cathedral. The exterior can be taken first, then the interior.

EXTERIOR. In the Perp rebuilding the extent of Lanfranc's nave and transepts was not increased: the nave of eight bays and transepts projecting by a single bay repeat the c 11 plan. The NAVE elevation is straightforwardly Perp, sober and dignified, with the minimum of unnecessary elaboration. The usual deep buttresses rise from a moulded plinth with a blank frieze. The second of their three set-offs admittedly supports a pedestal for a statue under a canopied niche, but the top pinnacles are quite standard, with crockets and panelling. Flying buttresses and clerestory pinnacles. The aisle windows, four-lighters, lofty for their breadth, yet occupy practically all the space between buttresses. Two transoms, and cinquecusped lights below them; at the top the lights group two and two, but above that is the most elementary panel tracery. Two-centred heads. Above that plain ashlar, with a quatrefoil gallery light in a neat square frame. Moulded parapet, above a string-course with inconspicuous square flowers. The clerestory windows, four-centred and of three lights, have slightly livelier tracery, with daggers standing on their heads. Plain moulded parapet here too.

The parapet carries round unbroken on to the N and s TRANSEPTS. Clerestory and aisle windows also correspond. String-courses do not, but range with the set-offs on the end buttresses. s transept s window of vast size, of eight lights grouped three, two, three, with two transoms. Panel tracery. N transept N window to match. The w buttresses of each transept hide a newel stair. That is why the s w pinnacle is extra large, with subsidiary pinnacles where it springs, and eight gabled faces higher up, and why the N w pinnacle echoes it. The Norman walling of the N transept rises almost to parapet level here, so the pinnacle stands above clasping buttresses. The Perp buttress takes a second, smaller pinnacle. The other external difference between the two transepts is not governed by Norman survivals, but a reminder that a third of a century separates their building. The s transept gable is all panelled; the N transept gable has three niches over a row of blank panelling. Recent restoration of the top of the s w transept gable is not precisely accurate (Tatton-Brown). Here the pre-Reformation golden angel stood before it was lassoed and felled by Cromwell's men.

ST MICHAEL'S CHAPEL, added to the E side of the S transept, breaks with the nave-transept design. Two bays by one, shorter than its predecessor, as shown by the projection outdoors of Langton's C 13 tomb. Two-storeyed elevation, for there is a second chapel above the main one. The lower windows have four lights, not grouped; the upper, of three cinquefoiled lights, have straight-sided heads.

The break that the SOUTH-WEST TOWER makes with the nave design is much more important. The tower is not especially tall (it must have been designed to match the height of the Norman N W tower), and only in the view from the s w does it stand up to the central tower. But Thomas Mapilton's preference for pretty little details like concave-sided gablets, panelled buttresses and ogee window labels ensures that the sobriety of the nave has a foil that stops it from falling into dullness. (Internally it is easy to see that the piers are part of the nave work, and that Mapilton built the s and w, i.e. the outer, walls, with slight changes in the base mouldings, and foliage on the shaft-rings, and the fan-vault.) The angle buttresses project so far that those on the s side almost enclose the porch. On the way up the depth is gradually consumed by four gableted and pinnacled set-offs, panelled below, with a string-course above, that sets up a syncopated rhythm of stages. Four-light main windows, two-light belfry windows in pairs in the top three stages. Elaborate skyline of panelled battlements and complex pinnacles, set lozenge-wise to the corners of the tower, their outlines fretted by two tiers of gablets. (The crockets in many places are, as old photographs show, modern enrichments.) The most sumptuous display is, however, reserved for the lowly SOUTH-WEST PORCH, which has two tiers of niches, carried on round the s w buttress, the lower square-headed, the upper gabled to the w, canopied towards the s. All renewed in 1862, and filled with statues by *Theodore Phyffers*. Internally the porch was not touched – its lierne vault, its carved bosses and shafted inner doorway. Larger niches, with *Phyffers* statuary, continue across the w front of the nave, which otherwise calls for little comment. Characteristically the shallow, lierne-vaulted w porch and doorway are inconspicuous, the w window huge. Seven lights, two transoms, panel tracery in three tiers. The gable is marked off by an enriched band, and is pierced by a large square window, with slightly convex sides, filled by tracery of quatrefoils in spherical triangles.

BELL HARRY. We now know that the crossing tower was built in two stages. Mr Tatton-Brown contributes the following, after examining the inside of the tower in 1976. Preliminaries early in the C 15 had included demolition (to vault-level) of the Norman central tower and new building work only up to roof-ridge-level, then work ceased between 1430 and c. 1490. During c. 1490–4 Archbishop Morton and his architect *John Wastell* built what they apparently then intended as a lantern tower, up to the deep band below the present upper windows (a prior's letter of 1494 mentions talk of intended pinnacles there, and timbers for a very low-pitched roof exist below the floor of the present upper chamber and above the fan-vault inside). But then they changed their minds and decided to double the tower's height, which was done at Morton's expense during 1494–8, perhaps to celebrate the cardinal's hat he received in 1493: he was 'capping' his cathedral. The angle turrets have Morton's rebus alternating with cardinal hats all the way up. The upper part of the tower is made of red bricks, with Caen stone only for facing, presumably to lessen weight at such height; smaller bricks had already been used in the earlier stage of Wastell's tower, visible in stair-turret walls; the earliest brickwork in the cathedral, in the N W transept gable, dates from about the 1470s. Inside the upper chamber of the crossing tower is an early C 19 walk-wheel, and in the small chamber below it and just above the vault is the original 'faulcon' or hand-spike windlass, almost certainly late C 15 (and so just older than a similar faulcon in King's College Chapel, Cambridge), and now used to raise and lower the great central boss of the fan-vault over the crossing. (Cf. treadmill at Salisbury.)

John Wastell's majestic crossing tower perfectly sets the seal on the cathedral, lofty enough to weigh against the enormous length of the building, magisterially forceful of outline, yet profusely decorated. The angles are buttressed by sheer octagonal turrets, the angles of which are further buttressed. (The other major towers erected c. 1500, at Magdalen College, Oxford, and Bath Abbey, are also handled in this way; but already the drawing for a proposed tower at King's College, Cambridge, has the same angle turrets, as early as c. 1448.) The turrets culminate in openwork lanterns, gableted and ringed by pinnacles. Those are the major vertical accents, for the shallow buttress in the centre of each face goes for little. Pairs of tall, slender two-light windows, with two-centred heads, at two levels. The lower windows light the crossing, so the belfry windows are very high up indeed. The wall surface that is left is all broken up with enriched bands and panels. The deep band below the belfry windows, of lozenges, embattled above, bordered by square flowers below, makes the strongest horizontal tie, much more important than the three inconspicuous string-courses, since this originally marked the top of the lantern tower intended until 1494. At the final parapet, pierced top battlements. The ogee-crocketed hoodmoulds to the lower windows, with luxuriant finials, are telling, and so are the quatrefoil- and trefoil-headed panels on the faces of the angle turrets.

So at last it is time to enter the s w porch and contemplate the INTERIOR of the nave. The design has, in its exterior, been criticized for a certain coolness; but inside one does not feel that any more. Whether *Yevele*'s design or not (see below; also the introduction to the nave, above), the nave is as nobly impressive as any Perp interior in the country, worked out with such thorough, final logic that one forgets that the length and width of nave and aisles and the bay-spacing were fixed by the Norman fabric. Only in height was there no restriction, so the designer raised the ridge as high as the chancel roof ridge; but as the nave does not stand on a crypt, the proportions of the nave are quite different from those of the chancel. (On another great contemporary nave conditioned by Norman work, see *Winchester* below.) Lanfranc's massive piers are cased and adorned with continuous double-wave mouldings and half-shafts in the cardinal directions, so that their bulk cuts off all but the briefest diagonal vistas. Yet the nave is brilliant with light. This result comes from the relationship of arcade arches to aisle windows. The windows are as tall and wide as the aisle walls and buttresses will allow; the arcade rises exactly as high. Above the arcades no gallery openings, but a panelled area of wall, the panels formed by the prolonged mullions of the clerestory windows. Nothing here to counterbalance the dominant verticals of the piers, for the double-wave is carried up from ground to vault up and over the clerestory windows. The pier shafts are interrupted by two sets of shaft-rings, but it is a mere whispered interruption. The fact that shaft-rings are used at all needs comment. Favourites in the c 13, by the mid-c 14 they were not used at all. But when Yevele, if it was he, in 1375 continued the unfinished nave of Westminster Abbey, he copied (very likely was required to copy) the c 13 design closely, shaft-rings and all. Here they are pressed into service for their own sakes, not for reasons of conformity. The high vault springs from the capitals of the main shafts, a cluster of ribs fanning out, major and minor, to join the ridge rib along the length of the nave. A network of lierne ribs, forming crosses bay by bay, with insignificant carved bosses, ceil the crown of the vault. Lierne vaults in the aisles too.

The strainer across the w crossing arch, a deep embattled stone band, pierced with rows of quatrefoils three deep, the middle row encircled, the upper row and lower row enclosed in blunt daggers, carried on a four-centred arch, was put in by *Wastell* to help the crossing piers carry the weight

of his tower. Identical strainer across the arch to the s transept. The choir screen does the same service for the E crossing arch. Nothing, however, on the N side, a risk taken, it has been suggested, lest the view to the place of Becket's martyrdom be obscured. The tower itself has a fan-vault incredibly high up, above the tower's lower windows. The vault is of brick and stone, and by *Wastell* (cf. King's College Chapel, Cambridge); the central boss is of wood with the arms of Christ Church on it, and four other bosses around it have the insignia of Henry VII, Cardinal Morton, Archbishop Warham and Prior Goldstone. (Goldstone's rebus is also on the strainer arch between nave and crossing.) The crossing is unusual in that much of it is floored by flights of steps.

The TRANSEPTS, in spite of certain irregularities caused by retaining parts of the Norman walls, follow the forms of the nave in all but trifling details. The gigantic end windows dominate.

Finally, the chapels added to the transepts. The LADY CHAPEL (or Deans' Chapel), built in the third quarter of the c 15, has a fan-vault, the first on a large scale in eastern England (for the next, see Peterborough retrochoir, which Mr Harvey attributes to Wastell). The chapel is only two bays long, but lofty. The vaulting has no special features, but the handling of the walls, as buttressing masses, projecting into the chapel, between the spacious windows, is a satisfying notion. To them many dainty shafts are applied, and on the canted splays shields and rows of quatrefoils. A double row of leaves on the E window splays, and canopied niches low down – part of a reredos? Ornate stone w screen built with the chapel. Restoration here in 1974–5 uncovered an engaged column from Lanfranc's chapel in the s wall (Tatton-Brown).

ST MICHAEL'S CHAPEL was built in 1437–9 E of the s transept. It has a lierne vault. Mouldings somewhat coarser than in the work attributed to Yevele. The E wall below the altar is arched over the foot of Langton's tomb, which, as we have seen, protrudes outside, the apse of Lanfranc's transept chapel having been deeper (see also *Furnishings*). Above the chapel, reached up a flight of steps within the thickness of the wall from the s choir aisle, is ALL SAINTS CHAPEL. Plain tierceron vault. Bosses at the ridge, three carved with cowled heads, one identified as Prior Thomas, i.e. Goldstone I, and so after 1449.

FURNISHINGS, E TO W

First, a short introduction to the STAINED GLASS. The cathedral is well endowed with furnishings and a fine series of monuments, but it is the stained glass that is unforgettable. A substantial part of the glass inserted in the newly rebuilt choir and in the Trinity Chapel has survived, and can be justly compared in quality with the finest c 12 and

C 13 French glass. Any history of glass painting in Europe must take account of it. Where the glass has gone, most of the iron armatures have not, and their strong geometrical patterns are an important element in the architectural effect of the Trinity Chapel aisles and the Corona in particular. As the glass is almost all not now where it was placed at first, and windows intended to form a series have been scattered up and down the cathedral, a brief résumé of the original layout of the glass must be made here. The glass in the clerestory of choir and Trinity Chapel formed a genealogy of Christ, as recorded in Luke, Chapter 3, beginning in the w bay on the N side, and continuing, with two figures per window, making eighty-four in all, clockwise to finish with Mary and Christ in the w window on the s. (We now have to imagine the grandeur of the ancestors all together at clerestory-level as an unbroken series large enough to be 'read' from the floor.) The sequence was broken in the apse by five windows, the centre three filled with scenes from the Life of Christ. The rose windows in the E transepts have panels illustrating the Old Dispensation (N) and the New Dispensation (s). In the choir aisles and E transepts were twelve 'Theological' windows, with medallions arranged in threes, two Old Testament scenes, coupled with the New Testament event they foreshadow. The scheme was a favourite one in English medieval art. The E window of the Corona is the culmination of this series, the 'types' and 'antitypes' here being confined to the Death, Resurrection and Glorification of Christ. It is a little later than the rest, as the border of stiff-leaf tufts shows. Of the twelve aisle windows of the Trinity Chapel, seven are partly or wholly intact. The medallions here depict miracles recorded to have happened in the years following Becket's murder, as set down by two monks of Christ Church, Benedict and William.

The dating of the glass has recently been clarified by Professor Caviness (1977), and her arguments from style and historical probability have such force that they are adopted here. She believes that the choir was fully glazed, both clerestory and aisles, between its completion in 1179 and the monks' entry into it at Easter 1180. It is recorded that this part was at that time closed off by a partition from the building under construction farther E. Glazing of the Trinity Chapel and Corona was slower, extending from c. 1185 to the years shortly before the erection of Becket's shrine in 1220, with a break in 1207–13 when the monks were in exile. The latest windows in style are some in the clerestory and ambulatory of the Trinity Chapel, but the whole programme of subjects must have been worked out at the beginning of the second phase. The glass will be described in its present positions among the rest of the furnishings.

In this description of furnishings, the crypt comes first, then the rest of the cathedral from E to w, taking N before s

where necessary. Structural sculpture, such as the carved capitals in Anselm's crypt, has been discussed in the architectural description above.

Crypt   Preserved in the crypt are the moveable remains of Reculver Church (demolished 1809; its surviving towers overlook the Thames estuary between Herne Bay and Margate). They are of national importance, speaking eloquently of the culture and refinement of Early Saxon art. The abbey of Reculver was founded in 669. In terms of ecclesiastical history that was a date when Canterbury was tied most closely to the rest of the civilized world. In 668 the great Theodore of Tarsus was consecrated Archbishop. He came to England with two assistants, Hadrian, an African monk who had been ruling a monastery near Naples, and Benedict Biscop, Northumbrian by birth but a monk of Lérins.

First the COLUMNS, two of them, that formed the chancel screen. They are monoliths, c. 20 ft high, their capitals a simplification of a Byzantine block capital, their bases (like a shaft-base from a Saxon church of St Pancras on the St Augustine's Abbey site in Canterbury) a form of classical Ionic, with an enriched moulding. In front of the columns there stood until at least the C 16 a lofty cross. Six sizeable fragments of the CROSS SHAFT are preserved in the crypt, together with two smaller pieces without figure sculpture. Leland's description helps to make sense of them: 'Yn the enteryng of the quyer [of Reculver Church] ys one of the fayrest, and the most auncyent crosse that ever I saw, a ix footes, as I ges, yn highte. It standeth lyke a fayr column. The base great stone is not wrought. The second stone being rownd hath curiusly wrought and paynted the images of Christ, Peter, Paule, John and James, as I remember. Christ sayeth *Ego sum Alpha et Ω*. Peter sayith *Tu es Christus filius Deo vivi*. The saing of the other iii wher painted *majusculis literis Ro.* but now obliterated. The second stone is of the Passion. The iii conteineth the xii Apostles. The iiii hath the image of Christ hanging and fastened with iiii nayles, and *sub pedibus sustentaculum*. The hiest part of the pyller hath the figure of a crosse.' In excavating Reculver Church Sir Charles Peers discovered that the original plaster floor of the nave stopped against a masonry foundation just where the cross according to Leland stood; moreover, a C 13 record mentions 'magnam crucem lapideam inter ecclesiam et cancellum'. If the base was contemporary with the church, so probably but not necessarily was the cross shaft. In spite of recent attempts to date the shaft to the C 10, a date in the C 7 is, however one looks at it, the more probable. C 7 sculptured crosses are familiar from Ireland and Northumbria. But in the south, apart from two shafts with sculptured figures at Glastonbury, one of them at least set up late in the C 7, we know of nothing like the Reculver Cross. The position of

27. CANTERBURY Lady Chapel vault, completed after 1468

the Reculver Cross in front of the chancel screen has no parallel in Britain or on the Continent.

There are eight fragments of cross shaft altogether, two without any decipherable carving, and six containing figure sculpture. These six fragments are part of two round shafts, one about 18 in. in diameter, the other about 15 in. The other early British crosses (e.g. Bewcastle and Ruthwell) have square shafts. An Early Christian forerunner, comparable with Reculver in more than the roundness of its shaft, is the ciborium of St Mark's at Venice. The biggest fragment, which is also the best preserved and artistically the highest in quality, has the lower half of two standing frontal figures, and part of a third, in quite high relief. This must have come from the lowest tier. There are two other pieces of large diameter carved with figures only, one with a side-view figure, and the hand of someone else stretching out towards his feet; the other with a figure striding nimbly on two knolls, and apparently reaching upwards. The latter must depict the Ascension. Christ strides uphill in just this pose, his hand grasped by the hand of God extended from a cloud, in the Ascension on the famous ivory diptych at Munich. The heads of both these are, alas, gone too. The fourth big piece does include faces, of busts set in a foliage scroll; and also a broad border of interlace. The two small fragments have figures between colonnettes, and seem to fit together. So here we have four of the twelve Apostles, or rather their ghosts, so damaged is the surface of the stone.

Figure sculpture, foliage scrolls, interlace: where else are all three found together in c 7 Europe? The answer is nowhere, except in the two great Northumbrian crosses, the Ruthwell Cross in Dumfriesshire and the Bewcastle Cross in Cumberland, the latter datable after 670. Yet monasticism in Northumbria was Irish monasticism. Ecclesiastically Reculver depended on Canterbury, and Canterbury had been colonized from Italy. It is to the Mediterranean too that we must look for the sources of the Reculver sculpture. The figures of course imply Antique sources ultimately. Of that more in a moment. The interlacing strands, which look so un-Antique, are at least Early Christian. They can be found on the low choir screens, the *cancelli*, of S. Clemente and S. Sabina in Rome, both of the c 6; though one should not forget that contemporary Kentish pagan jewellery is carved in such knotty strands. Now for the scrolls. Vine-scroll ornament can be found in the c 6 too, on the Throne of Maximian at Ravenna, for example. The scrolls there are inhabited by birds and beasts. So are the vine-scrolls on the Bewcastle Cross. But the Reculver scrolls are not recognizably vine branches, and the inhabitants are not animals, but half-length young men like the busts in wreaths familiar from Late Roman ivory consular diptychs. As for the standing figures, it must be confessed that to find anything as good in quality

as these, one must go back at least to the c 5. Where else in c 6 or c 7 art are there drapery folds as delicately carved as these are, or folds that tell as much of the limbs beneath them as these do? Where can one find poses so lively and convincing? It is tempting to suggest that the Reculver Cross was carved by workmen who had portable objects beside them as models; as we have seen already, ivories yield the best comparisons. The technique of carving too, the hair-breadth incisions that indicate hems or a rolled parchment, is a miniaturist's technique, quite unlike the bold simplifications of the northern crosses. But that is not a full explanation. A c 7 craftsman could not emulate the style of a c 5 ivory merely by looking at it; he needed training. And that implies that there were other c 7 works of art as expert as the Reculver Cross. What they were and where they were made, whether in Britain, in Italy or in the Eastern Mediterranean, we do not know. Time has destroyed them all. But the Reculver Cross testifies that they existed.

WALL PAINTINGS IN THE CRYPT. The apse of St Gabriel's Chapel (SE) has its complete set of wall paintings of *c*. 1130, an outstanding series in quality, extent and state of preservation (having been walled up from the late c 12 to the c 19). In the apse vault, Christ in Majesty flanked by four angels. On the walls to either side, scenes of the annunciations of the archangel and their results; on the N the annunciation to Zachariah, his dumbness and the naming of John; on the S the annunciation to Mary and the Nativity. On the soffit of the outer arch is depicted the vision of St John the Evangelist of the angels of the seven churches of Asia, and at the bottom at the N end, the Evangelist writing. The hieratic presentation and strict symmetry, as well as the convention for modelling faces, suggest a Byzantine source for the style that probably reached England via Norman Sicily. – In the Jesus Chapel (E end) c 14 vault decoration, crowned Is and Ms, recently repainted. – STAINED GLASS. E window (Jesus Chapel), original border, and top panel of the Virgin enthroned, *c*. 1200. The early c 13 figures lower down, Isaiah, Jeremiah, Jacob and Isaac, came from Petham Church, where they belonged. The Crucifixion is made up, some of it with old glass; the lowest panel started life perhaps in one of the Trinity Chapel aisles. – NE transept (crypt): in the N apse, a c 13 French panel recently inserted; four further panels, with scenes from the life of St Nicholas, in the S apse. – St Gabriel's Chapel: c 13 French medallion, set in French c 14 grisaille glass. Also a c 13 figure of St Dunstan, much restored. – MONUMENTS. Indent of a large brass of an archbishop (Morton's; for his tomb, see below). – Lady Mohun, before 1375. Alabaster effigy, badly damaged, of a lady fashionably dressed. – 'Countess of Atholl': this damaged effigy in St Gabriel's Chapel was identified by St John Hope as being not of the Countess but of Lady Tryvet

28. CANTERBURY Stained glass, late C12/early C13 Corona east window. The Grapes of Eshcol

† 1431. – Cardinal Archbishop Morton † 1501. Recumbent effigy, with little canons kneeling, three on this side, three on that. Splayed faces to the arch above, and attached to the faces small figures of saints, well carved but almost all now headless.

Corona In 1977 St Augustine's Chair was moved back to its original C13 position between Becket's shrine and the high altar (see Trinity Chapel below), having stood in the Corona from just before or just after 1800. – STAINED GLASS. The E window illustrates the main events from Good Friday to Pentecost, with the Old Testament episodes that foreshadow them grouped in fours, of semicircles round the square panels, of circular medallions around the lozenge-shaped ones. The sequence goes from bottom to top, as follows (the Crucifixion and the Resurrection are mostly modern):

Crucifixion	Moses striking the Rock
	Sacrifice of Isaac
	Preparing the Passover Lamb
	The Grapes of Eshcol
Entombment	Joseph in the Pit
	Samson and Delilah in bed
	Jonah cast overboard
	Daniel in the Lions' Den

Resurrection	Noah in the Ark (mostly modern)
	Jonah disgorged by the Whale
	Michal and David (mostly modern)
	Moses and the Burning Bush
Ascension	The High Priest enters the Holy of Holies
	Elijah carried up to Heaven
	The Sundial of Ahaz
	Enoch translated to Heaven
Pentecost	Consecration of Aaron and his sons
	Christ in Glory (to be read with the Pentecost panel)
	Moses and Jethro judging the people
	Moses receiving the Tables of the Law

In the N window part of a late C12 Jesse Tree, just the figures of Josiah and the Virgin, majestically conceived though small in size. The leaves of the tree are entirely Romanesque in form. The next window, a whole Jesse Tree, was made by *George Austin Jr* in 1861. More C19 glass, very muddy, in the SE window. C13 panel of Christ in Majesty in the S window. – MONUMENTS. Cardinal Reginald Pole † 1558, the last archbishop's tomb to be placed in the cathedral till the late C19. Plastered brick, with the words 'Depositum Cardinalis Poli' picked out in gold. Heraldic cartouche on the wall over it, presented in

1897 by Cardinal Vaughan, Archbishop of Westminster (Canon Ingram Hill). – Archbishop Temple † 1902. Kneeling figure, signed by *F. W. Pomeroy*, under a busy Gothic canopy by *W. D. Caröe*. – In the N part of the raised floor of the Corona two late C 13 TILE PAVEMENTS still *in situ*.

Henry IV's Chantry (Chapel of St Edward the Confessor) STAINED GLASS. Three delightful C 15 figures, St Christopher, St Edward, St Catherine. – There is some fine carpentery, 1430s, in front of this chapel.

Trinity Chapel PAVEMENT. St Thomas à Becket's shrine has gone, but not the pavement laid down in front of it *c.* 1220. It is a most handsome affair, a complicated geometrical pattern, a lozenge in a quatrefoil, in a square, in a much bigger lozenge overlapping four circles; executed in marble tesserae, the technique called opus alexandrinum. N and S of it are thirty-six roundels, in rows of six, of yellow oolite, on which designs are cut, and filled with red mastic. Now muddled up, they include the Signs of the Zodiac, Labours of the Months, and Virtues trampling Vices. Four more roundels, very worn, farther E. E of the opus alexandrinum pavement a rectangular wear-mark shows where the bottom step of the shrine was. The actual steps, re-used, are set N–S in the floor. There were three steps all round originally, and evidence of the wear patterns enables us to reconstruct them on paper (Tatton-Brown). Three pink marble fragments from the shrine itself are in the cathedral library. – W of the pavement now the ARCHBISHOP'S THRONE, 'St Augustine's Chair', C 13, of Purbeck marble. (It stood in the Corona *c.* 1800–1977.) It replaced the pre-fire 'patriarchal seat formed out of a single stone' described by Gervase as standing eight steps above and behind the high altar before 1174 (cf. Wilfrid's throne at Hexham and the fragmentary C 7 throne at Norwich Cathedral). – MONUMENTS. Prince Edward, the Black Prince, † 1376. Formal and withdrawn. Stiff recumbent effigy, of copper gilt, of the Prince in full armour, on a high tomb-chest, with shields in multifoils against its sides. Above, a flat wooden canopy painted with a large figure of God the Father holding his crucified Son, this too treated hieratically (facsimile in the aisle nearby). Above that hang replicas of the Prince's funeral achievement, a set of armour, tabard etc.; the originals, now decayed and fragile, are at present shown in the crypt treasury. – Archbishop Courtenay † 1396. Alabaster tomb-chest, with niches for weepers, and an alabaster recumbent effigy, already a drop in quality from the early alabaster effigy of Archbishop Stratford (see S *choir aisle* below). Podgy, self-indulgent face, perhaps not a portrait, for the effigy of William of Wykeham († 1404) at Winchester is almost a duplicate (bishops, for the use of?). Crisp, shallow drapery folds. Small angels hold the cushions under his head. – King Henry IV † 1413, and Queen Joan of Navarre † 1437, and probably erected after her death. One of the most am-

bitious alabaster monuments ever executed. Tomb-chest with canopied niches. Crowned recumbent effigies, set under elaborate vaulted tabernacles. His features are clearly a portrait. Much expertise in rendering their jewelled robes, but no joy. This is not art of a high order. Oak canopy, flat, originally painted on the underside, with demi-angels along the sides. Coronation of the Virgin painted on a panel at the foot, and the Murder of Becket painted at the head. – Dean Nicholas Wotton † 1567. He kneels in prayer on a bulgy tomb-chest, before a 'reredos'. Corinthian side columns, notably pure in form for the date. Obelisk at the other end. The total effect is already of Late Elizabethan showiness.

Trinity Chapel ambulatory STAINED GLASS. Of the twelve windows all keep their original armatures, eight their stained glass. The subjects are all of miracles worked by the blood or intervention of St Thomas. As the windows are at eye-level, there is a chance, all too rare, to study the glass close up, to see the delicacy with which designs are drawn, and how the lead glazing bars clarify them; to appreciate the colours, ruby, blue, green, amber, and brown, and the intensity of each; and to attempt to distinguish the hands of the different masters who designed and made the glass – though one needs to be aware that, besides the modern panels, numerous piecemeal renewals have been made in the late C 19 and C 20, many of them detectable only by technical examination.

The description of the windows starts at the W end on the N side and proceeds clockwise. – Window I. Only the border is in its original place. All the panels, mostly made up of old glass, have been put in during the C 20. Four medallions down the middle belong to the miracle series. – Window II. By *Clayton & Bell*. – Window III. Ten scenes, in lozenges and paired part-circles. The top three scenes show a riding accident; No. 4, Stephen of Hoyland delivered from nightmares; 5, 6, 7, pilgrimage scenes; 8, a young man's vision; 9, William the Priest cured by a drop of St Thomas's blood; 10, curing the blind and sick. – Window IV. Eight cures in eight pairs of medallions. The backgrounds here are picked out with delicious scrollwork. No. 1 (top l.), pilgrims with healing water; 2, St Thomas visits a sick man; 3, 4, Petronilla of Polesworth cured of epilepsy; 5, 6, 7, modern; 8, the dream of Louis VII of France; 9, 10, the healing of Robert of Cricklade, who suffered from swollen feet; 11, 12, the cure of a woman; 13, 14, a maniac cured; 15, 16, Audrey of Canterbury cured of quartan fever. – Window V. The iron armature, forming large circles for quatrefoils, is especially monumental here. This makes four scenes per circle, and two further scenes in the interspaces below before the next circle begins. No. 1, St Thomas appears from his shrine to a sleeping monk; 2, 3, miracles at the saint's tomb; 4, Godwin of Boxgrove (?) gives his shirt to a poor man; 5, 6, a woman with dropsy visits the tomb; 7, 8, 9, modern; 10, 11, 12, the lame daughters of Godbold of Boxley; 13–18, i.e. the third circle and the two panels below, illustrate the punishment and healing of Eilward of Westoning. 13 does not belong to the story. For stealing gloves and a whetstone Eilward is sentenced (14), blinded and mutilated (15). St Thomas cures him (17) and he walks and points to his restored eyes (16). In the last panel Eilward gives thanks at the tomb of the saint. 19, 20, 21, Hugh of Jervaulx cured, after drinking holy water, of a generous flow of blood from his nose; 22, modern. – Window VI. The design, providing thirty-three panels in three and a half stylized flowers, is the most complicated of all. The stories run from l. to r., filling for the most part trios of panels. Only the lowest 'flower' is filled with a single nine-scene story. As usual, description starts top l. Nos. 1–3, healing the blind Juliana of Rochester; 4–9, Richard Sunieve cured of leprosy; 10–12, modern; 13–15, Rodbertulus, a boy of eight, drowned in the Medway while stoning frogs. In 14 two boys tell his parents, and in 15 his body is rescued. His resuscitation is missing, and 16–18 are modern. 19–21, a mad woman healed; 22–4, modern; 25–33, plague in the house of Sir Jordan Fitz-eisulf. The story-sequence begins in the bottom row, continues in the top row, and ends in the centre. So – 31, the funeral of the first victim, the nurse; 32, funeral of Sir Jordan's son; 33, Water of St Thomas used to revive him; 25, Sir Jordan given coins to place in his son's hands; 26, the son sits up and eats, and his parents give thanks – but, says the inscription, they do not thank the martyr Thomas; 27, Gimp, a blind and lame leper, being bidden in a dream to warn Sir Jordan of his omission; 28, Gimp giving his warning; 29, as the warning is ignored, another of Sir Jordan's sons dies; 30, at last Sir Jordan accomplishes his vow, pouring gold and silver pieces on the tomb. – Window VII (the E window on the s side). The top eight medallions made up of old glass in 1893. Nos. 9–12, the story of William of Kellett, the carpenter. 9, he cuts his shin at the bench; 10, St Thomas appears to him in a dream; 11, unbandaged, his leg is miraculously healed; 12, William leaves Canterbury, rejoicing. 13, Adam the Forester shot by a poacher; 14, a man in bed drinks the Water of St Thomas; 15, a man in bed; 16, Adam's thank-offering at the tomb. – Window IX. Borders and two panels, one of pilgrims on the road, the other showing them at the tomb. – Window XI. No. 1, John, the Groom of Roxburgh, thrown from his horse into the Tweed; 2, St Thomas rescues him; 3, two men in a boat search for his body; 4, John is revived by lying beside a fire; 5, pilgrims; 6, a young man kneeling; 7, a dying man healed; 8, two men lowering a coffin into a tomb; 9, pilgrims; 10, an offering at the tomb; 11, a man lying on the ground, with a priest and a woman; 12, an offering at the tomb; 13, a girl restored to life; 14, 15, a boy restored to life; 16, funeral; 17, 18,

scenes at St Thomas's tomb. – Window XII. A pretty design, a tier of fan-shaped compartments, making twenty-two panels in all. At the bottom the shrine, set up in 1220, is depicted again. Nos. 1–6, the miraculous preservation of the child Geoffrey of Winchester, first from a fever, then when the wall of the house falls down; 7, 8, James, son of the Earl of Clare, cured of a hernia, by a rag of St Thomas's hairshirt; 9, 10, a lame youth (Eilwin of Berkhamsted?) healed; 11, a leprous monk and two pilgrims; 12, tending a leprous priest. 13–20, the story of William of Gloucester, a workman of Archbishop Pont-l'Évêque of York. 13, William buried by a fall of earth; 14, eye-witnesses tell a priest; 15, a woman telling of her vision that William is still alive; 16, the bailiff, ear to the ground, hears William's groans; 17, mostly modern; 18, the bailiff reports to the priest; 19, a party with shovels sets off; 20, and digs William out; 21, 22, offerings at the shrine.

MONUMENT. Archbishop Walter † 1205. Gabled Purbeck marble tomb-chest. The shrine of St Thomas must have looked something like this, though a great deal more gorgeous. In style too a date c. 1220 would suit this monument very happily. It is the earliest archiepiscopal tomb now in the cathedral (the next being Langton's, sw transept, E chapel). The gable decoration, of heads in quatrefoils within lozenges that overlap circles, plays with geometrical forms just like the pavement and the Trinity Chapel window armatures. Filleted mouldings, undercut where they overlap. The heads too are in notably high relief, with vivaciously incised wrinkles and curls. Shafted arcading, trefoiled, on the sides of the tomb-chest, with tufts of stiff-leaf in the spandrels.

St Anselm's Chapel CRUCIFIX and CANDLESTICKS, c. 1951 by *Andor Mészáros*. – CHANDELIER. C 18. Brass. Shell-shaped sconces. – WALL PAINTING. High up in the NW corner of the apse, the majestic mid-C 12 figure of St Paul shaking off the viper at Melita, on an intense blue

29. CANTERBURY Wall painting, mid- C 12.
St Anselm's Chapel. St Paul and the Viper

background (preserved by walling up in the C12 until 1889). It must be contemporary with the most splendid illuminated manuscripts of the Canterbury scriptoria, such as the Edwine Psalter and the Dover Bible; but in style, especially in the clinging draperies articulated by sparing S-curved folds, which give the figure its mass and rhythm, the closest parallel is with the Bury Bible. Such a comparison emphasizes the monumentality of this figure of St Paul. Naturally one looks for some large-scale source for the style. Dr Saxl has found it in the mosaics of Norman Sicily, specifically in those of the Cappella Palatina in Palermo. What wouldn't one have given to have some more of the painted decoration of Conrad's choir? (On Pearson's recovery of this much, see *The late* C12 *rebuilding* above, on the interior of this chapel; also cf. paintings similarly uncovered in St Gabriel's Chapel beneath: see *Crypt* above.) – STAINED GLASS. Disastrously glaring glass inserted in the Dec s window in 1959, by *H. J. Stammers* of York. – MONUMENT. Archbishop Meopham † 1333. A mighty structure, making a screen across the chapel entrance, with original wrought-iron gates. The s window, inserted in 1336, was put in to light it, no doubt. All of black marble or touch except the vaulting that grows from the gable of the tomb-chest. Lofty vaulted canopy, on lofty clustered shafts, that obscure the sculptured panels on the tomb-chest. The canopy was clearly an afterthought, for the coping of the tomb-chest is roughly cut away for its shafts. Altogether, the monument is a peculiar design, of a wilful, very Dec, oddness. Its joy is the sculpture, confined to reliefs in the spandrels, and all in little, but delightfully freshly carved. In the trefoils and half-trefoils on the canopy, monks seated at their desks. In the trefoils on the tomb-chest vault, ogeed and split-cusped these, smiling angels holding scrolls and symbols of the Evangelists.

In the tower room above St Anselm's Chapel are kept the magnificent fragments of mid–late C12 sculpture found when the cloister gables were dismantled recently for restoration. They probably belonged to the Norman pulpitum. Delicate demi-figures in quatrefoils and grotesque heads in roundels.

Choir SCREENS. Erected under Prior Eastry in 1304–5. Of stone, enclosing the choir on three sides. The idiom is Dec, the handling remarkable for its orderliness. So there are ogees all over the tracery, i.e. in the paired trefoiled lights and the cinquefoil in a circle over them, and split cusps in the spandrel trefoils; but the even row of windows is topped with a straight parapet, decorated just with a row of big square leaves, a row of pierced trefoils, and a crest of minuscule battlements. Ballflower on the s doorway. The w side, treated a little more richly, is hidden now by the C15 pulpitum, but *Scott* uncovered it temporarily and found much original colouring, red, blue, green and gold. – N and s, IRON GATES. C19 (probably by *Scott*), smooth-

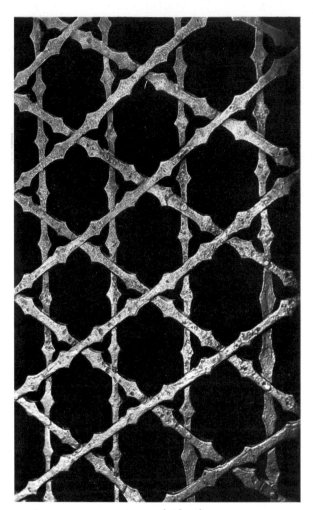

30. CANTERBURY C14 ironwork (detail),
west gate to pulpitum

faced imitations of Eastry's original w gate, which is C14, reset in a C15 frame in the C15 pulpitum doorway. The original C14 ironwork is a hexagonal 'Islamic' patterned grille rebated at its intersections as though by a carpenter (Dr Geddes). – PULPITUM. This screen, far more bulky and impenetrable than Prior Eastry's, was set up in Prior Chillenden's time (1390–1411). (Yet its entrance vault looks early C14, not early C15.) Its w face is treated as a setting for figures in elaborately vaulted niches. Fussy when seen close to, the main lines, typically, read in the distance as a grid, with the doorway in the centre enlarged visually because of its sloping reveals. The important part is the surviving sculpture. Six figures of kings survive in the main register. The kings l. and r. of the doorway are Ethelbert and Edward the Confessor (dated by a benefaction during 1411–27). The others are usually identified as Henry V and Richard II on the l., Henry IV and Henry VI on the r. (Canon Ingram Hill), but they are certainly not portraits. All six seem to have been set up together; there is no difference in style. These then are the major surviving examples of early C15 sculpture in England, apart from monuments; so thoroughly have other screens and reredoses been despoiled. What about the style? They stand impassively, holding their insignia in constrained poses, dignified but not noble. On their small, neat heads they wear rich crowns; their robes, falling in long unbroken folds to crumple at their feet, are clearly made of some heavy material. C14 figures, say the kings on the w front at Lincoln, or at Exeter (the earlier row), are more animated, their robes not so all-enveloping. The change in style is both a change in ideals, from Dec to Perp, and also a change brought about by knowledge of the most advanced sculptural style in Europe c. 1400, that of Claus Sluter, and his followers, in Burgundy. That knowledge affects only the draperies; it does not animate the cool-blooded figures. (Woodman (1981) surprisingly places this screen in the 1450s as Lancastrian propaganda; for another C15 and debatably dated screen of king-figures, see York pulpitum.) – ARCHBISHOP'S THRONE. 1843–4 by *George Austin*. Convincingly Gothic. CHOIR STALLS. The return stalls at the w are by *Roger Davis*, 1682, and just like the woodwork in a Wren church. The rest are by *Sir G. G. Scott's* office, 1879. (Older stalls, without canopies, were shown in Thomas Johnson's painting of the choir in 1657: *Age of Charles I* exhibition, Tate Gallery, 1972.) – LECTERN. Brass eagle of 1663 by *William Burroughs* of London: cf. his lecterns at Lincoln and Wells. – STAINED GLASS. In the clerestory, C19 copies of the genealogical windows. Original borders in three windows on the N side. – MONUMENTS. Described under N and S choir aisles, below.

North-east transept STAINED GLASS. Rose window, late C12. The Old Dispensation, represented by Moses and the Synagogue in the centre square. Four triangular panels surround this, with figures of the Cardinal Virtues, and then four semicircles with prophets. All this is set within a circle, which is the full extent of the old glass. – In the clerestory windows nearest the aisle four genealogical figures from the earlier series, Shem above and Isaac below, and two unidentified patriarchs. A much restored figure of Heber in the NW corner. – The main windows, except for the restored roundel of St Martin in the NE apse, are all modern, imitating the C13 glass. That in the w wall is by *Clayton & Bell*, that in the SE apse by *John Baker*, 1956. – MONUMENT. Archbishop Tait † 1882. Recumbent figure carved by *Sir J. E. Boehm*.

North choir aisle The door here is C12 (John Fletcher) with C12 C-shaped hinges overlying C11 ironwork (Jane

Geddes; both via Tim Tatton-Brown). – PAINTINGS. Restored C15 fresco of the Vision of St Eustace. Also a curiosity, the Vision of King Charles the Martyr, c. 1660. – STAINED GLASS. Here is what is left of the series of twelve 'Theological' windows, with scenes from the New Testament (anti-types) flanked by pairs of Old Testament types, i.e. events that foreshadowed them. The surviving glass fills only two windows, but the complete arrangement is known from a C14 key in the Chapter Library. The glass must have been made c. 1200, for the leafage is no longer the majestic Romanesque fronds of the earliest style, nor the springy scrolls with stiff-leaf of the Miracle windows, but something in between. For pure pictorial charm these are perhaps the pick, covering a much wider range of subject than the Miracle windows; so e.g. the Sower, or the miraculous Draught of Fishes, shows to perfection the graceful but ruthless schematization of early medieval art, so easy to comprehend. Some of the triplets are intact, as follows. Centre window (Window II), reading from top to bottom: the Magi riding, with, in the l. panel, Balaam on his ass, and to the r., Isaiah at the gate of Jerusalem; Herod and the Magi, between Pharaoh dismissing Moses, and the Conversion of the Heathens from Idolatry; Adoration of the Magi, between Solomon and the Queen of Sheba, and Joseph and his brothers in Egypt; the Magi warned in a dream not to return to Herod, between Lot's escape from Sodom, and Jeroboam sacrificing; Presentation in the Temple and Samuel received in the Temple by Eli (the other Old Testament panel of this triplet is missing. In its place is the Parable of the Sower). The two lowest rows are also mixed up: Ecclesia, with the three sons of Noah, the Pharisees leaving Jesus; the three blameless states of life, Virginity, Continence and Marriage; the Rich Men of this world; the Parable of the Sower (second scene); Daniel, Job and Noah, the three righteous men (Ezekiel XIV).

NE window (Window III). Only the top triplet, the medallion with the half-medallions below, is in the place made for it. The subjects are: Jesus among the doctors, and the types, to the l., Moses advised by Jethro, and to the r., Daniel among the Elders. The panels continue downwards as follows: the Miracle of Cana (six waterpots turned to wine); the Six Ages of the World; the Six Ages of Man. These form a triplet. The rest are out of context: the Miraculous Draught of Fishes; Noah in the Ark receiving the Dove; St Peter and the Jews; the Calling of Nathanael; Gentiles hearing the Word; Pharisees despising the Word.

The clerestory windows of the aisle each enclose three medallions. In the NW and centre windows, scenes from the life of St Dunstan; in the NE, the story of St Alphege. – MONUMENTS. Archbishop Chichele † 1443. Very sumptuous, the polygonal piers for the canopy covered in tiers of canopied niches. Recumbent effigy on a tomb-chest, and a gisant below. Straight-topped canopy fringed with angels.

All the colour and the niche statues are modern. – Archbishop Bourchier † 1486. As sumptuous as the last, but more imaginative and carved as crisply as can be, mostly in Bethersden marble (the browner and shellier, the rest being Purbeck). Small-scale tabernacles on the side of the tomb-chest. Lofty vaulted canopy carrying a loft with pierced panelling and niches. No effigy. – Alexander Chapman † 1629. Big, restrained architectural wall-monument, of black marble and alabaster. Frontal half-length scholar figure, under looped-up curtains. Side niches. (Moved here in 1970 from the N W transept.) – Archbishop Howley † 1848. The monument lives up to its companions in splendour, though inevitably the style of the tall open canopy is Dec, not Perp. *R. Westmacott Jr* carved the recumbent figure. Who designed the rest?

South-east transept STAINED GLASS. Genealogical figures in the E clerestory windows which are nearest the aisle: Neri and Rhesa, Juda and Phares, and, in the next window to the S, an unidentified figure. – Apse windows by *G. Austin Jr*, 1852. – S windows 1956 by *Erwin Bossanyi*. Symbolic of Peace and Salvation (below), Faith and Action (above). Scalding colours, jagged shapes, but sugary faces. Deeply felt by the artist, no doubt, but Expressionism of this sort does not fit in here. – In St John's Chapel, PAINTING 'Adoration of the Shepherds' by *Bartolomeo Schidoni* (1570–1615).

South choir aisle STAINED GLASS. In the three main windows, panels, seventeen in all, of C 13 French glass, inserted, in modern borders, in 1958 and 1962. It is good to be able to compare them with the English glass, e.g. with the medallions in the aisle clerestory windows immediately above, although these are worn and restored: S E window, Dormition, Assumption and Coronation of the Virgin; centre and S W window, Scenes from the Life of Christ, from the Nativity to the Resurrection.

MONUMENTS. Prior Eastry † 1331. Fine realistic recumbent figure. Notice e.g. his sunken cheek and neck, and even a detail like the shape of his toes within the shoes. Battlements to the tomb-chest, and, effective this, the ends canted forward to make room for niches, with panels of reticulated tracery above. Vaulted canopy on shafts with leaf capitals, pure Dec, like everything else. – Archbishop Reynolds † 1328. This must have been similar, but the canopy has gone, and the effigy, of Purbeck marble, is battered. – Archbishop Stratford † 1348. The effigy is as fine as Prior Eastry's, boldly and realistically carved, but it is of alabaster, one of the earlier alabaster effigies known, preceded by John of Eltham's at Westminster Abbey and Edward II's at Gloucester. On the tomb-chest, alabaster mixes charmingly with Purbeck marble. Vaulted canopy of stone on Purbeck shafts. The whole thing is a work of great sensibility, with dainty forms much broken up; but what makes it historically so interesting is that the vocabulary is

Perp. So the tomb-chest is panelled, the verticality of the canopy shafts stressed. – Archbishop Sudbury † 1381, murdered in the Peasants' Revolt. A very long tomb-chest, of Purbeck marble, oddly shaped with its end pieces and deep niches on the S side. Vaulted stone canopy. The monument seems coarse and plain after Archbishop Stratford's. – Archbishop Kempe † 1456. The standard panelled marble tomb-chest, under a wooden canopy that is anything but standard. So the mid-C 15 was capable of flights of fancy as delectable as anything in the early C 14. Four pairs of exceedingly slim shafts rise to carry, far above the tomb-chest, a flat-topped canopy, vaulted with three two-centred arches, and a half-arch each end, so that it seems about to fly away. – Dean Neville † 1615. Mutilated Jacobean monument of the standard kind, with kneeling figures. – Anna Milles † 1714. Tablet with seated putti and a bad, flat, half-length figure.

North-west (main) transept STAINED GLASS. The N window in its entirety was filled with glass, as the gift of Edward IV, who with his wife and children appear as donors. The window was finished in 1482. *William Neve* was royal glazier at the time. Prophets, Apostles and Saints in the tracery; the main lights all destroyed except for the donor portraits, and angels bearing shields of arms. Clearly the two parts are by different hands, the tracery figures by some not specially distinguished artist, typical mid-C 15 hack-work. In the main lights the colours are much stronger, applied with subtle shadowing, the leads enclosing daringly large areas. This almost watercolourist technique is hard to appreciate except in reproductions. So, standing in the transept, one tends to underestimate its quality and condemn the figures as limp and inexpressive. Of the royal faces, only the King's and Queen's are genuine. The panel between the King and the Queen is Rhenish, early C 16. – In the W window, the Annunciation in the tracery and the main lights by *Comper*, 1954, but with three C 15 coats of arms, all that remains of original glass given in memory of Thomas Barnewell by his son John † 1478, purveyor of fish and wine to the monastery, hence the arms of the City of London, the Fishmongers' Company and Barnewell (Canon Ingram Hill).

MONUMENTS. Indents of several great brasses. – Archbishop Peckham † 1292. One of the earliest pieces anywhere that can be called pure Dec. The recumbent effigy is of wood, idealized, not realistic, his hand raised in blessing, his robes falling in heavy, placid folds. Tomb-chest with niches and a row of stocky little weepers. The canopy, with a subcusped arch, a crocketed gable and side pinnacles, was to be a favourite form. At the sides niches with ogees, one of the very first appearances of the form (Hardingstone Cross, Crouchback monument in Westminster Abbey). Pretty borders of leaves stylized into Dec bumpiness. – Archbishop Warham † 1532. Reclining effigy on a tomb-chest, under a colossal vaulted triple canopy, drastically retooled in the C19. No hint of a Renaissance taint to the Gothic forms, because the tomb (with adjoining chantry demolished in the C19) is documented as made in 1507. If it were not for this foresight, one doubts if Warham, whose death in 1532 came so opportunely for Henry VIII, would have had such an expensive and confident monument on the brink of the Reformation.

Lady Chapel WALL PAINTING under the E window. A fragment of medieval painting recently uncovered, a scroll-bearing angel in the midst of a frieze of angels. – STAINED GLASS. In the E window armorial glass and the badge of Archbishop Bourchier, *c.* 1455. – A deanery of MONUMENTS. Dean Rogers (Bishop of Dover). Altar tomb, 1597. – Dean Fotherby † 1619. Tomb-chest, its sides covered with a charnel-house array of skulls and bones. – Dean Boys † 1625. Alabaster standing wall-monument transformed into the Dean's study. Seated at a table, the figure of the Dean half turns to look towards the altar. A book is open on a sphinx-ended rest, and books line the 'walls' on three sides. The motifs of a standard Jacobean monument are re-used with a new sense of realism. – Dean Bargrave. *c.* 1640. Portrait on copper by *Cornelius Jansen*. – Dean Turner † 1672. Baroque wall tablet

South west (main) transept STAINED GLASS. The great S window contains a good deal of C15 glass, figures and shields of arms, some C13 foliage, and, far more important, three rows of the late C12 ancestors of Christ from the choir and Trinity Chapel clerestory. Where they are now, they are easily within eye-shot. All figures are seated, the earlier ones (by 1180) under arches, the later (after 1185) in shaped surrounds – quatrefoils, almonds or stretched hexagons. The earlier figures are undoubtedly finer, the poses more animated and secure, the heads turned or cocked alertly, the hands in expressive gestures. Perhaps the noblest of all is Methuselah, in the centre of the bottom row. The complicated draperies, drawn, sometimes twisted in a multitude of folds, this way and that across the bodies, but in the best figures not obscuring the poses, have their closest parallels in sculpture in the (somewhat earlier) stone reliefs at Chichester Cathedral (S choir aisle). – W window 1903 by *Christopher Whall*.

St Michael's Chapel The principal fitment here predates the C15 chapel. The tomb of Cardinal Stephen Langton † 1228 is partly hidden under the modern altar and the Perp E wall of the chapel is arched over the foot of the tomb, placed here originally in Lanfranc's deeper apse. Simple Purbeck marble slab with a cross on it, in touching contrast to other contents of what is now called the Warriors' Chapel. – The chapel is full up with MONUMENTS, a riot of colour after their recent touching up. – Margaret Holland † 1437, between the two husbands who pre-

31. CANTERBURY Stained glass, by 1180, for choir clerestory, now main transept south window. Abraham

deceased her (the second was the Duke of Clarence, son of Henry IV). Three excellently preserved alabaster effigies on a single, low, broad tomb-chest set up, it seems, in 1440, the chapel having been consecrated in 1439 (Selby Whittingham). They all wear coronets, the men heavy plate armour. – Lady Thornhurst †1609. Typical Jacobean standing wall-monument, with columns, obelisks and loud heraldry at the top among strapwork, the frame for two figures, she reclining on her side in a 'toothache' attitude, her husband kneeling behind. Small kneeling daughters below. – Dorothy Thornhurst †1620. Hanging monument, with a large kneeling woman in prayer, and the usual trappings. – Thomas Thornhurst †1627. A more lavish affair in the same coarse idiom. He half reclines, gazing up; his wife lies supine. At the side stand soldiers in contemporary armour, holding curtains back. Kneeling children below. – William Prude †1632. Again the same sort of thing, a kneeling knight this time, hand on breast, with Ionic columns each side and standing soldiers, one drawing his sword. Allegorical females higher up. – Sir George Rooke †1708. Standing wall-monument, with a long bust on a pedestal, possibly by *Edward Stanton*. Ships in relief below, and an inscription recounting his naval exploits (one of them the capture of Gibraltar) in Ciceronian phrases. – Francis Godfrey †1712. Architectural wall-monument with trophies of arms.

Crossing　For the pulpitum, see *Choir* above.

Nave　FONT and FONT COVER. An outstanding piece of Laudian display given in 1639 by Bishop Warner of Rochester, torn down by Puritans, and reassembled with new sculpture in 1662. The font itself, of black and white marble, is memorably pure and unmannered in its classicism. Shallow, octagonal, gadrooned and fluted bowl on a stem with figures of the four Evangelists standing between Tuscan colonnettes. Cover of wood, in two stages, with small figures of the twelve Apostles; Christ blessing as the finial at the top. Metal pulley bracket, with the Royal Arms of Charles II. – ARCHBISHOP'S THRONE. Only the CANOPY, of wood, remains of the throne presented by Archbishop Tenison in 1704. *Grinling Gibbons* carved it, but the designer of this monumental columned structure may well have been *Hawksmoor*. This play with curved forms in three dimensions is just what he enjoyed. Trios of fluted Corinthian columns carry pieces of entablature with concave sides. These are linked by an arch with pierced scroll brackets carrying urns and a cloth of honour. – PULPIT. 1898; designed by *Bodley*. Of wood, coloured; in a Perp style, with a tester. Prim, tight outline, conventional handling. – PAINTING. Early C16 transferred fresco of St Christopher, by the Ferrarese painter *Garofalo*. Very Venetian in style. – STAINED GLASS. The W window (after restoration is completed) has the rest of the late C12 genealogical figures reset in the lowest two tiers of lights.

32. CANTERBURY Throne canopy, 1704.
Designed by Hawksmoor (?), carved by Gibbons.
North-west nave bay

Thirteen in all, they include the splendid figure of Adam delving. The upper parts of the window keep much of the glass inserted here in the C15. The tracery lights, however, are datable 1396–9. Armorial glass, and figures of prophets, saints and apostles here. In the main lights Kings of England and Archbishops, and a good deal of armorial glass. The subdued colours, browns, greens and mauves, and plenty of plain glass, are quite different from the strong, glowing C12 colours, and different too from the later C15 glass in the NW transept. – MONUMENTS. N AISLE. Hales family, after 1596. A bizarre narrative wall-monument. At the bottom a man kneels at a prayer-desk. Above him a kneeling woman, between obelisks, with, behind her, a painting of Sir James Hales's suicide in the river Stour. At the top, a second family tragedy, the committal at sea of the body of the younger Sir James, who led the disastrous expedition to Spain in 1589, meant to be a reprisal for the Armada, in which the crews were decimated by disease. – Sir John Boys † 1612. Big standing wall-monument, much too big for the effigy, a figure in scholar's robe reclining on one elbow and frowning hard. Two little children kneel below. – Orlando Gibbons † 1625. The famous organist and composer, who died while at Canterbury composing music for Charles I's reception of his bride Henrietta Maria. *Nicholas Stone* made the monument, in 1626, for £32. Black and white marble tablet, with an outstandingly fine bust, white against the plain black niche. The bust, cut short at the shoulders and set on a pedestal, is an elegant Continental form, new to England. Top-heavy segmental pediment on an eared surround, robustly Jacobean in feeling, but this too a form picked up by Stone in the Low Countries. Charming little swags at the bottom. – Dr Thomas Lawrence. 1806 by *Flaxman*. Just a tablet with a medallion portrait in profile. – Officers and Men of the 50th Regiment, 1848. 'Geo. Nelson sculp. from a sketch by the late *M. L. Watson*.' Large classical female in very high relief. She holds a flag and reclines on a cannon. Well designed; carved in a dead sort of way. – Dean Lyall † 1857. Medievalizing wall-monument, with a recumbent effigy, tomb-chest and canopy. One notes that the stone used is not marble. Archbishop Sumner, 1866 by *H. Weekes*. Similar, minus the canopy. – Bishop Parry † 1889. Recumbent effigy, 1881 by *James Forsyth*, of marble, on an alabaster tomb-chest, with E. E. arcading and allegorical figures. This too is completely conventional. Archbishop Benson † 1896. Designed by *Sir T. G. Jackson*. Alabaster recumbent effigy under a heavy Gothic canopy. It is rather surprising that at a time when in architecture novelty of effect, admittedly within the styles of the past, was so highly prized, monumental design should have remained quite uninspired by any feeling for experiment.

SOUTH AISLE. John Sympson. By *Rysbrack*, 1752. Standing wall-monument with two putti by a broken column. Grey pyramid at the back. Not carved with much gusto. – Officers and Privates of the 16th Queen's Lancers. Big relief, with a wounded soldier, carved by *Edward Richardson*, 1848. Very impersonal. – Sir George Gipps. Bushy-browed bust in classical drapery, by *H. Weekes*, 1849. – Lt-Col. John Stuart. With a relief of Minerva attending to a soldier with a headache. – Bishop Broughton. 1855 by *J. G. Lough*. Recumbent marble effigy in drapery that seems part shroud, part episcopal lawn. – Lt-Col. Frederick Mackeson. 1856, also by *Lough* (Gunnis 1953). Relief still in the Flaxman tradition, but mixing

allegory and realism with its classical female and Indian and English soldier by an urn. But the surround is Gothic. Lough seems to have been pretty muddle-headed. – Hon. James Beaney. Fussy Gothic wall-monument with a relief and a portrait medallion, carved by *J. Forsyth*, 1893.

West and south-west porches IRON GATES made up from a C13 14 grille made for the w crossing arch at the E end of the nave. – WOODWORK (sw porch) made up by *Seely & Paget*, incorporating fragments of *Roger Davis's* choir stalls of 1676.

CLOISTERS, CHAPTER HOUSE ETC.

Lanfranc made the monastery of Christ Church the largest in the country. The buildings he erected on the N side of the cathedral, a great cloister with chapter house and dormitory E of it, refectory to the N, and cellarer's lodgings to the w, fell into the normal Benedictine pattern, but of course on a grand scale. During the first half of the C12 much was added. A famous drawing at Trinity College, Cambridge, records the state of the waterworks, and so of the whole layout, at some time between 1153 and 1170. Prior Eastry at the start of the C14 and Prior Chillenden at the end of it were the great rebuilders. One can still grasp the great extent of this private world in the C12, though not its privacy, now that the refectory and necessarium have all but gone. They would have presented long, almost windowless walls towards the N; and the gates that let in from the secular world were kept locked or guarded. (On the great gate between the cathedral precincts and the town, see below.)

At the heart of the monastic enclosure is the GREAT CLOISTER. The walks were rebuilt under Prior Chillenden (1390–1411) to a consistent design. The s wall of the s walk, i.e. the vaulting shafts and springers of the vault, was built at the same time as the nave of the cathedral. The w walk was started in 1397. Lierne vaults, the ribs made the framework of cusped panels. Heraldic bosses, 825 of them altogether. A few in the s walk have grotesque heads, woman and fox etc. Four-light windows towards the garth, under crocketed ogee gables that rose above the roof-line with finials, eventually crumbling away, and now replaced. The exterior stonework of all four walks had to be entirely renewed. The gables rise again, not quite precise copies, as evidence existed for shorter pinnacles (Tatton-Brown). The tracery is of hexagons enclosing sub-cusped quatrefoils, surprisingly retardataire and not like the nave windows. The s walk was glazed in the late C15; for this was where the novices were taught. See the rebated mullions and tracery. In the w walk a stone bench for the monks to rest on, ending at the N with a stone seat with arms. By it, a contemporary doorway to the cellarer's lodging, with an octagonal opening beside it, identified as a 'turn', i.e. a hatch for handing food and beer unseen to exhausted monks. There are similar doorways at the s end.

The N cloister walls are E.E., rebuilt when the refectory N of it was reconstructed in 1226–36. Above a continuous bench, arcading, shafted, with moulded trefoiled arches, runs all along, with a band above of sunk circles and quatrefoils. Mutilated stiff-leaf here and there. The doorways to the refectory, one in the centre, the other at the E end, have luxuriant leaf capitals, the former of stiff-leaf, the latter crockets, upright leaves and grapes. Multiple shafts in the deep reveals of both. Keeled mouldings. Perp doorway set under the latter. The shafts of the Perp vaulting have so cut into the arcading that it is not easy to see that the E.E. decoration is organized into a pattern, of four bays and one bay of arcading alternately, the stiff-leaf coming at the ends of a group, moulded capitals in the middle. Opposite the main doorway to the refectory was the LAVATORIUM, where the monks washed before meals. See the panelled base and the truncated canopy that was set into the tracery at this point.

The doorways from the E walk are a more varied bunch. Continuing from the N end, the C12 doorway to the dormitory undercroft (and nowadays to the library) comes first. It has renewed scallop capitals, zigzag round the arch, an outer moulding with pellet, and an embattled hood-mould. Interlocked circles on a side shaft. After this the following: the Perp doorway to the Dark Entry; the chapter-house doorway with a window each side, erected in 1304–5 (see below); a second Perp doorway, to the slype; and finally the great monks' doorway into the N transept. The doorway is now Perp, but with its square surround is set, with callous indifference, into the centre of three sumptuous E.E. arches, which the vaulting further interferes with. They have many shafts with bunchy stiff-leaf. The rich, undercut foliage frieze of the centre arch remains, the winged demi-angel in the r. spandrel, and a good deal of colouring, red, blue and gold. Pointed cinquefoiled side arches, with dogtooth made of leaves around them. A date c. 1270 would fit this ripe production. The sumptuousness is explained by the fact that the Archbishop, coming from his palace, regularly used it. The monks reached the choir from their dormitory by way of the NE transept. In the cloister garth MONUMENTS with noteworthy lettering: Archbishop Temple, an early work of *Eric Gill*, 1904. – Hugh Sheppard. Also by *Gill*, 1938. – Dean Hewlett Johnson † 1966. Lettering by *W. C. Day*.

The CHAPTER HOUSE was rebuilt, probably re-using Lanfranc's walling, and made longer, by Prior Eastry in 1304. It was given end gables, a new roof and new windows by Prior Chillenden a century later. The doorway is easy to recognize as Eastry's, by its row of square flowers, with bumpy petals, round the arch, and by the four glazed arches l. and r. These are trefoil-headed, on shafts quatre-foil in plan, and over the capitals crawl knobbly, no longer naturalistic, leaves. All this leads one to expect a room more fanciful and florid, i.e. more Dec in spirit, than the one that appears. In fact the vastly lofty, oblong interior, 90 ft by 35 ft, impresses just because its majestic proportions are left to speak for themselves. There is no vestibule, so the wall-shafts divide the room into four equal bays. A double stone seat runs round all four walls, and closely spaced arcading above it, the spandrels filled with four-petalled flowers below a band of quatrefoils and embattling. One recognizes the sober vocabulary of Prior Eastry's choir screens. Clearly the same mason designed them both. Leaf-capitals to the shafts along the E wall – and the Prior's seat, in the centre, does, it must be admitted, shelter beneath a canted canopy gabled in three directions, with crockets and pinnacles, and the frieze has to climb up to clear it. But all that is undemonstrative enough too. The wall-shafts go with the arcading, but what the early C14 fenestration was like we do not know, for Prior Chillenden changed it all. His four-light windows, blank in the N wall, have one transom, the end windows, seven-lighters, two transoms, and tracery which starts like the cloister tracery, and continues with simple panelling. They flood the room with light. Finally the boarded ceiling, in seven cants (which produces a strange, mansard effect outside). This is covered with ribs that make patterns of cusped stars, as discreet as the Dec arcading. In the chapter house Dec and Perp combine in complete harmony.

To round off this account, CHRIST CHURCH GATE is the entrance to the precincts from the town. It makes a fittingly splendid prelude – and finale – to the cathedral. The date inscribed as the date of construction is 1517 (wrongly restored as 1507), which means that in time the Christ Church Gate is the last gesture of triumphant pride, an expression of royal patronage, a bare two decades before the King dissolved the monasteries. According to Mr P. H. Blake's researches, the heraldic shields which adorn the gate in profusion commemorate Prince Arthur, Henry VIII's elder brother, who died in 1502 and had visited Canterbury two years before (for his chantry, see Worcester). Mr Blake discovered that work certainly did not begin in Arthur's lifetime; but that it was under way in 1517, and concluded in 1520–1. The historical importance of this finishing date concerns the pilasters that flank the two entrance arches, for they are decorated with panels of Renaissance motifs. The closest parallel in England is of terracotta, on the windows at Layer Marney Towers, c. 1520. Several other buildings of the 1520s have such Early Renaissance touches in terracotta. The Christ Church Gate seems unique in that here they are of stone (and earlier than the stone capital at Chelsea Old Church of 1528). But Woodman has shown that the pilasters are very like those on a magnificent set of tapestries made for the cathedral in 1511 and hung in the choir until the Commonwealth (now, except for some recently stolen, in the cathedral at Aix-en-Provence).

For the rest Christ Church Gate is ornate but unoriginal, a square building, with octagonal angle turrets carried up above the panelled parapet. Lierne-vaulted ground storey entered through a wide four-centred arch, and a tiny, almost flat-topped, arch by those on foot. Rooms at two levels above the vault. All wall surfaces are panelled, the floor-levels marked by broad horizontal bands, the lower with shields on quatrefoils, the upper with half-length angels carrying shields. Big empty niche in the centre. The material is ragstone, which had crumbled so badly that *Caröe*'s restoration in 1931–7 involved a great deal of refacing, much of it in artificial stone. The splendid wooden doors to both archways bear the arms of Archbishop Juxon, which dates them 1660–3. Visible in the shops to l. and r. are the unrestored side elevations, where, surprisingly, brick predominates (but see *Bell Harry* under *Main transepts* above for C 15 use of brickwork).

For the precincts in detail, with the remaining monastic buildings, see the latest edition of B of E *North East and East Kent*.

Chelmsford

CATHEDRAL CHURCH OF ST MARY *Anglican*

(Based on B of E *Essex*, 1965, revised.)

Cathedral since 1913. But the church continues, whatever adjustments are made, to retain the look of a prosperous late medieval parish church: cf. e.g. Leicester, Bradford or Wakefield. (It was of Chelmsford that Pevsner commented in the 1950s that perhaps Liverpool and Guildford were 'wiser to build new temples'; Chelmsford's diocese is one of the most heavily populated in the country.)

The best impression of the building is the outside from the S E, with the commanding late C 15 W tower, the spectacular S porch, the nave, aisle and chancel, and the new E end of *Sir Charles Nicholson*'s, a little higher than the chancel. Its date is 1923, but *Sir Arthur Blomfield*'s E window of 1878 was re-used. The W tower has set-back buttresses, but the angles are chamfered. The battlements are decorated with flushwork – i.e. patterned flint and stonework – and carry eight small pinnacles. The charming open lantern is of 1749, when the leaded needle spire was also rebuilt. W doorway with ogee gable and tracery and shields in the spandrels, three-light W window, three-light bell-openings. The rest of the church over-restored. The outer N aisle and N transept are an addition of 1873. The

chapter house, muniment room and vestries, very much more attractive in design, date from 1926 and are also due to *Sir Charles Nicholson*. On the S side the S porch has plenty of flushwork decoration and inside a ceiling re-using blank tracery perhaps from bench-fronts. E of it the last two bays of the nave are alone ashlar-faced.

The interior reveals one earlier restoration, of 1801–3 by *John Johnson*, who had built the 'thoroughly civilized' Shire Hall nearby. In the nave he rebuilt the late C 15 piers with their characteristic lozenge shape and their mouldings and on the S side used Coade & Seely's *Coade* stone for the purpose. The clerestory windows were renewed by Johnson and the prettily ribbed, coved Tudor ceiling of the nave is also by him. Subsequently *Dent Hepper* added N and S galleries, the latter in 1818 (Colvin). The aisles embrace the tower, the chancel aisles the chancel. The N chapel opens in an early C 15 arcade of two bays which has an unusual shape: round arch divided into two pointed arches with openwork panel tracery in the spandrel. The thin pier has four shafts and four hollows in the diagonals.

FURNISHINGS

ALTAR by *Wykeham Chancellor*, 1931. – BISHOP'S THRONE with high Gothic canopy by *Sir Charles Nicholson*. – PROVOST'S STALL with simpler square canopy by *Wykeham Chancellor*, 1936. – COMMUNION RAIL with thick openwork foliage and cherubs, c. 1675, said to come from Holland. – PULPIT. 1872. – STAINED GLASS. Some by *A. K. Nicholson* and rather prosaic with its realistic figures on a ground of clear glass. – E window by *Clayton & Bell*, 1858. – W end of S wall, incised window by *John Hutton*. – MONUMENTS. Thomas Mildmay, erected 1571, a standing wall-monument of a curious shape, and without any major figures; but Mr P J Oldfield convincingly suggests that major figures originally existed. Base with colonnettes and small figures of kneeling children. Above this zone one with two steep triangular pediments and one semicircular pediment and above that zone a big ogee top with strapwork decoration. – Matthew Rudd † 1615. Small mural incised slab. Attributed by Mrs Esdaile to *Epiphanius Evesham*. – Robert Bownd † 1696 (N aisle), with fine flower garlands. – Earl Fitzwalter (Benjamin Mildmay) † 1756. Large standing wall-monument with an oversized urn in the centre flanked by Corinthian columns, and big cherubs standing to the l. and r. Signed by *James Lovell*. – Mary Mash † 1757. Of various marbles with an urn and fine Rococo decoration.

Remarkably, this busy industrial county town of Essex still has a quiet dignified centre near the cathedral. The large churchyard contains old tombstones and room to stand back and look. Further on surroundings, see the latest edition of B of E *Essex*.

Chichester

(Based on B of E *Sussex*, 1965, by Ian Nairn with NP, considerably revised, with information from Dean Holtby, Julian Munby, Jane Geddes, Thomas Cocke, Jeffrey West, Michael Gillingham, Anthony Quiney, George McHardy and Canon Lowther Clarke.)

Plan, Fig. 34, from the *Builder*, 1892, by A. Beresford Pite after a plan by Joseph Butler; not showing the Arundel Screen, in store 1859–1960 and now standing before the nave E bay.

Some references (see Recent Literature): Munby 1981; Quiney 1979; Singleton 1978.

INTRODUCTION

Chichester from the Selsey peninsula is like Chartres from the Beauce: perhaps no other English cathedral (though devotees of others might disagree) exerts such a continuous presence on the flat surrounding countryside, and it is the continuity which is the important thing; the spire becomes as invariable and natural as the sky and sun. What Chichester has in addition, on any kind of clear day – and there are a lot of clear days in Sussex – is the gently-rising backcloth of the South Downs two or three miles away, so that God, man and nature always seem to be in equilibrium. And from anywhere on those slopes, behind Goodwood or on Bow Hill, the effect is unforgettable: the plain like a sea, tipped with a glitter or a shimmer which really is the sea, punctuated only by one slim spire. And this spire can be seen from the sea, too. Nothing of the same height must ever be built near Chichester: spire and countryside form an equation or a symbol experienced by millions of people every year, which cannot be given a value purely in terms of landscape or architecture.

Closer to, the famous view of the cathedral seen across fields from the by-pass to the S W cannot be matched in England. And this can still just be carried through on foot over the railway, to the walls of the close, still in rough pasture (or in reverse, a walk of two hundred yards out of the busy South Street leads to fields, still partly walled with Roman bastions – fields from which, turning round suddenly, the image of the cathedral almost knocks the viewer over). But in 1960, after a long struggle, the Westgate Fields were designated for a future ring road and two schools; yet, as of the early 1980s, the view is still there.

In near views of the cathedral, the whole proportions, medium-long and medium-low, building up to the central spire, seem directed to make a single point like an outstretched hand. The W towers do not interfere (though they would if Pearson's scheme for reconstructing them with spires had materialized) and the detached bell-tower, the only medieval one remaining with an English cathedral, can hardly be seen from this side. Chichester has a different plan from Salisbury (no E transepts), yet it seems as single-minded as Salisbury.

But in temperament, Chichester and Salisbury are exactly opposite. Salisbury's single-mindedness is the result of one ruthless design, Chichester's the result of repeated piecemeal accommodations and repairs and additions. A history of English medieval architecture could be written without mentioning any single part of Chichester, yet as a whole, as the most typical English cathedral, it could never be left out. Nothing to excess, a bit of this and a bit of that, tolerance without servility, have over the centuries produced an effect as penetrating as Ely but in a completely different way. Without any doubt it is one of the most lovable English cathedrals: this is partly the architecture, partly the way in which city and church flow together easily (the Market Cross is just N E of the cathedral), partly the way in which the church authorities make you free of the cloisters and passages without harangue or stuffiness.

Chichester close is halfway between the miniature towns of Norwich close and Salisbury close and the traffic-laden fragments at Worcester and Lincoln. It is small and grew up casually (as the cathedral was never monastic, there was no need for a formal precinct), but it is free of through traffic, it is a good mixture of public and private space, and it has an enchanting plan, contained within the S W segment of the city walls, which also includes the big private

33. CHICHESTER View from the south-west

gardens of the Bishop's Palace, Chantry and Deanery. The spine is a cul-de-sac called Canon Lane, leading from South Street to the Palace grounds, but in the easy-going and civilized Chichester way it can also be reached through the cloister and down an alley. The cloister itself, a short cut between West Street and South Street, is almost a public space. Apart from the cloisters and palace the precinct's charm is townscape, not architecture.

Chichester Cathedral, like Norwich and others, was the result of the Norman centralization of sees. It had been founded at Selsey, about eight miles away by the sea, and was moved in 1075 (also perhaps because of erosion there) and established on a site which already contained a Saxon church of St Peter (liturgically this became incorporated in the N transept and was not given a separate building until 1850, in West Street). Bishop Ralph de Luffa succeeded to

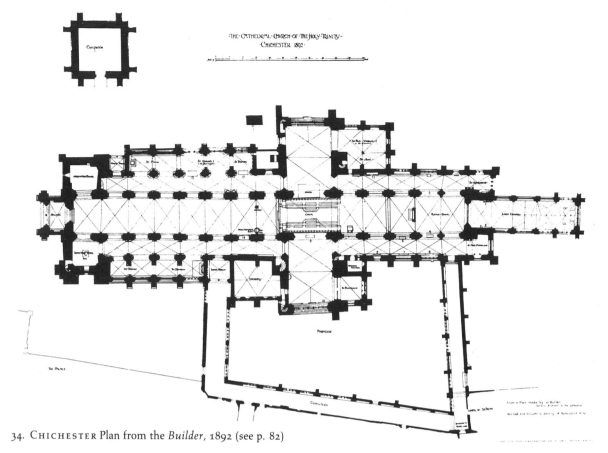

34. CHICHESTER Plan from the *Builder*, 1892 (see p. 82)

the see in 1091 and built the church 'a novo', as William of Malmesbury writes. There was a dedication in 1108, and building continued throughout the C 12, retarded by a fire in 1114. Bishop Seffrid consecrated it in 1184. In spite of additions, this forms the whole structure of the present church, except for the E end – i.e. eight-bay nave, transepts each with an E chapel, crossing and three bays of the choir. Luffa's church had an ambulatory and probably radiating chapels, and apparently just before the great fire of 20 October 1187 this had been extended eastwards to form the first two bays of the Lady Chapel.

After the fire, Seffrid II rebuilt rapidly and could reconsecrate in 1199. He and his successors used and sometimes ornamented the earlier work, providing a new clerestory and quadripartite vaults throughout. At the same time the chapels in the transepts, which had been apsidal, were enlarged and squared off. The ambulatory was replaced by a new retrochoir of two bays with E chapels l. and r. of the Lady Chapel. Work went on well into the C 13. A royal licence to the then bishop to carry Purbeck marble by sea was granted in 1206. A storm in 1210 wrecked two towers,

probably the s tower of the w front and the central tower. A statute of 1232 speaks of the church as 'needing manifold repair', Bishop Nevill, who died in 1244, left 130 marks to the building, and Bishop de Wych – subsequently St Richard – left £40 in 1253. An important study of the cathedral roofs (Munby 1981) dates them to the second half of the C 13. In 1279 Bishop Richard's remains were reburied in the retrochoir behind the high altar in the presence of Edward I. Then the Lady Chapel was lengthened by Bishop Gilbert (1288–1304) 'a fundamentis', the s transept was remodelled and given its big s window by Bishop Langton (1305–37), the cloisters were built c. 1400, the detached bell-tower added c. 1375–1430, the spire added some time in the C 15. The N W tower, engraved by Hollar, was called ruinous in 1658 (rebuilt 1897–1901 by *Frank Pearson* to his father's design, based on the s w tower). In the C 18 Bishop Mawson sponsored extensive repair and refitting of choir and Lady Chapel, completed 1759 with 'old Gothic ornaments all repaired and new ones added' (Cocke). The main C 19 restoration, which was mild, was carried out by *R. C. Carpenter* and *Joseph Butler* in the

1840s and 1850s. In 1861 the central tower telescoped in a spectacular way and was reconstructed in replica by (Sir) *Gilbert Scott* and *William Slater*.

The original building material is almost entirely a greenish limestone from Quarr Abbey on the Isle of Wight. The late C12 and C13 work used Caen stone. The overall external length of the cathedral is *c*. 295 ft.

Finally, before beginning description, to summarize the whole design. In spirit Chichester is a Romanesque building from end to end. Even the outside, with its big central tower – which is after all almost exactly the size and shape of Norwich – has preserved the measured, leisurely bay-to-bay rhythm of the original C12 design. The existence after the fire of 1187 of a recently completed shell must have been a strong inducement to continue the rhythm, but only if the builders were already temperamentally prepared for it. Only this can explain why, when the Lady Chapel was extended, a hundred years later, the designer maintained the rhythm of the heavy late C12 corbel table and completely defeated the original purpose of his bigger windows. Adapt and re-use, rather than sweep away and rebuild, has been the cathedral's leitmotif.

So, inside, the space is still basically Bishop Luffa's of *c*. 1091–1108. His design was straightforward, with no mannerisms and no *terribilità*, paying for its balance and reasonableness with a lack of intensity: good committee-man's Romanesque. The bay unit, with arcade, gallery and clerestory of almost equal height, was used again and again in Norman England, and achieved for example at Norwich and Ely a much greater power than it does here. But in relating it there is a missing building which ought to be given a bigger place in the history of English architecture. In realizing that the best Norman buildings were built in England, not France, we may have over-reached common-sense. The natural source of Norman ideas immediately after the Conquest was William the Conqueror's capital of Caen, particularly as so much building stone was imported from there; and it certainly seems fair to look to the Abbaye aux Hommes, built in 1066–86, as the father of the family of designs like Chichester. If engravings are compared, the proportions are identical, and the only big difference in the Chichester scheme is that the gallery is subdivided. Luffa's clerestory, however, nowhere survived the fire unaltered.

Luffa's design, without being austere, had hardly any ornament. It must indeed have looked bleak and officially impersonal to the designers of the late C12, because that is the only way to explain the extraordinary things that happened to it after the fire of 1187. (See also *Postscript on the E.E. style* after *Interior* below.) Though they maintained the Romanesque space unimpaired (the quadripartite vault with which they replaced the original flat wooden ceilings is barely pointed, and the clerestory is just a paraphrase of the standard Norman pattern of one big and two small openings), they embroidered the Norman design delicately and liberally, adding Purbeck marble shafts and string-courses, quickening the rhythm without altering the basic design. Later medieval architects faced with conversion or addition were usually more bold (Gloucester and Winchester) and occasionally more discreet (Yevele at Westminster Abbey, if it was he). An equivalent operation today would be to slow up the rhythm of a Victorian building by taking off ornament. It is no recipe for distinction, and whilst Chichester nave is friendlier for it, the remodelling has no more basic force than the original design.

The two-bay eastward extension of the choir, i.e. the C13 retrochoir, is a different matter altogether. The Norman rhythm and proportions are kept, but within that framework everything is new – though gentle even here; round arches in the arcade, round arches enclosing pointed ones in the gallery. The design is returned around the E end, where the gallery shrinks to a wall-passage with a sliding rhythm (of layered arcading which NP at Lincoln called syncopated arcading, or one might call it contrapuntal). This makes a splendid enclosed box in which the proportions are impeccable – no upward eager Gothic thrust but an exact balance, very typical of Chichester, between round arch and pointed arch – a dynamic living balance, where Luffa's High Romanesque was static and dead: the difference if you like between a good committee and a bad one. The thick expressive sculpture here must be later; yet again, a wish to quicken the rhythm, and yet again, addition instead of rebuilding. The two middle piers, composed of a central core and four detached shafts, are a classic solution to the problem of expressing the different loads that have to be borne (main vault, aisle vault, main walls, subsidiary arcade mouldings). Inspired by the work of 1175–84 at Canterbury, a chain of a sort can be made out from Canterbury to Chichester via New Shoreham.

The next part of the story at Chichester is purely English: three porches, using the fully developed E.E. style to do one of its favourite jobs, the single sharply defined bay. St Richard's Porch, now the entrance from the cloisters, is a classic example, in both design and carving: yet it must also be a hybrid, compounded of *c*. 1200 and *c*. 1240. And there the story peters out abruptly. The Dec style, in the Lady Chapel, was completely alien to Sussex, and only with the straightforward Early Perp cloisters was there again a consonance between the inherent virtues of a style and the temperament of the designers who were using it.

EXTERIOR

This description starts with Luffa's work, i.e. the chancel, the crossing and the transepts, then works continuously westwards to the W end. Thereafter it returns to the post-fire parts of the choir and works E; then St Richard's Porch; then the bell-tower. The rest of the cloisters follow *Furnishings* below.

Bishop Luffa would probably recognize his cathedral today, because of the continuity of proportions and spaces. But externally there are not many details to be picked up. As usual, they are around the CHANCEL, the TRANSEPTS and the CROSSING – the evidence complicated little by *Scott & Slater*'s rebuilding after the crossing tower fell. Their work is an accurate copy, and the join of old and new stonework is quite clear. Luffa's style was astonishingly consistent from the chancel to the NW tower, and astonishingly plain: his masons cannot have got much fun out of their work. They used a standard type of window that recurs throughout the building: a big opening with jamb shafts and cushion capitals, the arch with a thick roll moulding and an outer label of two rows of billet ornament. This can only be seen easily in one place – the W side of the N transept. (Less easy places are: the treasury (N transept E chapel) for one in the chancel aisle, and above in the library for another, vergers' vestry for one S transept E window, S aisle E bay for two blocked ones, N aisle W bay inside for another.) In spite of the plainness and blandness it makes a surprisingly rich window unit. The outer walls have massive clasping buttresses, themselves given nook-shafts, and a low string-course made up of chains of billets. Above the ground-floor windows followed small round-headed windows to light the gallery. A little higher up is a slight recession in the wall which probably marks the position of the original roof. The heavy corbel table above with its multiple repeated trefoiled heads between the corbels (also visible from the library over the treasury) is probably late C 13. Professor Willis suggested that its purpose was to raise the wooden roof off the stone vaults, which allowed no room for tie-beams (cf. Munby 1981). The earlier corbel table can be seen on the S choir aisle, ornamented with grotesque heads which are now badly weathered (and very like the heads in the corbel table of the S transept at Winchester, carved *c.* 1110). Also, above the S choir aisle, three blocked windows of the gallery. Their details can only be seen from certain places (one of the N chancel aisle from the library, one of the N nave aisle outside the first bay W of the transept): they had a plain single-step moulding. Immediately E of the easternmost of the three blocked gallery windows, the walling can be seen to turn inwards slightly. From this Willis deduced that Luffa's E end was an apse with ambulatory, and from the asymmetrical spacing of this third window that there was a radiating chapel. (This sounds convincing, but trial digging has shown no sign of any.) The clerestory windows of the Norman chancel are intact (i.e. outside; for fire damage, see inside), with shaft and billet in the hoodmould. Otherwise there is more C 12 evidence in the transepts, especially

the stump of a very broad centre buttress in the N transept N wall and clerestory windows like those of the chancel in the W and E walls of the S transept. Evidence of the apsidal chapels in the transepts are traces of the arch of an upper floor and the roof-line on the S side, an actual fragment of the curve of the apse on the N side (visible from the library).

Later work must start with the CROSSING TOWER, which, as has been said already, is now a replica of 1861–6. It is a comfortable, unaspiring design: big twin bell-openings consisting of two lights enclosing a trefoil with blind arcading below and a heavy corbel table above – so heavy that it is almost blind arcading also. The battlements and squat polygonal embattled pinnacles and the spire above are probably C 15, the latter a fine, light design that does more for the distant views of Chichester than anything else. Octagonal, with two bands of panelling, approximately one-third and two-thirds of the way up. At the base, four free-standing octagonal spirelets with firm, rich details in the diagonals between spire and pinnacles. The whole will stand a long and close look, yet its great virtue is that it never asserts itself. (But words like 'unassertive' and 'unaspiring' are too negative for so noble a structure. Its character may lie partly in this: unlike Norwich tower, which is square on plan, Chichester's on plan is oblong E W, unlike Winchester's, which is oblong N S; at Chichester the tower affirms the long axis of the cathedral plan.)

The SOUTH TRANSEPT is surrounded by the cloister, an extremely unusual thing, an irregular cloister and, in fact, not a normal cloister at all (described below after *Furnishings*). The main feature in the transept is the big S window put in by Bishop Langton, say about 1330, and heavily restored. It is an unsympathetic and wiry design, even discounting the restoration. The overall flickering effect is killed by the big spherical triangle in the head. Seven lights, formed into 3–1–3 sub-heads under the spherical triangle; all filled with reticulated tracery and cusped and foiled dagger-shapes. Plenty of technique but no understanding of the style. Above, in the gable, a small rose-window filled with equally clever and equally inorganic shapes, and between them a corbel table, recut in 1932, including recognizable heads of King George V and Lloyd George.

On the E side of the transept is St Pantaleon's Chapel, rebuilt in the C 13, now the canons' vestry. Simple E.E. detail with E window of three stepped lancet lights under a round-headed arch. On the W side is the externally three-storeyed-looking sacristy, now Song School and Chapter Room, an impressive hybrid. Inside, a small Norman doorway is preserved, but the two lower stages of the room are C 13, with narrow lancet windows, more vigorous than most C 13 details in the cathedral, to the S as well as the W, the latter visible in the cloister. It must have been built after St Richard's Porch because it incorporates a buttress from it in its w wall. The difference in the masonry (seen inside the cloister) is unmistakable (Willis). The top stage is Late Perp, clipped and effective. It has to the s two segment-headed windows of three lights without any mouldings at all.

The NORTH TRANSEPT is less complicated. It also has a show end window, Perp and assigned without documentary authority to the time of Bishop William Rede (1368–85), spurred on perhaps by its equivalent on the s side. It has seven lights and shows an uneasy compromise between Dec forms and the newly arrived straight lines of the Perp style. The lights are grouped 2–3–2, the outer pairs with steep heads, the inner trio meeting the apex of the arch in a flattened head containing an octofoil which ruins the overall pattern, bathos where there should have been climax. Above this a repaired c 13 corbel table, above again a c 19 gable and rose-window. Both E and w sides have clerestory windows typical of the E.E. repair and enlargement – pointed arches with obtuse heads, jamb shafts with stiff foliage capitals, the proportions almost exactly the same as Luffa's windows. The same windows recur in the Library, i.e. the upper floor of the E chapel (now treasury) off this transept, on the site of the Norman transeptal chapel, making an impressive two-storey composition at the E end. Below, a lancet on either side of a buttress. The buttress projects upwards and makes a stepped triplet out of the lancets in the upper storey: but it is not set centrally, so that one is at a loss to know whether any deliberate effect was intended. Perhaps it was an emergency repair. To the N the E chapel has two Perp four-light windows, later evidently than the great N window.

Now for the NAVE. Starting on the s side, the bays w of the crossing are partly obscured by the former sacristy (see above), but on the N the first bay is the best place to get the feel of Luffa's scheme. The clerestory window is a c 13 repair, but the gallery window is authentic, with its single-step moulding exactly as in the chancel (see above). Below it, the main window is later c 12, and pointed. But it has an outer label of billet ornament, like the Romanesque windows, and the capitals to the shafts are stunted and uneasy. It is obviously an earlier stage than most of the E.E. work at Chichester. The question is – something which will recur inside – whether in fact it was part of a remodelling which started before the fire of 1187.

Westwards of this the outer aisle begins: one bay with two lancets, above them, in plain plate tracery, a quatrefoil, and above this, in the bit of wall left, a tiny sexfoil. Then four bays whose windows now make an impressive show, with three lancets under two large circles under a smaller one, the circles originally unfoiled. In fact, the shafts and arches are authentic, but the tracery is an early c 19 repair

(by *Carpenter*, 1847) which repeated the original design but added the foiling inside the circles. The tracery is all of the bar, not plate, kind, and this appeared first at Westminster Abbey soon after 1245, but at e.g. Salisbury only about 1270. (It is not safe to date this tracery at Chichester by the founding in 1269 of a chantry 'in the north part', Dr Munby says, as that may refer to the N transept.) The s aisle consists of St Richard's Porch (see *Porches* below) and four bays almost identical with the earlier bay on the N side, but for reasons of Victorian imitation not of original contemporaneity. Fragments of string-courses show that both aisles originally had a gable over each bay, as many Continental churches still do; the buttresses between the bays are capped with heavy octagonal turrets, those on the N side just a little later and more ornate than those on the s.

Above, the clerestory is Luffa from end to end, with his unvarying big round-arched windows. In the c 13 flying buttresses were added for the new vault, one tier visible, another, on the s side only, below the roof of the aisle gallery. In the c 14 the nave roof was heightened, like all others, to prevent the load bearing directly on the stone vault, and here a functional makeshift led to one of the oddest features of Chichester, a second corbel table on the N side, about 3 ft below the normal position. The reason for this is that the clerestory walls had gradually sagged towards the s so that the N wall was concave and the s wall convex. To keep the parapets straight the concavity had to be reduced, and a single corbel table was not sufficient, so that a second had to be used. It runs westward from the central tower for five bays and then dies into the wall to reappear inside (as can be seen in the nave gallery – so there was a double sag, convex and concave). On the s side a simple set-back of the masonry was sufficient.

With that, except for the porches (see below), we are at the WEST END. And a very typical English west end it is too, an unreflecting stopping-up of the nave space which is neither a showpiece in its own right nor a crisp expression of the nave and aisles behind. There is plenty of compensation at Chichester in the overwhelming sense of mass of the whole cathedral enduring through all the alterations and restorations; but that need not have inhibited a more eloquent design. It is very English, too, in its patchwork. Luffa's front clearly had two w towers. The top of the s w tower was blown down by a storm in 1210 and replaced by an E.E. design; the N w tower fell down in the c 17 and was not replaced until 1896–1901, when *J. L. Pearson* designed and his son executed a near-copy of the s w tower. (He included funny openings high up on the s w buttress. Did he have any evidence for them? If so, they were the only bits of Chichester to reflect the extraordinary Late Norman details at Climping.) But Luffa's buttresses pop up everywhere, and the s face of the s w tower is one of the best places to see his style close to – or rather, the style he bequeathed to his successors, assuming that the w front was one of the last parts to be finished. Three storeys survive, two with the familiar windows, the ground floor with a blocked doorway which represents the limit that C 12 Chichester permitted itself in the way of ornamentation. Two orders of zigzag are separated by a thin rope-like moulding decorated with chevrons. It does not represent much slackening of the reins. The only similar work is the doorway in Canon Lane and, near Chichester, at Tortington. The C 13 re-working began with a single lancet and went on to the fine deep paired bell-openings, each of three orders with jamb shafts, carrying on a way of designing that is as common in Normandy as in England. The heavy parapet brings things back firmly to this side of the Channel, however. The part between the towers was almost rebuilt then or a little later; above the porch (see below) there is a three-bay arcade, in the gable are two lancets on a diapered background; between them the main w window, Early Dec in style, is *Carpenter's*, of 1849, replacing C 17 and C 18 repairs. That completes our description of the exterior w of the crossing, except for the porches described below after the Lady Chapel.

To follow in detail what went on at the E end, resulting in the RETROCHOIR, the story must be taken up again at the third bay of the chancel, the present sanctuary, where according to Willis the Norman ambulatory had started. In its stead, after the fire, the choir was lengthened by two bays, the change being reflected only in the shape of the clerestory windows, round to pointed, and the shafts and capitals, not in any alteration of the proportions. The flying buttresses, one tier only, as it is everywhere except on the s aisle length, are massive, as they must be, being as early as they are. They are, of course, a reflection of Canterbury, which can boast flying buttresses hardly, if at all, later than the earliest in France. Those at Chichester are very like the later examples at Boxgrove. The E ending is a group of the high choir, the partly older Lady Chapel (see below) sticking out far eastward, and the two short flanking E chapels finishing the chancel aisles. This arrangement occurs at about the same time – earlier? later? – in the work at Winchester under Bishops de Lucy † 1204 and des Roches † 1238 – work begun by 1202. The E wall of the high choir has a group of three widely spaced stepped lancets and above it a big rose-window of the later C 13, terribly renewed (the latter visible only outside, i.e. above the vault). The pattern is that of six circles surrounding a seventh, i.e. exactly the pattern of the E window of the Angel Choir at Lincoln, which was completed in 1280. The Chichester rose is flanked by a pair of turrets of utterly un-Gothic solidity which effectively anchor down the eastern mass (and are reinforced by another pair of C 19 turrets lower down flanking the ends of the aisles). Both are octagonal, and both are renewed: the N E has shafts

supporting a flat lintel, looking as much C 19 as C 13: the S E is later and has trefoiled heads between the shafts. The choir aisles have an assortment of C 13 to C 15 windows. One of these deserves a moment's attention. It has five lights and the intersecting tracery typical of about 1300. But the mullions are not medieval, thin square piers set diagonally, and so this was perhaps a replacement after the siege of 1643. On the N side are two Perp windows, similar to those of the N transept E chapel. One more puzzle occurs at the N E corner, that is outside St John's Chapel. Here the main window is of c. 1180, but above it is a small round-headed light which should belong to the early C 12 (though it has a chamfered surround, while the Early Norman ones had a single step). If the original choir aisles in fact continued in an ambulatory, why was such an insignificant detail moved to the new alignment or imitated? The E walls of both N and s chapels have small octofoiled openings, again probably of the later C 13, high up in the gable.

The LADY CHAPEL, to the E of this, is no kind of culmination. At best, it provides one more stepped stage to articulate the long spread-out volume. Four bays are visible outside; the first two were in fact built in the later C 12 as we shall see, and as the flat Norman buttresses suggest, but the details are otherwise all of c. 1290–1300, identical in N and s walls, distressingly mechanical in design and distressingly casual in arrangement – the windows are rarely fixed centrally in the bays and do not match each other in size. It looks as though window designs were ordered blindfold and the masonry then bodged to fit. Historically the windows have all the same some importance. They are typical of the most progressive work of the last decade of the century and can, as we have seen, be firmly dated to before 1304. Bay 2 was the first to get its windows, which are a little bigger and just a little more strait-laced than bays 1, 3 and 4, which are almost identical. The basic pattern is three stepped lights roughly dividing the window into a grid with trefoil and quatrefoil shapes in the tracery heads – a scheme which has neither the flow of mature Dec tracery nor the vigorous pattern of Perp windows. In bay 2 the trefoils and quatrefoils are enclosed in circles, in the others they are unleashed; the E window has exactly the same scheme as the later bays, but extended to five lights.

Next, three PORCHES: at the w end (also called galilee), at the w end of the N aisle, and halfway along the s aisle, forming one entrance from the cloister. They are all E.E., and all of the same basic pattern – a portal, preceded by a single quadripartite-vaulted bay and with the entrance subdivided into two bays by a central column. But within this framework, they are absorbingly different in detail and in quality. The earliest of them, St Richard's Porch to the s aisle, is easily the best, up to the level of units like the N porch at Christchurch or the little w porch at Lichfield, a way of designing in which England excelled. But it is itself a composite design, and the parts are not easily dated. The vault is early E.E. on the strength of the mouldings of the ribs and the corbels on which they rest, especially the two heads. But the capitals of the S entrance are lush stiff-leaf, and the unequal quatrefoil above the *trumeau* and the thick crude foliage corbel underneath it must all be of *c.* 1230–40 at the earliest. The statue of St Richard which it now carries is by *Hems* of Exeter, 1894, and does no violence to its surroundings. Inside on the l. (w) is a small wall arcade of four bays in the same style (what for?), then the inner doorway, in the usual Sussex C 13 style, well done: two orders of shafts with moulded capitals, circular abaci, and an inner order of dogtooth ornament. On the cloister, from which this is the nave entrance, see after *Furnishings* below.

The N porch has the same character as this inner doorway, but is skimped where the other was ample – especially in the (re-used?) cramped crocket capitals. The inner doorway has one roll on shafts and one continuous chamfer, the outer arches have two complicated roll mouldings on shafts with dogtooth ornament on both the extrados and the soffit of the arches. Again blank arcading was started on one side and not continued. Outside on the l. is a steep gabled niche, above head height, of *c.* 1260.

Finally the W porch, its outer entrance now glass-enclosed. Here the outer arches are a disappointment; for the tympanum and *trumeau* are almost all redone. The inner doorway has three orders of shafts with late-C 13-looking moulded capitals and arches starting just like those of the lancets above, in the W wall of the nave, with a bit of an extremely fat roll for each order and then developing finer mouldings out of them (or alternatively the finer mouldings dying into the fat stumps). The shafts of the W doorway are Purbeck marble which has weathered a deep brown to give an almost Northants striped effect. The sides of the porch have three blank arches each side with pointed-trefoiled heads and in the spandrels above them rounded quatrefoils, two complete and, l. and r., one half each – a curious, somewhat heavy, but quite forceful motif, comparable to the treatment of the N and S walls of the Winchester Lady Chapel (which, by comparison with plate tracery at Salisbury and elsewhere, might date *c.* 1225–35; see Winchester, *Interior*, below). Both sides have been cut into for tomb recesses, no longer identifiable – a gabled tomb of *c.* 1300 on the S, a square-headed tomb of the C 15 on the N.

The last part of the outside is the detached BELL-TOWER, which in fact is what most people notice first at Chichester. Such bell-towers were not as unusual as it must seem to us today. We know of their existence, as substantial as at Chichester, at Westminster Abbey, Salisbury, Norwich, Worcester, St Augustine Canterbury, and

35. CHICHESTER Detached bell-tower, C 14–15

Tewkesbury. The Chichester bell-tower stands a few feet N of the W end of the nave, and was probably built to house the bells as a result of some subsidence or movement in the central tower. It is a lumpish, unlovable building – nothing like the splendid, much slimmer bell-tower at Evesham, for example – but if it had been any taller it would have had a disastrous effect on the proportions of the whole cathedral. As the only remaining example close to a cathedral it is a precious relic, but one can see Wyatt's point of view when he removed the Salisbury one. Money was left for the Chichester campanile in 1375, the early C 15, and 1436, and this may correspond to the two stages: the lower heavy and blank, with small windows of typical late C14 design and big set-back buttresses, the upper a squat, thinner octagonal lantern with octagonal corner pinnacles, and bell-openings which are equally typical of the years around 1440. (Was the small w doorway, which is clearly early C14, re-set or proof of an earlier start?) They make a disproportionate match. Was any sort of spire intended on top, or should the lantern have been taller? The very different relative proportions of (say) Boston Stump, attached to its church, are not comparable.

INTERIOR

On going in by the w door, the immediate impression, just like the outside, is that this is still entirely a Romanesque church, comfortably spread out under its quadripartite vault, easy-going and balanced and very English. The second impression is of the admirable balance of spatial tensions created by replacing (and opening up) the Arundel Screen (see *Furnishings*, Nave). The choir is neither shut in nor opened out, but a mixture of both. Through the openings the eye sees the bottom of the reredos, above the screen the eye sees the lancets at the E end of the retrochoir, and the screen loft performs a beautiful conjuring trick by obscuring the top of the reredos and hence the fact that it is not in the same plane as the lancets but two bays to the w of it. Space filters away benignly forwards and sideways without compelling or coercing (and therefore, perhaps inevitably, without drama or rapture). Only the retrochoir would fix itself in the memory so strongly as to force a second visit, yet after two dozen visits there are a multitude of tiny, friendly sensations which add up in the end to something memorable. In its even temperament it was the perfect Anglican cathedral long before there was a Church of England.

A detailed look ought to start in the CHANCEL; for cathedrals were as a rule built from E to w, and of Bishop Luffa's E end further E we know no details. (The C13 retrochoir is described in chronological order after the nave.) The Norman chancel has a three-storeyed elevation, arcade, gallery and clerestory, and it had no doubt an open timber roof or a wooden ceiling. To study the details it is not advisable to look too closely at the w bay; for this is pretty completely a replacement of after the fall of the crossing tower in 1861. As for the other bays, of the arcade enough remains for us to visualize its late C11 sturdiness. The piers probably had demi-shafts towards the chancel, mast-like as in the Winchester transepts or at Ely. They have been replaced, but the thick demi-shafts to the arch openings are there, with heavy single-scallop capitals, and towards the aisle a strong nook-shaft which originally had its companion towards the chancel. To the aisle was

another demi-shaft whose stump exists still. It must have been for a transverse arch. The arcade arches have two slight chamfers to the chancel, one to the aisle. The gallery has survived unchanged. A twin opening for each bay, low and broad, the responds with high, coarse capitals with vestigial volutes and elementary leaves, probably early C12 in style (Jeffrey West). The thick mid-shafts have two-scallop capitals, the super-arches two strong rolls to the nave, and the tympana lozenge pattern of alternatingly grey and brown stone, an Early Norman motif. (Cf. e.g. Westminster Abbey on remains of the C11 reredorter.) Transverse arches were thrown across the gallery. (It is mysterious that the w bay of the E.E. retrochoir on the N side has part of a Norman arch above the E.E. arch, higher than the other gallery arches: was this the start of a different system for the ambulatory gallery?) Of the Norman clerestory only the windows are preserved and low arches at r. angles to the wall which belong to the wall-passage, now E.E. They prove, however, that the Norman clerestory also had such a wall-passage, and that it had the stepped tripartite arrangement which exists at Winchester and Ely and which one would have expected anyway.

The E.E. adjustments after the fire of 1187 are telling. Willis has shown most ingeniously why they are most extensive in the clerestory, less so on the ground level, and absent in the gallery. In a fire the roof will produce the worst heat. So the top storey will go most thoroughly. Then the timbers crash to the ground and damage the arcade. The gallery is less in danger. At Chichester what was done is this. The subsidiary order of the main arcade which faced inwards was replaced by detached Purbeck marble shafts and capitals (leaf crocket capitals typical of all the Purbeck work at Chichester), the arch moulding of this order delicately elaborated, and the bays were linked by a Purbeck string-course. The clerestory was rebuilt in an E.E. transcription of the Norman three-part division, one big and two small. Here the side arches are pointed, the central arch still round (perhaps because it had to incorporate the existing windows), and the supports between made up of three clustered Purbeck shafts. The vault above is quadripartite with carved bosses at the intersections (on one boss an angel with the arms of St Richard – a Perp replacement, it seems). In general the ribs are slim and have the section of rolls, keeled and unkeeled and hollow. (For more on this, see *Postscript on the E.E. style* below.) The vaulting cells or webs are plastered, but on the evidence of the exposed ones in the nave and the N porch it can be assumed that they were filled in the French (and Canterbury) not the English way, that is by cutting the stones of the courses of infilling so that they met at the crown or apex in a straight, not a sawtooth joint. The vaulting-shafts are triple, one round, two keeled, running up to the same kind of Purbeck capital poised halfway between crocket and stiff-leaf. The aisle vaults and shafts repeat this pattern on a smaller scale, the N aisle distinctly earlier than the S (again, see *Postscript* below). These aisles can of course not really be seen independent of the new retrochoir of after the fire and its aisles and E chapels, but there is good reason why these parts should be treated later.

So we move on to the TRANSEPTS first and again the Norman work there. It is of that Early Norman plainness and severity, as it is in the transepts of so many cathedrals. Each has two bays, each had a two-storey apsidal E chapel, later extended, and plain W walls. The galleries from nave and chancel ended in heavy two-light openings, all four renewed, again because of the fall of the spire. The apsidal chapels each had an unmoulded round opening to both storeys of two orders, much more severe than the other Norman work in the cathedral. It survives in the N transept. In the S transept it had from the beginning a slight chamfer towards the chapel, and the face towards the transept was redone with a very modest kind of embellishment – a roll moulding on the soffit, supported by corbels carved with primitive leaves – which may even have been part of the remodelling begun just before the fire of 1187. Both the upper openings of the chapels were redone E.E. The W wall of the N transept has two impressively severe Norman windows at ground level. Above, the details of clerestory and vault are those of the chancel. The only things to notice specially are that the outer bays have a five-part vault, with a rib of different section running from the intersection of the outer wall. This may have been an alteration done in the C 14 when the big N and S transept windows were put in. (The surround of the great S window has shafts with capitals carrying sparse leaves, abaci with fleurons, and a hoodmould on large heads.) The ribs in the S transept have dogtooth ornament on the soffit (cf. Boxgrove and Aldingbourne) and are hence probably slightly later than the other vaults in the cathedral.

The various spaces opening off the transepts had better be described here, although they break the general historical flow. The two apsidal chapels were both given square ends in the late C 12 or early C 13. That on the S (St Pantaleon), still one bay, has a quadripartite vault, that on the N (now treasury, former Chapel of the Four Virgins) was enlarged on the S to give a four-bay room squeezed against the choir aisle – part of one blocked Norman window has already been noticed – and hence with awkwardly stilted vault-ribs. The new vault in the original chapel has some but not all of its ribs given zigzag ornament in a puzzling way. Was this, one could speculate, something which was in progress before the fire, was it re-used material, was it conservatism, or were the various ornaments more interchangeable in time than we like to think? Such zigzag does not occur anywhere else, but it

does occur in the work of 1175–84 at Canterbury, and this essentially was the most go-ahead work of that moment in England. The foliage capitals and responds which support the ribs with the zigzag are indeed not specially early.

On the W side of the S transept is the SACRISTY, now SONG SCHOOL. This has already been noticed (*Exterior*, S transept) as being quite different from other E.E. parts in the cathedral, and the inside is just as individual; a sober, effective two-bay room with a five- – not six- – part vault, all the ribs single-chamfered, resting on corbels with rich, yet flattish stiff-leaf foliage, among the richest in the cathedral (cf. *Postscript* on style). (A small Norman doorway preserved here has been mentioned.) The upper storey, now the Chapter Room, is C 15.

To come back to the CROSSING, or to Scott's reconstruction of it, Luffa's firm, impersonal scheme becomes much more evident. One major unmoulded order and two minor roll mouldings, corresponding to one major half-column and two minor shafts, careful and ordered. The E arch has the major moulding elaborated with rolls and its column subdivided into two demi-columns with a cable moulding in between, sharing the same scalloped capital. The roll mouldings on E and W arches are decorated with cable ornament, and the E arch in addition has the sides of the orders decorated with chip-carved St Andrew's crosses. That is all; and the replica of the quadripartite C 13 vault above is just as plain. Whether these Norman details are pre-1108 or post-1108 is anybody's guess.

From catching the rhythm here, it is easy to move on to the NAVE. Nothing essential distinguishes it from the chancel. The system is the same, the changes concern only details, but these details do give an indication of historical sequence. The first bay again is of *Scott's* making. Part of the original Norman arcade arch, differing in size from Scott's, is exposed on the N side. Where the original work of the nave is not exactly like that of the chancel is in these minor ways: The thick demi-shafts to the arcade openings have two-scallop capitals like the gallery, not the arcade in the chancel (of one-scallop just one N and one S respond in different situations). Also, to the aisle, the arcade arches have a thick roll instead of the slight chamfer. On the gallery the responds have no longer the primitive volute capitals. The capitals now have one or two scallops.

More changes from the fifth bay onwards show that here really a revised plan must have been followed. The piers are now a bit thinner, the arches a bit wider, as Willis has spotted. The transverse arches to the aisles – so their plinths, if nothing else, show – had twin demi-shafts instead of single demi-shafts. This arrangement was then carried on with the arches between aisle and W tower bays. Incidentally there are two more details which may be of significance. In the W bay of the N aisle by the entrance from the E.E. N porch is a trace of what looks like the usual

Norman wall-arcading. Was there more of this? And in the w bay of the s aisle in the angle between the arch to the tower just referred to and the arcade arch is an extra angle-shaft. Its function must have been the support of a vault. Were the Norman aisles then vaulted, perhaps from the start? We cannot say, but there would be nothing surprising in it, as the aisles of Winchester and Ely were also vaulted – groin-vaulted, of course – before 1100. Then, in the gallery, the decoration of the tympana changes from the flat pattern to motifs in relief : fish-scales, studs, diamonds.

Curiously enough small changes were made again when the E.E. work reached the nave after the fire. Here the Purbeck shafts of the arcades acquire shaft-rings, from the w respond of the fourth bay onwards. In the clerestory, right from the crossing, the clusters of Purbeck shafts are replaced by taller single shafts (cf. the retrochoir, below). The wall arches show some of the odd faults so frequent in medieval work and so naïvely corrected.

The last bay of the nave connects with the TOWERS. The system of elevation still remains the same, but the gallery arch now has three rolls towards the nave instead of two. As for the E.E. contribution, the most interesting detail is that on the intermediate shafts of the group of lancets in the w wall the arches start with a fat, shapeless stump of an upright roll, out of which the finer mouldings then develop. The base of the sw tower, which was presumably less affected by the fire, is as completely Norman as anything at Chichester, with one tall and wide blank arch and to s, w and e a billet string-course. *Pearson* copied and matched up for his reconstruction job on the NW tower.

In the NAVE AISLES the c 13 work is almost exactly what it had been in the chancel aisles, bafflingly so; for even the capitals of the wall-shafts and the bosses are unchanged and that means as early as any of the post-fire renewal. This even applies – yet more bafflingly – to the entrance arches into the outer chapel at the e end of the n aisle (in spite of the plate tracery of the window) and the two two-bay outer chapels of the s aisle. The capitals are different here from any of the others, but undeniably early: high, crude crocket capitals of the most primitive kind (in stone). Yet on the s side these arches interrupt the string-course of the aisle wall, i.e. are not contemporary with it.

The two two-bay s chapels incidentally were originally separated from one another by a solid wall but later thrown into one to make an outer aisle, with a crude pointed arch (which in a village church would be dated *c.* 1200, another puzzle) and have now been separated again. The transverse arches in each chapel have the same mouldings as those opening from the nave, but the capitals are obviously late, with the same luxuriant elaboration of a basically crocketed shape as in St Richard's Porch (see *Postscript* below). The vaults are quadripartite, as everywhere, and they slope up

to the windows to allow these a larger size. The e wall of St Clement's Chapel (the easternmost) keeps a noble RERE-DOS of two pointed arches flanking one wider trefoiled arch and two quatrefoils over, with new statues inserted. In the arch once dividing the w from the e chapel one jamb shaft, fairly high up, tells of the former existence of another REREDOS. In the outer n aisle the easternmost bay was originally an isolated chapel, i.e. had a solid w wall. Against the remains of that wall in the next bay another REREDOS just like that of the SE chapel. The remaining four bays – two chapels – were added later in the c 13 and show this by subtler, more complex mouldings of the arches. The bosses on the other hand are of the simplest and must be re-used. The vaults again slope up to the windows. The e chapel of the two, i.e. where there was the solid wall mentioned before, had yet another REREDOS, and the lowish screen wall once separating the two chapels one more. Again it is the outer shafts which are preserved.

Now back to the e end. The present modern platform behind the high altar, i.e. in the RETROCHOIR, is said to mark the site of St Richard's shrine, dedicated in 1279. Though that spiritual and financial generator arrived some decades after the architecture, the placing of relics here was perhaps hopefully envisaged when rebuilding of the Norman ambulatory began. At any rate, the two-bay retrochoir is the aesthetic and spatial climax of the cathedral, the exact point of balance, perhaps in the whole of England, between Romanesque and Gothic, the point where stylistic transition and national temperament were exactly in step. The designer had to keep the Romanesque proportions and bay width to within a few feet (in fact the gallery is a little shallower, the arcade a little deeper). Many big churches tried this and failed – e.g. Romsey. But here, pointed and round arches are harmonized exactly. The arcade has to be round-arched, the gallery has two pointed arches under a round arch. The returned e end has one wide, slightly pointed arch and above it, to connect the N with the s gallery, a narrow wall-passage. To the chancel there are here also paired two-light openings, but immediately behind them appears a wall arcade which is given a sliding rhythm compared with the main arches (i.e. the two-layered counterpoint found at Lincoln, e transepts and choir aisles from *c.* 1200, and at Worcester, triforium of e end begun 1224). The clerestory has the same tripartite rhythm as the adjoining chancel, except that the intermediate Purbeck shafts are much taller and hence the outer little arches are vastly stilted on their outer sides. In each part of the design, curves and points answer each other, all in the comfortable overall volume which is still Romanesque. It is like a medieval debate made visible. The details generally are the same as in the other E.E. parts of the cathedral – complicated moulded arches with flat grooved soffits, crocket capitals interspersed with stiffly formal leaf pat-

terns, sometimes bending a little, but never submitting like the capitals in a cathedral like Wells. There are two exceptions: one is the sculpture, which is a problem on its own and will be discussed presently; the other is the design of the intermediate piers. These are both mighty and brilliant, consisting of a big central Purbeck shaft surrounded by four smaller free-standing Purbeck shafts, corresponding (in a way which would have delighted the logicians of the Île de France) to the main load of the walls and the subsidiary loads delivered by the inner orders of the arches, the nave vault, and the aisle vault. The idea is inspired by Canterbury, but not expressed so elegantly or concisely, even to the point of varying the depth of capital according to the width of the column: a misunderstanding of this principle may explain the occasional stunted or squashed-up capitals found at Chichester. (The abacus of the pier follows the division of core and shafts, and that has led to an awkward junction with the arch mouldings. Where there was not space for the diagonals to land safely on the abacus, deft little stiff-leaf sprays of stone are introduced to mediate.)

What sets the seal on this harmonization of diverse elements is the SCULPTURE and decoration in the gallery stage, and this is probably the biggest single puzzle at Chichester. It consists of spirited figures in the spandrels of each two-light opening, small in size but large in scale, and a good deal more foliage and even chains of monsters around the arches at the E end, forming complete openwork bands inside the main arch mouldings. All this is lush, curly, vivid, naturalistic, impossible to reconcile with c. 1200, easy to reconcile with the second third of the century, especially the figures. These deserve extra study. In the N and S bays they are small, in moderate relief, and set in fancy foiled shapes of ever varied detail, including pointed foils. In the E bays instead they come boldly forward out of their trefoils. In the N and S bays they are two angels and two and one seated figures. Much is C 19 renewal, but what is original has draperies clearly in the French style of 1230-40 (i.e. like the end of the Chartres workshop and the Villard-de-Honnecourt-like parts of Reims). Only the one seated king has been given a Romanesque head. Now these draperies and also the foiled shapes and the openwork stiff-leaf band confirm a date after 1240. So it must have been inserted; a brilliant job both technically and aesthetically, for it catches the earlier rhythms exactly. (On C 13 spandrel decoration with angels etc., see also Lincoln, Salisbury, Worcester and Westminster Abbey.)

Only a few words are necessary on the aisles and chapels of the retrochoir. The aisles are just a continuation of the chancel aisles, except that the bosses in the S aisle are lusher, bigger and later than those further W and in the N aisle. That also applies to the boss in the S chapel. Both chapels are of an awkward internal shape, due to the strange discrepancy between their responds. Those on the S in the N chapel and on the N in the S chapel are a flat projecting piece of wall with a row of three detached Purbeck shafts in front. Was the intention to do the same on the facing sides? Anyway, it was not done. In the S aisle the Perp doorway into the E walk of the cloister. It has the arms of William of Wykeham and can be dated c. 1400.

So, in conclusion, the LADY CHAPEL of c. 1300. It can only be a disappointment. Even for the best of designers it would have presented a problem – how to make a long, low building more striking than the taller and richer main parts of the cathedral. Extreme structural ingenuity and ornamental virtuosity is needed, and it is sadly lacking here. The first two bays must antedate the fire of 1187, and certainly the S capital to the first bay is more archaic than any other late C 12 detail at Chichester, being still in effect a Norman scallop capital with the mouldings made lighter (it occurs also in the crossing tower at Boxgrove). The remainder is hoist with the low late C 12 ridge-line and can find no better solution than to multiply the intermediate ribs and ram the large windows into spaces that are really too small for them, producing ungainly stilted rere-arches. The best details are probably the flickering, bossy capitals of windows, vaulting shafts, PISCINA, and SEDILIA. Perhaps this is an inevitable price to pay for the classical balance of the rest of Chichester. In turbulent times, nothing-to-excess often produces the best results; when the artistic pressure slackens, it may easily degenerate into dullness.

POSTSCRIPT ON THE E.E. STYLE AT CHICHESTER

It cannot have been easy, in the whole of this account, to separate in one's mind the Norman work from the E.E. work, and, while the Norman work is all of a piece, the E.E. work differs in its details so much that it should perhaps be summed up once more and a chronological order be attempted, even if not achieved. Willis, than whom no one ever could observe and interpret details better, says that the phases are 'much alike in style' and Walter Godfrey in the VCH that it is 'not easy to place the exact sequence'. And Julian Munby in the light of his recent study of the timber roofs of both E and W arms and related stonework, concludes that the stylistic sequence is still cloudy.

At least one knows where to start: in the W bays of the Lady Chapel; for here one capital is still entirely Late Norman. Another marks the beginning of the leaf development, two tiers of small, close, bud-like leaves, not yet stiff-leaf. The vault on the other hand has close, flat, small stiff-leaf bosses. So the first question is: Was the vaulting done before or immediately after the fire? In any case it is the earliest rib-vault in the cathedral. Transverse arches and ribs have profiles which do not exactly repeat anywhere, but the character and the proportions remain standard throughout the work.

An example is the vaulting-shafts. They are triple, two round and one keeled. Go further w and, in the variation of all three keeled, this continues in the chancel chapels, chancel aisles, the high parts of retrochoir and chancel, the transepts (in the N again exactly like the Lady Chapel) and even the nave. Then there are the bosses. Flat, small stiff-leaf bosses also continue more or less unchanged from the chancel chapels (N only; see below), to the aisles of the retrochoir (N only; see below), the chancel aisles and the nave aisles. These bosses go well with the small, close stiff-leaf capitals of the vaulting-shafts in the aisle walls, again of identical type in the aisles from E to w (small bosses also in the N outer chapels of the nave). So it looks as if the repair after the fire began with the aisles and their vaulting, not an unreasonable idea, if one thought straight away, as a fire insurance, of future high vaults for chancel and nave. Such vaults would need support against their thrust. Flying buttresses on the Canterbury example were decided on, and so they needed new buttresses and the vaulting (or perhaps re-vaulting) of the aisles would be the first stage in the realization of the programme.

The one exception to the small, close bosses is the SE chapel and the aisle bays s of the retrochoir. They are rich, larger, much looser and more rhythmically composed. In this they tally with the bosses of the high vaults of retrochoir, choir and nave, bosses which for obvious reasons must have been set up much later. Now this freedom in the treatment of stiff-leaf also applies to the gallery of the retrochoir. So here work took longest, up to c. 1230–40, as we have seen.

Other parts of the cathedral which show evidence of one kind or another of this late date are the following: first the entrance to St Richard's Porch (but the vault inside, i.e. the porch itself, is earlier), see the corbel under the statue of St Richard with several not strictly separated tiers of stiff-leaf, and see the irregular elongated quatrefoil for the statue. The parallel to this would be the odd foiled shapes of the N and s gallery arcades of the retrochoir. The closest parallel to the lush corbel is the yet lusher corbels in the chapel of the Bishop's Palace (though the chapel itself could be earlier and indeed of before 1204) and, among capitals in the cathedral, those of the sacristy (i.e. Song School; see s *transept*) which we know were a later addition to the E.E. work on the aisles and also to St Richard's Porch itself. A further parallel to the quatrefoil of St Richard is the elongated pointed quatrefoil of the entrance to the w porch flanked by two round quatrefoils. The inner arcading of this porch, also with pointed trefoils side by side with round quatrefoils, can be compared to the reredoses in the NE and SE chapels of the outer nave aisles. The former has plate tracery, i.e. a stage after the untraceried windows

38. CHICHESTER St Richard's Porch, c. 1230–40

everywhere else in the cathedral (except for the bar tracery of the other, later, N chapels).

However, there is a catch here. The NE aisle chapel and the s aisle chapels have capitals in the responds towards the aisles which, while they cut through their E.E. motifs (string-courses), are of the crudest crocket type, tall and inelegant. Crocket capitals otherwise were specially liked by the Purbeck marblers, and wherever they were busy for the cathedral, they used them, either as crockets proper or as leaf crockets, i.e. crockets with stiff-leaf characteristics.

Chichester is not a place to see stiff-leaf in its most luxuriant 'wind-swept' varieties, the varieties of, say, Wells about 1230–40. The freest stiff-leaf at Chichester is again in the entrance to St Richard's Porch and again in the chapels along the s aisle (the transverse arches). Otherwise not much can be made chronologically of the capitals, except that it can be stated that moulded capitals come late in the story. This does not apply without reservation; for the Purbeck shafts of the transverse arches in the chancel aisles and nave aisles have moulded capitals. Otherwise they were used in the arches to the N chapels and in the N chapels, in the w porch throughout, in the doorway inside St Richard's Porch, where they have dogtooth, and in the arches from aisles and chancel aisles to transepts (mostly of

1861, but there was enough evidence), which were clearly a later embellishment.

Dogtooth has just been mentioned, and this is also a sign of late date at Chichester. The earliest probably is in the vault of the s transept (cf. the small, close bosses – and cf. Boxgrove). Those in the E bay of the retrochoir are bigger and later. Another late occurrence is the rose-window in the E gable. Yet others, perhaps in date between s transept and retrochoir, are in the N porch entrance and the E windows of the N transept E chapel.

The profiles of ribs and transverse arches help little. They are thin and have fine mouldings everywhere in the cathedral, and the roll, the keeled roll, the filleted roll, the spur, the small hollow seem to have been used *ad libitum*. To give one example, the same transverse arches are found in the chancel aisles, the high vaults of retrochoir and chancel, the N transept and the chapel E of it. On the other hand the ribs of the chancel aisles start with a profile slightly different from that adopted in their more westerly parts, and this second profile is then carried on in the nave aisles, the E chapel of the N aisle, the s chapels, and even the w porch. An only fairly convincing criterion is that ribs with more than three principal members are likely to be late: four in the nave, five in the Bishop's Palace chapel and in the N chapels; but four also in the s porch, where the corbels prove an early date.

If one tries in conclusion to link early and late with actual dates, one can only point to 1187, the year of the fire, and 1279, the year of the shrine's dedication, as outer limits of the campaign. Dates in between can only be estimated from comparisons.

FURNISHINGS

Clockwise from the N W corner: N W tower, N nave aisle, N transept and crossing, N choir aisle and choir, retrochoir, Lady Chapel, s choir aisle, s transept, s nave aisle and s w tower.

Chichester is in fact not rich in furnishings, and it is not easy to see why. This was not by any means a poor diocese, and it has never been sacked or drastically restored, though some furnishings must have gone in the fall of the tower. Monuments are few and small, especially after the C 16, which is true of Sussex as a whole. Much Victorian stained glass has now gone, and not all of what remains is mentioned here; replacements of the 1940s and early 1950s are not worth mentioning. Furnishings added in the 1960s and since are much bolder and reflect Dean Hussey's interest in modern art.

North-west tower   MONUMENTS. A kind of Sailors' Corner, hence several late C 18 reliefs under inscriptions: Lt Pigot Alms † 1782 by *Charles Harris*, Sir George Murray † 1819 by *Joseph Kendrick*, Capt. Thomas Allen

39. CHICHESTER Fitzalan monument, C 14 and C 19: 'Whom the restorer has joined together'

† 1781 also by *Harris*. All are pleasant and none is remarkable.

North aisle and outer aisle   Second (first outer) bay. MONUMENTS. Joseph Baker † 1789 by *Hickey*. Female leaning on a pedestal with portrait medallion; urn on top, but still in the Rococo tradition. – A really terrible *Flaxman* to Vice-Admiral Frankland † 1823 (female in profile, heavily draped and looking up sentimentally). – William Huskisson † 1830 by *J. E. Carew*. M.P. for Chichester and a leading light in the Reform Bill movement, Huskisson was the first person to be run over by a railway train. Nevertheless (as also in *John Gibson's* statue of him in Pimlico) he is still shown in Roman dress, a life-size standing figure with a noble face. Mrs Huskisson: N transept.

Third bay. MONUMENTS. Richard Fitzalan, fourteenth or fifteenth Earl, † 1376 or 1397 and wife. Stiff conventional figures, originally separate, their hands touchingly joined only in 1844 by *Edward Richardson*, a restoring sculptor (Canon Lowther Clarke) – an example of an Early Victorian approach to restoration. – Rev. Thomas Ball, erected 1819. *Flaxman* again, but better, with a design as flowing and melting as those of his friend Blake but without any of Blake's force. Mourning lady, comforting angel: more lines curved down than up.

Between fifth and sixth bays. MONUMENT. Edmund Woods †1833. Standing monument, all white. Standing female by a plinth, soulless and with illiterate inscriptions. By *J. E. Carew.*

Sixth bay. MONUMENTS. Presumed Maude, Countess of Arundel, †1270, but must be of *c.* 1300 or a little later. Badly worn, but a fine, taut figure, all the rhythms caught and contained. All the subsidiary carving is done with meaning, not mechanically. Tomb-chest with quatrefoils alternately filled with standing figures and shields against a leaf background. The figures are early examples of 'weepers', though not earlier than those on the Crouchback tombs at Westminster. The leaves cannot be earlier than 1300. Chapel restored to use in memory of Lt Abbey †1918 by *Goodhart-Rendel;* refurbished 1978 as memorial to F. W. Steer, cathedral librarian.

Seventh bay. Here, across the nave, stretches the ARUNDEL SCREEN, luckily taken out in 1859, stored under the bell-tower, and put back in 1960. From neglecting it, appreciation has now almost swung too far the other way, and it is floodlit and set off at the expense of the more important spaces around. John Arundel was bishop from 1458 to 1477. His screen is an odd mixture of spatial lightness and decorative heaviness: the three arched openings, two wide and one narrow, promise well with their multiple continuous mouldings, but are defeated by the heavy lierne vault supporting the loft with its repeating pattern of ogee-headed niches. The mixture is typically English – France or Germany would not have been so undecided. The bosses of the vault are carved with foliage and with vivid human and animal faces. This is very English too. (Presumably the wider side arches were originally closed at the back, for nave altars; cf. Exeter.)

North transept　WALL PAINTING. Fragmentary remains of medieval painting on the s underside of the arch between the transept and its E chapel, now treasury (see below), also traces midway along the N wall of the latter. – PANEL PAINTING. Immense wooden panel, one of a pair by *Lambert Bernard, c.* 1520 (the other in the s transept). This one has the bishops from St Wilfrid to Sherbourne, all in roundels, all apparently drawn from the same model, and as uniform as the heads in a pack of cigarette cards. Restored by *Tremaine, c.* 1747, at Bishop Mawson's expense; jolly but nothing more. – WEATHERCOCK, 1638. It fell with the spire in 1861, was re-erected 1866, and replaced 1978 by a Victorian one previously on the bell-tower. – MONUMENTS. Bishop Grove †1696. Two cherubs holding the mitre and a proud well-carved bust above. – Bishop King †1669, the poet and friend of Donne but, it would seem, commemorated by an C18 monument. No figures, cold urn at the top. – Bishop Carlton †1685. Two more cherubs hold the mitre against an obelisk. Coy looks from both: they seem to have had the Baroque

equivalent of a perm. – Eliza, Huskisson's widow, †1856, by *John Gibson.* From the inscription, Gibson's grief was personal as well as professional, yet the angel and supplicant are fearfully void of feeling. Neoclassicism's influence had succeeded only too well.

CHAPEL off N transept, now treasury, designed by *Stefan Buzas,* 1976, for the display of cathedral treasures and parish plate. (On traces of medieval painting, see N transept above.)

North choir aisle　MONUMENTS. Two shoddy C16 tomb recesses with the brass effigies gone, the type of many Purbeck and Petworth marble monuments: a tomb-chest and a back panel for brasses, flanked by solid side walls and with, at the top, a flat arch or a lintel on curved pieces connecting with the side walls; top cresting. – PAINTING. Remains of vault decoration by *Lambert Bernard;* see also Lady Chapel below.

Choir and *sanctuary*　The reredos usually hidden by TAPESTRY, 1966. Designed by *John Piper,* woven by *Pinton Frères,* Aubusson. Seven panels, central three with

40. CHICHESTER Tapestry, 1966. Designed by John Piper

symbols of the Trinity in brilliant colours, outer ones with the four elements and signs of the Evangelists in cooler colours. – A new bishop's throne to replace that of *Slater & Carpenter* (after 1861) is projected. – STALLS, *c.* 1330 but much wrought about after the damage of 1861 (at first condemned but saved by *Scott*'s pupil *Bodley,* according to Canon Lowther Clarke). Repeating design of ogee arches on thin detached shafts. The more ornate canopied stalls at the w end are modern. Still on the rescued and restored stalls, thirty-eight MISERICORDS, all but one (eighth from the E on the N side, C15) of *c.* 1330, vivid and varied: e.g. a musician kissing a dancer, a finely carved mermaid with mirror, fox playing a harp, etc. – ORGAN CASE by the organ-builder and antiquary *Dr Arthur Hill*, 1888, the great case with remains of painted pipes from *R. Harris's* organ of 1678, the *chaire* case also incorporating fragments of woodwork from that former case destroyed by the fall of the tower: an elegant Gothic essay, acoustically as well as visually correct (Gillingham). Its iron spiral staircase behind in the N transept. – CHANDELIERS. Two of brass, two tiers, given 1752. Many of this highly suitable type now hang in the cathedral. – LECTERN of aluminium by *Geoffrey Clarke*. – MONUMENT. Bishop Story † 1503, N side. Stiff alabaster effigy on a panelled tomb-chest. Canopy modern.

Retrochoir, north aisle and *north-east chapel* CHEST. About 8 ft 6 in. long, with C13 ironwork. – MONUMENTS. Mrs Margaret Miller † 1701 (chapel). A good straightforward mason's monument; architectural frame with open scrolly pediment and mourning cherubs on either side. – Sarah Peckham † 1784 by *Harris*. Elegant shape, elegant use of marble, but fatally lackadaisical mourning woman juxta urn. – Bishop Otter † 1840, by *Joseph Towne*, 1844. Not a bad bust, no attempt at any deep interpretation, but not putting a false gloss on things either. This is provided immediately by the terrible monument next door by *John Tweed* to Bishop Wilberforce † 1907. – STAINED GLASS (aisle). Designed by *Marc Chagall*, made by *Charles Marq*, 1978, on the theme of praise, Psalm 150. Mostly in luscious reds with little figures. Dean Hussey's last commission to a living artist before his retirement.

RETROCHOIR. STAINED GLASS. E windows by *Kempe*, and deeper and richer than he usually is. – MONUMENTS. Two plain tomb-chests to Bishops Day † 1557 and Barlow † 1568; not a sign of the Renaissance, or of anything else.

Lady Chapel IRONWORK. Entrance gates incorporating panels originally in the Arundel Screen (see nave furnishings above, seventh bay). Thin nervous pattern of quatrefoils – a pattern thickened and repeated in C19 and C20 ironwork in the cathedral – the original surprisingly wispy and appealing. Related panels, found in a builder's yard 1891–6 and now in the Victoria and Albert Museum, have the quatrefoils rebated where they intersect and held by rivets, techniques that could well be of the 1470s, and also incorporate C13 stamped work (Jane Geddes). – LECTERN. Victorian brass pelican. – TILES. Medieval tiles now set in a single row in the floor alongside the E wall either side of the altar. Victorian tiles in the floor before the altar. – PAINTING. The second bay of the vault is decorated with a pretty foliage pattern, early C16, by *Lambert Bernard*. This and traces in the N choir aisle are all that survive from his decoration of all the vaults in the cathedral, which included roses and pomegranates of Catherine of Aragon, with shields and mottoes and Bishop Sherbourne's initials;

41. CHICHESTER Stained glass, 1978.
Designed by Marc Chagall

there were texts on the piers and lettering on the stalls by Bernard, as well as his panels in the transepts, q.v. (Croft-Murray 1962; for other Spenserian decoration by Bernard for the bishop, see Amberley, Boxgrove, and Chichester, Bishop's Palace, in B of E *Sussex*). – STAINED GLASS. A complete Victorian set which does not stand a close look but which makes an effective colour-pattern out of the space, taken all together. Dark colours: reds, browns, and blues. The E window is the best. All this is by *Clayton & Bell*, and carefully designed to fit in with the general internal refitting of 1870–2 by *Slater & Carpenter*. – MONUMENTS. Early C14 tomb recess on the S side. In it two coffin-lids of early bishops. The same type is represented better preserved in the coffin-lid on the N side which belonged to the monument of Bishop Luffa, the cathedral builder, † 1123 – see the inscription on the w side. The lid has a flat-topped hipped roof and carved on it, as effectively as if it were a trade mark, are a crozier and mitre. – CHAMBER ORGAN, c. 1780.

Retrochoir, south aisle and *south-east chapel* STAINED GLASS in the chapel by *Kempe* (memorial † 1894). Much disliked by Ian Nairn but, according to Canon Lowther Clarke, Kempe said it was meant to be seen from a distance (indeed all along the s aisles from the w end), and the glass was not of course conceived in the same spirit as *Graham Sutherland*'s self-conscious PAINTING of the Noli Me Tangere placed below it; their blue-green colourings harmonize somewhat. – Altar, communion-rail and candlesticks of 1961 by *Robert Potter* and *Geoffrey Clarke*, good examples of the bold religious arts of the 1960s (see also *Nave* s aisle, pulpit, below). – MONUMENTS. Mrs Frances Waddington † 1728. Plain architectural frame, all idea of the Baroque gone already. – Rev. G. P. Farhill † 1790 (chapel). *Harris* of London again. The usual mourner by an urn. His mourners really do not inspire confidence. – Also a thumping great C 14 GARGOYLE which puts the later sculptural inanities to shame, used as a collecting box. – Roman MOSAIC, c. C 2, part of a domestic floor discovered 1968 and shown *in situ* c. 5 ft below aisle-floor level.

Choir, south aisle SCULPTURE. Two famous Romanesque panels, the most memorable things in the cathedral. They were found re-used as building stones behind the choir stalls in 1829, and were almost certainly part of a C 12 choir screen which was known to have existed here. (According to Dr Zarnecki's convincing suggestion, part of a screen in the sense of a German *Chorschranken*, not of a rood screen.) The stone comes from Caen. The reliefs show Christ coming to the House of Mary of Bethany and the Raising of Lazarus. For a long time they were thought to date from c. 1000, and it is hardly surprising, because the architectural scenery looks Carolingian, the impassioned awkwardness of the figures and the empathy between them seems nowhere near the sculptural order and emotional calmness of most later Romanesque sculpture. Yet Dr Zarnecki and others have proved beyond doubt that the panels must date from c. 1125–50 and that their details depend on such things as the St Alban's Psalter (now at Hildesheim) of c. 1120 and German ivories of c. 1130. If this is true, then the gestures and proportions of German Romanesque – already more personal than France – were perhaps refracted by a sculptor who was still thinking in Anglo-Saxon terms. It would be a fair parallel to the case of mid-C 12 sculptures like those at Kilpeck, which undoubtedly depend on Poitou and Saintonge but

42. CHICHESTER Sculpture, c. 1125–50.
Christ at the House of Mary

which were carried out by a designer working in the old style and ended up looking more like Viking ornament. That is the old spirit using new techniques, but how it managed to survive for almost a century in an area like Sussex is a mystery. Of all the parts of Britain, it would have been most open to Norman–French influence. (Pite's plan for the *Builder*, 1892, which we reproduce, called these 'sculptures from Selsey', i.e. from the pre-1075 cathedral there, but their mid-C 12 date disproves that.)

The panels are wonderfully preserved: all that is missing is the coloured inlay that would have been set in the eyes, and even here the present empty deep sockets seem to add to the depth of expression. To assess them is not easy or simple. The sculptor was obviously impatient of details, and there is no point in trying to compare the quality of parts, such as folds of drapery around knees, with the first-rate pieces of orthodox Romanesque sculpture of the time (best represented in England by the porch at Malmesbury Abbey). The designer's care and love was all for the heads, for the relationship between heads and for the shades of feeling expressed in the faces. Beside this, the rest becomes irrelevant. In the first panel, Christ and the disciples are approaching the house – a house which looks like a Carolingian folly, a crazy and rustic Pierrefonds.

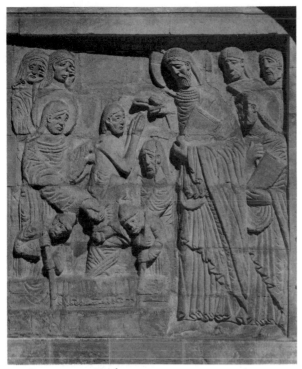

43. CHICHESTER Sculpture, c. 1125–50.
The Raising of Lazarus

Under the porch are Mary and Martha, in frozen dumb supplication. Christ's face is as preoccupied as that of a surgeon before the operation gathering up strength in himself; hurrying on to the door, already working out technical details. Two of his disciples are compassionate but composed, the third frankly distraught, even to the straining cords in the neck.

In the second panel are recognizably the same characters, like a still from the first and last acts of a play (Dr Zarnecki suggests that in fact the sculptor was influenced by the plays). But the work is completed, and Christ stands fulfilled and almost exhausted, raising up the still immobile Lazarus. His feeling is all outwards, now, where it was self-contained before, which is a miracle of expressiveness. And what adds understanding and wisdom to expressiveness is the treatment of the other actors. There is no simple relief, but a medley of different emotions, just as there would be after a miracle. Mary and Martha, their faces as agonized as Grünewald would have made them, are torn between continuing grief, newly-awakened hope and simple amazement. Lazarus himself is still: he cannot think and feel yet. The two disciples who raise him are compassionate but do not understand; to the two little lay figures underneath who have brought the coffin it is all in a day's

work. And, in the top right-hand corner, two more disciples (one of them was the distraught person in the first panel) are almost troubled, seeing further than the first pair, to what must now inevitably follow in persecution and crucifixion. (Parts of a third relief are in the library.)

MONUMENTS (s choir aisle continued). Bishop Sherbourne † 1536. Between the two panels. In such a situation, what on earth can be said, except that a cathedral must accommodate contrasts? Bishop Sherbourne was an astute, politically-minded bishop, a type which does not seem to die out. He was instrumental in arranging the marriage of Henry VIII and Catherine of Aragon, and himself lived in state second only to Henry's and Wolsey's, while steering his careful course. He was over ninety when he died, and the tomb was probably made well before. Stiff, elaborate effigy in a panelled tomb recess of odd shape, with sides. Two angels hold up the mitre, two more gaze down, all could have been carved out of cheese. There is no hint of Renaissance detail, which would be especially odd for a county whose tombs have so much of it, unless it was indeed made long before Sherbourne's death – another politic move (cf. Archbishop Warham's at Canterbury, N transept). Restored in 1847. – Dean Hook † 1875, by *Sir George Gilbert Scott*. This is, surprisingly, almost the best monument in the cathedral. Simple tomb-chest without figures, ornamented with different marbles used richly, soberly and discriminatingly, far removed from mechanical piety. The colours are deep red, olive green, olive grey and black, with a little inlaid mosaic. One of the best things about it is that, like a Victorian drawing-room, it could belong to no other time.

South transept STAINED GLASS. The huge s window entirely filled with glass of 1877. Bright colours and weak faces. Said to have been designed by *C. Parish* and made by *Maréchal* of Metz. – WOODWORK. Tall c 17 cupboard with a slit for coins. Presumably it contained relics. The ogee headed top is authentic but does not look it; the whole object is neither better nor worse than if it had been built in 1875. Willis, with his usual prescience, called it a 'machine'. – PAINTING. Large early c 16 wood panels by *Bernard*, companions to his bishops in the N transept. Medallion heads of kings of England from William the Conqueror, with two bigger scenes above. Cædwalla granting the see of Selsey to St Wilfrid, and Henry VIII confirming to Sherbourne the royal protection of Chichester. This last is an engaging diplomatic myth: oh, shrewd trimmer Sherbourne! The style (found during recent examination to have been little altered in the c 18 restoration by *Tremaine*) is already platitudinous, company boardroom painting. It could have slipped imperceptibly into an R.A. exhibition of the mid-1840s. – MONUMENTS. Sacellum between transept and crossing, i.e. a three-bay stone screen which was perhaps the original pulpitum, before the

Arundel Screen was put up. Taken down in 1860 (before the tower fell); replaced in 1904. It was originally put up by Bishop Stratford (1337–62) and encloses what is supposed to be his tomb, a weathered effigy, more than life-size, in a style which has blossomed into humane naturalism – a few years snatched between stylization and mechanical mass production. So the bishop is a real person, and the dog at his feet is prepared to bark. The tomb-chest is modern. Also under the canopy a brass to Dean Burgon † 1888, by *C. E. Kempe*, surprisingly honest and vivid, and a tablet to Kempe himself, who † 1907, also vivid and unaffected, and presumably by the firm's designer *John W. Lisle*. The screen itself is of the same family (although of stone) as the choir stalls (i.e. Dec work put up far away from the mainsprings of the Dec style), but much better done – the pinnacles are new but must represent what was there before. Canopy of three ogee arches, given especial bite by the double curve put in them close to the piers. The bosses thus provided have vivid grotesque carvings, human and animal. Inside, a firm but delicate quadripartite vault, showing where the sympathies of the designer really lay. In many ways Sussex jumped straight from E.E. to Perp. – Bishop Langton † 1337. A terribly weathered effigy which must originally have been very fine, under a fat ogee canopy which tries and fails to be sensuous and opulent. – Two bad tomb recesses of *c.* 1500, the same style as those in the N choir aisle. – J. Abel Smith, erected 1848, by *Edward Richardson*, under a C 19 canopy like Langton's. – The E chapel of the S transept is now used for the display of embroideries. – On the W side, in the entry to the Song School, two medieval DOORS. The one facing the transept has two bracing straps with a C 12 scalloped pattern and hinges that seem tailor-made for it, but the other straps were perhaps salvaged from the fire of 1187. The other, mightier door, facing the Song School and much bigger than its doorway, is clearly re-used and may have come from any of the cathedral entrances from the dedication of 1108 to the consecration of 1184 (Jane Geddes).

Nave south aisle and *chapels* Seventh bay. Spiral STAIRCASE entrance to the top of the Arundel Screen, 1960. Like the other new things in the cathedral, it is fresh and modern, with steps cantilevered from a steel stem. By *Robert Potter*. – Nearby the PULPIT, 1966, by *Robert Potter* and *Geoffrey Clarke*, is aluminium-faced and uncompromisingly of its time.

Sixth bay. Traces of another 'marble' MONUMENT of the recess type.

Between fifth and fourth bays. A small early NICHE of *c.* 1535 or so, square-headed, with tiny crude putti and arabesques mixed with the Gothic detail – the only sign of the Renaissance in the whole cathedral.

Fourth bay. MONUMENT. Bishop Durnford † 1895, by *Bodley & Garner*. Effigy, canopy, applied piety. Stone dead.

44. CHICHESTER Pulpit, 1966.
Designed by Robert Potter and Geoffrey Clarke

Third bay (chapel). Two sad *Flaxman* MONUMENTS: Francis Dear and his wife Bridget, erected 1802 (Whinney (1964) dates it 1800), and Sarah Udny † 1811 – 'Udny! How few thy excellence transcend' and so on, in both verse and stone. But Agnes Cromwell † 1797, also by *Flaxman*, has hopes of nobler things in its free-flowing design, which is again a faint echo of Blake.

SW TOWER (Baptistery). The FONT is trying to be bold and Romanesque and ends up worse than the most soulless of Victorian fittings. Erected 1894. On the E wall, PAINTING by *Hans Feibusch*, 1951. More modern in style than most English paintings of this date and position, yet nowhere near a truly C 20 religious expression. – Painting on the W wall: 'The Tribute Money', by *Ribera*, or said to be. There are indeed Riberesque gleams on furrowed brows. – Finally, a small set of odd MONUMENTS to take away in the memory: Ernest Udny † 1808 by *Henry Westmacott* (Sir Richard's brother), Jane Smith † 1780 by *Flaxman*, and

William Collins the poet ('How sleep the brave') † 1759 but buried in St Andrew's Church, this tablet by *Flaxman* erected 1795. More than a cathedral's-length away from the great feeling faces of the Lazarus panels in the s choir aisle.

Before leaving, a look at the WEST WINDOW. It was done by *Wailes* in 1848, using a newly invented rolled-glass technique which 'reproduced the unequal surface of medieval glass'. – A handsome three-light window made for the cathedral by *Wailes* in 1842, one of the earliest Victorian memorial windows anywhere, is now in St Peter's, West Street (Sewter 1974).

WEST DOORS, inner and outer, glass and iron, by *Geoffrey Clarke* and *Robert Potter*, 1965.

CLOISTERS

The plan of the Chichester cloisters is unique among English cathedral cloister plans in not being fitted into the angle between nave and transept, though it is a bit like a fusion of the E range of the Bishop's Cloister and the passage to the Vicars' Cloister at Hereford. At Chichester the three walks span the s transept, with one entrance into the nave (St Richard's Porch) and the other into the retrochoir. The reason is typical of Chichester, where everything is accommodating and nothing is imposed. The cloisters were apparently built new in c. 1400 (perhaps as a consequence of the rebuilding and enlargement of the accommodation for the vicars?) and had to fit St Richard's Porch, a graveyard on the s side called Paradise, and the line of existing buildings on the s side which in fact became the s wall of the cloister. The only encroachment was that in the s E corner the cloisters bit ten feet into the w front of St Faith's Chapel. But even here, the upper part was kept in its old place with its w lancet still in position. The s walk is now part of the cathedral, a short cut for the town, and a front door to two or three houses. Everything flows together, as it should.

The design is just as reasonable and unpretentious. It is supposed to date from c. 1400 because of William of Wykeham's arms over the NE door (the then Dean was a Wykehamist). If so, he was a Wykehamist in his architecture as well as his politics, for the cloister is firmly in the court style of Wykeham's architect William Wynford. Large-scale, bold and as humane and as extrovert as Chaucer (but much restored in 1890). Tall and wide four-light windows, the lights forming two sub-windows, and panel tracery. The roof is a subtle but unfussy timber construction, where almost every other cathedral in England would have had vaulting. Barn and church were always close together in Sussex. A simple trussed rafter roof is given great elegance by a system of braces forming four-centred arches. In the E walk, which was perhaps built

first, there is also a moulded beam along the ridge of the four-centred arches. It is a wonderful relief after the overloaded decoration of some Perp architecture. Good simple doorway of c. 1400 into the retrochoir in exactly the same spirit, square-headed, with bold deep carving of tracery and shields (William of Wykeham's arms – see above) in the spandrels. Where the bottom of St Faith's w front was taken out (i.e. at the s E corner) it was patched up again with wooden panelling and a wooden door, as nice a surprise as a friendly hello on a formal occasion. – MONUMENTS. A lot of c18 and early c19 tablets, and an earlier one to Percival Smalpage † 1595, with a frontal bust. – In the garth, recumbent (or stricken) figure, 'Fallen Warrior', by *Henry Moore*.

The c12 to c19 Bishop's Palace s w of the cathedral – with its c13 chapel and kitchen (the latter notable for its earliest known use of hammerbeams), c14 gatehouse, c15–16 Sherbourne wing, early c18 staircase, and late c18/early c19 vestibule – along with the early c18 Deanery and other private buildings in and around Canon Lane and the cloisters, are described in the latest edition of B of E *Sussex*.

Clifton: see *Bristol: Clifton*.

Exeter

CATHEDRAL CHURCH OF ST PETER *Anglican*

(Based on B of E *South Devon*, 1952, much revised and expanded, with information from the late Rev. V. Hope, Mrs Audrey Erskine, Bridget Cherry, Michael Gillingham, Peter Gundry, Michael Laithwaite and Michael Swanton.)

*Mid-*c *14* (before Black Death): nave roofed and vaulting begun? w front sculpture screen begun

*Mid-*c *14* (after Black Death): nave vaulting completed, w front sculpture continued

Late c *14*: w front sculpture continued and porches made; great E window rebuilt; N w chapel vaulted; and see *Cloisters* below

c *15*: w front sculpture completed; rebuilding of chapter house (upper part), front of N porch, tops of towers

Furnishings, E to W   116

Cloisters   123

  Originally c 13, rebuilt late c 14, demolished late c 17, partly rebuilt c 19

Plan, Fig. 45, from the *Builder*, 1891, after one of 1797 by John Carter, so showing the pulpitum with inner side arches unpierced and stairs not yet rearranged by *Scott*, the S E cloisters not yet rebuilt by *Pearson*, and without the stairs from S transept to chapter house, added in 1814.

Some references (see Recent Literature): Bony 1979; Coldstream 1976; Colvin 1978; Erskine 1981–2; Glasscoe and Swanton 1978; Hope and Lloyd 1973; Matthews n.d.; Norris 1978; Swanton 1979.

INTRODUCTION

This cathedral quietly dominates its city's hill, though less magnificently than Lincoln and Durham do. Exeter on its ridge once overlooked a busy river port where barges came with goods, including stone from coastal quarries. The fine ivory tone of the cathedral's walls came out of quarries on Devon's eastern shore, dark marble for its piers from Dorset's Isle of Purbeck (further on materials below). The cathedral is a surprisingly isolated phenomenon against the warm red sandstone of parish churches and the red brick of Georgian houses. Its bulk and its miraculous perfection inside have no echoes in the parish churches, none of which compares with St Peter Mancroft at Norwich or St Cuthbert at Wells.

Exeter is a visual exception in another way. Almost as much as Salisbury it differs from the general rule that English cathedrals are assortments of architectural styles. Except for its Norman towers, Exeter appears all of a piece as the work of three generations. As this work was begun after Salisbury was finished, they are very different, inside especially; where Salisbury is all concision, Exeter all profusion. Outside Salisbury added its vital c 14 spire, but Exeter's massive towers, like twin keeps, never sought great height.

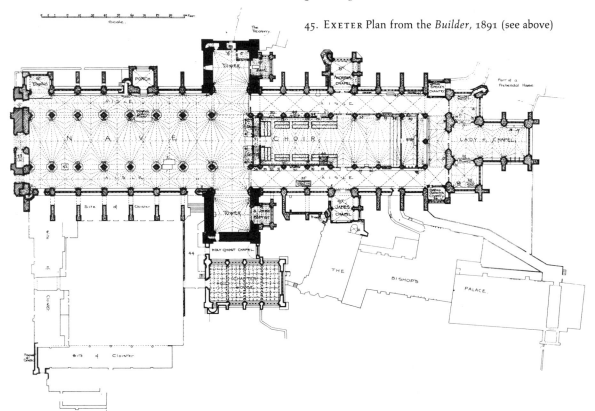

45. EXETER Plan from the *Builder*, 1891 (see above)

46. EXETER The west front in 1825

The close, not gated as it was before 1835 but still in effect a close, no longer contains the Victorian parish church of St Mary Major which until recently elbowed the cathedral's w front. Excavation on St Mary's site has discovered remains of a church thought to be the cathedral's Saxon predecessor. Remains of its monastery and the site of a spring, possibly a holy well (compare the one at Wells), have been found s E of the cathedral's eastern arm. Remains of the Roman town have been found in the close: medieval Exeter rested on Roman foundations. German bombers found Exeter primarily a medieval city with Georgian and Early Victorian fringes, and left it primarily a Georgian and Early Victorian city with holes in the middle. Postwar development took it from there. The cathedral itself in 1942 received a direct hit on the s side of the choir. But, like the Norman castle and the late medieval guildhall, it survived.

To go back to the beginning, a Benedictine monastery dedicated to St Mary and St Peter was founded here in the c7, reputedly refounded by Athelstan in the c10, de-stroyed by the Danes in 1003, and rebuilt by Cnut in 1018. The bishop's seat for the diocese of Devon and Cornwall, however, was from 909 to 1050 at Crediton, a few miles N of Exeter. But in 1050 Leofric was installed as bishop at Exeter in the presence of Edward the Confessor and his queen in the c11 monastery church, which served also for Leofric's successor. After the Conqueror's nephew William Warelwast gained the see in 1107, an entirely new building was vigorously begun c. 1112. Traces of the c12 apse were found (but not preserved) during *Gilbert Scott*'s restoration in the bay between the present choir and presbytery. Warelwast's eastern arm, up to the w end of a choir extending into the second bay of the nave, was consecrated in 1133. This building period included the unique twin towers flanking that choir. The rest of the nave was perhaps finished c. 1160. Then there was a pause. After 1225 the chapter house was built, and probably a cloister. Carved misericords now attached to Scott's choir stalls indicate that in the mid-c13 new seating was installed in the then century-old choir. These misericords, long divorced from their original stalls, are the oldest complete set in the country (the slightly older stalls at Rochester lack misericords).

The rebuilding of the Norman cathedral was a major programme lasting from the 1270s to the 1370s, held up only by the Black Death of 1348–9 and its aftermath of economic depression. The chief building bishops were Branscombe 1258–80, Quivil 1280–91, Bitton 1292–1307, Stapledon 1307–26, and Grandisson 1327–69, the first especially celebrated for his initial impetus to the grand design, the last two of national importance as patrons of art. The main building periods are: c. 1275–1328, eastern arm, conversion of existing towers to transepts, and E bay of nave; 1329–c. 1369 (with a gap c. 1349–53), nave, w front and beginning of its image screen, followed by rebuilding of cloisters from 1377 and the w front sculpture continuing into the C 15.

Master masons included *Master Roger* from before 1297 to 1310, *William Luve* 1310–16, *Thomas of Witney* 1316–42 (thought to be the same as Thomas of Winton, active at Winchester, Wells and elsewhere), *William Joy* 1342–52, previously at Wells and thought to be of Bristol origin, followed by *Richard Farleigh*, who had built the Salisbury spire, and from 1377 by *Robert Lesyngham* from Gloucester. But the origins of the Exeter master who initiated the whole design in the 1270s are not known: his style is summed up at the end of our description of the medieval architecture. More recently came pre-Victorian restoration work by *John Kendall*, c. 1805–29, probably the last man of his trade to combine design and execution as medieval masons had (Colvin). The principal Victorian restoration, mainly inside, was that of 1870–7 by *Sir George Gilbert Scott*. Some external restoration in 1906 was deplored by Lethaby (in *Country Life*, 15 December 1906). Restoration of war-damage 1940s–50s etc., and in the 1970s an eye-opening stone-cleaning etc.

Besides the cream Beer stone used for walls, and unpolished Purbeck marble for the piers, local red sandstone was used for vaulting cells and, in the early C 13, for the walls of the chapter house. Portland stone, the present master mason says, was used for some details in the choir. It is known that eight quarries in Devon, one in Somerset and one at Caen in Normandy were supplying stone in the 1320s. In the late C 20 a quarry at Salcombe has been reopened for the cathedral. Purbeck was also used for vaulting-shafts in the Lady Chapel but not later, i.e. not after 1290, but kept for pier shafts throughout: the nave piers shaped at Corfe were paid for in 1332. On a smaller scale, a metal (local latten or brass) was called upon for a pair of free-standing slender shafts on the presbytery sedilia (a unique usage?). For bishops' effigies, polished Purbeck marble was used mainly in the late C 12–early C 13; one important late C 13 effigy is of (local?) basalt,

covered with contemporary paint. Vaults, corbels and bosses, as well as effigies, were painted and gilded: lately the bosses and corbels have, in some cases, been quietly touched up in keeping with original colour found under later layers, but in other cases brightly, even garishly, repainted. While to our Renaissance-trained eyes painting stonework is a debatable procedure, it was a medieval one. (Although not invariably: see Southwell.) It is known that the figures on the w front here, as at Wells, were coloured. Yet perhaps circus colouring with vegetable pigments slowly fading was one thing, modern hard and fast applications another? Authenticity of medium may best ensure authenticity of effect.

EXTERIOR AND INTERIOR

The Norman cathedral had a five-sided main apse, according to remains of foundations seen during the restoration of 1870–7 in the presbytery bay nearest the choir, although no signs of such remains were found when the pavement was relaid in 1962. After the air-raid of 1942 a circular scalloped capital of impressive girth was found among the ruins of the 'S E transept', i.e. St James's Chapel. This would seem to have come from a thick column, comparable to West Country examples of c. 1100–20 at Tewkesbury, Gloucester and Hereford, apparently from the Norman chancel demolished before the late C 13 construction began and, with other such fragments, re-used in the new work. (On the above capital and fragments of two others now in the cloisters, Mrs Cherry reports that one may have shafts at the back, the other what could be rib-springers, all very suggestive of the Tewkesbury choir type; cf. also Exeter Castle gatehouse. Of other fragments preserved in the room over the N porch, she reports three voussoirs with a large roll, clearly from a C 12 rib-vault, and a small curved fragment, presumably from a column, with faint painted patterns of addorsed lions, which was found embedded in the N porch stair-turret.) Norman walling up to window-sill-level is still present in the nave and in the two bays E of the crossing. Flat buttresses remain outside the N wall of the nave, and on the s side marks where they were cut back for the C 13 cloisters can be seen. Inside the nave (lower walls) are indications of responds with characteristic alternating red and white stonework. The Norman nave is thought to have been as long as the present one. The Norman pulpitum stood in the nave, second bay w from the crossing.

The unique Norman feature now is the position of the TOWERS. Known parallels for towers flanking a choir are in the Burgundian orbit: Murbach in Alsace of the C 11 and the cathedral choirs of Lyons (from 1174 on) and Geneva (after 1185). But one English precedent for transeptal towers may just possibly have existed in the late C 11

47. EXETER View from the north-east. Tower, early C 12

cathedral at Old Sarum (see *Salisbury*) with its surviving ground-plan of thick-walled transepts and no proper crossing. (Gundulf's late C 11 tower N of his choir at Rochester remains puzzling.) The elevations of Exeter are severely unadorned and indeed as inaccessible as keeps. The N or St Paul's Tower is the earlier, with its lowest band of tall blank arcading only above the (presumed) height of the Norman nave and chancel roofs. The S or St John's Tower starts the first band lower down. Above the first (on the S second) stage of arcading is a frieze of intersected arches on the N, of circular windows on the S. Also the S arcading on this stage has zigzag decoration, which was not common yet when the N tower had reached that height (introduced into English architecture c. 1110–20). The next stage of blank arcading has zigzag N and S, the last

stage with alternations of arched bell-openings and blank arcades. The whole top storey of the N tower and the battlements and square pinnacles of the S tower are late C 15: the N tower was made slightly higher to house the great Peter bell given by Bishop Courtenay in 1484. The original C 12 tops must be imagined with low pyramidal spires.

The original inside openings to the towers were of course low and round-headed (cf. Crediton). The opening up of the present tall arches into what was then the Norman choir was done in the 1280s, e.g. the fabric roll for 1285 records the throwing down of the wall of St Paul's Tower, and in 1287 that of St John's Tower, also the making of the large S window, which contains an early example of a transom. The opening up of the towers implies the making of the high linking bays between the towers and what was to be the new crossing, even if rebuilding of the crossing itself, as of the choir and nave bays E and W of it, was yet to come. To each transept was added an E chapel, of two shallow bays and one narrow window N and S as well as an E window. The two chapels were probably begun in the 1280s, when altars were removed from the transepts themselves, and the chapel vaults, like the Lady Chapel's in little, completed nearer 1300. On the E and W walls of the transepts charming early C 14 balconies, in place of a triforium, resting on little demi-vaults like the covings of later Devon screens and cantilevered into the old walls. Each transept has a wooden ceiling originally painted to look like vaulting, and with oaken bosses.

To return to chronological order, about sixty-five years after the Norman cathedral was finished, and about fifty years before its C 13 rebuilding began, additions were made on the S for the clergy, this being by then an establishment of secular canons, not of monks. The lower parts of the CHAPTER HOUSE belong to the time of Bishop Bruere or Brewer (1224–44), begun c. 1225 as proved at once by its 'wind-blown' stiff-leaf capitals. The chapter house is a four-bay rectangle on the E side of cloisters that were apparently built (E and N walks at least) about the same time. The doorway from the cloisters has a finely moulded arch on shafts with wind-blown stiff-leaf caps (but the approach for visitors now is from the S transept directly into the chapter house). Inside, the ground-floor stage is plain (and of red sandstone as revealed by restoration in 1969) except for the main Purbeck marble vaulting-shafts, groups of three with stiff-leaf caps, meant for transverse arches and diagonal ribs, and with shaft-rings at sill-level of the next stage. On this stage the wall is enriched by blank arcades forming two niches per bay, again with grouped shafts. The original blue lias columns of the arcades, replaced by Purbeck marble in 1970, showed the effects of a fire presumed to have destroyed the upper parts of the chapter house in 1413. Those parts were redone from 1413 onwards, the main shafts replaced by shafts leading up to pretty niches for figure sculpture (not surviving) and then the timber braces supporting the tie-beams of the low-pitched roof, charmingly decorated with a painted rendering of small fan-vault effects, of the time of Bishop Bothe (1465–78). Early C 13 windows were replaced by four-light (E end seven-light) Perp windows with standard tracery. In the C 13 niches below, arresting C 20 sculpture (see *Furnishings* below). From the C 13 cloister walks the only survivals are two doorways, the one to the chapter house (above) and one known as Bishop Brewer's door leading into the E bay of the nave S aisle, round-headed of two orders outside, with a depressed pointed arch inside and wind-blown stiff-leaf capitals. (On further history, see *Cloisters* below.)

So much for the cathedral before rebuilding began. In 1258 Bishop Bronescombe (or Branscombe) was enthroned in April and probably attended with great interest the new Salisbury Cathedral's consecration in September. The 1260s, that uneasy time in England, must have been a time of scheming at Exeter. Before work could start on a longer E end, the Norman eastern arm was to be demolished and its materials used to level the ground E of it. This ground sloped considerably from N to S: the only part of the new cathedral to be built on a crypt was St James's Chapel on the S side near the spring. (That chapel and chambers above and below it rebuilt after the bombing of 1942.) Preparations may have been begun by c. 1270, and actual building by c. 1275. St Andrew's and St James's Chapels flanking the site of the future chancel were ready for glazing in 1279, and the Lady Chapel at the E end, mentioned in 1280, was still under construction in 1289. From 1279 on, the fabric rolls survive to document much of the work, though tantalizingly not all of it.

The general plan W to E, as the visitor usually travels, is this: nave of seven bays with aisles and N porch, crossing flanked by main transepts in the Norman towers, square-ended eastern arm of, first from the crossing, one narrow bay for the pulpitum, then seven bays (three choir, four presbytery) with aisles, and flanking the middle bay to N and S the two chapels (St Andrew's and St James's) in E transept position, then beyond the high altar a straight ambulatory one bay deep and the three-bay Lady Chapel flanked by aisle-end chapels. The E transeptal chapels, as well as all three eastern chapels and the ambulatory, are much lower than the clerestories of the eastern arm. Exeter's high vault runs straight through E to W, and both nave and east arm have flying buttresses.

To continue with the documentary evidence, Bishop Branscombe left instructions for his tomb between the Lady Chapel and the S E aisle-end Chapel of St Gabriel, both partway up when he died in 1280 (see *Furnishings* E *of the crossing*, Monuments, below). His successor, Bishop Quivil or Quinil, is thought to have completed the Lady Chapel in time to be buried in it in 1291. He had been present at Lincoln in 1280 when the Angel Choir was consecrated, and must have had a good look at the palm-frond effect of the nave vaults there (though he may have known Westminster Abbey's first nave bays with their tiercerons and fully developed N–S ridge ribs, unlike Lincoln nave's and Ely presbytery's transverse ridge ribs, which are incomplete). Work on the Exeter presbytery, i.e. the beginning of the main vessel, was perhaps started by the year of Quivil's death and structurally completed in 1299. (On a fabric-roll entry indicating that the roofs of the E end were covered with lead only in 1303, see below.) The presbytery vaults were painted in 1301 and its clerestory glazed in 1301–2. Bosses for the choir vaults were already

48. EXETER Looking from the nave, c. 1329–69, to the presbytery, c. 1291–9

being carved in the workshop in 1303, but those vaults were painted only in 1309. Structurally the whole eastern arm was complete by 1310, after about thirty-five years of work. As we shall see, there were afterthoughts in the presbytery in 1317. By then the first bay of the nave, between the crossing and the Norman pulpitum, was being rebuilt, and splendid sanctuary and choir fittings were being made. The high altar was dedicated in December 1328 and services were transferred from the old nave, where demolition down to windowsill-level then took place. New stone for the nave walls had been bought as early as 1324–5. Marble from workshops at Corfe for the main piers was paid for in 1332.

Work on a new w front also began in 1329, and the w gable was completed by 1342. Exact dates for the figure-screen are missing. The nave was roofed but (except for its E bay) we cannot be sure whether it was vaulted before the interruption of the Black Death. Nave vaulting, whether interrupted or newly begun, may have been the 'novum opus' mentioned in 1353. Much carved work of the 1330s–40s appears to have been stored in the cathedral workshops (see nave corbels and bosses below). No exact date for completion is known, probably by 1369, when Bishop Grandisson was buried in his little chapel behind the w front. The N porch was first added to the Norman nave c. 1280 (Hope), although re-used Norman stones have come to light (see above on Norman remains), but the porch exterior, much renewed, is partly late C 15. Over the porch proper are two rooms, one over the other: the lower room with large fireplace and adjacent oven and what seems to be a garderobe, the upper room with a small fireplace; in the C 19 this was the home of the cathedral dog-whipper. It shares a spiral staircase with the Minstrels' Gallery room over the corresponding nave aisle (see *Furnishings*). On the puzzle of St Edmund's Chapel just inside the N w front door, see below (after description of w front).

To return to the E end after our quick tour of the documents. Stylistic evidence confirms that of the rolls. Stiff-leaf foliage is still used in the piscina and sedilia of the LADY CHAPEL (and on one boss of the s transept chapel). Then we find at once everywhere bosses of enchanting realism in the rendering of foliage – vine, rose, hawthorn, oak, etc. – and on the elaborate corbels carrying the presbytery vaulting-shafts. The closest possible study of the Exeter bosses and corbels, preferably with glasses and a strong torch, will amply repay the effort wherever modern repainting does not obscure the carving. (The late C. J. P. Cave photographed them some years ago for a now rare King Penguin book; and see Swanton 1979 at the cathedral.) The Lady Chapel vault has longitudinal and transverse ridge ribs and *two* pairs of tierceron ribs in the N and s cells of each bay, one pair more than in Lincoln nave (or its followers mentioned above: by 1280 there was more

than one model to outdo). The vaulting-shafts here consist of clusters of five slim shafts, three of Purbeck marble and the two in the angles filleted. Alternate shafts in entrances and archways of the E chapels are of Purbeck. The Lady Chapel is divided from the N E and s E chapels by two pairs of half-quatrefoil responds.

The tracery of the Lady Chapel, N E and s E chapels, and the presbytery aisles and clerestories is essentially in advance of Westminster and Lincoln and Salisbury, although there are some similar elements in the E cloister walk, N end, at Westminster Abbey, presumably direct from France. (Exeter's great E window was to be rebuilt; see below with description of w window.) But Exeter's tracery that was bound to have been initiated before 1279 was entirely in keeping with contemporary London court-style tracery, particularly that of Old St Paul's E arm which was reflecting recent French work by the 1270s. Exeter was ahead of St Etheldreda's Chapel in Ely Place, London (?1286 to after 1290), and London-influenced tracery such as that in Merton College choir (1289–94). At Exeter, apart from the usual trefoils, quatrefoils and sexfoils in circles characteristic of geometrical tracery, are also trefoils and quatrefoils unencircled, pointed trefoils and quatrefoils, pointed cusping at the tops of individual window-lights, intersected mullions, spheric triangles and quadrangles – all in inexhaustible variations, with only the one limitation that corresponding windows (e.g. clerestory same bay N and s, or N E chapel E window and s E chapel E window) have the same patterns. The internal elevation of the Lady Chapel and flanking chapels shows blank arcading (pointed trefoil heads) on the ground stage with pointed trefoils in the spandrels, and tomb recesses with cusped arcading have also cusped circles in the spandrels. A small s door is a replacement of 1437, with a nodding-ogee canopy conservative for that date and so perhaps copying an earlier one, although the motif usually appears in this cathedral only in fittings. (For small-scale decorative use of it, see w front and *Furnishings* below.)

Outside the E end, the battlements enclosing low invisible roofs are early examples in the West Country of an initially royal decorative usage. An entry in the accounts for workmen spending three weeks and three days leading the roof of the Lady Chapel and other new-built roofs in 1303 (over a decade after building was finished) may simply mean a new lead covering after leaks in the first, almost flat roofing: an example of new styles new problems? Roofs generally precede vaults, and in style the Lady Chapel vaults precede the presbytery vaults that were finished by 1299. In the similarly low-roofed retrochoir or ambulatory, the vaults of the three central bays play minor variations on the tierceron theme.

The four PRESBYTERY bays of 1291–9 set the pier vaulting pattern for the rest of the cathedral: piers of

49. EXETER Presbytery, *c*. 1291–9, and choir, *c*. 1300–10

lozenge shape with sixteen close-set shafts (as already at St Paul's in London), correspondingly multiple arch mouldings, vaulting-shafts on corbels starting immediately above the piers but not connected with them, large clerestory windows and comparatively low broad vaults with ridge ribs and *three* pairs of tiercerons (again more than anywhere before) in the N and S cells of each bay. The luxuriant palm-branch effect is unforgettable. In only one respect does the appearance today differ from that of *c.* 1300, and it was corrected seventeen years later. These four bays were first given a two-storey elevation, with clerestory windowsills sloping like oblique aprons to the top of the main arcade. Two-tier chancels were rare in great C 13 churches, though not unknown (Southwell, Pershore and the not wholly similar, unaisled case of Rochester). Incidentally, Exeter presbytery as first built offered no halfway foothold for scaffold platforms from which the more easily to rig up centering for making vaults (on which point in general, see Fitchen 1961). The three CHOIR bays next built were completed in 1309 with the same vaulting, but with elevations in three tiers, the triforium a low trefoil-headed intermittent arcade of four arches per bay, carrying a clerestory passage with a pierced-quatrefoil parapet. As for the presbytery, soon the urge to homogeneity characteristic of this building was felt: in 1317–18 a shallow triforium with mock passage above was inserted in the four presbytery bays. 'For thirty-eight marble columns . . . for the galleries between the high altar and the quire £10 9s. at 5s. 6d. per column' (fabric rolls). Some juggling with the relative position of choir and presbytery piers had already occurred to allow for the width of the choir's real passage. And signs of old clerestory mouldings at presbytery triforium level can be detected. But a consistent pattern was now ready to be continued in the nave.

Another significant if slighter change in style occurs in progression from presbytery to choir in the design of the great corbels: leaves begin to lose freshness and tend to undulate or congeal into stylized knobbliness (see Swanton 1979). This happened all over England. It marks the end of classic Gothic perfection and the coming sophistication of the Dec style. But Exeter on the whole, in its architecture though not in its fittings, avoided Dec vagaries.

In the NAVE the style set before 1300 remained valid, with the full sets of tiercerons and ridge ribs already developed. Evolution can be seen only in details. The lierne ribs of the little vault subsequently added to St Edmund's Chapel, at the W end of the nave N aisle, appear elsewhere in the cathedral only in tiny vaults under the pulpitum of the 1320s (on both of which, see below). In the nave window tracery more complex motifs now occur, yet in consistent development from the eastern chapels. There are large spheric triangles filled with smaller ones, lozenges

with two sides concave and two convex, circles with a wheel of curved fish-bladders (mouchettes), and various spoke motifs in circles. Ogee arches occur only sparingly, though elsewhere in England a standard early C 14 motif. The great W window and the great E window at opposite ends of the splendid tunnel demonstrate the changes of the C 14. The W window, in a sense summarizing development all the way from the Lady Chapel, was probably designed by *Thomas Witney* †1342, and completed by his successor *William Joy*, with nine lights, the centre one wider, under a big encircled star-cluster of cusped lozenges etc. (Although the *Gentleman's Magazine* in 1817 reported that this window was redone in Coade stone *c.* 1810 to a design by John Carter under the supervision of Sir John Soane, it must have been an intention merely, as no sign of that long-lasting material survives, nor was any recorded during reglazing in 1904.) The great E window of the 1290s, however, was rebuilt in 1389–90 (perhaps partly in keeping with the C 13 tracery, as some of the original glass was re-used; see *Furnishings*), and its new Perp elements – centre panels rising straight to the arch – were presumably designed by *Robert Lesyngham*, the mason then in charge.

Change of style in the nave is also marked in bosses and corbels. There were many different hands busy on them. The best in the nave are as characteristic of the 1330s–40s, when they seem to have been made (and the bosses stored away?), as the best of the eastern arm had been of the 1290s. Two nave bosses may be singled out: second bay from the E, Christ in Majesty in the cross-legged pose of certain kings on the W front (see below); second bay from the W, the Murder of St Thomas à Becket, whose biographer Bishop Grandisson was. Earlier than these at the crossing, four great corbels were carved during 1309–13, possibly by *William Montacute*. the mason's head supporting St Catherine on the S E corbel is sometimes called his self-portrait, on no documentary grounds whatever, only out of romanticism (as Swanton makes clear). But on the nave corbels of the 1330s cutting is shallower; there is graceful variety but less vitality. (On corbels below the Minstrels' Gallery, see *Furnishings*.)

The WEST FRONT of the cathedral is at first puzzling to the visitor. It consists of a façade, apparently on the site of the Norman one, and a two-tiered figure screen in front of and structurally interconnected with the lower half of the façade. If the screen was an afterthought (as suggested by a string-course revealed by recent cleaning behind the lower statues), it was started soon after the façade was. The façade itself has the large central window described above, and steep lean-to aisle-fronts with rows of climbing slender blank arches (and almost a false-perspective effect). Aisle and nave tops are embattled, running horizontally above the nave window. Charming little figures (restored) peep through and over the battlements above the entrances.

Above and behind these battlements is the steep-pitched nave roof with a window (to the space over the nave vaults) of spheric-triangular shape and tracery of mouchettes, and a niche crowning the gable with the figure of St Peter (or Bishop Grandisson as St Peter). The image screen is like a reredos, crowned by its own pierced battlements. The figures in both tiers are under canopies with three-dimensional arches (the upper tier nodding ogees). The lower-tier canopies are now shown to have been truncated; the upper tier, therefore, was an afterthought. Some of the standing figures in the upper tier – shorter, thick-set, large-headed, and placid in type – would seem to be of the c 15 in style. The lower figures represent kings seated, many with their knees intently crossed, on pedestals enriched with demi-figures. The faces, figure-types and gar-

51. EXETER South-east crossing corbel, 1309–13

ment-folds of these kings are characteristic of c. 1340–50 and very similar to some of the nave bosses, with long thin bodies, stiffly tortuous attitudes, not at all placid. The cross-legged king motif first appeared in English art in early c 14 manuscripts. (See also on the w fronts of Lincoln and Lichfield.)

The central doorway has angels in very shallow relief in the spandrels. Inside this doorway and the N and s side doorways are porches to fill the space between screen and w front proper. In addition there is off the central porch Bishop Grandisson's tiny funeral chapel with pointed barrel-vault carrying an unusually large boss; the arches on the w and E have no capitals between jambs and voussoirs, and there are charming leaf-scrolls and fleurons in the arch mouldings. Both motifs were later going to be much used all over Devon. The porch of the s doorway has especially attractive (badly decayed) figure sculpture on the walls: Nativity and Adoration of the Magi in the 1330–50 style (note ox and ass below the Nativity). Inside the N doorway a fan-vault, almost certainly by *Robert Lesyngham*, in charge at Exeter after completing the E cloister walk at Gloucester. The three inner doorways between porches and nave have also no capitals between jambs and voussoirs. The same applies to a small door, again with fleurons, from the s aisle into the former cloister just E of the w front.

St Edmund's Chapel (now Devon Regiment chapel), off the N aisle just E of the w front, is a puzzle. A reference in 1279 to glazing in a chapel of that dedication seems to mean that a chapel was added to the Norman nave here while the eastern arm was closed for rebuilding. Its E window has plate tracery (late for 1279), its w window has Y-tracery (early for 1279), the N window is a c 14 replacement (in keeping with the aisle windows), and none is set symmetrically. Its vault with the only lierne ribs in the cathedral (aside from the pulpitum's) is not centred over the space. The s E vaulting-shafts do not go down to the floor but rest on a head-corbel. Externally, ill-fitting stonework could relate partly to addition to existing structure in the 1270s and partly to nave rebuilding in the 1330s with changes in the w front. When the chapel's N window and vault were inserted, they were not only not quite centred on the available space, but not centred either on each other or on the neighbouring aisle bay for viewing from the nave (see plan). Everything is just a bit off. We can only say of the medieval sequence here that the vault must have been the last afterthought of all. (The glazing is not original.) The cathedral archivist and master mason together confirm our bafflement. But now we must sum up.

At Exeter, any symptoms of a style in advance of that initially adopted are unimportant. The main architectural design of the cathedral remained unaltered from its conception c. 1275 to the death of Grandisson in 1369 – five active

52. EXETER Sculpture screen, c. 1340–50 and C 15, west front

bishops later – and the completion of the building. It was a very personal design, of much character. One would wish to be able to ascribe its inception to a designer known by name and circumstance of life. The *Master of Exeter* felt driven to the *nec plus ultra* of an existing style, the style of 1250–60, rather than to the creation of a new style. Such artists exist at all times. In his vaults he used more tiercerons than anybody before, on his piers more shafts than anyone except the St Paul's master (but at St Paul's the vaults were less rich). This multiplication makes for richness, and the Exeter master handled it with a sense of luxuriance, the epitome of late C 13 tendencies. His work makes even the Angel Choir at Lincoln appear restrained. (Had he worked at Lincoln? in London?) He did not abandon the accepted type of vault or pier. For his main vaults he did not conceive the next innovation after the tierceron, the lierne and the networks it led to, nor the pier leading up without complete break into the vaulting zone, nor the pier wholly or partially without capitals, nor curvilinear tracery. His tracery is particularly personal, composed of motifs of immediate London derivation. The unencircled trefoil and quatrefoil and spheric triangle and quadrangle and elementary mouchettes in spandrels were, indeed, the favourites of French designers about and after 1250 (Sainte Chapelle, Notre Dame s transept, etc.), and they became the main standby in French cathedrals of the late c 13 and early c 14 (e.g. Nevers, Carcassonne, Bordeaux). The Exeter master could have seen them in France. But nearer home by the 1270s there had developed the court-style work of London and centres influenced by London. He could see spheric triangles in the Westminster Abbey gallery, Hereford N transept, Lichfield nave. He could see the sixteen-shafted piers and the tracery at St Paul's. For he was emphatically an Englishman. The proportions of his main vessel are utterly un-French, generously broad, and the weight of the profuse palm-branch ribs from l. and r. makes the interior appear decidedly low. The proportionately short piers are also wholly against French c 13 ideals, and the abundance of sculptured bosses has no parallel the other side of the Channel. Given these English characteristics of the building and its impressive scale and richness of architectural conception, it is extremely surprising that it had so little influence in the diocese, either in Devon or in Cornwall. The s w English parish church is of great consistency of style, but its style, except in details, is not that of Exeter Cathedral.

For the last pre-Reformation construction at Exeter, see under *Monuments* E *of the crossing* for the c 16 Speke and Oldham Chantries, which structurally, very slightly, extended the retrochoir to N and s.

FURNISHINGS, E TO W

E of the crossing The early c 14 fittings are characterized by far more fanciful treatment than the carvers were allowed in the architecture itself. (For bosses and corbels, as integral with structure, see above.) Stonecarving and woodcarving are followed by metalwork, wall painting, stained glass and finally monuments.

The PULPITUM is thought to have been designed by *Thomas of Witney.* (Payments to William Canon of Corfe may have been for stone and for columns only.) Completed 1324. Of triple-arcade veranda type (i.e. the front arches always open), originally with side altars against rear partitions that flanked a central archway and enclosed a pair of staircases to the loft (staircases removed and their walls opened up by *Scott*, who substituted his charming spiral stair in the s choir aisle; cf. Ely). The front arcade is of three depressed ogee arches on piers with moulded capitals, the spandrels decorated with fantastically elongated quatrefoils packed with knobbly foliage. At the outer angles diagonal niches, a typically Dec conceit. The prominent parapet a cusped and crocketed blank arcade of thirteen ogee-topped compartments originally framing stone images, now with early c 17 painted scenes from the Old and New Testaments, provincial versions of the taste for Venetian art (Croft-Murray 1962). The parapet had elaborate cresting in wood, replaced with stonework by *Kendall* in 1819, with two compartments to each one below (pre-1868 photograph in the Matthews *Organs* booklet (Matthews n.d.) at the cathedral). Under the 'veranda' little vaults with liernes on a scheme somewhat similar to that of Bristol choir, and the central E bay (between the former stair-bays) vaulted on the scheme of Tewkesbury nave (1322–6) in miniature: in fact, this small single bay at Exeter has been called a try-out for the Tewkesbury vault (Bock 1961). The unusual plinths of the pulpitum's front piers are identical to those of the retrochoir piers at Wells (Coldstream 1976). So this pulpitum was a compendium of up-to-date West Country references. As early as the c 14, organs are thought to have been placed on it. The present ORGAN CASE, 1665, by *John Loosemore* (its side-towers of pipes removed from the NE and SE crossing piers in the 1870s, the case raised and deepened 1891): an important case, the central tower on its E face comparable in outline and position to that at Gloucester, and both probably modelled on *Thomas Harris's* then recently re-erected organ at Salisbury (Gillingham; Matthews n.d.).

SEDILIA. (1) In the Lady Chapel: three seats stepped up, with simple pointed-trefoil heads; and two-light piscina with six-foiled circle on top. (2) In the presbytery, s of the high altar, and far more elaborate than (1): three canopied seats of Beer stone, the slender central pair of colonnettes (unusually) of brass or latten: one a renewal, the other said to be original. The whole unavoidably much restored, having been smashed in 1942 and finely reassembled by Exeter craftsmen; previously restored by *Scott*, by *Kendall*, and earlier. Still most impressive proof of the nature of the development from the presbytery's vigorous bosses and corbels of the 1290s to the sedilia's probable date of *c.* 1320. Originally no doubt part of the larger composition of the great altar screen in a relationship now only conjectural (P. Morris, *Antiquaries Journal*, 1943–4, saw the whole as possible source for the Neville Screen at Durham). The sedilia composition has all the intricacy and unrestrained spatial play characteristic of the early c 14, say at Ely or Bristol, but absent on an architectural scale at Exeter. (The most sophisticated E. E. version of such a set of canopies on slim supports, Aquablanca's tomb of fifty years earlier at Hereford, is neither intricate nor unrestrained.) Here, as seen from the front, the seats have tall plain concave backs painted to represent hanging cloth, with tiny heads on top, and above these backs open to the s aisle. Each seat is crowned by a seven-sided canopy, two sides for the back, one each for the sides, and three for the front – the front unsupported, the back and sides borne by the pair of metal colonnettes and by outer walls (with matching but attached stone-shafted colonnettes). Minute star-vault inside each canopy. The gables ogee-shaped and sumptuously crocketed. (Three modern statues have been inserted.) On top of the canopies another set of tall, fragile three-sided canopies, with the point of the triangle towards the aisle. From the aisle one sees the elaborate shaft-work, with unexpected shafts and gables peeping through a gossamer of finely carved forms. The clue to the composition is that the gables towards the aisle are placed so that each shaft between them corresponds to the centre of a gable on the seat-front, as if playing the Lincoln arcaded counterpoint theme of over a century before. In a sense this multiple canopy is comparable in spirit to Exeter's vaulting: a top-heavy exploration of ultimate possibilities in stonework, though on this smaller scale going nearer to the edge, as it were, so needing stronger material for otherwise impractically slender supports. It is more easily seen than described.

CANOPY (remains) from some early C14 tomb, Easter sepulchre, altar screen or reredos. Now at N wall of NE transept (St Andrew's Chapel). Three gabled compartments (empty) separated by three-quarter angels and with steep gables crocketed and pinnacled, and between the gables two well-carved faces. The gables and their ogee-shaped pierced trefoils are on a similar though simpler pattern, and of the same overall width, as the aisle-front of the high-altar sedilia (above), raising conjectures as to this canopy's part in the great complex of sanctuary fittings. Scott thought it part of the original high-altar reredos; though a hypothetical Easter sepulchre on the N side, before Stapledon's tomb was put there, was tentatively suggested by Morris (*Antiquaries Journal*, 1944). If, on the other hand, it was originally intended for St Andrew's Chapel, which became Dean Kilkenny's chantry chapel in 1305, then the fitment incorporating this canopy would have had to be added a decade or more after that. At any rate this fragment shows what quality has been lost.

Stone SCREENS, erected c. 1420, to the Lady Chapel and its flanking chapels (see also *Monuments* E *of the crossing,* Bishop Stafford, below). Very slim four-light sections with standard Devon tracery and entrances headed by a boldly cusped arch below the tracery of one four-light section. That to the Lady Chapel much restored since damage c. 1657 when the chapel was used as a library.

CHOIR STALLS, Victorian. The stalls made in 1309–10 for the new choir were replaced during the Civil War by pews for Presbyterians. The pews were turned out at the Restoration and new stalls made in C17 Gothic. Those in their turn, 'obscured by incongruous accompaniments', were replaced by *Scott* in the 1870s with the present set, modelled on the Winchester stalls (contemporary with Exeter's C14 set) and carved by *Thomas Farmer*. (One back

53. EXETER Sedilia canopy, c. 1320 (detail), from the south presbytery aisle

panel from the C14 stalls survives as door to the Sylke chantry in the N transept.) The C14 stalls apparently replaced a C13 set of stalls whose presence in the Norman choir is indicated by the style of the MISERICORDS originally attached to them and miraculously preserved through all these changes. (One can understand individual stallholders becoming attached to them in another sense, as Dr Swanton has pointed out: 'In some churches it was customary for clergy to turn round to kneel, the upright seat forming something of a desk', its carving becoming a matter of 'proprietary concern' to its regular occupant; and so at Exeter seven centuries of fond occupants have ensured the survival of the oldest set of misericords in England.) In style forty-eight of them date from c. 1230–70, i.e. begun in Bishop Brewer's time; of two others one is of the early C14 and one of the C15 (see Glasscoe and Swanton 1978 at the cathedral; Remnant 1969). Some still have stiff-leaf foliage; in others leaves are naturalistic. Figures include a lion, a mermaid, a siren, a centaur, Apocalyptic locusts, the Swan Knight, and an elephant. The elephant (N side) could have been carved from a drawing imperfectly made from life: in 1255 Louis IX of France gave Henry III an elephant, which was kept in the Tower of London; sketches of it

54. EXETER Misericord, *c.* 1260, north row of stalls

appear in the margins of Matthew Paris's contemporary chronicle of its arrival (in Westminster Abbey library).

BISHOP'S THRONE, or, rather, architectural throne canopy, 1313–16, of oak from Bishop Stapledon's estates at Chudleigh and Newton St Cyres. The most exquisite piece of woodwork of its date in England and perhaps in Europe. Fortunately removed before the bombing of 1942. *Thomas of Winchester* came for a month in 1313 to supervise selection of the timber and his high wage of 3s. a week suggests that he was the designer and that the reputation of the Winchester choir stalls of 1308 was high. But the Exeter 'throne' is not a copy of them; it is rather an advance from them. On a basically square plan, the lowest and largest stage has big crocketed gables over cusped nodding-ogee arches (with finely carved human heads): these arches are some of the earliest nodding ogees in the country. The upper stages recede like an extended telescope, fantastically loftily pinnacled. The tall triangular aedicules on each side with tracery behind may originally have extended higher. Despite the difference in material, the aesthetic effect is much like that of the sedilia. Originally all painted and gilded. Harvey, in more than one of his works, says that Thomas of Winchester was very likely the same as *Thomas of Witney*, who returned to Exeter in 1316 and was in charge of building here until 1342.

Wooden SCREENS, C 15, between chancel and aisles at the 'E transept' bay, also at w end of choir aisles. Four-light doors with standard Devon screen tracery, the flanking sections of two lights only, and pierced cresting of slender upright birds (pheasants?) between foliage. Screens to St Andrew's Chapel (or NE transept) and to St James's Chapel on the SE, the former reconstructed and the latter replaced

after the bombing of 1942. In the Lady Chapel, other woodcarvings: group of shepherds, one piping with angel above, from an early C 15 Nativity scene, possibly from work discarded in the early C 19, impressive even though fragmentary; Virgin and Child with St Anne, possibly Flemish C 19? For chantry-screen carvings, see *Monuments* below.

LECTERN in the choir, brass eagle, given to the cathedral in the C 17 and probably medieval (Oman, *Archaeological Journal*, 87, 1930). For memorial brasses, see *Monuments* below.

WALL PAINTING, E wall of retrochoir s of entrance to Lady Chapel. Assumption and Coronation of the Virgin in the presence of the Trinity attended by the nine orders of angels with wall of Celestial City below, and once probably continuing down to the floor. Croft-Murray (1962) dates a similar painting in the N transept early C 16. Restored by *E. W. Tristram*, 1930. (See also early C 14 painting in the roof of the Stapledon tomb canopy, *Monuments* below.)

STAINED GLASS. In 1644 one Richard Symons noted down 150 coats of arms in windows. Fewer than twenty of these remain. The earliest surviving glass is in the NE and SE chapels flanking the Lady Chapel: grisailles, very neat and geometrical work, dating from the first years of the C 14, as borne out by the fabric rolls (glass bought 1303; also some from Rouen in 1317; in the E window of the NE chapel three inserted C 15 figures of kneeling canons). The early windows have the same naturalistic foliage as the earliest bosses: oak, hawthorn, ivy. Also early C 14 but a little later, the clerestory window facing the bishop's throne: also grisaille, but with a row of (headless) figures of saints under tall canopies (the choir clerestory glass was in place by 1311). – Similar figures and canopies in the six side-lights of the great E window, which, as we have seen, was partly rebuilt in 1389–90. Its centre lights were then conscientiously renewed by *Robert Lyen* of Exeter. He used yellow stain, still absent in the very early C 14, but his canopies are in imitation of the Dec predecessors. The whole window is a rich assembly of saints, patriarchs and heraldry. It has some later insertions, perhaps from C 18 restoration by *William Peckitt*. – In the Lady Chapel, nine biblical panels of French and Flemish C 16 glass collected in the C 18 by Sir William Jerningham and placed here in 1955. (For other glass, see nave furnishings below.)

MONUMENTS E of the crossing. LADY CHAPEL, SE recess. Coffin-shaped Purbeck marble slab of a bishop, probably 1170s–80s, when native Purbeck was supplanting imported Tournai marble. Sometimes assigned to Bishop Bartholomeus Iscanus † 1184, or, as sometimes suggested, retrospectively made for Leofric, the cathedral's first bishop, i.e. probably made well after Warelwast translated

Leofric's bones to the new Norman cathedral in 1133. (A lead coffin of bones brought to light in the ruins of St James's Chapel in 1942, and thought to have been Leofric's as retranslated to the C 13 cathedral, has been reburied there in his name; incidentally a spurious monument to Leofric made up in 1568 was removed from the cathedral in 1885: a commentary upon relative antiquarian sensibilities.) This slab in the Lady Chapel is one of the earliest sculptures in Purbeck marble in the country: cf. the one at Salisbury (nave s aisle) assigned to Bishop Joscelin † 1184, also the somewhat later abbots' effigies in local marble at Peterborough. Very flat relief obtained by carving away the background between the figure and the framing arch, which is triangular and only slightly curved; angels in spandrels. The draperies still with the few 'telescoped' folds usual in France fifty years before. – SW recess: Bishop Simon of Apulia † 1223, also in Purbeck but now with the higher relief, easier attitude and finer garment folds of the early C 13. – Set in the floor, incised marble slab with

55. EXETER Tomb of Bishop Branscombe from St Gabriel's Chapel. Effigy *c.* 1280, chest and canopy 1442

foliated cross to Bishop Quivil † 1291, under whom the Lady Chapel was finished. – The N pair of recesses, in high contrast to the S pair, are occupied by Sir John and Lady Doderidge † 1628 and 1614, he in the scarlet gown of a judge in the Court of King's Bench, she in flowered brocade.

Between the Lady Chapel and St Gabriel's (SE) Chapel. Bishop Branscombe † 1280; the chest, canopy and angels at foot are of 1442 (see Stafford's below), but the delicate workmanship of the effigy of painted basalt was presumably produced during the first flush of the cathedral's rebuilding initiated by him. Composition similar to the earlier bishops' slabs, but no longer coffin-shaped, the capitals and leaves of the framing arch still pre-naturalistic, draperies with fewer, heavier folds, and the position of his hands should be compared with Simon of Apulia (above). (Possibly of a Devon black basalt referred to by Clifton-Taylor (1972) as in structural use by Romans and Normans at Exeter.) – Opposite, between Lady Chapel and St John Evangelist's (NE) Chapel. Bishop Stafford † 1419, the earliest surviving monument of a type which became a pattern for the whole C 15 (the chest and canopy copied for Branscombe's tomb opposite). Tomb-chest with cusped quatrefoils, cusped 'Tudor' arch, traceried spandrels, cornice with hovering angels, broad quatrefoil cresting. Alabaster effigy with tabernacle at his head, thought to have been carved near the quarry at Chellaston, Derbyshire. Incidentally, dated graffiti by cathedral visitors began, it would seem, soon after the Reformation. – On the floor of the NE chapel beside Stafford's tomb, a fine BRASS to his kinsman Canon William Langton † 1413. Kneeling figure with scroll coming from his praying hands, and dressed in a cope, its form well represented, also the orphreys embroidered with his personal device, the Stafford knot (Norris 1978). For the cathedral's other surviving medieval monumental brass, see S presbytery aisle below. – Still in the NE chapel, Carew family monument, erected 1589, proudly ambitious with much heraldry: with all the quartering, 357 coats of arms represent marriages with fifty-one families (Hope and Lloyd 1973). Sir Gawen Carew and wife recumbent behind low colonnade, and below, as in a truckle-bed, their nephew Sir Peter, wearing armour and ruff like his uncle but also a C 13 surcoat and shield – and represented cross-legged! It must be one of the earliest instances in sculpture of a conscious medieval revival (and just contemporary with the spurious Leofric mentioned above). For Sir Peter by himself, see S transept.

Near these E chapels, at the N and S ends of the ambulatory or retrochoir, the early C 16 SPEKE AND OLDHAM CHANTRIES, built out between the easternmost pairs of aisle buttresses. Sir John Speke † 1518, Bishop Oldham † 1519; the latter founded Manchester Grammar School and (with his friend Bishop Fox of Winchester) Corpus Christi College, Oxford. In design the two chapels are very

similar outside, but quite different inside. The front walls of four sections with outer uprights decorated with small statuary (St Anne teaching the Virgin to read at l. of Speke Chantry entrance). Tracery and details of doorway as in contemporary stone screens. The large openings guarded by contemporary iron bars. Contemporary wooden door to the Oldham Chantry. Quatrefoil tomb-chests inside both. The Speke chapel inside has fully panelled walls, figures of angels in niches above, and a gently vaulted ceiling with pendants; not an inch left unadorned (it is said also to contain the arms of Vesey, precentor 1508–9). The Oldham chapel has an unusually elaborate reredos with three figure-scenes, Annunciation, Mass of St Gregory, Nativity; less decoration otherwise, but incorporating owls, Oldham's rebus. – Flanking the Lady Chapel entrance, a pair: John Bidgood † 1691 and James Raillard † 1692, quite grand and sombre, with black and gold epitaphs of a type found in Exeter parish churches.

PRESBYTERY. Tombs in this prime position, some also visible from the aisles, include the following, taken clockwise from the presbytery's N side entry. Bishop Marshall † 1206, Purbeck marble coffin-shaped slab with effigy, transitional in type between those of 'Leofric' and Simon in the Lady Chapel. It rests on a Purbeck chest thought to be slightly later, with three seated figures in quatrefoils (Christ in Majesty, St Peter, St Paul); separate side-slabs propped up in the N aisle nearby are more likely to be part of Marshall's original tomb-chest. – Bishop Lacy † 1453, tomb-chest with marble slab bearing matrix of a brass. – Bishop Bradbridge † 1578, Elizabethan tomb-chest, no effigy. – Bishop Stapledon † 1326, next to the high altar and opposite the sedilia. Walter Stapledon founded Exeter College, Oxford. As Lord High Treasurer of England he was murdered by a London mob. The first of the canopied tombs, but only a low canopy (was it originally higher?). To the presbytery a depressed, cusped and crocketed ogee arch, fleurons in jambs and voussoirs, to the aisle three trefoiled openings. Hovering angels in the frieze. Recumbent effigy looking up at a contemporary painting in the roof of Christ displaying his wounds. At the E end a little carved donor figure. C 18 iron railings to the aisle. (For his brother Robert opposite, see N aisle below.) – On the S side of the presbytery next to the sedilia, Bishop Woolton † 1594, Elizabethan tomb-chest with strapwork and pilasters, black marble slab on top, no effigy (see also wall-tablet, N transept, below). – Bishop Berkeley (for three months) † 1327, tomb-chest with Purbeck marble slab bearing circular matrix for brass.

SOUTH PRESBYTERY AISLE and CHOIR AISLE. In the bay W of the above, in arched recesses with carved label-stop heads between and at ends, two recumbent cross-legged armoured knights: on the l. Sir Humphrey de Bohun, Earl of Hereford † 1322 (whose arms are in Bristol's E window), on the r. probably Sir Henry de Raleigh † 1303. – On the aisle floor, E end, one of the cathedral's two large medieval brasses (cf. Langton above): Sir Peter Courtenay K.G. † 1409, formerly in the nave (cf. Courtenay tomb now in s transept). Nearly life-size, much worn; said to be one of only six brasses representing Knights of the Garter, though he does not seem to be wearing the Garter (Norris 1978). The armour a mixture of mail and plate, as on the effigy of the Black Prince at Canterbury. The border mostly reconstruction, but in the upper corners remnants of badges with falcons attacking a duck and a heron. – The other principal monuments in this aisle are post-Reformation, and are given chronologically. Bishop William Cotton † 1621 (symmetrically opposite his successor Bishop Carey's on the N side of the choir). Of alabaster, with bearded recumbent figure in typical early C 17 episcopal dress under an arched canopy on columns with symbols of fame, time and death. – Nearby wall-monument to Dr Edward Cotton † 1675, cathedral treasurer. Restrained and with a good portrait bust (the sculptor

56. EXETER Monument to Dr Edward Cotton † 1675. South choir aisle

deserves to be known). – Wall-monument to Dr Nicholas Hall † 1709, cathedral treasurer. Less restrained, richly ornamented with broken pediment, armorial cartouche and winged cherub heads. – Near w end of aisle, wall-monument to Bishop Weston † 1742, his wife † 1741 and daughter † 1762 by *Thomas Ady*, tablet with arms above and sarcophagus below, and kneeling angel pointing to inscription. – Lt-Gen. John G. Simcoe † 1806 by *John Flaxman*, wall-tablet with figures of a soldier with reversed musket and a Canadian Indian with tomahawk. General Simcoe was the first Lt-Gov. of Upper Canada, and founded Toronto.

NORTH PRESBYTERY AISLE and CHOIR AISLE. N wall near E end, opposite Bishop Stapledon, his brother Sir Robert Stapledon † 1320 in ogee-arched recess with angel heads as cusps of the arch: recumbent cross-legged effigy in contemporary mail armour, shown unusually between two enchanting figures, his squire and his groom, the latter holding a horse (damaged). If all this were in its original early C 14 state, we should know better how exquisite English C 14 carving could be. – Nearby, C 16 cadaver or emaciated corpse in shroud, in recess with little forward-tipped vault, perhaps *ex situ* but behind a grille of contemporary ironwork: was it once the *memento mori* of Anthony Harvey † 1564, tomb-chest (next to R. Stapledon) with mixed Gothic-classic details and no effigy? – In contrast the principal C 17 monument of the N aisle, corresponding to Bishop Cotton's on the s side of the choir, Bishop Valentine Carey † 1626, again of alabaster and a bearded recumbent figure in early C 17 episcopal dress under arched canopy on columns, here simply with putti. – Wall-tablet to Robert Hall † 1667 with broken pediment, coats of arms and attached columns. – Wall-tablet to Rachel Charlotte, wife of Capt. O'Brien of the 24th Regiment, † 1800 saving her child from fire, in coloured marbles, seated female figure with reversed torch, signed *J. Kendall*, the cathedral surveyor.

Transepts and Crossing For the great pulpitum screen, see *Furnishings* E *of the crossing* above. – At the crossing, large two tiered brass CHANDELIER dated 1691. – Stone SCREENS (1422) to the E chapel of each transept, closely similar to the E end chapel screens (above).

WALL PAINTING, N wall of N transept. Resurrection, early C 16 and like the painting in the retrochoir. Christ holding a banner steps out of the tomb surrounded by sleeping soldiers; in l. distance three women, on r. contemporary sexton and wife carrying spade and lantern (bringing scripture home to the people), in the background Jerusalem with circular church. As accomplished and with the same 'woodcut' feeling as prophets on a screen at Ashton, i.e. of an important Devon school of late medieval painting (Croft-Murray 1962, Hope and Lloyd 1973).

CLOCK, N wall of N transept. Late C 15, traditionally given by Bishop Peter Courtenay †1487; much restored and redecorated, notably in 1760, the works now on view are a mixture of several centuries in between. Large dial with central globe round which revolves the moon, also the sun represented by a fleur-de-lys, with inscription 'Pereunt et imputantur' from Martial's *Epigrams* V.20. References to earlier clocks in the cathedral records date from the late C 13 to the C 15. (For the two C 14 cathedral clocks, see *Salisbury* and *Wells*.)

MONUMENTS. NORTH TRANSEPT. NE corner, chantry of Precentor Sylke †1508. Tomb surmounted by cadaver or *memento mori* (cf. better-preserved example in N choir aisle, above). Surrounded by Perp stone screens with small (now mostly headless) figures against the uprights and crisp tracery. The wooden door is a sole remnant of the early C 14 choir stalls (see Glasscoe and Swanton 1978). – N wall, high-set wall-tablet to Bishop John Woolton †1594, pedimented with inscription between columns: was it originally part of his tomb in the presbytery? – W wall, Dr Edmund Davy †1692, bust in niche encircled by a wreath. – E wall, Capt. Benjamin Dollen †1700, portrait bust in medallion and naval tail-piece scene. – Near W wall, James Northcote †1831 by *Francis Chantrey*, life-size seated figure on high pedestal. – Crimean War memorial tablet on E wall to members of the 20th or East Devonshire Regiment †1854–5, flanked by bronze figures of riflemen.

SOUTH TRANSEPT. SE corner, two slabs, one of Tournai marble, one of Purbeck, rest on what may be a late C 14 tomb-chest. One or both slabs may relate to Bishop John 'the Chanter' †1191. – Hugh Courtenay second Earl of Devon †1377 and wife Margaret de Bohun †1391, free-standing tomb-chest with effigies, said to have been heavily restored after removal in the early C 19 from a Courtenay chantry formerly in the nave (S arcade, between the piers of the second bay from the E, also the original site of the Courtenay brass now in the S presbytery aisle). She with intertwined Bohun swans at her feet. The effigies' value as costume evidence no doubt diminished with restoration, unless pre-C 19 engravings survive. – S wall, Sir Peter Carew †1575 with kneeling figure (see also his uncle's display in the NE chapel above). – Sir John Gilbert †1596 and wife, recumbent figures behind low arches (similar in this to the Bampfield monument at Poltimore). – Very Rev. Joseph Palmer, Dean of Cashel, †1829 by *Humphrey Hopper*, female figure leaning on draped urn with reversed torch: cold.

Nave For bosses and corbels, see nave interior above.

MINSTRELS' GALLERY, above N arcade at bay corresponding to N porch. The most popular fitment at Exeter, but neither architecturally nor sculpturally of a high order. Presumably erected only after removal of scaffolds for centering of the nave vaults. The fact that the two corbels below, carrying the vaulting-shafts either side of this bay, differ in shape from all others in the nave suggests that this so-called gallery was an afterthought, possibly of the 1360s (but C 20 figures on the corbels). What is seen from the nave is the carved stone balcony of a hidden large high room – big enough for an orchestra or antiphonal choir – over the N aisle. The pierced parapet takes the place of both triforium and clerestory parapet for this bay. Fourteen angels, including one at each end, in tiny flattish recesses, the twelve on the front with musical instruments: citole, bagpipe, recorder, viol, harp, jews' harp, trumpet, portative organ, gittern, shawm, timbrel, cymbals. Recent conservation has shown that the angels were trimmed to fit the recesses. Trumpeters and choristers still use the gallery, and the *trompes militaires* of the organ are here.

Timber SCREEN to St Edmund's Chapel by the NW entrance. Possibly late C 14 and contemporary with the vault within, it is the earliest in style of the cathedral's wooden screens. Simple and substantial in solid oak, its only decoration pierced ornament along the top. Traces of bright red paint.

FONT, near W end of S arcade. Late C 17, of Sicilian marble with carved oak cover. First used in 1687. The pedestal of 1891. – The pulpit designed by *Scott* was set up in 1877.

STAINED GLASS. The great W window has been re-glazed at least three times since the Reformation: by *William Peckitt* in 1766 (heraldic panels – now predominantly yellow, their painted technique having led to fading – preserved in the Cloister Room); by *Burlison & Grylls* to *Bodley*'s design in 1904 (destroyed 1942); and since the war by *Reginald Bell* and *M. C. Farrer Bell*. – Much Victorian and Edwardian glass was lost in the war, but the S aisle still retains windows by *Powell* (Turner window), *Clayton & Bell* (South African War) and *Burlison & Grylls* (Tanner), as well as replacements by *A. F. Erridge*, *G. C. Abbs* and *Christopher Webb*. The Blackmore window by Erridge is in the N aisle (for the novelist's monument, see below).

MONUMENTS. Wall-tablets in the NAVE aisles, chiefly C 19 or C 20 with the following exception. N aisle: Matthew Godwin †1586, aged eighteen, organist and master of the music at Canterbury and Exeter cathedrals, said to be the earliest monument to a musician in England. Kneeling in profile among instruments, organ, lute, theorbo and trumpet; charming and full of feeling. – Also N aisle: officers and men of the Ninth Queen's Royal Lancers in India by *Baron Marochetti*, erected 1860, flanked by bronze horsemen. – W wall of N aisle: Richard Doddridge Blackmore †1900, author of *Lorna Doone*, portrait head in relief, signed by *Harry Hems*. – S aisle, includes other tablets signed by London sculptors: to Saccharissa Hibbert †1828, roses within a sickle, by *Richard Westmacott Jr* of Wilton Place; and to Sophia Charlotte Hennis † 1834, seated female and draped urn, by *E. Gaffin* of Regent Street.

Chapter house SCULPTURE. In the C 13 paired niches Croft-Murray (1962) noted remains of C 15 wall paintings of feigned sculpture, no longer visible. The niches are now occupied, in some cases leapt from, by a set of sculptures in aluminium and fibreglass on the theme of the Creation by *Kenneth Carter*, 1974. New Testament figures on the S wall are far more successful than Old Testament abstractions on the N wall, which in such precise materials and such a setting may connote the debris of 1942 more than the Book of Genesis.

CLOISTERS

In 1225 Bishop Brewer gave up part of his garden for the building of a chapter house (described in the main text above). The W wall of the chapter house was on the boundary between his garden and the cloister area (Hope and Lloyd 1973). Whether cloisters actually existed already is not clear, but surviving cloister doorways, one to the chapter house and one to the E end of the S nave aisle, are of Brewer's time, and the cloisters may have been built by him as well. From 1377 they were being rebuilt under *Robert Lesyngham*, who had finished the F walk of Gloucester cloisters (after it had been begun by Thomas of Cambridge with perhaps the first fan-vaults in England). So the late C 14 Exeter cloisters may have resembled Gloucester's E walk (Harvey 1978). The Exeter cloisters were demolished in 1656–7, either by a private owner, John Embree, who had got hold of them, or more probably by the Exeter city corporation, to which he sold them and which set up the town serge market here (Summerson 1975). In 1887 the S E corner, with library above on the site of the C 14 library, was rebuilt by *J. L. Pearson*, basing his cloister-bays on surviving fragments, with 'star-vault' and large Perp window each (Quiney 1979). These cloister-bays were glazed with *Peckitt* glass from the great W window, and a screen and doors were added *c.* 1960 to form the 'cloister room' under the library.

For the rest of the precinct and surroundings, see the forthcoming B of E *South Devon*.

Guildford

CATHEDRAL CHURCH OF THE HOLY SPIRIT
Anglican

(Based on B of E *Surrey*, 1971, entry by Ian Nairn, revised.)

On Stag Hill, N W of the town centre. Guildford was nominated as a suffragan bishopric to Winchester by Henry VIII in 1534, but his scheme never came into effect. Increased population finally forced an independent see in 1927, using Holy Trinity, the mainly C 18 parish church on the High Street, as the pro-cathedral. The job of designing the new cathedral was won in open competition by *Sir Edward Maufe* in 1932; it was begun in 1936, chancel and crossing were opened in 1954, the nave in 1961. The porches at the W end were completed in 1965–6. Maufe's style was sweet-tempered, undramatic Curvi-linear Gothic, very much like Temple Moore's. The result is a cruciform church with bulky central tower, tripartite W front and two low side wings enclosing garths to N and S of it, all in brick with a minimum of stone dressings. At the E end is a Lady Chapel, lower than the chancel, flanked by sacristy and chapter house. Long narrow windows with mildly fancy tracery heads. It was conservative when it was designed – even by English standards – and without any of the genuine fervour of Liverpool. The outside is no more than a well-mannered, even mealy-mouthed, postscript to the Gothic Revival. The next step was to be Coventry (see companion volume).

But Maufe's ability to create interior spaces (as in the Cooper's Hill Memorial at Runnymede) expresses itself in spite of the style. The result is a very impressive and sober free-Gothic central 'vessel' treated with white plaster rendering and a minimum of Doulting limestone dressings, with deep, narrow window splays (so deep that no direct light is visible looking E from the crossing) between piers without capitals running up into transverse 'bows' or arches crossing the vault. Beyond, a stumpy ambulatory with a lot of spatial play with knife-thin pointed arches. This leads to vestries at the sides and to the Lady Chapel at the E end, an austere enclosed room (contrasting with the long vistas of the rest of the building), with plain walls below high, broad, five-light clerestory windows with angular arch-heads. Five-sided apse, low pitched roof. The floor of choir and sanctuary finely paved with Purbeck limestone (Clifton-Taylor 1972). W of the choir, on either side, transverse barrel-vaulted transepts and hence a complex roof shape at the crossing. The nave has tall arcades, tall narrow aisles and tiny clerestory windows high up. The result is noble and subtle, and has a queer power of compelling, not reverence, but contemplation. Best of all probably are the views down the aisles from the crossing. It is a great loss to the development of English architecture

57. GUILDFORD Designed 1932 by Sir Edward Maufe

that Maufe felt impelled to harness this spatial imagination to a period style. (In some ways this tall interior could be called a version, diluted by two generations, of Arundel.)

The nobility is partly dispelled by the architect's own fittings in a sub-Comper style, e.g. the gilded tester high up over the altar and the strangely domestic (temporary) lamp-shades. Most of the other fittings also show the depressingly low standard of 1950s religious ornament. The exceptions are perhaps ENGRAVED GLASS by *John Hutton* in the S transept and W doors, and a large CARPET (designed by *Maufe*) in the sanctuary. – For the rest, there is some *Eric Gill* STATUARY, but of very poor quality: St John Baptist over the S transept doors, and a Christ in

Majesty on the E wall (executed after Gill's death by *Anthony Forster*). – On the S exterior of the Lady Chapel, Archangel Gabriel by *Alan Collins*, and on the Lady Chapel buttresses, St Martha and St Catherine by *Alan Collins*, St Cecilia and Lady Margaret Beaufort by *Dennis Huntley*. – Virgin and Child, of wood, in the Lady Chapel, by *Douglas Stephen*. – IRON GATES (N transept) and BRONZE DOORS (S transept), both designed by *Maufe*, the bronze doors made by *Vernon Hill*. – STAINED GLASS roundel at the E end by *Moira Forsyth*.

For the cathedral's new neighbour, the University of Surrey, and the town of Guildford, see the latest edition of B of E *Surrey*.

58. GUILDFORD Nave, completed 1961

London: the City

CATHEDRAL CHURCH OF ST PAUL *Anglican*

(Based on B of E *London 1: The Cities of London and Westminster*, 1973, further revised, with information from the Dean, Sir John Summerson, John Clark, Michael Gillingham, Ralph Hyde and J. Mordaunt Crook.)

Plan, Fig. 60, from the *Builder*, 1892, when the Wellington tomb was in the S W chapel, the font in the nave, and *Bodley's* altar screen in place; shows remains of the medieval chapter house.

Some references (see Recent Literature): Colvin 1978; Crook 1980, 1981; Downes 1971; Physick 1970; Summerson 1964, 1975; *Victorian Church Art* 1971; Whinney 1964, 1971.

INTRODUCTION

If Salisbury spire is one of the national icons, so is the dome of St Paul's. The famous photographic image of it in December 1940, calm as a rock among flames and smoke, was a tract for the times. The placing of the cathedral on a hill above city and river has always enhanced its authority, although C 20 commercial towers try to diminish it. But it stands there – where one can still see it – diminishing them. This was the first Protestant cathedral built in England, the first English cathedral completed in one man's working lifetime and to that one man's design, and the only one with a dome. It did not ape the style of its medieval predecessor: when the new St Paul's was built it was a modern building. Its predecessor, too, in each of its stages, was of its own time. Old St Paul's with its C 14 spire, until lightning struck in the C 16, was also visible from afar.

No Roman temple has yet emerged from early evidences found on this prominent site. And though one of the British bishops at the Council of Arles in 314 came from London, his church's site is unknown. The first cathedral here is assigned to the year 604, when Mellitus was bishop of London and Ethelbert king of Kent. If that building was later enlarged, as no doubt it was, we have no record of it. Nor do we know what Mellitus' church looked like. A fire destroyed it in 1087, and a completely new cathedral was begun by Bishop Maurice. It was built slowly, a fire damaged it in 1136, and appeals for support of the building are dated as late as *c.* 1175. Yet already in the early C 12 William of Malmesbury praised its 'capacitas' and its 'decoris magnificentia'. It was lengthened twice in the C 13. By the C 13, as was the case with most Norman cathedrals in England, the E end proved too small to hold the increased numbers of the clergy. Rebuilding and lengthening took place at St Paul's apparently between *c.* 1221 and a consecration in 1241. In 1256 a second lengthening was undertaken, for which the Chapel of St Faith had to be demolished. It was transferred to the crypt of the cathedral, which is to this day known as the Chapel of St Faith. The extension did not receive its pavement until 1312, and the first High Mass was said before the high altar only in 1327. The shrine of St Erkenwald behind the high altar was enriched in the C 14: its presence was undoubtedly a reason for the extension of space (Dugdale said the tomb of this C 7 bishop of London was first translated 'from the body of the church' in 1148, i.e. to behind the Norman high altar). The tower over the crossing carried a spire. In 1315, a time fond of tall needle-spires, the spire was renewed in a form similar to that of the mid-C 14 at Salisbury (and cf. Lichfield's; but Norwich spire is of the C 15). Also in the 1330s new cloisters and chapter house were added. That the medieval cathedral lay on a slightly different axis, more N W–S E than now, can be seen on our plan from remains in the S W angle of the old crossing.

In its completed form the cathedral was one of the largest in England. It was 585 ft long, that is, longer even than Winchester, and to the top of the spire 489 ft high. The C 14 chapter house lay on the S side, W of the S transept, and was surrounded by a two-storeyed cloister. W of it, that is S of the W front, was the parish church of St Gregory. To the N of the W front was the bishop's residence, E of it the Pardon Churchyard surrounded by a cloister in which were paintings of the Dance of Death. E of this followed the College of Minor Canons and then Paul's Cross (see *Precinct* below). The Jesus bell-tower, a detached campanile such as Westminster Abbey and several cathedrals also possessed, stood in the S E part of the precinct. The whole of the precinct was surrounded by a high wall (Paternoster Row, Carter Lane, Old Change, etc.).

We know the appearance of nave and chancel and spire from outside as well as inside from Hollar's engravings used as illustrations in Dugdale's *History of St Paul's Cathedral*. The nave was twelve bays long and had two W towers placed outside the aisles. Each transept was five bays long, with aisles, and the chancel altogether twelve bays. The fifth of these was given more width and prominence as a kind of undeveloped E transept: between choir and presbytery, this wider bay must have facilitated processional entry from the aisles. The Norman nave had composite

59. LONDON: OLD ST PAUL's East end begun 1256. Engraving by Hollar, 1658

60. LONDON: ST PAUL'S
Plan from the *Builder*, 1892 (see p. 126)

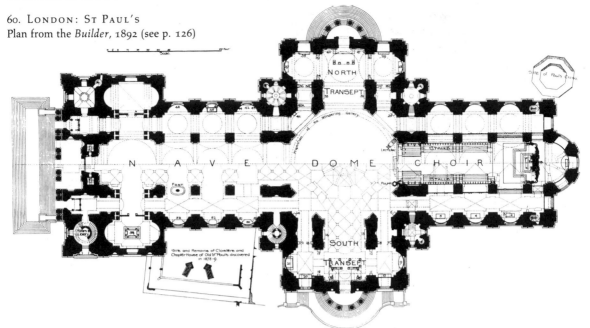

piers, identical in each bay, with three shafts carrying arches of complex moulding and three reaching straight up to the originally flat ceiling. A rib-vault was apparently put in early in the C13, and at that time also the clerestory windows were altered. The Norman gallery was large and entirely unsubdivided (as at St-Étienne at Caen). The clerestory had a wall-passage.

The C13 work on the eastern arm is less easily described. Hollar may here not be quite so accurate. In the arcade and the gallery differences in the tracery between 1220–40 and the new work after 1256 are recognizable (five W bays, piers with eight attached shafts; seven E bays, piers with sixteen attached shafts), but the upper parts appear all in a style later than Westminster Abbey (begun in 1245) and even later than the Angel Choir at Lincoln (begun in 1256). The chief symptom is the tracery of the windows. If this can be relied upon in Hollar's reproduction it introduced an irregularity in the relation between lancet and foiled circles which is, over the whole of England, more characteristic of the late than of the mid-C13. The vaults had in each bay one pair of tiercerons in each direction, but oddly enough no ridge ribs. Even so, this pattern of vaulting is clearly of an English type (the Westminster nave, begun by 1255, has tiercerons with ridge ribs), and St Paul's was indeed a design in the English tradition without any of those French incursions which are the hallmark of Westminster Abbey. Another proof of that is the design of the piers. To use a multitude of attached shafts is English, and was to be done at Exeter, probably influenced by St Paul's, whereas the

Abbey uses the classic French arrangement of four shafts round a circular core. Also the E end of St Paul's was straight in the English way, not apsed with an ambulatory and radiating chapels in the French way as at Westminster, and it had one huge window just like the Angel Choir at Lincoln. But that window consisted of seven lancets of equal height and a large rose above glazed even in the spandrels between it and the lancets. This motif comes clearly from the N transept of Westminster Abbey in its original form. The detail of the rose, however, differed from Westminster. It is not known when the E end of the cathedral was complete.

The next date to be mentioned is 1332. In this year, we hear, the chapter house was under construction. The mason in charge was *William de Ramsey*. A few scanty remains of foundations of the chapter house and cloister can still be seen in the garden W of the present S transept, and fragments of masonry are preserved inside the cathedral. The work was of great historical importance in that it had motifs clearly of the Perp style: blank panel tracery in the spandrels of the undercroft, descending mullions, straightened-out reticulated tracery, etc. The date 1332 means that the chapter house is actually of exactly the same years as the earliest Perp work at Gloucester, the S transept, built between 1331 and 1337. Both designs are probably based on St Stephen's Chapel in the Palace of Westminster. St Paul's chapter house, like those at York and Southwell, had no central pier. Its undercroft was entered from the lower cloister. Another unusual feature was that the chapter house stood in the garth, instead of projecting from the outside cloister wall; whatever the reason, this made it more private in such an urban setting.

No dates need be mentioned in the two centuries between the chapter house and the Reformation. In 1561, lightning destroyed the spire of the cathedral. It was not rebuilt, but a drawing of 1562 for its rebuilding exists at the Society of Antiquaries. Altogether little trouble was taken over the upkeep of the building at that time. The nave had in the course of the c 16 deteriorated into a public meeting-place, where business was transacted, where lawyers met their clients, and Sir John Falstaff could hire a servant.

Efforts to restore the cathedral began in the year 1620, when a Royal Commission was appointed to consider necessary measures. Nothing was however done until Laud became bishop of London. Then, in 1631, a new commission was called together. Work started in 1633, and *Inigo Jones* was in charge. He refaced the w, N and s walls of the nave and the walls of the transept, modernizing the Romanesque details by giving the walls heavy cornices, classical windows, and pilasters instead of buttresses, and hiding the angle between aisles and clerestory at the w front and the transept front by volutes of the Italian kind. (The choir, on the other hand, was restored externally without changing the Gothic details, as Summerson has shown.) Jones did little to make all this appear a coherent composition. The only exception is the giant portico which he placed in front of the w façade and which was a gift of the King. This with its columns 60 ft high and its cornice and balustrade must have looked truly magnificent to anyone walking up Ludgate Hill – more so no doubt than Wren's front. John Evelyn called it 'comparable with any in Europe' and Roger Pratt one of the two 'only remarkable buildings in England' – the other being the Banqueting House.

After Inigo Jones's death and the restoration of the monarchy yet another commission was appointed, and for this *Christopher Wren* wrote a report on 1 May 1666 on the defects of the old building and the steps to be taken. He suggested recasing the inside of the nave 'after a good Roman Manner' instead of 'the Gothick Rudeness of ye old Design'. But his principal suggestion was to replace the crossing tower by a dome – it would have been the first dome in England – and to give that dome a diameter as wide as nave and aisles together. This would have resulted in a closing of the nave aisles, transept aisles, and chancel aisles by big L-shaped blocks of masonry, and they were to receive niches in the corners. The dome was to be uncommonly steep in outline and to consist of two separate domes, the inner of masonry and open in the middle, the outer of timber. In this project of 1 May 1666 there were thus already several features which Wren was to introduce into the future cathedral. Other features kept included the covering of the nave with saucer domes with penetrations from the clerestory windows. Estimates for the work were ordered on 27 August. But on 2 September the Fire broke out and raged until 7 September. 'The stones of Paul's flew like grenados, the melting lead running down the streets in a stream', from sheets of lead that had roofed a cathedral 'no less than six acres by measure' (Evelyn's Diary).

WREN'S CATHEDRAL

There was some confusion after the Fire as to what ought to be done. The warrant to pull down what remained of the E parts was issued only in 1668, and it needed the collapse of a pier in the nave, in which services were still held (and continued to be held until 1673), to reach the decision to rebuild the whole cathedral. In 1669 Wren was made Surveyor-General, and in the spring of the following year he completed his first design. (It was only in 1673, when he was knighted, that he resigned as Savilian Professor of Astronomy at Oxford.) This design met with the general approval of the King, but was criticized by men of greater architectural experience, like Sir Roger Pratt, who called the design 'wholly different from that of all the Cathedrals of the whole Worlde'. The design was indeed strange, if ingenious. It consisted of a domed w end – Wren was convinced of the necessity of the dome as a sign of cathedral superiority – and then an odd choir with arcades which opened to the outside and not into the church, and galleries above the arcade open towards the nave. The outer arcades were no doubt meant to be a replacement of Paul's Walk for those who were used to regard the nave of the cathedral as fit for perambulating. Their architectural source is perhaps the s transept of Westminster Abbey, where a similar arrangement occurs (E cloister walk in w aisle). A fragmentary model of this nave remains at St Paul's.

But c. 1672, it seems, Wren realized that something grander ought to be suggested, and so he produced what can be regarded as his ideal of a cathedral church, the Greek cross design and its variant, the so-called Great Model, made in 1673 (recently in process of removal from the trophy room to the crypt). It is of wood and nearly 20 ft long. It is centrally planned with a w addition in front of which was to rise a portico as splendid as Jones's, though with a pediment. The w anteroom was to be oval and have a dome, and the main body of the church was to be crowned by a large dome on a drum, majestic enough to dominate the skyline of London as the medieval spire had done. The dome was to rest on eight arches on eight piers, and extending from this central space there were to be four cross-arms of equal length. The diagonal openings led into sub-centres. The four arms of the cross were to be connected by sweeping concave quarter-circles, the one element of surprise in a design which is otherwise evidently based on a study of the various designs made for St Peter's in Rome in the early c 16 and on projected and recently erected domed churches in Paris. Wren had visited Paris in 1665. The quarter-circles are indeed also a French motif, though not of ecclesiastical architecture. They occur in one of the fantastic palace plans of Antoine Lepautre published in 1652. But Wren probably knew John Webb's drawing for an ideal church on a Greek cross plan with convex curves between the arms (Whinney 1971), perhaps based on Lepautre.

However, this domed structure was too contrary to English tradition to find favour with the clergy. Wren had to abandon it, and to make an effort (as *Parentalia* has it) 'to reconcile as near as possible the Gothick to a better Manner of Architecture'. What he substituted was indeed much more in accordance with tradition, but it was also much less satisfactory aesthetically. The new design had a long nave, long transepts and a long chancel with straight aisle ends and an apsed chancel end, very much like an English Norman cathedral. All that Wren tried to keep was his large domed central space, and even that he made more palatable to the conservatives by raising on the top a crazily elongated spire – the oddest mongrel product ever recommended by a great architect. This plan received the Royal Warrant in May 1675. It is therefore known as the Warrant Design. According to it work started at the E end in June 1675. Fortunately, however, it was laid down in the warrant that Wren would have 'the liberty, in the prosecution of his work, to make some variations, rather ornamental than essential, as from time to time he should see proper'. He certainly took advantage of this clause, and he was liberal in calling ornamental what he considered essential. The disposition of the walls was altered almost at once, and in the end the transept fronts were different, the dome was different, and the w front was different. And, as already indicated, he did not build on the medieval foundations but on a newly excavated axis more s w–n e (the crossings did not even exactly coincide), nor did he seek to emulate the medieval length.

The principal dates marking the progress of the new building are as follows: foundation stone 21 June 1675; the transept ends were started in 1681, the outer walls of the nave in 1684, the foundations of the w front were dug in 1686. The pediments of the two transepts date from 1698. But the designs for the w towers and the dome, as carried out, are later than 1702. By then the chancel was at last completed. It had been furnished between 1694 and 1697 and was consecrated in 1697. St Dunstan's Chapel was opened in 1699. The w towers were built in 1705–8. The dome was finished in 1710 and the whole building declared complete by Parliament in 1711. Wren had been thirty-four at the time of the fire; he was seventy-nine now. In the last years he had much trouble with his commission,

which blamed him for deliberately delaying completion. He had perhaps really no longer been always watchful enough with the workmen, but it was mostly a matter of politics. In the end, in 1718, Wren was dismissed as Surveyor General. Still – he lived to see his cathedral complete, which is more than was granted to Bramante and Michelangelo.

The cathedral surveyors after Wren included in the c 18 *John James, Henry Flitcroft* and *Robert Mylne*, in the c 19 *S. P. Cockerell, C. R. Cockerell* and *F. C. Penrose*, and in the c 20 *Sir Mervyn Macartney*, who had to reinforce the crossing piers 1925–30, and *Godfrey Allen*, who had to deal with damage from the Second World War. This came chiefly from two direct hits, on the choir in 1940 and on the n transept in 1941 (on repairs, *R.I.B.A. Journal*, December 1948). Cleansing the fabric of its crust of coal dust has proceeded since 1964, giving new views of fine c 17 carving outside, and since 1974 of Victorian gold-ground mosaic on the chancel vaults inside. The chief material Wren used was Portland stone, from quarries already opened up by Inigo Jones. The cathedral is 510 ft long, and to the top of the lantern, including the cross, 366 ft high. The outer walls are 111 ft high. The nave inside is 89 ft high.

EXTERIOR

As building proceeded from e to w, so we will describe it. It has already been said that the first alteration made by Wren between Warrant Design and execution concerned the disposition of the outer walls. It was to affect the appearance of the whole building. The Warrant Design had a nave with clerestory windows and lower aisles like a medieval English cathedral. In the execution Wren carried up the outer aisle wall to nave height, as a screen wall, that is he erected an outer two-storey elevation which in its upper storey was wholly a make-believe. In this he established himself at once as a man of the Baroque and not of the Renaissance. He must have felt that this additional height of the outer walls was necessary to add dignity to the whole structure and act as a broad unbroken podium for the all-dominating dome. One can walk behind the upper screen wall and see the nave wall with its windows and indeed a row of flying buttresses. Wren did not mind using this medieval method of counteracting the thrust of the vaults, as long as it was not evident to the eye.

His wall unit then for the whole building is two-storeyed. The wall is rusticated and there are coupled pilasters on both floors. The ground floor has a round-headed window in an eared frame with garlands and cherubs above. The upper floor has a blank window with a niche in an aedicule with Corinthian columns and a pediment. (Below the blank window in the base of the aedicule a real window, into the roof space over the aisle vaults and

61. LONDON: ST PAUL'S 1675–1711. Designed by Sir Christopher Wren. View from the south after 1945

invisible from the aisles below – more of Wren's pragmatism.) As an enrichment garlands are introduced below the frieze at the E end, the transept fronts, and the N W and S W chapels. A balustrade finished the unit. Wren would have preferred a parapet, but his commission insisted. He was cross about it and said: 'Ladies think nothing well without an edging.' Stylistically the origin of the unit as a whole is the Banqueting House and Inigo Jones's and John Webb's Palladianism altogether.

The unit is repeated all along the building with four modifications. The first is that at the E end the upper storey has columns instead of pilasters and the balustrade rises by two volutes into an attic. The second concerns the TRANSEPTS. Here, first of all, in the re-entrant angles between aisles and transepts and chancel aisles and transepts are square additions containing a staircase and three vestries. Secondly, the fronts of the transepts have in the middle semicircular porches composed of six columns, a motif known to Wren from an engraving of the façade of Pietro da Cortona's S. Maria della Pace in Rome carried out in 1656. Above the porch is a window with more decoration than used otherwise and then, instead of the balustrade, a pediment and five statues. The doorways into the transepts have the odd motif of halved columns l. and r., a motif more familiar from the work of such less erudite architects as Peter Mills than from the Court style. Towards the w end, with more radical changes from the Warrant Design, there are also more irregularities in the exterior. They

131

62. LONDON: ST PAUL'S West towers, 1706–8, and the City before 1939

reflect the fact that Wren had decided – harking back to the Great Model – to precede his nave by a cross structure almost like the w transept of Ely with a centre bay larger than the nave bays and oval chapels much longer than the aisles. These chapels are of course expressed in the exterior. But without knowledge of the interior the projection does not make sense. The ground floor has to the N and s one of the usual windows flanked by niches and then one small arched window in a coffered niche. This asymmetrical bay ought to be read as the base of the w towers which stand on it. The w façade continues the system of the sides for the bays of the w towers. But in the middle is a two-storeyed portico of coupled columns. Earlier designs for single-storey 90-ft giant columns had not allowed for the stone-sizes available for the entablature at the Portland quarries (Jones's portico had been on a lesser scale).

In this portico again Wren's affinity with the Continental Baroque is obvious. On the ground floor the portico has six pairs of columns, on the first floor only four, i.e. the outer pairs below merge with the bays belonging to the towers. They carry coupled pilasters (the unit motif) whereas the others carry the free-standing columns of the first-floor balcony. Above this is a pediment with a relief of the Conversion of St Paul and again statuary. The WEST TOWERS are the most Baroque of all Wren's spires, broader and more substantial than any of the others, with, above the clock stage, coupled columns projecting in the diagonals and convex bays with columns between them, then complex volutes leading up to an octagonal lantern and an ogee cap. The whole is much more intricate than this description can convey (on the towers' design history 1701–4, see Whinney 1971).

And now the DOME. (On its structure, see *Interior* below.) St Paul's on its hill is so often seen and photographed from below, foreshortening the dome, and the front view in particular is so warped by the length of the

63 LONDON: St Paul's The dome, begun after 1702, completed 1710. View before 1914

nave, the dome's true shape can seem subjectively variable and has been much misrepresented by artists and even by cameras. The dome is in the most telling contrast to the w front – though not well seen from there – achieving a final repose far more convincing than St Peter's, where the *slancio* upward never ceases. Wren, just as he relished variety in his City churches, could consciously develop this contrast between Baroque dynamics and an ultimate end in peace and harmony. The base of the drum at St Paul's, below the colonnade, is left entirely plain. The drum is a direct descendant of that designed by Bramante for St Peter's, illustrated by Serlio and never built. It is only when we look very carefully that in one way at least Wren even here betrays his faith in the style of a different century. Bramante intended an even colonnade all round his drum. Wren's is not even. In eight places the columns do not stand free, but pieces of wall reach out towards them and appear, adorned with niches, between them. The

reason is structural, the effect is Baroque. Above the colonnade is a balustrade, and then the drum rises yet higher, continuing the diameter of the wall behind the colonnade. This attic has windows. (It may be that engravings of Bramante's Tempietto influenced Wren's treatment of drum and attic.) Above this follows the cupola, with rib-like ridges to lead the eye upward, though without the lucarnes of St Peter's as built. St Paul's cupola is of an elongated section. The 'lift' of this dome, compared to St Peter's, arises because each of the four accompanying elements (base, drum, attic and, above all, St Paul's leaner lantern) is taller in proportion to the cupola than those elements are at St Peter's. And so at St Paul's Wren adjusted his ratios to generate an alert and confident repose – an Anglican *O altitudo!*

Wren's crowning lantern is a glorious and indeed decidedly Baroque design, with piers and coupled columns projecting on the four sides, a little cupola and a ball with cross – all no more than a final weight on the great dome, heavy enough and not too heavy. The ball is in fact 6 ft in diameter. The first ball and cross had to be replaced in 1821 and were relegated to Thomas Horner's panorama in the Colosseum, Regent's Park, where the cross proved to be too corroded and a facsimile was exhibited, though the ball was restorable, its later fate unknown (Ralph Hyde).

ARCHITECTURAL SCULPTURE. A few figures, where erosion from almost three centuries of London weather has gone too far, have been replaced by replicas, an acceptable restoration here as part of the effect Wren intended. The w pediment (1706) and the statues of the w and transept fronts (1721) are by *Francis Bird*. The sculpture in the transept pediments (1698) is by *Grinling Gibbons* (N) and *Caius Cibber* (S, with phoenix rising from flames). The superb stone carvings on the exterior were made by *Gibbons, Edward Pearce, Jonathan Maine* and others. This wealth of carved reliefs probably grew from Wren's memory of Paris buildings such as the Great Court of the Louvre and the Hôtel de Sully. (For free-standing statues, see *Precinct* below.) The principal masons engaged on the cathedral were at first *Joshua Marshall* (1678) and *Thomas Strong* (1681). From 1679 the chief mason was Thomas's brother *Edward Strong*. Masons in addition *Jasper Latham, Thomas Wise*, later *Christopher Kempster* and later still *William Kempster* and *Edward Strong Jr*. The same masons and carvers were responsible for the equally excellent decorations of the interior. The chief plasterers were *Henry Doogood* and *Chrystom Wilkins*.

INTERIOR

On entering the cathedral, the first impression is one of ordered spaciousness and somewhat cool perfection. The colour of the stone is beautiful, and the exquisite quality of the carving is at once felt. First the w bay with its oval chapels l. and r. acts as a kind of forebuilding (reminiscent of Lincoln: compare their plans), then the nave of three bays with aisles, a domed crossing as wide as nave and aisles together and with supporting bays on all four sides and beyond them one-bay transepts with aisles and a three-bay eastern arm with aisles, plus apse: basically it is the plan of Ely, i.e. a Norman cathedral with an enlarged crossing. Indeed, when the oval w chapels, intended for (N) morning prayer and (S) consistory court, were begun in 1687, anti-Jacobite propaganda ascribed this provision of chapels to James II's devious Catholicism. (On the spaces under the w towers, see below.)

The NAVE has arcades set out with single pilasters towards the nave and lower coupled pilasters between the arches – piers not unlike those of the Val-de-Grâce, which Wren had seen in Paris. The pilasters towards the nave are continued by short pilasters in the blank zone between

arcade and clerestory. This zone is adorned by a narrow balcony with a fine wrought-iron railing which projects with the projections of the entablature above the arcade pilasters. On the upper pilasters rest the transverse arches of the nave vault. The bays between the arches are domed, and as there are also large clerestory windows (invisible from outside because of the aisle screen-wall), there are penetrations in the form of three-dimensional arches curving forward until they touch the saucer domes. The use of saucer domes, Wren said, derived from (engravings of) Hagia Sophia at Constantinople (Downes 1971), and his lining them with softer Oxfordshire stone suggests that he intended mosaics there (Crook 1980). The AISLES also have domes, and their windows are placed in coffered niches. The ambiguity between niche and window as well as the more noticeable ambiguity between w-e vault and transverse penetrations are once again a sign of the C 17, the Baroque century. Over the larger w bay is a larger dome, and the arch on each side into the aisle is here set out with coupled columns. Another arch with a pair of coupled columns on each side leads into the oval side chapels. They have richly decorated groin-vaults.

Between the nave and the domed crossing a piece of solid wall had to be inserted, here as well as at the inner ends of transepts and chancel, to provide a massive enough support for the dome. These pieces of solid wall are tunnel-vaulted and coffered and help to create a feeling of suspense before the whole width and height of the domed space are revealed. The DOME rests on eight arches of even height but uneven width, and to obtain these Wren had to invent some Baroque intricacies which are aesthetically not wholly successful. The domed space has a diameter equal to nave and aisles together. That means that nave aisles, transept aisles and chancel aisles meet within the domed space. Wren has treated the corners as niches. But as the aisle openings are low compared with the giant arches he needed to carry his dome, he gave these niches their own arches, segmental arches, repeated the niche motif above, that is at clerestory level, by means of a kind of box or balcony, and then gave these niches arches of the height and width which he required for his dome. The segmental below the semicircular arch is a distracting motif. Four square projections in the angles between nave and transepts and chancel and transepts (visible outside and on plan) serve to buttress the dome and contain the vestries of the Lord Mayor (NW), the Minor Canons (NE) and the Dean (SE), and the staircase (SW). Woodwork in the vestries by *Maine*, 1696.

The drum is visible from inside with its windows separated by pilasters and with eight C 19 statues. The dome which one sees above it is in fact the innermost of three domes. It is of brick and has a circular opening at its top, and through this one looks into what seems a second dome.

This was an effect much favoured by the Baroque architects of Italy and France. The second dome is not a dome at all, but a brick cone which carries the weight of the lantern. It has circular openings which give on to the space behind the outer dome, the dome which makes the skyline of London. This third dome is built of timbers resting on the brick cone and the stone drum and covered with lead. It is an ingenious solution of the engineering problem in hand, a scientist's solution rather than a born architect's who might have taken exception to the ugliness of the cone, regardless of the fact that it is not visible (on which Summerson comments: 'This seems an extraordinary statement!').

Finally, the spaces under the w towers flanking the portico and entrance lobbies. Under the sw tower the GEOMETRICAL STAIRCASE (mason *W. Kempster*), an elegant piece of construction, circular, with an open well and cantilevered all the way. Inigo Jones had done the same on a smaller scale at the Queen's House at Greenwich. The balustrade is of wrought iron. The staircase gives access to the LIBRARY above the sw chapel, a room with fine panelling and original bookcases. Woodwork by *Jonathan Maine*, 1709. Under the nw tower is the Chapel of All Souls (see *Furnishings*).

FURNISHINGS, W TO E

St Paul's Cathedral was left with its original c17–18 furnishings and without monuments other than those from the old building until after 1790. Then it was decided to place four statues of national benefactors in the corners under the dome and to pay for them out of public funds (see *Crossing* below). After that monuments multiplied. Most of the early ones are to the naval and military heroes of the Napoleonic wars. They are remarkably unified in style, to the detriment of personal expression of the character of those who made them or those who are commemorated. Mrs Esdaile called them the Peninsular School. They are of white marble, frigid and allegorical, with a varying degree of realism in clothes and incident. Where personality is more conspicuous, it will be emphasized in due course. With the swing of the pendulum a century later, Baedeker in 1892 found many of them 'remarkable for egregiously bad taste'. On the Victorian interior decoration of St Paul's, bedevilled by objections religious and aesthetic, see Crook 1980; also Physick 1970 and *Victorian Church Art* 1971; and below on mosaic decoration.

The furnishings are here described in topographical order from the nw entrance; n aisle; nave; s aisle; crossing; n transept; s transept; chancel and chancel aisles. (See also under *Crypt* below.)

Chapel of All Souls (n of the nw entrance) KIT-CHENER MEMORIAL, by *Detmar Blow* and *Sir Mervyn*

Macartney. Recumbent marble effigy with two stone statues and a large stone Pietà, all by *Sir W. Reid Dick*, 1925.

North aisle, Chapel of St Dunstan Exquisitely designed and carved wooden SCREEN, with fine Corinthian columns and a centre with two Corinthian pillars with Corinthian columns in front, broken pediment, vases and coat of arms. Carved by *Jonathan Maine* in 1698. – On the aisle, MONUMENTS. Lord Leighton, recumbent effigy high up on a sarcophagus, two seated allegorical bronze figures below. They represent Painting and Sculpture. Sculpture is holding Leighton's 'Sluggard'. By *Brock*, 1902. – Behind, memorial relief to Non-commissioned Officers and Privates killed in the Crimean War, l. by *Forsyth*, centre and r. by *Noble*. – General Gordon † 1885, bronze effigy on bronze sarcophagus, by *Boehm*. – The reliefs behind (l. to r.) by *Forsyth*, *Boehm* and *Marochetti*. – William and Frederick Viscounts Melbourne † 1848 and 1853, black doorway, studded with gold, and two white ample-bodied angels of marble l. and r.; by *Marochetti*.

Nave Two large bronze CANDELABRA, 1898 by *Henry Pegram*. – MONUMENT to the Duke of Wellington † 1852, *Alfred Stevens's* magnum opus. The composition is based on such tombs as that of Queen Elizabeth at Westminster Abbey, that is 'four-poster' with big middle arch. Columns also set in front of the four main ones in an e and w as well as a n and s direction, making a total of twelve columns. The decoration of the shafts is typically Victorian. Sarcophagus with bronze effigy, two large groups of allegorical bronze figures on the arch (Valour and Cowardice, Truth and Falsehood), and equestrian statue on top, under Wren's arch. Begun 1857, completed 1912. (Statue completed by *John Tweed* after Stevens's death in 1875.) Till 1893 the whole unfinished work stood in the sw chapel, former consistory court, now of St Michael and St George. Completed on its present site, n side of the nave (on its complicated history, see Physick 1970). One small but widely familiar feature, copied in many materials all over England: the little lions sitting upright on the railing, originally designed by Stevens (based on the lion at the foot of the Bargello staircase in Florence) for railings to guard entrance lodges at the British Museum, where they stood until 1896 (J. M. Crook, *The British Museum*, 1972).

South aisle, Chapel of St Michael and St George SCREEN as in the chapel opposite. By *Maine*, 1706. The furnishings inside partly (throne, stalls in w apse) made from original WOODWORK removed from *Gibbons's* choir stalls in the 1860s (the new arrangement designed by *Sir Mervyn Macartney*), partly new woodwork of 1932–3 by *James Walker*. – On the aisle, MONUMENTS. Capt. Richard Rundle Burges, by *Thomas Banks*, 1802. The youthful hero is nearly naked. Victory on the other side, across a cannon. Relief figures on the plinth. – The reliefs

65. LONDON: ST PAUL'S Wellington monument, 1857–1912. By Alfred Stevens

66. LONDON: ST PAUL'S Relief on monument to John Howard, 1795, by John Bacon Sr

in the niche behind by *Woodington*, 1862. – Bishop Middleton. By *J. G. Lough*, 1832. He blesses with a grand solemn gesture a kneeling youth and a kneeling maiden – The reliefs in the niche behind by *W. C. Marshall*, 1862–3. – Capt. Westcott, 1802–5 by *Banks*. He swoons and is held by an angel. Diagonal composition of free-standing figures. On the plinth fine Father Nile with many little children. – Reliefs behind w by *Noble*, 1855, E by *Marochetti*, 1853. – PAINTING. *Holman Hunt's* 'Light of the World', signed and dated 1851–1900, i.e. a much later version of the painting in Keble College Chapel, Oxford.

Crossing In the four diagonals four marble STATUES of benefactors of the English people, 1794–5; the beginning of that rapid growth in the stone population of the cathedral which was to go on in the next twenty years. Sir Joshua Reynolds (NW) by *Flaxman*, 1803–13; John Howard (SE) by *John Bacon* the elder, 1795; Dr Johnson (NE) by the same, 1791–6; Sir William Jones (SW), who has been called 'the first European to open the treasures of Oriental learning, the poetry and wisdom of our Indian Empire', also by the same, 1799. Flaxman's Reynolds is dull. Bacon has dressed Dr Johnson as well as Howard as Roman heroes. Neither seems comfortable with his bare chest and bare legs. Fine reliefs against the pedestals of Howard and Jones; that of prison relief especially is done with much delicacy. Jones is a little more Rococo in attitude

and draperies. – PULPIT by *Lord Mottistone*, 1964, in the Wren style. Its predecessor of 1803 by *Mylne* and that of 1860 by *Penrose* are still preserved. – LECTERN. By *Jacob Sutton*, bought in 1720 for £241. A splendidly naturalistic spread eagle. Pedestal of candelabra form. – IRON BALCONIES in the 'boxes' in the diagonals of the crossing, and all along the cornice of the dome and other parts of the church; partly by *T. Robinson*, i.e. of Wren's time, partly given by Somers Clarke, c. 1900. – MOSAICS of the diagonal apses by *Sir William Richmond*. – MOSAICS of the spandrels of the dome. The four Prophets (w) from designs by *Alfred Stevens*, the four Evangelists (E) by *Watts* (St John, St Matthew) worked up by *W. E. T. Britten*. – FRESCOES in the dome (not under Wren's direction, as it seems he wanted mosaics there): stories from the life of St Paul, by *Sir James Thornhill*, 1716–19. They are in monochrome, set in feigned architecture. – SCULPTURE in the drum of the dome. The figures were designed by *Kempe* and made in 1892–4 by *Brindley & Farmer* (sculptor *Winnington*).

North transept MONUMENTS. In the w aisle reliefs high up: Gen. Hoghton † 1811 by *Chantrey* (w) and Col. Myers (E), by *Joseph Kendrick*, c. 1811. – Beneath them, *C. R. Cockerell*, the architect, † 1863, and Gen. Sir T. Picton † 1815 by *Gahagan*, 1816. Bust on top, figures of Roman soldier, big lion, and two female allegories below. –

In the nave of the transept: Capt. Faulknor, 1797–1803 by *Rossi* (W), Gen. Dundas, 1805 by *Bacon Jr* (E). Above them two reliefs to Generals Craufurd and Mackinnon † 1812 by *Bacon Jr* (W) and Generals Mackenzie and Langworth † 1809 by *Manning*. Against the N wall MONUMENTS of Gen. A. Hay † 1814 by *Hopper* and Generals Gore and Skerrett, designed by *W. Tallimache* and carved by *Chantrey*, 1825. The general in Hopper's monument sinks back on a naked athlete. – In the E aisle of the transept: Reliefs high up to Maj. Gen. Bowes (W) † 1812 by *Chantrey*, and Gen. Le Marchant (E) † 1812 by *Rossi* (designed by *J. Smith*). – Below, monuments to Sir Arthur Sullivan † 1900 by *Goscombe John* (W), and Sir J. Stainer by *H. Pegram*, 1903. – PAINTING. Virgin with St Luke and a donor, school of *Titian*, c. 1550 (N E chapel). – FONT. 1727 by *Francis Bird*. It cost £350. (Formerly in the nave, and now with new surround.)

South transept   INNER PORCH, made up in the C 19 from the original choir screen and organ gallery designed by Wren and carved by Gibbons, all of wood except two marble columns. (Corresponding parts at N transept door destroyed in the last war; see also choir fittings below.) One of the most glorious pieces of woodcarving in London, with noble fluted columns and all the enrichments of garlands. – MONUMENTS. In the W aisle one relief high up: Sir Isaac Brock † 1812 by *Westmacott*. – Statues to Admiral Lyons by *Noble*, 1862, and Dr W. Babington by *Behnes*, 1837. – Large group to Gen. Sir R. Abercromby † 1801 by *Westmacott*, 1802–5. Two big frontal sphinxes l. and r. and a splendidly vivacious group above, in a truly Baroque spirit. Prancing horse, fallen enemy below its front hoofs; the general is lowered from the horse by a soldier, yet he 'expired on board the Foudroyant', as the inscription tells us; both figures in contemporary dress. – Gen. Sir John Moore, by *Bacon Jr*, 1810–15 (S wall). Much gentler and more Rococo. A demi-nude man and an angel lower the general into his grave. Higher up a putto with a big flag. – To the r. of this, statue of Sir Astley Cooper † 1842 by *Baily*. – Statue between W aisle and nave: Capt. Sir W. Hoste by *Campbell*, 1833. – In the transept nave: Nelson by *Flaxman*, 1808–18. He stands on a big circular pedestal, a statue so convincingly a portrait that it makes most of the others around look dummies. Britannia presents two sailor boys to him. This group also is composed and carved with tender life. Lion on the r. – Opposite Marquis Cornwallis by *Rossi*, 1811. It is most illuminating to see how wooden in comparison with Flaxman Rossi's figures appear. – Above Nelson, relief to Capt. Hardinge † 1808 by *Manning*. Above Cornwallis, relief to Capt. Miller † 1805 by *Flaxman*. – Statues to the W and E of the doorcase: Gen. Gillespie † 1814, looking up in a romantic way, by *Chantrey*; Generals Pakenham and Walsh † 1815 by *Westmacott*, 1823, a convincing group of two friends. –

67. LONDON: ST PAUL'S Nelson monument, 1808–18. By John Flaxman

In the E aisle reliefs to Col. H. Cadogan † 1813 by *Chantrey* (W) and Gen. Ross † 1814 by *Kendrick* (E). – Statues to Sir H. Lawrence by *Lough*, 1862, and Gen. Sir J. Jones † 1843 by *Behnes*. – Large group against the E wall: Admiral Earl Howe † 1799 by *Flaxman*, 1803–11. Far less warm and convincing than the Nelson monument. Standing figure with Britannia and Fame. – Against the S wall Lord Collingwood † 1810 by *Westmacott*, 1813–17. He lies on the prow of his ship, a Victory behind him; a river-god in front. Charming detail, especially the medallions on the prow with putti in boats. – Statues between E aisle and nave: Gen. Lord Heathfield (with fine relief on the pedestal) by *Rossi*, 1823–5, and Turner, the painter, † 1851, by *MacDowell*.

Chancel   The general impression now is very different from what it was in Wren's day. The altar then stood in the E apse with a low wrought-iron screen enclosing the sanctuary. The stalls went W as far as the middle of the first bay E of the crossing, with return stalls against the choir

68. LONDON: ST PAUL'S Choir stalls, 1695–7, by Grinling Gibbons

screen and organ gallery which offered only a low, narrowed vista into the choir, with the organ placed centrally. Now the organ is split up (see below) and a low rail keeps the chancel space open to the eye. – The MOSAIC decoration of the chancel vaults is of the 1890s by *Sir William Richmond*, following an Early Christian style that Burges had hoped to invoke here twenty years before. The original decoration of the chancel dates from 1695–7. Exquisite metalwork and woodwork, amongst the finest done at the time anywhere in Europe. At the entrances to the N and S chancel aisles wrought-iron SCREENS by *Tijou*. Each screen is divided into three parts by openwork Corinthian pilasters. The panels between are also made predominantly of vertical pieces, but at the top scrolls and curly leaves unroll. The former sanctuary screens are now in the E bays of the chancel arcades. They are much scrollier in design. Broader iron screens in the next bay to the w. These were made in 1890 from the original GATES to the chancel from the w, where there is now instead a low, also original,

wrought-iron COMMUNION RAIL. – The ORGAN is a *Schmidt* instrument commissioned in 1694. The CASE is again a piece of miraculous carving, with angels and cherubs on three levels, apart from the usual ornament. It can still be enjoyed, though halved by *Penrose* in the C 19 between the N and S sides of the first bay of stalls, an arrangement summarized for us by Michael Gillingham as follows. The present N case is the old E front, with a facsimile *chaire* case. The present S case is the old w front, with the old E front *chaire* case before it. (On the original organ gallery and screen, see S transept inner porch above.) – The CHOIR STALLS were made by *Grinling Gibbons*. They are equally admirable seen from the front or the back (in the aisles). Here incidentally – as in the organ case, the doorcases and other places – smaller iron grilles are used to fill in openings, and these deserve study too. Each bay of the stalls at the back has a tripartite composition, with coupled Corinthian columns to emphasize the centres and exquisite flower wreaths and garlands. In the thickness of

the stalls are small rooms for various purposes. The fronts are gayer than any other part of the decoration, with openwork cupolas enriched by cherubs' heads and volutes, columns with ornamental shafts to mark the principal seats, and a top cresting of feathery curls.

At the E end BALDACCHINO by *S. E. Dykes Bower* (who also designed the altar cross) and *Godfrey Allen*. The idea of a baldacchino was suggested by existing Wren drawings for a baldacchino for St Paul's and a footnote in *Parentalia*. In any case, the baldacchino makes a fine effect, in keeping with the Baroque qualities of Wren's building. It replaces *Bodley*'s marble reredos of 1888 (great in size and, to some who remember it, in quality, but it over-enveloped Wren's space). It is one of the virtues of the present baldacchino that light from the E, blocked by Bodley for more than half a century, penetrates Wren's chancel as intended. – STAINED GLASS in the E window by *Brian Thomas*. – Behind the high altar, American Memorial Chapel in the apse. – Two standard CANDLESTICKS sometimes near the high altar, with rich Renaissance arabesque, are casts from a pair at St Bavon, Ghent, said to have been made by *Benedetto da Rovezzano* for Wolsey's tomb (see Crypt below).

MONUMENTS, chancel aisles. John Donne † 1631, Dean of St Paul's and poet, by *Nicholas Stone*. Standing upright in his shroud on an urn, like a spectre. Dame Helen Gardner has convincingly questioned Izaak Walton's story of the dying Donne literally posing for it thus (Wellek and Ribeiro, *Evidence in Literary Scholarship*, 1979): Donne may indeed have been painted in his shroud, but head-and-shoulders only, as later engraved by Droeshout; Stone appears to have originally designed the figure recumbent but for lack of room placed it upright on the separately carved urn, as engraved by Hollar before the Great Fire. It lay with other relics in the new crypt until inserted in the present niche *c.* 1818. The epitaph above the figure was undoubtedly composed by Donne. – Dean Milman, asleep on a sarcophagus, by *F. J. Williamson*, 1876. – Bishop Blomfield † 1857, of the same type, by *Richmond*. – Bishop Creighton † 1901 (his tomb is at Peterborough): bronze statue, one hand raised in blessing, by *Sir Hamo Thornycroft*, 1905. – Archbishop Temple, plaque by *F. W. Pomeroy*, 1905.

69. LONDON: ST PAUL's High altar and baldacchino, 1958, by S. E. Dykes Bower and Godfrey Allen

70. LONDON: ST PAUL's Monument to John Donne † 1631, by Nicholas Stone

71. LONDON: ST PAUL'S Wolsey–Nelson sarcophagus,
1524–9, by Benedetto da Rovezzano

CRYPT

In course of rearrangement 1983. Wren's models for the
design of St Paul's are being moved here from the trophy
room. The crypt extends under the whole church, low,
with extremely massive piers and groin- or tunnel-vaults.
The area under the dome is singled out for a more distinguished treatment. A circle of eight Tuscan columns carries
the vault here. At the E end CHAPEL for the Order of the
British Empire, designed by *Lord Mottistone* (of *Seely &
Paget*), 1959–60.

FURNISHINGS from E to W (subject to recent change). In
the N aisle John Martin † 1680 and wife. Reredos back. The
two figures kneel facing each other, but instead of the
traditional prayer desk there is a pile of books. He kneels
elegantly on one knee. On the base two babies and some
cherubs' heads. – Further W Sir William Orchardson, with
bronze figures, one of an Edwardian lady, the other, oddly,
of Napoleon. By *W. Reynolds-Stephens*, 1913. – Then on
the S side, Jane Wren, Sir Christopher Wren's only daughter, † 1702, by *Francis Bird*. Relief of St Cecilia with angels,
of an almost Rococo delicacy. – Opposite, Randolph
Caldecott † 1886 by *Gilbert*. – Nearby, black marble slab to
Sir Christopher Wren † 1723 and, on the wall above,
big inscription panel with the famous: 'Si monumentum
requiris, circumspice.' – Then Sir Edwin Landseer, by
Woolner, 1882, with a relief of the 'Chief Mourner'. –
Near this, in the passage to the nave, Benjamin Webb
† 1885 by *Armstead*: demi-figure in niche. – On the N wall
of the nave opposite, John Singer Sargent † 1925, large
modernistic bronze figures in relief, by *Sargent*. – Further
W in the nave, Wellington † 1852, free-standing Cornish

porphyry sarcophagus by *F. C. Penrose.* – Back in the s aisle Earl of Lytton †1891 by *Gilbert*, with complicated bronze relief. – Under the dome Nelson †1805. The splendid black marble sarcophagus of generously curved outline was made by *Benedetto da Rovezzano* for the tomb of Cardinal Wolsey at Windsor in 1524–9. – To the s e, Florence Nightingale †1910 by *C. A. Walker.* – To the w Capt. J. Cooke †1805, by *Sir Richard Westmacott* (Gunnis), and Capt. G. Duff †1805, by *John Bacon Jr.* – In the n transept, Sir Stafford Cripps by *Jacob Epstein*, 1953, a very expressive bronze bust with hands. – Nearby, R. J. Seddon †1906, with marble portrait relief and allegorical figures of Justice and Administration. By *Frampton*, 1909. – Also by *Frampton* two other monuments under the dome near Nelson: E. V. Neale †1892 and Sir W. Besant †1901, both with portrait reliefs. – Nearby are also Admiral Lord Beresford †1919, by *Tweed*, Sir F. W. Richards †1912, by *Pomeroy*, and Field Marshal Lord Napier, by *F. Woodington*, 1891. – In the s transept, W. E. Henley †1903, bronze head by *Rodin*. Back in the nave, first, on the n wall, Sir G. Williams †1905 by *Frampton*, with two seated allegorical figures. – Then statues of General W. F. P. Napier †1860 by *G. G. Adams*, C. J. Napier †1853, also by *Adams*, and Admiral Sir P. Malcolm by *E. Baily*, 1842. – Opposite, the former PULPIT by *Penrose*, 1860, in coloured marbles, in the Italian medieval tradition. – Then Admiral Lord Rodney by *Rossi*, 1811. Standing figure in contemporary dress; standing demi-nude Victory to the l., seated History to the r., somewhat chilly figures. – Opposite, fragments of monuments from Old St Paul's: upper half of the recumbent effigy of Sir Nicholas Bacon †1579, his head on a half-rolled-up mat; recumbent effigy of Sir William Cokain †1626; upper half of the recumbent effigy of William Hewit †1599; Sir John Wolley †1595 and wife, damaged seated figures; Sir Thomas Heneage †1594 and wife, upper halves of recumbent effigies. – Then statue of Henry Hallum by *Theed*, 1862. – Opposite, Lord St Vincent by *Baily*, 1826. – Then Maj. Gen. Sir W. Ponsonby †1815, designed by *Theed* and carved by *Baily*; large group. Fallen horse; the hero, half-naked, has sunk from it and lies towards us. A Victory bends down and offers a wreath. – Opposite, Captains Mosse and Riou, by *Rossi*, 1805. Two demi-nude allegorical figures holding two portrait medallions. – N of the w end statue of Admiral Lord Duncan †1804 by *Westmacott*. – S of the w end, statue of the Hon. M. Elphinstone †1859 by *Noble*, 1863. – Finally, on the n wall of the nave s aisle, Thomas Newton †1807. Nice relief of charity by *Sir Richard Westmacott*. – On the s side of the crypt, Bishop Heber †1826, by *Chantrey*.

(Wellington's FUNERAL CARRIAGE of 1852 by *Semper* has gone to Stratfield Saye, Hampshire.)

This is a very old urban site. Four Roman pottery kilns were discovered in the churchyard in 1672 at a depth of 26 ft. They were arranged in the form of a cross and were each 5 ft wide by 5 ft high. A number of 'moulds of Earth, some exhibiting Figures of Men, of Lions, of Leaves of Trees, and other Things', were also discovered. Since the C17 many Roman burials have been discovered under the cathedral and N of it. They may have formed part of a large single cemetery, embracing finds from Warwick Square, Paternoster Row, St Martin's-le-Grand, and Cheapside. The burials are early, probably C1. Wren's workmen also found medieval burials in woollen shrouds with wooden pins. On the s side of the churchyard on the Cook warehouse site (now open space; see below) there was found in 1852 the fine Anglo-Scandinavian grave-slab with a fantastic beast in relief, now at the Museum of London.

The early C18 RAILINGS round the cathedral partially remain (supporting wall lowered 1879; some resiting C19 –20). Very early examples of cast ironwork, disliked by Wren, who wanted wrought iron. Made 1710–14 at Lamberhurst in Kent, close to the Sussex border. That then well-wooded area was the centre of iron smelting. – Before the w front, MONUMENT to Queen Anne, 1886, copy of the original (by *Francis Bird*, 1709–11, acquired by Augustus Hare, who installed it at St Mary's Place, Holmhurst, Sussex). The four attendant figures are England, Ireland, France and America. – On the n e in the leafy churchyard PAUL'S CROSS, rebuilt 1910 by *Sir Reginald Blomfield*. The original, torn down 1642, was a wooden preaching cross, or combination of roofed pulpit and cross. – s of the nave in a narrow strip of garden, remains of the C14 chapter house (buttress foundations etc.) with bronze FIGURE, by *Bainbridge Copnall*, 1973, shown as if violently fallen back: in this place one might expect it to represent St Paul on the road to Damascus, but it is St Thomas à Becket struck down at Canterbury, for Becket as native of Cheapside qualifies as a local saint.

St Paul's Churchyard only partly resembles a close. It is closed to traffic on the N, but on the s busy traffic flows all too near the cathedral and especially the s w tower. The opening of the s side of the churchyard between Ludgate Hill and Cannon Street, as an essential link in a main route between the City and Westminster, came of Victorian planning. Few buildings remain from the C19 or before. Opposite the cathedral's s porch, instead of the former (highly secular) enclosure of the stream of traffic by textile warehouses, there are strips of lawn and a processional way leading down to Queen Victoria Street. To the s w in Dean's Court and behind a high wall, the former DEANERY, 1670. – N of the cathedral, the CHAPTER HOUSE, 1712–14. Beside it, early C19 PUMP, not *in situ*. –

Farther E, opposite the cathedral's N porch, the former Canon Alley used to enter the churchyard, framing an axial view of the cathedral in a breathtaking slit from ground to

72. LONDON: ST PAUL'S The dome from below. The north view from Canon Alley before 1939

cross. But the alley was rebuilt in the 1950s and the view heedlessly blocked by the Paternoster Precinct developers.

E of the cathedral the CHOIR SCHOOL, 1962–7, by the late *Leo de Syllas* of *Architects' Co-Partnership*. The decision of dean and chapter to have the choir school so close to the cathedral, on such expensive ground, is much to be lauded. The way the architect achieved a small scale close to the huge scale of the cathedral is equally to be lauded. At the S end the building attaches itself to the remaining tower of Wren's St Augustine Old Change, with spire reconstructed in original shape by *Seely & Paget*.

For other postwar buildings and the surrounding streets, see the latest edition of B of E *London 1: The Cities of London and Westminster*.

London: Southwark

CATHEDRAL CHURCH OF ST SAVIOUR AND ST MARY OVERIE *Anglican*

(Based on B of E *London 2: Except the Cities of London and Westminster*, 1952, rewritten and extended, and on Dollman's folio (see below), with information from Ronald Sims and Bridget Cherry.)

Plan, Fig. 75, from RCHM *East London*, 1930, which also takes in Southwark. Some divergences from Dollman; e.g. RCHM alleges survival of the Norman N end of the N transept; Dollman's evidence was based on first-hand material from *Gwilt* and *Wallace* on their restorations.

References (see Recent Literature) include Cobb 1980.

The *Furnishings* section as rewritten by PM (below) also appears in B of E *London 2: South*, 1983.

INTRODUCTION

Long a landmark by the Thames and the S approach to London Bridge, at the ancient entrance to the City from Kent and the Continent, the cathedral straddles the line of a Roman road from the Lambeth shore opposite Westminster and stands close to the junction of Roman roads from Dover and Chichester, all converging on the Roman bridge. From 1866 hemmed in on the S by railways converging on London Bridge Station. On the N the church tower continued to overlook the river reach of the sinister opening scene of *Our Mutual Friend*. During 1940–4, when bridges and railways were enemy targets, the cathedral lost only some glass. Medieval Southwark, the old Surrey bridgehead, with its travellers' inns and bishops' town houses, its theatres and brothels and prisons, its riverside business and special relation to City and bridge, had a flavour unique in London.

Priory buildings N of the church, nearer the river, were replaced in the C 17 by Montague Close and that by C 19 warehouses and wharves, now mostly cleared to give a bald view of the cathedral from the river. Whether the resulting space, which leads nowhere, is to be a field for vandals or an inviting retreat remains to be seen. Just upstream is St Mary Overie Dock, where the priory had moorage rights

73. LONDON: SOUTHWARK (ANGL.)
East end, C 13, and tower, C 14–15, from the bridge-approach

(not the same as St Saviour's Dock downstream in Bermondsey). On the s side, still some churchyard character, surprisingly, despite trains rumbling at clerestory level.

A pre-Conquest minster mentioned in Domesday Book may have stood on this site. The Augustinian priory of St Mary Overie (meaning either 'over the water' or 'at the bankside') was founded here in 1106. The two main building periods were: 1106–1212, of which little survived a fire in 1212; and from then until the c 15, of which all but the nave and two chapels survive. From c 12 to c 17, the priory's bankside powerhouse of patronage was the London palace of the bishops of Winchester nearby upstream. To summarize evidences of their interest: in the early c 12 Bishop Giffard is said to have begun the first priory church, burnt in 1212; Bishop Peter des Roches (or de Rupibus; † 1238) is said to have initiated the rebuilding of which the E arm remains; and, John Harvey suggests, in the late c 14 Bishop William of Wykeham may have employed the mason-architect *Henry Yevele* on the w front, since rebuilt, and on the lower stages of the tower. (Yevele dined with the bishop nine times in early summer 1393 and, incidentally, owned property in Southwark himself.) In the early c 15 Bishop (Cardinal) Beaufort set up his arms in the s transept, and in the early c 16 Bishop Fox gave a new reredos. Before the Reformation, St Mary's canons held the rectories of two parish churches, that of St Margaret in the High Street and that of St Mary Magdalene established in the c 13 in a corner of the priory church itself (the latter a typical monastic arrangement). After the dissolution of monasteries, these parishes joined in 1539, aided by Bishop Gardiner, to buy the former priory church for their parish church, dedicated to St Saviour, so preserving it from destruction. In the early c 17 Bishop Andrewes was buried here; and still in the early c 19 Bishop Sumner led a successful protest against sacrificing the retrochoir to the new London Bridge approach. (Railways in the churchyard were to be another matter.) Southwark lay in the diocese of Winchester until the mid-c 19, then briefly until 1905 in that of Rochester. Renamed in 1897 the collegiate church of St Saviour, this became in 1905 the cathedral church of a new diocese carved from that of Winchester. By then its main architectural history was over.

There were serious fires in 1212, *c.* 1393 and 1676. The c 13 nave's stone vaults fell in 1469 (probably owing to c 14 removal of nave buttresses) and were replaced by lower-pitched timber vaults (for bosses, see *Furnishings* below). After the Reformation the retrochoir was let off as bakehouse and pig-sty until reclaimed in 1624 (Lancelot Andrewes possibly having an eye to his burial-place). In 1703 the sanctuary was embellished with carved wooden fittings like those in Wren's City churches. A century later the architectural critic John Carter found the medieval fabric 'splendid work, and very entire' but much dilapi-

dated, and it continued to deteriorate, with part of the nave shut off and left to ruin. Restoration began piecemeal (the ratepayers being divided on the subject) early in the c 19: of the tower in 1818, the choir in 1822–4 and the retrochoir in 1832–3 (the last without fee) by *George Gwilt*, F.S.A., the most scholarly member of a local family of architects; and of the transepts in 1830 and the reredos in 1833 by *Robert Wallace*. The c 13 nave, pulled down in 1838 as unsafe, was rebuilt in 1839–40 by *Henry Rose*, a classicist out of his depth, in a feeble Gothic caricatured in Pugin's *Contrasts*. Blomfield said Rose placed the nave floor nine feet above the transept floors (possibly trying to imitate the two-storey St Stephen's at Westminster, in the news after the fire of 1834 at the Houses of Parliament). This nave was replaced 1890–7 by *Sir Arthur Blomfield's* nave designed in carefully understated imitation of the choir. Further work by Blomfield's office on transepts, reredos and Harvard Chapel.

A folio of measured drawings reconstructing the medieval church, mainly from drawings by Gwilt, was published in 1881 by Francis T. Dollman, a scholarly architect taught by the elder Pugin: the most detailed record we have of 'Old Moll', as irreverent c 18 churchwardens had called St Mary Overie's remains. Today, like St Bartholomew's Smithfield, the building is a battered but noble survivor from medieval London's proud parade of monastic churches. Much is still left to respect, as well as questions still to resolve.

EXTERIOR

This is a central-towered plan on a small-cathedral scale (overall length *c.* 260 ft) with three-bay transepts, five-bay choir with aisles leading to a rectangular retrochoir, and seven-bay nave, originally with a cloister on its N side. A Norman tower projected in 1106 may never have gone above roof-level, especially after Winchester's fell in 1107. The dominant feature from river, opposite shore and passing trains is the tower completed in the early c 15. Its two top stages (ringers' and bell chambers, refaced by Gwilt) each have two two-light transomed openings in each face; if the ringers' stage was begun under *Yevele*, the window-pattern was set before 1400. The tower's c 15 embattled parapet with flint-and-stone chequered work, and pinnacles (shown in Norden's 1600 view and rebuilt on taller bases in 1689) with wind-vanes, were all renewed by *Gwilt*. The clock may be Gwilt's. An intended medieval spire (to answer old St Paul's?) was never carried out, probably because of the alluvial ground's inability to support it. The tower is now our oldest South Bank landmark downstream of Lambeth.

The E end stands close to the bridge-approach road viaduct which in 1830 required removal of a c 14 chapel,

74. LONDON: SOUTHWARK (ANGL.) View from the south, showing Blomfield's nave

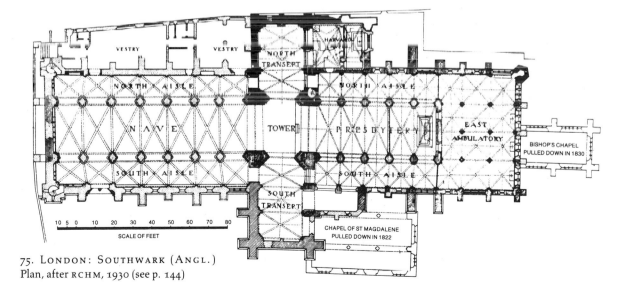

75. LONDON: SOUTHWARK (ANGL.)
Plan, after RCHM, 1930 (see p. 144)

built originally as a Lady Chapel E of the retrochoir and known as the Bishop's Chapel when Andrewes' C 17 tomb stood in it. From the bridge-approach a dramatic piled-up close view of tower, choir and four-gabled retrochoir, C 13–15 limbs resuscitated in the C 19. One descends to the churchyard by two flights of steps beside the railway viaduct. Except for the ashlar of tower and transepts, the exterior is faced with knapped flints (two sorts) with stone dressings: *Gwilt*, setting the course for Blomfield, may have reproduced earlier flintwork (not earlier than the C 14, when knapping began). For external carved work *Blomfield* used Weldon stone. Flying buttresses for the choir clerestory were applied in the C 14 and renewed by Gwilt. No remains of the late C 14 W front. From the N riverside space, part of the curve of the C 12 apse to the N transept's E chapel (now the Harvard Chapel; see below) is visible.

INTERIOR

The late Victorian N A V E (see below) holds a few C 12 traces. At E and W ends of the N aisle, remnants of doorways from the former cloister, the western door for canons a plain round-headed arch, the eastern door for the prior more elaborate: there one must step through and turn round to see the outer jambs and lower ground-level; shaft-rings, with evidence from early C 19 drawings of three carved orders, suggest a late C 12 date (Mrs Cherry). Also a wall recess near the W end of the N aisle. These, with C 12 remains in the N transept, tell us that the C 13 nave, crossing and transepts were built on the C 12 foundation; but of the C 12 E end we are ignorant. Remains of a wall arcade just W of the S door of the nave are thought to belong to the C 13 rebuilding (though Mrs Cherry suggests that capitals of Canterbury type may mean a late C 12 date); it is hard to make out now that one out of three supports in this wall arcade was a console instead of a shaft – the master mason here had his quirks. (A more impressive vanished feature of the C 13 nave was recorded by Dollman, as drawn by Gwilt: a pair of extra-heavy piers two bays from the W end of the nave arcade, suggesting some sort of intended westwork, narthex or tower, and possibly recasing C 12 work.) E responds of the nave arcade remain from the C 13–14 rebuilding of the crossing. The W responds may be Blomfield's or, according to the R C H M plan, Norman. The main evidences of the C 13 are E of the crossing.

The C 13 rebuilding of the CHOIR is thought to have begun soon after 1212. Winchester's new E end was being added to a Norman choir from c. 1202 at the latest. By c. 1225 the Temple Church's E end had been begun and Salisbury Cathedral's E end had taken its final form, both much more sophisticated 'hall' designs than the Southwark priory's retrochoir. There was less money available here, no doubt. Rebuilding must have started at the high-gable end of the sanctuary, with the choir roofed over before the retrochoir was started at its lower level behind the high altar, for there was no pilgrimage shrine to hurry up and plant there. Mrs Cherry suggests a C 13 chronology that runs: lower walls of choir aisles and N arcade, then retrochoir walls and S arcade and upper part of N arcade. Yet the place in that sequence of the separately roofed and floored retrochoir had better wait for detailed study of documents. The once open arches (a pair, as at Exeter) behind the high altar do imply that a retrochoir was part of the early C 13 programme. And both choir and retrochoir in their even tempo and comfortable (that is, English not French) proportions were clearly planned together. The profile of vaulting ribs and transverse arches is similar throughout, and building must have been continuous. Enough was done at any rate for a bishop of London to be consecrated in the choir in 1260, when St Paul's was also in the builders' hands.

In the choir alternately round and octagonal piers probably derive from the Canterbury choir, but with vaulting-shafts brought down to the floor as in the Rochester presbytery completed by 1214. There are some differences between the N and S arcades, e.g. on the S the inner arch mouldings rest upon corbels, on the N upon attached shafts, and the S triforium arcade is plainer. On both sides, what is in fact a series of separate arcaded bays at first-floor level gives the effect of a triforium, which only the most progressive French cathedrals (Chartres, Reims) then had, though arcading in the Canterbury E transepts may have had some influence. Here, piercing the piers at this level may have seemed structurally unwise on riverbank ground, and the working passage is behind out of sight; this triforium construction also appears in Worcester's W nave bays and in Gloucester nave. The clerestory at Southwark is wholly English, with wall-passage and stepped-triplet arches in front of single lancet windows. Moulded capitals throughout, and for other ornament the occasional line of dogtooth, suiting the somewhat puritanical spirit here (yet Dollman shows sketches of much former stiff-leaf carving from the C 13 nave aisles, built slightly later). The vaults of choir, aisles and retrochoir are quadripartite (more French than English), although the cells are filled on the English not the French principle (assuming Gwilt followed what he found). The C 13 designer here would seem to have been an Englishman who had very recently been in France. The choir vaults had to be rebuilt by *Gwilt*, using old ribs as much as he could, though vestry parsimony forced him to lower the pitch of the roof above them. As a 'scientific man' (epitaph in retrochoir) he was using cast-iron roof trusses above the vaults there in 1822–4. The present E window in the high gable, remodelled by Gwilt in a C 13 manner, supplanted a C 16 window above Fox's reredos.

76. LONDON: SOUTHWARK (ANGL.) Choir and sanctuary, after 1212, with (renewed) C16 reredos

77. LONDON: SOUTHWARK (ANGL.) Retrochoir, after 1212

The RETROCHOIR (called Lady Chapel C17–19) is a rectangular space subdivided into twelve nearly equal bays by six free-standing piers, as in a crypt or hall-church, supporting quadripartite vaults of nearly equal height and forming the four aisles indicated by the four roofs we saw outside. Departing from Winchester retrochoir's triple plan, it follows the dictates of choir and aisles (two-bay sanctuary-width plus two aisle-widths), as no focal shrine needed centring behind the high altar. The two inner aisles, or naves, of this retrochoir are slightly higher than the outer ones (a refinement rediscovered by Gwilt), and all four bays nearest the choir are slightly narrower E–W than the rest, which makes for some wrenching of the outer vaults to meet the choir-aisle vaults. The piers are of elementary shape, with four attached thin shafts and four diagonal wide hollows: such hollows, so popular later, were unusual though not unlikely for the C13, and early C19 drawings show that Gwilt did not tamper. The bases seem botched a bit by changes at some time in floor-level (late

C19 views show no step from the choir aisles). Sets of stepped-triplet lancets along the E, restored by Gwilt (especially the second from the S, site of the entrance to the C14 chapel chopped off in 1830). On N and S, and also in the choir aisles, single lancets alternate oddly irregularly with bar tracery of three unfoiled circles, apparently faithfully reconstructed here by Gwilt. He also rebuilt the S choir aisle's S wall after removing the parochial chapel of St Mary Magdalene from the angle between choir and S transept.

On the W side of the retrochoir is C14 flowing blank tracery within the two filled-in arches: apparently open tracery was inserted (with triplet openings below) behind the C13 high altar after the retrochoir was finished, and filled in when the C16 reredos was installed; two small postern doors, as seen from the retrochoir, were part of the C16 design on the other side (see *Furnishings* below). This C14 tracery was repeated in the window at the E end of the N side of the retrochoir, in the corner where consistory courts were held (hence the term 'spiritual court' sometimes used of the whole retrochoir), whence Bishop Gardiner in the C16 is said to have dispatched martyrs for burning. Under the choir a barrel-vaulted cellar (not open), made in 1703 for coffins, was excavated in 1977, when an important group of Roman sculptures was found in a C3 well. Medieval riverside undercrofts were made only at ground-level (lower, of course, than now), as the nearby remains of Winchester House testify. The cathedral has no medieval crypt.

And so to the CROSSING under the tower. The wider C13 arches toward choir and nave rest on brackets against sheer wall with no shafts to the floor, so as to accommodate monks' stalls (filling the crossing and part of the nave as well as the choir), the masons allowing ahead for the carpenters: C12 pier formations like this in other monastic churches, e.g. at Smithfield and Romsey, suggest C12 precedent for it here too. And the N and S openings may already have been made narrower here in the C12 as Winchester's were narrowed following the tower's fall there in 1107. Here the N and S arches rest on grouped fat shafts that run to the floor on the S side, but on the N only two-thirds of the way down with unarticulated piers below – the N transept was probably intended to be screened off entirely. High up on all four sides of the crossing, C14 arcaded passages. Ceiling redesigned by *Ronald Sims* using thirty-six of the C15 wooden nave bosses.

The TRANSEPTS are of three bays each, two-storey in elevation with wall arcades and deep clerestories, and quadripartite vaulted. The late C13 rebuilders of the N TRANSEPT used Purbeck marble, so popular in E.E. work, for wall-shafts upon the partly C12 core, but the entire N bay and all the stone vaulting were gone by 1830, when they were reinstated by *Wallace* (with vaults and arches in cement, Dollman says). The RCHM plan takes this bay as Norman: possibly the old lower walls remained. Wallace, less possessed by the *genius loci* than Gwilt, modelled the N window tracery on that of the Salisbury chapter house. Further restoration by *Blomfield*. Two openings in the E wall have C12 imposts and reinstated round arches. The transept's pointed arch to the N choir aisle is abruptly stilted on the side toward the crossing's NE pier (containing a staircase), probably ever since C13–14 work on the tower's lowest stage. On this arch traces of medieval decorative painting. – The HARVARD CHAPEL in the N transept's E chapel, long a sacristy and now entered from the N choir aisle, was installed in 1907 by *Blomfield*'s office for the tercentenary of the birth in Southwark of Harvard University's first benefactor (*not* founder), John Harvard. The C12 chapel's originally rounded E apse (see *Exterior*) was apparently extended and squared off in the C13 rebuilding. A C12 wall-shaft was at some time moved and inserted in the NE corner. Window tracery revised by *Gwilt*

in cast iron was again revised in stone by *Blomfield*. – The S TRANSEPT, without Purbeck marble, is C14: a mysterious documentary reference of 1303 to some parts of the Southwark fabric being 'for thirty years a ruin', probably after a grant in 1273 of indulgences for contributors to the building fund, may refer to this transept. Vaulting renewed by *Blomfield*. Side windows Dec with Perp leanings, but renewed, and the S window, already 'miserably modernized' in Carter's day and once again by *Wallace*, redone by *Blomfield*. Two E arches once opened into the now vanished parochial chapel, thought to have been part of the early C13 building with further work of the early C15 (on Beaufort's arms, see *Furnishings*).

For *Blomfield*'s NAVE of 1890–7 we should be grateful after all. He was not being asked to add to the work of a medieval genius as Street had been at Bristol, but to replace Rose's inept work while managing not to upstage the surviving C13 work Gwilt saved. Yet this nave – though a Blomfield is not a Street – is, like Bristol's, a preparation for a more interesting medieval E end. It should be emphasized that Blomfield was designing 'in harmony with' the choir and purposely, as indeed he said, not reproducing the full character of the C13 nave, which was available to him in Dollman's folio. So this was a consciously tactful operation, as Street's was. On medieval survivals in the nave, see above. Rose had replaced a C16 W window; Blomfield designed the present five lancets with three glazed lights and outer lancets blind, like Gwilt's over the high altar. *Blomfield* abolished the W door below, no longer the nearest way in from Winchester House, only facing the rear of Borough Market. His S door replaced a much rebuilt S porch. Stone used internally is Ancaster to the top of the nave arcade, Bath above.

FURNISHINGS, W TO E

The accumulated monuments and other furnishings, though giving only a slight idea of the rich deposits silted up in London's churches before the Reformation, do suggest that St Saviour's in its time was no mean parish.

Nave Left of the S door, marble FONT with towering wooden cover, by *G. F. Bodley* with all the stops out. Tall Pascal CANDLESTICK by *Sims*. – On the high sill of the W window, spirited carved wooden STATUES of King David with harp and pair of trumpeting angels, from the organ of 1703. – STAINED GLASS: W, Creation window by *Henry Holiday*, 1893; N aisle, glass 1900–9 by *Kempe & Co.*, whose S aisle glass went in the last war. – At the W end of the N aisle, display of oaken BOSSES from the nave's timber vaults of 1469, carved with symbols and foliage and showing how such bosses looked before being plugged in, rather like champagne corks except that each stump has slots for ribs. – MONUMENTS. C15? *memento mori* or

78. LONDON: SOUTHWARK (ANGL.) Monument to William Austin and Lady Clerke, 1633, by Nicholas Stone

gisant effigy of emaciated corpse, probably from the lower deck of a more worldly memorial. – Near the E end of the N aisle, John Gower, *Anglorum Poeta celeberrimus*, † 1408, recumbent figure on tomb-chest in recess with canopy of three cusped ogee arches, his head resting on his books, *Vox Clamantis*, *Speculum Meditantis* and *Confessio Amantis*: carving not of high quality and much repainted. – At the E end of the S aisle, Shakespeare memorial, 1911, by *H. W. McCarthy*. Reclining figure in gelatinous brown alabaster, with background relief showing old Southwark, celebrating the neighbourhood of the Globe Theatre. (The poet's younger brother Edmond, 'player', was buried in the church in 1607, as were the playwrights John Fletcher † 1625 and Philip Massinger † 1640, in graves no longer marked.)

Crossing   C 20 portable ALTAR with bishop's chair and other mobile sedilia by *Ronald Sims*, 1976–7, in keeping with the new liturgical scene. The brass three-tiered CHANDELIER of 1680, on elaborate chain with crown and mitre, represents continuity. (The chandelier much envied at Westminster Abbey, according to memoirs of the late sacrist Jocelyn Perkins.)

North transept   On the W wall, the Austin MONUMENT, the most rewarding in the cathedral, by *Nicholas Stone*, erected by a literary-minded lawyer, William Austin, in 1633 and also commemorating his mother, a benefactress of the church, who had become Lady Clerke. based on the parable of the sower and related themes, with (now brightly gilded) angel of Resurrection pointing to the sun of righteousness while supported by the rock of Christ, from which issue a stream and a serpent, with standing corn below bound by a scroll lettered 'Si non moriatur, non reviviscit', between two resting figures with haying implements and sun-hats, and below them a winnowing fan with inscription; in short, Stone was gracefully expressing an allegorical epigram in the manner of the metaphysical poets. – Nearby (but mobile) early C 17 ALTAR TABLE with carved frontispiece and twisted legs, gift of the same Lady Clerke. – On the N wall, MONUMENT to Lionel Lockyer † 1672, reclining gawkily to the tune of a claim that 'His virtues & his Pills are soe well known / That envy can't confine them under stone / . . . his Pill Embalmes him safe / To future times without an Epitaph'. – Richard Blisse † 1703. Lively full-wigged bust under looped drapery inside an aedicule with curved pediment, all skilfully designed. – Lord Mayor's SWORD-REST, 1674, from St Olave's demolished church downstream of the bridge, proof of ritual visits from the City to Bridge Ward Without.

Harvard Chapel   Oddly enough, its treasure is by *A. W. N. Pugin*: a spired TABERNACLE for enshrining the Sacrament. Painted and gilded stone and plaster surround a brass door set with gems. Shown in Pugin's Medieval Court at the 1851 Exhibition and then given to his church of St Augustine Ramsgate, translated here *via* the Victoria and Albert Museum in 1971. As the fiercely Catholic Pugin would hardly have approved of a Protestant migrant to Massachusetts, or John Harvard of Pugin, its presence here implies the ecumenical commonsense of two broad-minded institutions, the Church of England and Harvard University. – PAINTING. *Pietà* by the C 16 Ferrarese *Garofalo*. Small but with whole figures. – STAINED GLASS, *c.* 1907, designed late in the career of *John Lafarge*, the American pioneer of modern pictorial glass technique.

North choir aisle   MONUMENTS. Wall-monument to John Trehearne † 1618, 'Gentleman Portar to James I', and wife, two frontal half-figures and offspring below (original colouring restored 1977–8). – Oaken effigy of a recumbent cross-legged knight, possibly of the Warenne family, *c.* 1275 (making it, if that is the case, the oldest movable object in the cathedral), but considerably restored, especially and saccharinely in the face. – Free-standing tomb, in prime spot (doubtless cleared at the Reformation) between aisle and high altar, of Alderman Richard Humble † 1616, kneeling with two wives under a coffered arch with obelisks and achievements on top, probably by *William Cure II* (Esdaile). – STAINED GLASS in two lancets, † 1856 and † 1867, by *Powell* of Whitefriars.

Choir and sanctuary   Filling the E wall, the progressively restored remains of the early C 16 stone REREDOS given by Bishop Fox † 1528, tiers of canopied niches with figures in the richly packed manner of the Henry VII Chapel walls at Westminster or of the similar altar screens at Winchester and St Albans. As much as survived the Reformation here was hidden after 1703 by a carved-wood altarpiece (very like the one at St Magnus just over the bridge), removed during Gwilt's work on the choir. By then, of the C 16 reredos carvings no figures, no canopies, and only two string-courses remained. In 1833 canopies, friezes and demi-angels only were restored to it by *Wallace* (Dollman plates based on Wallace's before-and-after drawings). Images being still popish then, the niches stayed empty until *Blomfield* inserted figures in 1907 (so in the end this was even more like the Tudor screens, repeopled in the C 19, at St Albans and Winchester). Central figures recently gilded. – Gwilt's WINDOW above is filled with C 20 glass by *Sir Ninian Comper*. – PULPIT and STALLS by *Blomfield*, THRONE by *Bodley*.

Retrochoir   At the N wall, Elizabethan CHEST with much intricate architectural and heraldic detail in wood-carving and inlay, given by a treasurer of St Thomas's Hospital, the City Alderman Hugh Offley in *c.* 1588, the year he was elected sheriff, but incorporating with his own the arms and initials of his father-in-law Robert Harding † 1568, so perhaps dating from years when they were in business together: a museum piece. – C 20 ALTARS and

SCREENS (1930s) and E WINDOW (1950) by *Comper*. – At the E end of the N wall, GLASS of the Martyrs' Window, 1890s, by *Ward & Hughes* of Frith Street, Soho. On the s, window of the 1920s to Thomas Francis Rider, Blomfield's builder.

South choir aisle MONUMENTS. Between aisle and sanctuary, free-standing tomb of the great Bishop Lancelot Andrewes † 1626, the last to live at Winchester House; the tomb was placed first in the now gone Bishop's Chapel E of the retrochoir and moved to the W side of the retrochoir after the fire of 1676, when the canopy was lost; present canopy by *Comper*. Well-modelled draperies but face much restored. – W of it, tomb of Edward Talbot † 1923, first Bishop of Southwark (1905–11), afterwards of Winchester, by *Cecil Thomas*. – On the s wall, chaste Greek tablet to Abraham Newland † 1807, chief cashier for thirty years to the Bank of England, by *John Soane* when architect to the Bank. – At the steps to the s transept, Roman MOSAIC found in the churchyard, set in the floor.

South transept MONUMENTS. W side, slightly hallucinatory wall-monument to William Emerson † 1575, with miniature emaciated corpse on a mat rolled under his head. – Above it, John Bingham † 1625, saddler to Elizabeth and to James I, half-figure in arched recess. – Below, part of a C 13 coffin-lid, tapered with foliated cross. – Skied on the W wall, tablet to Richard Benefeld with bust in mid-C 17 dress. – On the s, Rev. Thomas Jones † 1770 by *William Tyler*, one of the founders of the Royal Academy. – At left, two early C 18 wall-monuments translated in 1901 from St Thomas's, one to Thomas Cole † 1715, with charming cherub heads. – Between E wall arches, Bishop Beaufort's arms with cardinal's hat (conferred 1426), set up perhaps to celebrate both the hat and building work in St Mary Magdalene Chapel, then entered through those arches; he may also have presided over the finishing of the tower. – ORGAN CASE, free-Renaissance design by *Blomfield*.

CHURCHYARD

The only remaining tomb is Gwilt's † 1856, between buttresses of the s choir aisle, beside the cathedral's eastern arm that he made safe. – From 1907 the CHAPTER HOUSE was the former church of St Thomas (1702; master mason *Thomas Cartwright*) c. 100 yards SE in St Thomas Street, adapted by *A. E. Bartlett*. (A suitable use for it, because St Thomas's Hospital, moved up-river in the C 19 to the Albert Embankment, was first founded in the C 12 within the newly founded priory precinct.) But a new chapter house is rising in the new close N of the cathedral near the river.

For further description of the neighbourhood, see B of E *London 2: South* by Bridget Cherry: e.g. on surviving remains of the medieval bishops' palace.

London: Southwark

CATHEDRAL CHURCH OF ST GEORGE
Roman Catholic

(Based on B of E *London 2: South*, 1983, by Bridget Cherry, slightly revised.)

Cathedral since 1850. In 1780, when this was open ground called St George's Fields, the anti-Catholic Gordon rioters assembled here. In 1850, England's first C 19 cardinal was enthroned as Archbishop of Westminster here. A suitable site for the old religion's return to status. To place it in South London: the cathedral stands near St George's Circus in the irregular network of roads converging from the Thames bridges, its principal neighbour now the Imperial War Museum. As with other post-Reformation cathedrals inserted into built-up areas, compass directions in this text are ritual, not geographical. The 'E' end actually points NW; the main 'W' door on Lambeth Road is on the SE; the 'N' aisle along St George's Road is on the SW, and the 's' aisle towards Barbel Street (now closed) on the NE. Badly bombed in 1940; surviving arcades and turrets, also an engraving of its prior state, are shown in Richards and Summerson, *Bombed Buildings of Britain*, 1947.

This is *A. W. N. Pugin*'s most important church in London and as such has always attracted much criticism, notably from Ruskin. It was built with great financial difficulty between 1841 and 1848, and was from the outset a compromise. In Pugin's own words 'it was to hold 3,000 people on the floor at a limited price: in consequence, height, proportion, everything was sacrificed to meet these conditions'. The E end, the lowest part of the W tower, the long yellow brick aisle walls and a few details inside are all that now remain of Pugin's church. The rest of rebuilding and extension by *Romilly Craze* after war damage. But the result, although essentially a C 20 Gothic-revival building, still depends on Pugin's plans.

In 1838 Pugin was introduced by his patron, the Earl of Shrewsbury, to the church committee then discussing the replacement of an inadequate chapel in London Road. He produced an ambitious design for a major church with three-storey elevation, stone vaults and a huge central crossing tower, a splendid expression of Catholic hopes after Emancipation. It was always intended to be an important church, though not officially a cathedral until 1850. But this scheme was rejected as too expensive, and in 1839 a competition was held. In December Pugin was declared the winner. His new, much more modest plan, with a chancel, N and s chapels, a very long nave with gabled aisles and W tower, was dictated by the present restricted site, which had built-up roads on all sides. A rather dull exterior was to have been redeemed by a magnificent tower and spire, which takes pride of place in

79. LONDON: SOUTHWARK (R.C.) Designed 1838–9 by A. W. N. Pugin, and partly redesigned by Romilly Craze after C20 war damage

the frontispiece to Pugin's *An Apology for Christian Architecture* (1843). But the great W tower and spire were never built. The cathedral was restored and redecorated in 1888–1905 by F. A. Walters, who reassembled many dispersed Pugin fittings.

Inside it is easy to pick out the remains of Pugin's work: the large Dec E windows, and the N aisle windows all to a different pattern, and the carefully accurate Perp medievalizing of the Petre Chantry of 1848–9 (S aisle), complete with its original furnishings apart from the stained glass. The Hon. Edward Petre † 1848 was one of the main benefactors of the church. His chantry is a tiny enclosed chapel with table tomb, carved altarpiece with Virgin and Child, angels, and its own stone vault. The addition of the new Lady Chapel beyond has effectively made the chapel free-standing, like those little medieval chantries at, say, Gloucester or Winchester. – At the E end of the N aisle,

Pugin's Blessed Sacrament Chapel with original fittings (see *Furnishings* below). – Within the N aisle the Knill Chantry of 1856–7, to relatives of Pugin's third wife, designed after Pugin's death in 1852 by his son, E. W. Pugin, in a delicately refined Gothic with a vault supported by thin internal piers linked to the outer walls by transoms. It is based on a design by him for a chapel at Ushaw, Durham, of 1855. Well-carved capitals with birds and frieze, stone reredos. – W of the Petre Chantry: St Patrick's Chapel, begun in 1854 as the Talbot Chantry, completed as a relics chapel in 1905 and largely reconstructed since the war. – St Joseph's Chapel, with a stone vault, converted from the Weld Chantry of 1890.

After relishing the C19 work, any medievalist will wince at the details of the C20 rebuilding, with its effort to marry the, by then, desiccated traditions of Arts and Crafts free Gothic to Pugin's fragments. Yet the scale is noble; the

long nave is undoubtedly improved in proportion by the addition of a clerestory, while the pseudo-transepts created by heightening the E bays of the aisles add spatial interest lacking in the original building. *Romilly Craze* was clearly influenced by Pugin's first design. Craze's early proposals of 1943 already suggested the addition of a clerestory. Those of 1949 proposed an elaborate stone vault with liernes and bosses over the nave. This was still intended when final plans were accepted in 1953 and rebuilding began, which explains the massive nature of the piers which replaced Pugin's. The aisles were built as planned, with the illusion of a vault created by flying ribs *à la* Bristol, but the upper parts were completed to a simpler design, so that the piers support only stone transverse arches with a boarded ceiling in between (a failure of intent not uncommon in the Middle Ages as well). A chronological pursuit of the rest of the building is rather like tracing the decline of Perp in the C16–17. The very peculiar clerestory window design with semicircular transom (an echo of the curved rood beam in Pugin's first design?) is also a post-1953 modification, as is the design of the equally unmedieval W window. The Lady Chapel, with yawning rectangular openings with uncusped lights, dates from 1961–3. The baptistery at the W end with its faintly C20 exterior S of the entrance was completed in 1966. The extension of the chancel into one bay of the nave dates from the 1953 designs; the reorientation of the Lady Chapel is an experiment of 1977.

FURNISHINGS

In the Blessed Sacrament Chapel (NE) original Pugin fittings: gate by *Hardman*, encaustic tiles, altar and reredos. – STAINED GLASS. E and W windows by *Henry Clarke Studios* of Dublin. Brilliant colours, dull drawing, best seen from a distance. – SCULPTURE. Virgin and Child (Lady Chapel), small Flemish C18. – MONUMENTS. Two table tombs with effigies: Thomas, Provost Doyle, † 1879, chiefly responsible for the building of the church; Bishop Amigo † 1949. The contrast in quality of detail echoes the building history.

Beyond the E end, filling the apex of the triangular site, clergy houses rebuilt by *F. A. Walters*, 1886–7, to a uniform battlemented height, destroying the picturesque variety of roof-line achieved by Pugin's original group of clergy house and schools.

Further on surroundings, see B of E *London 2: South* by Bridget Cherry.

80. LONDON: SOUTHWARK (R.C.)
Pugin's arcades redesigned with modern clerestory

London: Westminster

COLLEGIATE CHURCH OF ST PETER (WESTMINSTER ABBEY), Royal Peculiar, the Coronation church since 1066, cathedral 1540–50(–56)   *Anglican*

(Based on B of E *London 1: The Cities of London and Westminster*, 1973, further considerably revised, with information from Stephen Dykes Bower, Peter Foster, N. H. MacMichael, the late Howard Nixon and the late Lawrence Tanner at the abbey.)

Introduction   158
Exterior   163
   C11 12: monastic remains (below). *Early* C13: Lady Chapel (demolished). *Mid-*C13: eastern arm, transepts, chapter house, nave E bays. C14–16: nave W bays, W front, W towers to roof-level (completed C18). *Early* C16: Henry VII Chapel
Interior   167
   C13: eastern arm with ambulatory and chapels, gallery, clerestory, high vault; S transept, Muniment Room, St Faith's Chapel; N transept, crossing, nave E bays. C14–16: nave W bays, tower bays and W end. *Early* C16: Henry VII Chapel
Furnishings and monuments   176
   Preface on attitudes. Sequence mainly E–W but starting with feretory and sanctuary, then ambulatory and chapels, and Henry VII Chapel; crossing; S transept (Poets' Corner) with St Benedict's and St Faith's Chapels (for Muniment Room, see *Cloisters, Library* below); N transept; nave and choir. N aisle, main nave and choir, S aisle; gallery
Cloisters etc.   201
   Cloisters, C13–14 etc. Chapter house, C13, C19. Library and Muniment Room, C13–17. Chapel of the Pyx and museum, C11 etc. Other monastic remains: refectory, C11–14 (demolished); Dark Cloister, C11; Farmery or Little Cloister, C14–17 (infirmary chapel remains, C12); Deanery (Abbot's Lodging), Jerusalem Chamber etc., C13–18 etc. Dean's Yard and College Garden

Plan, Fig. 81, from *Building News*, 1909; although not hatched to show building periods like that in the *Builder*, 1894, it shows vaulting more clearly; remains S of cloisters not shown.

Some references (see Recent Literature): Bony 1979; Colvin 1963, 1966, 1971, 1975, 1978; E. Eames 1980; P. Eames 1977; Harrison 1980; Hunting 1981; Jordan 1980; Leedy 1975; McLees 1973; Norris 1978; Quiney 1979; *Official Guide*; Rigold 1976; Whinney 1964.

Warning: we follow a mainly chronological path from the E, but the abbey's tourist traffic-flow usually proceeds from

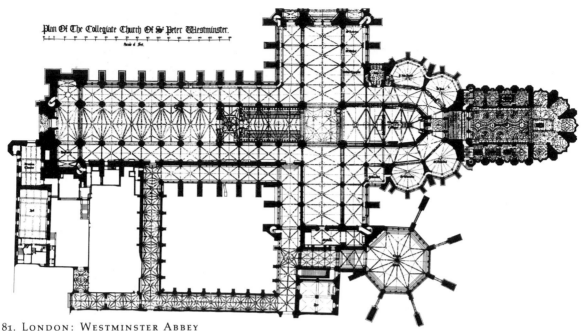

81. LONDON: WESTMINSTER ABBEY
Plan from *Building News*, 1909 (see p. 157)

the W end into the nave, N choir aisle, N transept (or from the nave directly into the choir); crossing with choir and sanctuary, N ambulatory and N chapels, Henry VII Chapel, by modern bridge and Henry V Chantry to and from the feretory; S ambulatory and S chapels, S transept and S choir aisle, to cloisters, chapter house and museum.

INTRODUCTION

Westminster Abbey as approached from the N today is excellently seen from the S end of Whitehall (as continued by Parliament Street), a view opened up only in the C19. With Parliament Square in front, the trees and St Margaret's give scale and the Houses of Parliament lead into a larger picture. Only the abbey's skyline is disappointing. Both the low pyramid roof of the crossing tower and the rather strait-laced W towers lack strength to counterbalance the body of the building. Yet it is as dignified as its nearest present equivalent with those features, Beverley Minster, and is further anchored on the E by the Henry VII Chapel. When approached from the W along Victoria Street or Tothill Street, the W front would seem a little too discrepant and slight to impress if it were not for its narrow height. These features will be better understood from their history.

The abbey (that is, the abbey church) as it appears today has little relation to the picture a traveller would have seen at the time of the Reformation. Then the abbey lay partly in the fields, with streets and houses only on the smallest scale to N and W. Its monastic ranges lay S of it, its close, known as Sanctuary, on the N. One entered the precinct from the N through the Great Gate from King Street at the foot of Whitehall or from the W through the gate from Tothill Street. An isolated bell-tower (built 1224–53, removed 1750) stood between the two gates where the former Middlesex Guildhall stands now: it was a stone tower, 75 ft square and 60 ft high, with a leaded spire above; Salisbury and other cathedrals once had such towers, and Chichester still has. Close by the church to the E lay the Palace of Westminster, a complex and not at all orderly group of structures on the bank of the Thames, which runs N–S here. (From the river's fishermen the abbey of St Peter once took tithe of salmon.) The medieval palace, the church and the monastery formed one whole to the eye. Still in Canaletto's mid-C18 river views the church loomed high above the house-tops of Westminster. Plans and views of that neighbourhood are to be found in Colvin (1966) and Hunting (1981).

We are entirely in the dark about the earliest history of Westminster Abbey. The site had certainly been used by the Romans: a Roman sarcophagus dug up in 1869 N of the nave is now in the chapter-house vestibule; Roman fragments were found in 1878 when Sir George Gilbert Scott's grave was dug in the nave; in 1883 other such fragments

82. LONDON: WESTMINSTER ABBEY
West front, lower stages C14–16, towers C18, in the 1930s

were found in the abbey garden and also, it is said, in the cloister. But the founding of the abbey itself here at Thorney (Isle of Thorns) close to the marshy bank of the Thames: was it in the c 7, or only in the c 10? The first trustworthy records do not date back further than about 970, the time of St Dunstan, the great reformer of monasticism in England. The first connection with royalty is the recorded burial of Harold Harefoot in the abbey precincts in 1040. Edward the Confessor rebuilt or began to rebuild the church and monastic buildings c. 1050–65; the date of the nave is uncertain, possibly c. 1110–50. Of the church itself no traces are visible now above ground, but out of excavations and odd references in chronicles it has been possible to establish much about this church where the Conqueror was crowned on Christmas Day 1066. The choir had solid side walls and an apse, and there were no doubt chancel aisles and probably also E apses to the transepts. The existence of transepts and a crossing tower can safely be assumed. The W end had two towers and the nave six double bays, that is, alternating supports. The whole church was longer than any of the remaining Norman churches of Normandy.

A good deal more survives of the Norman monastery. Fragments are visible above ground of the undercroft of the E range of buildings, of the dormitory on the first floor of that range, of the reredorter or latrines to its S, and of the S range, which contained the refectory. In addition small fragments, especially from the cloister, survive, including a c 12 capital with a dramatic representation of the Judgement of Solomon, now in the undercroft museum (see *Chapel of the Pyx and museum*).

Next in date comes the ruinous former infirmary chapel of St Katharine (E side of the Little Cloister), which can be dated c. 1165–70 and is in a typical Transitional style. The main new building after that, Henry III's first building, is lost to us: the Lady Chapel added to the E of the Norman E end. It was begun in 1220, and stood for almost three centuries until replaced by the Henry VII Chapel. Excavations indicate an elongated plan with polygonal apse, like that of Amiens (started in the same year) but yet longer. The plan of Lichfield's Lady Chapel, although a century later, gives us an idea of the Westminster chapel plan, which it apparently followed. (Gloucester's Lady Chapel of 1227, later rebuilt, may have resembled it too.)

The foundation stone of the new abbey church was laid on 6 July 1245. Building proceeded fast, very fast at the beginning. It seems that after ten years the whole chancel and transepts and the first bay of the nave were complete. Then, after a slowing down for a few years, four more bays of the nave were built in the sixties. On 13 October 1269 the body of St Edward the Confessor was translated to its present resting-place E of the high altar.

In its plan and proportions the abbey is the most French of all English Gothic churches. At Canterbury under William of Sens in 1175 the new style of the north French cathedrals had been introduced into England. Less than twenty years later, at Wells and Lincoln, that alien style had been englished entirely, and a more national Gothic style was current in England in the first half of the c 13 than in Germany or the Netherlands or Spain or Italy. Only Westminster Abbey is an exception. Not that it has not plenty of English features – they will be pointed out as we go on – but essentially, no doubt thanks to Henry's French upbringing and sympathies, the abbey is French. French and similar to Reims is the plan with polygonal apse, ambulatory and radiating chapels. (The first E end with this plan in England had been William the Conqueror's Battle Abbey church, modelled on St Martin's at Tours, if excavations at Battle are clear.) French and dependent on Reims are the wall-passages at the foot of the aisle and chapel windows and these windows themselves with their bar tracery, an innovation introduced at Reims shortly after 1210. French also are the proportions. The abbey, with an interior height of 103 ft (nave), is higher than any other medieval English church. Lincoln choir is 74 ft high (its nave 82 ft), Salisbury 84 ft, Wells 67 ft; but the height of Reims is 117 ft, of Amiens 144 ft. The relation of height to width of the chancel 'nave' is 101½ by 38½ ft at Westminster, 74 by 38 ft at Lincoln. French and of course a consequence of the great height is the abutment with flying buttresses in two tiers. (The earliest English flying buttresses had been of the late c 12 at Canterbury.)

The source of other features at Westminster Abbey is some even more recent French work. From Amiens and the Sainte Chapelle come windows in the form of spherical triangles (i.e. in convex-curved triangular frames), consistent diapering of such flat surfaces as spandrels, capitals with naturalistic foliage (also at Reims), spandrels with censing angels (transepts), four-light windows with geometrical tracery (chapter house), tracery of unencircled trefoils and quatrefoils (N E cloisters). Now the nave at Amiens dates from 1220–39, but the Sainte Chapelle only from 1243–8. So no one could have been internationally more up-to-date than the master of Westminster Abbey.

Who was he? Or, if there were several, who were they? The abbey was built at the king's expense, and so we must look for the king's masons. Now the king's mason in 1243 and thereafter was *Henry of Reyns*, and it would surely be asking a great deal of accident to presume that he came from Rayne or Raynes in Essex rather than from Reims in France. He disappears from the documents in 1253. It is tempting to make him the harbinger of the new ideas of Reims and altogether of the French High Gothic style, but work strikingly similar to that at the abbey in its earliest years exists at Windsor, a wall arcade of the chapel begun in 1239–40 (visible in the E ambulatory of St George's

Chapel); however, bar tracery at Binham Abbey in Norfolk, once thought to pre-date Westminster's, was probably inserted later. The king himself cannot have been responsible; for though he knew Gascony well, he saw the Sainte Chapelle for himself for the first time in 1254, Amiens in 1254, and Reims in 1262. Moreover, even the earliest work at the abbey is not entirely French. The cell-filling of the vaults is done in the English, not the better French technique (see *Interior*, high vault, below), the chancel vault has a ridge rib, an English fashion of Lincoln, and, even more conspicuous, the whole ambulatory with its radiating chapels has a gallery over. It is in the outer windows of this gallery that the spherical triangle first occurs in England. While Reims and Amiens merely have triforium passages over their arcades, the royal abbey church at Royaumont near Paris had recently been given galleries (see *Interior*, E end, below).

There are two possibilities to explain this situation. Henry may have been an Englishman who had worked at Reims (just as the master of Bamberg in Germany, clearly a German, had) and for that reason received the appellation of Reims. He may also later, perhaps in 1243, have revisited France and seen Amiens, the Sainte Chapelle and Royaumont. Or Henry was indeed a Henri, and the English elements are due (1) to his masons being used to English cell-filling rather than French, (2) to the choices of his patrons, king or clergy, and (3) to the high vault being done after his death.

Details of the early building history cannot be charted bay by bay, but the main stages can be inferred since publication of the first volumes of *The History of the King's Works* (Colvin 1963) and also of the surviving accounts (Colvin 1971); these include some week-by-week particulars of the employment of craftsmen e.g. in 1253, but not a continuous series. We have a large number of photographs of details by the late C. J. P. Cave and the late R. P. Howgrave-Graham, and a thesis by Dr P. Wynn-Reeves (later Tudor-Craig), University of London, 1952, on stiff leaf foliage development in England, all of which help to establish sequence.

For the purposes of this book it is perhaps sufficient to say that it looks as if building started at the E end, the E walls of the cloister, and the chapter house all at the same time. The ambulatory, chancel aisles and chapels would of course have to be completed and vaulted before the upper walls of the chancel could be built. Work in the cloister is recorded for 1248-9; a lectern for the chapter house was commissioned in 1249, in 1250 Matthew Paris speaks of the 'incomparable chapter house', statuary for it was paid for in 1253; in 1252 timber was ordered for the roof of the chancel and the stalls for the monks; in 1254 Henry III, all the time pressing for increased speed, expressed the wish to see the work completed by 13 October 1255. We do not

know whether it was; but the history of the following fifteen years makes it probable.

Henry of Reyns was followed in 1253 or 1254 by *John of Gloucester*. He seems to have been less consistently busy at the abbey. Perhaps he closed the chancel vaults with their ridge ribs. To him also the modified details W of the crossing seem to be due, for in 1258 the king ordered him to take down part of the old church as far as the vestry 'juxta sedem regis'. Just where the 'sedem regis' may have been is discussed below (*Interior*, S transept and nave). That may indicate the beginning of work W of the E bay of the nave. The E bay itself had of course to be put up at least partly when the crossing was erected. John of Gloucester disappeared in 1260-1 and was replaced by *Robert of Beverley*, who remained in his job as king's mason until 1284 at least. The differences of detail between nave and chancel and within the C13 bays of the nave will be discussed later.

We can be briefer here for the rest. Under Abbot Byrcheston (1344-9) the E walk of the cloister was rebuilt in the Dec style which plays a small part in the whole of the abbey, the S and W walks followed under Litlyngton, first prior (1350-62), then abbot (1362-86). He did much more. He rebuilt the abbot's house S of the W front of the abbey with its hall and the Jerusalem Chamber, rebuilt the infirmary now and made a start on the new nave. Master mason is thought to have been *Henry Yevele* (after 1360; † 1400), although this has been strongly challenged (by McLees (1973), who questions Yevele's hand in Canterbury nave too). Plans for continuing Westminster nave may go back to the early 1360s (when Langham was abbot), and work began with demolition of the remaining bays of the Norman nave in 1375; in 1388-9 five windows were ready for glazing. The style is self effacing to an amazing degree. No major Perp motifs – just minor modifications of the system laid down in the C13. This conservative procedure appears signally English because so respectful of the past. It had indeed been done in England, in the nave of Beverley Minster during the second quarter of the C14, and see also Chester nave. But it is all the same extremely rare even in England (cf. St Albans nave). The W front at Westminster with its porch is very similar to Yevele's Westminster Hall, and also similar to the W façade of Winchester. Here the Perp was given its due – with consistent panelling ('grating-like', said Willis), over wall surfaces as well as windows.

Abbot Islip's is the last work before the Reformation. He completed the nave and built the W towers up to roof-level, also his own burial chapel N of the chancel, and added the Jericho Parlour to his house and the Abbot's Pew above the S nave aisle. And the building of Henry VII's Chapel took place in his time. So Islip finished his church at both ends. What may be his portrait bust is in the abbey museum.

We are so used to this cathedral-like building in the middle of London that we may forget to ask why it is that so many other great English abbeys lie in ruins and Westminster stands undamaged, except by time and air pollution, and by the restorers who had to deal with their effects. The answer is the unique connection of the abbey with the king and the state. The church was in a sense the Reims and the St-Denis of England together, coronation church and often burial church of sovereigns, and the Chapel of the Pyx was the royal treasury. Already in *Piers Plowman* the chapter house was called the parliament house: the original House of Commons sat there, mainly in the c13–14. The abbey church was till the Reformation exempt from episcopal jurisdiction, even from Canterbury. Then it became one of Henry VIII's six new cathedrals: for ten years only, 1540–50, there was a bishop of Westminster; for six further years, however, it remained a cathedral church in the bishop of London's diocese. Briefly restored to monastic status under Mary I, it was handed over to the Crown upon the accession of Elizabeth I. Its charter as a collegiate foundation directly under the sovereign and exempt from the jurisdiction of both Canterbury and London was granted in 1560. Its unique architectural authority, not its administrative peculiarity, accounts for its presence in this book.

The restorers of the fabric of the abbey have had much to contend with, not least the contents of London air and the susceptibilities to it of the various stones used by their predecessors: e.g. Chilmark limestone, sound at Salisbury after seven centuries, decaying at Westminster after one. Restorers have themselves done what was later regarded as great damage, though it was perhaps often more pugnaciously recorded than that of the medieval cathedrals. At the abbey a repair fund was set up by Dean Lancelot Andrewes (1601–5, later, as Bishop of Winchester, to do much good to the fabric of Southwark), and extensive rebuilding and refacing was done by Dean Williams (1620–44; see Jerusalem Chamber under *Cloisters etc.* below). In 1698 *Christopher Wren* was appointed to the newly created post of Surveyor to the Fabric (though of course there were lesser-titled surveyors on hand before that). In 1713 he presented to the Dean a memorandum to explain what he had already done in the way of restoration, what remained to be done, and what in addition he wished might be done (forty-five years, incidentally, after his similar report to the Bishop of Salisbury). It is an extremely interesting document. He calls the abbey 'Gothick' but explains why he would prefer the term 'Saracen'. He speaks of the building in a businesslike way, neither with enthusiasm nor with antipathy. He recommends that the w towers should be completed and a crossing tower built. They ought to be 'in the Gothick form', because 'to deviate from the old form, would be to run into a Disagreeable Mixture,

which no person of good Taste could relish'. Wren's assistant was *William Dickinson*, a man evidently seriously interested in the Gothic style. Wren's successor as Surveyor to the Fabric was *Nicholas Hawksmoor*, to whose design the w towers were at last begun in 1734. But Hawksmoor died two years later, and the w towers were completed c. 1745 by his successor *John James*. The base for a crossing tower, a low lantern, was built in 1727 but got no further. Wren wanted an elongated dome with Gothic detail and then a slim lantern and spirelet. (A dome was placed over the crossing at Beverley in the 1720s: see Cobb 1980.) But Hawksmoor and James may have intended a tall needle spire of c14 type like the wooden model shown in the N transept made to an earlier design by Wren.

The restorations under Wren were quite considerable. (It was his and Dickinson's treatment of the N transept that Scott and then Pearson took in hand, theirs in turn being redone in 1981.) After Hawksmoor and James, Surveyors to the Fabric were *Henry Keene, James Wyatt* (who restored Henry VII's Chapel), *Benjamin Wyatt, Edward Blore, Sir George Gilbert Scott* (on his work, see Jordan 1980), *J. L. Pearson* (Quiney 1979), *J. T. Micklethwaite, W. R. Lethaby* (who wrote two fine books on the abbey), *Sir Walter Tapper, Sir Charles Peers, S. E. Dykes Bower* (under whom the interior has been cleaned, a revelation), and since 1973 *Peter Foster*, under whom the exterior is being rehabilitated, the N side emerging finely from scaffolding in 1981 (and especially striking under night spotlights during the snows of early 1982). At the abbey the great change of heart from restoring to preserving came only with Micklethwaite and Lethaby, the latter a pupil of Norman Shaw yet an ardent, sensitive and highly intelligent disciple of William Morris. Morris had preached the 'anti-scrape' ideal since 1877; his letter of protest about the restoration of the abbey dates from 1892 and his S.P.A.B. pamphlet *Concerning Westminster Abbey* from 1893. (For Morris on the abbey monuments, see the preface to *Furnishings* below.) War destruction in 1941 took the lantern roof over the crossing, part of the Deanery, and certain houses in the Little Cloister, all since rebuilt.

Westminster Abbey was built of Reigate stone, Henry VII's Chapel of Huddleston and Caen, its plinth of Kentish stone and interior screens of Reigate, but Wren used Burford stone on the main vessel, Wyatt used Bath stone on the Henry VII Chapel, the Victorian work on the N transept was in Chilmark stone, and restoration now is in Portland stone, already in the c18 used for the upper towers. Like the London plane tree, Portland stone, so far, stands up to London air better than most. The abbey with Henry VII's Chapel is 511 ft long, four feet less than Canterbury, longer than Lincoln or York or Peterborough, shorter than Ely or St Albans or Winchester or Old St Paul's.

Before starting to study the exterior of the abbey in detail one ought to remember that it is, as already implied and as Lethaby put it, 'so completely recased that to describe it will be to describe a series of modern works'.

We start with the EAST END, that is, the whole eastern arm. (For the E Lady Chapel added in 1220 to the Norman church, see *Interior*, E end; for Henry VII's Chapel that replaced it, see below after W front.) Here the French plan is evident at once, the ambulatory with its radiating chapels, the buttresses (originally apparently with statues under canopies) and the flying buttresses, and the tall two-light windows with their bar tracery. The arch above the two lights and below the window arch is pierced and adorned by a circle enclosing a sexfoil, all of openwork. The same pattern repeats high up in the tall clerestory windows, though the circle has a cinquefoil here. (Originally there may have been blank lancets l. and r. of the clerestory

windows.) The windows are all thoroughly renewed. The best-preserved lower window is in the sheltered corner just SW of Henry VII's Chapel. The windows originally had nook-shafts. It is at first surprising that between the chapel windows and the clerestory a second tier is inserted, its windows in the shape of a spherical triangle with an eight-foiled circle, also nook-shafted. The arches on the nook-shafts have a typically depressed two-centred shape which repeats in other parts of the abbey. These windows belong to the gallery, which in a unique way repeats the combined plan of both ambulatory and chapels. The spherical triangles are an impressive proof of how completely up-to-date the master of this work was. Bar tracery had been conceived at Reims between 1210 and 1220, but windows in convex triangular frames had only been introduced, it seems, on the W front at Amiens c. 1230–35 and, more prominently, at the Sainte Chapelle in Paris, begun 1243, two years before Westminster Abbey. (Above each ambulatory chapel also, besides the triangular windows,

83. LONDON: WESTMINSTER ABBEY South transept and chapter house, 1245–c. 1253, from the cloister garth in c. 1930

one narrower bay has a gallery window of two lights and an encircled quatrefoil: a similar design occurs in the Sainte Chapelle's lower apse.) The high vaults are supported by two tiers of flying buttresses. The transept E aisles continue the E-end design.

The CHAPTER HOUSE adjoins the S transept. As this must have been begun soon after 1245, and structurally completed by 1250 or by 1253 at the latest, the master of Westminster was keenly up-to-date and in addition very resourceful as to when and how to use newly introduced elements here (on which in full, see Cloisters etc. below). The prominent flying buttresses were added as a necessary strengthening in the C 14. The roof of the chapter house may have been originally nearly flat, like Salisbury's, but unlike Lincoln's. The present tent roof at Westminster is Scott's.

The NORTH TRANSEPT is fully exposed, and its N front was royalty's state entrance from the adjacent palace; especially during the long building works on the nave, this was the way in for processions (see Solomon's Porch below). The pattern for the façade was such transept fronts as those of Chartres, and it provided a correspondingly important setting for sculpture. As there have been three major restorations, almost no detail can be called original. Hollar's N view of 1654 shows the general design before the first restoration under Wren, for whom Dickinson drew before-and-after details in 1719 (Hollar and Dickinson both shown in Hunting 1981, the former also in Bony 1979, the latter in Jordan 1980). In the restoration of 1875–86 Scott was responsible for the porches, Pearson for the parts higher up. In the restoration of 1980–1 much crumbling stonework had to be renewed. We must here try to re-evoke its original appearance. The front is tripartite, expressing the fact that the transepts have E and W aisles. There are three gables and ample porches below them. The middle one has a double doorway originally no doubt with a figure of Christ. It is likely that the W porch was dedicated to the Virgin. There is no doorway in the E porch. The ornamental details are all renewed or new. Only the boss of the W porch is original. It has stiff-leaf foliage. The corbels against the sides of the porches represent original corbels. They carried life-size statues, a very different, much less dramatic arrangement than the statues in French cathedrals, where their array in canted jambs leads one irresistibly into the doorways and through into the church. The Westminster arrangement is much more static, the arrangement of a country which liked large porches to linger in and also of a country which liked the decoration of flat surfaces. This same liking is responsible for the decoration of the tympana. In France they had figure scenes in tiers or strips, full of drama. Here in the E and W porches are tiers of cinquefoils in circles, geometrical pattern rather than human action. For the middle porch the original

arrangement is not certain. At the top was no doubt the figure of Christ in Majesty in a large quatrefoil (as at the S chancel portal at Lincoln, which was greatly influenced by Westminster). Below this seem to have been two tiers of pointed arches on top of each other, filled with smaller figures, perhaps a Doom. (Scott in his Gleanings (1863 ed.) said statues of the apostles and many minor figures were then still in situ, but Jordan (1980) seems to doubt this. Much 'time-eaten sculpture', it was said in 1723, was 'pared away' by Dickinson.)

Above and behind the gables are groups of lancet windows under deep superordinate arches of depressed pointed form, and above these a tier of twin openings with bar tracery all of even height and design, three to each aisle, and five in the middle. Lethaby has proved that the original arrangement was 2-4-2, just as at Amiens in the W front of c. 1220–40. Above that stage the flying buttresses of the aisles appear, and in the middle a rose-window which is entirely Scott's but must once have been of great beauty and daring. For its design see Interior, N transept. It was again Lethaby who established that the rose had its spandrels glazed above as well as below (as in the above-mentioned Dickinson drawing), an innovation made in France and no earlier than c. 1240 (at St Germain-en-Laye). In design the Westminster rose (and that of certain tiles in the chapter house, q.v.) is considerably closer to the S transept of Notre Dame in Paris, which was begun only in 1258, a date probably too late for Westminster. The gable originally had blank geometrical tracery of a design hardly probable before c. 1290. The pinnacles are now C 20.

Under Abbot Litlyngton (1362–86) a tall galilee called Solomon's Porch was placed in front of the N transept's middle portal. According to Hollar it had a stepped group of three tall slender Perp windows. It will have sheltered the forming of processions (like the temporary pavilion put up at the W front for the Coronation in 1953; see below). Removed by Wren.

The SOUTH TRANSEPT's front, partly hidden from public view by the monastic range to its S, was made safe in 1981–2. The rose-window is of c. 1890 but seems to represent an insertion of c. 1460 (glazed 1462). At various times, eroded pinnacles on both transept fronts have had to be renewed, in the C 16–17 with curved turret-tips and then at various times replaced again by Gothic ones: photographs of c. 1860 show a mixture (Cobb 1980).

The NAVE continues the system of the E parts, and the only change noticeable at first is that the spherical triangles of the gallery windows are replaced by windows shaped like pointed arches pure and simple, that is, with straight not convex bases. The windows are filled with three small cinquefoiled circles instead of one large octofoiled one. With this small alteration the design was preserved to the end of the C 13 building campaign, that is, probably to

1269. This campaign is represented by the first four windowed bays w of the crossing (in addition to that bay corresponding to the transept w aisles, built when the crossing was).

After this, building stopped, until a new start was made in 1375. It is astonishing and without parallel outside England that the master (*Henry Yevele*, if it was he) did not insist on something in his own style or the style of his day. (Yet not so astonishing here, considering royal reverence for Edward the Confessor's shrine and the status of the chancel as setting for coronations: further on this conservatism, see *Interior*, Nave, below.) At any rate, they continued the system laid down more than a hundred years before with such small changes that the whole abbey from the chancel to the w towers looks to this day very much as if it were built to one plan during a short period. The main changes are at once visible in the sixth bay from the E. In aisles and clerestory the lancet lights are cusped instead of plain, and the foiled circles are replaced by unencircled quatrefoils. There are also slight changes in the buttress details. It may, or may not, be strange that what motifs the C14 master chose to use were by no means of a convincedly Perp character, and did not really depart from C13 precedent. The nave originally had a battlemented parapet.

From the s side, i.e. from the cloister, the same observations can be made. The only difference is that to support the nave and gallery wall here flying buttresses in three tiers are used (in addition to the two tiers of the clerestory). They are carried down to sturdy detached buttresses forming part of the s wall of the N walk of the cloister – a splendid arrangement proving that flying buttresses were by no means regarded as a necessary evil, necessary to obtain for the faithful inside the building the effect of miraculous height and transparence of wall. The terse resilience of these tiers upon tiers of flyers must have been appreciated as a positive value when they were built.

Now for the WEST FRONT. This appears to belong in its lower parts to *Yevele's* work, and was continued until c. 1532, but the towers above roof-level were built only under Dean Wilcocks in 1735–45 (as celebrated on his monument, nave, s aisle). They were designed by *Nicholas Hawksmoor*. The façade was never as grand as that of the N transept. It is tripartite, and the lower stages of the towers carry on the design of the nave and aisles. The four buttresses have broad flat faces with blank panelling. In the centre, serving as the main w entrance, is a porch slightly projecting in front of the wall but still contained between the buttresses. It has a pretty little vault with thin ribs and canted sides decorated by blank arcading with Perp tracery. To the l. and r. of the porch are two niches each, and above them and the porch runs a row of niches for statues. Then follows the w window, of seven lights, with a two-centred arch, Perp panel tracery of no special interest, and four

transoms. The upper two are connected by a band of quatrefoils. The third stage of the towers also has Perp windows. They are of three lights. Up to here all seems to be the C14 design. The similarity to the porch of Westminster Hall is remarkable. The w window was completed later, under Abbot Esteney (1474 etc., rebuilt by *Hawksmoor*). Work on the towers continued until Abbot Islip's death in 1532 (portions above eaves-level in Hollar's view were rebuilt to the C18 design).

Higher up the work of the C18 begins. At Wren's time the nave gable was still weatherboarded. The first motif of the C18 is a parapet in forms entirely in the Late-Wren–Hawksmoor style. Above the parapet, however, Hawksmoor attempted seriously to be in keeping with the Gothic style of the abbey. It is true that the clock in the N tower and the stage in the s tower corresponding to it exhibit Baroque curly open pediments, but the buttresses carry on with squared-up panelling consisting of Gothic elements, and the large three-light windows at the bell-stage are also in a squared-up Perp manner. They have ogee heads, ending, however, instead of a point, in a horizontal ledge carrying a crocket. The towers finish in a parapet and polygonal pinnacles. (It is worth remembering that Hawksmoor knew Beverley Minster well, having supervised repairs there 1716–20.) Still in Hollar's mid-C17 views there was no central tower nor any visible base for one (though massive crossing piers inside mean that one was intended). Canaletto's mid-C18 views show the present lantern added in 1727 by *Hawksmoor*. The low pyramid roof added by *Wyatt* was burnt in 1941 and rebuilt.

Those who remember the Coronation of 1953 will recall the annexe put up by the then Ministry of Works before the w door, like a temporary Solomon's Porch (N transept, above). Luckily, a 'narthex' designed 1942 by *Lutyens* to stand permanently here – in his very own gothic, arrogant in size – was never built.

Finally HENRY VII's CHAPEL. This was begun by Henry VII as a new Lady Chapel in 1503 and completed as Henry VII's chantry chapel by Henry VIII c. 1512. The designer is not known for certain, but is now thought to have been *Robert Janyns Jr*, a royal mason with experience at Windsor, and of a Burford family of masons with experience at Oxford (Leedy (1975) shows this to be much likelier than previous attributions to the Vertues). The exterior is Late Perp at its best, both sturdy and sumptuous. Lethaby rightly calls the structure 'frank and energetic', Wren equally rightly the decoration 'nice embroidered work'. The chapel has nave and aisles and five radiating E chapels (like the abbey itself). The buttressing of the clerestory is made the principal motif of the structure. The buttresses are complete octagonal turrets rising up nearly as high as the clerestory. Their lower parts are closely panelled, above the aisle and chapel parapet they have statue niches – three

statues over the aisles, four over the chapels – and they end in crocketed domes with finials. The aisle and chapel windows are given a delightfully broken plan. In the aisles each window is a bow flanked by two half-bows; in the chapels it has canted sides and a V-projection in the middle. The predecessor of this fanciful plan of bay-windows was Henry VII's Tower at Windsor, on which Janyns is known to have worked. Similar though a little later is the great s bay at Thornbury (c. 1511–21). The mullions and transoms of the bays follow the same close panelling as the blank tracery of the turrets. High pierced parapet. Clerestory with five-light windows. Between them flying buttresses which again succeed in looking massive, although they are of openwork design. They are of two bars rising from the turrets to the clerestory with tracery between. The bar at the bottom of each buttress is a straight diagonal, that at the top curves up to meet the wall. Broad, panelled, solid parapet crowned by an early c 19 pierced parapet with pinnacles. The buttress turrets were originally provided with coloured statuary, and on the top of the turrets gyrated metal weathervanes. Credit for the external refacing under *Wyatt*, 1807–22, should go to *Gayfere* the mason.

INTERIOR

What distinguishes the interior of Westminster Abbey from the interior of most English medieval churches is its height in relation to width. No other major English church has proportions so similar to those of the c 13 cathedrals of France. It is true that the abbey is not as high as Reims or Amiens nor provided with an elevation designed so single-mindedly to emphasize height. But compared with Lincoln or Wells the difference is indeed startling. Equally startling in comparison with Lincoln or Wells are the height and relative narrowness of the arcade openings and the height of the clerestory. A further distinctive feature of Westminster Abbey is the dark grey, greenish or purplish piers of Purbeck marble. They were never painted. Otherwise to try to conjure up a picture of the abbey in the c 13, one must think of plain stone surfaces painted white with red lines to imitate ashlaring and rosettes in the middle of the ashlar blocks, and decorated stone surfaces and stone carving all in a blaze of colour (lit by flickering candles, of course, not the unblinking stare of electricity). The colours probably were of the character familiar from stained glass and illuminated manuscripts, strong and clear and warm, and with much gilt. Enough fragments, even if very small fragments, have been noticed to be sure of that. Foliage capitals e.g. were green on red or gold on red, roll mouldings red or other colours, etc.

In addition, to distil out of the present-day appearance of the abbey its original appearance, one must blot out all the monuments save a very few in the chancel. The abbey is architecturally so much of a piece that it ought to be visualized pure, not as a mixture of styles and scales (on the difficulty, see *Furnishings and monuments*, Preface, below).

We must now examine the interior in detail, starting at the EAST END (except for Henry VII's Chapel, which is treated chronologically after the nave). The chancel ends in five sides of an octagon and is, just as at Reims, surrounded by an ambulatory with radiating chapels. The ambulatory has trapeze-shaped bays with quadripartite vaults. The shape of each chapel is of six sides of an octagon, with the rest open to the ambulatory. Each of the eastern pair of chapels has two sides solid and four pierced by windows, the easternmost window in each darkened by the Henry VII Chapel. (As the earlier Lady Chapel was narrower, these windows were originally more telling at the end of the aisle vistas, as at Reims.) The chapels of the other pair have three solid sides and three windows each. The bar tracery of the windows has been described with the exterior. In front of the windows inside runs a continuous wall-passage, another feature taken over from Reims, and now much camouflaged by tombs. The chapel vaults have seven ribs carried up to one boss. The central E chapel was the Lady Chapel built by Henry III before the new abbey church was begun, as an addition to the Norman church, on an elongated plan with polygonal apse as shown by excavation. It disappeared entirely when Henry VII's Chapel was built. All we can now see is that it had an oblong vestibule. (The very beginning of the continuation of the wall-passages into the vestibule can still be traced.) The ambulatory bays have their vaulting cells filled in the English not the French manner. The ribs have complex mouldings, including fillets. Tie rods were inserted to strengthen the structure; although the French had more confidence in their masonry than the English in the c 13, Reims also received iron bars (in England these had first appeared in the E parts of Canterbury). In the centre of each bay a big boss. The four remaining original chapels have or had a lower stage of blank arcading with pointed-trefoil cusping, much of it mutilated. In the spandrels remains of foliage, both stiff-leaf and naturalistic, and a few remains of figures and demi-figures. Some of these are winged, some oddly twisted, one part of an angel-holding-two-crowns motif, just enough for us to see here precursors of Lincoln's Angel Choir reliefs. (A possibly influential earlier set of angels, if their attributes are original, may be those of the Worcester s choir triforium.) Above the blank arcades where there are windows they fill the walls, and their slim tall transparence creates a feeling of height and light that sets the scene for the chancel.

The CHANCEL (in this church containing the sanctuary and the feretory, or place of the shrine, but not the choir)

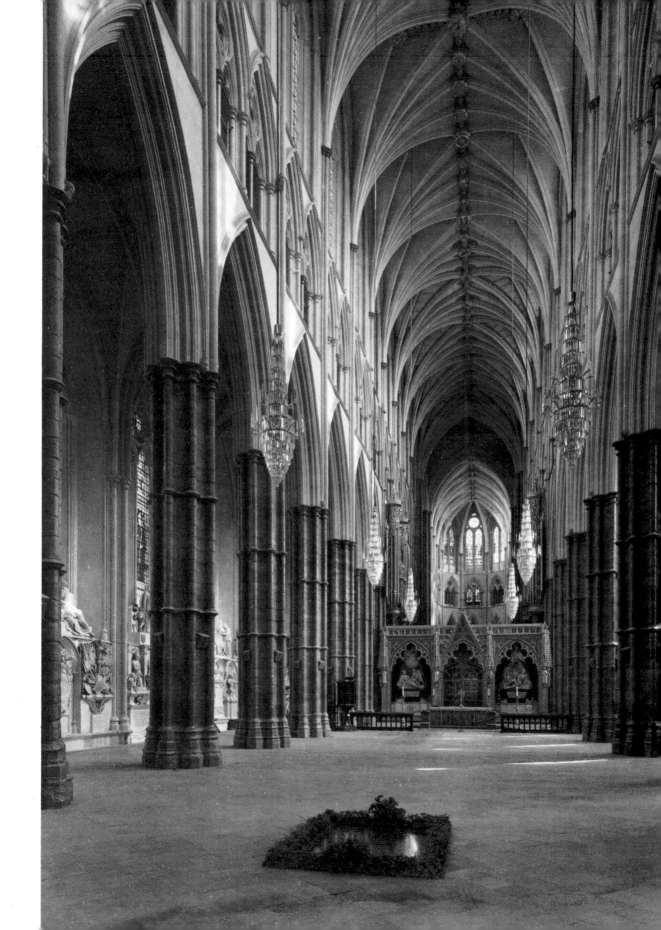

has slender arcades with strong circular piers provided with four slim detached shafts (with two shaft-rings) in the four main directions. This shape is again that of Reims (and before Reims of Chartres and after Reims of Amiens). But the piers at Westminster are of Purbeck marble, and that anglicizes their character effectively. The arches are of extremely complex section. Original tie rods run between them. The spandrels to their l. and r. are all decorated with diaper, a motif derived probably from the w front of Amiens, but applied with a thoroughness at Westminster which reflects the Anglo-Norman liking for all-over surface patterning. On the shallow moulded capitals of the piers stand single vaulting-shafts of Purbeck marble. One shaft-ring at the sill height of the gallery.

The existence of a GALLERY at Westminster Abbey is a national English contribution. (Local habit at the abbey itself persists in calling this 'triforium', but gallery it is.) Galleries were characteristic of English Norman churches and those of large areas of France in the c 11 and c 12. But in France they had been replaced by triforia when the High Gothic style was created just before 1200. In England they were kept, e.g. at Lincoln and in the Ely retrochoir, to mention only two Gothic designs of the c 13 preceding Westminster. One might have thought that a building so French as the abbey in its proportions, its plan and in many details might have dispensed with the gallery. But that was not so, perhaps at the request of the king or chapter rather than the architect. The gallery has the same width as the ambulatory and extends through all four radiating chapels (cf. Norman Norwich). Towards the 'nave' of the chancel each bay has two twin openings, each of them with a middle shaft of Purbeck marble and bar tracery above with a cinquefoil in a circle. The whole of these openings is duplicated in depth, one complete range facing into the 'nave' and one, independent of it, facing into the gallery. It was a very lavish thing to do, but now that the abbey's internal stonework has been cleaned, it has become clear that it paid the doing. It is less effective than the double tracery in the clerestory of the Angel Choir at Lincoln, where more direct light comes through the outer layer and the changing relation of the two layers tells as one moves along. Yet even though the light from the abbey's gallery windows is less direct, the refinement is no longer lost in gloom. (A source of the idea, Professor Branner suggests in his study St Louis and the Court Style, 1965, may have been the double arcades of the gallery inside the w front of Notre Dame in Paris, c. 1230.) The voussoirs of the arches of the openings are in some cases given stiff-leaf decoration, in some sharply cut leaves in square panels, in some they are left unenriched. Diapering in the spandrels. The outer windows of the gallery are spherical triangles with foiled circles (see Exterior). What appears of arches and concealed flying buttresses on the gallery is simply double-chamfered, frankly utilitarian. In contradiction to this, the beams of the timber roof of the gallery towards the e end rest at the back of the wall to the chancel on beautifully carved figures, demi-figures of men, a demi-figure of a woman wearing a wimple, a ram, a monster and so on. They give a first indication of the two main styles or workshops of stone-carving that appear in the forties, fifties and sixties at the abbey, one favouring full, round forms, the other sharp, hard lines. The first tends to be more lyrical, the second more dramatic. (Does this decoration of the gallery mean some liturgical function here?)

The CLERESTORY has the same two-light windows with bar tracery as the chapels. The HIGH VAULT consists of oblong bays with quadripartite ribbing to which, however, is added a longitudinal ridge rib, broader than the others and given special prominence by stiff-leaf decoration. Big leaf bosses. The ridge rib is an English device, introduced partly for technical, partly for aesthetic reasons. The English way of filling vaulting cells as illustrated in the high vault of the Westminster chancel leads at the crown to an untidy edge. The bands of grey stones across the cells of chalk show that clearly. In France all stones for a cell were shaped individually so that, where the two halves of the cell would meet at the crown, they would lie snugly parallel to each other. The ridge rib in England hid the jagged edge. But at the same time it also established a connection from bay to bay which was the outcome of an English desire to break the logically impeccable isolation of the French bay with its quadripartite vault. The French in the c 13 (and even later) insisted on the finality of these divisions, the English wished to blur them and achieve spatial unity. So much for the ridge ribs of the Westminster chancel.

There are few published dates as to what was done from year to year at the abbey (see Colvin 1963, 1971). It seems, however, that the s transept, the e walls of the cloister, and the chapter house were all begun concurrently with the e end of the church, and arguments in favour of this will be offered as we proceed. For the moment all that can be done is to point out small differences within the chancel which indicate the progress of building. Most of them are enumerated in Lethaby's books. Pier bases in the apse and the first three N bays are more deeply hollowed out (i.e. again more like Reims) than pier bases in other parts. Instead of iron bars wooden bars were used here. They were also used on the s side between the ambulatory and the chapels of St Edmund and St Nicholas. In the three s bays of the arcade between chancel and ambulatory iron bars appear, running into the capitals. From the first straight bay of the chancel on the N side (counted from the e) and the second on the s side they were attached to iron hooks. Moreover, a difference in the size of the diapering in the spandrels can readily be noticed. The larger diaper is later. The smaller runs along the e end, the s side of the chancel, and the E side of the s transept. On the N side of the chancel within two of the spandrels the 'masons' muddle' of the meeting of the two sizes is unconcealed. The s transept also continues the voussoir enrichments of the galleries as in the chancel; the N transept has different foliage there, as we shall see later. Foliage altogether is a promising element to study for the tracing of the building development. It has recently been done in greater detail than can be attempted here. All that can be said is that from the beginning (e.g. in the capitals of the wall arcades in the various parts) three different types of foliage occur: crockets of the well-known French type, stiff-leaf of the English type and naturalistic leaves. Naturalistic leaves were an innovation in France of about 1240–5. They occur at the Sainte Chapelle and at Reims and represent in visual terms the turn towards an interest in nature, man and incident – also noticeable in C 13 philosophy, science, and poetry – and so fully exemplified in Southwell chapter house later in the century.

To sum up. What is likely as the sequence of events in these first five or six years is this: the N piers and arches of the chancel are a little earlier than those on the s, but then the s spandrels and galleries and the s transept were built – how far we do not yet know – before the N transept. If, as we assume, both transepts, and the crossing, and the first bay of the nave were ready or nearly ready by 1255, the differences in time are in any case very small. It should be added that Westminster Abbey may be more closely connected with royal workshops in and around Paris than with Reims. The E end plan, the tall narrow elevation, the gallery and clerestory could all come from Royaumont Abbey, dedicated 1236.

We must now proceed to the SOUTH TRANSEPT. It is, like the N transept, four bays deep and has E and w aisles. To the E of the first bay of the E aisle is a square chapel in the angle between chancel and transept, the Chapel of St Benedict. The aisle and s wall of the transept continue the system of the chancel. On the w side of the s transept, however, a strange irregularity is that the w aisle is occupied by part of the E walk of the cloister. (This also occurs elsewhere on a smaller scale, e.g. at Oxford Cathedral.) A solid wall to the height of the cloister roof, which is considerably lower than aisle height, separates this 'aisle' from the main transept. On the roof of the cloister walk, that is, still inside the aisle, is an extra (as it were, entresol) storey partly open to nave and transept. The function of that open part, like a deep balcony, has been much debated: although Lethaby thought it might be the royal pew (see also *Nave* below), both access and view of the altar were too poor for that, as the Abbey Librarian points out. Possibly it was used by the abbot or by musicians. Now it is part of the Muniment Room, reached via the Library and cloisters. The screen-wall below it (w side

of transept) is given two tiers of blank arcading with stiff-leaf capitals and some diapering in the spandrels, still visible behind the monuments. From the elevated position of the Muniment Room it is ideally easy to study the bosses of the w aisle vault above it, bosses about 30 in. in diameter. They have, unlike anything in the E parts of the building, figures and scenes, as also a Coronation of the Virgin in the E bay of the nave's s aisle, just N of the Muniment Room. They are not completely preserved, but there are three more bosses which can be studied in comfort in the Muniment Room, and these are amongst the most perfect works of sculpture at Westminster Abbey. They are in the rib-vaulted soffits of a group of three stepped lancet windows to the s, part of the transept s wall, and distantly visible from the floor of the s transept. The scenes represented are unexplained, combats of a man and a centaur, a dragon and a centaur, etc. The carving is precise and angular, the faces and draperies are sharply lined, and the actions conducted with great energy.

At ground-floor level, blank arcading is carried on in the transept E aisle. Here on the E side, close to the s end, is a doorway with one of the typical Westminster arches: depressed pointed arches raised by inserted vertical pieces above the jamb-shaft capitals. (Variants on the Westminster arch occur at Salisbury Cathedral, where they may relate to Henry III's masons' work at Clarendon Palace.) The doorway, though small, may have had an important function as the king's private entrance from Westminster Palace, not far from the Shrine. (But the remains of a very narrow staircase visible on the E and s sides of the transept do not suggest access to a royal pew in the Muniment Room.)

The treatment of the s wall of the transept 'nave' is as follows. The ground floor has five blank arches on shafts. The voussoirs are ornamented with rosettes. Diapered spandrels. Some capitals with leaf carvings. Wall-passage above with pointed-cusped arches, decorated cusp spandrels and diapered main spandrels. Above the wall-passage a tier of six lancet windows with deep embrasures, and above that, on a level with the gallery, three pairs of lancet windows continue the design of the gallery openings. There is, however, one motif which singles out this wall. The spandrels above the twin openings have, instead of simple diapering, figures of censing angels on the l. and r., and (damaged) figures of St Edward and the Pilgrim in the middle. The angels are the best pieces of large C 13 figure sculpture in the abbey, in their facial type obviously derived from Reims, and more exactly from the style of the master of the Joseph, the Anna, and the smiling Angels of the Reims w front, figures that must date from about 1245. The English carver – the same who did the bosses in the window soffits of the Muniment Room – has given their limbs and the folds of their mantles an almost alabaster-

87. LONDON: WESTMINSTER ABBEY
Censing angel, c. 1250–5, south transept south wall

like sharpness and an emphasis on line typical of his country. Nothing could be more characteristic than the rendering of the bones in the foot of the l. angel. The rose-window above was renewed c. 1890, but its forms are so convincingly of the c 15 that it probably represents the design introduced c. 1460. For the s transept as Poets' Corner, see *Furnishings* below.

ST FAITH'S CHAPEL, now usually entered here, was built c. 1250 between the s wall of the s transept and the chapter-house vestibule. Uncommonly well preserved. Of irregular shape (as an afterthought), consisting of a w part of two bays and an E part of one. The two are separated by a two-centred arch. At the w end runs a gallery on a tunnel-vault, which connected the dormitory with the night stairs in the s transept. In the w part the N wall has three bays of large blank arcading with Westminster arches. It is covered by quadripartite rib-vaulting. The E part has an irregular sexpartite vault. Mouldings as in the adjacent chapter-house vestibule. The ribs spring from head-corbels of remarkable eloquence. They are amongst the best and certainly the best-preserved in the abbey. Why are those on the N side so evil-looking? Could they represent the executioners at the martyrdom of the saint? On the wall painting, see *Furnishings*.

The system of the NORTH TRANSEPT is the same as that of the s transept. The chapel corresponding to that of St Benedict was in its lower part filled in the early c 16 with Abbot Islip's Chapel, and the loft of this allows a close view of the ribs and vault of the c 13 chapel. The E and w aisles have excellent blank arcading with leaf decoration in the spandrels, partly stiff-leaf, partly naturalistic, and also with dragons (w aisle) and figure scenes (w aisle, e.g. a

censing angel; also E aisle, N wall). Even the earlier French form of the crocket survives (E aisle N wall). In the w aisle, as in that of the s transept, are bosses with figures too, e.g. King David with the harp, Moses and Aaron, and an exquisite Annunciation. In the E aisle corresponding to the royal door is another small doorway. It has again the Westminster arch with its vertical pieces above the capitals of the jamb-shafts.

The gallery is essentially like those of chancel and s transept, but the leaf decoration of the voussoirs is noticeably deeper in the cutting and richer in the foliage design. Also it will be remembered that the size of the diapers below the gallery openings is larger than in the s transept E wall and the chancel.

The N wall is similar to the s transept s wall, but the portals to the N make some adjustments necessary. The double doorway in the middle again has Westminster arches. So has the single N doorway in the w aisle. The voussoirs are again given fleuron-like studding with rosettes. The spandrels have figures as well as leaves. The arrangement of wall-passage, tier of six windows, paired windows at gallery-level, and rose-window is the same as in the s. But in the E and w walls of the tier of six windows are two standing figures in relief, unconvincingly called Edward the Confessor and Henry III. In the soffits of the six windows is a beautiful chorus of angels, busts in medallions, altogether twenty-four, making music, censing, holding a dial (?), and so on. They are outstanding examples of the soft, full, rounded style of sculpture which runs parallel at Westminster with the sharp style of the censing angels of the s transept. Of the corresponding N transept spandrel figures only the two outer ones remain, also considerably less slim and alabaster-like. The middle spandrels have thick stiff-leaf scrolls and corbels for lost figures. One of these is enriched by an extremely telling bearded head.

The rose-window is most unfortunately renewed. Its original shape is known. It had sixteen lancet lights radiating from the hub, on which stood thirty-two lancet lights in sixteen twin groups. The spandrels had foiled circles, all motifs organically belonging to the architecture of Westminster and at the same time developed from French precedent. The four spandrels above and below the rose were glazed, an exceedingly 'modern' thing to do at that moment.

The CROSSING is marked by four big soaring Purbeck piers, enriched by shafts. Each of the four arches stands on one strong round shaft. Between them in the diagonals are groups of three thin shafts. On these high up rise round shafts connected with the projected design of the lantern. The piers have only one tier of shaft-rings. The lantern is in a highly temporary-looking state: Wyatt's vault here was destroyed in the last war. We do not know what the

C 13 masters wanted it to look like, as the lantern was only added in the C 18 (see *Exterior*). The choir originally occupied the crossing as well as the C 13 nave bays w of it. Stone screens behind the C 13 choir stalls cut off the crossing from the transepts till 1775.

The NAVE dates partly from the C 13, probably from before 1269, and partly from the time of the resumption of work under Abbot Litlyngton. The master then, as we said, may have been *Henry Yevele*. Work started in 1375 and went on into the C 16. The joint between the two periods can easily be detected if one looks for it, but it remains remarkable that the design did not alter more. One might expect work of the resoundingly Perp character of the Winchester and Canterbury naves, so different in elements and proportions. But reverence for the C 13 – and for the abbey's unique status – was preferred by mason and abbot. Or was it especially the preference of Cardinal Langham († 1376), former Abbot of Westminster, former Archbishop of Canterbury, and source of some of the money? The present Keeper of the Muniments considers Abbot Litlyngton the chief influence, as he is known to have been responsible for continuing the use of Purbeck for columns. At any rate, these men continued with a minimum of change what had been done, and we have every reason to be grateful to them, since four bays of this nave were already built. A radical change of style as we see it in the E parts of Ely or the w parts of St Albans may be historically very instructive, but it ruins almost without exception the aesthetic value of the interior in which it happens (though not the poignant survival value in what is unevenly embedded at St Albans, q.v.; see also the General Introduction above on different sorts of reverence and the matter of consistency *versus* the organic view of development). At Westminster, thanks to an actively conservative attitude of mind in 1375 and after, we can maintain the illusion of a work all of one design – indeed an English Reims or Chartres.

The first job of a detailed survey of the nave must be to compare its C 13 bays with the transepts and the chancel. Such a comparison will show how French forms were progressively englished. The first bay of the nave (corresponding to the transept w aisles, not a windowed bay) had of course for the sake of the safety of the crossing to be erected at the same time as the bays N, S and E of the crossing. So there are still some features in common with the other parts of 1245–c. 1255, which are then at once modified or dropped. The piers e.g. have marble shaft-rings. From the second pair of piers they were to be of bronze. The vaulting-shafts stand on the capitals and abaci of the arcade piers. From the second piers they have no intervening capitals, and of the abaci only one roll moulding, exactly like a shaft-ring, is kept. Also the voussoirs of the gallery arches have leaf enrichments, which were then

given up. On the other hand already the first pier has eight instead of four shafts, four detached and four attached, the wall arcades have shields (perhaps the earliest architectural heraldry in England, but see below) in the spandrels instead of foliage and figures as in chancel and transepts, the gallery windows are different (see *Exterior*) and, above all, the high vault is different. But vaulting need not of course have been done at once.

Although the first bay, as we have seen, belongs to before 1255, the next bays were only begun after the king in 1258 ordered demolition 'juxta sedem regis', that is of the Norman work beyond the royal pew, which seems to have been at or near the crossing. But if the wall arcades of the aisles with the spandrel shields were ready by 1264, the latest admissible date because of inclusion of Simon de Montfort's shield (N aisle, third bay from E), and if all the C 13 work was ready and vaulted in 1269, we can date the vaults safely within the years of *Robert of Beverley*. It has been suggested that the heraldic details were added later; but it has also been suggested that all the C 13 aisle bays with their shields were made before 1258 and the demolition order of that year concerned bays farther w, not rebuilt till the C 14. The high vaults have, in addition to the longitudinal ridge ribs of chancel and transepts, transverse ridge ribs and one tierceron in each cell. That is almost the system of Lincoln nave and Ely presbytery, except that their transverse ridge ribs stop partway, whereas Westminster nave's N–S ridge ribs are fully developed. In the aisles the wall-passage continues in front of the windows. The S aisle at its very beginning, below the Muniment Room, has an exceedingly fine doorway into the cloister with another of those Westminster arches with almost straight-sided depressed head and vertical pieces above the capitals of the jamb columnettes. These pieces are exceptionally high here. The voussoirs have leaf scrolls forming medallions. To the l. and r. of the doorway a blank stilted lancet arch. Above the whole group three large blank quatrefoils, in the same somewhat coarse style as the N cloister walk.

The joint between C 13 and C 14 runs about the fifth bay (fourth windowed bay) from the crossing. The sixth piers have polygonal bases and capitals to the attached shafts, and a different moulding of the shaft-rings. The arch mouldings also differ. But all that is negligible in the general impression. More noticeable are the differences in aisle and clerestory windows. From the sixth bay (fifth windowed bay) the two lancet lights of each window now receive cusps, and the foiled circle is replaced by an uncircled quatrefoil – both motifs which are in no way opposed to C 13 custom. (But the fifth clerestory bay is unlike those E and w of it. There are both Purbeck and stone shafts. The window has uncusped lights and an encircled quatrefoil, but the window opening is of the same shape as those farther w. Dr D. M. Palliser suggests that this window could be of intermediate date between the c 13 and c 14 work, providing a starting-point for the c 14 interpretation.) The outer walls of the aisles carry on their blank arcading, but the shields are now painted and not carved, and the foliage and small-scale sculpture are clearly of a different age, especially the charming small figure of a saint in the seventh bay from the E on the N side. In the gallery the level changes slightly, the details of the twin openings differ a little and – most obvious of all changes – the diapering of the spandrels ceases. The design of the high vaults remains the same, but the bosses from the end of the fourth bay onwards are Perp in detail and no longer c 13. It is thus clear that the time of Henry III saw the building of the aisles and the nave walls five bays from the crossing, but the vaulting of only four bays. These four bays, incidentally, now contain (first three bays) the choir stalls and (fourth bay) the organ loft.

The bays under the WEST TOWERS are set off by a bigger and more elaborate pair of piers. The upper walls continue their system except that the gallery arches are subdivided by quatrefoil instead of single shafts, and the clerestory tracery differs. (In the s w tower on the first floor a c 17 brick fireplace was found, and this has been connected with the Civil War rumour that John Bradshaw, when living in the Deanery, built himself a study 'on the roof' of the abbey.) The w wall of the nave has Perp blank arcading round the doorway and above it the seven-light window with four transoms (renewed in the c 18). Willis called the design 'the merest stone grating'. The whole wall is framed by canted panelling. The w end was begun and probably in its entirety designed by the c 14 master whom we suppose to have been *Yevele* (see *Exterior*, w front), but it was not completed until after 1500 (w window glazed 1506–12).

While we do not usually mention the carpentery of great church roofs invisible to the visitor above the vaulting, it can be said that the abbey's original ROOFS remained until (very necessary) mid-c 20 reconstruction. Unfortunately no record of the nave and s transept timberwork was made before its removal, but the Royal Commission on Historical Monuments in 1964 was able to record the roofs of the chancel and N transept, then still extant. According to Lethaby, the c 15 nave roof had 'stout rafters about 9 in. square', with collar purlins carried by crown-posts, and straight braces. Tie-beams were added at the time of Wren's restoration. The c 13 roofs over choir, transepts and the E bays of the nave had upper and lower collars with scissor-braces crossing the lower collars. In the N transept there were additional longitudinal diagonal braces. Scissor-braced roofs were already being constructed c. 1200. The Royal Commission's survey concludes that the technique of the c 13 roof construction 'lacked any of the spirit of

innovation and any of the French influence which characterised the masons' work in the abbey' (*Archaeologia*, Vol. 100, 1966). Innovations in roofing were yet to be an entirely English development.

HENRY VII's CHAPEL, 1503–c. 1512, is the last medieval work at Westminster (on *Janyns*, the probable mason, see *Exterior*). The chapel was begun with a view to being a shrine of Henry VI, who Henry VII hoped might be canonized, and at the same time a chantry chapel for himself. In his will Henry VII stipulated that in the chapel 10,000 masses should be said for his soul. The chapel is detached except for its vestibule, which (cf. the relation between the side doorways and the vault below Henry V's Chantry) has the same width as that of the c 13 Lady Chapel. The vestibule is entered by three doorways. In it a broad staircase of twelve steps rises to a level only a little below that of the chapel pavement. The walls of the vestibule are fully panelled and traceried. A transverse depressed four-centred tunnel-vault covers it. Small side entries lead into the aisles of the chapel, which are to the eye wholly cut off from the nave by the chapel stalls. The chapel itself is entered by another triple doorway.

It consists of a nave with aisles of four bays and a polygonal chancel with five radiating chapels. The arcade has depressed four-centred arches. The windows of the aisles and chapels have been described (see *Exterior*). From inside, their fanciful and broken shapes are even more attractive than from outside. The clerestory has five-light windows. The w window over the entrance is of fifteen lights. The walls are clothed with a wealth of sculpture unparalleled in any English church interior – perhaps only because so infinitely much was destroyed everywhere in the country in the c 16 and c 17. There are tiers of figures above the arcade, figures against the E walls of the aisles, figures against the walls of the five E chapels, small figures in two tiers on the panelling of the broad arch between nave and chancel. There were more than 100 figures in the chapel originally, and nearly all of them survive. The chapel was intended to sparkle with colour and gilding, but there is no sign of the king's instructions to paint the figures ever having been carried out (Colvin (1975) quoting Micklethwaite).

The aisles and chapels are fan-vaulted with pendants, and the nave and chancel have a vault which is without doubt the climax and triumphant symphony of this chapel. It seems a fan-vault of the most glorious richness and size, but it is not – it is a superbly ingenious fantasy on the theme of fan-vaulting. The vault is in fact a groin-vault divided into bays by strong transverse arches with a fringe of cusping. These are given a form similar to (and influenced by) the arched braces of timber roofs. Thence also comes the openwork tracery in the spandrels. Then, however, at a certain height, these transverse arches dis-

88. LONDON: WESTMINSTER ABBEY Henry VII Chapel, 1503–c. 1512, looking west

appear in the solid vault and only their cusping remains visible. The place where this change occurs is marked by huge pendants of fan shape. They are structurally in fact part of the wedge-stones of the arches or braces but appear like fans suspended in the air. The rest of the vault is panelled all the way through as if it were a normal fan-vault. One can almost call the whole design of this vault a design for nave and aisles with the arcade piers removed. The wealth of detail especially at the chancel end defeats description. Technically it is all a spectacular *tour de force*. The thickness of the vault is pared down to a mere 3½ in., the same as Bath Abbey's, though at St George's Windsor it was thinner – and proved unsound (Leedy 1975). The source of the conception of the vault was undoubtedly at Oxford, partly in the Divinity School vault of 1480–3 but more in its subtler successor of *c.* 1500 at Christ Church (see *Oxford Cathedral*) – grafted on to the mason's long family experience of fan-vaulting. For two interpenetrating systems are uniquely combined here.

So far as the ARCHITECTURAL SCULPTURE is concerned an immediately prior and seemingly preparatory work should be noted in passing, much smaller and not well documented: Prince Arthur's Chantry, begun 1504, at Worcester Cathedral (q.v.). The sculpture of Henry VII's Chapel deserves more comment. In the chapels and against the E walls of the aisles stand large figures, and below them run friezes with demi-figures of angels. Above the arcade runs again a frieze of demi-figures of angels and then a tier of smaller figures, five for each bay. (A frieze of demi-angels on the w wall over the entrance is at present silhouetted against c 20 strip-lighting.) It is clear at once that more than one master was active here and more than one workshop. There are two styles side by side, one of long, erect, nobly placid figures, one of nimbly moving figures with angular broken drapery folds. Some figures even still have the heavily hanging mantles with thick rounded folds which go back to the Burgundian style of 1400 and after. Specially good examples of the erect placid type are the figures at the E end of the N aisle, specially good examples of the lively type the five small figures above the opening of the NE chapel. We do not know the names of individual carvers. What is certain, however, is that amongst the imagers and the craftsmen recorded as carving at the beginning of the c 16 for the King's Works there were quite a number of men with Netherlandish names, *Derrick van Grobe, Giles van Casteel, Nicholas Delphin.*

FURNISHINGS AND MONUMENTS

Preface

First a few words on changing attitudes to the abbey's crowd of monuments. It is hard to visualize this interior as

it was in the c 13, the purity of its architecture nowhere concealed (save for painting and gilding, but that is another matter). The Shrine of the Confessor stood behind the high altar, and there were altars in the ambulatory chapels. A pulpitum ran across the nave w of the choir, but otherwise there was nothing to deflect attention from the building and the enrichments belonging immediately to it. In the c 14 a garland of royal tombs appeared round the Confessor's shrine, and then tombs were put up in the chapels. They were of relatives of the kings, of abbots and former abbots, some bishops and a few others. How few there were still about 1600 is evident from Camden's description. Besides, the tombs were of modest size in relation to the height of the arcades and the whole building.

The first megalomaniac monuments were Late Elizabethan, on the sites of pre-Reformation altars recently made available. Some tombs of Elizabeth's and James I's courtiers were more sumptuous, more massive and higher than the tomb of Elizabeth herself. The types of Elizabethan monuments are basically few: such motifs as coffered arches, flanking columns, obelisks and strapwork cartouches repeat time and again. Then the first half of the c 17 brought a great liberation of iconography. *Nicholas Stone*'s inventiveness on a small as on the largest scale is astounding. The abbey has five of his larger works. He was trained on the Continent, and from the Continent also came *Le Sueur* (four works in the abbey). After the Commonwealth a move towards simplicity of monuments was noticeable: quite a number of those in the abbey dispensed with effigies and figures altogether. About 1700 a new aspiration to grandeur and eloquence appeared, and the final outcome was the spectacular allegorical machines of *Roubiliac* and his like, heavy in weight, ingenious in conceit, brilliant in execution. (The abbey has seven Roubiliacs, sixteen *Scheemakers*, seventeen *Rysbracks*.) The transition from this Baroque to a Classical Revival and finally a Grecian taste can be followed in all shades. Yet John Wesley († 1791) could still admire Roubiliac's Hargrave and Nightingale monuments. (Perhaps a comparison could be drawn with the exuberant certainties of early Methodist hymns.) A guide-book of 1835 still says of the Nightingale monument (N transept E aisle) that it was 'a capital performance'. But John Carter, in so many antiquarian matters ahead of his time, had written in 1799 foretelling that Lord Bourchier's c 15 tomb (NE ambulatory) might soon have to make way for 'the statue of some overgrown nabob or some harpy fattened on widows' and orphans' tears'. While that is not a strictly aesthetic objection, Carter no doubt meant to voice one. (In 1772 the c 14 Aymer de Valence monument in the sanctuary had indeed been in danger of replacement by General Wolfe's giant memorial.) In 1807 Robert Southey wrote that 'most of the monuments' in the abbey 'are wholly worthless in their design and execution', but he added: 'the few which have any merit are the work of foreigners' – so Roubiliac and Rysbrack were probably exempt from censure. (Southey's own monument of the 1840s in Bristol Cathedral was to be by the English *Baily*.)

The C 19 preferred statues to larger compositions. A feeling that damage was done to the abbey by such crowding does not seem to have arisen until the medieval revival had reached the stage when ritual demands and demands for architectural purity were made. That was with Pugin and the Cambridge Camden Society. The tone becomes vehement with Pugin. (But no monument in the Abbey was designed by him.) He speaks of 'the incongruous and detestable monuments' (1835), the 'cumbrous groups of pagan divinities', the *Ecclesiologist* in its second volume of 'revolting monuments' and 'wax dolls', John Weale in 1851 of 'the most odious that mute matter could by any torture be made to embody' (compare the 1920s on the contents of the 1851 Exhibition), Bohn's *Pictorial Handbook* (1851) of 'vulgar ostentation', the 'advertising van' and 'Madame Tussaud', Ruskin of the 'ignoble incoherent fillings of the aisles'. And Dickens in *Our Mutual Friend* (1865, Book 3, Chapter 17) described the 'full-length engraving of the sublime Snigsworth . . . snorting at a Corinthian column, with an enormous roll of paper at his feet, and a heavy curtain going to tumble down on his head; those accessories being understood to represent the noble lord as somehow in the act of saving his country'.

Fortunately nothing came of a grand Late Victorian fuss over provision for monuments in some new Campo Santo. This was heralded by a Scott report as early as 1854, and culminated in a Royal Commission in 1890 to consider proposals by Pearson, Seddon and others for new cloisters or great towers dwarfing the abbey (Jordan 1980; Physick and Darby, *Marble Halls*, 1973; and Sir Herbert Baker even designed a memorial cloister for the F end in the C 20). More fortunately for England's treatment of its past, there was William Morris. From him there is plenty to choose from on the subject of the monuments: 'idiocies', 'monstrous and ghastly pieces of perversity and bluntness of feeling', 'aberration of the human intellect', 'Cockney nightmares' (N P asks 'why Cockney?', but the Baroque still flourished in the City of London), 'pieces of undertakers' upholstery', 'the most hideous specimens of false art that can be found in the whole world'. Yet Morris was a wise as well as an honest man and he did not recommend that the monuments should be removed, as misguided medieval enthusiasts do to this day. For he knew that the monuments had become part of the structure of the fabric and that to remove them would mean 'making good' with imitation-Gothic. That is the truth of the matter.

It is sheer perversity to deny that the monuments lessen the impact of the architecture. One can see the building as a

building only from a few vantage-points, in the chancel looking across and up, looking E through the crossing from the choir, or obliquely from the Muniment Room, and so on. The architecture of the abbey possesses an uncommon unity of style. Variety is as good a principle of art as unity. But variety must be contrived and controlled. With the monuments it is the outcome of accident, of actions not in the least concerned with aesthetic value. Such places as the E aisle of the N transept or the N W tower bay are no more than overcrowded repositories of figures (at monument-level, for the architecture remains overhead). The nave aisles are frankly an exhibition of monuments. One walks along them as one walks through the rooms of the Royal Academy. If in doing that one succeeds in forgetting where one is, one may well derive a great deal of enjoyment from the artistry of many of the monuments. (There speaks the great art historian. Perhaps for some of us in this place, aesthetic enjoyment is inseparable from remembering where one is: the subjects of the epitaphs walked here in life, the monuments have roots here, just as every English parish church would be less than itself without its memorials. And so pure aesthetics may never be enough; one may prefer to relish the abbey's peculiar complexity.)

However, the attempt must now be made to appreciate the monuments on their merits, not on the merits or demerits of their appearance in this place. Yet how can literally hundreds of them be discussed in the compass of a book such as this? To the author it would have been very tempting to describe them historically. The result would have been a fairly full history of English monumental sculpture from the C 13 to the C 19. But no user could find his way from one monument to the next without covering in the process many miles forward and backward. So the descriptions are arranged topographically, entailing some cross-referencing. As the abbey contains so much of furnishings also, a division between furnishings and monuments is not consistently maintained.

First, to recall the topography. E of the high altar, at the heart of the apse and with the floor-level raised high above the ambulatory, is the feretory (from Latin *feretrum*, bier or shrine), i.e. the Chapel of St Edward the Confessor. Enclosing the shrine on N, S and E, the ambulatory chapels culminate in the Henry VII Chapel. W of the reredos, high altar and sanctuary are immediately E of the crossing. The crossing and transepts, originally separated by screens, are now visually continuous. The choir, never E of the crossing, used to occupy both the crossing and the first three bays of the nave, but now only those bays with the organ loft over the fourth bay. The nave proper occupies only the bays W of that. Our sequence goes: feretory, including Henry V Chantry; sanctuary; ambulatory S W–N W, then ambulatory chapels, S W–N W but ending with Henry VII Chapel; crossing (for choir, see *Nave*); S transept (Poets'

Corner) with St Benedict's and St Faith's Chapels; N transept; nave and choir: N aisle E to w with N choir aisle, main nave w to E with pulpitum and choir, s aisle w to E with s choir aisle; gallery. (Monuments in the cloisters etc. are in the following section.) On the visitor's rather different sequence, enforced by tourist-traffic rules, see the warning at the head of our text on the abbey. The plans in the *Official Guide*, placing the monuments, are a great help. A reminder: the C13 architectural sculpture of the transept end-walls and the ambulatory chapels, like that of the C16 in the Henry VII Chapel, is treated with the architecture (*Interior* above).

Feretory   The back of the REREDOS forms the w side of the feretory. This is work of the C15, probably second quarter, and has a frieze with stories from the life of Edward the Confessor. Trefoils between the scenes, and a ribbon running below the scenes and around the trefoils to link them all up. Originally statues stood below the frieze. Elaborately vaulted canopies are above their places. The wall otherwise is panelled, and there are two doorways. (For the front of the reredos, and figures originally above it, see *Sanctuary* below.) – Some C13 TILES below the reredos.

The SHRINE and PAVEMENT now to be described remind us that at Canterbury St Thomas à Becket's costly shrine, consecrated there in 1220 with its inlaid pavement, provided an example to outdo at Westminster. PAVEMENT. Abbot Richard Ware (1258–83), in 1268, obtained from Rome porphyry, jasper and marble for a pavement and apparently also Italian masters to lay it down and do other work. The pavement, a document says, came from 'the court of Rome', i.e. the Pope, 'to the King's use in the church at Westminster before the great altar'. That refers to the sanctuary. But the feretory has a pavement of the same entirely Roman type, the type known as Cosmati work and characterized by a mixture of porphyry slabs in red and green and glass mosaic. The most frequent forms are circles surrounded by ribbons intertwined or plaited. A payment in 1267–8 for the 'caementarii pavatorum' before the feretory may refer to the pavement here or to that w of the high altar. Another payment of 1271–2 speaks of paving before the altars. There was in the feretory indeed an altar of the Confessor, and a celebrated Relic Altar once stood at the E end. The pavement is mostly covered up, the hard Italian stones and softer Purbeck having worn unevenly. A difficulty arises over the name or names of the workman or workmen who came to work in distant England. The sanctuary pavement was signed by *Odericus* in 1268, the base of the Shrine itself by *Petrus Romanus* in 1270. Petrus was probably the son of Odericus (see *Shrine* below). These two practised the craft of Roman decorators known as the Cosmati. At the abbey they made not only

89. LONDON: WESTMINSTER ABBEY
Shrine of Edward the Confessor, 1268–70 and 1555

two pavements and the Shrine but also tomb-chests for Henry III (below) and his children (s ambulatory).

SHRINE OF EDWARD THE CONFESSOR. Henry III commissioned the shrine, before he began the new abbey, in 1241. It was a coffer with a saddleback roof, as we know from illustrations in illuminated manuscripts and as was the custom of C12 and C13 shrines. It was of 'purest gold and precious stones' (so Matthew Paris writes) and decorated with images. It stood high up on a tall base which survives, visible from the w above a high altar with a much lower reredos than the present one. The Venetian Ambassador Trevisani about 1500 wrote that not even the shrine of St Martin at Tours could compare with it. It is unrecorded when the shrine was destroyed. To the N and s of the base stood two pillars with the statues of the Confessor and the Pilgrim. The base is Cosmati work and was, as has just been said, signed by *Peter of Rome* and dated 1270. It has all the features of the pavement and in addition such typical Cosmati features as the twisted pillars at the corners meant to carry candles and the twisted colonnettes flanking the recesses – for kneeling in – below. The walls separating the recesses from each other and those on the N from those on the s are only about 5 in. thick. The recesses have trefoil-pointed heads, a Northern and Gothic motif probably unknown before 1270 in Italy. It recurs for the first time in the canopy under the equally Northern crocketed gable of the tomb of Pope Clement IV at Viterbo by *Petrus Oderisi*. This was completed in 1274, and we may assume from the signature that our Petrus Romanus was the son of Odericus and that both were in London together. Petrus later worked with Arnolfo di Cambio on the ciborium for S. Paolo fuori le Mura in Rome (1285). (Twisted pillars at a shrine may refer to the 'salomonic' columns – said to have come from Solomon's temple – at the name-saint's shrine in Old St Peter's, Rome: the perhaps similarly derived spiral-tooled Norman piers in Durham choir and Norwich nave are on quite a different scale and earlier than Westminster's shrine, which, however, is far more directly derived from Rome. On revivals of the 1630s, see *Salisbury*, Gorges tomb.) The shrine base, in addition to its exotic materials, is made of Purbeck marble. St Edward's coffin is now inside the base. The wooden superstructure that replaced the shrine is of two orders of Renaissance arches separated by pilasters, and dates from Mary I's time. E of the shrine an altar of relics stood where Henry V's Chantry is now.

CORONATION CHAIR. The chair was made by Master *Walter of Durham*, the King's Painter, in 1300–1 (P. Eames: 1299) to contain the Stone of Scone brought by Edward I from Scotland. It is of oak with arms curving up to the back. In the middle of the back rises a steep gable. The chair is decorated with blank arcading with circles, quatrefoils and trefoils, and was once entirely covered with decoration of *c.* 1330–50 in glass mosaic and gold leaf (P. Eames 1977). Naturalistic leaf patterns visible on the l. arm outside. The lions are not original; they may be of Tudor date.

STAINED GLASS. The three E windows of the clerestory have glass of many periods skilfully assembled. In the SE and E windows four large C 15 figures, in the NE window two large figures made up of fragments. Four shields may be essentially of the time of Henry III. But the only stained glass representing that time in its full glory is in the Jerusalem Chamber (see *Cloisters etc.*, other monastic remains, below). The assembling of the windows was done by Wren's glazier *Edward Drew*.

MONUMENTS. Edward I † 1307, large, completely undecorated black Purbeck tomb-chest, no effigy; the inscrip-

tion is mid-c 16. – Henry III † 1272. The base, much higher of course from the ambulatory than from the feretory, and the tomb-chest are the last of the Cosmati jobs in England. They cannot be dated with accuracy. Twisted columns at the angles arranged differently on the base and tomb-chest. On the s, towards the feretory, two trefoiled kneeling-niches l. and r., flanked by pilasters, and in the middle a pediment on pilasters, more 'Renaissance' than anything in England before Henry VIII. The arrangement is very similar to that of the Cosmati altar at S. Cesareo in Rome, where the side parts, however, are round-headed and not trefoiled. The effigy is of bronze gilded and was made by *William Torel* in 1291 (i.e. only added when Edward I was commissioning his queen's tomb; see below). Thin later

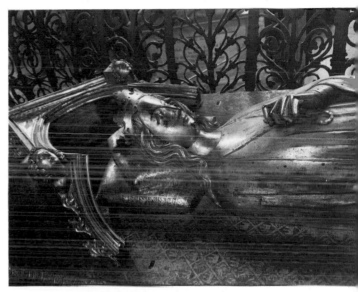

90. LONDON: WESTMINSTER ABBEY
Tomb of Eleanor of Castile, 1291, by William Torel

tester of timber. The figure is slim and frail with long limp hands and long feet with pointed shoes. Drapery with long parallel folds on the l. and r. and a few quiet loops across. Sensitive, far from vigorous face. The style is not like any surviving English or Continental late c 13 sculpture. The figure originally held the sceptre and another attribute. To its head was a canopy. The king's crown was enriched with jewels. – Elizabeth Tudor, daughter of Henry VII, † 1492. Small. Tomb-chest of Purbeck marble, lid of dark Lydian marble. The effigy has disappeared. – Queen Eleanor † 1290. Edward I's queen died at Hardby in Lincolnshire, and to mark the resting-places of the funeral cortège back to the abbey the Eleanor Crosses were erected, the last at Charing Cross. The tomb-chest of Purbeck marble has cusped blank arches under crocketed gables. Shields are suspended under the arches. They hung originally from branches of oak, maple, thorn etc. The effigy is again of gilded bronze and was made by *Torel* in the same year as Henry III's. The queen lies on a gilded bronze top plate nicely powdered with lions and castles (for Castile) and with marginal inscription in Norman French. Her robe and mantle flow down in the same long, fine, even, parallel folds as Henry III's. The face also has the same tender and vulnerable character. One hand held a sceptre. Above the head a pointed trefoiled arch projecting from the back plate and crowned by a simple gable. The small leaf crockets on the arch and gable are already no longer naturalistic. They have the knobbly shapes of the C14. The wooden tester is C15. Towards the ambulatory, curved IRON GRATE, made by *Thomas of Leighton*, 1294 (found in pieces and restored by *Scott*). The composition is in vertical bands of pairs of 'affronted' foliage scrolls, still resembling the stiff-leaf conventions of the earlier C13 (see similar work at Lincoln). A row of trident spikes on top. Also towards the ambulatory the tomb-chest stands on a plinth which is painted. The PAINTING represents a tomb-chest, with Sir Otes de Grandison (see the *Official Guide*) kneeling on the r. in front of the Virgin, and on the l. four courtiers or clerks (not monks).

For Henry V's Chantry at the E edge of the feretory, see below. Between it and St Edward's shrine, in the pavement, remains of two brass and glass mosaic tombstones, John de Valence and Margaret de Valence, † 1277 and 1276 respectively, part of the work of the Cosmati. They have crosses inlaid on the slabs.

Queen Philippa of Hainault † 1369. By *Hennequin de Liège*, a sculptor living in Paris and famous there. Blue marble tomb-chest with very damaged, originally daintily embroidered white marble niche-work. The difference from the treatment of tomb-chests forty and thirty years before is remarkable (see Aymer de Valence in the sanctuary and John of Eltham in St Edmund's Chapel). Equally remarkable is the difference in sculptural style. The elegant stylizing of the early C14 is here replaced by a new veracity, both in portrait and in costume. This is specially noticeable in the face of the queen and in the two happily preserved weepers at the NE end, recovered by Scott's detective work (Jordan 1980, and *Official Guide*). The figures are of marble and were originally painted and decorated with gold, glass and beads. To the l. and r. of the queen buttress strips with four tiers of niches for figures. Pretty filigree canopy. The wooden tester may be original. It is very modest. – Edward III † 1377. (By *Henry Yevele*?) Tomb-chest of Purbeck marble with six flat recesses separated by two-tier panelling. In the recesses exquisite little, rather toy-like, yet very realistic bronze figures of weepers (representing the king's children, according to shields be-

low). The effigy also is of bronze gilded. The bronze-work (or latten-work) was probably done by *John Orchard*, 'latoner', who worked in 1377 for Philippa's tomb. The effigy is impressive in the new calm way of which Chaucer's age was capable. None of the alluring mannerisms of the age of Edward II, nor anything of the (no less Chaucerian) liveliness of the image of Queen Philippa. Placid face with hair and beard in long even flow. The king's hands held two sceptres. The effigy is flanked by flat strips instead of buttresses, and on these are four tiers of small bronze angels. Simple three-sided canopy above the head of the effigy with concave-sided steep gables; vaulting inside. Oak tester in the form of a row of ogee-sided decorated gables and an openwork cusping. – Margaret of York, infant daughter of Edward IV, † 1472. Small dark marble tomb-chest; the brass effigy is missing. – Richard II and Anne of Bohemia, made in 1394–5, the stonework by *Yevele* and *Stephen Lote*, the effigies by *Nicholas Broker* and *Godfrey Prest*, coppersmiths. Tomb-chest of Purbeck marble so similar to that of Edward III that one is inclined to attribute that also to *Yevele*. The chest is decorated with buttresses and canopied recesses. The gilded bronze top plate, the pillows and the effigies have exquisite engraved decoration with fleur-de-lys, lions, the white hart of Richard II, eagles, leopards, ostriches, broom-pods etc. The style of the effigies is still that of gentle long parallel folds – a surprising evenness of tradition over a hundred years. Dare one call it English? Excellently characterized faces. Two separate plain canopies above their heads. Simple wooden tester with faded PAINTING by *John Hardy* of the Coronation of the Virgin, Christ in Majesty, and two pairs of angels.

HENRY V's CHANTRY. The plan was made in the form in which it was executed, as early as 1415, when the king made his will. The idea is most ingenious and succeeds in fitting a complete and quite roomy chantry chapel into the congested space along the margin of the feretory. The tomb is placed at r. angles to the apse and projects with its base a little into the ambulatory. Above it, and carried as a bridge across the ambulatory to the entrance of the former Lady Chapel, is the loft or upper stage with the altar. (On the new bridge over the ambulatory and under the loft, see *Henry VII Chapel* below.) Two spiral staircases lead up to it, placed in front of the two E piers of the apse. The little vaults at their tops are fans. The idea of such a tribune came from the relic tribune at the E end of the Sainte Chapelle. The king died in 1422 and the tomb was made in 1422–c. 1430. Purbeck tomb-chest with recesses with (rather French) depressed segmental heads, and effigy of a wooden core formerly sheathed with gilt silver. A new head and hands of polyester resin, by *Louisa Bolt*, were added to the effigy in 1971 (the silver originals disappeared during the Reformation): justified restoration to a body that had become a mutilated block of oak. The chantry stonework was prepared by 1440 and still unfinished in 1448. A mason working on the chapel is mentioned even as late as 1458. The staircase turrets are all of Perp openwork, the vault below the loft has elaborate lierne enrichments (closely visible from the new bridge below it), and the loft has parapets and an altar wall encrusted with ornament and statuary. Life-size figures against the stair-turrets. Frieze of small figures between the turrets. Two more such friezes against the outer walls of the N and S parapets, doubled, i.e. two tiers, at the E end to link up with the height of the reredos on the l. On the reredos one tier of larger figures. Two tiers again as a continuation of these, to the N and S, that is above the side entrances into the vestibule to the Chapel of Henry VII. Henry V appears twice on horseback, and twice crowned. The style of the sculpture is far from uniform. It ranges from a continuation of the conventions of c. 1300 (e.g. the so-called King Sebert, N turret, S W face; cf. Aveline, Sanctuary, Monuments) to the broken jagged angular draperies introduced in the Netherlands about 1430 (e.g. Annunciation above the altar). The small figures with the broken folds are on the whole of better quality than the long, stiff and lifeless, more traditional figures against the turrets. With the best in France and Germany hardly any can compare. – IRON GATE, made by Roger Johnson of London from 1428 to after 1431. With close diapering below, and Perp tracery above, said to be the earliest example in England of iron tracery. Scott found this and the C13 grating of Queen Eleanor's tomb broken and scattered, casualties of George IV's coronation (Jordan 1980).

When Henry V's Chantry was built, the available space in the feretory was filled. Queen Katherine, Henry V's queen, was buried in the former Lady Chapel, Henry VI at Chertsey Abbey (removed to Windsor).

Sanctuary

At the abbey the whole space before the high altar is called either the sanctuary or the presbytery, and we follow the *Official Guide*. The front of the REREDOS is of 1866–73 (for the C15 back, see Feretory above). Scott was 'much criticized for its outrageous confidence and richness' (Jordan 1980, pointing out that Scott replaced, not ancient work, but a plaster remodelling of 1824 by *Bernasconi* under Benjamin Wyatt, although Scott was able to find remains of an original recess and old cresting to guide him). He used sumptuous materials for this backdrop to the altar at the heart of Empire (the latter doubtless the prose of Dean Stanley): alabaster, marbles, cedar, porphyry and jewels, with a Last Supper in mosaic by *Salviati* to the design of *J. R. Clayton* of Clayton & Bell, and statues by *H. H. Armstead*. Before the Reformation there stood on the cornice of the reredos a kind of triptych with large figures of St Peter and St Paul to l. and r. Above this a tester was suspended from the rood-beam on which were the Crucifixus, the Virgin, St John and seraphim. (An early C16 view of it is preserved on the Islip Roll showing that abbot's funeral). See also the C13 retable in the S ambulatory.

PAVEMENT. The largest work of Abbot Ware's Cosmati, signed originally by *Odericus Romanus* and dated 1268. The signature and other long inscriptions were in bronze. The pattern of the mosaic corresponds to those in the feretory (see above; and cf. the pavement of c. 1220 at Canterbury).

SEDILIA. c. 1308. Made in conjunction with the monument to the legendary Sebert (see S ambulatory). To the ambulatory four tall cusped pointed arches with steep gables and encircled quatrefoils below them. To the sanctuary gabled canopies with encircled openwork trefoils below the gables. Finely carved small heads between the canopies. The most important thing about the sedilia is, however, the surviving PAINTINGS, perhaps by *Thomas of Durham*. There are three whole figures, 8 ft tall, and two more half-figures, all in the characteristic style of the earliest C14, more familiar from illuminated manuscripts than from monumental painting. At Westminster this style appears clearly as a somewhat more vigorously stylized development of that of the retable in the S ambulatory and the wall paintings of the S transept S wall. Strong, dark colours. Towards the altar two kings, towards the ambulatory more fragmentary figures including Edward the Confessor and the Annunciation.

MONUMENT. Anne of Cleves †1557. Only the base exists, low and long with four short broad pilasters with busy decoration still in the Early Renaissance, that is Quattrocento, style. But in the middle panels also more up-to-date motifs such as tapering pilasters. – Above the monument TAPESTRY with thick twisted columns flanking a composition with flowers in vases in a colonnaded architecture in perspective; Brussels, late C16. – PAINTING. Triptych by *Bicci di Lorenzo* (†1452), bequeathed by Lord Lee of Fareham. In the centre the Virgin with two angels, l. and r. saints. Frame with two medallions on top of the side wings. – Three brass chandeliers, C17, small in scale for this place.

MONUMENTS. Also visible from the ambulatory. Edmund Crouchback, Earl of Lancaster, brother of Edward I, †1296. The prototype of a considerable group of architecturally ambitious monuments made by the court workshops (possibly by *Michael of Canterbury*) for churches outside London as well (e.g. Archbishop Peckham †1292 at Canterbury, Bishop de Luda †1299 at Ely). Tomb-chest with small figures of weepers in recesses under crocketed gables, and large tripartite canopy, with

91. LONDON: WESTMINSTER ABBEY
Tombs of Edmund Crouchback † 1296 (r.), Aymer de Valence † 1324 (centre), and Edmund's wife Aveline † 1274 (l.)

small quadripartite vault inside. The centre has a cusped arch with leaf decoration of C 14 character in the cusps, a steep crocketed gable, and in the space below it diapering and a trefoil with a figure of a man on horseback. The side parts are narrow but similar in design. Under the gables towards the ambulatory, in a quite inconspicuous position, are the earliest ogee arches of the abbey. The weepers are in style so close to the large figures on the Eleanor Crosses, especially the Waltham Cross, that the same carver may well be responsible for both. The Waltham carver was *Alexander of Abingdon*, Imagour or Imaginator, a man traceable till 1312. The earl is represented cross-legged; two angels hold his pillow. The effigy, the weepers and the architecture were all painted and gilded. On the curiously clumsy brackets of the middle gable stood angels holding candles. Sumptuous big top finial. Base towards the

ambulatory with a frieze of painted knights, standing on a brown ground with small flowers. Dark green background as if meant to represent the dense leafage of a wood. – Aveline, Countess of Lancaster, Edmund's wife, † 1274, but the monument of about the same time as his. Almost the same composition, though with only one gable. Excellent quality of sculpture, though badly preserved. The countess wears a wimple, effigy in long robes, the Y-shape of the curves across and the main diagonals from the l. hip to the r. foot typical of the style of 1300. Two angels hold the pillow. This monument also was fully painted and gilt originally. – Aymer de Valence † 1324, Earl of Pembroke and cousin of Edward I. Again of the same type, but now characteristically adapted to the wishes of the Dec style. The main arch is cusped and sub-cusped, and cusps and sub-cusps have ogee forms. The foliage is richer, lusher and in fuller relief. High relief also for the recesses of the weepers. Circles between the gables of the recesses foiled and barbed. The weepers are more agile, suppler figures than those of Crouchback's tomb, a generation before. They are smaller below their arches, turn more easily into profile and demi-profile, and there is a certain irresponsibility and sensuality in the way they let their weight rest on one hip. The effigy is again cross-legged. At his head two angels holding a small figure which represents his soul.

Ambulatory, s w to n w

Although perambulating the ambulatory and its chapels is one performance, we separate the descriptions of their contents, starting with the ambulatory, as entered from the s transept. For the s chapels (except St Benedict's, for which see s *transept*) see *Chapels of St Edmund and St Nicholas*, and for the N chapels see *Chapels of St Paul, St John Baptist, Our Lady of the Pew*, and *Abbot Islip's Chapel* (which corresponds to St Benedict's but is shut off from the N transept), all below. For Henry VII's Chapel, see after Islip's. For royal monuments visible above the ambulatory, see *Feretory* and *Sanctuary* above.

IRON GATES, s w and n w. 1733, designed by *John James*, Surveyor to the Dean and Chapter from 1725 and to the Abbey from 1736.

MONUMENTS. King Sebert, forming part of the substructure of the sedilia (see *Sanctuary* above), 1308, niche with segmental arch; back wall with panelled tracery, including some straight-sided lozenge shapes. – Children of Henry III and Edward I. Tomb-chest of Purbeck marble, originally in the feretory. Cosmati decoration of *c*. 1270. Moved *c*. 1394. – Richard Tufton † 1631, hanging monument with white marble bust in oval niche, curved open pediment.

RETABLE, below Philippa's tomb and opposite the Chapel of St Nicholas. In spite of its fragmentary state, the finest piece of panel painting of its date in Northern Europe. Originally it may have been the retable or reredos of the high altar, or of another altar, or indeed (F Wormald) an antependium and not a retable at all. The size is 11 by 3 ft, the date quite uncertain. It may be of the time of the transfer of the body of the Confessor in 1269, or as late as the 1290s. The former opinion has been argued by Professor Wormald, the latter by Dr Margaret Rickert. Professor Wormald compared with manuscripts, Dr Rickert emphasized connections with Italian painting and sculpture and, in the decoration, with the Cosmati work in the abbey. Whether it is English or French work, it will perhaps never be possible to say. Even if made in London, foreign workmanship is by no means impossible. Amongst the court painters of Henry III were *John of St Omer, Peter de Hispania* (first mentioned in 1251), and *William of Florence*, but also *William*, a monk of Westminster, and *Walter of Durham* (who in 1262 painted in the Painted Chamber in the Palace of Westminster). The exquisite quality of the retable cannot discount either side. It is sufficient to look at English illumination of *c*. 1270 to credit England with work of the highest order. The retable consists of five parts. Parts one and five are (or were) St Peter and St Paul, under cusped arches and gables, parts two and four are sets of four star-shaped panels arranged as two tiers of two, and part three, i.e. the centre of the retable, has three cusped arches with gables. In the middle stands Christ, blessing with his r. hand and in his l. holding the world (with a minute landscape with animals, birds, and fishes). To the l. and r. are the Virgin and St John. The panels contain stories of the miracles of Christ. The three scenes which are still recognizable are the Raising of Jairus's Daughter, the Healing of the Blind, and the Feeding of the Hungry. The retable is enriched by painted glass in imitation of mosaic and by imitation cameos. The style of painting is very close to that of the illuminators. One must go close to it to appreciate the delicacy of transitions, especially in the modelling of the faces. What can be recognized of action is of great tenderness. The proportions of the figures are elongated, and the heads very small. The whole very small in scale (worth taking a magnifying glass) compared to the sedilia paintings in the sanctuary and the wall paintings in the s transept.

MONUMENTS. Sir Robert Ayton † 1638. Hanging monument of black and white marble, with a bronze bust in an oval niche. According to its style it seems to be by *Francesco Fanelli*. To its l. and r. standing stone figures of Apollo and Athene, very classical and sedate. Two mourning putti on the pediment. – Then we go under the bridge. At the entrance to the Chapel of St Paul: Lord Bourchier (see *Chapel of St Paul* below). – William Pulteney, Earl of Bath, † 1764 by *Wilton*, erected 1767. Reredos back with pilasters and pediment. Against the entablature portrait medallion with thin garlands. The main representations are the figures of Wisdom and Poetry, l. and r. of a big urn, one seated, the other standing. Strongly diagonal composition, but calm figures. – Admiral Holmes † 1761, also by *Wilton*. A late case of representation in Roman dress. The admiral is in an elegant pose with one hand on his hip, the other on a big gun, draped with a huge banner. Grey obelisk behind. – Lady Jane Crewe † 1639. Small relief of the young woman expiring on her bed; disconsolate husband and four children. The figures in a classical style, the atmosphere Italianate, the feeling genuine. Pilasters l. and r., and open pediment on top. – Against the N wall to the E of the Wolfe monument, another general, Sir J. Oughton † 1780, signed by *R. Hayward*.

Sir John Harpenden † 1457. Brass on Purbeck slab below the tomb of Aymer de Valence; knight, 4 ft 6 in. long. –

Earl Ligonier, 1773 by *J. F. Moore*. Dull, symmetrical composition. Fame stands in the middle, urn with portrait medallion on the l. below, trophies behind. – Abbot Esteney † 1498, brass on Purbeck slab, the figure 4 ft long, tripartite, 3 ft high gable above his head. – General Wolfe † 1759, by *Wilton*, erected 1772. Larger than any monument so far inspected. Battle relief of bronze on the plinth, two big lions at the angles. Huge pyramid shape behind made up of drapery against trees. The general reclines dying and semi-nude, tended by two soldiers. Fame flies in from on high on the l. The back of the monument faces into the E aisle of the N transept.

Chapel of St Edmund (S Ambulatory)

SCREEN. C 15, of wood, straight-topped. – MONUMENTS. Late thirteenth and fourteenth centuries: William de Valence † 1296, half-brother of Henry III. On a tomb-chest with shields in quatrefoils. On this an oak chest with scanty remains of architectural decoration, some of it with its original metal sheathing. The effigy is of copper plates on an oaken core, partly engraved and partly enamelled. The work was in all probability done at Limoges (cf. Bishop Maurice † 1238 at Burgos Cathedral in Spain, and Blanche de Champagne † 1283, Paris, Louvre), and so the only Limoges work remaining in England (other than the little portable shrine now at Hereford Cathedral). – John of Eltham, Earl of Cornwall, † 1337, brother of Edward III. Tomb-chest originally with tall slim tripartite canopy, the central gable taller than the others. Chest as well as effigy are of alabaster. It is one of the earliest monuments in that material. It seems that in the beginning alabaster was considered specially precious and used only for very special occasions; cf. Edward II, Gloucester Cathedral. Tomb-chest with niches for weepers, grouped in threes. The little figures are best preserved towards the ambulatory. They are very outré in the sway of their hips, and they step out as if dancing. (For the reaction against this excessive courtliness, see the natural, matter-of-fact little figures of Edward III's tomb of forty years later in the feretory, above.) Armoured effigy with crossed legs; two angels at the pillow. – Blanche of the Tower and William of Windsor † 1342 and 1348, made *c.* 1370–5, tiny tomb-chest with alabaster figures of a boy and a girl. – Earl of Stafford † 1762. Large white marble wall-tablet with painted inscription and coats of arms, signed by *Robert Chambers*.

Fifteenth century: in the middle of the chapel BRASSES, the first two the finest in the abbey. Eleanor Duchess of Gloucester † 1399, daughter of Humphrey de Bohun and wife of Edward III's youngest son; 5-ft figure in widow's dress; architectural surround with tripartite canopy and Bohun swan badge. – Robert Waldeby, Archbishop of York, † 1397, friend of the Black Prince; 5-ft figure and single canopy. – Humphrey Bourchier † 1471, tomb-chest with quatrefoils, with largely decayed brass, figure in armour. – Above this Sir Bernard Brocas † 1396. The effigy is characteristically different from that of John of Eltham, stiff and solid and no longer aspiring to elegance. Recess with straight top; l. and r. ogee-gabled niches. Over the centre three arches with ogee gables.

The other monuments from E to w: Frances Duchess of Suffolk, 1563. An important memento of what monuments of a high order were like at the beginning of Queen Elizabeth's reign. Still the free-standing tomb-chest of the Middle Ages, and still the recumbent effigy. Still reposeful attitude, no activity in the draperies. All marble. The tall tomb-chest, however, has panels with a little strapwork, and they are separated by pilasters. Roman colonnettes at the angles. The figure lies, after the new Netherlandish fashion, on a mat with the rolled-up top as her pillow. – Behind her feet to the l. Bishop Monck by *William Woodman*, 1723; obelisk and no effigy. – To the r. Francis Holles † 1622, aged eighteen, but already a soldier. By *Nicholas Stone* and with all the originality of that great sculptor. Seated figure in Roman dress, like a young Mars, on a drum-shaped pedestal with much Roman detail. The position of the figure is derived from Michelangelo's Medici effigies at S. Lorenzo in Florence. Inscription plate and thick garlands hanging down from female heads. – To his r. Elizabeth Russell † 1601. She died of consumption, aged twenty-six. Godchild of Queen Elizabeth and Leicester. Here already, before Stone, was a seated figure, though one that looks as if taken out of the context of a wall-monument where such seated figures do occur. And here also is the circular pedestal, though with much simpler detail. Bucrania, eagle, garland. – John Lord Russell † 1584. Standing wall-monument. He reclines stiffly on his side, hand against cheek, lying on a bulgy sarcophagus. A baby is placed against his feet. Shallow arch between columns, in the spandrels Victories. Against the back, shield held by two bedeswomen. – Farther w Sir Richard Pecksall † 1571, large tripartite standing wall-monument with four Corinthian columns. Three kneeling profile figures in niches, he higher up than his two wives. – Edward Talbot eighth Earl of Shrewsbury † 1618 and wife. The latest and the most ambitious monument in the chapel. Coffered arch on columns and an arch on each side. Big top achievement. Bulgy sarcophagus behind three pairs of black Ionic columns. Two recumbent effigies, his behind and a little above hers. One child kneels at her feet, turning away from the monument.

Chapel of St Nicholas (S Ambulatory)

SCREEN. Tall and plain, of stone, with three tiers of panelling, the lowest partly solid, the others pierced. Embattled top. From the time of Abbot William of Colchester (1386–1420).

MONUMENTS. To the r. of the entrance Philippa Duchess of York † 1431. Recumbent effigy on a tomb-chest with quatrefoiled and cusped panels carrying shields. – In the middle Sir George Villiers and his second wife, parents of the Duke of Buckingham. Made for £560 in 1631 by *Nicholas Stone*. Very big white marble sarcophagus with inscription and shields. Black marble top with white marble effigies, he in armour. Podgy and stodgy.

To the l. of the entrance Lady Cecil † 1591, wife of Sir Robert, later Earl of Salisbury. Small tomb-chest of alabaster with angle pilasters, the top obviously not belonging. – Then on, to the r., Lady Jane Clifford † 1679, black and white marble without any figures. Big square urn on feet to which cherubs' heads are attached. The inscription as if it were written on two pieces of parchment nailed to the tomb (cf. *Stone*'s for Julius Caesar † 1636, in Great St Helen's, City). – Countess of Beverley † 1812 by *Nollekens*. Large, very simple neo-Greek tablet. – Duchess of Somerset, widow of Protector Somerset, † 1587. Large standing wall-monument. Recumbent effigy, the mantle from one side draped with lovely folds across her legs. Shallow coffered arch flanked by coupled columns. Back with sumptuous strapwork cartouche. Big superstructure with obelisks, and achievement between coupled columns. – Nicholas Bagenall † 1688, free-standing, small, steep, black pyramid with urn. – Behind this, hanging monument to Lady Fane † 1618 (restored 1764). Frontally kneeling figures under baldacchino of drapery, looped to columns on the l. and r. Outside the columns small standing angels.

Mildred Cecil Lady Burghley † 1589, and daughter Tall and big tripartite monument with two good recumbent effigies. Shallow coffered arch, back with strapwork cartouche. To the l. and r square compartments with red columns. In these, children kneeling and facing E. Lady Burghley was William Cecil Lord Burghley's wife. The kneeling man represents their son Sir Robert Cecil. Above, a flat upper storey with another kneeling figure. – Then W. Dudley, Bishop of Durham, † 1483. Indent of brass on tomb-chest with quatrefoils and shields. Canopy with lierne vaulting inside and suspended arches with ogee gables. Pierced parapet of pointed arches and finely decorated cornice. – Anne Harlay † 1605, daughter of a French ambassador. Obelisk on square pedestal. A plain obelisk as a funeral monument was erected at the same time to Margaret Hoby † 1605 at Bisham. – Marchioness of Winchester † 1586. Recumbent effigy on a tomb-chest against which kneel her children. Columns l. and r., back with two arches and two inscription plates. Nothing special. – Elizabeth Cecil Countess of Exeter † 1591, semi-reclining figure above the previous monument. Fragment of a larger tomb. She wears an unusually large hood. – Duchess of Northumberland † 1776. Designed by *Robert Adam* and made by *Nicholas Read*. Large, flat, standing wall monument of

an unusual composition. Tripartite; the arch in the middle with black inscription plate is the entrance to the Northumberland vault. Above this a fluted straight-sided sarcophagus with a delightful relief of Charity. Above this, obelisk with urn and putti. To the l. and r., at the height of the sarcophagus, stand Faith and Hope, against tall pedestals with urns. Large inscription: 'Esperance en Dieu'.

Chapel of St Paul (N Ambulatory)

SCREEN similar to that of the Chapel of St Nicholas, but cut into by the Bourchier monument. – MONUMENTS. Lord Bourchier † 1430 and wife. With the screen brightly repainted and gilded. Tomb-chest with cusped quatrefoils containing shields and, at the angles, large figures of eagles and lions bearing standards. Depressed four-centred arch and small lierne vault inside. – In the middle of the chapel Sir Giles Daubeny † 1507 and wife, with alabaster effigies, two tiny bedesmen at his feet.

Against the walls mostly monuments of between c. 1580 and c. 1650. From the SE: Lord Cottington † 1652 and his wife † 1634. The monument is mostly black. Upper part, with Lady Cottington's frontal bust in metal in a circular niche surrounded by a metal wreath, by *Le Sueur*, contract 1634. Lower part by *Fanelli* after Lord Cottington's remains were brought back from Spain in 1679. recumbent effigy on a sarcophagus standing on a very high base. – Countess of Sussex † 1589. Possibly designed by *Ralph Symons*, architect of Sidney Sussex College, her foundation at Cambridge (*Official Guide*); probably carved by *Richard Stevens* (Whinney 1964). The typical monument of its date with recumbent effigy, shallow arch between columns with a strapwork inscription plate behind, and on the top an achievement between obelisks. – Dudley Carleton Viscount Dorchester, 1640 by *Nicholas Stone* (price £200). The same type, but now in a much more classical taste. Tomb-chest with semi-reclining effigy, comfortable and at ease. Probably the earliest example in England of this new courtly and elegant version of a familiar attitude. Tall fluted columns l. and r., broad open segmental pediment. Sir Thomas Bromley † 1587. Tomb-chest with children kneeling against it. Recumbent effigy on partly-rolled-up mat. Shallow arch, columns l. and r., strapwork inscription plate. – Sir James Fullerton † 1632 and wife. Again (in spite of the late date) tomb-chest and recumbent effigies, he behind her and a little higher up. Shallow arch. The inscription plate no longer with strapwork. – Sir John Puckering † 1596 and wife. Large monument of the accepted type. Tomb-chest with the children kneeling against it. Two recumbent effigies, he behind and a little higher. Coffered arch with elaborate strapwork cartouche, columns l. and r. Big upper storey with figures of a Purse Bearer and a Mace Bearer, and obelisks.

Finally Sir Henry Belasyse † 1717; erected 1731 (R. Gunnis). Plain obelisk with urn. On a sarcophagus, against the back of the monument to the Earl of Bath. By *Scheemakers*.

Chapel of Our Lady of the Pew (N Ambulatory)

Hollowed out of the wall beside the Chapel of St John Baptist, but not originally opening into it. Still only 9 by 6 ft in size. The date is late c 14 and the chapel may be that founded as a chantry for Aymer de Valence Earl of Pembroke (see his tomb in the sanctuary) by his widow, the foundress of Pembroke College, Cambridge, who died in 1377. The space enlarged *c*. 1502 for an altar to St Erasmus when his chapel was demolished for the Henry VII Chapel. Originally with none of the lobby character which one now regrets; only after 1524 was it made the entrance to St John's Chapel. Doorway from the ambulatory with two-centred cusped and sub-cusped arch. Square hoodmould on two busts of angels. Original painted wooden half-gates and iron cresting. Two bays inside, the first with panelled walls, both with tierceron vaults. Good boss of the Assumption. Remains of PAINTING, brocade patterns, etc. SCULPTURE on the N wall, new though hieratic in style, a Virgin and Child in alabaster (like aspic) by *Sister Concordia Scott*, 1971.

A richly canopied empty frame above the outer doorway facing the ambulatory seems unconnected with either chapel.

Chapel of St John Baptist (N Ambulatory)

MONUMENTS. At the back of the Holmes monument in the ambulatory tomb-chest of Abbot William of Colchester † 1420. Quatrefoiled tomb-chest with shields, recumbent stone effigy, two angels by the pillow. – Above this small hanging monument to Lt-Col. MacLeod † 1812 by *Nollekens*. – Next to these on the r. Thomas Ruthall, Bishop of Durham, 1524. Tomb-chest with quatrefoils containing shields. The effigy in poor condition. Two angels at the pillow. – To the r. of this Abbot Fascet † 1500. Similar tomb-chest; no effigy. Big canopy, the l. wall of which is panelled outside and serves as a back behind the head of Bishop Ruthall, where it is dated 1520. The canopy has a depressed four-centred arch, a plain straight top, and panel vaulting inside.

By far the largest monument in the chapel, and the tallest in the abbey, is Lord Hunsdon † 1596 and wife. The height is 36 ft. Oversized sarcophagus under deep coffered arch. Obelisks l. and r. To the l. and r. of these big coupled red columns and in front of them taller obelisks. Then a complete upper tier, again with columns and obelisks. The obelisks stand on six-poster bases. The third tier with an octagonal domed structure in the middle. Very curious in many details. – To the r., in the corner, Countess of Mexborough † 1821, hanging monument with a female figure weeping over an urn. It might be in any village church.

To the l. of the Hunsdon monument Humphrey and Mary de Bohun † 1304 and 1305, tomb-chest with blank pointed trefoiled arcading, rather late c 13 than early c 14 in style. – Two straight-headed c 13 RECESSES, originally a double locker with wooden doors (P. Eames 1977).

Col. Popham † 1651 and wife. Black and white. Two standing figures l. and r. of and leaning on a pedestal with a helmet. Pilasters l. and r., baldacchino above. – Sir Thomas Vaughan † 1483. Plain tomb-chest with damaged 3-ft brass of knight in armour under a big ugly four-centred arch. – Mary Kendall † 1710. Kneeling in a Baroque attitude between two columns.

In the middle of the chapel Thomas Cecil Earl of Exeter † 1623 and wife. Big square tomb-chest with large recumbent effigies. Space left for the Earl's second wife. The tomb-chest has three compartments on all but the E side with shields in wreaths, separated by pilasters.

Abbot Islip's Chapel (N Ambulatory)

The chapel was built into the Jesus(?) Chapel by Abbot Islip, who died in 1532. It is two-storeyed, with a narrow straight staircase in the wall to the N transept on the w. Three-bay panelled SCREEN to the ambulatory. Entrance to the chapel and the staircase in the narrower l. bay. Cornice and tall parapet with panelling and small figure niches. The walls inside are panelled, with blank tracery. Central lierne vault with defaced boss. To its l. and r. shallow bays with depressed panelled tunnel-vault. – MONUMENT to Abbot Islip in the upper storey (since 1950 the Nurses' Memorial Chapel) now used as the altar. In a very fragmentary state. Table-top on bronze columns of Renaissance character. – STAINED GLASS by *Hugh Easton*, 1948. All this postwar stained glass in Westminster Abbey, as indeed most stained glass in England of this time, suffers from the same faults. Lack of force in the design and the colouring, a water-colour gentleness rather than the glow one expects from stained glass. Lines which are too fine and have none of the strength of which leading is capable. And finally a curious and alarming unconcern for any of the new c 20 tendencies in painting, sculpture and design.

For the N transept E aisle w of the Islip Chapel, see N *transept* below.

Henry VII Chapel

BRIDGE of aluminium, steel and plastic over the ambulatory. Erected 1970 to link the feretory with Henry VII's Chapel, taking tourist traffic through the lower stage of Henry V's Chantry (see above). – DOORS. Three original

w doors of oak entirely plated with bronze panels, with such emblems as the rose and portcullis, the fleur-de-lys, the falcon and fetterlock, the three leopards. – FONT. Seems to be c 15 (or early c 16 for Islip's baptistery under the s w tower). Much renewed by *Scott*. Cover by *Farmer & Brindley*, 1872. – ALTAR. 1933–4 by *Sir Walter Tapper*, incorporating two pillars with close Early Renaissance decoration and a part of the frieze of *Torrigiani*'s original altar, made c. 1520–2. – The PAINTING of the Virgin and Child is by *Bartolommeo Vivarini*, c. 1480 (given by Lord Lee of Fareham).

STALLS. c. 1520. Two rows, the back row with tall canopies, the Flamboyant detail decidedly Flemish in character. Pretty lierne vaulting under the canopies and, in the lower row, under the book-rests of the upper row. The stalls of the E bay are an addition of 1725, when this was made chapel to the new Order of the Bath. – Since that date, on all the stalls heraldic STALL PLATES of brass or copper, enamelled or painted, of Knights of the Bath and their esquires (cf. Garter stall plates at Windsor, B of E *Berkshire*). – Plenty of entertaining MISERICORDS (Mermaid and Merman, monsters, monkeys, Wife beating Husband, David and Goliath, Judgement of Solomon). One of the misericords dates from the abbey's c 13 stalls (s side, first to the l. of second stair from w). It has stiff-leaf foliage. The return stalls in the N W and s W corners have vintage scenes, and in one of them the new Renaissance interest in the nude body is evident. – For the so-called 'Cranmer pulpit', probably made for this chapel, see *Nave*.

STAINED GLASS. Of the original rich and splendid glass (by glaziers whose work can still be seen in King's College Chapel, Cambridge, and possibly in the Lady Chapel at Gloucester) no fragments are at present to be seen. It has been suggested that the glass which has been since the c 18 in the E window of St Margaret's Church next door was part of Catherine of Aragon's dowry, and meant for the Henry VII Chapel but never used there. For c 20 glass, see E *chapel* below.

MONUMENT of Henry VII and Elizabeth of York. A report on the cost of the stonework for the proposed tomb was signed in 1506 by the King's Masons *Robert Vertue*, *Robert Jenyns* and *John Lebons*. The design was intended to be by *Guido Mazzoni*, known as *Paganino* or Pageny, who worked for the king of France. Henry was to kneel – a type of monument established for the kings of France. The plan came to nothing. The brazen screen had, however, been begun before the king's death. It is referred to as unfinished in 1509. It was designed by *Thomas Dutchman*. The monument was in the end begun in 1512, to the design and models of *Pietro Torrigiani*. It was to cost £1,500. The images were cast by *Nicholas Ewen*. It was completed, it seems, in 1518. The monument is in the Renaissance style, but the SCREEN is entirely English and Perp. Elaborate openwork tracery in two tiers. Pierced, ribbed coving to the outside as well as the inside. Pierced parapet with, in the middle of each side, a big candle bracket coming forward, carrying a crowned rose. At the angles of the screen are heavy hexagonal turrets, also of openwork. Doors under depressed segmental arches on the N and s sides. Statuettes in two tiers stood in niches flanking the turrets and the doorways. Six of them survive. Amongst them are some in a style which might be called a truly English Renaissance, that is a new calm and evenness of fall in the draperies achieved without any borrowings from Italy (e.g. Edward the Confessor, St John the Baptist).

The MONUMENT itself was made by *Torrigiani*, who had been a pupil of Ghirlandaio at the same time as Michelangelo. He is best known as the rowdy youth who knocked Michelangelo's nose in. That does not detract from the value of his sculpture in London, quite apart from the fact that Michelangelo no doubt was a trying boy. Torrigiani has of course none of Michelangelo's overawing genius, but for delicate, sensitive work in a Late Quattrocento style Henry VIII could not have made a better choice. The monument is a tomb-chest with recumbent effigies and in that respect does not differ from the traditions of English funeral art. It differs in every other respect, and it must be remembered that in 1512 there was nothing in existence anywhere in England (except some stained glass and perhaps the monument of the Lady Margaret, s aisle of the chapel) that could represent the new taste which Torrigiani brought with him. The tomb-chest is a sarcophagus and has instead of buttresses pilasters decorated with pretty candelabra shapes. Instead of canopied niches it has medallions surrounded by wreaths, instead of angels winged putti (l. and r. of the shields on the E side), and instead of gaunt figures in angular draperies figures in mantles which give them amply rounded contours. St George and St Michael are Roman soldiers, and the Virgin to the l. of St Michael is a Madonna. The effigies with praying hands are more what the English Court might have expected. Yet here also there is a gentleness and tenderness and a unison of lifelikeness with sheer beauty of modelling unprecedented in England. The monument is of black and white marble, and the figures of bronze gilt. At the four angles four seated fully dressed angels, their faces childlike yet of supreme dignity.

Chapel of Henry VII, Apsidal Chapels, from s to N
FIRST CHAPEL. Low stone SCREEN, of three pretty bows curving forward into the chancel of the chapel, an echo of the window shapes of the aisles of the chapel. Free-standing large MONUMENT to the Duke of Lennox and Richmond, cousin of James I, † 1624 and his wife † 1639. By *Hubert Le Sueur*. A composition developed from precedent in the Netherlands and France. Black and gilt,

almost filling the chapel. Sarcophagus with recumbent gilt effigies. At the angles four over-life-size bronze caryatids. They represent Faith, Hope, Charity and Prudence. They carry gilt Ionic capitals. On the capitals big entablature and rising from this big openwork gilt dome like that of an arbour. On the top figure of Fame with two trumpets, balancing on one foot, much like such French work as Biard's Fame of 1597. Large caryatids were an accepted motif in France too, cf. e.g. the balcony by Goujon in the Louvre, though free-standing for tombs they were rather a Flemish tradition. The nearest parallel is Cornelis Floris's tomb of Frederick I of Denmark at Schleswig of *c*. 1550.

SECOND CHAPEL. Duc de Montpensier, brother of Louis Philippe. By *Westmacott*, 1830. Tomb-chest with recumbent effigy. – Dean Stanley † 1881. Designed by *J. L. Pearson* and carved by *Boehm*. Tomb-chest with recumbent effigy.

EAST CHAPEL. STAINED GLASS. Battle of Britain window, 1946–9 by *Hugh Easton*.

FOURTH CHAPEL. John Sheffield Duke of Buckingham and Normanby † 1721. Designed by *Plumière* and made by *Scheemakers* and *Delvaux*. Buckingham House was built for him, and he paid for the monument to Dryden erected in Poets' Corner. Large, of lively composition, and the first in the abbey to proclaim such independence of iconographical traditions. The duke semi-reclining on a sarcophagus, trophies to the l. and r. At his feet the duchess, a natural daughter of James II. Higher up, on a pedestal, Father Time (by *Delvaux*) with medallion of the duke's children. Weeping putto to his l.

FIFTH CHAPEL. Low SCREEN exactly like that of the chapel opposite. There were originally such screens also in the end bays of the two aisles, where now the C18 E extensions of the stalls are. – MONUMENT. George Villiers Duke of Buckingham † 1628, James I's favourite. By *Le Sueur*. Attached with its w side to the chapel w wall. The rest free-standing. Tomb-chest with seated mourning figures at the corners facing E. Specially good Neptune and Mars. Also at the corners big obelisks. The two recumbent effigies are gilt. At their feet small bronze statue of Fame also facing E (the trumpets have vanished). Back wall (w) with three kneeling children, and one child behind, reclining. Allegorical figures higher up. (See also Portsmouth.)

Chapel of Henry VII, Aisles

NORTH AISLE. MONUMENTS. Queen Elizabeth I † 1603 (in burial joining her half-sister Queen Mary I † 1558; only a heap of broken altars marked the spot in the long interval). By *Maximilian Colt*, completed 1606 for £765. (Whinney 1964: Colt paid 1605 and 1607, *John Critz* paid for painting 1607.) Free-standing, and nothing like as sumptuous (or vulgar) as the monuments erected by her courtiers. Nothing could be more characteristic of the

93. LONDON: WESTMINSTER ABBEY
Tomb of Elizabeth I † 1603, by Maximilian Colt, completed 1606

queen. Four by three black columns, i.e. a total of ten. They carry two straight-topped side pieces and a coffered middle arch rising much higher. White marble effigy brilliantly characterized. Mary has no effigy, but see the ecumenical inscription recently inserted in the pavement w of the tomb. – To the E the 'Innocents' Corner' with the monuments to the Princesses Sophia and Mary, daughters of James I. Princess Sophia † 1606, three days old. By *Maximilian Colt*, who was paid £170 for it. The questionable conceit of an alabaster cradle, accurately portrayed with its embroidered velvet cover. The baby faces E; so one has to go round the hood of the cradle to peep in. – Princess Mary † 1607, two years old. Tomb-chest with seated putti at the angles. On the top semi-reclining girl. – Set in the E wall above: Edward V and Richard Duke of York, the princes said to have been murdered at Richard III's request. The bones were found in 1678. The monument is by *Joshua Marshall*, master mason to Charles II. Pedestal with broad low urn. No effigies. – Further w on the s wall: Sir George Savile † 1695. Plain sarcophagus with medallion and two putti. Restrained white 'reredos' back. – Earl of Halifax † 1715. Big obelisk – On the s wall, three *Morris* tapestries, in the manner of the c 13 sedilia paintings.

SOUTH AISLE. The ALTAR is by *Detmar Blow*, 1929. – In front of the altar Charles II, William and Mary, and Anne are interred. For the MONUMENTS it is best to start near the altar with the Lady Margaret Beaufort, Countess of Richmond and Derby, Henry VII's mother, † 1509. By *Pietro Torrigiani*, though 'counsel in devising' the monument was given by the then Prior of St Bartholomew-the-Great, *William Bolton*, and drawings were provided by a Flemish painter, *Maynart Wewyck*. Yet what matters most in the monument must be Torrigiani's. It is in all probability the earliest work in the Italian Renaissance style in England. Torrigiani signed the contract in 1511 and undertook to finish in 1513. Black tomb-chest with pilasters and shields in wreaths. The inscription in Roman lettering. Recumbent effigy, again – as in the tomb of Henry VII – with a wonderful understanding of character, lifelike and yet spiritualized. The effigy is flanked by buttress strips still in the Gothic taste and has over its head a Gothic canopy with pierced tracery.

The GRATE (put back in place in 1915) was made by *Cornelius Symondson* and originally carried much decoration. It was paid for (£25) by St John's College, Cambridge, founded by the Lady Margaret, and completed in 1529. It is of Spanish iron. – One of the Lady Margaret's executors, Sir Thomas Lovell, is recorded by a portrait medallion in a wreath with heraldic roses, against the N wall. It is of bronze in a wooden frame and also by *Torrigiani*. Lovell died in 1524. – Free-standing further w Mary Queen of Scots, c. 1607–12, by *Cornelius Cure*. Two groups of four columns carrying straight ceilings, and connecting the groups a big coffered arch with a superstructure bigger and heavier than that of Queen Elizabeth's tomb. White marble effigy of superb craftsmanship high up on a sarcophagus. (Surrounded by the original iron grille, like Lady Margaret's rescued and put back in the early c 20). – Yet further w Countess of Lennox † 1578. Free-standing tomb-chest with decorated pilasters. At the corners obelisks. Kneeling children against the tomb-chest. Recumbent effigy, her mantle draped across her legs.

Other monuments from E to w: To the l. of the altar General Monk Duke of Albemarle † 1670, erected in 1730, designed by *Kent* and made by *Scheemakers*. Black obelisk and *columna rostrata* (cf. Vice-Admiral Baker, nave N aisle). The duke stands to the r. in armour. To the l. seated female figure leaning on a portrait medallion of

Monk's son. – Catherine Lady Walpole † 1737, Horace Walpole's mother. Ordered by him; delivered 1743. A very original monument if one compares it with the various conventions then current in England, remarkably pure in its classical taste. Statue by *Filippo della Valle*, copied in the draperies from the Modestia figure in Rome. The exquisitely simple square pedestal with inscription plate framed by leaf scrolls is by *Rysbrack*, 1754. – Earl of Cromer † 1917. Small tablet by *Sir W. Goscombe John*.

Crossing

PULPIT, early c 17. Tapering pillars and bits of fretwork, but also garlands. Pedestal and sounding-board by *Tapper*, 1935, iron steps by *Bainbridge Reynolds*. – LECTERN. Neo-Georgian, 1949, by *Sir Albert Richardson*. For the choir, see *Nave*, E bays.

South Transept

From the end of the c 16 a cluster of poets' memorials began to form round the nucleus of those to Chaucer and Spenser in the E aisle. The name Poets' Corner seems to have developed in the c 18, and came to be applied to the whole transept.

EAST AISLE N WALL, that is, on the back of the sanctuary s side. MONUMENTS. Dr Busby, Head Master of Westminster School. By *Francis Bird*, dated by Vertue 1703. White marble, with reredos background and semi-reclining figure with scholar's cap. A very telling portrait. – Dr South, Archdeacon of Westminster, † 1716. The same composition, but black and white, and with a fuller, bigger figure. At the top of the inscription plate on the 'reredos' three cherubs' heads and rays. Also by *Bird*. – At the corner of St Benedict's Chapel bust of Archbishop Tait † 1882 by *Armstead*.

CHAPEL OF ST BENEDICT. STAINED GLASS, s window. By *Hugh Easton*, 1948. – MONUMENT to Cardinal Simon Langham † 1376, Abbot of Westminster till 1362. Tomb by *Henry Yevele* and *Stephen Lote*, chest with shields in quatrefoils. Recumbent alabaster effigy with two angels by the pillow. Original plain iron grille to the ambulatory. Original canopy destroyed in the c 18. – Countess of Hertford † 1598. High wall-monument (28 ft). Recumbent effigy; groups of three columns l. and r. Back wall with two arches and strapwork cartouches. Second tier above the centre, with coupled columns and achievement. Obelisks at the top. – Dean Goodman † 1601, large kneeling figure in a niche, facing E. – Earl of Middlesex † 1645 and wife. Black and white marble. Big plain free-standing tomb-chest with recumbent effigies, still with animals at their feet. – Next to this on a low tomb-chest brass to Dean Bill † 1561, 2-ft figure. – Behind Dean

Goodman's tomb in 1936 a RECESS was found with piscina and squints, connected with an anker house or anchorite's cell made in the C 14 in the angle of the Chapel of St Benedict and the s transept. – TILES probably of the C 13 at the E end of the chapel.

EAST AISLE E WALL. John Dryden, erected 1720. The excellent bust, 1731, by *Scheemakers*. – H. W. Longfellow, bust by *Brock*, 1884. – Abraham Cowley † 1667 by *Bushnell*. With a big urn and no effigy. The design breaks ruthlessly through the C 13 arcading. – Geoffrey Chaucer († 1400, buried nearby). The monument was erected here in 1556, but it looks as if the tomb-chest with its shields in quatrefoils and the canopy of four ogee arches, and the circular pillars l. and r. with their trellis decoration might come from an earlier monument, re-used perhaps after the Dissolution. So complete a survival of Gothic forms thirty-five years after the tomb of Henry VII is improbable. – Above this John Roberts † 1776 by *R. Hayward*. Simple but of great finesse. It would be the pride of any village church. – John Philips † 1708. Portrait medallion in profile, with trees and branches. – Barton Booth, 1772 by *William Tyler*. Bulgy pedestal and portrait medallion with two putti. – Michael Drayton † 1631. Hanging monument with bust between the open sides of a segmental pediment above the inscription plate. By *Edward Marshall*. – Though we seldom mention plain lettered stones (for which see the *Official Guide*), an evocative cluster on the floor before Chaucer: to (chronologically by dates of death) Byron, George Eliot, G. M. Hopkins, Browning (in Italian marbles), Tennyson, Henry James, Dylan Thomas, T. S. Eliot, Masefield and Auden; Lewis Carroll lately added. (Dickens, Kipling and Hardy form a separate literary nucleus near the door to St Faith's.)

EAST AISLE S WALL. The DOOR into the chapter-house crypt is a fragment of the original doors to the N transept. – MONUMENTS Ben Jonson, designed by *Gibbs* and carved by *Rysbrack*, c. 1737. Simple with fine bust. Erected at the expense of the Earl of Oxford. – Samuel Butler † 1680. Frontal bust against black obelisk. Erected in 1721 at the expense of John Barber, Lord Mayor in 1733 and by trade a printer. The bust is probably by *Rysbrack*. – John Milton, erected 1737, by *William Benson*, Wren's successor as Surveyor General, with bust by *Rysbrack*, whose name forms part of the lengthy inscription. The bust was made independent of, and earlier than, the monument. – Edmund Spenser † 1599. By *Nicholas Stone*, erected 1620 and renewed 1778, quite big, but very simple. – Thomas Gray † 1771 by *Bacon*, placed as if it were the base of Milton's monument. Seated figure holding a portrait medallion.

EAST AISLE W WALL. In the centre Matthew Prior † 1721, designed by *Gibbs* and carved by *Rysbrack*, except for the portrait bust, c. 1700, by *Coysevox* Black sarcopha-gus, standing figures of Thalia and Clio and bust in circular recess. Top pediment with two reclining putti. – To the l. William Mason † 1797. A typical *Bacon*. Poetry mourning over a portrait medallion. – Above Thomas Shadwell † 1692 by *Bird*. Bust in front of obelisk. (According to Mr de Beer, erected after 1700.) – To the r. of Prior: Granville Sharp † 1813 by *Chantrey*. – Above this Charles de St Denis † 1703, with small bust on top. – At the N corner eloquent bust of Tennyson by *Woolner*, 1857.

MAIN TRANSEPT E SIDE. From the N the following: on NE pier, William Blake, bronze bust by *Epstein*, 1957. – The rest at the s spur wall. Adam Lindsay Gordon † 1870, large impressionistic bust by *K. Scott*. – Thomas Campbell, statue, 1848 by *Calder Marshall*. – William Wordsworth, seated figure by *Thrupp*, 1854. – Dr Johnson † 1784, fine bust by *Nollekens*, 1777, given to the abbey in 1939. – Robert Southey † 1843, bust by *Weekes*; good. – S. T. Coleridge † 1834, bust by *Thornycroft*. – Shakespeare, designed by *Kent*, statue by *Scheemakers*, 1740. The money for the memorial was publicly collected, the committee consisting of Lord Burlington, Pope and Dr Mead. The background is a richly detailed blank doorway with pediment. Shakespeare stands, with his legs elegantly crossed, pointing to a scroll while leaning on a pile of books which are placed on a tall pedestal. On this the heads of Henry V, Richard III and Queen Elizabeth. On the scroll lines varying Prospero's in *The Tempest* to form a memento mori suited to this place. Above: Keats and Shelley, two tablets with inscriptions connected by a thick garland of flowers, put up in 1954. By *Frank Dobson*. – James Thomson, erected 1762 to the design of *Robert Adam*. Seated figure in a toga, a book in one hand, the Cap of Liberty in the other. A putto on the r. On the circular pedestal on which Thomson's arm rests, fine relief of the Seasons. The sculptor was *M. H. Spang*. – Above: Robert Burns, bust by *Sir John Steell*, 1885.

SOUTH WALL. Here, screened off, was the Chapel of St Blaise, dismantled in the C 18. Two WALL PAINTINGS were discovered in 1936: St Christopher and the Incredulity of St Thomas. The figures are nearly 9 ft tall and stand below the blank arches of the wall arcade, extremely elongated figures much in the style of contemporary English illumination and similar also to that of the retable in the s ambulatory (cf. also the figure in St Faith's, below, and the slightly later sedilia paintings of sanctuary and ambulatory, above). The forms (perhaps because of the different scale and technique) are broader and flatter and the outlines stronger. They are the most monumental C 13 wall paintings in England. Their exact date is unknown. Professor Wormald pleaded for c. 1260–70, Dr Rickert for c. 1300. – STAINED GLASS. Rose-window and two tiers of lancets below. 1902 by *Burlison & Grylls* to *Bodley's* designs, and certainly giving a more appropriate light than

Within these sacred Walls
the Memory of HANDEL
was celebrated
under the patronage
and in the presence
of his most Gracious Majesty
GEORGE the III
on the XXVI and XXIX of May
and on the III and V of June
MDCCLXXXIV
The Band consisting
of DCCXXV vocal & Instrumental Performers
was conducted by
JOAH BATES Esq.

the Musick performed
on this Solemnity
was selected from his own Works
under the direction of
BROWNLOW Earl of Exeter
JOHN Earl of Sandwich
HENRY Earl of Uxbridge
Sir WATKIN WILLIAMS WYNN Bar.
and
Sir RICHARD JEBB Bart.

GEORGE FREDERICK HANDEL Esq.
born February XXIII MDCLXXXIV
died April XIV MDCCLIX

94. LONDON: WESTMINSTER ABBEY The west wall of the south transept with monuments

the Comper and Easton windows. – For architectural sculpture, see *Interior*, s transept, above.

MONUMENTS. Oliver Goldsmith † 1774, above the door to the Chapel of St Faith (for which see below). Inscription and oval portrait medallion, with attributes around. By *Nollekens*. – Sir Walter Scott. Copy of *Chantrey*'s bust at Abbotsford. – Above: John Ruskin † 1900. Bronze medallion by *Onslow Ford*. – John Duke of Argyll and Greenwich. By *Roubiliac*, 1748–9 (terracotta model, V & A, dated 1745). Nowhere in the abbey does he appear greater as a sculptor. The conceits of the Nightingale and Hargrave monuments may be more ingenious, but in spirited portraiture and delicacy of draperies the Argyll monument is supreme and need indeed not fear comparison with any contemporary monument in France or Italy. The source of the composition is clearly Italy. Big black base with relief of Liberty with the Phrygian cap and Magna Carta and putti against a background of lightly indicated architecture. To the l. Eloquence standing and looking and gesticulating towards us; to the r. Minerva seated and looking up to the main group. The figures establish at once the diagonal movement so essential for Baroque composition. Above, on the sarcophagus, semi-reclining, the duke, his head to the r., carrying on the movement from below. His elbow rests on the thigh of Fame standing to the r. and writing his name and titles on an obelisk at the back of the composition. She stops short at the Gr of Greenwich to indicate that the title died out with him. The obelisk with the figure of Fame writing was taken by Roubiliac from the Mitrovitz monument at Prague, dated 1714, designed by Fischer von Erlach and illustrated in his *Historische Architektur*, of which an English edition came out in 1730.

WEST WALL, that is cloister wall, below the Muniment Room. Mostly smaller, often hanging, monuments. They profit from being contained in the C13 wall-arcading. – J. S. Mackenzie † 1800, by *Nollekens*. – Sir Edward Atkyns and others, before 1750, by *Sir Henry Cheere*. No effigies, but pretty ornament, light brown, white and pink marble. Sarcophagus below, inscription plate above, crowned by a shield in a rocaille cartouche. – Above: Sir Archibald Campbell, by *Wilton*, 1795. Large, with Fame, a portrait medallion, and putto. – Sir Thomas Robinson and his wife, *c.* 1778 by *John Walsh*. With two well-characterized busts. Otherwise nothing special. – Above: Handel. By *Roubiliac*, 1761. Another instance of Roubiliac's psychological insight. Handel appears here the type of the ageing theatrical manager. Yet an opportunity for closer study reveals in his face the signs of inspiration. Above his head an angel in clouds is playing the harp. An organ also in the background, all this very lightly carved so as to convey distance. Before Handel lies a piece of music. It is 'I know that my Redeemer liveth'. Roubiliac's Gothick surround must not be missed. – Thackeray † 1863. Bust by

Marochetti. – Addison. Statue on circular base with classical figures. By *Westmacott*, 1806 (Whinney 1964: 'proclaims himself clearly as the pupil of Canova'); Addison himself died in 1719 and was buried in the Henry VII Chapel N aisle, but with no monument before this. His *Spectator* paper on the abbey monuments is much quoted.

Second bay. William Outram † 1679. Urn, but no figures, a fashion of those years (cf. e.g. Cowley, E aisle E wall, above). – Above: Dr Stephen Hales † 1761, by *Wilton*. Figures of Religion and Botany, the latter with a portrait medallion, and at her feet the winds on a globe (Hales invented the ventilator, a blessing for prisons, ships, etc.). The use of one standing and one seated allegory is still typically Baroque. – Dr Isaac Barrow † 1677, with bust on top. – Dr Wetenhall † 1733, tablet by *Woodman*. – John Keble, bust by *Woolner*, 1872. – Sir John Pringle † 1782, by *Nollekens*.

Third bay. William Camden, the antiquary, † 1623. Frontal bust on tall pedestal. – Sir Robert Taylor, the architect, † 1788. No figures; various marbles; urn and partly erroneous inscription (aged seventy-four). – Dr Grabe † 1711. Seated in his Geneva robes on his sarcophagus. Excellent figure, remarkably informal. By *Francis Bird*. – Garrick by *H. Webber*, 1797. Two coarse allegories representing Tragedy and Comedy. He stands, a resilient figure, with a cynical face, and opens a curtain. It is a brilliant piece of characterization and shows what surprises the works of the lesser-known English c 18 sculptors may hold in store. – Busts at the end of the third bay: Bishop Thirlwall † 1875 by *E. Davis*. – George Grote by *C. Bacon*; unveiled 1855 (R. Gunnis).

Tablets also to architects Chambers, Adam and Wyatt. On the 'balcony' above, see *Cloisters, Library*.

ST FAITH'S CHAPEL (between s transept s wall and chapter-house vestibule) is usually entered from the transept. WALL PAINTING (were there more originally? Cf. those on the transept wall next door). What remains now is, in a recess in the E wall, a large figure of St Faith, a commanding figure if not of attractive features. The very elongated proportions and the small head point to a date late in the C13 rather than the sometimes suggested 1260 or 1275. Below the figure a 'predella' of eight-pointed stars, and in the centre a small defaced Crucifixion. Zigzag decoration in the reveals and, on the l., painted panel of a kneeling monk with inscription. – PAVEMENT. Many original C13 tiles survive in the E part of the chapel.

North Transept

EAST AISLE. At present visible mainly from the N ambulatory. This aisle was once three chapels, of St John Evangelist (s bay), St Michael (middle bay) and St Andrew (N bay). The whole is locally called 'Nightingale' after its most startling monument (middle bay; see below). Between the s bay and the main transept, a late c 15 stone screen. The MONUMENTS are taken roughly s to N.

Against the back of General Wolfe's tomb, COFFIN LID with foliated cross, late c 13. – Sir Francis Vere † 1609. A novel conceit in England, followed a few years later for Lord Salisbury at Hatfield († 1612). Free-standing, of black marble and alabaster. Four kneeling knights supporting a slab on which is placed Sir Francis's armour, carved carefully piece by piece. Below, recumbent effigy on half-rolled-up mat. The carving of faces and dress is of the highest competence (illustrated in the *Official Guide*). Perhaps by *Maximilian Colt*, the artist of the Salisbury tomb. The immediate source of the composition is the Nassau monument at Breda, made a good two generations earlier. – To the N of his feet Lady St John † 1614, alabaster figure reclining on her side; not *in situ*. – s of the Vere monument, to the l. of the coffin lid: Captain Cooke † 1799, by *Bacon Jr*. Tall and white against the back of the Wolfe monument. High base to reach above the Vere monument. The captain has a sail behind him and is attended by a half-naked sailor. Relief of sea battle below.

Against the E wall Admiral Storr † 1783, bust, unsigned. – Between Wolfe and the E wall, John Beresford † 1812, simple monument with trophies by *Henry Westmacott*. – Sir George Holles † 1626. By *Nicholas Stone*. Base with relief of horseman. Two sloping sides of an open pediment with volute ends, and on these Bellona and Minerva, rather huddled and pinched. The model, as for the other Holles monument, is Michelangelo's Medici tombs. Fat garland between the figures. In the middle on a pedestal the standing figure of Sir George, a conceit still very rare at the time in England. – To the l. of this, almost as if part of it, Admiral Sir George Pocock by *Bacon*, 1796. Large seated figure of Britannia, holding a thunderbolt. Her elbow rests on a portrait medallion.

At w screen, Sir John Franklin † 1847 when completing the discovery of the North West Passage. By *M. Noble*, 1875. Nice relief of a ship buffeted in ice and wind. – Sir W. Webb Follett † 1845; statue by *Behnes*. – Next to it Earl and Countess of Mountrath, erected 1771 after her death, designed by *Sir William Chambers*, carved by *Wilton*. (Upper part, with the earl awaiting her on high, removed.) Sarcophagus; the countess kneels on it in a thin dress, revealing the form of the body. Large angel on clouds from the l. – Against its N side Admiral Kempenfelt, by *Bacon Jr*, 1808. Small; a rounded obelisk with reliefs of a sinking ship, the admiral rising in profile, three-quarter naked, and an angel holding a crown.

At the centre of the E wall, J. G. Nightingale † 1752 and his wife † 1731 at the age of twenty-seven. When walking on the terrace at Mamhead a flash of lightning gave her such a shock that she had a miscarriage and died. One of *Roubiliac*'s most famous works; made in 1761 (figure of Death carved by *Nicholas Read*). Against an arch rusticated in the Wren manner and with canted sides stands Mr Nightingale holding his wife and in vain trying to ward off Death in the form of a gruesome skeleton pointing a lance

95. LONDON: WESTMINSTER ABBEY
Death, by Nicholas Read, detail of the Nightingale monument by L. F. Roubiliac, 1761

at her. It stands below, on the ground (where we stand, looking at the monument), having just slipped out of the heavy door of a vault below. The skeleton is of hideous realism yet carries the same fantastic conviction as late medieval demons and monsters (the whole work, if not yet visible to visitors, is shown in the *Official Guide*). One may grumble at so sensational an effect in so noble and restrained a building, and also, from the Christian point of view, at such a cruel representation of grave's victory and death's sting. John Wesley had no such qualms. He wrote of this and Roubiliac's Hargrave monument (nave s aisle): 'Here indeed the marble seems to speak. None of the other [abbey monuments can] be compared.' Whatever one's reaction to the conceit, on the sculptural mastery there can be no two voices. – To the l. three fragmentary c 15 niches, remains of the REREDOS of the chapel; richly canopied. – Below Duchess of Somerset † 1692. Semi-reclining on a sarcophagus as if it were a couch. Eyes turned to heaven, pleading gesture. To the l. and r. two kneeling charity boys. The duchess devoted much money to charitable and educational enterprises. By *Grinling Gibbons*.

Lord Norris † 1601. Made probably after 1606, and, it seems, by *Isaac James*. Free-standing, of the new, Late Elizabethan size. Large eight-poster. Two recumbent effigies on a sarcophagus. On the N and S sides three and three sons kneeling against it. At the w and E ends arch on piers between the columns. The centre has a solid upper storey, with military reliefs to N and S. – Opposite, on the w wall, many minor monuments, e.g. Charles Stuart † 1801, by *Nollekens*, and the Forbes Brothers, 1803 by the *younger Bacon*. – Statues of Telford, the engineer, by *Baily*, 1839, and John Kemble, the actor, † 1823, by *Hinchliffe* to a design of *Flaxman*'s. – On the N wall bust of Dr Baillie on a Grecian pedestal, by *Chantrey*, 1827. – Statue of Mrs Siddons by *Thomas Campbell*, 1845.

MAIN TRANSEPT E SIDE. Mostly statues of statesmen, a ghostly assembly: Sir Robert Peel † 1850 by *John Gibson* of Rome. – Gladstone † 1898 by *Brock*. Then a *Roubiliac* Admiral Sir Peter Warren, 1753. Excellent and not big. Curved pedestal. Seated figure of Navigation on the r., Hercules standing on the l. and bending tenderly over the bust. Originally there was behind the monument a big falling flag. – Disraeli † 1881, statue by *Boehm*. – Sir John Malcolm, statue by *Chantrey*, 1838. – First Duke of Newcastle † 1676 and his literary Duchess. Base with inscription and trophies in relief. Sarcophagus with two recumbent effigies still on a half-rolled-up mat. Black and white reredos back with columns. Big looped draperies and big segmental pediment. – Then three Canning statues: Viscount Stratford de Redcliffe † 1880 by *Boehm*; Earl Canning † 1862 by *Foley*; George Canning, the Prime Minister, by *Chantrey*, 1834.

John Holles Duke of Newcastle † 1711 designed by *Gibbs* (final designs 1721), carved by *Bird* (signed). Erected in 1723. Called by a guide-book of 1834 'perhaps the most magnificent as well as the most costly, of any in the Abbey'. Large, tripartite, convex architectural background. In the centre the duke, white marble, on a black marble sarcophagus. He is in armour and looks to heaven. To the l. and r. Wisdom and Sincerity, both standing. Open pediment at the top with angels. The pediment breaks boldly back in the middle, a wholly Baroque effect. Upper storey over this middle part, with putti above.

NORTH WALL. MODEL in oak and pearwood, c18, of *Wren*'s or *Hawksmoor*'s design for tower and spire. – STAINED GLASS. N rose-window by *Joshua Price*, 1722, to designs by *Thornhill*. Radially arranged figures in the pictorial technique of the c18. – In six lancets below, Six

Acts of Mercy, 1958, by *Brian Thomas*, replacing Indian Mutiny memorials bombed in the last war. – MONUMENTS. Admiral Vernon by *Rysbrack*, 1763. Fame crowning with laurels a bust of the admiral. – Sir Charles Wager by *Scheemakers*, 1747. Base with relief of sea battle. Seated Fame holding portrait medallion supported by the infant Hercules. Grey obelisk back.

MAIN TRANSEPT W SIDE. William Pitt Earl of Chatham † 1778, by *Bacon*, 1779–83. He was paid £6,000 for it; and it is huge enough. The type is that of the Guildhall and St Paul's monuments, a type which, in the long run, the abbey could clearly not contain. Large obelisk. In it, in a niche, statue of Pitt, haranguing. Below big group of five allegories pyramidally (i.e. classically) arranged. They are Prudence and Fortitude, Britannia, Earth, and Ocean. – Statue of Palmerston, 1870 by *Robert Jackson*. – Captains Bayne, Blair and Lord Robert Manners, by *Nollekens*, commissioned 1782, completed 1793, based on a sketch by *Reynolds*. Again of a type shortly to invade St Paul's. Huge black obelisk. At the top Fame on a Doric *columna rostrata*, with the three portrait medallions suspended. Below standing Britannia with lion, and reclining Neptune with sea-horse. – Viscount Castlereagh second Marquis of Londonderry † 1822. Statue by *J. Evan Thomas*.

WEST AISLE E SIDE. Earl of Aberdeen, Prime Minister, bust by *Noble*, 1874. – Mrs Warren, philanthropist, † 1816. A moving statue of a seated beggar girl, one breast bare, and holding her baby. By *Westmacott*. – Sir G Cornewall Lewis † 1863, bust by *Weekes*. – General Sir Eyre Coote † 1783, by *Thomas Banks*, 1784–9. Erected by the East India Company. Obelisk as huge as that of the three Captains, against which it stands. Victory hanging up on a palm-tree a trophy with the portrait of Sir Eyre. Weeping Mahratta captive on the l. Classical detail and draperies. – Charles Buller † 1848. Bust by *Weekes*. – Francis Horner. Statue by *Chantrey*, 1820.

In the centre of the aisle: Lord Mansfield, Lord Chief Justice, 1801 by *Flaxman* at a cost of £2,500. Seated in robes with wig on a tall circular pedestal. Wisdom and Justice standing to the l. and r. At the back of the monument Death as a naked youth leaning on an extinguished torch. How different a conceit from that of Death on Roubiliac's Nightingale monument – but not for that reason more Christian.

East side (continued). Smaller monuments, e.g. General Hope by *Bacon*, 1793, with a mourning Indian woman; in the carving Bacon's usual finesse. – Jonas Hanway † 1786, by *J. F. and J. Moore*. Relief on sarcophagus with seated woman clothing boys. Portrait medallion at the foot. – Above Major-General Edwardes † 1868, by *Theed*. Bust on pedestal with two seated angels – an c18 composition interpreted with Victorian sentiment. – Sir Clifton Wintringham † 1794, by *Banks*. Mourning wife with hair hanging down. Above, relief of Sir Clifton as a Roman doctor visiting the sick. – Above: bust of Cobden † 1865, by *Woolner*.

WEST AISLE N WALL. Earl of Halifax by *Bacon*, 1782. Lively and pretty; with eloquent Rococo bust and two putti at different levels. – Admiral Watson † 1757. Designed by *James Stuart* and carved by *Scheemakers*. James Stuart is known as Athenian Stuart, but there is not an inkling of Grecian leanings in this composition. The admiral stands in the middle, in a Roman toga. (Formerly he stood beneath a classical arcade with palm-tree columns; *Official Guide*.) On the r. a kneeling figure symbolic of the survivors of the Black Hole of Calcutta. On the l., seated Indian prisoner in chains symbolic of those captured at Ghereah by Watson in 1756. – Sir William Sanderson † 1676, small, with telling bust on curly pediment; by *Edward Marshall*.

WEST AISLE W WALL. STAINED GLASS. Bunyan Window, 1912 by *Comper*. – Disaster of HMS *Captain* window, 1870, by *Clayton & Bell*. – All the MONUMENTS are contained in the C 13 arcading. General Guest, 1752 by *Sir Robert Taylor* (inv. et sc.). Lively Rococo ornament and lifeless bust. – Admiral Sir John Balchen † 1744, by *Scheemakers*. Storm relief and trophies; no figures. – Bishop Warren † 1800, by *Westmacott*. No portrait. Standing figures of Religion and an Angel; somewhat dull. – Lord Aubrey Beauclerk † 1740, by *Scheemakers*. Bust and trophies; not interesting. – Gen. Kirk † 1741, by *Scheemakers*, erected after 1743. Bust and two putti; no more attractive. – Richard Kane † 1736, by *Rysbrack*. Simple pedestal with volutes on the l. and r.; excellent bust. – Bishop Bradford † 1731. By *Cheere*; no figures. – Bishop Boulter † 1742. By *Cheere*, with sarcophagus on which an oak garland. Trophies and bust.

Nave and Choir

North Aisle, E *to* W

SOUTH WALL (back of the choir stalls). MONUMENTS. Sir T. Fowell Buxton † 1845, seated statue by *Thrupp*. – Sir T. Hesketh † 1605. Reclining stiffly on his side. Columns l. and r. and big heavy strapwork at the back. Not a courtly work. – Mrs James † 1677. Urn on pedestal; no effigy.

Second bay: Dr H. Chamberlen, 1731. By *Scheemakers*. A cultured scholarly face; semi-reclining figure on black sarcophagus; Physic and Longevity stand to the l. and r. One of these two is by *Delvaux*. Reredos back. – Orlando Gibbons, the composer. Black marble bust by *A. G. Walker*. – In the floor brass to Bishop Monk † 1856.

Third bay: Sir T. Stamford Raffles by *Chantrey*, 1832; seated statue. – Above: cartouche to Purcell † 1695. – Nice little hanging monument to Capt. Bryan † 1809, by *Bacon Jr*. – Almeric de Courcy Lord Courcy and Kinsale † 1719.

Black sarcophagus carried by two putti. On it semi-reclining figure in Roman dress wearing a periwig. Looped baldacchino on the reredos back. Fluted Corinthian pilasters l. and r. – William Wilberforce. By *S. Joseph*, 1838. Seated statue, the face so violently characterized that it is almost a caricature.

Fourth bay: Lord John Thynne † 1881, designed by *Pearson*, effigy by *H. H. Armstead*. Recumbent effigy in pink alabaster recess. – Above and to the side five portrait medallions, e.g. G. Stokes † 1903, by *Thornycroft*, and Lord Lister † 1912, by *Brock*.

IRON GATE. 1764 by *Wood*.

NORTH WALL. STAINED GLASS. Eight windows by *Sir Ninian Comper*, begun before the First World War to a scheme drawn up in 1907 and completed since the last war. – E window N choir aisle to the Stephensons, with architectural and engineering works ancient and modern (the Ark, the Menai Bridge, Nineveh, Newcastle High-Level Bridge) and portraits of engineers. By *Wailes*, 1862. – MONUMENTS in the first three bays keep to the medieval wall-arcading. Philip de Sausmarez † 1747. By *Cheere*. Excellent Rococo pedestal with sea battle in relief. Oval medallion and two putti; very lively and elegant. – Dr Blow, the composer, † 1708. Cartouche with two cherub heads. Open music book at the foot showing a canon composed by Dr Blow. – Dr Croft † 1727, also a composer. An organ on the base; bust at the top.

Admiral Temple West, 1761 by *Wilton* (signed I. W.), with a very convincing bust. – Richard Le Neve † 1673; no figure. – Sir Edmund Prideaux † 1728 and wife † 1741. By *Cheere*. Fine Rococo detail; two putti, double portrait medallion above. – Above these on the wall-passage: Sir G. L. Staunton by *Chantrey*, 1823. Neo-Greek. Relief of Staunton seated expounding the law to an Indian. – E. L. Sutton † 1834. Also neo-Greek. Mourning woman lying over some books. By *Chantrey*.

Earl of Normanton, Archbishop of Dublin. By *Bacon Jr*, 1815. The archbishop stands above in high relief. Cathedral in low relief on the pedestal below. To the l. charity folk, to the r. clergymen.

Philip Carteret † 1710, aged nineteen. Signed by *Claudius David Eques*. An odd composition with a bust against the back wall, but free of it and below a figure of Father Time.

Admiral Priestman † 1712. By *F. Bird*. Obelisk, dull portrait head and trophies, but according to Dr Whinney the earliest example of the type of monument with a head in a medallion set against an obelisk. – Vice-Admiral Baker † 1716. Also by *Bird*. With *columna rostrata* on sarcophagus. Trophies, but no effigy.

Dr Richard Mead, the celebrated physician, † 1754. By *Scheemakers*. Bust on a pedestal with caduceus and books. – Robert and Richard Cholmondeley † 1678 and 1680; no figures. – Edward Mansell † 1681, by *W. Woodman*. Cartouche; no figure. – On the wall-passage above: Spencer Perceval, Prime Minister, assassinated in 1812. By *Westmacott*, 1816. Recumbent effigy on half-rolled-up mat; a remarkable archaism. Seated Power (with fasces) at his head; Truth and Temperance at his feet. Relief of the murder above. A disjointed composition.

William Morgan † 1683 and Thomas Mansell † 1684. Two inscriptions in oval medallions, flanked by twisted columns (otherwise absent from the abbey except in the C 13 Cosmati work); scrolly open pediment with urn. – Mrs Jane Hill † 1631. She kneels towards the E. Against the back wall small figure of skeleton in shroud ('Mors mihi lucrum') and of tree of life ('solus Christus mihi sola salus'). – Mrs Mary Beaufoy † 1705, by *Grinling Gibbons*, signed; not at all good. She kneels between two pilasters and is crowned by cherubs. Two putti l. and r. seated outside lamenting her. – On the wall-passage: Governor Loten by *Banks*, 1793. Large standing allegorical figure, very Grecian. With one hand she holds a lion, the other rests on a portrait medallion.

Robert Killigrew † 1707. By *Bird*. Cut out of one stone, with a large trophy of arms arranged fan-wise; no figure. – On the wall-passage Captains Harvey and Hutt † 1794, by *Bacon Jr*, 1804. Seated figures of Britannia and Fame, l. and r. of an urn with double portrait in medallion.

Dr Woodward † 1728. By *Scheemakers*. Seated female figure holding a portrait medallion. – Lady Price † 1678. Probably by *Gibbons*. Big cartouche; no figures. – Dowager Countess of Clanrickard † 1732. Semi-reclining effigy on sarcophagus.

General Stringer Lawrence † 1775. By *W. Tyler*. Erected by the East India Company. Tall pedestal with relief of the relief of Trichinopoli. Seated and standing allegories of the E.I.C. and of Fame; bust on top. – Sir Henry Campbell-Bannerman † 1908, with bronze bust by *Paul Montford*.

West end of the aisle: Charles James Fox, 1810–15 by *Westmacott*. A brilliant piece. Fox expiring on a couch, Liberty holding him, Peace mourning at his feet, a Negro praying for him.

Under the NW tower: STAINED GLASS. Impressive large figure made up of assembled fragments of *c.* 1400. – MONUMENTS. E side. Viscount Howe † 1758, designed by *James Stuart* and carved by *Scheemakers*. Large, noble inscription plate on lions. Seated on top, perhaps a little too small, mourning figure of Massachusetts Bay province, which put up the monument, as a few years later it would not have done. – Sir James Mackintosh, 1855 by *Theed*. Base with allegorical figures; pedestal with bust on top. – George Tierney † 1830, by *R. Westmacott Jr*, with allegories on pedestal and bust on top. – Above this Col. Lake † 1808, by *J. Smith*, sarcophagus with draped banner against obelisk with rounded sides.

North wall. Third Lord Holland † 1840. By *Baily*. Illustrated in the *Illustrated London News* in 1848 as 'The Prisonhouse of Death'. Big doorway with tapering sides. Realistic arched door. Bust on top. Three large seated allegories below. No inscription. – To the l. and r. two busts, Marquess of Lansdowne † 1863, and Earl Russell † 1878, both by *Boehm*.

West wall. Col. Sir R. Fletcher † 1813. By *Baily*. Good, with two standing soldiers. – Joseph Chamberlain † 1914, bust by *Tweed*. – Zachary Macaulay by *Weekes*, 1842. Bust and relief referring to his work for the abolition of slavery. – Above the doorway to the tower stairs: General Gordon, bust with shield and scrolls below. Bronze, 1892 by *Onslow Ford*. – On the wall-passage Major Rennell † 1830, bust by *T. Hagbolt*. – Dr Arnold of Rugby † 1842, demi-figure with hands, by *Pinker*. – In the middle between these two, William Horneck † 1746, by *Scheemakers*. Portrait medallion with standing allegory r. and putto l.

In the middle of the chapel. Capt. Montagu by *Flaxman*, 1804. Circular base with lions l. and r. Standing figure crowned by Victory. Probably the last naval monument erected in the abbey, just when St Paul's was becoming the favoured anchorage.

Main Nave and Choir, W to E

WEST WALL. Seventh Earl of Shaftesbury † 1885, the philanthropist. Design by *Pearson*, statue by *Boehm* – John Conduitt and wife † 1737 and 1739. By *Cheere*. Sarcophagus and obelisk. The portrait medallion and the putti below and above are of bronze. – Over the W door William Pitt, son of the Earl of Chatham, † 1806. By *Westmacott*, 1807–13. Rather a dull performance. He stands and addresses an invisible crowd. To the l. Anarchy subdued and chained, a muscular male body turned towards us, to the r. History, a female figure, with her back towards us. – Admiral Sir Thomas Hardy † 1732, by *Cheere*. Semi-reclining against an obelisk, a fine figure in a telling attitude.

STAINED GLASS. W window. 1735 by *Joshua Price*, possibly to a design by *Thornhill*.

PAINTING. Against the NE pier of the S tower large portrait of Richard II (thought to have been his votive gift to St Edward's shrine). The date seems to be *c.* 1385–90. The king appears seated in full regalia on a flimsy Gothic throne painted without a real sense of structure and of volume. The same is true of the body and especially the legs of the king. The modelling is softly graded, and in this volume is convincingly expressed. The head is clearly lifelike, as comparisons with the Wilton Diptych (National Gallery) and the effigy in the feretory (see above) prove. But the interest in realism does not yet go beyond that. The painting is still entirely C 14 in character and indeed more closely related to Bohemia and North Germany than to the progressive courts of Dijon and Paris. It was once attributed to *André Beauneveu*, but is now generally accepted as English.

Two FLOOR SLABS near the w door: of black Belgian marble, to the Unknown Soldier buried here 1920; of green marble, to Winston Churchill †1965, lettering by *Reynolds Stone*. – CANDELABRA. By *Benno Elkan*, 1940 and 1943, Old Testament l., New Testament r. It was a bold thing to do for the abbey to commission these; for though the general form is not in any contrast to medieval traditions, the modelling of the figures has little of that sentimentality which is so irritating in the stained glass of the 1940s in the abbey. – ALMSBOXES. Two early C18 boxes of wood with scrolly volutes on the sides.

PULPIT, called 'Cranmer's' for no documented reason. With linenfold panelling; probably early C16. Formerly in the Henry VII Chapel and possibly made for it. Canopy restored by *Dykes Bower*, and steps by him.

CHANDELIERS. Made by *Pilkingtons* of Waterford glass and put up in 1965, given by the Guinness family. Curiously French (or at any rate secular) in effect. Whether this is desirable is another matter. An aim was to conceal the light-bulbs.

MONUMENTS in the nave. N side, tower bay: Marquess of Salisbury, the Prime Minister, designed by *Bodley*, made in 1909 by *Sir W. Goscombe John*. Black marble sarcophagus with recumbent bronze effigy. Bronze figures against the sides of the sarcophagus, in freely Baroque niches. – Farther E, BRASSES in the floor: Robert Stephenson †1859, with large figure, by *Sir G. G. Scott* and *Hardman*. – Sir George Gilbert Scott †1878, by *Street* (made 1881 by *Barkentin & Krall*), with cross flanked by a knight and a figure of architecture. – Sir Charles Barry †1860, with cross flanked by a plan of the Houses of Parliament and an elevation of the Victoria Tower. – G. E. Street by *Bodley*, 1884. – J. L. Pearson †1897, by *Caröe*.

PULPITUM. The choir with its stalls extends three bays into the nave. It is closed to the w by a pulpitum or choir screen one further bay in depth. In c. 1725 the medieval pulpitum was demolished (though some of the masonry may still be C13) and rebuilt by *Hawksmoor* in his Gothic taste. Ceiling under organ loft improved probably by *Keene* in 1775 with fan-vaulting 'of less quality than Hawksmoor would have exacted' (Dykes Bower). *Blore* in 1834 put a new w front on the pulpitum. Iron gates by Hawksmoor, with overthrow by *Tapper*, c. 1930, successfully in keeping. – The ORGAN CASES are by *J. L. Pearson*, 1895–7, restored to their original position by *Dykes Bower*.

Against the pulpitum l. and r. of the doorway two large MONUMENTS designed by *Kent* (for £50 each) and with sculpture by *Rysbrack*, fitting well into their recesses (then

in Hawksmoor's screen). To the l. Sir Isaac Newton, 1731. Black sarcophagus on fat scrolly feet. The relief on it with its putti refers to the discovery of the law of gravitation, to optics and to the new fixed standards of coinage. Sir Isaac appears semi-reclining on the sarcophagus, a noble figure with intelligent, vigorous features. His elbow rests on four books: Divinity, Chronology, Optics and Phil. Princ. Math. Above, a large globe on which the course of the comet of 1680 is shown, with signs, constellations and planets. Two putti to the r., Astronomy reclining on the globe. The composition is entirely Baroque, yet there is nothing sensational or indeed operatic about this monument. What it has of oratory is nowhere excessive. – Lord Stanhope, Secretary of State, 1733. A similar composition, obviously meant as a counterpart to the Newton. The figure (in Roman armour) also semi-reclining, one putto with shield on the l., a tent behind, and Minerva on top.

CHOIR STALLS. 1848 by *Blore* (the medieval stalls having been destroyed in 1775 and replaced by *Keene*; for one surviving C13 misericord, see *Henry VII Chapel* above).

Nave and Choir South Aisle, w to e

Under the s w tower: to the E, SCREEN of stone erected by Abbot Islip; early C16. The chapel was originally used as the baptistery of the abbey, and the Consistory Court also met here. In 1925 it was converted into a memorial of the First World War and called the CHAPEL OF ST GEORGE. The architect was *Sir Ninian Comper*. By him the heavy wrought-iron SCREENS and other fittings. The erection of the N screen necessitated the removal of one of the largest C18 monuments in the abbey, the Capt. Cornewall monument (see *Cloisters*, exit to Dean's yard), a dangerous precedent. – STAINED GLASS. Large, not well-preserved figure of St George, C15, and more bits of old glass. – MONUMENTS. s wall: Henry Fawcett †1884 by *Alfred Gilbert*. With seven small, somewhat fantastic bronze figures. – Above James Craggs, Secretary of State, the son of a shoemaker, designed by *Gibbs*; carved by *Guelfi* in 1727, assisted by *Bird*. Standing figure leaning on an urn. The commission was secured for his protégé Guelfi by Lord Burlington; the inscription was composed by Pope. The monument is Guelfi's most conspicuous work in England. Not in its original position; the pedimented background not preserved. The attitude of the figure became very popular and was imitated by Rysbrack and others (cf. Kent's design for Shakespeare in the s transept). – William Booth, founder of the Salvation Army, †1912. Small marble bust by *Albert Siegenthaler* after a model of 1905 by *Mary Booth*. – On the w wall busts of F. D. Maurice †1872 and Charles Kingsley †1875, both by *Woolner*.

SOUTH WALL. Congreve †1729. By *F. Bird*. Sarcophagus with books, masks etc., and above demi-figure in relief

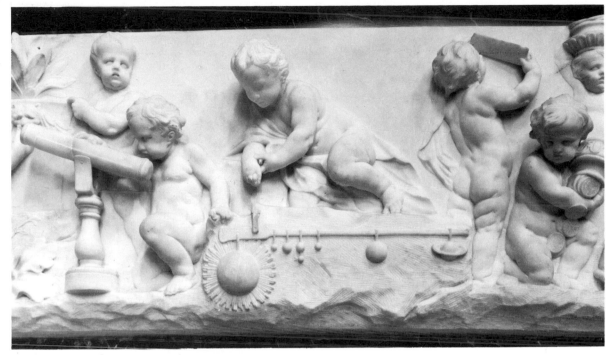

96. LONDON: WESTMINSTER ABBEY
Relief on monument to Sir Isaac Newton, designed by William Kent, made by J. M. Rysbrack, 1731

in oval medallion, an extremely telling character study. –
Dr John Freind † 1728, designed by *Gibbs* and carved by
Rysbrack. Very simple; bust on pedestal, black and white
reredos back, contained within the C 14 wall arcade. –
Above: ABBOT'S PEW, a wooden gallery with simple Perp
blank arcading. Early C 16. Erected by Islip.   STAINED
GLASS. British Flying Corps window, 1922 by *Burlison &
Grylls*.

Dean Sprat, Bishop of Rochester, † 1713. By *Bird*. Tablet
with inscription in plain architectural setting. – Dean
Wilcocks † 1756. By *Cheere*. Rococo base with relief showing the abbey completed by the two w towers built while
Wilcocks was dean. Pretty, free group of two putti above,
and pretty, loose garlands and cartouche above in the
wall-arcading. – Above: Admiral Tyrrell † 1766. By
Nicholas Read. A vast machine with plenty of rock and
clouds, the figures of History, Navigation and Hibernia, a
globe, a very Rococo anchor, and the stern of the *Buckingham*. Originally (figure removed) the admiral in the middle of this turmoil ascended to heaven. – STAINED GLASS.
Brunel memorial window, figures designed by *Holiday*,
arcaded setting by *Norman Shaw*, early for both: 1869,
clearly influenced by Morris and Burne-Jones, and 'easily
the finest in the Abbey' (Harrison 1980). Made by *Heaton,
Butler & Bayne*.

Dean Pearce † 1774, Bishop of Rochester. By *W. Tyler*.
Bust on pedestal. The same decorative elements as in the
Rococo monuments, but no longer the spirit of the Rococo.
– Mrs Bovey † 1724, signed by *Gibbs*, sculpture by
Rysbrack. Sarcophagus and above allegories of Faith and
Wisdom with portrait medallion between. The reredos
back reaches into the window zone with an open scrolly
pediment. – Dean Thomas † 1793, Bishop of Rochester.
The composition similar to Dean Pearce's. By *Bacon Jr*. –
Above: busts of Dean Buckland † 1856 by *Weekes*, and
Dean Ireland † 1842 by *Ternouth*. – STAINED GLASS.
Y.M.C.A. window, by *J. D. Forsyth*, 1921.

Lord Lawrence † 1879, bust by *Woolner*. – Col. Herries
† 1819, relief signed *R. Smirke, inv^t*, bust above by *Chantrey*. – Above: Ann Whytell by *Bacon*, 1791. Pedestal and
urn; charmingly carved figures of Innocence and Peace. –
Field-Marshal Wade, 1750 by *Roubiliac*. Portrait in relief
in an oval medallion. Below and over the sarcophagus
loosely hanging garlands. Higher up big composition of
Fame pushing away Time, who is trying to pull down a
pillar decorated with a trophy. The field-marshal left £500
for the erection of this monument. – Gen. Sir James
Outram † 1863, by *M. Noble*. Bust on square pedestal with
relief. On the relief Gen. Havelock between Outram and
Clyde. Seated mourning Scind and Bhil chiefs l. and r.

Carola Harsnett Lady Morland † 1674, and Ann Filding second Lady Morland † 1680, both by *William Stanton*, almost identical memorials with inscriptions in Hebrew, Greek, Ethiopic and English. The earlier inscription plate is flanked by halved columns, the later by full columns. Garlands and shields on top. – Between the two John Smith † 1718. Designed by *Gibbs*. Sarcophagus and obelisk. The c 14 wall-arcading had to be raised for the obelisk. On the sarcophagus rather saucily placed female figure weeping over a portrait medallion. – Above this: Gen. Fleming † 1751. Obelisk with bulgy double-curved sides and portrait medallion. Trees grow l. and r. of it. Below Hercules and Minerva tying together emblems of wisdom, prudence and valour. By *Roubiliac*.

Sir Charles Harbord and Clement Cottrell † 1672. Double inscription plate and relief of sea battle. Open segmental pediment. – Earl of Godolphin † 1712, the statesman. By *Bird*. Scrolly bracket and well-characterized portrait. – Above: Gen. Hargrave. Like the monument to Hargrave's friend Fleming, by *Roubiliac*. Signed and dated 1757. Perhaps his most famous and certainly his most sensational work. Crashing-down pyramid of massive stone blocks. The general climbing out of his tomb. Time on the r. defeats Death, a skeleton. The often encountered disgust or at least impatience with such displays is a c 19 feeling. It is food for thought that John Wesley admired this and the Nightingale monument (N transept E aisle) more than any other in the abbey.

Col. Townshend † 1759. Designed by *Robert Adam* and carved by *T. and B. Carter* and *J. Eckstein*. The coarse caryatids, two Indians, carrying the fluted straight-sided sarcophagus are the work of the Carters. The finely and floridly carved relief of Townshend's death is by Eckstein. Trophy above and obelisk. – Sir Palmes Fairborne † 1680, with urn and no figures. By *Bushnell*. – Major André, hanged as a spy by the Americans in 1780. Designed by *Robert Adam* and carved by *P. M. van Gelder*. Straight-sided sarcophagus with relief of Washington receiving André's petition. Reclining allegorical figure on the sarcophagus. – Above: Sir John Chardin † 1713 by *Cheere* (his cousin), 1746. An unusual design with very large bronze lettering: 'Soli deo gloria', 'Resurgam' etc. Large obelisk reaching high into the window space. At the foot of the obelisk globe, geographical instruments and books: he was a travel writer, merchant and diplomat.

IRON GATES. 1764 by *Wood*. – MONUMENTS against the N WALL of this bay, that is the back of the choir stalls: Thomas Thynne † 1682, by *Arnold Quellin*. Semi-reclining figure with pleading gesture and looking to heaven, on a sarcophagus decorated by a relief with the scene of Thynne's murder by hired highwaymen in Pall Mall. Back architecture with cloth draped over the pediment. – On the s wall: Gen. Strode † 1776. By *R. Hay-*

ward. Very chastely designed tablet. Small mourning figure: relief and trophies in the pediment. – Admiral George Churchill † 1710, brother of the Duke of Marlborough. By *Grinling Gibbons*. White architecture. Urn on pedestal in arched niche. Two putti l. and r. – Martin Folkes, P.R.S., F.S.A., † 1754. Designed by *W. Tyler* and executed by *R. Ashton*. Very staid and classical, in a style more suited to the date of its erection, 1788. Seated statue on the l., group of two putti on the r. busy with a microscope and compasses. A third putto by an urn on a pedestal higher up in the middle.

Next bay on the N wall: Thomas Owen † 1598. Stiff on his side. Flat arch, strapwork cartouche, columns l. and r. – an ordinary composition. – Pasquale de Paoli, the Corsican patriot, † 1807. Bust by *Flaxman*, exhibited at the Academy in 1798. – James Kendall † 1708, a typical cartouche of the time about 1700. Excellently carved. – On the s wall: Isaac Watts, 1779 by *Banks*. Charming hanging monument. Square base with fine circular relief of Dr Watts, pen in hand, listening to an angel. Fine foliage in the spandrels. Bust and two small putti on top. – George Stepney † 1707. Attributed to *Gibbons*. Bust under baldacchino of curtains. Two weeping putti; obelisks l. and r. – John and Charles Wesley, 1875 by *J. Adams-Acton*. Circular medallion with double portrait, and relief below. – Thomas Knipe † 1711. Typical large tablet with fluted pilasters and metope frieze and no figures. – Above: John and Sir Paul Methuen, by *Rysbrack*. Contracted for in 1758. Large hanging monument with elaborate cornucopia at the foot. No figures except two putti.

Against the N wall: Dame Grace Gethin † 1697, in her twenty-first year. Hanging monument. She kneels tightly between two angels standing against two black columns. Open scrolly pediment with two small allegorical figures. – Elizabeth Freke and Judith Austin † 1714 and 1716. Hanging monument. Simple architecture with two portrait reliefs in oval medallions on the l. and r. – On the s wall: William Wragg, 1779. Nice, small, classical monument with relief of shipwreck. Mourning figure on the l. (Signed R. H.; i.e. probably *Richard Hayward*.) – Above: Lord Clive, medallion, 1919 by *John Tweed*. – In the centre Sir Cloudesley Shovell † 1707. By *Grinling Gibbons*. Price £387 10s. Base with trophies and relief of shipwreck. Large semi-reclining figure in Roman dress with wig, lying on sarcophagus. Addison complained: 'Instead of the brave rough admiral, he is depicted in a long periwig, reposing himself upon a velvet cushion under a canopy of state'; and Horace Walpole said: 'Men of honour dread such honour.' (Lady Walpole's monument in the Henry VII Chapel, s aisle, is indeed in a very different vein.) Coupled black Corinthian columns. Two putti on the entablature. Inscription plate under baldacchino of curtains. – Above: Sir Godfrey Kneller by *Rysbrack*, 1730. Originally intended for Twickenham Church, Middlesex, Kneller's country house being near Twickenham. The model was probably made in 1722 or 1723. Bust between two putti, the principal feature of a big hanging monument.

Last bay of the N wall: Sir Thomas Richardson † 1635. Black marble monument with bronze bust in oval recess. Signed by *Le Sueur*. Baroque bulgy form of base and pediment. – William Thynne † 1584. Tomb-chest with recumbent effigy in armour on a half-rolled-up mat. – Dr A. Bell † 1832 by *Behnes*. Nice relief of school-teaching. The inscription praises Dr Bell's so-called Madras scheme of monitorial education which 'reduced to successful practice the plan of mutual instruction founded upon the multiplication of power and division of labour in the moral and intellectual world'. – On the S wall: Marchioness of Annandale † 1716. Signed by *Gibbs*. Very restrained architecture; no figures.

Postscript: Gallery

Certain MONUMENTS have been transferred to the gallery. The first two formerly hid the medieval paintings rediscovered on the S wall of the S transept.

On the S transept E gallery: Nicholas Rowe † 1739, by *Rysbrack*. High pedestal with bust. Seated female figure mourning. On the obelisk behind portrait of Rowe's daughter in profile. – John Gay † 1732, by *Rysbrack*, erected 1736. Standing putto on pedestal holding a portrait medallion. Obelisk at the back. On the front of the monument two lines by Gay: 'Life is a jest, and all things shew it: I thought so once, and now I know it.'

On the E gallery, above St Edmund's Chapel: G. L. Johnstone by *Flaxman*, 1815. Prostrate mourning woman over sarcophagus.

On the N transept E gallery: Sir Christopher Hatton Jr † 1619. Transferred from the Islip Chapel. Not in its original state. Sir Christopher and his wife, rather stodgy figures, recline on the sloping sides of a former pediment or sarcophagus.

CLOISTERS ETC.

The CLOISTERS must have been begun at the NE corner, apparently at the very beginning of Henry III's work, i.e. c. 1245–50. The earliest remaining part is the N bays of the E walk (i.e. under the Muniment Room), and then the E bays of the N walk, which look of 1250 rather than of the sixties. The latter date would have to be expected considering the dates of the nave. It is, however, quite possible that the outer aisle walls to the height of the cloister roof were put up before the demolition of the Norman nave and outside it. In any case the wall tracery of E and N walks (and the tracery above the inner side of the E doorway from nave to cloister) have a coarseness (or bold plainness) not otherwise

found in the abbey. The DOORWAY just referred to, in its face towards the cloister, on the other hand must be by a different workman. It is an exquisite piece of decoration, with two orders of Purbeck shafts, rosettes up the hollow moulding between them, diapering closer to the door itself, foliage roundels in the voussoirs, and a hoodmould on crowned heads. The l. side capitals of the shafts are of the French early C 13 variety known as crocket capitals. The N bays of the E walk take the place of the W aisle of the S transept, as has been explained before. The wall arcade of the E walk has blank tracery corresponding in design to that of the openings towards the cloister garth: broad openings of three lights with pointed-trefoiled heads, and above three unencircled trefoils, a motif invented, it seems, only two or three years before at the Sainte Chapelle in Paris. In the N walk the wall arcade has unencircled quatrefoils, but the openings to the garth, less squat than those of the E walk, return to the normal shapes in other parts of the abbey and have tracery of three encircled cinquefoils for each three-light opening. The quadripartite vaults with the same bands of grey stone as in the high vaults and aisle vaults. The three bays of the E walk described are followed by one bay of three plain blank arches (W wall of St Faith's) followed by the chapter-house entrance (see below). After that the contemporary doorway to the chapter library (former day stairs to the dormitory). The doorway has one order of columns and a tympanum with two blank archheads and a quatrefoil filled by a stiff-leaf arrangement of symmetrical cross-shape. Then the entrance to the Chapel of the Pyx (see below).

Meanwhile the E walk of the cloister itself had been continued southward only in the middle of the C 14. The work (much restored by *Blore*, c. 1835) is characterized by quadripartite vaults enriched by ridge ribs and transverse ridge ribs and by openings towards the garth with elaborate reticulated tracery. But the bay of the chapter-house entrance is distinguished from the others by a lierne vault and a sumptuous display of Dec tracery in the four-light opening towards the cloister garth. The tracery consists of two types of quatrefoil, each with spikes projecting from the junctions of the four lobes. Each is inscribed in an ogee quatrefoil. These motifs, bristling with sharp points, are repeated seven and four times apart from the fragmentary forms which result from the fitting of the system into the main arch.

The rest of the cloister was begun by Abbot Litlyngton before 1352, when he was still Prior. It was finished in 1366. The joint in the N walk is easily seen. The vaults lie lower, and blank tracery between the W bay and the bay adjoining it to the E overcomes the difference. Litlyngton's bays have tierceron vaults with ridge ribs and transverse ridge ribs and broad Perp tracery in the openings towards the garth. The tracery (heavily restored) consists of straight-sided panels, a kind of rectilinear reticulation. The w walk has four-light openings and therefore five of these panels in each bay, the s walk (much re-done by *Scott*) three-light openings with two panels. Good figure corbel in the w walk, demi-figure in late c14 clothes. Both walks have flat roofs, lower than the other work. Behind them to the w appear the two modest and informal houses which form the Deanery, behind to the s the remaining N wall of the refectory with its blocked windows (see below). Near the w end of the s walk a mid-c14 doorway (now into the Song School) with handsome cusped and sub-cusped opening, and next to it a recess of four lancet openings with large blank reticulated tracery above. At the N end of the w walk late c14 doorway into the s aisle, with two-centred arch and four circles with tracery above, two with mouchette wheels. – The unfortunate postwar tower visible from the w walk is part of Westminster School, not treated in this book. – There are two sets of good mid-c18 IRON GATES in the cloisters (s end, E and w walks) showing how direct *Keene* could be in Gothic.

MONUMENTS in the cloisters. Most are modest tablets not mentioned here, though a number are signed. The most touching inscription in the abbey (E walk): 'Iane Lister, dear childe, died Oct. 7th 1688.' EAST WALK. S. and A. Duroure † 1745 and 1765. Designed by the *younger Dance*. Plain, rather dry panel with urn on top. – Daniel Pulteney † 1731. Designed by *Giacomo Leoni*, sculpture by *Rysbrack*. Big sarcophagus and obelisk. Semi-reclining figure on it, reading.

SOUTH WALK. Below benches three early effigies of abbots: Laurence † 1173, the figure now utterly unrecognizable, Gilbert Crispin † 1121?, of black Tournai marble, in sunk relief, and William de Humez † 1222, again very defaced, effigy not sunk but in high relief. – Later monuments: Edward Tufnell † 1719, with bust and inscription referring to his refacing of large parts of the abbey building. – John Hay † 1751, tablet with urn at the top, signed by *Rysbrack*. – Magdalen Walsh † 1747, tablet with urn, signed by *Scheemakers*. – Wall tablet in coloured marbles, 1979, to the great c16, c18 and c20 circumnavigators Drake, Cook and Chichester.

Then down the so-called Parlour towards the w exit to Dean's Yard. On the r. Capt. Cornewall † 1743, erected 1744. Removed in 1925 to this back-door position from just inside the nave w door, where it stood 36 ft high; cut down for its present site. The young sculptor (later the architect Sir) *Robert Taylor* instead of architectural features here used rocks: the grotto style, not new to gardens in 1744, was new to the abbey. These frame a naval battle in low relief, and above is a medallion between Fame and Minerva –Britannia, the two allegorical figures carved by *B. Cheney*. This was the first monument to a naval hero voted by Parliament.

WEST WALK. Below the c14 corbel, W. R. Lethaby † 1931, a plain floor slab. – Lord Fraser of Lonsdale † 1974. The tablet by *David McFall* includes braille lettering, fingered smoother by blind visitors. – Sir Richard Jebb † 1787. Obelisk with portrait medallion and below, roundel with mourning woman. – W. Buchan † 1805, tablet by *Flaxman*. – William Woollett, the engraver, † 1785. By *Banks*. Relief of artist with muses and genii; bust on top. – Arthur O'Keeffe † 1756. By *Benjamin Palmer*, with bust on top. – Charles Godolphin † 1720 and his wife. Reredos back with Corinthian pilasters and open pediment. Long inscription and above it four cherubs' heads. – George Vertue † 1756, the antiquarian, tablet in architectural frame. – Edward Wortley Montagu † 1777. Tablet of *Coade* stone.

NORTH WALK. Two plain little tablets signed by *Scheemakers*: Mrs F. Meyrick † 1734, and T. Jordan † 1736.

Chapter House

The chapter house was built concurrently with the E parts of the abbey (see *Exterior* of the eastern arm). Its crypt must have been begun at once and the superstructure continued without break, for already in 1249 a lectern was ordered for the chapter house; in 1250 Matthew Paris spoke of the 'incomparable chapter house'; and in 1253 money was spent on its sculptural decoration. The first royal council recorded here was in 1257, so the tile pavement was probably laid by then. Flying buttresses were added in the c14. The original vault was destroyed in the c18. Use of the chapter house as a government record repository ended with the building of the Public Records Office in Chancery Lane in the 1850s. (On early use by the House of Commons, see *Introduction* above and Rigold 1976; on *Scott*'s restoration, Jordan 1980.)

The entrance from the cloister is by a low double doorway gathered together under a tall blank arch the height of the cloister. It has three orders of Purbeck shafts with sprays of foliage between. The outer order carries the arches and ribs of the cloister, the inner two are combined by archivolts with small-scale carved decoration, one with foliage, the other with fragmentary seated figures representing the Tree of Jesse. The doorways themselves have no capitals or abaci or any other hiatus between jambs and arches. They have a hollow chamfer decorated with sprays of stiff-leaf foliage. Above the doorways and below the superordinate arch is a large tympanum. This is given the unusual and typically Westminster all-over enrichment of large scrolls of stiff-leaf. In the spandrel between the two doorways rises a large bracket with crockets. It originally carried a big figure. Smaller brackets are above the apexes of the doorways. On these stand two angels, and of the r. one enough is preserved to recognize in him the Westminster features of slender proportions and long, sharply cut, parallel vertical folds.

The doorway leads into a low, dark OUTER VESTIBULE. The height could not be increased because of the floor-level of the dormitory above. Nor would the designer probably have wished to make it loftier, as we shall see presently. The outer vestibule is two bays wide and three bays deep. It has circular Purbeck shafts with moulded capitals, ribs of an elegant complex section, stiff-leaf bosses (the vaulting-cells partly renewed by *Scott*), and along the walls blank arcading with pointed arches of so shallow a curve that they are almost straight-sided.

The outer vestibule is followed by the INNER VESTI-BULE. This is as wide as the outer vestibule but has no subdivision into two aisles. The quadripartite vaults also run across the whole width. The space thus seems wider; it is also considerably higher (and was originally full of light, before *Scott* closed up the open tympanum of the entrance arch ahead). A staircase ascends in it to the chapter house proper. There can be no doubt that the designer was conscious of the *crescendo* he was here achieving. The ribs rest on Purbeck wall-shafts. The wall towards the outer vestibule again has two doorways with no hiatus between jambs and arches, but with stiff-leaf sprays all up both. Above the doorways against the wall is blank arcading just like that of the cloister N walk: three lancets and three unencircled quatrefoils. In the lancets are brackets for statues. The whole of this composition is, like that of the entrance from the cloister to the outer vestibule, enclosed by an arch of three orders on three orders of tall Purbeck shafts. Stiff-leaf sprays up the jambs between the shafts, and in the arch one order of voussoirs with stiff-leaf foliage too. In the s wall is one three-light and one slim lancet window. The three-light window is so typical of *c.* 1300 that it must be part of the repairs done after the fire of 1298. — STAINED GLASS, James Russell Lowell memorial, 1891, the poet having been American Minister in London. By *Clayton & Bell*. — ROMAN SARCOPHAGUS with inscription: 'Memoriae Valer(i) Amandini Valeri Superventor et Marcellus patri fecer(unt)'. It is of oolite and measures approximately 7 by 2½ ft, with a depth of 1½ ft. The inscription is well cut and well spaced, and is flanked by two peltate decorations. The sarcophagus itself is of the later Roman period, but its coped lid, which bears a large cross in relief, is early medieval. It was found in the churchyard, containing the bones of a young man, evidently not the original occupant.

It has already been said that the CHAPTER HOUSE must have been one of the earliest parts of the abbey begun by Henry III. The blind arcading behind the stone bench indeed has trefoiled arches which are not pointed, an early C 13 motif not otherwise used architecturally anywhere in the abbey. The chapter house is of an exceptional

architectural purity. It is octagonal, like the earlier chapter house at Beverley (demolished; Worcester's was then round, Lincoln's ten-sided, Lichfield's an elongated eight). But whereas before Westminster the walls of chapter houses had had no larger openings than lancets, the master of Westminster Abbey made use of the recent invention of the nave of Amiens (1220–39) and the Sainte Chapelle (1243–8) and filled the whole wall space of six of his eight sides with broad four-light windows nearly 40 ft tall and 20 ft wide. The seventh has blank tracery, the eighth the entrance. As at Amiens, one large foiled circle crowns and dominates each window. Below it are two arches, each containing a quatrefoil, and below these are the four even cusped lights, divided by the mullions of the window. It is a perfectly logical design, and a logical development from the bar tracery of Reims and the E parts of the abbey. It was bound to appeal to the Westminster master. Below the windows in the dado zone whose trefoiled blank arches have already been referred to, the capitals of the Purbeck shafts and the diapering of the spandrels also deserve careful study. Most of the capitals are moulded, but there is also stiff-leaf from the simplest upright leaves to the later 'wind-blown' variety. Most of the spandrels have stylized diapering, but occasionally more natural motifs are introduced (E bay, right of Christ in Majesty, S E bay, S W bay), especially a rose motif with leaves growing on a trellis. At the eight angles the Purbeck shafting gets very rich; for in the dado zone the strong vaulting shaft is flanked by one shaft each side for the lower blank arcading, and in the window zone by three nook-shafts either side for the windows. In addition the centre of the room is taken by a tall slim compound pier of eight shafts tied together by two shaft-rings. This pier which carries the vault was rebuilt by *Scott*. The vault (completely rebuilt) is evolved on the pattern of the Lincoln chapter house, with three ribs and a boss in each of the eight triangular cells.

The entrance wall has been sadly tampered with. It has a large, tall arch on two orders of Purbeck shafts. There are two doorways, and the inner order carries these. Between the two orders on the l. side a chain of seated figures, only nine in all, but well preserved and a reminder of how exquisite the carving even of minor details must originally have been at Westminster. The capitals are all C 19. The arch has one order of voussoirs with seated figures of the Tree of Jesse connected by foliage scrolls. The *trumeau* of the double doorway is all C 19, as is alas the large seated figure of Christ in a quatrefoiled circle. The narrow blank arches to the l. and r. of the doorway are original. They are pointed-trefoiled, and above them in two round-trefoiled recesses stand the two figures of the Annunciation, which will be discussed a little later. The spandrels between the recesses and the main arch are filled somewhat awkwardly by two trefoils with figures of angels of two different sizes, according to the spaces available. The remaining wall space again has diapering. It is curious that such cacophony as the meeting of the pointed main arch with the trefoils and trefoiled heads of the recesses and altogether the bitty disposition of forms on this entrance wall should have been devised by the same artist who conceived the tall, airy, spacious whole of this chapter house, the pattern for many to come (notably at Salisbury, c. 1260, also at Wells, laid out c. 1250 though not completed until c. 1307).

A last word here on *Scott* and his much attacked restorations. There is one thing at least that ought to be remembered. He found the chapter house full of bookcases, staircases, galleries (see the illustration in his *Gleanings*). If we have an idea today of its noble original beauty, Scott has given it us.

SCULPTURE. Annunciation, w wall. Probably the two figures paid for, according to documents, in 1253. They are slender figures, rather stiffly erect, with the sharp ridges in the drapery which we know from the angels in the transept, but with less elegance of action. The arm of the angel is decidedly unfortunate; it seems withered. The attitude and drapery of the Virgin is derived from Reims, but from the stage preceding that of the Joseph and Anna, that is, from the Queen of Sheba etc. The elongation is English (cf. Wells). See also *Interior*, s transept, angels.

PAINTINGS. At the back of the seats of the Chapter, that is in the blank arches of the dado zone. Not much of the whole scheme remains, and what remains is damaged or badly restored, and in any case does not seem to have been of very high quality. The E wall seems to have been a Last Judgement. The paintings were probably done about the middle of the C 14. Seated Christ in the centre. Angels and Instruments of the Passion l. and r. In the N W bay later c 14 scenes from the Revelation of St John. The first arch deals with the legend of St John, the second, third and fourth with the events of the Apocalypse. Below these must have been a Bestiary. Such animals appear as the reindeer and roe, the wild ass and tame ass, the dromedary and camel. These are dated by Dr Rickert as late as the beginning of the C 16. The inscriptions are in black letter and written on parchment and pasted on. Minor traces in the s E bay, s bay and s w bay. The source of the composition of the Apocalypse is illuminated manuscripts (possibly Camb. Trin. Coll. 102 or 213), the source of the style probably Hanseatic (Master Bertram); 'the damned' possibly the monkish view of the Commons meeting here (Rigold 1976).

STAINED GLASS. With pieces of the 1882 glass by *Clayton & Bell*, reset and added to after the Second World War by *Joan Howson*.

TILES. The pavement consists mostly of original mid-C 13 tiles, the majority with foliage, but there are also shields, an archer, a horseman, St Edward and the Pilgrim, a king, a queen, a bishop, fish (probably pike), and an often

repeated rose-window which is architecturally of special interest as it represents fairly accurately what the N transept rose was like originally – an eminently up-to-date design, not only from the English point of view. In the pavement Henry III placed the proud and lovely inscription: 'Ut rosa flos florum sic est domus ista domorum'. The floor was relaid by *Scott* but little restored, as it had long been covered by a wooden floor.

CRYPT. Below the chapter house is an octagonal crypt, accessible from the s transept E aisle. It has a low vault, springing from a thick circular pier. The ribs are simply chamfered. The windows are square and heavily barred and the walls are extremely thick.

Library and Muniment Room

Entrance s of the chapter house, up the former day stairs to the dormitory. Furnished c. 1620. Like a college library with presses on the l. and r. at r. angles to the walls. Some little strapwork decoration at the top of the ends of the presses. Heavy, strictly utilitarian hammerbeam roof, c 15. In the N wall blocked doorway to the w gallery of St Faith's Chapel, leading to the night stairs into the s transept. In the E wall of the N bay the rear of the blank tracery over the chapter-house vestibule.

MUNIMENT ROOM (on its position and sculpture, see *Interior*, s transept). Upon a wooden screen wall of the late C 14, large PAINTING of Richard II's white hart. – TILES. Very well preserved. Ascribed to the late C 14. – FURNITURE. A remarkable collection of sound utilitarian pieces. Two late C 12 chests, a C 13 chest, and one chest of the C 14 or C 15. Also a large tripartite cupboard standing under the C 14 white hart painting and dated by Eames to the C 15, when painted star devices were added on cupboard and screen (P. Eames 1977). – STAINED GLASS. Mid-C 13 roundel with the Resurrection. Formerly in the Jerusalem Chamber, where there are six other medallions of the same date, no doubt originally all from the abbey church (see *Jerusalem Chamber* below).

Chapel of the Pyx and museum

These were originally one and formed the undercroft of the dormitory. They date from the second half of the C 11. The room continued a little further N than the N wall of the Pyx Chapel, but that part was cut off in the late C 12 (Rigold 1976), when the day stair was constructed from the cloister to the dormitory. The outer walls are C 11. So are the circular piers, those capitals which are undecorated, the groined vaults, and some of the plain transverse arches. One blocked original E window in the museum. Several capitals were enriched in the late C 12 by foliage carving, partly with plain upright leaves, partly with stiff-leaf and some more richly lobed leaf shapes. One E arch of the museum has some painted zigzag decoration in red. – In

the museum CAPITAL, c. 1140, from the Norman cloister, with lively carvings of scenes from the Judgement of Solomon. – Stone HEAD of an abbot, very likely Islip and c. 1520, a striking portrait of an individual, used as filling in a N transept buttress c. 1720–c. 1890.

Other monastic remains

The range bounding the S cloister walk was the REFEC-TORY. (The House of Commons met here in the C15 and early C16.) Its site now forms part of a yard behind Ashburnham House (Westminster School). The lower part of the N wall shows C11 blank arcading with plain block capitals, continued in the Song School W of the refectory. The upper part has nine tall blocked early C14 windows (originally overlooking the S cloister roof) with transoms and cusped Y-tracery: repairs are recorded for 1301 etc. The lower arcading of the E wall (backing on to the Dark Cloister, below) is mid-C14 and much ruined. Angel corbels to support a timber roof still exist.

Continuing the E cloister walk southward (now to Little Dean's Yard, Westminster School), the DARK CLOISTER. This is a late C11 N–S passage flanked at first by the walls of the refectory and dormitory, and after that by walling of the C11 on the E and the late C14 on the W, the latter with a long strip of wooden-framed window of twenty lights. To the E a completely plain tunnel-vaulted C11 passage leads to the infirmary cloister (below). Farther S the Dark Cloister originally turned E to skirt the reredorter or latrine range (below).

Normally only the W walk of the FARMERY (i.e. infirmary) or LITTLE CLOISTER is accessible. This cloister is to the eye essentially late C17, though much had to be rebuilt after the Second World War and the masonry of the surrounding ranges is of Litlyngton's time, i.e. the later C14. The whole or most of it stands on the site of the later C12 INFIRMARY. Of this nothing at all remains above ground, but it was continued to the E, just as at Canterbury, Ely and in other monastic establishments, by the INFIRM-ARY CHAPEL. This, called Chapel of St Katherine, is still clearly recognizable. It lies beyond a fine DOORWAY made by Litlyngton in 1371–2. Two-centred arch with two orders of clustered shafts, and the canted reveal between them decorated with a chain of quatrefoils running up the jambs and into the arch without any break. The chapel had a nave with aisles of five bays and an oblong chancel. On the N side there are only stumps, but on the S, built into the wall, are the piers, alternately circular and octagonal, with multi-scalloped capitals and arches with three-dimensional zigzag and crenellation motifs. The octagonal piers have an edge, not a side towards the nave and the aisle. In the remaining S wall of the S aisle a round-headed window with roll moulding. All these forms point to a date c. 1170.

The cloister has an arcade of probably 1680–1, with segmental arches on oblong piers. Good IRON GATE into the garth. The N and S walks and the S part of the W walk were rebuilt after the Second World War by *Seely & Paget*. The N part of the W walk keeps some original C14 masonry features. The same is true of the part of the E range, which was the INFIRMARER'S HALL. E windows with transoms and early or mid-C14 tracery. In a wall some C14 tiles. At the S end of the W walk in the W wall a precious fragment of the C11 E wall of the REREDORTER with a small round-headed window and above it square facing-stones and square tiles set diamond-wise to make a two-colour pattern (such two-colour work is a feature also of Early Norman gallery tympana of the chancel at Chichester).

W of the great cloisters lies the Deanery. The S walk at its W end is continued by a passage (to Dean's Yard, below) which was originally the monks' parlour. It is in two parts, each of two bays with tierceron vaults of the later C14 identical with those of the cloister W and S walks. (For the Cornewall monument, see *Cloisters* above.) Above the parlour was probably the ABBOT'S CAMERA (called Cheynegates, the early name of the abbot's house). A recent staircase leads up to it. It is also in two parts. In the E part original segmental-headed N window reveals and TILES on the windowsills which belonged to the former floor, in the W part two two-centred arches to the S which connect with the Cellarer's Building (facing Dean's Yard), and in the SE corner remains of the original outer NW corner of the C11 refectory. The wall (like the reredorter remains in the Little Cloister) is faced with square stones laid diamond-wise, some grey and some red. Above them the C14 cornice.

The ABBOT'S LODGING extended NW of the Camera round an oblong courtyard. This is reached from the parlour by another tierceron-vaulted passage. The buildings all belong essentially to 1370 etc., though they have been added to at various times. The S wall is C13 masonry, the W wall clearly later C14. Here lay the Abbot's Hall, now COLLEGE HALL of Westminster School. It has two-light windows with tracery similar to that of Litlyngton's cloister walks. They were glazed in 1375–6. Roof of low pitch on corbels with angels holding shields. Partly original heavy tie-beams on arched braces with traceried spandrels and small kingposts. The braces rest on angel corbels of stone. The transomed windows are renewed. At the S end is a plain mid-C17 SCREEN with gallery over. Odd straight-sided blank tracery of lozenge or diamond shapes between the doorways, ordinary blank arching on the gallery parapet above. S of the hall is the KITCHEN with a large fireplace in the E wall, N of the hall the Jerusalem Chamber.

The JERUSALEM CHAMBER was so called perhaps after wall paintings or tapestries originally to be seen here (a comparable case being an Antioch Chamber at Clarendon Palace). It has renewed W windows of two lights, and a renewed early c 16 N window of four lights. The low-pitched roof rests on tie-beams on small arched braces. – FIREPLACE with coupled Tuscan columns flanking the opening and two more orders of columns in the overmantel. Set up by Dean Williams in honour of the betrothal of Charles I to Henrietta Maria in 1624, and including the arms of Westminster and Lincoln, of which Williams was also bishop from 1621. – TAPESTRIES. Five parts of two large pieces woven by *W. Pannemaeker c.* 1540–50 at Brussels to *B. van Orley's* design, related to a set hanging in the Great Hall at Hampton Court. On the s wall 'St Peter Healing the Lame Man', probably c 17 English, much simplified from the original scene in the Acts of the Apostles series. – STAINED GLASS. Six medallions of outstandingly good mid-c 13 glass, no doubt from the abbey church, and no doubt completed by the time of the consecration of 1269. One pair of somewhat irregular quatrefoils represents the Ascension of Christ and the Descent of the Holy Spirit. The Martyrdoms of St John the Baptist (?) and St Stephen are framed by pointed quatre-foils, the Murder of the Innocents and a miracle of St Nicholas by vesica shapes. All these shapes are usual in c 13 glass in France and England. Deep blue backgrounds, ruby-coloured borders. The glass may be by *William le Verrer*, who is mentioned in a charter in 1272. A seventh medallion is now in the Muniment Room (see *Library* etc. above).

The basement of the Jerusalem Chamber is divided by a row of oaken posts. From the Jerusalem Chamber, going E, one enters a small lobby (original niche for a lamp) communicating on the s with the Abbot's Hall and on the E with the Jericho Parlour, part of a range leaning against the abbey nave and put up by Abbot Islip in the early c 16. The difference in date is at once visible from outside. The stone is buff as against the grey of the late c 14 buildings, and the windows are typical of their date; mullioned, of two, three, four and eight lights, segmental-headed. The principal room, with linenfold panelling inside, is on the first floor (level with the Jerusalem Chamber) and reached via another small lobby from a (later) outside staircase. In the basement below runs a late c 14 w–E wall. Here also a small room with an early c 16 brick vault. The second floor has three rooms, two with original early c 16 moulded ceiling ribs. c 16 and c 17 panelling.

The E range of the courtyard is the present DEANERY. Its s half was rebuilt after the Second World War by *Seely & Paget*, its N half consists of two unassuming brick houses of late c 17 and Early Georgian date, now all painted white. There is a small private garden towards the w walk of the cloister (on the outer w cloister wall, i.e. E garden wall, remains of two arches). The houses are of two and three storeys. On the s and w sides the three-storeyed part has two pretty oriel windows, one of them pedimented. The Deanery also extends into the s range. Here on the first floor a room with renewed c 14 windows and a handsome FIREPLACE with a late c 18 surround and overmantel of *c.* 1740 with open scrolly pediment. Below is the passage from the parlour through which we entered. At the w end of the parlour lies Dean's Yard.

DEAN'S YARD is a large and sheltered space, once partly filled by medieval bakehouse, brewhouse and granary, now with a lawn and trees, and a variety of buildings around. On the s side visual character is diminished by CHURCH HOUSE, 1937–40 by *Sir Herbert Baker*. On the N side, the backs of *Scott's* Sanctuary Buildings (with some good Victorian ironwork) and the kitchen range of College Hall. The w side mixed 1860s and 1930s. The E side mixed c 14 and c 18. For Westminster School, see B of E *London 1*.

The COLLEGE GARDEN is bounded on the s to Great College Street by the PRECINCT WALL of the abbey. It dates from *c.* 1374 and stands 20 ft high. The garden is much older (open for band concerts in summer; impressive close view of Barry's Victoria Tower). The wall also stands to the E, where on the outside Abingdon Street's former c 18 houses have been replaced by an underground garage and municipal lawn. In the garden four STATUES (two male and two female, saints?) from *Wren's* great marble altarpiece which was executed by *Gibbons* and *Quellin* for James II's Catholic chapel at Whitehall Palace, and quickly relegated to Hampton Court in 1688, so saved from the subsequent Whitehall fire. Installed in the abbey 1706–1820 with some damage to the sanctuary, the altarpiece was ousted for George IV's coronation. The heads of these sadly weathered standing figures are probably by *Quellin*.

The triangular 'square' before the abbey's w front is the SE half of the space called Broad Sanctuary at the E end of Victoria Street. Immediately s w of the abbey's w porch and attached to the exterior of the Jerusalem Chamber's basement, the ABBEY SHOP. Built *c.* 1880 as the chapter office, converted *c.* 1955 with hybrid fenestration. (NP: 'regrettable', yet there is a need for such a shop at the w door in this touring age, and the shop's visual effect in its mixed surroundings at this prominent spot is fairly null.) The s side of the square is formed by *Scott's* SANCTUARY BUILDINGS of 1854, a Gothic asymmetrical row with gateway to Dean's Yard. In the centre of the space in front of the abbey is *Scott's* MEMORIAL COLUMN of 1859–61 to Westminster School's Crimean War dead. Red granite column with shaft-ring from which hang shields, a big Gothic capital, lantern-cross top on that and a statue above that – a High Victorian piling-up of effects. Sculpture by *J. B. Philip*. On Lutyens's 'narthex' design for this space, see *Exterior*, w *front*, above.

For more details on the abbey precinct and environs, see the latest edition of B of E *London 1: The Cities of London and Westminster*.

London: Westminster

METROPOLITAN CATHEDRAL CHURCH OF THE MOST PRECIOUS BLOOD, ST MARY, ST JOSEPH, AND ST PETER *Roman Catholic*

(Based on B of E *London 1: The Cities of London and Westminster*, 1973, partly rewritten with information from Monsignor Canon Bartlett, Peter Howell, George McHardy, John Phillips and *Victorian Church Art* 1971.)

Cathedral since 1903. Until the redevelopment of Victoria Street in the 1970s, the site lay among narrow side streets. Beyond them, for three-quarters of a century, only the tower revealed the cathedral's presence. In 1976 a piazza was opened up between the w front and Victoria Street, greatly enhancing both. The newly visible and newly cleaned cathedral is at last shown to be one of London's noblest buildings.

Built 1895–1903 to designs by *John Francis Bentley* (1839–1902). Another site had been bought by Cardinal Manning in 1867, and between then and 1873 Henry Clutton (related by marriage to Manning) made several designs for a Gothic cathedral, variously inspired by Cologne, Amiens, Notre Dame in Paris, etc. Nothing came of them, nor of a proposal in 1882 to get Ferstel to build a replica of the Vienna Votivkirche here. In 1884 Manning

bought the present site, which was part of that of the Westminster New Bridewell (1830–85), but it was left to his successor to build the new cathedral. In 1894 Cardinal Vaughan asked for designs from Bentley who, as it happened, had trained in Clutton's office, and whose fine church of the Holy Rood at Watford had recently been completed. Against Bentley's preference for Gothic, Vaughan insisted upon an Italian basilica, partly so as not to compete with Westminster Abbey only half a mile away. But Bentley loathed the basilican style and won Vaughan over to Byzantine. So Bentley went off to look round. He saw Rome, Pisa, S. Ambrogio in Milan, Ravenna, Padua, Venice, Torcello and other places, but was prevented by a cholera outbreak in Constantinople from going there. Yet the roots of his design are more St Sophia and St Irene even than St Mark's in Venice. Bentley said that Lethaby and Swainson's book on St Sophia, published in 1894, and his visit to S. Vitale at Ravenna 'really told me all I wanted', according to his daughter Mrs de l'Hopital's book on Westminster Cathedral (1919).

The EXTERIOR is red brick with ample bands or stripes of stone. Although such striping is parodied on neighbouring blocks of flats of similar date, the superiority of the cathedral's brickwork, especially since recent cleaning, is clear. The dome over the sanctuary is entirely Byzantine in its peculiar fenestration, and the large tripartite semicircular

98. LONDON: WESTMINSTER CATHEDRAL Final plan by J. F. Bentley, 1896. R.I.B.A. Drawings Collection

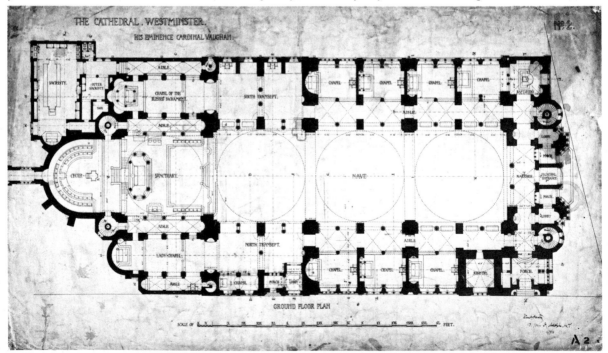

99. LONDON: WESTMINSTER CATHEDRAL
Built 1895–1903. The main front from Victoria Street, *c.* 1980

windows come from the same source. The campanile, however, is more Italian. It is 284 ft high, almost precisely the height of the most similar Italian campanile, that of Siena Cathedral, and it is placed asymmetrically over the first bay of the N range of chapels. Bentley wanted two towers (Collcutt's Imperial Institute with three, also Mediterranean in feeling, had just been completed). The initial credit for this most inspiring element of the design must therefore go to Cardinal Vaughan. In its slender sheerness it has established itself as one of the beacons of London, and the way in which, at the top, it climbs up by small pinnacles from the square into the octagonal lantern was brilliantly managed by Bentley. This as well as much of the detail lower down is not at all imitative – see for instance such curious motifs as the 'bricknogging' and the segmental windows with garlands of the outer chapels. The NW porch and the big W portal are Italian Renaissance. Although when Bentley died in 1902 some of the carving on these remained to be done, all the drawings of the W front were signed by him, and the façade was finished by 1902.

It is important to remember, now our view of the front is opened up, that originally the front of this major building was only to be seen sideways. Mr Phillips, the present cathedral architect, says 'innumerable difficulties with the London Building Acts', settled by Bentley well before 1900, concerned angles of light to buildings then closely opposite. Externally the cathedral is 360 ft long, 156 ft wide, and up to the top of the main dome 117 ft high. Inside, the span of the vaults is 60 ft and the height of the main arches 90 ft. As usual with C19 churches on urban sites, 'W' and 'E' here are ritual not compass directions.

Westminster Cathedral is a longitudinal domed building, and in this alone Bentley's freedom of adaptation appears. It is really the Gesù scheme of nave with outer chapels, domed crossing, transepts not projecting, and chancel, but translated into Byzantine. There are other equally original features. The cathedral consists of a narthex, a nave of three domed bays (the third forming the crossing), narrow low aisles with vastly high galleries above, and low outer chapels a little higher than the aisles. Each aisle bay is subdivided into two by a square pier, and each of these half-bays is screened from the nave and from the chapels by pairs of smaller arches on columns, which carry the gallery. The vaulting of each aisle bay also is subdivided. Above the gallery there are two high transverse tunnel-vaults for each bay. The aisle itself is vaulted by a tunnel-vault running E–W, interpenetrated by the arches which carry the gallery. The domed crossing is as wide as the other nave bays. The N and S crossing arches are again subdivided in the same way as the nave bays, but the two pairs of arches carry a balcony instead of a gallery.

Moreover the division of the transepts is continued in a N–S direction by an arched screen separating a W from an E half of the transept. Each half of the transept has a high tunnel-vault running N–S, like those of the aisle galleries. This division of the transepts Bentley may have seen and liked in churches such as Pearson's St Augustine Kilburn. The sanctuary bay is domed too, but here the dome has small windows. The sanctuary bay is accompanied to N and S by long apsed chapels – a Romanesque motif. E of the high altar is the main apse. There is a crypt beneath the sanctuary and two bridges connecting the E end with the Archbishop's House and the Clergy House. SE of the main apse and at right angles to it, the sacristy, large and tunnel-vaulted.

The INTERIOR of Westminster Cathedral is without a doubt one of the most moving of any church in London. This is – it is true – to some extent due to the fact that it is unfinished. Bentley wanted to cover all the walls and vaults with marble and mosaic. As it still is, higher up, the absolutely bare rough brickwork, emphasizing the straightness of the uprights and the vast curves of the arches and domes, helps to keep Bentley's structural statement clear and unblurred (even if primeval grandeur was not entirely the atmosphere he had in mind). However, when the cathedral opened, one of its admirers, the architect Philip Webb, according to his biographer Lethaby, thought that 'the splendid rashness of design in the inter-buttressing of the domes . . . can hardly be spoiled by the future decorative work', and that 'even if the finishing work to be done on the surface be too inferior, it can hardly kill the effect of the great skeleton'. Today, up the main piers and in the chapels marble and mosaic facing has been completed or begun. The marbles are splendid and their various colours and patterns are an ideal architectural enrichment, because they are smooth and do not introduce anything small, as the mosaics with their figures and stories do. Perhaps that would be different if artists of Ravennate calibre had been used or available. As it is, Lethaby as early as 1902 complained of the mosaics' 'weakness' and 'sentimental vulgarity'. But the marbles are wonderful. (There used to be a joke that the best foreign marbles in London were to be found here and in the Lyons Corner Houses, but the latter were never as good as this.) The green for some of the columns is from Thessaly, the same, it is said, which Justinian used for St Sophia; there is a green-patterned Cipollino from Euboea; the yellow is mostly from Siena, with one fine column from Var and the baldacchino columns Veronese, the red Languedoc, and the white for capitals Carrara. Greys in superb shades are from Hymettus, also Italian 'dove'. Where on the other hand the mosaic decoration is complete, as in some of the chapels described below, it looks – maybe for associational reasons – Early Christian Revival.

This is even more obviously so in the case of the PULPIT, made by *Aristide Leonori* in 1899 in Rome, frankly on the pattern of medieval Italian pulpits; original base changed to columns by *L. H. Shattock* in 1934. – The altar BALDAC-CHINO was designed in 1901 by *Bentley* and made after his death by *Farmer & Brindley*, the well-known firm who were responsible for much of the decoration and detailing of the cathedral.

The most valuable work of art in the cathedral is the series of *Eric Gill*'s STATIONS OF THE CROSS, made in 1913–18 (Bentley had wanted opus sectile for these). Eric Gill's work in relief always tends to be more graphic than strictly sculptural. One finds oneself time and again reading these stories as if they were wood engravings. In that respect Gill is yet another illustration of that curious English leaning towards line rather than shaped mass. But with these limitations the Stations are memorable as one of the first works of religious art in England to abandon sentimental naturalism and seek for a deeper expression of feeling in intensified line and rhythm of lines. – At the foot of the twelfth, burial slab of Cardinal Heenan †1975, with LETTERING by *Nicolete Gray*. By her also, in the tympanum of the N W porch, MOSAIC 1981.

The other FURNISHINGS etc. can be taken topographically, starting with the first chapel on the l., that is from the N W, and ending with the S W chapel. The HOLY SOULS' CHAPEL is one of those completely decorated and the one giving the best idea of what Bentley wanted. The mosaics by *W. C. Symons* are remarkable for their silver ground and almost Art Nouveau designs. Fine marble revetment and floor. – Bronze screen designed by *Bentley*. – CHAPEL OF ST GEORGE AND THE ENGLISH MARTYRS. Reliefs by *L. Clarke* and (above the altar) *Eric Gill*, his last work before his death. Bronze screen by *L. H. Shattock*. – Then the Chapel of St Joseph. Iron screen by *Seymour Lindsay* with metal grille below by *J. A. Marshall*. – Then on the outer wall of the l. transept mosaic of Joan of Arc by *Symons*. The chapel on the r. of the transept porch is the VAUGHAN CHANTRY, with monument designed by *Marshall*. Effigy by *J. Adams-Acton*, and metal screen by *Marshall*. – BLESSED SACRAMENT CHAPEL. Altar, canopy and bronze screen by *Marshall*, reckoned to be his masterpiece. Mosaics by *Boris Anrep*, 1953–61. They depict types and antitypes of the Mass. – To the N is the small SACRED HEART CHAPEL with mosaic of the Holy Face on the w wall by *W. C. Symons*, 1911. – SANCTUARY. The relief of Christ is by *Lindsay Clarke*; the prettily inlaid stalls were designed by *L. H. Shattock*; the throne is a facsimile of the one at St John Lateran. – The ROOD high up was designed by *Bentley* and made in Bruges, with paintings by *Symons*, the green line round the edge suggested by *John Singer Sargent*. – LADY CHAPEL. The mosaic decoration of the vault was carried out in 1931–2

and is by *G. A. Pownall*. The four alcove conches and altarpiece are earlier. They are by *Anning Bell*. – The CRYPT can be reached from behind the Lady Chapel. It has an impressive semicircle of monolithic columns of red granite with four Ionic capitals and above the altar a mosaic of St Edmund by *Symons*. In it also the MONUMENTS of Cardinal Wiseman by *E. Pugin* (transferred here from Kensal Green) and of Cardinal Manning, designed by *Bentley* with effigy by *J. Adams-Acton*, and, above, an early mosaic by *Anrep*, 1914. – On the middle pier of the N side of the SOUTH TRANSEPT a bronze plaque of St Teresa of Lisieux by *Manzù*, a slender swaying figure. Opposite, the Canadian Air Force War Memorial: a plaque of silvered nails forming a X P monogram, by *David Partridge*. An inscription by *Edward Wright* is to be added. Also in the S transept, C 15 alabaster sculpture of the Virgin and Child. The first chapel on the S is the CHAPEL OF ST PAUL. Mosaics by *Justin Vulliamy* with assistance from *Boris Anrep*, 1964. Cosmati pavement by *Edward Hutton*, author of many books on Italy. – The second chapel is the CHAPEL OF ST ANDREW, designed by *R. Weir Schultz*, completed 1915. The blue-grey marble is Hymettian, the white Pentelic. The mosaics designed by *George Jack* were executed by Debenham's men (who did the mosaics in his Addison Road house), directed by *Gaetano Meo*. The screen is by *W. Bainbridge Reynolds*. The sculpture is by *Stirling Lee*. The execution of the stalls of c. 1912, designed by *Schultz*, is one of the finest works of *Ernest Gimson*, indeed amongst the best decorative woodwork of its date anywhere in Europe. Slender upright forms and crisp dainty inlay of ebony and ivory. The remarkable hanging light-fitting incorporates an ostrich egg. – The next S chapel is the CHAPEL OF ST PATRICK with Connemara green marble and Cork red marble. The altar is by *Marshall*, the statue of St Patrick by *Arthur Pollen*, and the mosaic on the wall to the w of the chapel by *Boris Anrep*. – Next the CHAPEL OF SS. GREGORY AND AUGUSTINE. Its marblework, designed by *Bentley*, was partly set up before his death (the only revetment he saw). Opus sectile panels made by *Clayton & Bell* to designs by *J. R. Clayton*; also mosaics designed by him, made by *George Bridge*, 1902–4. – At the S W corner (corresponding to the porch at the N W corner of the w end) the BAPTISTERY, with large marble font designed by *Bentley*. – The nave chandeliers date from 1909, and there is no definite evidence that Bentley himself designed any of the electric light-fittings in the cathedral, but those most characteristic of him are in the Lady Chapel sanctuary (*Victorian Church Art* 1971, No. J11).

For surrounding buildings and streets, see the latest edition of B of E *London 1: The Cities of London and Westminster*.

101. London: Westminster Cathedral The sanctuary

Oxford

CATHEDRAL CHURCH OF CHRIST
(CHRIST CHURCH CATHEDRAL) *Anglican*

(Based on B of E *Oxfordshire*, 1974, revised with information from Thomas Cocke, Michael Gillingham, Martin Harrison, Peter Howell, George McHardy, Julian Munby.)

Plan, Fig. 104, from the *Builder*, 1892, by Roland Paul (who chose to treat *Scott's* E end as Norman).

References (see Recent Literature) include Sewter 1974–5.

INTRODUCTION

This cathedral which is also a college chapel stands with its own small cloister near the S E corner of Tom Quad, the great front quadrangle of the college called Christ Church. Visitors to the cathedral now enter from the S, from the Broad Walk through Meadow Buildings, by a one-way route that brings them into the cloister to the chapter house, which they are asked to look at first; and departure is through the W door of the church and Tom Quad. So the view of the C 13 spire from the cloister garth, the restored Late Perp cloister walks, and the C 13 chapter house with its Norman doorway are our introduction to this interesting building. Its exterior, set among private college buildings and gardens, is not easy to observe. On all sides college accretions make it difficult to establish the building's scale and character. One should not indeed expect cathedral character here. Even before some W bays were cut off by Wolsey to make his college quadrangle, some twenty years before the church became a cathedral, it was only a little over 200 ft long; now, since *Gilbert Scott*, it is a little over 180 ft (as against, say, the 290 ft of King's College Chapel, Cambridge). Its spired crossing tower as seen from Tom Quad reads with the quad as other college towers do. On Oxford's skyline St Mary's exuberant C 14 spire out-

dreams the cathedral spire, but the approaching railway traveller can single it out.

As for the town, the name of Oxford first occurs in the Anglo-Saxon Chronicle for the year 912, as if it were already a place of some importance. But record of students coming here in search of learning only appears in the second half of the C 12, and it was in the C 13 that a university began to establish itself. As for this church, however, first on the site was that of an Anglo-Saxon nunnery, though whether St Frideswide was the foundress – which would mean an early C 8 date – we shall never know for certain. In any case the church of this nunnery was burnt by the Danes in 1002. Of its rebuilding nothing architectural has come down to us. And we are only a little better off for evidence of the Augustinian priory established by Henry I in 1122 (see traces off the cloister and in the S transept). The building as we see it may have been begun in the 1170s, as St Frideswide's translation was recorded in 1180. There are two documentary references to building work in the 1190s: a sermon of Alexander Nequam and a papal bull of Celestine (Salter, *Medieval Oxford*, 1936, citing Frideswide's Cartulary published

103. OXFORD C 12 doorway to the chapter house in 1820

104. OXFORD
Plan from the *Builder*, 1892 (see p. 215)

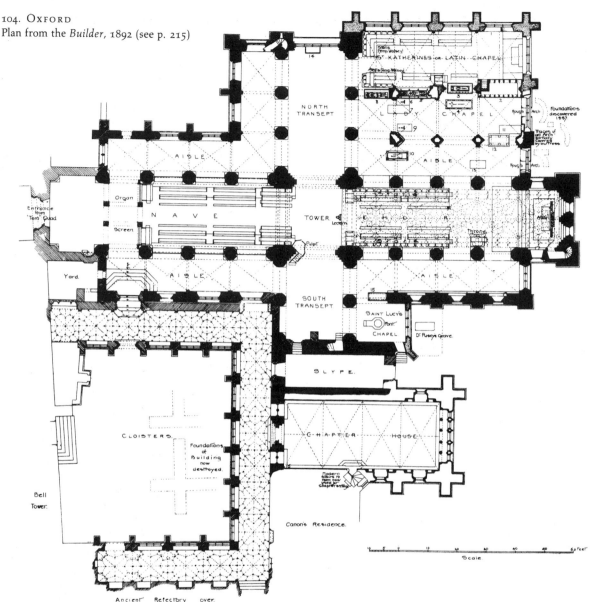

1894; reference from Julian Munby). Some aspects of the interior (see *Capitals* below) suggest that work went on into the early C13. Additions in the C13 and C14 (Lady Chapel, Latin Chapel) produced the present unusual width of the eastern arm. A chief architectural treasure was added *c.* 1500 when this was still a priory church: the pendant lierne vault over the choir, a vaulting system soon to be combined, even more ingeniously, with fan-vaulting over the Henry VII Chapel at Westminster. In 1525 Wolsey suppressed the priory and began building his Cardinal College here with the intention of demolishing the church

entirely. (His own unfinished college chapel N of Tom Quad was pulled down *c.* 1671.) After Wolsey's fall in 1529 the college, like his other projects, was taken over by Henry VIII. So the church, as Henry's college chapel, was unscathed at the Reformation. In 1542 the see was created, and in 1546 Osney Abbey, at first intended to be the cathedral, was supplanted by the present cathedral. In the choir a Laudian refurnishing of the 1630s was completed in time for Charles I's presence at Christ Church during 1642–6. Although Wren designed Tom Tower in 1681 to complete the main college gateway and to contain Great

Tom, the giant bell from Osney Abbey, he is not known to have done any work on the cathedral. Loggan's bird's-eye view of 1675 in his *Oxonia Illustrata* shows the pre-Victorian cathedral.

In the earlier Victorian years this was the cathedral where young Ruskin came daily as a Christ Church undergraduate and where subsequently Huxley's enemy Wilberforce was bishop, Alice Liddell's father was dean and Charles Dodgson was a canon. In the 1850s *Benjamin Woodward*, designer of the University Museum with its celebrated carvings by O'Shea, designed a new window for the cathedral's Latin Chapel, with carving by *O'Shea* and early *Burne-Jones* glass. The most considerable restoration of the cathedral was that of *Gilbert Scott* in 1870–6, when he drastically changed the E wall of the sanctuary, moved the organ and added fine new fittings. The *Burne-Jones/ Morris & Co.* windows of the 1870s are said to have convinced Morris that modern windows were not right for ancient churches (Lethaby's life of Webb), although this was part of the larger question of Morris's opposition to restoration expressed in his founding of the S.P.A.B. in 1877 in protest against Scott's doings elsewhere. Meanwhile, between the cathedral cloister and the college hall range, *Bodley & Garner* in 1876–9 built the sumptuous college bell-tower over the C17 hall staircase and also the lobby leading from Tom Quad to the W door of the cathedral, *Scott* having already added the west bay inside.

CLOISTER AND CHAPTER HOUSE

This description starts as the visitor does, in the CLOISTER, S of the nave. The cloister was rebuilt in 1499 and the following years. It has three-light openings and a tierceron vault with many bosses. Only the S part of the E walk and the S walk are original. (Part of the cloister was converted by *Keene* in 1772 into a Gothic muniment room: Cocke.) Inside the garth are exposed excavations of a building not identified. The W part of the cloister was destroyed for Cardinal College; here are the E exit from the hall staircase and the S end of the E range of Tom Quad. From the E walk

105 OXFORD C13 interior of the chapter house in 1820

of the cloister, between chapter house and s transept, is a tunnel-vaulted passage or slype belonging to the c 12 building, possibly that of 1122 rather than that of the 1170s, lying lower than the cloister and accessible now only from the s transept.

The CHAPTER HOUSE is rectangular, of four bays, E of the E cloister walk. The entrance is Norman and older than the main features of the chapter house. Two inner orders of continuous zigzag and two outer orders with columns carrying leaf and scallop capitals. An outer band of shallow segmental motifs. The side openings are said to have been restored by *Bodley & Garner* in 1881. The interior has on the N side half-chopped-off Norman blank arcading. Three bays are preserved. So that wall is Norman. The rest of what is seen belongs to the second quarter of the c 13 and is of classic perfection. It has at the E end five stepped lancets, to the N a single and to the s two lancets, with blank lancets l. and r. on N and s. This group of windows has boldly detached shafts inside, the E window also dainty dogtooth and in the spandrels spreading stiff-leaf. The w half of the room has no windows. There are vaulting-shafts against the walls standing on excellent busts. The capitals are stiff-leaf throughout. Quadripartite rib-vaults with fillets and bosses. The bosses show Christ seated, the Virgin (the finest), St Frideswide, and four lions with one head. All have stiff-leaf lapping around. The Perp s doorway and stairs up from it are recent. Some time between *c.* 1600 and *c.* 1800 the chapter house was given a fireplace. – In the N and s walls are re-set two small early stone PANELS in relief. In the E wall is the re-set FOUNDATION STONE of Cardinal Wolsey's college at Ipswich, started in 1528, one year before his fall. It was to be the grammar school for his college, on the Winchester–New College pattern. – PAINT-ING. In the vault of the E bay four exquisite medallions with figures, and one more in the next vault. – On the walls painted joint-lines survived *c.* 1240–1968 (Harvey 1974). – Outside in the cloister, on the window-reveal N of the doorway (straight jamb, N side), a faint fragmentary out-line of a (Norman?) draped figure survived both the c 18 transformation into an oval window and the c 19 (presum-ably Bodley's) restoration (Munby). – STAINED GLASS. N and s windows. These contain a small miscellaneous collec-tion of late c 15–c 16 glass, presumably *ex situ*. The most important panels are the Virgin and Child, the Assump-tion, Cardinal Wolsey's badge of the crossed pillars and cross staff, and Pilate washing his hands, this last Flemish work. – Staircase window, *ex situ*. Three large and most unusual roundels of the late c 15: first (and third with minor changes) a 'Maria' monogram with the Assumption depicted on the letter M; second the I.H.S. monogram with the Crucifixion depicted on the letters: a class of design suggesting knowledge of Continental woodcuts and engravings.

EXTERIOR

The approach through the cloister, with the view from the former garth, shows the s side of the nave. (On the tower, see view from Tom Quad, below.) The s aisle has Perp windows and battlements, the clerestory E.E. windows, shafted. All this is drastically restored. The w side of the s transept has better-preserved plain Norman windows below, shafted Norman windows above. Roll mouldings in the arches of the latter. The s window, high up because of the E range along the cloister, is of five lights and has cusped intersecting tracery, i.e. must be of *c.* 1300. (The E clere-story windows are like the w ones.) The Chapel of St Lucy on the E side of the s transept (not visible from the cloister garth) was an addition datable to *c.* 1330 or so by the tracery of the E window: two tiers of reticulation and then freer-flowing shapes. The choir exterior, not easily approachable this way, has a s aisle with shafted Norman windows, much renewed, and a clerestory of *c.* 1500 (see *Interior*) with three-light Perp windows, four-centred arches at their tops. Carvings on the string-course of the parapet. The E wall, where the sanctuary projects beyond the aisles, is all of the time of *Scott's* restoration, i.e. 1870–6, but the side windows of the sanctuary, one s and one N, are original though over-restored. Scott removed the large E window of 1853 (its date discovered by Peter Howell in the pages of the *Ecclesiologist* for that year), which had itself replaced the presumably medieval window dimly visible in Britton's view of 1820. Here Scott installed a Norman rose-window, with a pair of round-headed windows below it, on the strength of traces far from conclusive, and the details now are all his (in spite of Paul's plan of 1892, which calls it all Norman). Original are the square angle turrets, at least in their shape, and the shaft-ing above the rose-window. The turrets have blank arcad-ing, with round arches below and pointed arches above, and that Scott took from the N transept. (As for his rose-window, cf. *Stained glass*, s transept, St Lucy's Chapel, little c 17 scene with rose-window: might Scott have taken this as an older representation of the original E end?)

N of Scott's E wall is an evident extension of the original building. The E wall of the choir aisle is indeed Norman, though it has a Dec window. (A blank arch below may have been only a temporary access arch for workmen later on, according to David Sturdy.) Farther to the N follows the Dec window of the Lady Chapel with its flowing tracery, and then the Victorian Gothic window of the Latin Chapel, inserted in 1858 and evidently pre-Scott, heavier and cruder with its plate tracery. It is known that *Billing* did repairs in 1856, but this window is by *Woodward*. On this side is one genuine Norman buttress, shallow, as they were. The choir clerestory on this side is as on the other. The Latin Chapel to the N has four Dec windows with

106. OXFORD Choir C 12–13 and C 15–16, with C 15 east window in 1820

resourceful flowing tracery. The N transept is almost flush with the chapel. It has a large Perp N window of five lights, but Norman angle turrets with pointed blank arcading below, round arcading at the top stage, and recessed circular pinnacles, also with shafting, as the top motif. The W aisle of the transept has a Perp N window, a Norman clasping buttress at the angle, and two more Perp windows to the W. The clerestory has its northernmost W window Perp (and so is the opposite window, i.e. the one facing E, above the Latin Chapel), the others Norman and shafted with a roll in the arch as in the S transept. Perp carving along the string-course of the parapet. The nave continues the same system: Perp aisle windows (possibly of *c.* 1637) and shafted pointed-arched C13 clerestory windows.

The W porch with its twin entrance (which the visitor sees on leaving) is by *Bodley* and of 1872–3. One looks back from Tom Quad at the CROSSING TOWER, Norman and entirely plain with a few arched windows in the lower stage, and E.E., probably mid-C13, in the upper stages. Pairs of twin bell-openings with quatrefoils in plate tracery, flanked by blank lancet arcading. A pointed-arched top frieze ends the tower part. On the four corners are shafted pinnacles, and between rises the stone spire, comparatively short, with large, gabled lucarnes at the foot. They also have twin lights and a quatrefoil in plate tracery. This is one of three C13 central-tower spires in Oxfordshire; Witney and Bampton are taller.

INTERIOR

If one assumes that the priory church was built from E to W, as was the rule, one should begin in the CHOIR. It is of four bays, plus one-bay sanctuary. Here the system is at once established which was not to be changed to the end of building operations. It is a highly unusual, though not a unique system. Tall round piers carry arches, and there is a triforium, but not above the arches, as, say, in Gloucester nave, but below them, tucked into them. The aisles therefore are not as high as the piers, and so second arches are needed below the triforium. It is the system of Romsey in Hampshire and Jedburgh in Scotland, and originally of Tewkesbury apse (now partly rebuilt), and it leads to painful compromises. Description must indeed be more detailed. The piers have interesting, again unusual, capitals (see also *Capitals* below). They are shallow and have either loosely intertwined trails or (five times) crockets. Crocket capitals one does not expect before 1190, though they are earlier in France. The super-arches have strong roll mouldings. But the sub-arches are unmoulded, and there is no visual or structural logic in the way they touch the round piers. In the choir aisles the arcading is even more distressing. The half-capitals for the transverse arches cannot be excused. The aisles are rib-vaulted with wall-shafts against the outer walls, unmoulded transverse arches, and ribs of a thick roll moulding. One tiny boss in the S aisle. The S aisle's Dec E window has plenty of ballflower enrichment, a motif of which the West Country, notably Herefordshire, was particularly fond. Next to it is a Perp piscina. The N aisle must have been like its fellow, but the N wall went when the Lady Chapel was built. The Norman rib-vaults, however, remained.

The choir was also meant to be rib-vaulted, or perhaps was rib-vaulted. The transepts make that probable. In any case there are Norman vaulting-shafts, with heads at the bottom, though above them all was changed when the choir was vaulted or re-vaulted. When precisely that was we cannot say, but as the highly ingenious system of vaulting is very close to that of the Divinity School, i.e. apparently developed from it, and as the Divinity School was vaulted in 1480–3 by William Orchard, one can perhaps assume a date about 1500 for the priory choir and look to *Orchard* as its designer, especially as he was buried in the cathedral in 1504. The problem here was that the bays were oblong and the designer wanted to make them square. So he started from N and S by big and strong arches treated exactly as if a timber hammerbeam roof were intended, even with the pendants of such roofs. The areas between the hammerbeams towards the windows are panelled. The windows have a wall-passage, and their heads are panelled too. That left the designer his sequence of square bays in the middle, and they have complicated lierne star-vaults with many bosses. The thick arches seem to disappear above and behind that vault, a much more subtle use of the motif than at the Divinity School and soon exploited in Henry VII's Chapel at Westminster Abbey, begun in 1503. At the crossing, the square bays left a small strip across the vault just E of the crossing arch. The westernmost arch of that strip stands on a concave-sided wall-shaft of *c.* 1500 with a capital, though polygonal like the others, slightly different from them. It stands on figure corbels of the original building, one each side, called C14 by the RCHM, but they must be C13 and are of very good quality. Within the strip are four statues under canopies left, it seems, in their original state.

The CROSSING has tall piers with many shafts. Crocket capitals appear, but also waterleaf. The arches are round to E and W, but pointed to N and S. Inside the tower is first a wall-passage with low arcading of seven bays each side. Short columns. Then, between the Norman windows, there is thin and large blank arcading. The C13 stage is hidden by a ceiling.

The TRANSEPTS have aisles, E and W on the N side, only E on the S because of the cloister: the place of a W aisle bay is filled by the E cloister walk's N bay. (Our plan shows that the presence of E aisles has become with later additions rather ambiguous.) The system is the same as in the choir,

107. OXFORD Choir, with Scott's east end

only the exotic vaulting does not continue. The aisle bays are again separated by unmoulded transverse arches. The SOUTH TRANSEPTS bay of the aisle (extended eastward in the C14 as St Lucy's Chapel) has a ceiling. The clerestory here has the usual English tripartite arrangement with low arches flanking the high window arches. Short columns and, in the middle, short thinner nook columns on them. The original vaulting-shafts carry thin capitals here, and there is even the springing of the vault or for the vault, indicating transverse and diagonal members, all slim. The S wall of the S transept has a Victorian vestry in C13 Gothic. This belongs to *Scott's* work. Above, l. and r. of the window of *c.* 1300, one can still see that the clerestory arrangement carried on. In the W wall there is no change,

but one detail needs pointing out: the triforium in one bay has colonnettes which are earlier than anything we have yet seen. They are in fact the earliest architectural evidence. They have steep bases and two-scallop capitals. That one would call *c.* 1100, but it may be a little retardataire and belong to the building of 1122 (as perhaps does the slype on the other side of the S wall of this transept). The NORTH TRANSEPT has capitals different from those of choir and S transept. There are in some two rows of five-lobed early stiff-leaf, a little like Bourbon lilies. There is also waterleaf, more prominent. The E aisle has the transverse arches preserved, but only the southernmost ribs are original. The others were changed when additions were made in the C13 and C14. We can, however, say that what was then replaced included a chapel E of the middle of the aisle. In the later context one can still see the s w wall-shaft and capital of this and one bay farther E a nook-shaft. Excavations have shown that the chapel was narrower than the Latin Chapel is now, two bays deep, and straight-ended (Sturdy). The N transept w aisle is later, though only a little. This is clear from the transverse arches, which now have hollow-chamfered edges, and the thinner ribs with three slim rolls. This is the system that was to continue in the nave aisles. Both transepts have ceilings of c. 1500. Below the N window of the N transept is large blank panelling.

The NAVE modified but did not alter the system. It has alternating round and octagonal piers (as in the Canterbury choir of 1175–9), and the clerestory has pointed windows. The w bay, beyond the organ screen, is an addition by Scott. The wall-shafts to the nave have Perp shafts with concave-sided capitals, but the roof is panelled timber, on semicircular transverse arches that echo the w arch of the crossing. These timber arches are almost certainly C 19, though apparently a careful copy: the curve is a perfect semicircle and may be of softwood (Munby), and indeed the roof is said to have been renewed in 1816 (Harvey 1978), though it appeared much as now in Malton's view of 1804; but Loggan's view of 1675 shows old steep roof-lines against the w face of the tower, presumably of the medieval nave. So the present roof is likely to be early C 19 renewal of early C 16 work. (The 1804 view of the nave interior, incidentally, shows a balustrade inserted at clerestory level, clearly not original and since removed.) The aisle vaults are like those of the N transept. The N aisle has no wall-shafts, only corbels, and the w window is an early C 17 alteration. It has plain Y-tracery.

The CAPITALS throughout are of great variety, and few are run-of-the-mill. Those of the N transept in fact look earlier, but the w aisle vaulting excludes that. As crockets appear everywhere and waterleaf rarely, and as, moreover, broadly speaking, waterleaf was popular to about 1190 and crockets after 1190, a dating to the last quarter of the C 12 for the whole building seems too early, and something like 1190 to 1210 more probable. (Wilson 1978, n. 38, notes a strongly French Gothic flavour in detailing here and finds certain affinities with Sens as well as with Worcester and Wells.)

Of additions there are few. First, quite soon, came the LADY CHAPEL, N of the N choir aisle. The wall was replaced by piers with clusters of shafts, partly with fillets. All have small and pretty crocket capitals and finely moulded arches also with fillets. Four bays of vaulting (but the w bay is really part of the N transept E aisle), the rib section not much different from that of the choir aisle ribs. On the N side fragments of tripartite wall-shafts, interfered with c. 1320–30 when the LATIN CHAPEL was built, the one with the flowing tracery in its N windows. The capitals

here are all moulded, with a section obviously Dec, not E.E. The vault has ridge ribs and bosses. The carving of Woodward's E window is by O'Shea (Howell). In the s transept, as we have seen, the ST LUCY CHAPEL was added c. 1330 to the s bay of the E aisle.

FURNISHINGS AND MONUMENTS, E TO W

Stained glass is described separately below.

Choir and sanctuary RETABLE of 1881 by *Bodley* (recently reduced in height), the figure carving by *Farmer & Brindley*. – The STALLS and the fine iron SCREENS to the aisles are *Scott*'s (1872), the screens made by *Skidmore* of Coventry, the stalls by *Farmer & Brindley*. – BISHOP'S THRONE. The feeble canopy is by *Sebastian Comper*, c. 1955, replacing a sumptuous one by Scott. – Of Scott's time also is the PAVEMENT with roundels of seated Virtues. They are copies from those in the church of the Knights of St John on Malta and were made in 1871. (An earlier choir pavement was supplied with stonework by Nicholas Stone, 1631–3: Cocke.)

South choir aisle RETABLE by *H. S. Rogers*. – MONUMENTS. Leopold Duke of Albany. By *F. J. Williamson* of Esher, 1884. Williamson was much patronized by royalty. White marble with bust in oval recess; *Salon* type. – Bishop John F. Mackarness †1889. Bronze profile in shallow relief, by *George Frampton*, 1891. – Mrs Henry Acland †1878. Profile in oval. (Fine ceiling paintings recorded by Tristram here have suffered modern destruction: Munby.)

North choir aisle Between the aisle and the Lady Chapel, St Frideswide's SHRINE, probably 1289, the date of the second translation of the saint's body. Reconstructed 1889–91 by *J. Park Harrison*. Low tomb-chest with quatrefoils with faces, and others with foliage. The canopy is of two bays with arches all formerly cusped. Foliage with little heads in between in all spandrels, and it is naturalistic foliage, as fits a date c. 1290 perfectly. – BRASS in the floor, anonymous, 32-in. figure.

Lady Chapel PAINTING. One bay of the vaulting has eight censing angels, C 14. – MONUMENTS. Lady Elizabeth Montagu †1354. Founder of a chantry in 1348, which may be the date of the tomb. Tomb-chest with mourners, the most rewarding on the N side. To w and E a large quatrefoil with a standing figure between angels. The effigy has the typical coiffure of the time. The tomb retains much of its original painted gesso finish. – Prior Alexander Sutton †1316?. Recumbent effigy in prayer. Canopy at his head. Tomb canopy of three bays with much ballflower. – BRASS to John Fitzalyn †1452. A 14-in. figure. – BRASS to Edward Courtenay †1462, 14-in. figure. – Opposite the saint's shrine, WATCHING LOFT, half of it in the Latin Chapel. This curious piece, the upper part of which is of

108. OXFORD C 12–13 north choir aisle (r.) and C 13 Lady Chapel (l.)

109. OXFORD St Frideswide's Shrine (detail), c. 1290

† 1578. Palimpsest. On the back a large C 14 head. – In the E aisle William Goodwin † 1620. Demi-figure with book. L. and r. all manner of funerary objects, strung along ribbons. – Robert Burton † 1639. Bust in oval recess. Emblems l. and r., and there duly appears an inscription referring to Melancholy. – Sir George Nowers (?). Early C 15 recumbent effigy not apparently belonging to the tomb-chest. Alabaster and much repaired. His head on a big helmet with an ox crest. – In the W aisle, J. T. James † 1829. By R. Westmacott Jr. Profile in roundel. – Many cartouches here and elsewhere. Though mostly very provincial, they are worth surveying, because some are good, some are quaint and some are downright funny. In the N transept e.g. John Torksey † 1702. How provincial this is, if one compares it with the one to James Narbrough † 1707 in the S nave aisle by William Townesend! The C 18 was going to show so much more skill and wanted to appear more civilized.

South transept and aisle   Between the two bays of the E aisle (i.e. between St Lucy's Chapel and what appears to be the W bay of the S choir aisle): the tomb, no effigy, of Bishop Robert King † 1557, last abbot of Osney and first bishop of Oxford. Purbeck marble tomb-chest, still entirely without Renaissance motifs, very richly traceried. Canopy on a flat arch and with a straight cresting. To the S seven lights. Panelled E wall and traceried vault. – In St Lucy's Chapel: Richard Gardiner † 1670. Cartouche with piled-up books. – Viscount Grandison, signed by *J. Latham* and made probably c. 1670. High plinth, wreathed urn, sumptuous trophy behind. Quite splendid altogether. – Peter Wycher † 1643. Gristly cartouche with four flat putti. It looks later. – John Banks, by *John & Henry Stone*, 1654. Cartouche with cherub heads and drapery. – South transept S: Viscount Brouncker † 1645 and the Viscountess † 1649. Small, white marble tablet. Pilasters and an open curly pediment with putti. Relief of the two sitting by a table l. and r., with a skull between them. The background is a lightly indicated Gothic arch. – Edward Littleton, Lord Mounslowe; 1683. High pedestal. Urn and piled-up armour in front of it. Two detached Ionic columns and a big broken segmental pediment.

Crossing   PULPIT. Probably Laudian, though motifs still Elizabethan. Large, with a sounding board with open ogee ribs above. Apart from the stair rail (c. 1700?) the pulpit probably dates from the choir refitting of c. 1631–3 (Cocke). LECTERN. Splendidly elaborate, by *Scott*, 1873. Brass, lions at the feet bearing shields, the stem with figures of St Frideswide, Bishop King and Cardinal Wolsey beneath richly crocketed canopies (McHardy).

Nave and aisles   VICE-CHANCELLOR'S THRONE. Jacobean, but with some Victorian work. The canopy stands on thin shafts. – ORGAN. The double-fronted four-tower case survives, somewhat altered, from *Bernard Smith*'s organ of c. 1680. (It stood on a screen between

wood and served to watch the shrine (was it also a raised pew?), stands on a stone substructure like a tomb-chest with canopy. It may date from c. 1500; the watching loft at St Albans is earlier. Base with quatrefoil panels, and shafts supporting a cresting of small pendant arches. A fan-vault inside. Enclosed stairs at the N W end. Above two wooden stages, the lower solid, the upper open and vaulted. Pinnacles all along.

Latin Chapel   RETABLE by *Kempe*, late C 19. – STALLS, early C 16. The ones Scott replaced in the choir. No high backs or canopies (i.e. presumably of the front row of stalls), but very good poppyheads on the ends, the best in Oxford. One with cardinal's hat (Wolsey's). – BRASS to Frederick Barnes † 1859, in the medieval brass style.

North transept and aisles   Fragment of the COFFIN-LID of Ela, daughter of William Longespée, † 1297. She was buried in Osney Abbey. Two lines of lettering and a border of thin leaf trail. – Against the N wall, short TOMB-CHEST with quatrefoils. It is supposed to commemorate James Zouch † 1503. – BRASS to Henry Dowe choir and crossing until moved to its present position and enlarged by *Scott*.) The case was raised in 1979 to accommodate part of a new organ by *Rieger* of Austria, with anachronistic visual effect (Gillingham). The organ gallery by *H. W. Moore*, 1888, but altered, probably by *Caröe* in 1922 (Howell). – MONUMENTS. N side: George Berkeley, Bishop of Cloyne, the philosopher, † 1753. Epitaph by Pope. Sarcophagus with straight tapering sides. A black obelisk behind, with crozier, torch and palm-fronds. Very good. – s side: Dean Aldrich † 1710, but erected 1732 by the connoisseur George Clarke, who probably designed it (Colvin). Made by *Sir Henry Cheere*. Roundel with an excellent profile. A winged and crowned skull below. – Thomas Tanner, Bishop of St Asaph, † 1735. Architectural tablet, convex in plan. – Dr Fell † 1686. Standing monument; extremely unenriched. Two urns l. and r. on the base, achievement on top. – Opposite four Grecian tablets. Two of them have profile heads: Alexander Nicoll † 1828 and Edward Burton † 1836. – South aisle. Edward Pocock † 1691. Bust on top with mortarboard. – John Corbet † 1688. Cartouche with two putti. – James Narbrough † 1707, by *William Townesend*, cartouche. Specially good.

STAINED GLASS, E TO W

Separate chronological descriptions of the glass in this cathedral in B of E *Oxfordshire* (1974) are now merged and taken topographically. Notes on medieval and c 17 glass were contributed in 1974 by Peter Newton. Some notes on Victorian glass were contributed by Martin Harrison, and others have been drawn from A. C. Sewter's great catalogue of Morris glass (1974–5). See *Chapter house* above for glass there.

Choir   In *Scott's* three E windows, by *Clayton & Bell*.

South choir aisle   E window by *Morris & Co.*, designed by *Burne-Jones*, 1877–8. Three white figures, the angels with blue wings, demi-figures of angels in the tracery, stories of St Catherine below. A window of special range and subtlety of colour. – Third window from E. Figure of the c 16 Bishop King, probably of the choir refitting of the 1630s. Attributed to *Bernard van Linge*, c. 1630–40. With achievement of the arms of King impaled by shields of arms of the See and Osney Abbey.

North choir aisle   E window by *Morris* and *Burne-Jones*, 1874–5. Three white figures, angels in the foliage, stories of St Cecilia below.

Lady Chapel   Vyner memorial window, again *Morris* and *Burne-Jones*, four lights this time, of 1872–3. All white figures. The tracery and upper background mostly foliage.

Latin Chapel   The E window was glazed by *Powell's* to a design by *Burne-Jones* in 1859. This was done at the suggestion of *Woodward*, the restorer of the window,

110. OXFORD Stained glass, 1872–3. Vyner memorial, designed by Burne-Jones, made by Morris & Co.

friend of Ruskin and the Pre-Raphaelites. As Morris started his firm only in 1861, this is Burne-Jones pre-Morris, and one of his earliest works. It is much bolder and more forceful than Morris ever was. Scenes with many figures and genre details. Nothing statuesque as in his later windows here, but types straight from Rossetti. The colours are violent. The flaming red ship of St Ursula in the top roundel is the most easily remembered piece. – Three N windows contain mid-c 14 glass, somewhat restored. Their particular interest is that they show developments in the use of perspective in the canopy designs that are paralleled in contemporary manuscript painting. Second window from E: three saints in the main lights, border of the centre light, and Holy Dove in the apex of the tracery; otherwise mostly restoration. Third window from E: three figures in the main lights (Archangel Gabriel, an archbishop saint, Virgin Annunciate, not as originally arranged), borders of centre light with interesting grotesques of beasts and birds, and two lower tracery lights each with a human head against foliage; otherwise much restored, borders of outer

111. OXFORD Stained glass, c. 1630. Jonah contemplating Nineveh (detail), by Abraham van Linge

lights all restored. Fourth window from E: saints and Virgin and Child in the main lights, heads of a king and a bishop in the main tracery (their foliage surround not original), and Courtenay arms in the apex tracery light; otherwise mostly restored.

North transept   N window by *Clayton & Bell*, 1872. They are not happy on such a scale. The small scale of the choir E windows suits them much better. – The clerestory and W aisle windows contain mutilated fragments from windows by the *Van Linge* family, c. 1630–40.

South transept   St Lucy's Chapel, E window, the original tracery glass, a gorgeous display. Early C14, complete and *in situ*. (Ruskin will have known it.) The design is very striking, with unusual background diapers and deep-coloured glass throughout. The subjects include St Cuthbert holding the head of St Oswald, St Augustine preaching, the martyrdom of St Thomas à Becket, St Martin dividing his cloak, grotesque creatures, a kneeling donor canon and a kneeling donor monk, the arms of England and France, censing angels, and Christ in Majesty at the top. In the heads of the main lights parts of an

architectural background (showing, incidentally, a rose-window) from a window painted by *Abraham van Linge*, c. 1630–40. In the centre light fragments including a C14 donor and a C14 head of a monk. – Transept S window by *Clayton & Bell*, 1891.

Nave and aisles   N aisle W window. Jonah seated beneath the gourd-vine with Nineveh before him, signed by *Abraham van Linge*, 163?. Fabulous vegetation at l., the fabulous city climbing up r. – South aisle W window. By *Morris & Co.* to *Burne-Jones's* design, c. 1870–1. Faith, Hope and Charity in turquoise, red and blue. Background of foliage and fruit. Slim upright angels in the tracery. – Other windows include a single-light life of St Peter by *James E. Rogers* of Dublin, made by *Powell's*, 1864; and in the S wall S W one by *Wailes*, 1858 (Harrison).

The cloister and chapter house with their fittings have already been described. For former monastic buildings S of the cloister and for all other buildings of 'the House', as Wolsey's college is known in the university, see Oxford, Christ Church, in the latest edition of B of E *Oxfordshire*.

Plymouth

CATHEDRAL CHURCH OF ST MARY
AND ST BONIFACE *Roman Catholic*

(Based on B of E *South Devon*, 1952, and information from
Roderick O'Donnell.)

Diocese from 1850. Rebuilt 1856–8 by *Joseph Aloysius
Hansom* and his brother *Charles Francis Hansom*, probably designed by Charles. On a restricted site, and the
projection of the E end into Cecil Street gives a 'decidedly
Continental air' (Anthony New, *Cathedrals of Britain*,
1980). Tall slim tower and spire 205 ft high by Joseph
Hansom, 1866, striking a less rustic note than the simple
E.E. limestone exterior of the rest. The interior is a less
expensive version of Pugin's at Nottingham. Proportions
of arcades and open roofs tall and thin. The Lady Altar may
be original. The Blessed Sacrament Chapel in the S transept
has fine colourful work by *F. A. Walters*, who restored the
church 1920–7. There is much late *Hardman* glass. The W
window has good Arts and Crafts glass of *c.* 1900.

Further on the neighbourhood, see the forthcoming B of
E *South Devon*.

Portsmouth

CATHEDRAL CHURCH OF ST THOMAS
OF CANTERBURY *Anglican*

(Based on B of E *Hampshire*, 1967, entry by David Lloyd,
revised, with information from Rodney Hubbuck and
Anthony New.)

Introduction 227
The medieval church 228
  Medieval eastern arm: late C 12 chancel (now sanctuary),
  late C 12 and early C 13 transepts (now E transepts), and
  remains of crossing
The seventeenth century 231
  C 17 nave (now choir), tower (formerly w, now central
  tower) and fittings
The twentieth century 232
  C 20 extensions: nave and new transepts wrapped around
  C 17 parts on w, N and s, 1938–9 (bold plans of 1966 for
  further w extension not executed)
Furnishings 233

Plan, Fig. 112, based on a plan by the cathedral architect.

INTRODUCTION

Cathedral since 1927. This former parish church stands in
its churchyard at the foot of Old Portsmouth High Street,
not far from the harbour entrance and waterside ramparts.
Nearby still some pleasant C 17–18 houses among less
interesting redevelopments that followed the savage
bombings of the 1940s. The church was originally founded
c. 1180 as a chapel of ease to Portsea Island's parish church
of St Mary (medieval predecessor of the present St Mary,
Fratton Road, Kingston). St Thomas's itself became a
parish church in 1320.

The instigator of the original late C 12 chapel was John de
Gisors, a rich merchant and shipowner, possibly with
London connections, and lord of the manor of Titchfield.
His avowed interest was to build a chapel in honour of the
recently martyred Archbishop Thomas à Becket, but he
must also have had in mind the needs of the nascent
community at the mouth of the harbour. He entrusted the
building to the Augustinian canons of Southwick Priory a
few miles N. So the church was something special, a
testimonial of piety, a chapel for the needs of a growing
port (and those who passed through it), and, in the event, a
showpiece for a fairly powerful monastery. It was not
particularly big but, in many respects, it had more of the
character of a miniature cathedral or monastic church than
of a medium-sized parochial church. Architecturally it was
always perhaps a little patchy (and parts of it must have
been built piecemeal over a few decades), but much of the
building was of the first architectural quality, in the main-
stream of South English tradition – as exemplified in the
late C 12 reconstruction of Chichester Cathedral and the
somewhat similarly situated (though grander) parish
church of New Shoreham.

The medieval crossing tower, *c.* 70 ft E of the present
tower, served as a naval watch-tower, its lantern mentioned in records of Henry VIII's time, to guide ships into
Portsmouth harbour. After damage in the Civil War,
eventually in the late C 17 the tower and the nave were
taken down and replaced by a new nave with a tower at its
w end, the present central tower. C 19 restorations did not
alter the essential character of the building, but enlargements since 1927 to provide for its new role as the cathedral
of a populous diocese and, alas, to try to turn it into
something faintly like the traditional idea of a cathedral
have deprived it of much of its old character as a medium-
sized town church without making it seem in size or in
splendour anything even remotely reminiscent of York or
Lincoln. But, to be fair, the inter-war enlargements were
never finished, and an exciting postwar scheme for completion of the enlarged building in a very different style
was not carried out.

The description is split into three sections, relating to the
surviving medieval parts, the C 17 parts, and the C 20
enlargements, which corresponds to a description from E to
w. The medieval work is so good and so remarkable that it
needs detailed description.

THE MEDIEVAL CHURCH

One would dearly like to have seen the medieval St Thomas's in its entirety, and still more the vanished church of Southwick Priory, of which St Thomas's was a protégé. (For the priory's predecessor at Portchester Castle and for its church of c. 1133–44, see B of E *Hampshire*.) St Thomas's was never particularly large, but it was ambitiously conceived and has unusual features, most notably the arrangement of pairs of small arches within the chancel arcade contained within larger arched frames, the larger frames representing the width of the vaulting bays of the main space and the smaller arches the widths of the bays of the aisles. Only here and at Boxgrove Priory in Sussex is such an arrangement extant. Portsmouth also has affinities with Chichester and New Shoreham and with numerous lesser churches in Sussex and eastern Hampshire, and, in order to fit it properly into the regional architectural picture of c. 1150–1250, it is necessary to examine the evidence we have for its dating in relation to the other buildings. There is record that St Thomas was being built in 1185, that part was consecrated in 1188, and that in 1196 the churchyard and two transept altars were also consecrated. It is a reasonable assumption that work started with the E end, which would, at least, be under way by 1185; some of its architectural details support such a presumption. Parts at least of the transepts must have been built by 1196; stylistic evidence suggests that the S transept could have been built by then, but obviously much of the N transept, with its cusped windows and arch, is somewhat later. (The Garrison Church nearby, probably begun c. 1212, has cusped E lancets.) So we have a chancel probably of c. 1180–90, and transepts of c. 1190–1220; of the medieval nave we have no evidence. This must be set against New Shoreham, where building of the choir probably began about 1170 but continued over several decades; Chichester, where major remodelling followed the fire of 1187 (although some work, e.g. in the Lady Chapel, probably dates from just before); and Boxgrove, where the choir is probably of c. 1220. (For New Shoreham and Boxgrove, see B of E *Sussex*; for Chichester, see above.) Portsmouth then comes fairly early in the regional architectural sequence of the Transitional period: much of the chancel probably just pre-dates most of the work at Chichester, and the doubled arcading certainly pre-dates, by a fairly wide margin, the comparable arcading at Boxgrove. The missing link is Southwick Priory, and if we knew more about how that looked, the architectural history of Southern England during this important period might become clearer.

The medieval CHANCEL arcades attract attention first. There are only two main bays, each consisting of a broad blank round outer arch containing a pair of smaller, sharply pointed arches. The smaller arches are of two orders, heavily moulded, the moulding thicker and more incisive (and evidently slightly earlier) on the N than on the S, where it is subtler and more undulating. The intermediate piers within each pair of smaller arches are of black marble, dating in their present form from 1904 (the original Purbeck marble piers having crumbled, and some of them having been replaced by iron supports in 1843), with renewed moulded round capitals of stone, except in the S W main bay, where the original moulded capital of Purbeck marble has been preserved. The outer containing arches are of a single moulded order. The piers between the main bays are octagonal, big (out of structural necessity) and with simply moulded capitals. The responds are clustered, and have engaged shafts corresponding to the inner orders of the smaller arches, and slightly slenderer shafts, within square-angled recesses, corresponding to the outer orders of the smaller arches and to the single orders of the containing arches; each shaft has a capital of its own under a moulded square abacus. The W responds form continuous compositions with the adjoining responds of the W arches of the aisles, so that there is a continuous series of capitals and shafts (including five in a straight diagonal line) at the W end of each arcade, to striking effect. The W arches of the aisles are specially notable, of three orders, with beautifully formed mouldings – wide and narrow rolls, deep and shallow incisions, in undulating patterns, much as on the arches of the S arcade.

The aisle vaulting is quadripartite, with transverse arches of the same section as the diagonal ribs – thick rolls with hollow sides; the bays are beautifully balanced in their proportions, since each is related to the width of one of the lesser arches of the arcades, roughly equal to the width of the aisles, so that the awkward elongated effect which is obtained, e.g., at Chichester, is avoided. Furthermore the difficulty arising from the difference in the thicknesses of the main and intermediate capitals of the arcades is neatly mastered at Portsmouth by having the ribs springing in bunches from the smaller intermediate capitals but separately from the larger capitals. (At Boxgrove the solution to this problem was to be aesthetically much more clumsy.) On the outer sides of the aisles the ribs rise from corbels resting on trefoiled slightly keeled shafts, resembling those at Chichester and New Shoreham but, of course, on a much smaller scale than at Chichester. In the E angles of the aisles the diagonal ribs spring from small corbels resting on single shafts. The capitals and corbels of responds and vaulting-shafts in the aisles are intriguingly but haphazardly varied; some are straightforwardly round and moulded, but others are in varieties of simple, rather primitive foliage in the preliminary or early stages of development to stiff-leaf; the obviously early date of these lends support to the documentary evidence that

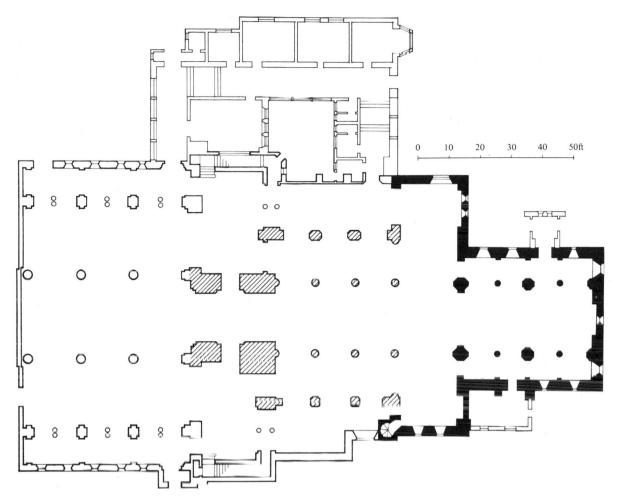

112. PORTSMOUTH (ANGL.) Plan, after Anthony New of Seely & Paget

the choir was built *c.* 1180–90. The most striking array is on the combined w respond of the s arcade and N respond of the w arch of the s aisle, where there are nine shafts in all, each with a capital (some damaged or partly renewed) of distinct Portsmouth types, having spearpoint leaves (i.e. with a straight broadening and then a gradual narrowing to points) with simple incisions usually following the shapes of the leaves, or, in some cases, broadening more roundly into the shape of spades (in the playing-card sense). The leaves have slight convex curves (suggestively anticipating crocket capitals), which seem to echo in miniature those of the vaulting-ribs. The corresponding pair of responds on the N side has ordinary round capitals and the total effect is not so memorable. The rest of the capitals and corbels are carved as follows. In the s aisle, the s respond of the w arch has spearpoint decoration as on the opposite respond, except for the capital of the inner order, which has a

contorted foliage pattern, with twirling stems and leaves. The corbel at the end of the first bay has crocket foliage; the next two corbels and the one in the s E corner of the aisle have dagger foliage (i.e. narrow leaves curving to points, without the initial widening from stems characteristic of spearpoint leaves), usually with simple incisions; the capitals of the E respond of the s arcade have crocket foliage. In the N aisle the capitals of the N respond of the w arch, and the corbels at the end of the first two bays and in the N E corner have varieties of dagger and spearpoint foliage, whereas the corbel at the end of the third bay and the capitals of the E respond of the N aisle are plain, round and moulded. These, on the whole, like the differences in the mouldings of the two arcades, suggest a slightly earlier date for the N aisle than for the s.

The medieval vaulting of the chancel's main vessel has disappeared. The present mock-vaulting in plaster is re-

113. PORTSMOUTH (ANGL.) Chancel, *c.* 1180–90, and choir, *c.* 1683–93

markably convincing work of 1843, year of restoration by *Thomas Ellis Owen* in collaboration with *Jacob Herbert*, surveyor to Winchester College (Colvin). It probably represents, pretty closely, the appearance of the medieval vault. The original corbels remain, with crocket foliage, with vaulting-shafts of the same trefoiled section as those in the aisles, ending at lower corbels, in the spandrels of the main bays of the arcades, which consist of half-rings of stiff-leaf foliage (the most fully developed in the cathedral) surmounting small brackets carved with grotesque human faces. There is a galleried clerestory, tall in relation to the height of the arches underneath, each main bay having an internal screen of three lancet-shaped arches, the centre ones wider and higher, with slender intermediate shafts of Purbeck marble and engaged end-shafts of stone, all with moulded round capitals, the end-shafts also with shafting-rings. The actual clerestory consists of one lancet window only over each bay, behind the central arch of each triple screen (much as at Chichester). The high E window, level with the clerestory, has a similar internal screen, but with rings halfway up the intermediate Purbeck marble shafts as well as on the end-shafts, and with rib-moulding round the arches. The window itself is a triple lancet, repeating the scale and shape of the screen. In its lower storey the E end terminates in a pointed-arched recess, with marble shafts and capitals entirely renewed, and flanked by a pair of miniature trefoiled arches on either side, about five feet up; this again is wholly renewed but may represent a medieval feature. Within the arched recess is a single, very slender, lancet window, a medieval feature revealed and re-opened in 1920. In the gable of the E wall a small circular window, visible outside, opens into the space above the vaulting. The aisle side windows were originally very thin lancets, one to each bay; one survives in the N aisle (E bay) and two in the S (two E bays). Other aisle windows are Victorian, including the two-light E windows.

The medieval (now E) TRANSEPTS are relatively tall and narrow, the S shallower than the N. The fenestration is in two tiers, corresponding to the two stages of the chancel; but windows and other architectural features are rather jumbled, suggesting that the transepts were built in a somewhat piecemeal way, the N transept being, on the whole, later than the S. The S transept has in its E wall a plain chamfered arched recess, containing a small blocked lancet window. Above, but to the N, is a larger lancet. The S wall has two fairly wide lancet windows in the lower tier and a wider one above. At the S W corner of the transept is a stairway leading into the clerestory passage, which continues round the transept and into the chancel. The transept was, or was intended to be, vaulted, and the corbels for the vaulting-ribs, together with short lengths of shafts below, remain in the S W and S E corners. The N transept has two arched recesses in its E wall. The northern one is like

that in the S transept, but contains a two-light window with quatrefoiled circle above; the southern one is trefoiled and roll-moulded and contains the remains of a WALL PAINTING of Christ in Majesty in a small vesica which is contained within the head of the arch, with a host of angels in the space below. The upper part is fairly distinct (it was touched up by *Tristram*), but the bottom of the painting is completely gone. The vesica suggests that the painting is coeval with the recess: early C 13. In the upper stage of the E transept wall are three trefoiled lancets, two paired towards the N and a single one to the S. The N transept wall has in its lower tier a three-light uncusped window in an arched frame, in its present form wholly Victorian, and three stepped trefoiled lancets above. In the gable is a small sexfoiled circle. The W transept wall has a single trefoiled lancet at upper level. (Such lancets are found in neighbouring village churches, e.g. Chalton and Soberton.) Of the medieval CROSSING there survive the two E piers (the chancel arch, above the piers, dates with the vaulting from 1843), with a series of rounded shafts facing diagonally N W and S W into the crossing; the original capitals, simply moulded and of hollow-sided octagonal shape, survive on the N side, but are renewed on the S (1843). The W arches of the chancel arcades and the aisles spring from the piers at much lower levels on other sides.

THE SEVENTEENTH CENTURY

The present choir was the C 17 nave. Although the medieval crossing tower and nave were damaged in the Civil War, they survived until c. 1683; between then and 1693 they were replaced by a new nave with aisles and W tower. *Ambrose Stanyford* † 1694, according to his epitaph, was 'the happy instrument of contriving, framing and finishing the inside beauty of this house'; *John Mitchell* (or Michell) having given up his contract, finding the job of reconstructing the old crossing space too difficult (Hubbuck, Colvin). The C 17 work, internally, is like a provincial adaptation of Wren's architecture: arcades with fairly slender round piers resting on tall octagonal bases (indicating the height of the original pews); Tuscan capitals; round arches with straightforward mouldings. The nave arcades proper are of three bays; there is a further E bay with wider and taller arches opening into the transepts and preserving something of the feel of the original crossing. Coved plaster ceiling with dentilled cornice, broken by dormer windows; there are other dormers lighting the aisles, and both sets of dormers appear outside, picturesquely, projecting from the tiled 'catslide' roof which sweeps over nave and aisles without a break. A WEST GALLERY was erected in 1706; it was extended along the aisles and into the transepts in 1750. The parts filling the transepts were removed in 1904. In 1938 the rest of the old galleries were removed and a new attenuated gallery, using parts of the fine panelled fronts of the old ones, was erected across the w end of the former nave and aisles a few feet in front of the w wall. It serves as part of the organ loft, and bears the exceptionally fine ROYAL ARMS of William III. By *Stanyford* probably the surviving late C17 fittings (Hubbuck). The PEWS of the former nave date in their present form from 1904, but it seems that much of the panelling of the C17 pews was re-used in the present much lower ones, especially in the roomy CORPORATION PEW, which is said to date from 1693 but has obviously been reduced in height. – The PULPIT is of 1693, in the same decent, solid but unostentatious style as the rest of the C17 features of the church; octagonal, with large vertical panels, tapering at the base in ogee curves to a stem; the splendid sounding-board with a gilded angel blowing a trumpet is a replica of 1904 of the original sounding-board cast out *c.* 1885 – a very telling example of how an act of iconoclasm can be regretted, and put right at considerable expense, less than a generation later. The former nave from 1904 till the enlargements of the late 1930s must have been very attractive and full of atmosphere, with the galleries wrapping round the aisles (but not then encumbering the transepts), the dark-stained fittings of the C17 and 1904 very much in keeping with the simple Renaissance architecture, and the walls abounding in monuments and wall-tablets; crowded but capacious. The aisles of the C17 nave had straightforward three-light square-headed windows, faintly, vestigially, Gothic, now re-set in the C20 outer aisles. Only a little of the pre-cathedral atmosphere can now be savoured.

The C17 W TOWER is now central in the enlarged cathedral (see below). Outside, we see it has small pairs of round-headed lights to the top storey and parapets slightly raised at the corners to give the suggestion of angle battlements. The unusual size of the attractive wooden cupola, added in 1702–3, is explained by the fact that it was built to take bells. It is octagonal, with louvres on each face, and a domical top with miniature second cupola, open-sided, rising at the top, ending in a tiny ogee spirelet and a golden ball. On the ball is a WEATHERVANE, a replica of one of 1710 which was blown down in 1954 and is now inside the cathedral (nave N outer aisle), a splendid piece of gilded metalwork, with the outline of a sailing ship and the date in openwork figures.

THE TWENTIETH CENTURY

Plans were first drawn up by *Sir Charles Nicholson* in 1935 for the enlargement of the newly-established cathedral, but the large-scale enlargements and alterations took place mostly in 1938–9. Nicholson in his early days designed churches using Gothic and Renaissance motifs which were yet original in general conception and sensitively composed in terms of colour and space; the Ascension, Southampton, and St Alban, Portsmouth, built in the tens and twenties, indicate this clearly. His restoration of St Peter and St Paul, Fareham, in the early thirties shows a diminution in sensitivity. His work at Portsmouth Cathedral suggests that he had lost almost all feeling for spatial composition and all stylistic conviction. Yet the problem was a difficult one; in fact few parish churches of comparable size could have seemed less suitable for enlargement. Eastward expansion was impossible because of the medieval work, and Lombard Street E of it; large-scale lateral expansion might have been possible but would have resulted in a weirdly-shaped building; straightforward western expansion would have been relatively easy, if the tower had been demolished – but this was unacceptable for the understandable reason that, with its cupola, it was a familiar and well-liked landmark in the city (more so then than now, with other tall buildings not far off). So somehow the church had to be expanded westward while retaining the tower. This was done by making the tower the focal point in the enlarged building, with new transepts and new double-aisled nave, turning the old nave and choir into a roomy choir and sanctuary for the enlarged building. But the tower still proved an obstruction; any opening through it was necessarily fairly narrow and very deep and, although an impressive effect could have been obtained if a tall crossing space had been formed under the tower, this was not done, owing to concern for the foundations. Instead a two-tiered space was created, the upper tier being taken by the organ and the lower consisting only of a low round arch giving a restricted view from nave to choir. The tower and the space under it, therefore, act as a pulpitum of unusual thickness, cutting the choir off, functionally, from the nave. An attempt was made to reduce the effect of this separation by having wide interconnecting spaces between nave and choir on either side of the tower – from the new nave aisles into the new transepts, from there into new second aisles added beyond the old aisles of the former nave (now choir), and so into the old building.

Such a flowing of one space into another provided a splendid challenge to which almost any medieval designer (consider what the masters of Bristol or Wells might have done) or the best Victorian architects like Street or Pearson or Scott would have risen – but Nicholson did not rise to it. Instead of an exciting series of oblique vistas there are just muddled views through arches of different shapes (or degrees of shapelessness) which simply confuse and do not satisfy. Furthermore the spatial qualities of the C17 nave have been largely destroyed by the addition of outer pairs of aisles. Of Nicholson's new nave and aisles only three bays out of an intended six were completed. The main arcades are in a sort of watered-down Romanesque, with tall circular piers, circular capitals with rounded protuberances and round arches, the roofs tunnel- or groin-vaulted and the arcades of the second aisles small, round and paired in bays (like a parody of the medieval choir arrangement); the windows (forming a kind of double clerestory, one range over the main arcades, one, more prominent, over the subsidiary arcades) in a sort of simplified Tudor style in segmental-arched frames.

The present (re-set) outside N W entrance to the N nave aisle has an open round pediment and representations of skulls and bones, the Portsmouth star and crescent, and the date 1691: it was originally the W doorway of the tower, until 1938 the main entrance to the church (for its inside doorway, see *Furnishings* nave, below).

Plans of 1966 for completion of the nave by Seely & Paget (architect in charge Anthony New) with, excitingly, Pier Luigi Nervi as consulting engineer, have since been abandoned. A cornerstone laid by Field-Marshal Viscount Montgomery stands now within the W end of Nicholson's nave. The intended reinforced-concrete construction, with external curtain glazing to the aisles, was to include a tunnel roof over the nave, with arched braces and concrete framing in web patterns in an unsupported span that was hoped to exceed all but that of St Peter's (though hard to envisage in the space available). With exquisite small-scale medieval work at one end, daring C 20 work at the other, and a perhaps rather endearing muddle in between (the 'perhaps' referring to Nicholson's linen traditionalism, the 'endearing' to the C 17 part), no other cathedral would have been quite like it. Nervi's roof may have been meant to compare in daring to, say, the Ely Octagon. Whether such discrepant parts would hang together, as the discrepant parts of Ely do, is the question.

FURNISHINGS

For wall painting, see the medieval N E transept, above. For C 17 fittings, see the present choir, and for the former weathervane now in the nave, see the C 17 tower above. – In Nicholson's N transept, the FONT is C 15, not very significant; octagonal with quatrefoil panels. – Near it the cathedral's artistic treasure, a majolica PLAQUE of the Virgin and Child, *c.* 1500 by *Andrea della Robbia*, the personal gift of Sir Charles Nicholson. – The ORGAN retains exquisite casework of 1718 by *Abraham Jordan Jr*, now facing the new nave. – Against the present W nave wall and now looking meaningless is the wooden DOOR SUR-ROUND formerly on the interior of the C 17 nave's W door, by *Lewis Allen*, 1694 (for its outer doorway, see the present N W nave entrance above). Two pairs of simple posts support a cross-beam surmounted by royal arms flanked by intricate carving. – In the S transept, PAINTING of the Miraculous Draught of Fishes, by *W. L. Wyllie*, the marine artist, who lived nearby. – STAINED GLASS. A few Victorian windows, many of them by *Clayton & Bell*, survived bomb blast. They are in the N choir aisle, the old N transept and elsewhere, mostly in small lancets.

MONUMENTS. Only the Buckingham monument is of any scale or special interest, but there are many tablets and cartouches of merit, probably most by local craftsmen. Only a brief selection can be made. In the S sanctuary aisle: Duke of Buckingham, murdered in 1628 in a house in the High Street, but buried in Westminster Abbey (see *Henry VII Chapel*, monument by Le Sueur). This one is by *Nicholas Stone*. Rather overloaded, with a large and extremely elongated urn in a black rounded recess, scroll work and military emblems to either side. An open pediment on top with cherubs. Lively allegories, one Fame blowing her trumpet, on either side of the tablet below. Originally at the E end of the chancel, now crowded in a bay of the aisle, and probably modified a little on removal. – Cartouches to Thomas Heather † 1696, with cherubs, and John Mellish † 1765. – Oval tablet with unusual surround to Thomas Spearing † 1779. – Wall-slab with heraldry, brightly repainted, to Robert Moulton † 1652 and William Willoughby † 1651. – In the N choir aisle: cartouche to Admiral John Cleland † 1795. – In the old S transept: five cartouches, to William Read † 1790, Thomas Stanyford † 1795, Robert Haswell † 1765, James Gee † 1762, the Hon. John Barrie † 1791. Henry Stanyford † 1735, with a miniature mourning figure. – In the old N transept: recumbent bronze figure in relief to William Thomas Wyllie † 1916, the son of W. L. Wyllie. – In the new N transept: tablet to Sir Charles Blount † 1600, flanked by free-standing Corinthian columns supporting a hood with miniature kneeling figure on top; military emblems on a coved shelf below. – In the new S transept: tablet to Richard Holford † 1703, draped, the folds and edges of the drapery indicated in a curious way. – Tablet to Philip Varlo † 1749, an elegant triangular composition enlivened by cherubs and garlands.

For the surroundings, including the remains of the Royal Garrison Church and, to northward, Her Majesty's Dockyard, as well as the vestiges of Old Portsmouth, see the latest edition of B of E *Hampshire*.

Portsmouth

CATHEDRAL CHURCH OF ST JOHN EVANGELIST
Roman Catholic

(Based on B of E *Hampshire*, entry by David Lloyd, revised with information from Roderick O'Donnell.)

Cathedral since 1882. On Edinburgh Road, hemmed in by traffic. Built 1877–82 to designs by *John Crawley* † 1880; completed by *J. S. Hansom*, 1886 and 1892, with W end –

narthex, angle turrets and porch – by Canon *A. J. C. Scoles*, 1906. Exterior in local Fareham red brick with white stone dressings. English Dec details on a French Gothic plan (polygonal apse). Designs for a tall, much enriched s w tower and spire over a porch not carried out. Nave, transepts and choir with tall roof-lines, lean-to aisles and chapels. Windows mainly neo-Dec, except for the s transept's conspicuous window with weirdly flowing tracery *à la* Bishop's Eye, Lincoln. Inside, immediately, an impression of moderate grandeur: this does feel like a cathedral (more than Portsmouth's Anglican cathedral does), albeit modest, thanks very largely to the exquisite proportions and shapes of Crawley's nave arcades. Timber roofs, bracketed, coved and inlaid with different woods. The sanctuary occupies the crossing, redesigned with furniture by *Fritz Steller*, 1971. The Victorian fittings suffered first from bomb damage in 1941 and then from the reordering of 1971 (architect *Austin Winkley*), when a marble baldacchino and much painting by *Nathaniel Westlake* were removed, but some Westlake decoration survives in the Lady Chapel. In the N transept three panels of stained glass by monks of *Pluscarden Priory* in Scotland, 1962: two heraldic and one with a portrait of Pope John XXIII, in shades from deep purple to red and blue, the features realistic and strong. Other windows by *Arthur Buss* of Goddard & Gibbs.

On surroundings see latest edition of B of E *Hampshire*.

Rochester

CATHEDRAL CHURCH OF CHRIST
AND THE BLESSED VIRGIN MARY
(formerly OF ST ANDREW) *Anglican*

(Based on B of E *West Kent and the Weald*, 1980, by John Newman, revised, with information from John Newman, Gerald Cobb, Thomas Cocke, Michael Gillingham and the late Emil Godfrey.)

Plan, Fig. 114, from the *Builder*, 1891, by W. H. St John Hope.

Some references (see Recent Literature): Harrison 1980; Quiney 1979; Swanton 1980.

INTRODUCTION

In any distant view of Rochester it is the castle that dominates. The cathedral lies lower, and its stocky tower and short, thick spire cannot match the masterful keep. From the w and N, from the railway, from the hills behind Strood and Frindsbury, the two grey shapes, the one upright, the other crouching, appear above the river, now one in front, now the other, but always so that the cathedral seems to shelter under the castle. And so it was at the beginning. Rochester is the second oldest see in England. In 604 St Augustine ordained Justus, one of the missionary band who had settled with him in Canterbury, as first bishop. King Ethelbert, says Bede, built a church, dedicated to St Andrew, and Justus placed it in the hands of secular canons. In 670 the bishop was referred to as the Bishop of the Castle of West Kent.

The cathedral occupies what had been the s w quarter of the Roman town, so that, although the monks managed to expand their precinct little by little towards the s, its dimensions were never large, and the s w corner of the Roman wall still stands, tightly hemming in the old Bishop's Palace. Today the cathedral precinct is the perfect antithesis to the High Street, small-scale, waywardly irregular, and almost free of traffic.

The present buildings belong largely to the c 12. In 1076 Lanfranc, Archbishop of Canterbury, appointed a reforming bishop, Gundulf, a monk of Bec, who had been his chamberlain. Benedictine monks replaced the secular canons. Gundulf made a great reputation as a builder, and by his death in 1108 had built a completely new cathedral church. Nothing of this can now be seen except the detached N tower, and part of the crypt. A consecration took place in 1130, it is said. Gervase records devastating fires in 1137 and 1179, but the latter at any rate cannot have been as serious as he makes out, for the present nave and w front are of the mid-c 12.

Early in the c 13, Rochester, like so many other cathedrals and abbeys, was reconstructed in its E parts, up to and including the transepts, and greatly enlarged, with a second pair of transepts between presbytery and choir. The work was done in several stages. The money for it came from the offerings at the shrine of St William of Perth, a baker murdered at Rochester in 1201 when on a pilgrimage to the Holy Land. After he was buried in the cathedral miracles conveniently began to occur at his tomb, and Rochester, like Canterbury, had a money-making martyr. William of

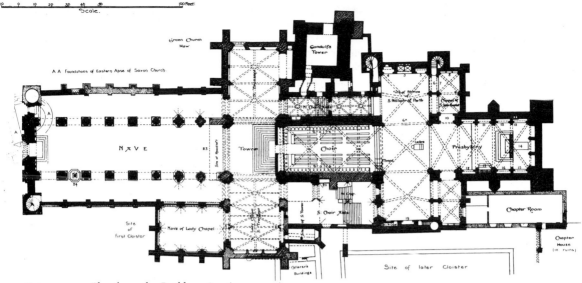

114. ROCHESTER Plan from the *Builder*, 1891 (see p. 234)

Hoo when sacrist built 'totum chorum' with these funds. The presbytery must have been vaulted by 1214, for Bishop de Glanvill, who died that year, was buried there. 1227: 'introitus in novum chorum'. No consecration, however, took place until 1240. After the c 13 no addition to the structure was made except the Lady Chapel w of the s transept, the occasional doorway here and there, a few larger windows, and a Perp w window and clerestory in the nave. In the c 17, before the Civil War, work was done on the w front, in 1664 the s aisle was restored, and in 1670 the N aisle was rebuilt from the ground (I. Cocke). But by the c 19 drastic restoration was necessary, to the exterior at any rate. The major c 19 campaigns were *Cottingham's* in 1825 (central tower rebuilt), *Sir G. G. Scott's c.* 1870 (much new stonework; E gables built up) and *Pearson's* in 1888 (w front underpinned and largely refaced; turrets and w end of aisles reconstructed). Finally in 1904–5 the central tower was again rebuilt, in accordance with c 17 prints, by *C. Hodgson Fowler.* (In the title-engraving, 1870 edition, of *Edwin Drood* – if it represented Rochester – the tower had no spire and presumably Cottingham's pinnacles.) The total length of the cathedral is 305 ft 6 in., of the choir and presbytery 147 ft 6 in. The main transept is 120 ft across, the E transept 88 ft.

THE SAXON CATHEDRAL

Justus's church of St Andrew, built *c.* 604, was, naturally enough, similar to the earliest churches of Canterbury (St Pancras, St Mary). Part of the stilted apse and the s E corner of the rectangular nave of a small stone building were found during excavation in 1889, under the N half of the w front of the present building. The outline of the apse is marked in the pavement. In 1876, under the outer wall of the s aisle, remains had already been found, with a floor of red *opus signinum*, just like the flooring of the other c 7 churches. St John Hope, in his architectural history of the cathedral (1900), interpreted the walling beside it as an apse with a wall to the w. Was that part of a second early church? St Augustine Canterbury had as many as four together, aligned along one axis (and a similar arrangement has been excavated at Wells). Did Rochester follow suit, in a less organized way? When the site was re-excavated in 1927 no trace of the apse was to be seen, so no certain answer can be given to these questions. As for the later, larger Saxon cathedral which superseded the c 7 building, the s w angle of its N transept was in 1968 identified by Dr Ralegh Radford below floor-level in the present N transept (information from the late Emil Godfrey). Loose in the crypt is a small fragment of Saxon carved stone, with interlace and the haunches of a four-legged beast.

THE NORMAN CATHEDRAL

Gundulf (1077–1108), encouraged and aided by Lanfranc at Canterbury, built a completely new church, and finished it 'in a few years'. GUNDULF'S TOWER, in the angle between N transept and N choir aisle, belongs by its construction as well as by its name to the earliest Norman period (contemporary with the White Tower of London, where Gundulf supervised building). It pre-dated the early c 12 keep of Rochester Castle nearby. It was built to stand

free, almost square, with heavy clasping buttresses. Before
c. 1779, when the top third was taken down, it rose about as
high as the transept, and was crowned with a ring of
machicoulis. These must have been an addition, of the c 14
perhaps, but the question remains whether defence was the
primary purpose of its building. Original windows, small
and deeply splayed, at three levels, and an arch at the s end
of the w wall at the highest level, a doorway it may be, to a
bridge by which the tower could be in private communi-
cation with the N transept. (On pairs of such towers
flanking a choir, see *Exeter*; also *Salisbury* on Old Sarum.
An oddity about Gundulf's Tower is that it is not quite
aligned with the supposed remains of the Norman choir.)

In the church itself Gundulf must be supposed to have
followed the general medieval practice and built from E to
w. Nothing that he did remains above ground, so the
CRYPT is the place to start. Mostly it is c 13, but the two w
bays remain of the Norman one, below the E, not the w end
of the present choir. Short, slender round shafts and
responds, groin-vaults without the normal transverse and
longitudinal arches. The capitals are very simple, shallow
without abaci, and making the transition from square to
round by means of keeled corners, i.e. not yet with the

block shape almost universal by c. 1100. Bases of two rude
rolls. Unmoulded tufa arches N and S lead into the crypt
aisles, also groin-vaulted, below the choir aisles. Hope
established that two bays further to the E were demolished,
and that originally the crypt and its aisles ended in a
straight line, with an immensely thick wall, and a one-bay
square E projection in the centre. Such a termination is
Saxon rather than Norman (before the Cistercians popu-
larized the square-ended plan); so Lanfranc and his
followers did not sweep away all earlier ecclesiastical
traditions, it seems. (It has recently been established that
the E end of Malling Abbey was similar.)

The interior of the NAVE must be considered next, or
rather the six bays, three-quarters of the whole, which
were left untouched when the enthusiasm for rebuilding,
which had been sustained throughout the c 13, finally gave
out. Inspection should begin in the s aisle. The outer wall is
largely that of Gundulf's church. A small piece of
stonework, exposed near the w end, shows the characteristic Early Norman herringbone lay of the rubble stone.
Internal pilaster buttresses, quite plain, with a plain string-
course carried round them at the level of the arcade capitals. At the level of the gallery they are cut off suddenly,

115. ROCHESTER View from the south-west   116 (*opposite*). ROCHESTER Nave, mid-c 12 and c 13

where the top of the wall has been rebuilt. But at least one can say that no aisle vaults were intended. Similar, somewhat shallower, buttresses in the N aisle. They are, however, a C 17 rebuilding. (Hope reported that he had excavated the footings of the four E bays of Gundulf's N wall.) The three E bays of the N aisle wall, not touched in the C 13, are Norman, but no longer in the early undecorated style. The pilaster buttresses have nook-shafts; the string-course is enriched with a succulent pattern of lozenges. Similar buttresses and string-course here outside, the sole surviving Norman features of the N and S nave walls. This mid-C 12 piece of wall, as Dr Fairweather has emphasized, is aligned, not with the rest of the nave, but with the crypt, the cloisters and the whole E end. So the conclusion is that Gundulf's nave, not just the S aisle wall, exists encased in the present arcades. The change of axis was effected by Ernulf's new cloisters after 1114.

The nave is strikingly broad and low and, it must be admitted, not a distinguished piece of architecture. The elevation is the normal for major Anglo-Norman churches: arcade – gallery – clerestory, though the clerestory is a Perp rebuilding. This mutilation apart, the Rochester treatment is a curiously unresolved and bitty one. In the first place the piers within each arcade are, all six of them, different, though answering one another N–S. Only the westernmost piers, in the form of an octagon stretched on the E–W axis, have a simple shape. The rest consist of shafts and fat half-columns attached to a basically square core. The gallery is subdivided, with shafts doubled in depth because there is a passage in the thickness of the wall. (Pointed tunnel-vault to the passage.) The wall-passage gives some circulation at the upper level, which is restricted by the very curious fact that the gallery has no floor. Some explanation of this peculiarity is needed, and yet what can it be? String-courses divide the three storeys horizontally; but the vertical division, by shafts, descends no lower than the arcade capitals. Upwards the shafts have been cut away at gallery-level. The string-courses continue across the w end, the upper one dropping a fraction, dividing into tiers the tight arcading with which the nave w wall was originally covered. Most of the upper part of the wall went when the immense eight-light Perp window took the place of the original one. Just enough is left to show that the proportions of the arches there bore no relation to the openings of gallery and clerestory.

The enrichment of the nave is, by contrast, pretty consistent. All capitals are scalloped, except for those in the two w bays of the gallery where the scallops turn into embryonic leaves. Round all the arches a simple row of zigzag runs, with nailhead on the arcade hoodmoulds, and half-pellets on the hoodmoulds of the gallery arches. The gallery tympana form the focus of the decoration filled with busy patterns of square stylized flowers. The w end

again dissents, with billet on the hoodmoulds, and a rope moulding round the inner arch of the central doorway. Embattling on the doorway to the s w turret. The other variations are trifling. The most important is the fact that the N arcade is given zigzag towards the aisle, but the s arcade is not. The four w bays of the N arcade have leaf spurs on the pier bases. On the s side, on the other hand, a start was made above the westernmost pier – giving the two arcade spandrels a pair of sunk roundels. Some of the pier bases are of brown local marble.

The WEST FRONT is logical, balanced, and well-proportioned, which can be said of very few Norman façades in England. The logic of it is that the nave and aisles are expressed by turrets at their outer angles. (This simple solution was apparently not hit on at once. Hope discovered foundations for two w towers, and the w piers of the arcades are enlarged as if to receive them. During *Pearson's* underpinning of the façade, footings of an earlier front were found, in the shape of a straight wall exactly below the present one and as wide.) Between the turrets, the aisle end walls are slightly recessed, but the nave is not. The outer turrets – the N square, the s octagonal in the top two stages – of five stages are stout enough to take stair-turrets, the slenderer inner ones, of seven shallower stages, just over-top them. Thick conical caps to them all. Each stage above the lowest is arcaded, with tiny arches on long shafts, the former decorated with stylized leaves, the capitals of the latter far more varied than those inside. On the inner turrets lintels appear at one level, and intersecting arches at the next. Variegation of the wall texture by laying the ashlar blocks lozenge-fashion in places. Even so at a distant view, the impression is of all-over homogeneity. The taste for this sort of façade treatment must have been learnt by English masons from West France and Poitou. Even the great Perp window does not upset the rhythm of closely spaced uprights – the many mullions carry on where the colonnettes leave off. N W doorway of 1327. *Pearson* in 1888–9 restored the turrets in accordance with King's engraving of 1655. He had to rebuild the whole of the N one, and the inner N and outer s turrets above the roof-line. He refaced much of the rest, but did not touch the sculpture; and that is what remains to be considered.

The SCULPTURE is concentrated on the central doorway, and decorates the jamb-shafts, tympanum and five orders of radiating voussoirs. On the tympanum is Christ in Majesty, supported by angels, flanked by the symbols of the Evangelists, with the twelve Apostles on the lintel, i.e. basically the scheme of the w portal at Chartres. The mere mention of it brings home how modest in ambition and attainment is the Rochester tympanum. The voussoirs are carved into violently curling leaves, transmogrified as often as not into beasts viciously biting their tails or their backs. The jamb-shafts, five each side, are plain, with

117. ROCHESTER West portal, mid-C12

carved capitals and bosses, except that the second shaft each side is developed into a column figure, Solomon on the l., the Queen of Sheba on the r. They are more worn even than the rest of the carving, but such figures were an invention of the Île de France, and first appeared at St-Denis in the 1140s. They and the tympanum make this doorway the most French piece of C12 sculpture in England. What is disconcerting is that elements should appear here in a combination that is unknown to France itself.

THE C13 CATHEDRAL

PRESBYTERY, CHOIR AND TRANSEPTS. Here the EX-TERIOR deserves to be examined first. Straight-ended presbytery. E transepts with E chapels projecting. From the E, one is at once struck by the massiveness of the architecture, especially the colossal buttressing angle-turrets, which are solid, up almost to the top. (The identical ones on the NE transept, on the other hand, contain stair-turrets.) There is far more sheer unrelieved wall than in the Norman parts. Above a blank storey, two levels of generously proportioned lancets in threes, with two rows of dogtooth on the reveals. The elevation, counting the crypt, reads as four-storeyed, with string-courses carried round everything and over the heads of the lancets, to separate each level from the one above. The upper two string-courses were introduced by *Scott*, who also replaced a Perp window by the upper trio of lancets. His treatment of the gable too is not authorized by early illustrations, and no reflection of the low-pitched roof behind it either. His alterations give the elevation a coherence it may not originally have had. Angle-turrets gabled at the top in all directions, with an absurdly small pinnacle set where the gables cross. There was evidence for the restoration like that.

The scheme established at the E end is carried on round the side walls of the presbytery, and in the NE transept, with the modifications necessitated by the transept E chapel. The presbytery is divided into two plus two bays by a far-projecting polygonal buttress with angles cut in to take shafts originally. Dec tracery inserted in the lower lancets here. Or should one call the designs in the middle two windows Early Perp? St John Hope thought this modernization of the presbytery went with the sedilia of the 1370s inside (see below). The SE transept, however, operated a different system, as it was interfered with by the cloisters. But complete refacing in the C19 leaves its original treatment in doubt. One or two Dec windows are inserted, with flowing tracery.

The exterior of the choir aisles is uninformative, but the MAIN TRANSEPTS introduce new motifs. Taking the N again first, one at once notices a decisive lightening of effect. The lancets are brought into a scheme of arcading, alternately wide and narrow, on both the N and W sides. Restrained use of Purbeck marble shafts. The buttressing is reduced to angle buttresses with regular set-offs. Early illustrations show three large foiled circles in the gable. All heavily restored by *Scott* again, faithfully this time, it seems. The S transept has bar tracery, Y-tracery in fact in the main S windows; and the same in the W clerestory before Scott's restoration. The E clerestory has a pointed quatrefoil over two trefoiled lights. By this we have reached the last decade or two of the C13. Angle buttresses and enriched gabled pinnacles.

Now for the INTERIOR of the C13 parts. The CRYPT, as has already been noted, was greatly enlarged to support the E.E. extension. It follows the outline of presbytery, E transepts and choir (i.e. both E and W of the two C11 bays). Short, slim piers, round and octagonal, with heavy, moulded capitals and bases. Quadripartite vaults, the ribs hollow-chamfered. The spacing of the piers is hardly greater than in the c12 crypt. Seven bays across the transept. PISCINA in the NE transept E bay. WALL PAINT-INGS in the SE transept E bays, terribly decayed but once rather beautiful. Medallions on the vaulting illustrative of the life of a saint. Figures on the entrance arches among stylized trees. They seem to have been executed early in the c14.

If one now ascends to the choir and stands at the junction of presbytery and E transepts, one is brought face to face with a fact that one may already have deduced. The PRESBYTERY is aisleless, with a two-storeyed, not a three-storeyed, elevation – a perhaps unique combination in an English great church at this date (by 1214), though it was to be followed in the E end at Southwell (begun 1234). Instead of aisles there are recesses, four to the N and four to the S, which at any rate since the c14 have contained tombs. Whether they were intended for tombs from the start cannot be proved, but it seems a natural explanation of this remarkable system. William the Englishman's Corona at Canterbury Cathedral must have suggested how it should be handled. As architecture the presbytery is remarkable for its coherence, harmony and lack of exaggeration, the E.E. style already fully-fledged in the first years of the c13. The four narrow bays are covered by sexpartite rib-vaults, direct from Canterbury, the ribs supported on shafts that go down to the ground, singletons or in threes, in conformity with the vaulting system but not throwing much emphasis on the alternating rhythm which the vaulting sets up. The fifth bay, that opens on to the transept chapels, is wider and has a quadripartite vault. In this bay, no clerestory because of the towers outside; just a row of arcading, instead of lancets and the tripartite shafted screen which comes at clerestory level everywhere else. Also everywhere at clerestory level there is a wall-passage. The main lancets, in the recesses, are shafted, and so are the arches that frame the recesses. Sparing dogtooth and billet moulding round the arches. What brings the design to life is the Purbeck marble used for all the shafts, but not for all the capitals, and for the horizontal mouldings, string-courses and abaci. Perp SEDILIA, gabled, with the arms of Bishop Brinton, 1373–9.

In the EAST TRANSEPTS the same system prevails without significant alteration. Sexpartite vault over each transept, quadripartite vaults to the E chapels. In the NE chapel shafts, not of Purbeck marble (except for the vaulting-shafts), on the E wall suggest that a revised scheme was toyed with here and abandoned. In the SE transept, E aisle, completely unexpected, is a sumptuous Dec doorway, to the Chapter Room. Its luxuriant sculpture, so at variance with the austere E.E. architecture around, does not, however, destroy its bold profile. Two-centred arch with

pinnacles, and an ogee super-arch from which colossal leaf crockets rear up, set against a diapered rectangular background. Round the arch, in a broad band, figures under tabernacle-work; standing females l. and r., Ecclesia and blindfold Synagogue, their heads c19; seated prophets at their desks holding up scrolls, in the niches higher up.

118. ROCHESTER
c14 doorway (detail) in south-east transept

Cottingham repaired the figures. Did he also retool the whole surface? It looks disturbingly mechanical.

So to the CHOIR. This has aisles, but they are separated by solid walls from the choir proper. Once more, this is a highly peculiar arrangement. There seem to be no c13 parallels, but Norman St Albans is planned like this; so perhaps the Norman choir at Rochester followed St Albans, and its walls were merely cased in the c13. The NE respond of the Norman crossing tower remains below the c13 base, but that is the most easterly piece of the Norman church visible above crypt-level. But that the c13 choir was at first intended to have had aisles is suggested by the Purbeck marble shaft base uncovered at the E end of the s choir wall. The choir stays faithful to sexpartite vaults, two double

119. ROCHESTER Presbytery, vaulted by 1214

bays long, though the transverse arches and ribs now have bands of dogtooth along them. The wall system is also recognizably what had been established further E, not any longer of course with wall recesses but with wall-arcading up to the same height, two arches of it per bay. Purbeck marble shafts, as before, but the main ones stopped at the level of the lowest string-course, on marble corbels carved with leaves, heads and in one place dragons. The clerestory lancets are larger than in the presbytery, the shafted arches in front of them of less squashed proportions. In the NORTH CHOIR AISLE a new feature is introduced, a ridge rib to the vault, which is quadripartite in each bay, with foliage bosses at the intersections. The mouldings here are finer than we have yet seen, and Purbeck marble is confined to the bases and caps of shafts. But in fact all this vaulting must be a Perp build or rebuild, as it is integral with the simple Perp windows which replace the lancets high up facing Gundulf's Tower. The SOUTH CHOIR AISLE, on the other hand, is most awkwardly managed. It is not in fact truly an aisle, for at the E end it opens into the transept by a mere door, and it is widened to occupy the whole space up to the N wall of the cloister. Various wall-shafts and buttressing for the choir vault, but no coherent system is established. E.E. doorway to the crypt. NP notes the two puzzling E.E. arches in the E wall of the S choir aisle, and points out that the masonry of the S wall seems Norman. Christopher Wilson suggests that a double aisle was originally intended on this side, and the blocking of the E arches and the compromise roof were expedients employed when the solid choir walls were built.

The choir was taken into use in 1227, but the remodelling of crossing and main transepts seems not to have been proceeded with at once. The E arch of the crossing, and the arches to the choir aisles, must have been built in one with the choir; further W there are substantial changes in design. Purbeck marble is abandoned except on the W piers of the crossing, and the arches into the nave aisles, and although dogtooth and billet mouldings survive, the shaft bases are no longer waterholding. Piers with multiple shafting at the crossing. On the W piers further development in detail, such as the profiles of caps and shaft-rings. Sexpartite rib-vault, with additional ridge ribs running N–S, to the NORTH TRANSEPT, with foliage bosses. Plenty of marble shafting round the lancets. On the W wall, blank arcading at the lowest level, on fine big head corbels; on the E side, a shallow chapel with a shafted PISCINA in the E wall, and stiff-leaf on the capitals of the N window. The most important innovation, however, is that the N wall at last introduces the normal three-storeyed cathedral elevation. The SOUTH TRANSEPT is clearly later, for the lower windows are Y-traceried. The vault was never fully constructed. The present vault is of wood. The E and W elevation is again two-storeyed. Within the blank arch on

120. ROCHESTER Choir, C13, casing C12 walls?

the E wall, part of an earlier arch not easy to account for. (NP notes the blocked doorway in the choir aisle, which, together with the partly preserved lancet, can only mean that the large arch in the transept was built as part of a plan not carried on with and so left filled in against a future knocking out.)

A start was made with remodelling the nave too. The lancet at the S W corner of the N transept suggests that aisles narrower than the Norman ones were envisaged. All that was in the end done was to rebuild the first two bays of the nave arcades on each side. Structurally, it was necessary to do this at the same time as the crossing was rebuilt, to provide buttressing. Extra buttressing mass left on the N side. The gallery openings were blocked, and the nave arcades raised in height. Had the whole nave been remodelled, the heightened arches still with the close C12 spacing, the piers, in fact little reduced in bulk, would have produced an uncomfortably claustrophobic effect. The piers were built up into a lozenge-shaped core, and sparse black shafts set against it. Arch mouldings with sunk quadrants; so the building programme was dragging on into the last decade or two of the C 13. The second pier each side was left half altered, the respond capital on the s side carved into fine naturalistic leaves. At the crossing the shafts spring from a height of 14 ft from the ground, i.e. above the level of the pulpitum.

That was the last structural alteration to the cathedral during the Middle Ages, except for the LADY CHAPEL, tucked into the angle between s aisle and s transept. It is Late Perp, possibly in course of completion in 1512–13. It is open to the aisle by three arches, replying to the windows, with stone screens across their lower parts, and open to the transept by a single arch double the size and considerably coarser in the mouldings. Was the s transept then intended to be the choir of the Lady Chapel, and the new work the nave of it? Windows set in reveals taken down almost to the floor, with a wave and hollow moulding. Slim clustered wall-shafts for vaulting, never carried out.

FURNISHINGS, E TO W

Presbytery   REREDOS. By *Sir G. G. Scott, c.* 1875. – MONUMENTS. First those on the N side, from E to W, then the s side similarly. Purbeck marble effigy of a bishop, identified as that of Bishop de St Martin † 1274, who was buried 'iuxta maius altare a parte boriali'. The effigy, with arms raised, is badly worn, and was originally flanked by slender shafts to support the exceedingly heavy gabled canopy. Plenty of delightful detail survives here, with bar tracery and even naturalistic leaves, decidedly advanced for the 1270s. – Gabled tomb-chest, traditionally that of Bishop de Glanvill † 1214. Purbeck marble. The front arcaded with seven pointed arches, and big upright leaves under them. The sloping lid almost broken, but keeping two sunk quatrefoils that frame half-length figures. Still Romanesque in feeling. It should be compared with the contemporary monument of Archbishop Walter at Canterbury.   Bishop John de Sheppey † 1360. The effigy was found in the wall in 1825; hence the original colouring is remarkably well preserved, so that it should be an object of pilgrimage to find what medieval freestone effigies were intended to look like. ('A drunken artist', said Cottingham in a letter, misunderstood his orders and started retouching the effigy, but when the repaint was taken off, not even 'the most fastidious antiquary' could find fault: information from Gerald Cobb.) There is great insistence on correct depiction of the details of the robes. C 16 iron railings. C 19 canopy palely copied from the superb pieces of the original canopy now kept in the crypt.

s side: Bishop Ingoldsthorpe † 1291, who was buried 'juxta magnum altare ex parte australi'. Purbeck marble. Reclining effigy under a gabled canopy. Ivy-leaf capitals of the side shafts. The pattern then is the same as the St Martin monument, and is no advance on it. Simplified canopy; heavier, coarser drapery folds. – Late C 13 gabled tomb-slab of Purbeck marble, carved with two croziers along the ridge, from which sprout oak and other simple leaves.

North-east transept   TILES. A few old patches, some with patterns. – STATUE. Figure of a bishop, removed in 1888 from the N turret of the W front. As the turret was an C 18 rebuild, the original position of the statue cannot now be discovered. Possibly the wider arches, now filled with modern statues, above the W portal, were meant to take statues from the first. The back of the figure proves that it has been cut from a wall, not lifted from a tomb. In style the figure belongs to the very end of the C 12, see the V-shaped folds of his cope, cut with a beginning of weighty plasticity, and the four-petalled flowers at the sides of his robe, in advance of anything on the W front. – PAINTING. St Sebastian and St Roch. Venetian, *c.* 1500. – MONUMENTS. Purbeck marble tomb-chest. Earliest C 13. Four quatrefoils on the sides, enclosing leaf crosses. Romanesque leaves in the spandrels. Foliated cross on top. It stands under a somewhat later arch, pointed, outlined with a keeled roll and set on fine, big, undercut corbels of trefoil leaves. Remains of WALL PAINTING by it, *c.* 1300, of trails of maple and vine leaves. – Bishop Walter de Merton † 1277. Vaulted double canopy on clustered marble shafts. Naturalistic leaf crockets and fine panels of oakleaves in quatrefoils on the gables. Once again, bang up to date. Much restored. The alabaster effigy is wholly new, designed in 1852 by R. C. Hussey. – Bishop John Lowe † 1467. Plain tomb-chest, with inscriptions and shields in quatrefoils on the side. – Bishop John Warner † 1666. Standing monument signed by *Joshua Marshall*. Segmental pediment on Corinthian columns. Black and white marble. A typical piece. – Archdeacon Lee Warner † 1679. Standing monument with scrolls and columns set back beside the large inscription. Urn between the ends of an open pediment. By *John Shorthose*. – Lee Warner † 1698. Similar standing monument, with putti at the top drawing back the curtains of a baldacchino.

Choir   SCREEN of stone. *Scott*, in 1876, placed the ORGAN on it; divided cases by him. (On the W side of the screen, by *Pearson*, see *Nave* below.) Original C 13 shafted W doorway. The E face retains original C 13 woodwork of the PULPITUM, with arcading on octagonal shafts, and the s doorpost, carved with the wing of an angel and trefoil leaves, part presumably of the canopy of the bishop's stall. – The back STALLS incorporate trefoiled arches on octagonal shafts, more of the original choir fittings of *c.* 1227, the earliest to survive in England. (They are without misericords.) *Scott's* stalls are quite simple. They incorporate Early Renaissance panelling. Hope mentions desks made in 1541. – WALL PAINTINGS. The w end and the N and s walls below the first string-course are completely painted, mostly in 1876, following traces that remained of a medieval design. The English lion and French fleur-de-lys, repeated again and again, i.e. the arms adopted by Edward III in 1340. – C13 framed panel, Wheel of Fortune, or rather half of it, on the SE pier. Very well preserved, and of quite high quality. The tall figure of Fortune stands within the wheel, while two figures scramble upwards among the spokes, and a king at the top is about to topple from his perch.

North choir aisle MONUMENTS. C14 tomb-chest under a canopy, assumed to commemorate Bishop Hamo de Hethe † 1352. The tomb-chest is panelled, the canopy cusped so that spiritedly carved heads among leaves come in the spandrels. Slightly concave-sided gable, and idiosyncratic crockets with square lobes growing from it. Compare and contrast with the Chapter-Room doorway. – William Streaton † 1609. Small hanging monument, with small figures kneeling in prayer, as usual.

South choir aisle WALL PAINTINGS. High in a niche on a buttress of the choir wall, a late C13 Crucifix. – Very faded St Christopher on the w wall. – MONUMENT. Headless Purbeck marble effigy of a bishop, flatter and so earlier than the St Martin and Ingoldsthorpe effigies, i.e. not later than the first half of the C13. It is set under a later arch, with cusps split back, and a trefoil at the apex also with split cusps. At the back, tiny naturalistic vine leaves. The cusping is exactly like the tracery at Chartham of *c.* 1294, especially in the way the points are turned over as if made of plasticine. It is datable a decade earlier, for it must cover the tomb of Bishop John de Bradfield † 1283, who was buried 'iuxta ostium crubitorum' (i.e. by the steps to the crypt).

North transept STAINED GLASS. Both tiers of lancets 1859 by *Clayton & Bell* (Harrison 1980). – MONUMENTS. Augustine Caesar † 1677. Large tablet with side-columns, and an inscription in Latin and Greek, worthy of his name. Very restrained. – John Parr † 1792. Hanging monument in yellow, white and grey marble. Sarcophagus, urns and pedimented obelisk.

South transept STAINED GLASS. E clerestory windows 1898 by *Kempe*. – MONUMENTS. Sir Richard Head † 1689. Attributed to *Gibbons* since the mid-C18 and a favourite design of his: a three-quarter-face relief portrait in an oval medallion, with a gadrooned projection below and a swag of flowers looped above it. – Richard Watts, 1736. The C16 benefactor is commemorated by a frontal bearded bust, a copy of a C16 original, set in a Gibbsian hanging frame. *Charles Easton* was paid £50 for making

both. – Sir Edmund Head, 1798, by *Flaxman*. Just a Grecian tablet. – Sir William Franklin † 1833. Fine aristocratic bust on a pedestal, by *Samuel Joseph*, 1837. – James Forbes † 1836. Heavy Grecian tablet, with a profile medallion. – Dean Hole, 1905, by *F. W. Pomeroy*. Marble recumbent effigy. The dean wrote the much-loved *Book about Roses* (1869).

Nave SCREEN. W face designed by *Pearson*. Niches with statues by *Nathaniel Hitch*. – FONT. Dedicated 1893, carved by *Earp*. – CHANDELIERS. 1957. Small cup-shaped shades, hanging at many different levels from a brass ring. They are by *Emil Godfrey*, the cathedral architect, and the sole addition to the furnishings that the C20 has yet made (except for new sculpture in the cloister garden). – STAINED GLASS. N aisle W window by *Kempe*, 1901. – MONUMENTS. NORTH AISLE. Francis Barrell † 1679. Elegant draped cartouche. – Francis Barrell † 1724. Large architectural tablet signed by *Robert Taylor*, i.e. *Sr.* – Ann Spice † 1795. Tablet with an urn on a yellow marble ground. – SOUTH AISLE. Richard Somer † 1682. Tablet with a scrolly open pediment. – Lady Ann Henniker † 1792. Grand standing monument under a Gothick arch. White sarcophagus in front of a black pyramid. A figure of Truth stands to the l., Time is seated to the r. These figures,

121. ROCHESTER Henniker monument, figure of Time, *c.* 1792, by Thomas Banks

of *Coade* stone, were designed by *Banks*. Time is an especially vivid creation, the complex pose and succulent detailing still wholly Baroque in feeling. – John Lord Henniker. By *J. Bacon Jr*, 1806, and a pompous affair. A pair to the last in scale, but altogether of marble. The symbolism, however, is Christian. A girl, holding a nest with a pelican in her piety, leans on a sarcophagus and is about to be wreathed with olive by a substantial crowned female. At the top rays and 'Sic itur ad astra'. Lord Henniker's medallion portrait at the bottom l. corner. – Traces of light graffiti for an extensive programme of WALL PAINTINGS have been detected on the C 12 W wall and nave piers (Swanton 1980), only on surviving Norman surfaces and possibly a scheme for restoration of paintings lost in the fire of 1179. Also a C 14 St Christopher on the westernmost pier of S nave arcade, N side.

CLOISTER AND CHAPTER-HOUSE REMAINS

It is most unusual for CLOISTERS to adjoin the chancel rather than the nave (but see *Salisbury* on Old Sarum; also *Chichester*). Gundulf, says the *Textus Roffensis*, 'constructed all the necessary offices for the monks'. Nothing of that is left, for the cloister remains, as we shall see, are no earlier than Ernulf's time. Did Ernulf then begin a second cloister, E of Gundulf's? That is the generally accepted explanation, though no trace of earlier cloisters has ever been found. Single-storeyed Perp GATEWAY at the SW corner, and beyond it, down a few steps, a square chamber with Norman shafts in trios at the angles. Springers of vaulting were found in 1938. It must have formed an undercroft to the cellarer's lodging.

From here a length of the Roman town wall runs eastwards. The refectory was built against its S side, over 124 ft long. Nothing of that except the entrance doorway, with a two-bay vaulted LAVATORY and a towel-recess on the r. behind a big trefoiled arch, built by Prior Helias during the first twenty years of the C 13.

The real rewards are on the E side, where the whole outer wall of the E cloister walk remains. Ernulf, bishop from 1114 to 1124, 'fecit dormitorium, capitulum, refectorium'. The cloister wall, behind which the first two of these lie, is decorated with intersecting blank arcading, a constant motif of the early C 12 work at Canterbury, executed when Ernulf was prior there. Even more tellingly Ernulfian is the treatment of the ashlar wall over the triple entrance arches to the CHAPTER HOUSE, with a diaper pattern, in which the diagonal bands are incised so that they seem double, one half overlapping at an intersection, while the other half underlaps, so to speak, a subtlety that occurs identically on the walls of the N passage to the crypt at Canterbury. The chapter-house façade is two-storeyed, with three shafted upper windows with zigzag, and three doorways below, the

outer ones blocked, the inner richly sculptured. The problem is whether such sculpture is possible as early as before 1125. The doorway to the dormitory stairs, to the r., with a tympanum carved with a terribly decayed relief of the Sacrifice of Isaac (the subject confirmed by the fragment of inscription: 'aries per cornua'), must be considered with it. There are Saxon overtones in the tympanum, such as the hand of God shooting out of a stylized puff of cloud; but everything else, much of it very peculiar and hard to parallel in England, suggests a date not before the mid-C 12 – in particular the black shafts (of Tournai marble), the greatest rarity in England before Canterbury Cathedral made such shafting popular. A capital of *c.* 1160 excavated at Faversham and the shafts at Iffley of *c.* 1170 are just about the only other examples. Prowling beasts in panels on the abaci, and, once, in roundels on the voussoirs. Birds in foliage on the capitals. Bases with claw-like spurs. The strangest motif is the heads, some with horns, that project fully in the round from the imposts. Such heads, however, do turn up in the Prior's Doorway at Ely, where they are datable *c.* 1140. These doorways then seem to be insertions, probably after the fire of 1137, which is recorded to have damaged the chapter house. Very clever insertions, for the diapered walling shows no signs of disturbance.

The CHAPTER HOUSE was rectangular. The E wall, inside the Deanery, has more intersecting arcading, on shafts, with sub-arches from shaft to shaft. The N and S walls show evidence of a Perp remodelling, demi angel corbels for a timber roof, and a jamb of a vaulted vestibule underneath a W gallery, over which a passage will have led from the dormitory to the choir of the cathedral, when at long last the monks could no longer endure descending into the night air of the cloisters in order to say their offices.

Further on the precinct and the town, see the latest edition of B of E *West Kent and the Weald*.

St Albans

CATHEDRAL CHURCH OF ST ALBAN *Anglican*

(Based on B of E *Hertfordshire*, 1977, as revised by Bridget Cherry with information from Eileen Roberts and Jane Geddes, and further revised, with information from Michael Gillingham, George McHardy and Christopher Wilson.)

Plan, Fig. 122, from RCHM guide, 1952.

Some references (see Recent Literature): Biddle and Brooke in Runcie 1977; Norris 1978; Roberts 1971; Skeat 1977. (Also Biddle, forthcoming, on excavations.)

INTRODUCTION

As one approaches St Albans, one's first sight from miles away is a long ship-like nave and stumpy tower on a hill. It is a typically English sight, as the approaches to Lincoln and Ely are, and the impression of the cathedral city is confirmed on entering the older streets with their well-to-do Georgian houses. Yet St Albans became the see of a bishop only in 1877, with dean and chapter only from 1899. The glorious history of the church is that of one of England's greatest abbeys. Its head was made premier abbot of England in 1154. Its artists and its chroniclers were famous all over England in the C 13. Of the domestic buildings of this powerful community hardly anything remains, and if it is always difficult to see with one's mind's eye what large Benedictine monasteries of the Middle Ages must have looked like, it is almost impossible at St Albans. We know that the monastic buildings extended south-westward down the hill from the abbey church towards the River Ver, the mill and the fishponds. To the N the medieval town grew from a nucleus around the market established by a C 10 abbot outside the abbey gate.

   The abbey had grown from a shrine on the site of St Alban's martyrdom outside the Roman city of Verulamium. On this site the cathedral still stands. The remains of Verulamium in the valley of the River Ver are, thanks to the excavations undertaken from the 1920s onwards, better known than the abbey. This was one of the biggest and most important Roman towns on English soil. St Alban died in 209, one of the earliest Christian martyrs in Latin Europe. The shrine on the hill on the site of his execution was replaced or enclosed by a monastic church already by the end of the C 4. Of this building and of its Anglo-Saxon successors no remains are left, although excavations could no doubt reveal something. The development of the site from simple Roman-Christian shrine to major medieval church must have been comparable to examples known from excavation in Germany (e.g. at Bonn and Xanten).

122. ST ALBANS Plan after RCHM, 1952

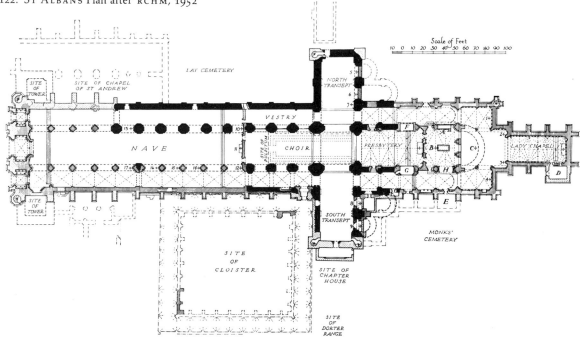

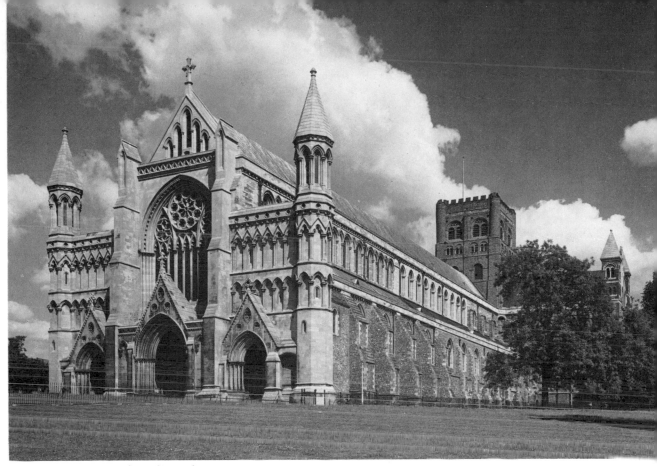

123. ST ALBANS View from the south-west

In England such continuity from Roman times may be unique, but may yet emerge elsewhere.

The first impression of the present church is one of unbalanced length: the nave alone nearly 300 ft long but unmatched by high towers. The whole building is only about 16 ft shorter than Winchester, where, however, the nave is less long in proportion to the whole and both nave and transepts are wider. St Alban's crossing tower is sturdy and seems squatter than it is, because of its uncommon bulk: square on plan, unlike Winchester's (which is wider N–S) and Chichester's (which is longer E–W), and bulkier than the one at Norwich. Doubtless too the fact that the C 19 raised the pitch of all the roofs lessened the grandeur with which the tower lorded it over the (c 15?) lower-pitched roofs. w towers are completely lacking. That is unfortunate; two w towers were planned in the late C 12, outside the width of the aisles, as was happening at Wells, but never built. And the crossing tower would have had a spire, as was indeed built in the C 13. A spike of Herts type was taken down in 1832. In a nearer view of the building's Norman parts, the most striking peculiarity is the russet and blackish-grey colouring of the Roman bricks and flints – originally all plastered white. As it is, the great building has a sombre tone.

Inside, we are never allowed to forget the overpowering weight of the walls. The Norman piers and arches seem cut into them, of materials so hard that no pier, no shaft becomes a being with an individual life. Despite the grim austerity of all this, there is much to respect and much to investigate. If the building's peculiar architectural history has been aesthetically somewhat lopsided, we must be intensely grateful for what did so impressively survive, embedded in later medieval work, and in spite of still later Victorian work.

The Norman church was probably built at one go or with one brief pause: of the works started in 1077, the E arm and transepts seem to have been done by 1088 and then the nave may have taken until 1115, when dedication took place (Biddle; see Runcie 1977). The site of the Anglo-Saxon church that had developed from St Alban's shrine was either in the Norman main apse, where the medieval shrine behind the present high altar is, or, perhaps more likely, below the present nave, to allow the older church to stand while building 1077–88 went on (Biddle, op. cit.):

from it remain only the baluster shafts high up in the Norman transepts. When building began in 1077, the first Norman abbot of St Albans was Paul of Caen, nephew of Lanfranc, Archbishop of Canterbury. Paul had been a monk of St-Étienne at Caen when his uncle was its abbot. Lanfranc is said to have had a good deal to do with inaugurating the building work at St Albans. (Professor Brooke (op. cit.) says both men were probably originally Lombard Italians, and so used to building in brick.) Paul's church was c. 360 ft long, with a nave of ten bays, a crossing with tower, transepts and an apsidal choir, flanked by shorter apsidal chapels and by apses of diminishing depth on the E sides of the transepts, two on the N and two on the S. Thus a stepped outline of seven apses was created, where Canterbury had only five. It must have been an impressive sight indeed, there on the hilltop. It was the richest development of a scheme first, it seems, conceived at Cluny in the C 10.

A hundred years after Paul of Caen, Abbot John of Cella (1195–1214) lengthened the nave by rebuilding the W bay and adding three further bays and began to erect a worthy W front with two towers outside the line of the aisles, just as was done at Wells, and also at Ripon outside a then aisleless nave, a little later. The style he used was E.E., and St Albans is amongst the earliest representatives of the style. However, John of Cella's finances were not of the soundest, and in 1197 work had to be suspended. The W parts were completed only c. 1230 under William of Trumpington, without the towers, and also without the intended nave vaults. So in 1230 the nave at St Albans had nine Norman bays and four E.E., aesthetically not a happy combination.

But worse happened. In 1323 five piers on the S side of the Norman nave collapsed, causing much further damage, and so, in a style blending with the E.E. W bays but conflicting with the Norman ones opposite, the S side of the Norman nave was rebuilt. There can be no peace for the eye where opposite arcades do not correspond. But when the money or the will to complete both sides at one go is not there, the ultimate alternative may be historicism; e.g. Chester nave, where the two arcades, visually alike, are a century apart. One could not expect the C 14 at St Albans to rebuild à la normande. There is, however, the consideration that pious care for the C 13 Crucifixion paintings on the Norman N piers may have prevented their deliberate destruction after those opposite had collapsed.

The E parts of the abbey had in the meantime also been completely rebuilt. The need for room and also for altars was so great that even the seven apsed spaces were not sufficient. It is the development we find in most English cathedrals. The rebuilding began with the S choir aisle before 1235. In 1257 a major rebuilding of the E end was begun and went on till the Lady Chapel was completed about 1320. This was slow work compared with that under Paul of Caen. His impetus was evidently lacking. Just as the builders of the W parts of the nave had given up the projected vaults, so the new chancel, retrochoir and Lady Chapel had all been begun with the intention of stone vaulting and all ended with wooden vaults or ceilings. Had money or enthusiasm returned after that, the nave might have been entirely rebuilt, as at Canterbury later in the C 14, or at least entirely remodelled, as at Winchester. What may seem to some a painful conflict between N and S may for others, however, make this nave interesting as an 'architectural peculiar'.

The separateness of parts of St Albans goes still further. The monks' choir extends for three bays into the nave, the traditional arrangement in the C 11 and C 12, preserved here, as the crossing tower was never rebuilt. The large C 14 screen of solid stone ends it to the W and thus cuts off part of the nave and the view towards the crossing tower and the E. And from the late C 15 another even bigger and heavier screen, the reredos, forms another division farther eastward.

St Albans is the only one of the major churches of England which has a W front completely, or almost completely, Victorian (i.e. not counting replacements of decayed stonework elsewhere). It is the work of *Lord Grimthorpe*, designed in 1879 and built at his own expense. The cathedral was indeed in a sad state early in the C 19. The Lady Chapel was walled off as a grammar school, a public way led through the retrochoir, and the W front was a ruin, with the lateral porches walled up. Indeed a century earlier, in 1721, *Hawksmoor*, about to make repairs, published an engraving of the abbey to 'Support this venerable pile from being Martyred by ye Neglect of a Slouthfull generation'. Minor repairs were made by *Cottingham* in the 1830s. Plans for restoration date from the 1850s, but nothing was done until 1871, when *Sir G. G. Scott* issued a report. He was responsible for repairing the nave S clerestory windows, the S aisle roof, the stonework of the Lady Chapel, and the central tower. But work had to be stopped after Scott's death in 1878 for lack of further funds. That was when Lord Grimthorpe, a lawyer, amateur theologian and amateur architect, aged sixty-three, intervened. He was dictatorial and rich, and is reputed to have spent £130,000 on the abbey. One can only speculate what Bodley or Pearson or even Oldrid Scott (of Hereford's W front) would have made of so responsible a job. It was within precisely the period between the creation of the bishopric and the authorizing of a dean and chapter that Lord Grimthorpe flourished here. On a carved spandrel inside the W porch he is represented as St Matthew, as if contemplating with satisfaction a camel's safe passage through the eye of a needle (must we add, these days, cf. Matthew 19:24?).

The earliest remains of the Norman style at St Albans belong to the years immediately after the Conquest. Paul of Caen began building probably as soon as he had been made abbot to reform the lax Saxon monastery. From 1077 until 1088 a substantial part was built, presumably the eastern arm, crossing and transepts, so that services could be transferred from the Saxon church while the nave was built, presumably by 1115, when there was a consecration. Of its E parts, described above, little survives. We have to go to the TRANSEPT and the crossing tower to receive the full impact of that mighty and graceless style. The building is of flint, with almost all the strengthening at the angles, round doors and windows, and in similar places by means of Roman bricks taken freely from old Verulamium. Only a very little stone was available, some of it brought from Caen, apparently the first use of Caen stone in England (Clifton-Taylor 1972). Arches and windows are completely unadorned (no more than one step back instead of any mouldings). The walls are articulated by strip-like flat buttresses without set-offs (rather than lesenes). Paul of Caen might have seen these at St-Étienne in Caen, begun in 1064 and consecrated about 1075–80. In the N and W walls of the N transept the ground-floor windows survive, and in both transepts the clerestory windows. Moreover, inside the transept the three equal openings to the apsidal chapels can still be seen. In the S transept two small windows remain above them. Of the S front of the S transept and the N front of the N transept we cannot say much, as *Lord Grimthorpe* gave the S transept a spectacular group of E.E. lancets, the N a large, rather thin rose-window (since sometimes called the Colander). In their stead there had been big Perp windows. Each transept end is now flanked by symmetrical staircase-turrets. On the S side formerly the W turret was circular, with twin round-headed windows on four sides, and the staircase only in the upper part. The E turret was small and octagonal, with no stairs. Between them were remains of blank arcading, with a small oculus at each end. The interior system of the transept is of a tall ground floor, a triforium and a clere-story with wall-passage. The triforium has for each bay two pairs of openings. The colonnettes are circular or octagonal, or of an odd, decidedly Saxon-looking baluster shape. Some of these have moulded bands. They support Norman cushion capitals. It seems likely that some of the shafts are Late Saxon work, perhaps forming part of the building materials collected before the Conquest, or from the pre-Conquest church. The tympana of the arches are filled by a criss-cross of bricks, which was no doubt once whitewashed, like all the rest. On the whitewash originally simple patterns were painted (an apparent alternation of red and white blocks of stone, for example, or a sham

124 ST ALBANS South transept,
late C11 with pre-Conquest triforium shafts

ashlaring by red lines to indicate joints, as once, e.g. in Oxford chapter house, or by zigzag lines).

The CROSSING TOWER rests on immensely high arches. The supporting piers have a double-stepped section for each side. Above this is a triforium of three twin openings, supported on colonnettes of different shapes (some perhaps re-used), and above this are two large windows. The rest is hidden by a painted wooden ceiling with pretty square panels (a copy of the early C16 one). The exterior of the crossing tower is entirely of brick. The builders did not trust flint for construction so high up in the air. Above the first stage of windows is an outer gallery of four arches of twin openings on each side, and above this the bell stage with two large twin openings with angle-

125. St Albans Crossing tower, late C 11

not true aisles because they were divided from the main part of the church by solid walls (as at the Trinité at Caen and at Rochester); therefore the bays did not have to correspond. Buckler discovered evidence surviving in the aisle roof space of pilasters which divided the bays, and also the remains of a triforium passage.

The NAVE remains complete in the first three bays from the crossing, at least at arcade and clerestory level. The flat ceiling is of the C 15 (see below) but of course replaces an equally flat Norman ceiling. w of the third bay only the N side is Norman. The nave has tall arcades with broad rectangular piers – in fact hardly piers at all, but chunks of solid wall masonry left standing. To appreciate the contrast between this raw treatment of the arcade and the articulate and elegant arcading of later styles one need only look at the C 13 work farther w. (See the westernmost Norman pier on the N, its lower portion spared – perhaps for the Crucifixion painted on it – with new carved work rising out of it.) The wall character of the Early Norman piers is emphasized by the pilaster strips or buttress strips which rise on their surface and go right up into the clerestory zone. Towards the arches the piers are double-stepped, a small progress against the single stepping farther E. There is also double stepping towards the pilasters on the aisle side. The projections above these pilasters suggest that there were quadrant arches across the aisles. There are not yet any further mouldings anywhere, nor any capitals, nor any ornament. This is perhaps explained by the use of flint and brick rather than stone. No other major Early Norman buildings in England are so plain (although cf. the nave of Elstow, Beds.). The only exceptions in the nave arcade are the fourth and fifth piers from the E on the N side. These have very coarse capitals, and the fifth one has rounded projections to S and W, giving the pier a composite shape similar to the type used in the naves of Ely and Peterborough, although much cruder. Is this the start of a new design for the nave which was then abandoned? The fifth pier in fact contained a very small staircase, which still survives between gallery and clerestory.

Almost equally unadorned no doubt was the storey above the arcade. But here some alterations have been made which obscure the original state, and make it difficult to appreciate fully the Norman design. As things are at present, one sees from inside a deep unmoulded arch above each arcade bay at the outer end of which is a cusped three-light C 15-looking window. These windows give no light, as they now lead into the roof of the aisle. The explanation seems to be that in the C 15 the pitch of the aisle roofs was lowered, and windows were inserted in the middle storey to make a second clerestory. Pre-restoration engravings show the low aisle roofs before they were heightened again by *Lord Grimthorpe*. To the l. and r. of the main upright pilaster strips shallow piers can still be

shafts, and a curious piercing of the tympana by rows of little triangles. At this level the central buttresses change from flat pilasters to paired shafts separated by an angular projection. The angles of the tower are strengthened by buttress strips which at the level of the bell-stage develop into circular angle supports. The use of rounded forms and shafts at this level shows that by the time the bell-stage was reached the austerity of the Early Norman work was being abandoned. The tower has later battlements (rebuilt by *Lord Grimthorpe*).

Of the EASTERN ARM as built by Paul of Caen, the beginning can be traced in the exterior of the N side and in the interior on both sides. The chancel aisles are groin-vaulted. On the S side a blocked arch in the first bay marks the former access from the chancel chapel to the inner transeptal chapel. In the second bay a pair of quite tall windows has been found and exposed. The Norman E arm was four bays long, with an apse, and was flanked by chapels of five bays, possibly with internal apses (traces of which were found in 1845 by Buckler). The chapels were

126. St Albans Choir and crossing, late C 11 etc, looking east

seen with their bases and imposts on which formerly the arches toward the nave must have rested. In the third bay from the E, on the N side, which was protected from alterations by the pulpitum, a little more is left, which shows that there were double-stepped orders as in the arcade below. That shows that the arrangement here was not identical to that of the transepts. There are no traces to be seen of any triforium passages, i.e. a passage in the thickness of the wall as exists in the transepts, and it seems that the middle storey of the nave was not a triforium but a gallery, although one which opened only into the space below the aisle roof, as there appears to be no evidence for outer aisle walls with upper windows. According to Sir Alfred Clapham and others there was one large arch for each arcade arch, as at St-Étienne at Caen (and in England at e.g. Blyth, Notts, in the C11, or Norwich in the C12). But at St-Étienne and Norwich the gallery openings are very lofty, which is not the case at St Albans, where the clerestory is taller than the middle storey. But neither is the latter of the very low type found e.g. in the nave of the Trinité at Caen, or in the Norman buildings in the west

country such as Gloucester or Tewkesbury. The proportions of St Albans are closer to Jumièges or Mont-Saint-Michel. Both these had subdivided galleries, and it is indeed possible that the St Albans nave gallery had subdivisions of some kind. The large brick arches visible in the roof space of the aisle could have been mere blank relieving arches. Details of the C11 gallery have no doubt to be visualized as being almost as raw and bare as the arcade. Some of the imposts are decorated with simple sunk star patterns, but this is hardly visible from below.

That St Albans, in the C12, did not shun ornament is proved by the SLYPE (lately shop), that is the passage between s transept and chapter house (see *Precincts* below), which is decorated with blank arcading with intersected arches. These arches have rings at close intervals so that they look like bent spinal cords, or strings of cotton reels. Some of the arcading is still *in situ*, but *Lord Grimthorpe* was busy here, and most of it has been re-erected against the s wall of the s transept. Below it is, also re-set, the highly ornate DOORWAY from the cloister into the slype. This has three orders, without any break between jambs and voussoirs, the outer of foliage scrolls, the middle one with two sets of round-headed crenellations, one on the intrados, the other on the extrados. The inner order is C19 reconstruction. Amongst architectural fragments exhibited in the slype, more pieces of C12 decoration.

127. ST ALBANS C12 cloister doorway
reset in south transept wall

THE THIRTEENTH AND FOURTEENTH CENTURIES

What reason can Abbot John de Cella (1195–1214) have had to lengthen yet farther the NAVE of the church, the nave being the least important part of an abbey church? Or was he only carrying out what had been planned from the beginning? He added three bays and started a proper w façade. The design is wholly in the Gothic style. No compromise with the existing nave is aimed at. Considering the fact that the Gothic chancel at Canterbury had been begun only twenty years before and Lincoln and Wells no more than five, John of Cella was certainly a modern-minded man. However, after only two years, work was stopped for lack of money, and much of what we see now goes back only to William of Trumpington (1214–35). The new bays of the nave have piers of an unusual section. They are basically square, with four attached shafts, but as the angles are broadly chamfered they appear as if they had semi-octagonal shafts in the diagonals. It is a somewhat heavy section, due perhaps to existing square Norman foundations for the lengthening of the nave? (Compare again the N arcade's pier with C13 work rising out of Norman work.) The arch mouldings are more complex than can here be described. The arches reach up higher than the Norman ones. Their apexes touch the sill-line of the triforium, for the E.E. extension has no proper gallery.

128. ST ALBANS Nave, early C12 (l.) and mid-C14 (r.)

The triforium is of two twin openings per bay, with ample dogtooth decoration along the sill and up the shafts, and with pierced quatrefoils in the spandrels. The most interesting thing about the triforium is, however, the fact that no differentiation is made between the curve of the inner arch of each light and that of the outer arch above both lights of one twin opening. Thus it looks as if the outer arch started with one broad complex set of mouldings from which some suddenly break off to form the smaller arch inside – a lack of articulation or logicality typically English. It exists at Worcester as well, probably a little earlier (retrochoir consecrated 1218). Most of the work on this stage belongs to the second building phase. During the first, that is between 1195 and 1197, vaulting-shafts of Purbeck marble had been attached to the spandrels of the arcade below. The triforium was prepared to receive their continuation up to the projected vault, but they were abandoned, as can clearly be seen, and with them the plan to vault the nave. The intention must have been for a sexpartite vault over each bay (see the bases of the shafts). The last bay to the E on the S side, adjoining the C14 work further E, has no vaulting-shafts; i.e. it was begun after the idea of vaulting had been given up. Also in the trioria of the last two bays there is a quatrefoil instead of a circle above the two sub-arches. So here, after the W extension was ready, a beginning was made on the rebuilding of the Norman nave. It could have been this work that weakened the Norman bays further E, causing the collapse of 1323 (or it may indicate that the nave already needed repairing in the C13).

The clerestory of the W extension continues the wall-passage of the Norman nave. On the outside it is handsomely shafted, with a larger arch for each lancet window and smaller, more pointed, blank arches between. The aisle windows were all altered by *Lord Grimthorpe*. Inside, the aisles have bare walls (none of the usual English blank arcading), but the S wall has tripartite vaulting-shafts along the wall, as if for aisle vaults. The existing vaults, however, are C19. Abbot de Cella's W end was meant to be a grand showpiece, with two W towers standing outside the nave to widen the façade, and with three deep porches. The idea of towers was given up; the rest was built but fell into such dismal decay that it was almost entirely rebuilt by Lord G. Of the upper parts of the façade nothing is C13: a nine-light Perp window was demolished by Lord G. to replace it by his Late Geometric one. The porches are original in their structure, but only in a few details. The long Purbeck shafts carrying an outer skin of arcading in front of the blank arcading against the back walls of the porches, however, can be ascribed to the late C12. The inside of the front towards nave and aisles is richly adorned with blank lancet arcades. The capitals are of the crocketed as well as the stiff-leaf type. The detail is much richer than in the nave,

which suggests that it belongs to the more ambitious scheme of Abbot de Cella.

The next addition to the church was the replacement of the Norman E end by one more spacious and more up to date. A beginning was made in Trumpington's time, when the S choir aisle was partly rebuilt (see the stiff-leaf capitals and dogtooth mouldings decorating the windows). Also of the early C13, some alterations to the W wall of the S transept: two lancet windows, added without regard for Norman proportions, project into the triforium, so that two triforium shafts had to be replaced; the RCHM suggests more light was wanted for sculpture placed in the transept then (e.g. a statue of the Virgin by *Walter of Colchester*). Part of the new work was again rebuilt when the major scheme for a new EASTERN ARM was started in 1257. This involved the rebuilding of both aisles, apart from the first bays, and the covering of the solid walls between aisles and choir (which were left standing) with tall blank arcades. The entrances to the aisles in the first bay from the crossing were partly blocked and replaced by smaller ones decorated with canopy work, later broken up. The present little balcony on the S side, with three canopies each with three pointed and cusped arches and three crocketed gables, is a C19 reconstruction. That on the N side is a copy (RCHM). Farther E, that is in the feretory or space for the shrine, behind the altar and reredos, the chancel arcades are open, with piers of four major and four minor shafts. The aisles have quadripartite rib-vaults. Above the arcade is a small, mostly blank triforium of even little cusped arches, and above that the clerestory with clusters of nook-shafts and wall-passage. The tracery is C19. Here also a stone vault was planned, but only a wooden vault carried out. It is of C13 timber, but was altered and repainted in the C15 (see *Wall paintings* below). The chancel ends to the E in an arcade of three bays. Into the springers of the arches odd little blank arcades have been carved, for no purpose which can now be understood. The shape of the springers also suggests that a vault was intended here at arcade level: difficult to understand, but perhaps the springers were made for another place. Above the arcade a large and excellent group of a four-light Geometric window and two flanking lancets. The large window has two trefoils and above them a splendid large octofoil, similar to the contemporary chapter house at Salisbury but a little more advanced (Salisbury has encircled quatrefoils where St Albans has unencircled trefoils).

E of this the building is carried on one-storeyed, and on its general outline, especially from far away, this lowering of the roof-line has an unfortunate effect. In plan the new E parts seem quite able to balance the long nave; in elevation they don't, except when the building is seen from the N E or S E. The E exterior consists of the RETROCHOIR and the LADY CHAPEL. Contrary to custom the Lady Chapel was

129. ST ALBANS C 13–14 Lady Chapel, retrochoir and choir from the south-east

the last undertaking. The retrochoir carries on the line of the chancel aisles, but uses an octagonal pier to separate the aisles from the roomy central span. This is not broader than the chancel but appears so because it is so much lower, and also because it has a flat ceiling. All this is not as it was originally intended. The foundations of sleeper walls have been found which would have divided the central span into three naves, as is the case at Salisbury. Against the outer wall is renewed blank arcading, and above it open the windows. The window decoration of the w bays is of the earliest bar-tracery type, two cusped lights with a foiled circle above. Others have the slightly later form of three unencircled quatrefoils above the two lights. Yet others (retrochoir N aisle E, Lady Chapel vestibule N and S) go a decisive step farther away from the purity of the E.E. style. These must have been the latest parts to be completed. (The retrochoir aisle walls of the second bay from the E are C 19.

This was where a passage ran through the building after the Reformation.)

The Lady Chapel itself must be called Dec, although it has none of the fantasies of East Anglia or Yorkshire. A special effort was made here (e.g. the outer walls of these E parts were intended to be, and were partly, stone-faced). A vault was also intended, but once more not carried out. (The present stone vault is C 19. Before it was wooden vaulting. Pre-restoration drawings show vaulted niches below the springing of the vault.) The walls again have blank arcading inside, all in its present form C 19. The original design was simpler. However, according to the RCIIM much of the internal stonework of the windows is original. The windows are sumptuously adorned. They have inside ballflower decoration, and in addition tier above tier of small figures on brackets (one with a canopy that is an embryonic nodding ogee). The window tracery is com-

130. St Albans Lady Chapel interior, early c 14

plex. It includes ogee reticulation and small ogee heads to the individual lights of the five-light E window. These are mostly oddly crowned by little crocketed gables, as if they were blank arches, although the glazing of the window goes on above them in the larger forms of the arch common to the whole five-light window. Otherwise there are intersections, unencircled trefoils, daggers arranged cross-wise so as to fill the oblong lozenge shape at the top of a four-light window, a wheel of six cusped daggers in a circle, with mouchettes in the spandrels, etc. If all these features are as early as *c.* 1308, the date suggested by the documentary evidence, then they are very early examples. (But Mr Christopher Wilson draws attention to e.g. crocketed gables at Merton College Chapel, Oxford, and York Minster chapter-house vestibule, and ogee reticulation in the Hatfield Chapel at Spalding, all of the very beginning of the C 14.) The *Gesta Abbatum* records that a bequest to the Lady Chapel was spent on roof, vault, and glass windows *c.* 1310. Was all the tracery complete by then? The middle window on the S side, with the Perp feature of two vertical lights in its head, can hardly be of this date.

The E bay on the S side has charming SEDILIA with two tiers of arcading (completely renewed at ground-level). The upper level has crocketed gables above ogee cusping, framed within the rere-arch of the window above, which is in the form of a spherical triangle. The room S of this bay is a replacement by *Lord Grimthorpe* of a C 15 chapel.

In 1323 part of the S side of the Norman nave came down, and instead of a complete rebuilding of the nave, only this side (five bays long) was redone. The designer decided to keep to the general scheme of the C 13 work farther W. He used piers of the same shape, and only adjusted his capitals and arch mouldings according to a different taste. He abandoned the C 13 vaulting-shafts in the arcade spandrels, as he never intended vaults, and introduced pretty label stops instead in the form of heads: a king, a queen, a mitred abbot, and a layman, perhaps the master mason *Henry Wy*. His triforium also differs from that of the C 13 in such details as the elongated cusping of the arches and the decoration of the spandrels. The earlier dogtooth ornament was replaced by knobbly foliage. The clerestory fenestration is different too, as can be seen outside from the S. In the aisles cinquepartite instead of tripartite shafts are used, and vaults were actually carried out.

Some time later in the C 14 vestries were built E of the S transept, where the Norman chapels had been. Their two doorways still exist, as does also the infinitely more elaborate late C 14 DOORWAY from the S aisle into the cloister. This is set in a square frame, as pleased the taste of those who believed in the new Perp style. The door arch is very cusped. In the spandrels are quatrefoils with shields as they appear in the W doors of so many parish churches. To the l.

and r. are slim niches with tiny lierne vaults inside. For the cloisters, see below.

The FIFTEENTH CENTURY, so prominent in most major churches, whatever their original dates, is almost absent at St Albans (except for the nave windows above the Norman arcades). The parochial church of St Andrew, N of the nave, was rebuilt at this time, but has completely disappeared. So has a C 15 chapel built by Abbot John of Wheathampstead to the S of the feretory. Another C 15 chapel S of the retrochoir was rebuilt by *Lord Grimthorpe*. Other Perp alterations, such as the N and S transept windows (the latter already rebuilt in the 1830s) and the great W window, were replaced by Lord G.'s version of the E.E. Of his completed W front the *Builder* wrote: 'it is very much the sort of Gothic which one meets with in competition designs for the larger class of Dissenting Chapels – effective in a showy way but totally devoid of refinement' (quoted by Peter Ferriday in his *Lord Grimthorpe*, 1957, which is rich in quotable matter).

FURNISHINGS

For wall paintings and monuments, see below.

First the two main screen partitions, the reredos between sanctuary and feretory, and the choir screen in the nave.

REREDOS. Erected by Abbot Wallingford, with completion recorded in 1484, though more money was contributed in 1487. As with the similar and contemporary reredos at Winchester, its great height signifies the declining importance of the shrine E of it (see below). As also at Winchester, the images are all Victorian. The St Albans reredos was built of clunch and suffered much ill-usage. The cresting and canopies are all renewed, and *Harry Hems*'s figures of 1884–90 give it an unmedieval air. But its structure is indeed essentially original, a solid stone wall with three tiers of niches. (Fragments of stonework said to have been removed during restoration are now in store.) The schematism of the uprights and horizontals is far stronger than the fancy of the details (a typical Late Perp feature). The relief now inserted in the reredos immediately above the altar is by *Sir Alfred Gilbert*. As the reredos cuts awkwardly into the chancel arcading short stone screens, with plain panelling, were inserted towards the aisles.

CHOIR SCREEN, former rood screen, behind the nave altar, three bays W of the crossing. It is also of stone and was probably built by Abbot de la Mare (1349–96) after the previous one had been damaged by the collapse of the S arcade. It has none of the grace and lightness of earlier C 14 screens such as those of Exeter and Southwell. In its solid squareness, with straight top and only a thin cresting, it is wholly in the new Perp spirit. It has two doorways, with original oak doors; on the spandrels of the rere-arches grotesque faces in foliage (a feature reflected on the Crowmer tombs at Aldenham). A lay altar between them, and above this seven closely set niches for images with tall canopies above. More niches, at a slightly lower sill-level, to the l. and r. of the doors. – The SCREEN across the N aisle is an addition by *Lord Grimthorpe*. – One bay E of the rood screen stood the pulpitum, which divided the monastic choir from the nave. It was usual in major medieval churches for the monks' choir to extend w of the crossing. In the C19, foundations were discovered which showed that the medieval choir stalls extended as far w as the pulpitum, leaving a vestibule between this and the rood screen. – On the choir screen, at the sides twin ORGAN CASES by *Oldrid Scott*, 1908, and in the centre facing E choir-organ case by *Cecil Brown*, 1963 (Gillingham; also booklet by Peter Hurford available at the cathedral). – (In the N transept a fragment of cresting said to come from a rood beam in the E crossing arch, i.e. between choir and presbytery.) – CHOIR STALLS. 1905, by *Oldrid Scott*. In the nave moveable stalls of 1973 by *George Pace* (*Grimthorpe*'s nave stalls and pulpit removed; parts of the pulpit's diapered stonework in the N transept.) – FONT and COVER, 1933, by *J. A. Randoll Blacking*.

SHRINE OF ST ALBAN, surviving base (behind the reredos in the E bay of the presbytery, i.e. the feretory). Erected *c.* 1302–8, destroyed 1539, base found in 2,000 pieces in 1872. Of the shrine on top nothing remains. The

131. ST ALBANS Shrine, *c.* 1302–8, and watching loft, *c.* 1413–29

shrine base, tall enough for the shrine to tower above the altar w of it until the late C15 reredos reared up, rests on a pedestal like a tomb-chest with the usual quatrefoil decoration. Around the shrine base detached post-like buttresses are linked with the structure only higher up. Bony (1979) compares these to a playful array of flag-poles, as in the upper w bays at Selby, or like the semi-detached framework on Wells w front; one might call them small-scale predecessors of the Ely Octagon lantern's finials. On the lower step remains of twisted columns, doubtless inspired by the C13 Cosmati work on St Edward's Shrine at Westminster (see *Furnishings*, Feretory, there). New railings around designed by *Pace*. The shrine base itself, mostly of Purbeck marble with some clunch, has four niches on each of the long sides and a canted niche at each end, decorated inside with blank ogee-reticulated tracery. Crocketed gables above the niches, the spandrels with excellently carved but badly damaged figures, seated saints, the martyrdom of St Alban, censing angels etc. The style of carving is close to that of the Eleanor Crosses (the nearest of which survives as Waltham Cross, begun 1291, heavily restored: see B of E *Hertfordshire*). – The shrine was from the C15 under the watchful eye of a *custos feretri*, for whom a special raised box or WATCHING LOFT was made probably between 1413 and 1429 (St John Hope, *per* P. Eames 1977). It has a parallel in wood and stonework at Oxford Cathedral (Lady Chapel). This one is entirely of timber, the ground floor made into cupboards for relics and gifts, with a narrow staircase, and the upper floor coved out like a rood-loft. On the beam dividing the two storeys carving of the Labours of the Months, with the Martyrdom in the centre. The upper floor is one chamber, open towards the shrine in eight twin-windows. The detail is all of the simplest Perp, again much like that of rood-screens. The designing and carving was probably done by a workshop usually engaged on such jobs. In one of the cupboards a limewood figure of Christ, probably C19 German. – Another reconstructed shrine-base, in the N chancel aisle, for the SHRINE OF ST AMPHIBALUS, originally centred in the retrochoir. Here also only the base remains, put together again in the C19. Mid-C14 work of clunch.

DOORS. N wall, N transept, with big iron hinges. C19, the design partly based on the original slype door now in the Victoria and Albert Museum. – From s aisle to cloister, richly traceried, late C14. – The original w doors, probably late C14 but simpler, are now kept at the w ends of the nave aisles: large leaf with small cat-door. – BREAD CUPBOARDS. Late C16, small, in a w recess of the s transept, with balusters to the doors. – TILES. A few of the C14–15 placed in front of the now blocked entrances to the N transept's former E chapels.

STAINED GLASS. Surprisingly little of interest (but see Skeat 1977 on St Albans glass). A few medieval fragments.

N transept, E side, S window: four shields C 14, possibly from the cloisters; nave N aisle: angels with shields, fragments, probably early C 15. – Lady Chapel: E window and second from E, 1881, by *Burlison & Grylls*; S W and N W windows by *Kempe*, 1896 and 1900. – Nave N aisle: w window and window over font, 1939, by *Christopher Webb*. – Nave w window, 1924, war memorial by *Comper*.

WALL PAINTINGS

St Albans possesses an amount of medieval wall painting unique among the major churches of England, even if far inferior to what, for example, some French and German churches possess (St-Savin, Reichenau). (For fuller details, see Roberts 1971.)

There are first of all traces in many places of the decorative motifs used to enliven the whitewashed wall surfaces: sham ashlaring, alternation of red or yellow and white courses, zigzag, foliage scrolls etc. The whole church must be visualized painted in this fashion. Of the late Middle Ages are the pretty vine scrolls in a N transept N window and the dark green Tudor roses on a strong red background on the piers to the S E of the Shrine of St Alban. There are also traces left of the major figure motifs which must originally have been everywhere in the most important positions. The best-preserved painting is the figure of St William of York, sophisticated work of high quality, datable *c.* 1330, in the N E corner of the feretory. It was probably part of an altarpiece above the Altar of the Relics which stood here. – In the S E corner is a fragment of an archbishop. – In the N chancel aisle, seated figure of King Offa, probably early C 15. – On the E side of the E crossing arch a mid-C 13 Christ in Majesty, flanked by saints in niches. Painted on top of this is a C 15 Eagle and Lamb (the badge of Abbot Wheathampstead), and shields. – S transept, E wall: early C 13 figure of an angel. – N transept E wall: a C 15 scene of Doubting Thomas, in an elaborate architectural setting. (This scene was mentioned in 1428 as intended for the instruction of pilgrims on their way from the N transept to the shrine.) – Between the nave clerestory windows, towards the E end, are several large standing figures of apostles (three uncovered on the N side, one on the S).

Next, the decoration of the Norman NAVE PIERS themselves. Five of them have or had paintings on both S and w sides. On the S sides, starting from the w: St Christopher, late C 13; then two piers with large C 14 figures, St Thomas of Canterbury and St Citha (?); on the fourth from the w two figures, possibly St Edward and the Pilgrim. – On the w sides of the piers the precious remains of C 13 paintings originally no doubt above altars. It is a most interesting fact in itself that altars should have stood against all these piers in the nave of an abbey church. Each painting is of two

132. ST ALBANS Crucifixion, C 13 painting on nave pier

tiers, and in each case the Crucifixion is on the upper tier. This repetition is again interesting, and equally interesting is the variety of treatment and sentiment, from the gentleness of the second of the painted piers (counting from the w) to the majesty of the third, and the terrible distortion of the fifth. In date they range from *c.* 1215 (first) to *c.* 1275 (fifth). The scenes below, from w to E, are: on the first two piers, the Virgin and Child; then the Annunciation, the Annunciation to Zacharias (?), and the Coronation of the Virgin.

CEILING PAINTINGS. Choir (i.e. w of the crossing over the E bays of the nave): late C 15 coffered panels, two with the Coronation of the Virgin, the rest with shields and monograms (repainted by *T. C. Rogers* and Professor *Tristram*). – Tower: a reconstruction of the early C 16 scheme (one original panel preserved). Tudor roses and shields. – N transept: *c.* 1550. Only the central panel showing the Martyrdom of St Alban survives. – Presbytery: the C 13 wooden vault repainted in the C 15, from which dates the present design of circular medallions enclosing the eagle and lamb, symbols of S S. John Evangelist and Baptist; repainted in the 1930s by *Rogers* and *Tristram*.

MONUMENTS

The most important are the three CHANTRY CHAPELS to the N and S of the high altar and the shrine. They are (S of the shrine) Humphrey Duke of Gloucester's † 1447; (S of the high altar) Abbot Wallingford's † 1484; and (N of the high altar) Abbot Ramryge's † 1519. There was also a chantry chapel of Abbot John of Wheathampstead † 1465. This projected to the S of the S aisle. Only the door and flanking niches survive. According to documents it was built by 1430. – One handsome feature of the GLOUCESTER CHANTRY may be late C 13: the IRON GRILLE of rectangular panels alternately built up of vertical, horizontal and diagonal bars, on the aisle side of the

133. ST ALBANS Iron grille, C 15?, Gloucester Chantry

chantry barring entry to St Alban's Shrine from the S, as the watching loft does from the N. Jane Geddes thinks the grille may be C 15, i.e. contemporary with the chantry, and RCHM, 1952, suggests the artist was *Johnson* of the gate to Henry V's Chantry at Westminster (see *Furnishings*, Feretory, there). The late Charles Oman called the grille's visual interference disastrous (*Archaeological Journal*, 136). The chantry itself has a large tripartite opening to the shrine, and above stonework of the design usual in screens, with piers between on which are three tiers of figures in niches. Prominently displayed are handsome shields and decorative bands of Duke Humphrey's device of plants in a

cup, signifying the Gardens of Adonis, a classical *memento mori* (the device perhaps suggested by his friend the humanist scholar Abbot Wheathampstead). There is no effigy and no tomb-chest. The vault is traceried. (Beneath the pavement is a panel-vaulted tomb chamber with a WALL PAINTING of the Crucifixion, in black outline. Dr Roberts.) – The WALLINGFORD CHANTRY has a wide four-centred arch closed by contemporary ironwork and a heavy, straight-topped superstructure with wheat ears and the device 'Valles Habundabunt', and above the rose in a sunburst, the badge of Edward IV. Despite the wheat ears, the records indicate that it was Abbot Wallingford who built a chantry in this position. The tomb does not survive. There is nothing fanciful about the architecture of this chantry; it is much less sumptuous than that erected by Wheathampstead to his patron the Duke of Gloucester. – The RAMRYGE CHANTRY of *c.* 1515–20 is the most elaborate of the three, a tall ground floor with a close stone screen, again of the patterns used for stone rood screens, and above finer and thinner decoration with ogee arches and polygonal turrets. Among the carvings appear, apart from shields and Ramryge's emblem, the ram, the Instruments of the Passion, and scenes from the Martyrdom of St Alban. To the aisle the chantry is of wood, four bays plus half-bay at each end and with upper part coved out. The interior is daintily fan-vaulted. On the floor an incised slab with the figure of the abbot. The door into the chapel is original. – The only other medieval stone memorial is a RECESS in the S aisle, arched and cusped, late C 13.

On the other hand, many BRASSES are preserved, and even more indents. Most of the figure brasses have been collected on a wooden board. These are of the C 15 and early C 16 and of no special merit. Remaining on the floor Ralph Rowlatt † 1543, merchant of the Staple of Calais, with children below (S chancel aisle), R. Beauver, *c.* 1460, a monk holding a bleeding heart, and Sir A. Grey † 1480, in armour (chancel). – In the chancel floor a fine tripartite brass canopy with concave sides belonging to the brass of Abbot Stone † 1451. – But the best brass at St Albans (S transept but subject to change) is the large plate of Flemish workmanship to Abbot de la Mare † 1396. The brass was made in his lifetime, probably *c.* 1360 (Norris 1978). Until recently it lay on the tomb-chest of Abbot Wallingford. It has broad buttresses on the sides of the figure with three tiers of pairs of small figures of saints under canopies and two of single figures above. In the low top canopy the Lord holding the Abbot's soul in a cloth, and four angels, the whole done exceedingly delicately.

Post-medieval monuments are scanty and not of great interest. Painted epitaph to Ralph Maynard † 1613 with kneeling figure (S chancel aisle) and, alongside and much more civilized, a wall-monument in alabaster and black marble to his son Charles Maynard † 1665. – J. Thrale

†1704, epitaph with two frontal busts against an altar back-plate with weeping putti l. and r. (s aisle). – W. King †1766, epitaph of variously coloured marbles and with charming cherubs' heads at the foot. By *Cheere* (s aisle). – The remaining monuments are in the N transept: Christopher Rawlinson †1733, by *William Woodman*. Large epitaph, with life-size figure of History seated on a sarcophagus against a black obelisk (N transept). – Mrs Frederica Mure †1834, by *Chantrey*, pure white, with a kneeling female allegory and Grecian detail. – Archdeacon Grant (bust) by *Theed*, 1884. – Bishop Claughton, designed by *Oldrid Scott*, the figure by *Forsyth*, 1895: alabaster tomb-chest with recumbent marble effigy. – Alfred Blomfield, suffragan bishop, †1894, designed by *Sir Arthur Blomfield* the architect: tomb-chest with tracery panels and poor figures between them.

THE PRECINCTS

Of the monastic buildings little survives. There is the SLYPE along the s wall of the s transept (on its rebuilding by *Grimthorpe*, see *The Norman Abbey* above). Then, along the E half of the s nave aisle, blank arcading and the springers of the vault of the CLOISTER: remains clearly of the early C14. The blank arcading (broken into by Lord Grimthorpe's buttresses) has three lights in each arch, each light containing a pointed trefoil above a triple cusp. s of the slype was the rectangular chapter house, recently excavated by Professor and Mrs Biddle before a new chapter house with visitors' centre was built in 1981 to the design of *W. Whitfield & Partners*.

w of the cathedral's w front the GATEHOUSE survives in all its bulk. It stands in a line with the s aisle of the church, c. 50 ft away from it, with the gateway leading from N to S into the abbey precincts. The building is due to Abbot de la Mare, and dates from the 1360s. It is of flint with stone dressings, a big, broad, fortress-like structure. The gateway is divided on the N side by a pier into a carriage-way and a pedestrian entrance, but on the s side there is only one very wide and high opening, flanked by rectangular turrets. The lierne vault has a central octagon of ribs inscribed into a four-pointed star. (In the second-floor room some much worn portrait corbels.) Details of construction suggests that the abbey WALLS and the gatehouse were part of the same project (Dr Roberts). For other surviving gatehouses, see Bristol, Bury St Edmunds, Carlisle, Chester.

For the remains of Verulamium and the town of St Albans, see the latest edition of B of E *Hertfordshire*.

St Paul's: see *London*.

Salisbury

CATHEDRAL CHURCH
OF THE BLESSED VIRGIN MARY *Anglican*

(Based on B of E *Wiltshire*, 1975, revised, with information from Dean Evans, J. Mordaunt Crook, Jane Geddes, George McHardy, Alan Rome, Clive Wainwright, Michael Gillingham and Anthony New.)

Plan, Fig. 134, from the *Builder*, 1891, by Roland Paul.

Some references (see Recent Literature): Bony 1979; Cobb 1980; Crook 1981; E. Eames 1980; Norris 1978.

INTRODUCTION

Salisbury Cathedral with its spire is one of the national icons. Celia Fiennes, who was born nearby, considered that 'the Cathedrall . . . is esteemed the finest in England in all respects it only lyes low in a watry meadow . . . yet notwithstanding its want of a riseing ground to stand on the steeple is seen many miles off the spire being so high it appeares to us below as sharpe as a Dagger . . .' River meadows and flat lawns are as different from the sites of Lincoln and Durham as could be imagined. It may well be said that Salisbury's is the most beautiful of English closes. Even Lord Torrington – and he never wrote but to nag – had to admit in 1782 that 'the close is comfortable and the divines well seated'. Well seated they are now too, and moreover in houses of absorbing architectural interest. The Salisbury close has more such houses than any other, that is certain. In the C13 the building of houses for the canons, choristers etc. began at once, though now the medieval remains have to be pieced together laboriously. A licence to build a wall round cathedral and houses and thus make the close a close was granted by Edward III in 1327. The open area to the w and N of the cathedral was a graveyard until Wyatt turfed it and thus created that smooth green expanse which goes so perfectly with the cathedral.

Trollope's visit to Salisbury in the early 1850s, 'wandering there one mid-summer evening round the purlieus of the cathedral', set off the novels placed in his blend of south-western cathedral towns, Barchester.

The cathedral was first built, not on this site, which is New Sarum, but at Old Sarum, 1¼ miles N of Salisbury, on a hill settled in 1075 when the see was transferred there from Sherborne. What now appears as an impressive earthwork became in the C12 a walled hill-town with cathedral, houses and the keep of a royal castle. The cathedral, begun c. 1075 and consecrated by St Osmund in 1092, was a mere 173 ft long, with a short apsed choir flanked by aisles (apparently with walls between, as at Rochester), thick-walled transepts which may have been transeptal towers (if so, earlier than Exeter's) and a nave of seven bays. The piers stood on cruciform plinths. The lack of a proper crossing for a central tower may help to confirm the possibility of towers over the transepts. Bishop Roger (1107–39) enlarged it to 316 ft long. He added a W façade, probably with twin towers, or possibly with an axial tower on a façade block (as at Ely), and replaced the E end with a more spacious one. The high choir ended straight, like that of New Sarum later, or that of Hereford in the C12. To the E of this was an ambulatory with three E chapels. Unlike the

French scheme of radiating chapels, as at Tours or Cluny or Rouen, the English sometimes tried to compromise between radiating and orientated chapels (Canterbury, Norwich, St Hugh's Choir at Lincoln). Bishop Roger's is the most convincing solution, the chapels attached to a straight-sided ambulatory, the wider middle apse having a straight outer wall, satisfying an English preference for straight-ended plans (e.g., in the C12, Romsey). It is likely that ambulatory and chapels were lower than the chancel; if so, that was again repeated at New Sarum.

Bishop Roger also added a cloister at Old Sarum. He placed it to the N, not, as more usual, the S, and N of his choir, not, as usual, the nave. This being so, it is indeed likely that a rectangular building immediately N of St Osmund's transept was the chapter house, even if chapter houses were more usually in the E, not the W range of the cloisters. It had an undercroft, and only this remains. Twice four bays with originally three round piers and rib-vaults. The arrangement was caused by the fall of the site to the N.

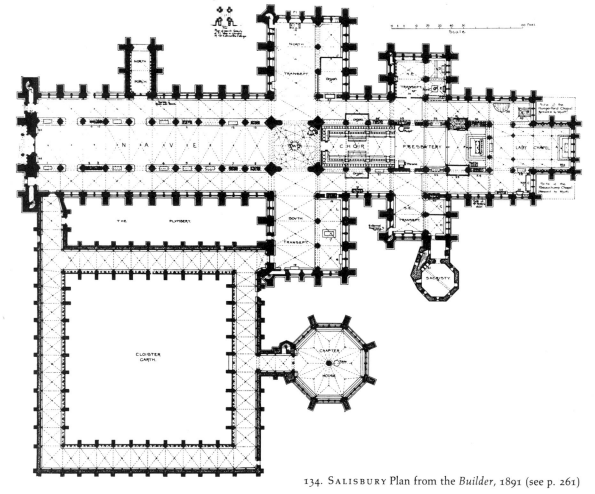

134. SALISBURY Plan from the *Builder*, 1891 (see p. 261)

135. SALISBURY View from the north-east

Old Sarum hill was poorly watered, and there were rows between castle and clergy. The move from there to the valley must have been decided already shortly before 1200.

Peter of Blois, a canon of Sarum, wrote in a letter, probably in 1198–9, that he was sorry not to be able to be present at the distribution of plots for canons' houses, but delighted that you have decided to transfer the site' from a place ventis expositus, sterilis, aridus, desertus'. The papal bull of Honorius III, dated 1219, finally authorizing the move, confirms all the disadvantages of Old Sarum: 'Let us descend joyfully to the plains, where the valley abounds in corn, where the fields are beautiful and where there is freedom from oppression.' Henry of Avranches, in a highly rhetorical poem, calls it 'mons maledictus', where nothing grows except 'absinthia amara', whereas in the valley are lilies, roses, violets, of course 'philomela', and plenty of springs 'cristallo clarior, auro purior, ambrosia dulcior'; in fact if Adam had gone here when he was expelled from Paradise, he would have preferred the exile.

If canons' houses were being laid out so early, one wonders how soon and in what detail the new cathedral was first laid out. We do not know who the designer was. Mr Harvey has suggested Nicholas of Ely, a mason who was granted a messuage E of the cloister by Bishop Poore. He is the most likely first master mason. But is he also the most likely designer? Elias de Dereham, Canon of Sarum, ought certainly to be considered seriously. Mr Harvey accepts him as an appreciative client. But he may well have been more; for what we know of him establishes him not only as an extremely able churchman and administrator, present at Runnymede in 1215, an executor, for instance, after the deaths of three archbishops and two bishops (Poore of Salisbury and des Roches of Winchester), and a personal friend of Bishop Jocelyn of Wells and Bishop Hugh II of Lincoln, but also as an artist and a man closely connected with architecture. In 1220 the shrine of St Thomas à Becket for Canterbury was made according to Matthew Paris by the 'incomparabilibus artificibus mag. Walter de Colecestria, sacrista de Sancto Albano, et Elya de Dereham, canonico Salisburiensi, quorum consilio et ingenio omnia quae ad artificium thecae . . . necessaria fuerant parabantur'. It would be unusual for an administrator to be called an incomparable artifex even in an age when faciebat applied to buildings often means 'was responsible for' and not 'designed'. Now Elias was also in charge of the king's works at Winchester and at Clarendon in the 1230s, had perhaps been busy on the king's works in London already in 1199, where an Elias Ingeniator appears, and at Salisbury he is called 'a prima fundatione rector novae fabricae'. Rector may well mean administrator only, but it stands to reason that an amateur artifex of high standing would also take more than a business interest in the new cathedral.

At any rate, Bishop Poore laid the foundation stones in 1220, one for the pope, one for Archbishop Stephen Langton, one for himself; and William Longespée, Earl of Sarum, and his countess, Ela, laid two more. In 1225 three altars could already be consecrated, those no doubt in the Lady Chapel (Trinity Chapel; see below) and at the E ends of the choir aisles. In the week following their consecration

the archbishop and the young King Henry III visited the church. In 1226 William Longespée was buried there. Building continued at the same uncommonly fast rate. Matthew Paris wrote of Bishop Bingham, who died in 1246, that he 'perfecit' the cathedral, including the W front and its lead-covered gable. This can hardly be true, though it was probably begun at that time. An indulgence was granted in 1244 to those who would contribute money to the building, without which money it could not be completed. And the consecration took place only under Bishop Bridport in 1258, and the leading of the roof (no doubt of the nave) is recorded only for 1266 (with vaults yet to be done?). At the same time a mighty campanile or bell-tower was added in the N W corner of the precinct, of stone, square and heavily buttressed below, then with a smaller square stage, in its detail much like the interior of the crossing tower, and, above that, with an octagonal top stage, probably of wood, and a short spire.

Of such campanili, Chichester's survives, but Westminster Abbey's and others have gone. One mason is mentioned by name at this time, when a *Richard* was left one mark by the cathedral treasurer in 1267. The cloisters were next begun under Bishop de la Wyle (1263–71), completed only c. 1300, while the chapter house was probably begun in or after 1279. In the 1330s the crossing tower was wonderfully heightened and the spire added: the contract for this work dates from 1334, between the chapter and *Richard of Farleigh*, who must have been a man of some reputation, as he insisted on also carrying on with commitments at Bath Abbey and Reading Abbey. Later he was to be in charge at Exeter. In the C 15 two low chantry chapels were added N and S of the Lady Chapel: the Beauchamp Chapel, very sumptuous inside, by Bishop Beauchamp (1450–81) and the Hungerford Chapel in 1464–77 (interiors pre-*Wyatt* are in Cobb 1980). The spire gave cause for worry, and Bishop Beauchamp put in the two strainer arches at the crossing. In 1668, when Seth Ward, mathematician and astronomer, was bishop, his friend and fellow astronomer *Christopher Wren* made a report on the state of the cathedral and praised the proportions of nave width to height and of nave to aisles, the presence of 'large planes' without too many ornaments to 'glut the eye', of windows without tracery (for 'nothing could add beauty to light'); but he criticized the inadequate foundations and inadequate buttressing. He recommended long-term measures for the future, but for the present only small adjustments, including 'the bracing ye Spire towards ye Top with Iron'. *Francis Price*, surveyor to the cathedral 1737–53, in his book on the cathedral (1753) reported more in detail and with quite exceptional sagacity and competence ('the first serious attempt to describe and analyse the structure of a major Gothic building': Colvin 1978). Then came *James Wyatt*, reporting in 1787 (Lichfield, Salisbury and Hereford were his first cathedral jobs). His restoration of 1789–92 has often been called disastrous, and was indeed both ruthless and biased. (Yet his clients were not uninvolved; the decision to remove the two Perp chapels had been taken by Bishop Shute Barrington before Wyatt appeared on the scene.) Also removed were the campanile and two small porches: one of these led to the aisle just s of the high altar and E of the S E transept; the other, to the N transept, is re-erected at Council House, Bourne Hill, former St Edmund's College (see B of E *Wiltshire*: Salisbury, Public buildings). Wyatt also refurbished the interior, tidying it up with depressing orderliness, and swept away a good deal of original glass. *Gilbert Scott* from 1863 swept away as much Wyatt as he could and replaced it by Scott. He also filled the empty niches on the façade. Inside, Scott's handsome iron screen, which did not obscure the view but only filtered it, and his reredos were in their turn swept away in 1959–60. (Some of Salisbury's C 13 glass found its way to the Winchester diocese: bits in the s retrochoir aisle of the cathedral, q.v.; and a fine Stoning of St Stephen in Grateley Church, s side.)

The building is 473 ft long outside. The vaults are only 84 ft high inside. The height of the spire is 404 ft. It leaves all other English spires behind, though not all Continental spires. The tallest of all, that of Ulm, completed only in the C 19, is 530 ft. Salisbury is built of Chilmark stone, an oolitic limestone quarried twelve miles away. Inside, influenced by Canterbury and Lincoln, Salisbury uses wherever possible long slender detached shafts of polished Purbeck marble, brought up in barges when the Avon was still navigable. The contrast of this dark grey shiny stone with the light, warm greyish-buff Chilmark stone, and indeed with the cool grey of unpolished Purbeck, is one of the two most readily remembered characteristics of Salisbury. The other is less easy to formulate. It is an impression of nothing done to excess. Proportions contribute to that, and the attempted balance between the verticalism of all Gothic forms and the stressed horizontalism of the somewhat squat gallery. A refusal to decorate contributes perhaps even more. Of all the major capitals inside, just two have leaves. All the others are moulded. If you are looking for stiff-leaf on areas more than an odd six inches square, you must lift your eyes right up to the vaulting bosses. The vaults incidentally are quadripartite, with nothing of the adventurous novelty of Lincoln, and the windows are consistently lancets, also in pairs and triplets, and a little later with some simple plate tracery. The only prominent place where variety is allowed is the piers. Here divers beautiful shapes have been developed, all by means of the contrast between a core and its detached Purbeck shafts, a delightful motif. Because of these qualities, light plays a special part in this cathedral (as Wren saw), especially in its reflections from polished stonework and espe-

cially where there is still grisaille glass. Perhaps there is no other great church in England, as Clifton-Taylor (1972) pointed out, where 'under the right conditions of light, reflections count for so much'. Today, at the end of the long vista of elegant coolness, a balance has been upset by the advent of the late C 20, so hot and anxious, in the new glass of the E windows. Perhaps, today, this is necessary.

EXTERIOR

The plan of Salisbury Cathedral is the *beau idéal* of the E.E. plan. On a virgin site the designer could do exactly what he thought best, and the outcome differs in every respect from the French ideal of Chartres, Reims and Amiens. At Salisbury all is rectangular and parts are kept neatly from parts. The Lady Chapel projects two bays. Then there are two bays of retrochoir. The high choir is seven bays long with an E transept projecting two bays and a main transept projecting three bays beyond the chancel aisles. The nave is of ten bays. A screen façade not organically growing out of nave and aisles finishes the building to the w. A tall N porch two bays deep is added, and this sticks out as straight and as detached from the rest as the two pairs of transepts and the E parts. In elevation the Lady Chapel and retrochoir are as low as the aisles.

Of all English cathedrals Salisbury is the most unified in appearance. It was built entirely in the course of sixty years except for its justly most famous feature, its spire. This, though of course far too high from the E.E. point of view, happens to be the work of a mason of the highest genius and fits the rest perfectly. The C 13 has certain motifs in common throughout which can be listed at once. The windows are lancets, mostly in pairs or triplets and nowhere excessively elongated and narrow. They are often shafted outside and mostly inside – nearly always with Purbeck marble shafts. The windows appear with and without tracery, the tracery being of the plate variety. (On plate tracery, see also *Winchester*, Retrochoir, interior.) The buttresses are characterized by a group of five closely-placed set-offs about two-thirds up. The base of the cathedral and the buttresses have also many set-offs, and at the sill-level of the windows there is yet another course with four set-offs. The top parapet is panelled with trefoil-headed panels. It rests on a frieze of pointed trefoils with a band of half-dogtooth between.

As building went on from E to w, we start our more detailed examination at the LADY CHAPEL (we keep the generic name, though it is called in the cathedral the Trinity Chapel). Its E wall has three consecration crosses in encircled quatrefoils below the windows. The windows are a group of three stepped lancets, shafted (the shafts with a shaft-ring). The top of the E wall carries three crocketed gables. The side gables have two low lancets with a quatrefoiled circle in plate tracery. In the centre is a group of five stepped lancets, the l. and r. ones being blank with pedestals for statues and curved-back panels. The pinnacles are *Scott*'s. The N and S sides have pairs of lancets not shafted but only double-chamfered. The chamfering of the middle post of each pair stops at the top.

The CHOIR AISLES have their E windows as groups of three stepped lancets, shafted, the shafts with a shaft-ring, and gables like the middle gable on the Lady Chapel. The pinnacles are again *Scott*'s. The N and S walls are of four bays, identical with those of the Lady Chapel, except that in the bays closest to the transepts the chamfering of the post between the two lancets has an inner hollow chamfer.

The HIGH CHOIR has a group of seven shafted stepped lancets in the gable, with the first and the last blank, a group of five shafted stepped lancets below, again with the first and last blank and flat buttresses embracing the angles. On them are Perp pinnacles. To the N and S the High Choir has clerestory windows of groups of three stepped shafted lancets. Between the trefoil frieze and the panelled parapet there is here no dogtooth, and that remains so throughout the clerestory. The E wall is steadied by steep flying buttresses on the N and the S side.

Now the EAST TRANSEPTS. To the E they have one pair of chamfered lancets continuing the details of the W bays of the chancel aisles and one group of three shafted stepped lancets. The N and S fronts of the transepts do not carry on the rhythm so far determining the exterior. The dogtooth frieze breaks off at the W end of the NE and SE buttresses. Then the E aisle has on the ground floor a pair of shafted lancets continued to the l. and r., towards the buttresses, by rising half-arches, an oddly fragmentary motif, hard to explain, and harder to appreciate. It is going to puzzle us more often as we go W. Above, under the roof, is just one small lancet. The centre of the transept front has on the ground floor three lancets of the same height, but greater width for the middle one. They are triple-shafted and have fine dogtooth in the arches. Again fragments of arches rise to the l. and r. On the first floor three pairs of smaller lancets, again the middle pair wider. Each pair has a quatrefoil circle in plate tracery over. The surrounds are shallowly moulded with hollow chamfers. A little stiff-leaf in the spandrels. The second floor has a stepped group of four shafted lancets, the centre pair again provided with a quatrefoiled circle. In the gable five stepped lancets, one and five being blank. These two have no proper arches but two rising half-arches, and two and four, though they have proper arches, have two rising blank half-arches above them. Simple polygonal pinnacles l. and r. On the S side the design is partly obscured by the addition of the Sacristy and (former) Muniment Room, which seems to date from the later C13. It is octagonal, partly of ashlar, partly of flint with irregular stone, two-storeyed with a flat roof. In the

corridor one lancet and one blocked lancet. In the building itself the lower windows have segmental heads, the upper ones end straight. (The upper room has a renewed octagonal central pier of wood and eight renewed curved, radiating braces of wood.) The W lancets of the E transepts have consistently hollow chamfers in their surrounds, and that now remains the rule for the parts further W. In the tucked-away bays of the choir aisles between E transepts and main transepts, the E bay has a sloping roof. With the W bay the friezes start again. These bays and those immediately W of the main transept are not in their original state, as the addition of the Dec spire made flying buttresses necessary in a N–S and E–W and in a diagonal direction. They carry square pinnacles with small blank Dec arches and tracery. In the S transept all three flying buttresses are of this type, in the N transept only the inner one, the outer two being thinner and steeper (and probably later).

The E side of the MAIN TRANSEPTS is in no way different from what precedes it, except for one minor detail: in the clerestory the flat C13 buttresses, as they finish, do not divide the trefoil frieze into sections, but run up into one awkwardly elongated arch. This motif is carried on all along the nave. The façades of the main transepts are unfortunate: as there is an E but no W aisle, the composition is lopsided. The dogtooth friezes break off as in the E transepts. The E aisle front has on the ground floor again the shafted two lancets with rising fragmentary arches l. and r. and on the first floor instead of a group of three shafted lancets, the same two shafts but instead of arches three, then four, then again four rising half-arches to follow the roof-line. The centre or 'nave' part of the transept front is made tripartite by thin buttresses with set-offs which rise through the ground floor and first floor. To their l. and r. are single lancets with rising fragmentary arches only outward. In the centre is just one lancet. On the first floor pairs with quatrefoiled circles in plate tracery and again rising fragmentary arches outward. On the second floor a group of five, the outer ones blank, the middle one wider and higher and with a two-light window with a sexfoiled circle (the first we have come across) in plate tracery. Above one and two and four and five a large blank pointed quatrefoil (also the first). In the gable are two pairs with quatrefoiled circles and above them a big octofoiled circle (the first again). The surrounds are chamfered in the N transept, but in the S transept they have thick and heavy roll mouldings apparently of a slightly later date. The W sides of the main transepts have nothing new. The pairs of lancets, the pairs with the quatrefoiled circle in plate tracery, the clerestory triplets, the frieze and parapet all continue, and continue into the nave as well. (On the crossing tower, see below, after the W front.)

The NAVE clerestory has flying buttresses not evenly distributed on N and S. The more easterly ones have the

136. SALISBURY View from the south-west

137. SALISBURY The west front in 1814

Dec pinnacles, the two further to the w are thinner. Originally the C 13 work had the flat buttress strips running awkwardly into the trefoil frieze which we have first met on the main transept E walls.

The NORTH PORCH is a very fine piece. Externally it continues the system of the nave, but the E and W walls are entirely blank, and the N wall has a tall and wide, richly shafted entrance. The innermost shafts are detached. One tier of shaft-rings. Richly moulded arch. On the first floor two pairs of shafted lancets with a quatrefoiled circle in plate tracery. However, the lancets now have pointed cusping in their heads (the first we have met in this cathedral). Small dogtooth in the arches, a quatrefoiled circle in the spandrel. In the crocketed gable two quatrefoiled arches with shafts carrying stiff-leaf capitals (the first, except for the tower – see below). Inside, the porch is vaulted in two bays and has noble erect proportions. On the ground stage vigorous blank arcading with detached shafts and relatively simple stiff-leaf capitals. The arcading has pointed cinquecusping in the heads. On the upper stage each bay has two pairs of blank lancets. All shafting is detached. The capitals are moulded here. The arches again have pointed cusping. The quatrefoils in the circles are also pointed. They must still be called blank plate tracery, but come very close to bar tracery. Above in the lunettes two quatrefoiled circles and a large octofoiled one. Bits of stiff-leaf in various places. Quadripartite vaults, resting on strong shafts which stand detached from the walls and indeed cut into the ground-floor arcading, even if they form an organic part of the first-floor system. Finely moulded ribs and stiff-leaf bosses. Terribly restored inner portal. Thick shafting l. and r. The stiff-leaf capitals are of Purbeck marble, and those on the l. seem original. *Trumeau* of four attached shafts with four small hollows in the diagonals – a section which became popular much later. Pointed trefoil arches. The C 19 figure of Christ in the tympanum is placed in a large pointed quatrefoil. Above a row of four short trefoiled arches, the shafts with stiff-leaf capitals, and one blank quatrefoiled circle over. The ribs as well as the large octofoil and the prominent pointed quatrefoils indicate a relatively late date, not too far indeed from cloister and chapter house. The floor of the porch, with its simple geometrical pattern of white and grey, could be original. The porch was restored by *G. E. Street* in 1880–1.

The FAÇADE of Salisbury Cathedral is a headache. There is so much in it which is perversely unbeautiful. There are also far too many motifs, and they are distributed without a comprehensible system. The façade is of the screen type, i.e. wider than nave and aisles (which the English had already done in Norman form e.g. at St Paul's Cathedral and at St Botolph Colchester), and it has no tower or towers. Instead there are two square turrets, hardly more than over-broad buttresses at the angles, and they carry a

spirelet each, hardly more than a pinnacle, each accompanied by four corner pinnacles. In the middle is a gable, but this has the nave width only and thus looks somewhat stunted. That the sculpture all over the façade is of the 1862 restoration (by *Redfern*) does not help either. (In fact, for admirable C 13 sculpture at Salisbury one must look at the former rood screen, now in the NE transept; see *Furnishings* below.) Indeed only six figures on the W front are old, and they are so over-restored that only the Peter and Paul to the l. and r. of the great W window can count. (The others are the two below Peter and Paul and two in the bottom row of the N tower.) Their style is decidedly C 14. Is this due to the restorers? It is not known whether the façade had all its statues before the C 19. An engraving by Hollar shows 22, but there is no record of their destruction. The same question arises with regard to the bases of the statues. Most of them have stiff-leaf brackets, but on the lowest tier the decoration is partly by ballflower. That again is impossible before 1300, and the façade cannot be as late as that. Are these motifs then again due to the restorers?

The great W window is the centre of the façade, a group of three stepped lancets, triple-shafted, the shafts with two shaft-rings. To the l. and r. rise once more the ununderstandable fragmentary arches. Much dogtooth. This window dwarfs all the rest and especially the triple porch below, a French motif with its three gables, but ridiculously insignificant, as the three together represent the nave, not the nave and the aisles. Moreover in all its details it is C 19. The side parts have no doors, just blank arcading, the middle part five shafts on each side in the jambs, two portals separated by a *trumeau*, filigree stiff-leaf in one order of the arch, and in the tympanum three C 19 figures beneath pointed-trefoiled arches with gablets over. The portal recess is much deeper than the side recesses. The latter being left blank proves of course that the designer used the French scheme of the three portal gables expressing nave and aisles without an inkling of its meaning. The real aisle fronts also have three gables each, but they are narrower and lower. Portal with cinquecusped arch. In the middle, above the porches a gallery of saints under trefoil-headed canopies. In the aisles pairs of lancets with the usual quatrefoiled circle in plate tracery and the perennial fragmentary side arches. In addition, the square angle-turrets which project beyond the aisles, and also the buttresses between nave and aisles, have two tiers of statues at this level, flanked by shafts which carry pointed-trefoiled, gabled canopies. These canopies, a new and most unfortunate motif, break round the corners. In outline they look bitten out. Also – and this makes one more doubtful about the capabilities of the designer than anything else – the buttresses project further than the turrets, and to even that out, the turrets in their inner quarter send out their own buttress to range with the other buttresses. That the niches and gables of the buttress part are cut off by the meeting with the turret part will by now hardly surprise. It applies to the other buttresses as well.

Above this level the familiar frieze of half-dogtooth comes round, the one (much too weak) motif that tries to tie the whole façade together. Then the great w window, and alas to its side, below the fragmentary arches, statues under their canopies, two l., two r., one on top of the other. They have so little space that the canopies cannot stand on shafts. In the aisle parts this tier of the elevation is much less high, just two pairs of lancets, with the indispensable quatrefoiled circles. Dogtooth in the arches. In the turrets on this level more statues, more shafted canopies, more gables and dogtooth. The aisles then come out with a broad band of quatrefoiled lozenges with trefoils in the spandrels. This motif is repeated, higher up, in the centre, above the great w window and moreover cut into by the raised middle lancet of the window. At this level, in the aisles and turrets are more pairs of lancets with the quatrefoiled circles. Shafts with stiff-leaf capitals. Finally aisles and turrets end with the panelled parapet familiar from the E part of the cathedral and battlements over, and the centre ends in a steep gable. Here once again two pairs of lancets with quatrefoiled circles. Above the circles a lozenge with a vesica inside. In this a Victorian Christ in Majesty and above the vesica, again rather squeezed in, a bird in profile, probably a Pelican. Is it original? It is not in the Grimm engraving of 1779, and Britton's view is vague. Very much dogtooth all around here.

As the turrets project beyond the aisles they have a visible E side, an awkward fact which spoils the view w along the nave and aisles. There is, for example, a supporting wall with a sloping-up t. ? as a kind of prop with rising blank arches. The repetition of the clerestory triplets on the E side of the screen wall, i.e. where the façade itself pretends to have upper aisle windows, on the other hand, is a happy solution.

The idea of the Salisbury façade must be derived from Wells on the one hand, Norman towerless screen façades on the other. Wells has the display of statuary, but mighty towers as well. The effect is baffling enough, even if not quite as baffling as that of Salisbury. The Wells façade seems to have been designed about 1235, i.e. earlier than the Salisbury façade.

After so much has been said against the Salisbury façade two redeeming features deserve to be noted. There is one major motif which ties the discrepant parts of the front together. If one draws a triangle connecting the top of the great w window with the tops of the aisle w windows, the two lines will be parallel to those of the top gable. And secondly, though this is not the merit of the designer of the façade, the crossing tower and spire, seen from a distance,

do not call for any greater emphasis on the w front than the spirelets of the turrets and the middle gable provide. Anything more prominent would compete, to the detriment of what must after all be considered the crowning glory of Salisbury.

So now, after this embarrassed criticism, we can indulge in the examination of the CROSSING TOWER and the STEEPLE. The E.E. cathedral was meant to have only a relatively low lantern tower. On top probably was a leaded pyramid spire. The C13 stage of the tower, the one against which the roofs abut, has tall blank E.E. arches with depressed trefoil heads. Shafts and stiff-leaf capitals (the earliest on the cathedral, other than retrochoir capitals inside). Then the Dec work begins. Its date, as has already been said, is 1334 etc. Ballflower frieze and blank battlements and then two tall stages. They are studded everywhere with ballflower. Tall two-light windows with circles over. In these, on the lower stage, undulating foiling, on the upper subcusped foiling. Friezes of cusped lozenges and trefoils. All these motifs are an intelligent, up-to-date restating of E.E. motifs of the cathedral. The angle buttresses start flat and set-back, but in the Dec work turn polygonal, with the same kind of fine blank arches, tracery and gables that we have found in the pinnacles of the flying buttresses added at the same time to help carry the tower and spire. (A useful article is W. A. Forsyth, 'The Structure of Salisbury Cathedral Tower and Spire', *R.I.B.A. Journal*, January 1946.)

The spire is wonderfully slender, and the solution of the problem of how to reach the octagon from the square is perfect. Short crocketed pinnacles on the buttresses, in the middles of the sides at the foot of the spire lucarnes under crocketed gables and with pinnacles, and again at the corners taller inner pinnacles rising higher than the lucarnes. They are square, with their own angle buttresses and angle pinnacles, as it were. From a distance the effect varies. If you are inside the Precinct the pinnacles keep close to the spire and the outline is almost like that of a broach spire, except for just the slightest barbs. If you are in the meadows to the S or w the pinnacles speak individually and form a subordinate preamble to the spectacular rise of the spire.

INTERIOR

The interior of Salisbury Cathedral is as unified as is the exterior. That (and *Wyatt's* tidying-up) gives it its perfection, but also a certain coolness. The whole interior (like the whole exterior) has certain motifs in common: particularly the slender, detached polished Purbeck shafts applied wherever possible. These, in conjunction with the consistently used lancet windows, endow the interior with a vertical vigour needed to counteract the relative lowness of

138. SALISBURY The east end, begun 1220 (as before 1980; see Fig. 142)

the vault and the strong stresses on horizontals, especially in the gallery. The result is poise, and so contributes to the perfection of the whole.

The LADY CHAPEL and RETROCHOIR with the E end of the choir aisles must be taken as one. They are all of the same height, considerably lower than the High Choir. This conception Salisbury Cathedral took over from Winchester, where it had been demonstrated in the new E end begun under Bishop de Lucy († 1204) and probably completed soon after Salisbury's was begun. (In fact, this influence on the planning of Salisbury is clear enough to show that the structure of Winchester retrochoir really was standing by 1220: Draper 1978.) The Lady Chapel as well as the retrochoir have narrow aisles (on the 'hall' principle), though those of the retrochoir are not at once noticed, because the chancel aisles act as more prominent, wider aisles. What distinguishes Salisbury at once from Winchester is the emphasis on the slenderest Purbeck shafts. In the Lady Chapel the piers separating nave and aisles are just single Purbeck shafts without any shaft-rings – like stove pipes, it has been said disrespectfully. In the retrochoir there is a cluster of five shafts instead, all detached. Between retrochoir aisles and choir aisles a similar cluster, but with stronger shafts and an extra shaft added to the inside to correspond with the detached wall-shafts of the Lady Chapel aisle walls. These detached wall shafts to carry the vaulting become a recurrent motif throughout. The windows moreover also have detached shafts throughout. In the vaults thin ribs and transverse arches no wider, though of a different moulding. The w bay of the Lady Chapel has small dogtooth in ribs and transverse arches. The w bays of the retrochoir aisles are a little irregular in shape to connect with the piers of the E High Choir wall.

A few further details may be noted. Most capitals – most capitals of Salisbury Cathedral – are moulded and of Purbeck marble. But the capitals of the piers to N and S between retrochoir 'nave' and retrochoir aisles have dainty stiff-leaf sprays, the earliest inside the cathedral, though slight and hard to see. The arches from the retrochoir to the E ends of the chancel aisles are enriched with big dogtooth.

Against the walls of the Lady Chapel Perp niches with little fan-vaults on head-stops, a foliage frieze, and cresting. In the retrochoir on the S side a fine double piscina with trefoil-cusped arches, on the N side double aumbry with shelf on triangular heads, heavily roll-moulded.

The CHOIR AISLES just carry on, though in the vaults there are now small stiff-leaf bosses. All this work so far probably belongs to 1220–5. There are five bays from E to w, i.e. to the stage of the E aisles of the E transepts. The E transepts will be examined a little later. To their w the choir aisles continue for another three bays. What is different now, and the sign of a slightly later date, is that the stiff-leaf bosses are decidedly bigger than further E.

The HIGH CHOIR has piers of beautiful grey unpolished Purbeck with black, polished, detached Purbeck shafts. The forms of the piers differ remarkably. First the E side. There are three arches. The piers consist of two strong grey shafts, just detached, and two slender black shafts to N and S. Arches with many thin rolls, those to the l. and r., i.e. those corresponding to the retrochoir aisles, a little higher than the middle one – the first of the minor oddities inside of which we have found so many outside. The reason is that the wide band of mouldings is the same for the three arches and that the steeper angle of the side arches pushes their apex up higher. The arches have hoodmoulds with stops consisting of two pellets, one above the other, a motif that was to become standard for a while. The N E and S E corner piers are stronger. They have four big detached grey shafts and four thin black ones. Now the N and S sides. The arches here have dogtooth. The first pier is quatrefoil with eight detached shafts, the next octagonal with concave sides into which black shafts fit nicely. Then the piers of the E crossing, again quatrefoil with eight shafts. The motif of detached Purbeck shafts round a pier was taken over from Canterbury and Lincoln. In St Hugh's Choir at Lincoln especially they are used in front of concave sides of a pier. But both Canterbury and Lincoln have foliage capitals, whereas at Salisbury only the w piers introduce any ornamentation in the capitals. They are of the crocket type. The arches are many-moulded, and they have the pellet stops like the E end; however, only on the N, not on the S side. We do not go further w yet, but first look at the upper parts.

Salisbury still has a gallery – like Lincoln and Westminster Abbey – though the Île de France had by that time given up galleries. Moreover, the gallery of Salisbury emphasizes the horizontal particularly strongly. The E wall at gallery-level has five arches, the middle one a little wider. They are thickly Purbeck-shafted, and the arches themselves are cinquecusped. The clerestory has a group of five stepped lancets. The outer bays have rising half-arches, of three curves outside, only one short one inside. The next bays have two and one, and only the middle one is a normal arch. In the spandrels stiff-leaf paterae.

The gallery has for each bay two pairs of two-light openings with trefoiled heads. They are low and much Purbeck-shafted. The two sub-tympana have foils in awkward areas, bordered by two sub-sub-arches and the sub-arch. The foils are quatrefoils, then octofoils, then again quatrefoils. In the main tympanum a quatrefoiled circle, then an octofoiled circle which has the foils pointed, then again a quatrefoiled circle. The super-arches are excessively depressed as though the designer wanted to do everything in his power to counterbalance the verticalism of all his shafts. The foils of the circles have little knob-like cusps, and the hoodmould stops, wherever they occur, are

139. SALISBURY C 14? strainer arch, east transept

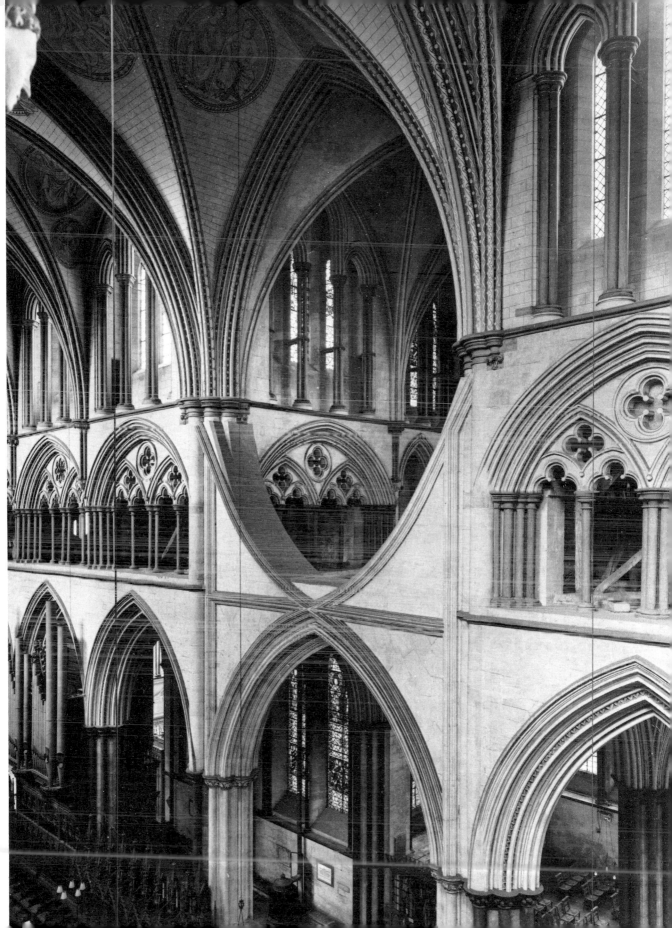

knobs too. The vaulting-shafts start only in the spandrels between the super-arches. They stand on heads and have rich stiff-leaf capitals, much richer than the few further E. The leaves are quite big, but arranged as only one tier. Clerestory with wall-passage and stepped triplet arcading – the Anglo-Norman tradition. Again all detached shafts. Spandrels with stiff-leaf paterae.

The vaults are quadripartite rib-vaults on an oblong plan, i.e. the French system of Chartres, Reims, Amiens etc. Ribs and transverse arches are, as in the E parts, very thin and of the same thickness, which is not usual in C 13 France. The mouldings again differ. Small stiff-leaf bosses, also in the E crossing.

The EAST TRANSEPTS are separated from the chancel – for safety's sake – by strainer arches inserted probably in the C 14. Their date is uncertain. They stand on Chilmark piers with attached shafts, deliberately similar to those of the C 13. Small Perp leaf capitals. Arch with many fine mouldings, and on its apex an inverted arch, the two together performing the shoring action. Vertical frame-like moulding and horizontal moulding across at the level where the arches meet.

The N E and S E transepts are essentially identical. (On the two-storey octagonal sacristy attached to the S E transept, S side, see Exterior, transepts, above, also the Muniment Room tiles under Furnishings below.) The inner bay of the E aisle is of course identical with the w bay of the E part of the chancel aisles. The bay has a stiff-leaf boss, the arches have dogtooth. The pellet stops are present, and in fact remain part of the system of decoration, until further notice. The first pair of the E aisle is of the octagonal type with concave sides and eight shafts, the next is of the type with two strong detached grey shafts and two thin black ones to N and S (see chancel E wall). The details differ a little. In the S transept the S E bay has bits of dogtooth in the window arches, the next bay to the N in the arcade arch. The S E bay has a stiff-leaf boss, the next has not. In the N transept the N E bay also has dogtooth in the windows but no boss, the next bay no dogtooth and no boss. But these variations are not relevant. The gallery continues as in the High Choir, except that some of the hoodmould stops have stiff-leaf instead of being simply knobs. The clerestory continues too, except that there are no paterae in the spandrels. In the aisle of the N E transept in the S wall double piscina, in the N wall double aumbry, exactly like the pair in the retrochoir. In the S E transept in the S wall double piscina, in the N wall double aumbry, the former with pointed-trefoil-cusped arches.

The S wall of the S E transept and the N wall of the N E transept have first three big lancets of even height with detached triple shafts and pellet hoodmould stops. However, where the triplet ends, another arch starts and has no space to carry on, a most disconcerting conceit. We shall see more of this than we want. At gallery-level there are three lower lancets, the middle one wider, and their capitals do not range with the gallery capitals, which is disconcerting again. At clerestory level, four windows but only three openings to the inside. The outer ones rise again by three half-arches and come down by only one (see E wall of the High Choir). To the w the two outer bays have single lancets delightfully detailed. Shallow niches fill the jambs, a tiny quadripartite rib-vault the intrados of the arch. The inner bays have the arches to the w parts of the chancel aisles. There is here the usual gallery opening over. Above the single lancets are paired windows with stiff-leaf hood-mould stops. The vaulting-shafts here start lower, close to the bottom of the windows. They also stand on heads. These heads are of Purbeck marble, whereas the corbel-heads on the E wall, which, like those in the choir and nave, are at capital-level, are of Chilmark stone. The details are very varied. (Selby Whittingham, in A Thirteenth Century Portrait Gallery of Salisbury Cathedral, argues that at least some of the heads are contemporary portraits.) The clerestory is like that of the E side, but with shaft-rings. The small bosses a little bigger than those of the chancel.

Now the w bays of the choir, i.e. the three bays w of the E crossing. They continue the system, i.e. have a pair of piers which are quatrefoil with eight shafts and one pair which is octagonal with concave sides and eight shafts. Arches with dogtooth, gallery with two quatrefoils in circles and the big circle octofoiled with pointed foils, clerestory without shaft-rings and paterae, and vaults with bosses. The one principal difference is that these bosses are emphatically bigger and more agitated than any so far (or any after).

So we have reached the main CROSSING. The piers have five shafts to each side. On the bases are slight bits of decoration, of stiff-leaf on the S E and S W piers, of an abstract kind (or never carved further?) on the N E and N W. The arches are studded with thick C 15 fleurons. A lierne vault was also put in in the C 15. It is thinly cusped. The geometrical patterns are such that the step to Elizabethan plaster patterns really is not wide. But above it is the lantern stage of the C 13, originally open from below. It has very tall blank twin arches with a quatrefoil in plate tracery. The dividing major shafts are quatrefoil, the minor ones single, and both types of Purbeck marble with shaft-rings. While this stage is closed to the space below by the lierne vault, it is open to the lower Dec stage. Between crossing and transepts strainer arches were put in in the C 15. They have wide jambs with tall, narrow image niches, embattled tops, and spandrels with open tracery. In the tracery straight and nearly straight diagonals play an important part. In addition the crossing tower and spire were steadied by flying buttresses in the gallery and the clerestory wall-passage to E, W, N and S.

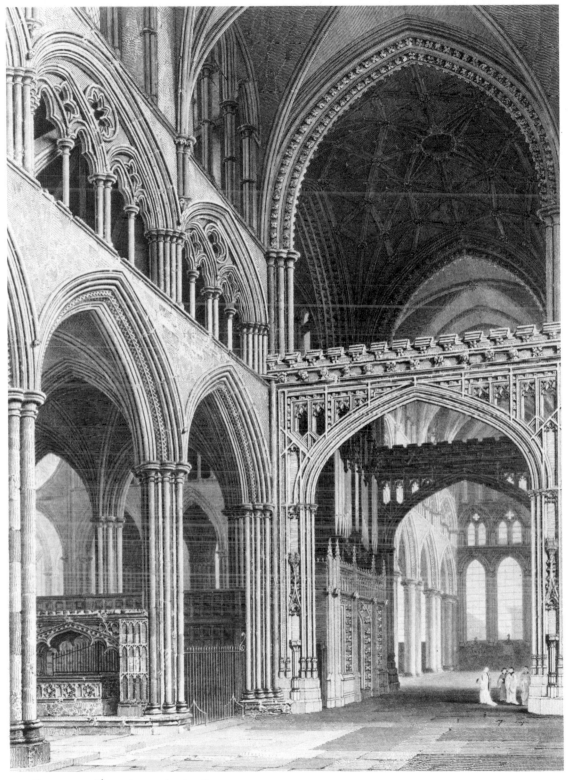

140. SALISBURY The main crossing in 1814

Back to the tower. Inside it iron tie-rods were placed by *Wren*, by *Price*, and later by *Scott*, and bronze ties in 1939. To see the inside of the SPIRE one must ascend high. But the climb is worth the effort. One can see the timber scaffolding put up for the construction of the spire and sensibly left standing as a steadying. It has a middle post with arms and braces. The stonework of the spire is 2 ft thick below, thinning up to 9 in. at a height of 20 ft. At the base of the spire is a C14 TREADMILL of 12 ft diameter, used to hoist the masonry and the timbers of the spire. Beverley has one. Cf. faulcon or windlass at Canterbury.

The MAIN TRANSEPTS are again nearly identical. The E arcade has first one of the octagonal piers, then piers of four strong grey shafts without black ones. Arches with some dogtooth. In the aisle vaults small stiff-leaf bosses. The gallery has for the first bay three quatrefoiled circles, for the rest two and the big upper one octofoiled. Hoodmould stops etc. with stiff-leaf instead of plain knobs. This, it will be remembered, was the same in the E transept gallery. The clerestory shafts have shaft-rings like the w walls of the E transepts, and this now becomes standard. The s transept s and N transept N walls are very similar to those of the E transept end walls. The triple shafts of the ground-floor windows are stronger, the three arches on the gallery-level of equal width, and the climbing arches of the clerestory are treated differently too. The centre here is a pair with pointed-trefoil heads and an octofoiled circle over. In the w walls are three pairs of lancets, then on the gallery-level three two-light pairs with stiff-leaf hoodmould stops. The vaulting-shafts, as in the E transepts, start close to the foot of the upper windows. They stand, like all the others, on heads. The clerestory with shaft-rings as on the E side. The vaulting bosses are smaller again, not as big as in the w part of the chancel. N and s transepts are identical, except for one minute detail: one hoodmould stop on the ground floor of the s transept w wall has stiff-leaf instead of the pellets. Actually, this does represent a deliberate change, as we shall see presently. In the s transept w wall doorway to the cloister. It is of Purbeck marble. The arch is very depressed, two-centred, and stands on short vertical pieces – a Westminster Abbey motif. A similar doorway, also Purbeck, but with an arch almost flattened out to be horizontal, in the N transept w wall. (See also such doorways in the cloister w walk, with which the transept doorways may be contemporary; are the two examples in the high choir, inner sides of aisle entrances, more recent?)

The NAVE continues the system without major revisions. What is different is only this: the arcade piers are now grey quatrefoils set diagonally with four black shafts in the main directions, a change made no doubt under the influence of the round piers with four shafts of Westminster Abbey (and the French cathedrals). Westminster Abbey was begun in 1245. Does that date this nave, or at least its design? The shafts have no shaft-rings, except for the w responds. The piers are placed on continuous sleeper-walls (actually pier-bases extended and merged), possibly with regard to the swampy terrain. For swampy it was – Philomela or no Philomela – and the nave floor is lower than the ground outside. (Enlarged pier-bases at Exeter provided seats for the infirm.) The richly moulded arches have no dogtooth, but hoodmould stops with stiff-leaf instead of pellets, i.e. what had been begun in one bay of the w wall of the transepts. On the gallery the foiling of the circles above the openings is now as follows: it alternates between four, four, four and four, four, eight; the eight being all pointed foils with stiff-leaf decoration in the little spandrels. Stiff-leaf also for hoodmould stops and cusps. The mouldings round the foiled circles are much deeper and more subdivided, i.e. on the way from plate to bar tracery. The clerestory continues as in the main transepts, i.e. with shaft-rings. The vaulting bosses are certainly smaller than those of the w parts of the chancel, though of about the same size and type as those of the main transepts.

The w wall is again an embarrassment. How can it be that the designer cared so little for any linking with the nave walls? Did the sense of keeping part from part as isolated units, as we have seen it at work in the whole exterior, go so far that even walls inside were not seen in conjunction? The ground floor has three blank arches, the middle one much wider. They have stiff-leaf stops, and their capitals are just a little below the shaft-rings of the nave w responds. Under the middle arch is another blank arch, and under this the two real arches of the portal. Stiff-leaf stop in the middle. The string-course finishing this ground-stage at the top is not at the level of the capitals or abaci of the nave piers. The next stage has four pairs of blank arches with quatrefoiled circles over. The arches are pointed-trefoiled. Then the great w window, amply shafted. The shafts have two tiers of shaft-rings. Here again the system of the nave walls is in no way continued. The sill of the great triplet is just that painfully little lower than the floor-level of the gallery.

FURNISHINGS, E TO W

Includes stained glass. Monuments are listed separately.

Lady Chapel (Trinity Chapel)   STAINED GLASS. In all five E lancets, 'Prisoners of Conscience of the C20', 1980, designed and made by *Gabriel Loire* of Chartres. Gorgeous deep rich blues with a little red, yellow and green. Designed on the medieval mosaic principle, with thick leading (for contrast, cf. Chagall at Chichester). Obscurely pent-up figures; poignant faces with both medieval and human feeling. (See also comment on p. 265.) C13–16 glass previously in these windows inserted elsewhere in the cathedral since 1981. – N windows

142. SALISBURY Stained glass, east end, 1980.
Prisoners of Conscience, by Gabriel Loire

by *Clayton & Bell, c.* 1901. – s windows by *Clayton & Bell,
c.* 1872, finer than the later ones opposite.

Retrochoir STAINED GLASS. N side, second from w:
c. 1900 by *Powell.* – s windows by *Clayton & Bell, c.* 1885.

South choir aisle, east part STAINED GLASS. Two
Radnor windows (near the family pew), very good, with
white and brownish single figures, under the influence of
the Pre-Raphaelites. By *Holiday,* made by *Powell,* 1881
and *c.* 1892.

North-east transept PISCINA (or IMMERSION
FONT?), s chapel. Perp. Panelled base with trough at the
top. Recess with little vault inside. Cusped ogee arch with
crockets. Straight top. – ROOD SCREEN. Part of the
original rood screen is here re-erected. Stone. Wonderfully
unrestored. Five plus five shallow niches for statues of
kings (there were originally seven plus seven) and a Perp
doorway in the middle. The doorway, tall and narrow with
a four-centred arch and a concave-sided gable against a
panelled background, comes from the Beauchamp Chapel.
Between the niches triple Purbeck shafts, flanked by thick
stiff-leaf sprays. Big, very agitated stiff-leaf capitals, dating the screen to *c.* 1235–50. The niches have nodding
trefoiled heads with little gablets partially over. The gablets stand on stiff-leaf stops. Arches on outstandingly
well-characterized heads above the gablets. In the spandrels small demi-figures of angels with spread wings. The
motif of the angels is familiar from the Westminster Abbey
transepts, but is later, on a larger scale and with whole
figures there. At Westminster it was taken over from the
exterior of the apsidal chapels at Reims Cathedral, at
Salisbury it is more probably derived from work on a
smaller scale. The demi-angels in the Lincoln choir-aisle

wall-arcade spandrels are earlier. The motif occurs already
in the C10 illumination of the Athelstan Psalter and in
stone e.g. in a fragment of *c.* 1200 in a private collection at
München Gladbach. – Another SCREEN, simple and panelled, w of the piscina; Perp. – STAINED GLASS. In the E
aisle the s windows by *Powell, c.* 1911; the N windows by
Burlison & Grylls, c. 1887. – The w single lancets by
Powell, 1920. – N window by *Powell, c.* 1907 (Heavenly
Jerusalem).

South-east transept (vestry) SCREEN to the N. Recent and incorporating rosewood carved openwork panels,
possibly Indo-Portuguese, C17 (McHardy). – CHEST.
Probably C13. 5 ft long. The feet were probably longer. –
STAINED GLASS. NE windows by *O'Connor,* 1859. – Then
to the s, *Clayton & Bell, c.* 1877. – The s windows have
C13 grisaille glass in geometrical patterns re-set in 1896. –
MUNIMENT ROOM (now Choir Practice Room) over the
sacristy off this transept. TILES on the floor of the upper
room and the staircase landings, probably of *c.* 1260. Remarkably complete and undisturbed pavement, similar to
tilework at Henry III's Clarendon Palace nearby (E. Eames
1980).

143. SALISBURY Rood screen (part), *c.* 1235–50, in 1813

North choir aisle, west part STAINED GLASS. Both windows by *Clayton & Bell, c.* 1884.

South choir aisle, west part STAINED GLASS. The E window by *Clayton & Bell, c.* 1885. – The W window by *Morris & Co.*, the amply draped figures by *Burne-Jones*, part of a series of the hierarchy of the angels. Background of scrolled foliage by *Morris*. 1878–9. The same composition was also woven as tapestry (see e.g. Eton College Chapel; Brockhampton Church, Herefordshire).

Choir Scott's REREDOS and IRON SCREEN were scrapped in 1960, a crime against the tenets of the Victorian Society, but the need of the C 13 cathedral was indeed greater than theirs – although a wide-open E crossing arch is no C 13 solution. Part of the screen was made into a communion rail for Alderbury Church. – STALLS. The lower parts (two rear rows) C 13–14, the MISERICORDS C 13 floral designs (Remnant 1969), also arm-rests decorated with heads, beasts and foliage. The upper parts, except for canopies of 1913–14 (New), are by *Scott, c.* 1870, as is the BISHOP'S THRONE. – The PULPIT is of *c.* 1950, by *Randoll Blacking.* The ORGAN CASES are of 1879–83 by *G. E. Street*, completed by his son. Rich and stuffy, in contrast to the architecture. The organ itself by *Willis*, 1865–77, a typical example of a Victorian divided organ (cf. Durham), made possible by the invention of pneumatic action (Gillingham). – PAINTING of the vault. Re-done *c.* 1870 on the general lines of the C 13 work. Medallions with figures and scenes, sparse scroll ornament, and masonry lines. The repainting is by *Clayton & Bell.* – STAINED GLASS. The E window of the Brazen Serpent, though it looks late C 16 or early C 17 Flemish in composition, colouring and Michelangelesque poses of the figures, is in fact of 1781, designed by *J. H. Mortimer* and made by *Pearson* (according to a system whereby the leading did not interrupt the figure-contours, displayed in 1781 at the Oxford Street Pantheon; *Architectural History*, 1982 on Selva's diary)

Crossing PULPIT. 1877, by *Scott.* – LECTERN by *Blacking.*

North transept REREDOS (Chapel of St Edmund Rich) by *A. Blomfield* with paintings by *C. Buckeridge.* – STAINED GLASS. In the E aisle N windows by *A. O. Hemming* and by *Ward & Hughes, c.* 1884. – The E windows by *Clayton & Bell, c.* 1880–5 (?). – CHESTS. Three iron-bound chests from the former Muniment Room. Also a cope chest, large semicircular, said to be C 13 (legs later?).

South transept STAINED GLASS. Of the S windows the centre light of the top tier contains C 13 grisaille glass from the chapter house. The rest is imitation, by *James Bell* (directed by *G. E. Street*), 1880. – Also some original grisaille glass in the northernmost twin window of the 'gallery' tier on the W side.

Nave and aisles COLLECTING TABLE (S aisle). This incorporates a MISERICORD with the story of the Virgin and the Unicorn. It was presented to the cathedral. – SCULPTURE. Abraham's Sacrifice, of elmwood, 1951, by *Ernst Blensdorf.* – CLOCK. *c.* 1386 or before, thought to be the oldest working mechanical clock, probably just preceding the one at Wells. Formerly in the bell-tower. Restored to its original working order in 1956. – STAINED GLASS. The nave W window is largely C 13 grisaille glass in the usual geometrical patterns, but it includes C 15 and early C 16 glass from France, arranged in 1824 by *John Beare.* – C 13 grisaille glass also in the aisle W windows. – S aisle third bay from the W excellent C 14 and C 15 glass with whole C 14 figures and some C 13 remains of a Tree of Jesse. It comes from the great W window. – Fifth bay from the W, 1891, by *Holiday.* – Easternmost by *Clayton & Bell*, 1886.

MONUMENTS

The monuments are described topographically from E to W. Salisbury is rich in monuments, but not rich in monuments of outstanding quality. After the C 14 they get in fact very few.

Retrochoir from N to S. Sir Thomas Gorges, the builder of Longford Castle, † 1610, but the monument erected in 1635 and very Baroque. Two recumbent effigies. Arches to all four sides, with flanking fluted pilasters. The decoration curiously Early Renaissance. At the corners large detached twisted Corinthian columns. (In the mid-1630s the twisted salomonic column suddenly reappeared in various forms in England, sometimes in grandiose forms traceable to Raphael's tapestry cartoons or to Rubens's Whitehall ceiling, but here probably fed by carvers' patterns from the Continent, used by craftsmen at Longford Castle?) Top with obelisks, various polyhedra, with square and hexagonal facets, pediments and four Virtues. The very top is formed of four semicircular members like the top of an arbour. Inside, above the effigies coved ceiling with circular reliefs of the seven *dona spiritus sancti* and cherubs' heads. Many inscriptions. The scenes have been identified to varying degrees of probability: Judgement of Solomon, Sacrifice of Manoah, David at Prayer?, Sacrifices of Cain and Abel, Samson slaying the Philistines, Joseph and his Brethren, Esther, Joseph warning Pharaoh. There are some felicitous inscriptions. – Bishop Wordsworth. By *Frampton*, 1914. White marble recumbent effigy on a black marble tomb-chest. – Jane Weigall † 1906. Brass plaque by *Omar Ramsden & Alwyn Carr.* – C. W. Holgate † 1903, also no doubt by them (McHardy). – St Osmund † 1099. Tapering black (Tournai?) marble lid of a coffin (see also part of his shrine, nave S side). – Earl of Hertford † 1621, son of the Protector, and his first wife † 1568, Catherine, sister of Lady Jane Grey. Very tall wall-monument, almost covering the E window of the S aisle. (The same splendid type as those the Earl erected in Westminster Abbey, one for his mother, Duchess of Somerset, in 1587 and one for his second wife, Frances, in 1598, with tall obelisks reasserting family pride after his and Catherine's stay in the Tower.) Tripartite centre. The lower side parts with two kneeling children between columns, facing the altar. Very big obelisks l. and r. The centre with the two recumbent effigies, she behind and above him. Coffered arch. Obelisks also on the side parts and curiously fragmentary bits of curved pediments with allegorical figures. Top structure in the centre with more allegorical figures and more obelisks. (cf. Mompesson monument, S choir aisle.) – William Wilton † 1523. Tomb-chest with cusped quatrefoils and lettering and a rebus. Recess with panelling. Frieze with inscription. – Bishop Moberly † 1885. Designed by *Sir A. Blomfield*. Rich, with big gabled arch and recumbent effigy. Against the back wall big quatrefoil with four scenes.

North choir aisle, east part Bishop Bingham † 1246. Excellent Purbeck effigy under nodding pointed-trefoiled head-canopy on thin shafts. His staff overlaps the canopy. Stiff-leaf border. The effigy belongs to a mid-C13 Purbeck type of which similar examples occur e.g. at Ely (Bishop Northwold † 1254, Bishop Kilkenny † 1256). The canopy over the tomb is rebuilt, but correctly. – Bishop Audley † 1524. Large, important chantry chapel. A tall stone screen surrounds it. To the aisle it has two tall transomed windows, polygonal buttresses and pinnacles with concave sides, and many niches for images. To the chancel the composition is much more restless. The two windows are subdivided differently, the W one into a doorway and a window, the E one into a tomb-chest with a canopy and a very pretty extra canopy over with pendants and a little fan-vault inside. The whole chapel has a fan-vault as well. Against the E wall lively reredos with niches. – Roger de Mortival † 1329. Tomb-chest. Black lid; the brass is missing. Ogee arch with openwork cusping and subcusping. A clan of charming little figures reclines on it. Enormous top finial. On top of this thin buttress canopy similar to those of Edward II at Gloucester and the Despencers at Tewkesbury. L. and r. pairs of slim openings with gables and a little Dec tracery. An original iron grille fills the main arch, similar to the W choir gates at Canterbury (Geddes).

South choir aisle, east part Bishop Kerr Hamilton † 1869. By *B. Pleydell Bouverie*. Recumbent effigy of white marble. Canopy in the C13 style. – Hungerford Chantry (of Walter Lord Hungerford † 1449, whose tomb-chest is in the nave). Known as 'the Cage' from its iron grilles, once painted blue and gold and vermilion. Moved here in 1778 from the nave. The removal was pre-*Wyatt*, unconnected with Wyatt's subsequent demolition of the Hungerford Chapel beside the Lady Chapel. (Presumably

this C15 chantry originally stood in the C15 chapel, before Gough recorded it in the nave, and presumably it contained one or both of the C15 Hungerford tombs now in the nave.) In 1778 Lord Radnor adapted the chantry for use as a family pew (with Gothick armchairs). To this date belongs the thin Gothic decoration of the stone base towards the chancel. The tall sides are entirely of iron, and the cresting, though it looks stone, is of wood (?). Pretty painted ceiling inside with shields undulatingly connected by cord. – Simon of Ghent † 1315. Tomb-chest. The brass has disappeared. Wide ogee arch, filled by an original iron grille (cf. the Mortival monument opposite). Jambs with ball-flower. Arch with fleuron trail in one order. Big crockets and very big finial. Buttress-shafts l. and r. – Between chancel aisle and E aisle of the SE transept, Bishop Giles de Bridport † 1262. A marvellous monument of Purbeck and stone. Purbeck effigy, beardless, under a pointed cinque-foiled head canopy. Turrets to its l. and r. Two angels also l. and r. The bishop holds his crozier and raises his other hand in blessing. The effigy lies in a shrine-like architecture open in two twin openings to N and S. To the N they are of Purbeck marble, to the S of stone. They consist each of pointed-trefoiled arches and a quatrefoiled circle over. All this is pierced work, i.e. bar tracery, and the earliest occurrence at Salisbury of this important motif, some five or ten years before the cloisters, though over fifteen years after Westminster Abbey. Stiff-leaf sprays. The upper parts are of stone on both sides. Gables on dragons, small heads between the arches and the gables. The gables again with leaf sprays, just on the point of abandoning the stiff-leaf convention. Scenes from the life of the bishop in the spandrels, again earlier than in the chapter house. The scenes are unrestored. Slender figures and much relished landscape elements. Shrine-like roof as a top. On it stiff-leaf crockets and finials.

North-east transept Brass to Bishop Wyville † 1375. An enormous piece, the actual brass plate 90 in. long. The composition is unusual. A fantastic tower or symbol of a fortress, with the bishop looking out. This commemorates his recovery of Sherborne Castle for the Church in a lawsuit against the Earl of Salisbury which nearly ended in a trial by combat. Below at the gate small figure of the bishop's champion, Richard Shawell: the sole representation on a brass of the equipment used in a trial by combat (a leather jack, a shield with a large boss, and a heavy military pick). Rabbits and hares represent Bere Chase, which was also at issue. Norris (1978) thinks the design possibly inspired by medieval romance on the theme of a lady in a keep watching combat at the gate. (A modern facsimile in the nave is for brass-rubbers.)

South-east transept On the E side: William Lisle Bowles, the poet, † 1850. Gothic tablet, no doubt by *Osmond* (see below). – J. H. Jacob † 1828. Grecian sar-

144. SALISBURY Tomb of Bishop Bridport † 1262, detail

cophagus in relief. – On the s side: Bishop Burgess † 1837. Standing wall-monument with canopy. By *Osmond*, Gothic of course. – On the w side: Dean Clarke † 1757. Astonishingly classical, without a touch of the Rococo, i.e. on the way from Rysbrack to Wilton. Below, a still-life of astronomical and geometrical instruments. This was originally above the inscription, and on top was a big urn inside an arch (Devizes Museum I, 49). – Bishop Seth Ward † 1689. Large tablet. A bad bust at the top. At the foot a still-life in the round of mathematical instruments. – Gothic tablets to Richard Hooker and William Chillingworth, both placed by Bowles in 1836 and both by *Osmond*.

North choir aisle, west part Thomas Bennett † 1558. Cadaver on a half-rolled-up straw mat. Tomb-chest with cusped quatrefoils and shields with initials. Recess with four-centred arch, panelled. Straight top, including

the date 1554. L. and r. re-used triple Purbeck shafts. In the E jamb Crucifixus. Not a trace of the Renaissance yet. George Sydenham † 1524. Cadaver, already on a half-rolled-up mat, which makes a date in the 1540s more likely. No tomb-chest. – Bishop Woodville † 1484. Purbeck tomb-chest with cusped quatrefoils. Much wider surround. Very broad panelled posts l. and r. Four-centred arch towards the top really straight-sided. Horizontal top. Rather plain.

South choir aisle, west part Bishop Selcot † 1557. Tomb-chest with quatrefoils, purely Gothic still. – Bishop Davenant † 1641. Standing monument, no longer Jacobean in style. Complicated architectural setting with, at the top, a segmental pediment and two fragments of a wider segmental pediment l. and r. – Sir Richard Mompesson † 1627. Probably by the master of the Hertford monument (retrochoir). Two recumbent effigies, he behind her and a little higher. Detached columns with vine wound round. Shallow back arch. Big obelisks outside, l. and r. Top with allegorical figures and obelisks. – Bishop Mitford † 1407. Alabaster. Tomb-chest with gabled niches. Recumbent effigy. Much wider surround. Four-centred panelled arch. In one of the orders martlets and very pretty columbines. In the spandrels shields with allegorical figures and arms. Top quatrefoil frieze.

North transept In the E aisle Walter Long † 1807, a surgeon. Marble tablet with Gothic details. L. and r. allegories of Science and Benevolence. It is signed by *John Flaxman*. – On the N wall: Sir Richard Colt Hoare. By *R. C. Lucas*, 1841 (of Leonardo da Vinci fame – the wax bust). Seated marble figure with a book. Heavy chair. – Bishop Blyth † 1499. Recumbent effigy. Tomb-chest with cusped quatrefoils. Tight-fitting plain canopy with horizontal top. – Sergeant-Major J. M. Peniston † 1858. Signed by *Osmond*. A composition of three gables, with a brass at the base by *Waller*. – On the w wall: William Benson Earle † 1796. By *Flaxman*. Big tablet with standing female figure unveiling a relief of the Good Samaritan. Obelisk background. – First Earl of Malmesbury. By *Chantrey*, 1823. Very Grecian semi-reclining figure with book. But the architectural details Gothic. – George Lawrence † 1861. By *Gaffin*. Still with a Georgian mourning woman, amazingly late, possibly ordered long before. – James Harris † 1780. By *Bacon*. Seated female holding a portrait medallion. Obelisk background. – John Britton, the architectural antiquarian, † 1857. Brass plate erected by the R.I.B.A. – Richard Jefferies † 1887, 'who observing the works of Almighty God with a poet's eye has enriched the literature of his country'. By *Margaret Thomas*, 1892.

South transept In the E aisle: J. H. Jacob † 1862. Designed by *Street*. Ornate table tomb with alabaster and mosaic. Low coped tomb-chest beneath. Under a canopy (added later). – Bishop Fisher † 1825. Made by *Osmond*, 1828. Tomb-chest and on it, instead of an effigy, a cushion, the Bible and the crozier. Canopy with four-centred arch. – On the s wall: tablet to Bishop Hume † 1782, by *King* of Bath. So small and so simple. – Poore family, 1817. Already in an archaeologically accurate Perp. Triple canopy. By *John Carline* of Shrewsbury, to a design of the *Rev. Hugh Owen*. – On the w wall: T. H. Hume † 1834. Gothic tablet by *Hopper*. – Sir Robert Hyde † 1665. Black and white marble. Bust in an oval medallion; bad. By *Besnier*.

Nave and aisles *Wyatt* transferred the monuments from the Lady Chapel and the Beauchamp and Hungerford Chapels to the nave and lined them all up neatly on the sleeper walls between the arcade piers. (He may have interfered with the tomb-chests as well.) We take them from the N E to the w and back to the s E. Sir John Cheney

† 1509. Tomb-chest with cusped fields. Alabaster effigy. – Walter Lord Hungerford † 1449. Two tomb-chests side by side, to appear as one very broad one. The brasses have been looted. – (A facsimile of the large C 14 Wyville brass here is for rubbers: for the original, see N E transept above.) – Sir John de Montacute † 1390. Damaged effigy of a formidable knight. The N side of the tomb-chest is of Purbeck marble and was the top of the canopy of a Hungerford monument. – Tomb-chest of a person unknown. Cusped quatrefoils. – William Geoffrey † 1558. Tomb-chest with on the N and s sides three small sexfoils enclosing shields. – William Longespée the Younger † 1250. Purbeck effigy of a cross-legged knight. One hand on the sword-hilt, the other holds the shield up high. – Miniature stone effigy of a bishop; C 13. Pointed-trefoiled, nodding head-canopy. Angels to its l. and r. – Tapering coffin-lid of an unknown bishop, C 12 or C 13.

Against the w wall: D'Aubigny Turberville † 1694. His wife died in 1704. Very tall black base with long inscription. On top putti, a shield and a vase. – Thomas Lord Wyndham † 1745, Lord High Chancellor of Ireland. By *Rysbrack*. Seated female figure (in the round) drying her tears and holding a staff and a harp. On the l. big urn. To the l. of this on the ground his official seal-bag with the arms of George II, in style consciously antiquated, i.e. of c. 1700.

s aisle from the w: black lid with tapering sides. Unknown whom it records. – Then two effigies from Old Sarum. The first is Bishop Roger's. He died in 1139. It is a lid with tapering sides. The carving is completely flat, except of the head, which is a C 14 replacement. Flat leaf border. Crozier on a dragon. The slab is of Tournai marble (i.e. imported) and may date from the mid-C 12. The head is Purbeck marble. Mr Hugh Shortt has pointed out the close similarity of the slab to that of St Memmie at Châlons-sur-Marne. The leaf border and the dragon are almost identical. – The other slab is Purbeck throughout. It is thought to commemorate Bishop Joscelin de Bohun † 1184. The head is bearded. The modelling is considerably rounder. The head in an odd two-lobed surround. Inscription on the orphrey of his chasuble: 'Quisquis es, affer opem, devenies in idem', i.e. 'Whoever you are, help [with prayer]. You will be like me.' A much longer rhymed inscription on the rim starts: 'Flent hodie Salesbirie quia decidit ensis/Justitiae, pater ecclesie Salesbiriensis'. The connection with Joscelin has been questioned, with a suggestion that it is a posthumous monument to St Osmund, perhaps made for Bishop Roger's new E end at Old Sarum. But the poem's reference to distinguished ancestors fits Joscelin better (claims for Osmund's were only made in the C 15), and it would have been unlikely for Osmund's early shrine to stand on a carved grave slab. At any rate, the monument seems to date from the later C 12. (cf. a contem-

145. SALISBURY
Effigy (detail) of Robert Lord Hungerford † 1459

146. SALISBURY
Effigy of William Longespée the Elder † 1226

porary one at Exeter: Lady Chapel, s E recess.) Tomb-chest with three cusped lozenges – Opposite against the s wall Alexander Ballantyne, 1783, designed by *Nicholas Revett*. Simple but very elegant tablet. – Bishop Beauchamp † 1481. Tomb-chest (which did not originally belong) with ornate quatrefoils, and for its lid an altar *mensa*. – Opposite tablet to Edward Davenant † 1639. Already entirely classical; black and white. – Robert Lord Hungerford † 1459. Purbeck tomb-chest with cusped fields. Alabaster effigy with meticulously detailed armour. – Opposite Mary Cooke † 1642, also classical. – St Osmund. Part of the shrine, probably c 13, with three kneeling-holes to the N, three to the s (see lid, retrochoir). – Bishop de la Wyle † 1271. Perp tomb-chest with quatre-foiled panels of Purbeck marble. These come from the canopy of the monument to Robert Lord Hungerford. Purbeck effigy with a pointed-trefoiled nodding head-canopy. It must have been of good quality once. – Opposite Sir Henry Hyde † 1650. With a militantly royalist inscription. Black columns with white Ionic capitals. – Elihonor Sadler † 1622. Kneeling figure with columns l. and r. – William Longespée † 1226, when he was buried at the very new E end. Tomb-chest of wood with wooden shafts carrying pointed-trefoiled arches. This was once covered with

gesso and painted. (cf. the table in the chapter house.) The effigy of freestone is not the earliest English military effigy, for Duke Robert's at Gloucester (of wood) may be c 12. Chain mail, also covering the one visible arm and hand. Long shield with six lions rampant.

Cloisters (For the architecture, see below.) Many Gothic tablets of stone, no doubt by *William Osmond*. There are tablets commemorating two Osmonds, one who died in 1875 aged eighty-four, the other who died in 1890 aged sixty-nine. One classical tablet († 1824) is also signed *Osmond*. – Tablet to Francis Price † 1753, the cathedral surveyor, who was buried in the cloisters. – Fine c 13 pier-head and base, s w corner: see *Chapter house* below.

CLOISTERS

Salisbury is a secular, not a monastic cathedral, and so, while a chapter house was needed, a cloister was not, and indeed the Salisbury cloister has no other ranges attached to it. It was an afterthought altogether. In dimensions and layout it is so similar to the original cloister layout at Wells, completed except for an intended N walk c. 1260, it was probably inspired by it; the unbuilt N walk at Wells was to be similarly separate from the nave aisle (Rodwell

147. SALISBURY Cloisters, c. 1270–c. 1300

1980b). At Salisbury no provision for a cloister was made when the s aisle was built. It is entirely isolated from the cathedral, except for the w side of the s transept and a corridor or branch passage continuing the w walk past the N walk to the aisle, i.e. the N walk is separated from the s aisle by an open space called the Plumbery (where lead roofing was once prepared; now plumbing and feeding for tourists). The cloisters were begun by Bishop de la Wyle, perhaps c. 1270. They are of twelve bays to each walk.

In the middle of the garth are two splendid cedar trees, beautifully framed by the broad openings of the cloister walks. The age of these patriarchal trees is unknown. Perhaps they were recommended to Bishop Ward by Sir Stephen Fox, donor of Farley Church and almshouses near Salisbury in the 1680s, when Fox was also planting evergreens at Chiswick, but that is only a supposition. The first cedars of Lebanon at Wilton House near Salisbury are thought to have been early c 17, the second planting there early c 18. Those in the Chelsea Physic Garden were planted in 1683.

The cloisters introduce the bar tracery of Westminster Abbey to Salisbury (although the Bridport monument in the s E choir aisle already had it on a smaller scale) and with it a sumptuousness so far quite absent from the design of the cathedral itself. The lancets which had dominated up to 1270, even with what plate tracery there is, emphasize height, the cloister openings breadth. They are framed by plain buttresses with plain set-offs. Each bay has two-light openings with a deeply moulded quatrefoiled circle. The *trumeaux* are of a centre shaft with two shafts at r. angles to the wall attached to it and two detached shafts in the direction of the wall – a subtle, wholly successful arrangement. The shafts were originally all of Purbeck. All capitals are moulded. In the lunette above the two pairs is a large circle alternately cinquefoiled and sexfoiled. Westminster Abbey in 1245–55 had taken this type of four-light bar tracery from Amiens, where it had occurred about 1235–40. Above the arcade runs a parapet with small quatrefoiled circles, two to each bay. Only in the E wall opposite the chapter-house entrance the system of the openings is interrupted. There are here simply two large openings into the garth without subdivision or tracery. Above the N half of the E walk is the LIBRARY, built in 1445. It has straight-headed cusped two-light windows to the W, i.e. the garth, as well as to the E. Actually what happened in 1445 is that the new accommodation on the upper floor was built as long as the whole E range. The surviving N part was the Chancellor's Schools. The library occupied the S part. This was demolished in 1756, and the library moved N.

The interior of the walks is rib-vaulted throughout, with quadripartite bays and bosses. The ribs and the transverse arches have the same thickness and mouldings. The bosses are mostly stiff-leaf in the E and N walks, though there is the occasional figure-motif, e.g. biting dragons by the chapter-house entrance and mermaids further S. At the S E corner the foliage turns naturalistic and goes on being so in the S walk. The vaulting of the W walk came last. The bosses here have more human figures and heads. The style is decidedly later, say of c. 1300–10, though the rib profiles do not change. At the N end of the W walk a branch runs N to connect with the S aisle of the cathedral W of the Plumbery. The walls of the cloister walks are all covered with blank arcading, echoing the openings with their bar tracery. Each bay has two arches with a big sexfoiled circle over. All shafts are detached. At the entrance to the S transept the S wall of the short passage to the entrance is canted, and the blind arcading cants with it in the same disconcerting way in which in the earlier C 13 work quatrefoils were broken round corners.

There are a number of C 13 DOORWAYS out of the cloister. That in the N E corner to the S transept is nine times cusped with stiff-leaf cusps and stiff leaf in the spandrels. To its S is a second, minor doorway, cinquecusped. Where did it originally lead? Another small doorway leads E from the S E corner. It is also cinquecusped. The entry to the cloister from the W is by a doorway at the N W corner. This has a type of arch frequent at Westminster Abbey. The arch is very depressed two-centred and stands on short vertical pieces. The doorway cuts into the blind wall arcading, though symmetrically. The same type in the doorway from the N branch of the W walk to the Plumbery, also cutting into the wall-arcading and also symmetrically. (See also *Interior*, transept doorways, above.) The doorway into the S aisle is cinquecusped with leaf cusps and cuts very awkwardly into the blank arcading. The exterior of the cloister ranges is very bare, without windows and only with simple buttresses, but the *leitmotif* of the parapet of blank trefoil-headed panels is preserved even here.

CHAPTER HOUSE

The chapter house was begun a little later than the cloisters, according to the discovery of Edward I pennies under the central pillar when that was rebuilt by *Clutton*, which would give 1279 as the earliest possible date. It is entered from the E walk by a two-bay corridor or vestibule with sexfoiled circular windows and the same small quatrefoiled circle over as the parapet of the cloisters. The chapter house itself is an octagon, with gloriously spacious windows of four lights with two quatrefoiled circles and a large octofoiled circle over. The pattern was of course Westminster Abbey, where the chapter house was apparently complete by 1253. On the exterior, frieze without dogtooth and parapet. Buttresses without the multiplied set-offs. Flat roof, unfortunately. Higher stair-turret N E of the vestibule. From the E one can also see the E wall of the library (see above), the passage leading to it at an angle, and the projection of the fireplace.

The portal from the cloister into the corridor is all C 19. The walls of the corridor have the same blank arcading as the walls of the cloister, except that here Purbeck shafts are used. Vault in two bays with ribs like those of the cloister and stiff-leaf bosses. The inner portal also has a *trumeau*. This is slender, of Purbeck marble, and consists of four shafts attached to a centre shaft. The detail is all C 19. The jambs l. and r. are thickly Purbeck-shafted. Purbeck stiff-leaf capitals, restored. The two arches are cinquecusped with stiff-leaf cusps, all this also of Purbeck. The super-arch has one order of little figure niches with trefoiled canopies. This also corresponds to Westminster Abbey. Drawings made before the restoration in 1856 (by J R *Philip*, under *Clutton*) show that the lively little figures (apart from some hands and heads, etc.) are largely original. They represent the Virtues and Vices.

Now the interior of the chapter house itself. It is 58 ft across. The large windows make it very light. Moreover the centre pier is very slender. Circular centre with eight thin detached Purbeck shafts. (The original top, base and splendid capitals – together looking exactly like a font – are happily preserved in the S W corner of the cloisters.) Two tiers of shaft-rings. Stiff-leaf capitals and on the base more stiff-leaf and a series of little animals. Vault with eight arches across and eight cells with 'triradial' ribs, i.e. ribs radiating to the centre and two corners. All ribs slender. Stiff-leaf bosses. Below the windows blank arcading with pointed cinquecusped arches. Quatrefoil Purbeck wall-shafts, and in front of them at the angles detached triple Purbeck shafts (the E wall with more elaborate arcading on even more detached sets of shafts like little spur walls for the dean's and six other seats). Rich stiff-leaf capitals, some with heads, birds, animals, grotesques. More heads as hoodmould stops – these indeed are most remarkable, and carry on the tradition of the rood screen. They are of all physiognomies, types and expressions, male and female, heads held up and leaning a little sideways, heads with the tongue out and with a distorted mouth, heads bearded and

148. Salisbury
Chapter house, head-stop by the dean's seat: Prudence

beardless, heads young and old. A triple-faced head by the dean's seat presumably represents the cardinal virtue of Prudence, much invoked in chapter houses, in its three aspects to past, present and future of memory, intelligence and foresight (while suggesting the tennis-watching effect on the dean of listening to his canons seated round). A Britton engraving confirms its pre-Victorian existence. On the spandrel carvings, see below.

The only disturbing element is the w wall. The blank arcading first continues one more bay, but the bay is wider and the arches hence round-cinquecusped. But the portal cuts into their mouldings. In the big main spandrel a large quatrefoiled circle with a c19 figure of Christ. This upper part of the portal cuts into an upper blank arcading of eight bays, necessary because the corridor has that height. Consequently the w window has no space to go down as low as the others. The row of blank arches has very rich stiff-leaf capitals. Head stops, shallow spandrels with stiff-leaf, dragons etc.

The spandrels of the blank arcading right round the chapter house have carved stories from Genesis, from the Creation to Moses, i.e. with Adam and Eve, Cain and Abel, Noah, Abraham, Esau, Jacob, Joseph. The carving was unfortunately savagely, i.e. sentimentally, restored in the

1860s, by *John Birnie Philip*. But iconographically the series remains extremely valuable all the same, a veritable picture book with any number of lively, well-observed genre details. In 1859 William Burges, in two articles in the *Ecclesiologist*, listed the subjects and noted the condition of all the chapter-house sculptures as they were before the restoration. Burges's role as 'art-architect' assistant to Henry Clutton here in 1855–6, before Clutton withdrew, and then under *Scott*, has been described by Dr Crook (1981), with all the nuances of Burges's iconographical researches and recreative influence.

There was also then some unspecified restoration of the wooden TABLE that stands here (possibly once fitted round the central pier: there is a pre-Scott drawing of the Westminster chapter house with such an arrangement). Eight sides pierced with trefoil-headed openings: work comparable to the wooden tomb-chest under the effigy of Longespée Sr in the nave, though that might have been tampered with by *Wyatt*. The table is shown in Britton's view of 1814. – STAINED GLASS. For some of the original glass, see *Furnishings*, s transept, above. The chapter house was given new windows in the 1860s, inoffensive copies by *Ward* of the c13 grisailles. In 1967 two of these Victorian windows were quite unjustifiably replaced by clear glass, with harsh effect on the appearance of the interior. Fortunately further destruction was stopped and the remaining windows repaired. May replacement of those two be suitable. – The original floor tiles replaced in the c19 were illustrated in Henry Shaw's *Specimens of Tile Pavements* (1858); they were similar to pavements at Clarendon Palace and at Winchester (E. Eames 1980).

On the lawn near the cathedral a seven-foot Walking Madonna by the sculptor *Dame Elisabeth Frink*, 1981.

For details of the close, its c14 walls and gates, its bishop's palace and its houses, see the latest edition of B of E *Wiltshire*.

Southwark: see *London*.

Truro

Cathedral Church of St Mary *Anglican*

(Based on B of E *Cornwall*, 1970, rewritten by Anthony Quiney, slightly extended, with information from John Phillips.)

This late Victorian cathedral rises out of a tight network of streets like a French cathedral. It owes its existence to the revival of the diocese of Cornwall (with separation from

149 SALISBURY Chapter house, begun *c.* 1279, interior in 1814

150. TRURO Design by J. L. Pearson completed 1879, built 1880–1910

that of Exeter) in 1876, and above all to the appointment in the following year of the redoubtable Edward White Benson as first bishop. He was determined to have a new cathedral to rival the achievements of the Middle Ages, and, coming from Lincoln, had that cathedral no doubt in mind. (Exeter he certainly did not have in mind.) He set up a building committee whose first act was to find an architect from among Bodley, Burges, Pearson, R. P. Pullan, J. P. St Aubyn, Oldrid Scott or Street. They recommended *John Loughborough Pearson*, who, incidentally, since 1870 had been chapter architect at Lincoln. His design was completed by the summer of 1879. The E parts of the cathedral together with its crossing (but not the upper parts of the tower) were built 1880–7. The nave and crossing tower followed after Pearson's death 1897–1903, the W towers were raised 1910, and a small part of the proposed cloister was begun only in 1935, all being executed to the original design (with slight modifications in the W towers) by Pearson's son, *Frank Loughborough Pearson*.

Pearson Sr gave Benson exactly what Benson wanted, a version of Lincoln: a traditional cathedral, that is, with a square-ended choir and retrochoir, two pairs of transepts with a tower over the main crossing, an aisled nave and a pair of W towers. 'Simply a medieval cathedral over again', grumbled the *Builder*, but it nevertheless perfectly suited the revived liturgy of the Oxford Movement which Benson wanted to establish here, and architecturally it is much more than that too, despite its medievalisms. The plan lacks the easy-going spread of Lincoln and is by contrast as tight and compact as a French cathedral. This was natural to Pearson's style, and here additionally forced on him by the constrictions of the site. Pearson was determined to retain the best part of the crumbling medieval church on the site, its S aisle, both as a link with the past and to serve as a side chapel, even though bishop and building committee called it 'tinkering up rotten stones'. Pearson was more a conservationist than his reputation at Westminster Abbey suggests. The retention of the old aisle, now called St Mary's aisle, together with the restraints imposed by the site, meant that he had to bend the axis of the cathedral slightly at the crossing; some believe this is only an example of his academic pedantry but in fact it shows how he could turn medieval precedent to profit. Another need imposed by the old aisle was to provide a further aisle between it and the choir to carry massive transverse arches to support the choir buttresses above. The extra spaces and piers give the cathedral the internal vistas so characteristic of Pearson's mature work. Another vista is provided by the richly decorated baptistery tightly placed in the re-entrant angle between S transept and nave aisle, and there are more vistas in the tall W tower halls opening towards the nave and in the arcading set before the aisle windows. The principal E–W vista leads to the tall reredos, of the same family as

151. TRURO South-east view, with the medieval south aisle

Bodley's of 1888 for St Paul's and Johnson's of *c*. 1882 for Newcastle, following C 15 precedent at St Albans and Winchester.

The cathedral is in the E.E. style, with details reminiscent of the northern abbeys like Whitby which Pearson had known and loved from his youth. Other details are French Gothic from Normandy, which he visited in the 1850s, notably the spires (cf. Bayeux, Bernières and St-Étienne Caen) and the placing of the w towers (cf. Jumièges). But compare also the former spires at Lincoln. Many complained that the cathedral was alien to Cornwall, where churches are low and usually without spires. That may be so but with its bounding silhouette the cathedral leaps upwards from its cramped site to dominate the town as a cathedral should.

The INTERIOR is in many ways an idealization of the E.E. style, perfected as against the proportions of, say, Salisbury Cathedral, and purged of the lovable irregularities of Lincoln. The nave elevation is built up on a grid of equal squares: each bay of the arcade is twice as high as long, the springing of the arches being halfway up, and takes two squares; the same goes for the clerestory; while the tribune bays, as high as long, take a single square each. The proportions of the transverse section of the nave and the details of the w wall make extensive use of the Golden Section. Here is Pearson's typical fusion of classical proportion into the Gothic style. Like his best churches, the cathedral is stone-vaulted throughout, mostly with quadripartite rib-vaults. The nave has sexpartite vaults, following the early Gothic of France, though such vaults appear at Lincoln. They are a logical conclusion to the system of double nave bays and help to slow down the sense of bay-by-bay progression eastwards in this none-too-long nave (a little over 125 ft). The total internal length of the cathedral, including the w towers, is *c*. 275 ft (to Lincoln's 482 ft).

The cathedral was intended to be carried out in Bath stone so that its decoration could be the more easily carved. After protests, Pearson was forced to use local granite for the ashlar inside and out, and the Bath was kept for the decorated parts. Much of these are no more than mouldings, cool and plain in the nave, enriched in choir and baptistery by nailhead. As so often in Pearson's later churches, the architectural sculpture is regrettably stiff, or, to be kinder, impersonally hierarchical, and exactly opposite to the free Arts and Crafts work of the time, which Pearson distrusted. Much of the carving is by *Nathaniel Hitch*. Pearson also used internally the Cornish marble-like stones, serpentine and polyphant, e.g. shafts of serpentine in the baptistery.

Of the former parish church of Truro, St Mary's, Pearson restored the s aisle and pulled down the rest, including a tower and spire. In its place he gave St Mary's aisle a tower of its own set against the s transept. The aisle, of 1504–18, is indeed one of the most ornate Gothic structures in Cornwall. Probably by the same masons as Probus tower, it has some of the decoration of the plinth in two tiers, the same use of niches for statuary, the same decorating of buttresses. The window spandrels have tracery, and the battlements also are adorned with quatrefoils. The s windows are large, of four lights, the E window of five. The interior has its arcade with piers of standard Cornish design, plain capitals and arches nearly semicircular. Some of the roof timbers are still in place, and a little old glass.

On the NE side of the cathedral a CHAPTER HOUSE combined with a memorial hall was built in 1967, architect *John Taylor*. The building is of concrete with surfaces of grit-blasted granite aggregate. The heaviness of the horizontal concrete members is in total contrast to the verticalism of the cathedral, and the tiny round arches of the vertical slit windows cut into the top slab – a fashionable motif initially derived from Le Corbusier's Maisons Jaoul – have no more convincing relation to the pointed arches of Pearson's building. Not that imitations of Pearson's C 13 style would have been preferable, but modern forms more consistent in vertical emphasis might have been chosen.

Many of the FURNISHINGS of the cathedral are dull, with too much of the 'church art-furniture shop'. Stained glass and other fittings are by *Clayton & Bell*, except for good glass of the 1840s in the old aisle s side by *Warrington*. The choir stalls and bishop's throne are to *Pearson's* design, as are the reredos (see above) and the marble mosaic floor in the choir, which is based on Early Christian examples he had seen in Italy on a visit in 1874; for other fine pavements by him, see especially Bristol and Peterborough. The original parish-church pulpit in St Mary's aisle is of a comfortably bulgy shape, with inlay of local workmanship. The pulpit of Hopton Wood stone at the crossing is by Pearson. – MONUMENTS. In the crypt two life-size kneeling figures of alabaster, *c*. 1620, not well carved. – In the N transept, tomb of John Robartes † 1614 ('of his age seventy or thereabouts'), and wife, a large affair with the two effigies reclining stiffly and behind each other, double columns l. and r., and on their entablatures two very good smaller figures of Father Time and Death; the carving of the larger figures is by no means good. – Some late C 18 and early C 19 monuments to Vyvyans, high up.

Among Gothic Revival conceptions of the cathedral, Truro is of the time and attitude that induced Carpenter's unbuilt design for Manchester, the senior Scott's St Mary's Edinburgh, and the younger Scotts' St John's Norwich (R.C.), all designs on a cathedral scale and proofs that traditional Gothic still had power in it. The last stop was to be at Liverpool (Anglican, q.v.).

For the town of Truro, see the latest edition of B of E *Cornwall*.

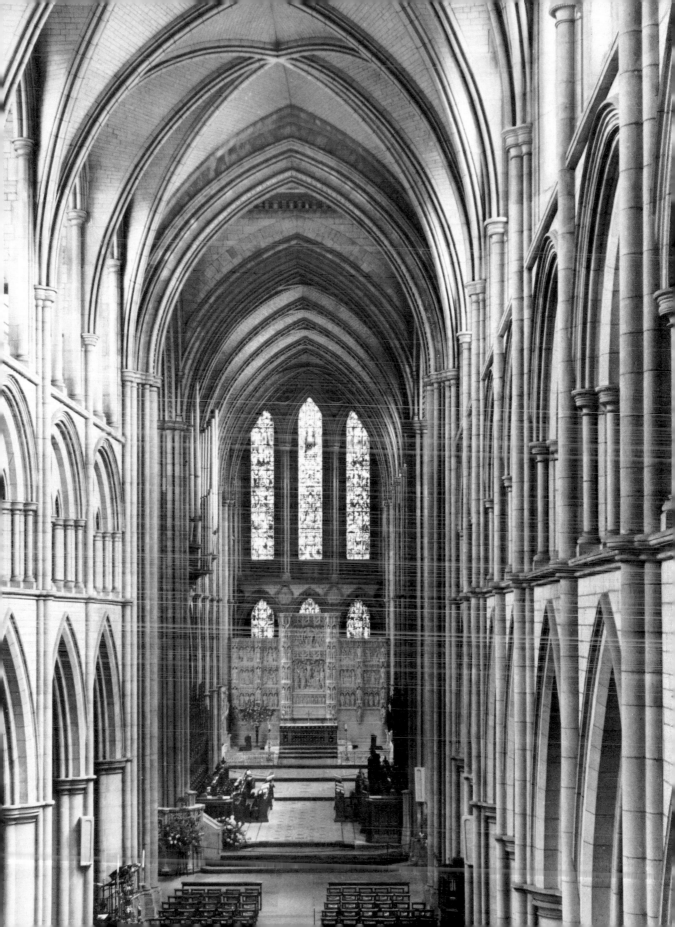

Wells

Plan, Fig. 154, from the *Builder*, 1891 by Roland Paul (after John Carter) before excavation in 1894 revealed the old alignment of the Saxon Lady Chapel E of the cloister; but shows the Saxon alignment of an underground chamber in the cloister garth (marked gong, or privy; see *Introduction* below on the 'dipping place').

Some references (see Recent Literature): Bony 1979; Colchester 1977, 1978; Colchester and Harvey 1974; Coldstream 1976; P. Eames 1977; Harvey 1978; Remnant 1969; Rodwell 1980a, 1980b, 1981; Tudor-Craig 1976. A new history of the cathedral edited by Mr Colchester, with articles by Harvey, Rodwell, Tudor-Craig *et al.*, came out in 1982.

INTRODUCTION

The ancient town named for its wells or springs sits partly surrounded by gentle hills at the southern edge of the Mendips in Somerset, about fifteen miles s of Bristol and five miles NE of Glastonbury. The cathedral's immediate surroundings include the Cathedral Green before the w front and, along the N side of green and cathedral, the C 15–17 Old Deanery, the C 16–19 Wells Museum, the C 13–19 Music School, the C 15 Chain Gate and bridge from the chapter house, and the C 14 Vicars' Close. s of cathedral and cloisters are the moated ruins of the C 13–16 Bishop's Palace in its romantic early C 19 setting of trees and lawn. Just SE of the cathedral's E end the water of St Andrew's Well still 'bubbles up so quick a spring' (Celia Fiennes in 1698). The earliest surviving written record of the church thought to have been founded here early in the C 8 is a charter of 766 referring to 'the minster near the Great Spring at Wells for the better service of God in the Church of St Andrew'. s w of cathedral and green the town market-place lies on a N E–S W axis that, as we now know, continued the alignment of Saxon cathedral buildings oriented, not on the sun as the present cathedral more nearly is, but on the springs. Such an alignment was first suggested in 1909 by W. H. St John Hope and sceptically ignored by all. But archaeological excavation in 1978–80 showed that the C 10 cathedral, as well as earlier buildings, lay obliquely across the site of the present cloisters, on the axis of a line from St Andrew's Well to the market-place. The town, now the City of Wells, is thought to have been laid out from that. So it seems we have here a partly preserved piece of Saxon town planning, a secular layout generated by a church layout, all oriented on a spring of possibly pre-Christian sanctity.

First to summarize the EXCAVATIONS. (The following four paragraphs were contributed by Dr Rodwell.) These were undertaken during 1978–80 in the Camery, an outdoor space adjacent to the E cloister range and s transept, on a site once occupied by the 'Lady Chapel by the Cloister'. A sequence of structures of great interest was found here, revealing for the first time parts of the cathedral and minster which preceded the present Gothic building and lay just to the s of it. In brief, the sequence was as follows. The earliest Christian evidence is an C 8 cemetery and chapel, of which only the w end has been excavated. Fifty metres to the E lies the 'holy' well dedicated to St Andrew. By the late Saxon period, the chapel, then dedicated to St Mary, had been rebuilt to the w of its former site, but at the same time it seems to have stood just E of a large apse, which is interpreted as the eastern termination of the Anglo-Saxon cathedral. The excavated building was thus a detached Lady Chapel, with an extensive cemetery around it. About the time of the Conquest a link was built between the chapel and the apse, and claustral buildings were erected on both sides by Bishop Giso. After a short life, these were demolished by Bishop John de Villula c. 1090. The Lady Chapel remained and it alone was saved when the rest of the old cathedral was swept away in the 1190s for the laying out of the cloister of the new church.

In 1196 the Chapel of St Mary was 'restored' and joined to the E range of the new cloister, thus acquiring the title Lady Chapel by the Cloister. Meanwhile, interest in the chapel grew: ordinations were held there, and it became packed with the burials of clergy and influential lay benefactors. In the years around 1276 it probably acquired

154. WELLS
Plan from the *Builder*, 1891 (see p. 292)

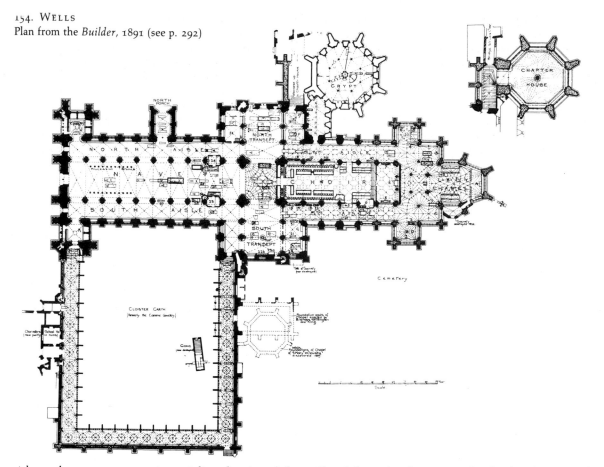

aisles and an eastern extension, tripling the size of the building. In the C 14 a small building with side benches was erected N of the chapel in the angle between the E cloister and S transept. Entrance was from the S transept and the structure is provisionally interpreted as a consistory court. In 1477 this building and the whole of the chapel were demolished and Bishop Stillington erected a large cruciform Lady Chapel designed by *William Smythe* and vaulted in the style of his contemporary vault under the cathedral's central tower and also of his vault at Sherborne Abbey. The wall-arcading inside the W end of the chapel may be seen on the E side of the cloister, and the present archway from the cloister to the Camery was formerly the entrance to the chapel. A series of carved bosses now exhibited in the S cloister, and parts of two vault-rings built on to the bench of the E cloister, are from the vaulting of Stillington's chapel. This chapel was completed in 1486 and Stillington was buried in it in 1491. In c. 1500, on the site of the former consistory court building, a chapel dedicated to the Holy Cross was built against the cloister, N of Stillington's chapel. A stone screen, of which the upper tracery survives *in situ*, divided the Holy Cross

Chapel from the cloister. Inside, the foundation for the altar has been discovered, together with a single tomb.

Since the C 13 the masons' yard has been sited in the Camery, adjoining the S E corner of the cloister, and here two rectangular workshops of the C 15 have been found in excavation. These workshops were apparently built for the masons engaged on Stillington's Lady Chapel. Upon completion of the chapel one workshop was demolished, while the other, according to a lease of 1541, was converted into a stable and hayloft (demolished in the C 18). By c. 1550 the dean and chapter were in financial difficulties and Edward VI was seeking revenue from the cathedral, so in 1552 the Lady Chapel by the Cloister was handed over to Sir John Gate, the king's collector of lead, whereupon demolition followed.

The excavations have also examined the medieval conduit which carried water from St Andrew's Well along beneath the cloister and into the town beyond. This conduit was constructed c. 1190–5 across the site of the demolished Saxon cathedral. An underground chamber in the cloister garth which gave access to the stream – the 'dipping place' remembered in the C 19 as a privy – may have been an early medieval baptistery below the site of the c 10 high altar, or some earlier holy feature. The font in the s transept of the present cathedral (see *Furnishings* below) is thought to be Anglo-Saxon of a late c 8 or c 9 type: did it once stand at the 'dipping place'? (A fuller account of the chapel excavation, Rodwell 1981, mentions Roman remains nearby and adds that in view of the proximity of the springs and the western British tradition of holy wells, it would not be surprising if a Roman shrine were eventually uncovered near the cathedral.)

The cathedral as we now see it is mainly the work of two building periods, c. 1180–c. 1260 and c. 1285–c. 1345. The first period achieved the creation of a completely English yet completely Gothic style: Wells was the first English Gothic building to use pointed arches exclusively. In its second period Wells – together with Bristol – represents the most original treatment of architectural space of which any country at that time was capable.

Wells became a cathedral in 909 on the site s of the present cathedral described above. It briefly suffered diminished status during the late c 11–early c 12 when the bishop's seat was at Bath (partly in preference for the warmer waters there?). But some building work at Wells was dedicated in 1148, and documents hint at new foundations on a new alignment. There is no proof yet that the later c 12 plan was influenced in position of piers and outer walls by that work. The building with which we are familiar was begun by Bishop Reginald (†1191), and the earliest documents relating to such work suggest a beginning c. 1180 (Colchester and Harvey 1974). Also, certain piers of a canons' barn (now incorporated in the Cathedral School, North Liberty), documented as of Reginald's time, are of the same (unusual) Chilcote stone as occurs here and there in the transepts and the e bay of the nave, just at a time when Glastonbury, after a fire of 1184, may have been monopolizing the Doulting quarry (see below). At Wells, enough nave walls to bolster the crossing will have been part of the choir–crossing–transept programme of Reginald's time, and the nave–cloisters layout projected. A period of unrest followed Reginald's death, yet new work in the late 1190s probably included the e walk of the intended cloisters on the site of the demolished Saxon cathedral (Rodwell 1980b).

The next prime mover of construction was Bishop Jocelyn (succeeded 1206, out of England 1209–13, †1242). The completed nave with n porch and w front form his chief memorial. The craftsman in charge is thought to have been *Adam Lock* (†1229) followed by *Thomas Norreys*. The cathedral was consecrated (not necessarily completed) in 1239. In 1248 the 'tholus' – probably a lantern on the crossing tower – fell in an earthquake, but there are few surviving traces of repairs (see *Interior*, n transept e aisle).

The work of the whole first period from c. 1180 into the c 13 comprised an e end with one-storey straight ambulatory, a straight-ended chancel, crossing with tower over, transepts, nave and n porch, w front with towers to the same height, the under-structure and staircase for a chapter house, and the cloisters completed c. 1260 (rebuilt c 15).

The work of the period c. 1285–c. 1345 comprises the chapter house itself, a new e end with Lady Chapel, e transepts and retrochoir, a new presbytery with renewed choir, and the completion and strutting of the crossing tower. In 1286 it had been decided to complete a 'nova structura' long since begun, which must be the chapter house; and a document of 1307 speaks of great expenses for it in the past tense. For the beginning of the Lady Chapel we have no date, but it was called 'newly constructed' in 1326 (and Colchester and Harvey (1974) cite reburial of Bishop Bytton there in 1319 as a more persuasive date than Dean Armitage Robinson's even earlier date based on stained glass that now appears to have been moved from elsewhere in the cathedral). The retrochoir, containing part of the Lady Chapel vaulting-structure, was necessarily built with it. In 1325 several documents mention a 'novum opus', most probably eastward extension of choir and presbytery to join the retrochoir. Bishop Drokensford's burial took place in 1329 in the e transept s of the Lady Chapel. When the high vault of the chancel was put in, we do not know, but presumably by c. 1340. The mason *William Joy*, who may have trained in Bristol, was in charge from 1329.

A new campanile (central tower) was begun in 1315 and there was a grant for roofing it in 1322. In 1338 the church is called 'enormiter confracta' and 'enormiter deformata'. It is thought that that refers solely to the effects of the new crossing tower on the crossing piers and that the astonishing strainer arches were the remedy. They can therefore be dated c. 1338–40. Colchester deduces from a document of 1356 on repair of the tower that underpinning, including scissors braces (the strainer arches), had already been done, starting soon after 1338, and assigns to 1356 the placing of stone grids – with the same wave mouldings as the scissor arches – inside the tower (above the c 15 fan-vault) as the last phase of *William Joy*'s plan for stabilizing the tower: i.e. grids and braces all designed c. 1338 but partly postponed by the Black Death, of which Joy may have died (Colchester and Harvey 1974).

By 1345, at the latest, it can be assumed that the whole eastern arm was complete. Later work was confined to the w towers, rebuilding of the cloisters with Stillington's chapel there, external remodelling of the crossing tower and insertion of vaults inside it, a raising of parapets on the c 13 part, and a thorough remodelling of the c 13 lancets by introducing simple two-light Perp tracery. For some at least of the c 15 work *William Smythe* is thought to have been the mason in charge.

The cathedral was built mainly of local oolitic limestone quarried at Doulting near Shepton Mallet. Polished stone shafting on the w front, originally of local blue lias (a dark grey limestone), is now mostly of c 19 Kilkenny 'black marble' (there is very little Purbeck outside). The w towers are 124 ft high, the crossing tower 182 ft. The whole cathedral is 415 ft long; the c 13 cathedral was *c.* 325 ft long. The Lady Chapel was restored by *Ferrey* in 1842, the choir by *Salvin* in 1848–54, the west front by *Ferrey* in 1870–3, with further restoration of the front in 1903 and 1925–31, as well as the most recent, and sensitive, restoration there. Almost 300 surviving figures (once nearly 400) on the great w sculpture screen, damaged by seven centuries of weather at its worst in westerly gales, by c 17 iconoclasts, and by the past century's varying modes of restoration, are in process of conservation as we write.

EXTERIOR

It is comparatively simple to appreciate the work of the first period outside. The subtler points of development come out more clearly inside. Church building as a rule started in the Middle Ages from the E. We will assume that that was so at Wells too, and begin where we can see what remains of the late c 12 CHANCEL. The best point is in the churchyard to the E of the cloister and the recent excavations. The broad aisle buttresses remain and the corbel table, and of the clerestory the narrower buttresses, the string-course which goes round the original windows like a hoodmould, and again the corbel table. The break between what we may for the moment call *c.* 1180–*c.* 1200 and what was done in the early c 14 is obvious enough, and it is equally obvious that it takes place in the clerestory one bay further w than in the aisle – proof of the fact already mentioned that the church of *c.* 1180–*c.* 1200 had a one-storeyed ambulatory.

The TRANSEPTS come next. They have both E and w aisles. But they differ in other ways. That on the s side is more easily visible than in monastic cathedrals, where extensive buildings usually rise to the E of the cloister. It has broad buttresses, three ground-floor windows, then a row of blank pointed arches with continuous roll moulding – the hallmark of Wells, as we shall see – cut into by the lowered sills of three stepped lancets above. The gable again has three stepped lancets, the central one wider and blank. On the buttresses stand tall polygonal pinnacles like chimneys, their long shafts with blank arcading, again without any capitals. The E aisle windows were enlarged in conjunction with the new presbytery, i.e. are not of the simple early c 15 forms that most other windows are.

At the s end of the s transept's w aisle is a doorway into the E walk of the cloister. It is a tall rather narrow doorway with an inner continuous chamfer, then two pairs of columns on each side separated by a step in the wall of the jamb. (The doorway's height suggests the loftiness of the earlier cloisters; it is later than the transept itself, probably of about 1240 replacing a smaller doorway to the primary E walk, according to Rodwell 1980b.) The columns have one shaft-ring and stiff-leaf capitals. The capitals (cf. below) are more developed than in the chancel, less than in the nave. Broad arch with filigree of stiff-leaf arranged in oblong shapes. The hoodmould on head-stops is damaged by the later cloister.

On the N transept the pinnacles on the buttresses are in three tiers, with blank panelling. The blank arcade below the main upper windows has six arches, of which the two outer ones are higher. The window zone consists of three tall arches of even height and two narrow blank bays l. and r. Under the tall arches are three stepped lancets, and above the lower of them paterae of stiff-leaf foliage, the first appearance of another *leitmotif* of Wells. In the gable finally there are twelve stepped blank arches with continuous moulding. Above the middle pair stiff-leaf in the spandrel. This description will show that the N transept has more variety of motifs than the s transept, perhaps a sign of later completion.

The system of the NAVE is again very simple. Broad buttresses below, narrow buttresses above. The lower buttresses have on the N side a stepping of the set-offs – four little steps on the first, three on the second set-off – which Salisbury took over and made a speciality. Corbel tables on aisle and clerestory. The window tracery again Perp and the parapet raised. More ornate only the doorways, and especially that leading into the church from the N under the porch. It is placed five bays from the crossing and six bays from the w front. This N entrance is a twin doorway with a middle post or *trumeau*. The *trumeau* has three shafts and two hollows between them, and shaft-rings to the shafts. Each doorway has a continuous moulding, which is, however, stopped short by the *trumeau*. The whole entrance is enriched by one order of columns with shaft-rings, one outer continuous keeled moulding, and a keeled hoodmould on two small busts. The capitals of the columns are decorated with the standing figures of a monk (with a scroll) and a bishop, with stiff-leaf behind them – the first figured capitals which we meet. The part of the arch which they carry has, to one's surprise, a Norman zigzag, set at an angle of 45°.

The doorway is preceded by the NORTH PORCH, treated so sumptuously that we cannot be in any doubt where the principal entrance to the cathedral was meant to be. The porch has externally completely plain sides (except for the Perp parapet of the same design as everywhere else; see below) but a highly enriched façade and interior. Two flat nook-shafted buttresses flank the entrance. They end in polygonal pinnacles, again with blank arcading without any capitals. The doorway has eight orders of columns with shaft-rings plus two facing into the interior. The arrangement of the columns follows an odd rhythm. From outside, the wall first comes out to form a polygonal attached shaft, then curves back and allows space for two columns. Then it comes forward again, and so on. The rhythm is shaft – column – column – shaft – column – shaft – column – column – shaft – column – shaft, and then the columns at the opening proper. The capitals are purely stiff-leaf on the r., but full of figures on the l. (five capitals represent the Martyrdom of King Edmund). The arch mouldings repeat the same rhythm: keeled rolls over the coupled columns, a frieze of the most puzzling ornament over the single columns. It is unquestionably again a paraphrase of the Norman motif of the zigzag and corresponds to a certain degree with what was done at the same time at Glastonbury. Two crenellations with triangular merlons at an angle of 45° to the surface meet in the middle a similar zigzag set at an angle of 90°, that is pointing straight at us. Stiff-leaf sprays inhabit this spiky frieze. The hoodmould is a filigree band of thin stiff-leaf scrolls. In the spandrels are two oblong panels with reliefs: one with a man and a beast, the other with a scaly mythical animal. The gable of the porch contains a group of six stepped blank lancets with continuous moulding. The highest pair in the middle has a short shaft on a corbel. Below it, inside this pair of blank arches, a group of three small stepped lancet windows (of the tracing house described below). Four bits of stiff-leaf and minor figure work above. The conception of all this is developed from the N rather than the S transept.

The inside of the porch is a masterpiece of the E.E. style, of a richness which is at the same time orderly and measured. Two rib-vaulted bays; on detached double shafts in the corners, on triple shafts in the middles. The shafts have shaft-rings and stiff-leaf capitals. The walls are covered with tiers of arcading, first a tier of four blank pointed arches per bay with continuous moulding and spandrels filled with symmetrical stiff-leaf arrangements, then the sill-moulding with hanging sprays of stiff-leaf. The moulding is cut off at the ends of each bay by tailed monsters biting into it (cf. Elder Lady Chapel, Bristol). The upper blank arcades are almost in two layers in so far as they have their own supporting shafts close to the wall but are separated from one another by two detached shafts standing behind one another. So there is much depth in this blank arcade, but depth in front of a clearly maintained back surface. That is E.E. at its best and most English, in the same spirit as contemporary work at Lincoln, the cathedral which was built by St Hugh of Avalon, Bishop of Lincoln. The shafts of this arcade again all have shaft-rings and stiff-leaf capitals. Arch mouldings with keels and fillets. The outer moulding of each arch intersects a little with that of the next immediately above the capitals. In the spandrels rings of stiff-leaf and also figure motifs. The lunettes above have blank windows with Y-tracery uncusped – and detached from the wall – once more the desire for a distinction between front layer and back layer. This must be one of the earliest appearances of the Y-motif anywhere. The vault makes no difference in girth or mouldings between transverse arch and diagonal rib. Fillet on the middle member of each rib and arch.

It can be mentioned here that the upper room over the N porch contains one of the two TRACING FLOORS known to survive in England (cf. York), with a maze of incised lines from generations of masons' working drawings set out on the smooth plaster (Colchester and Harvey 1974).

Now the WEST FRONT. If you approach it, as it is proposed here, immediately after the N porch, the impression will at once force itself upon you that here is the work of another designer, and what is more, not simply another man from the Wells lodge, trained in Wells traditions. Here the spirit is entirely different, different (if I may anticipate) from the whole interior too. The Wells style so far has been one of amplitude, of firmly rounded forms set against nobly sheer surfaces. Now we find something spare instead, harsh uprights and horizontals, angular gables, long marble poles almost, in their detachment from the wall, like steel scaffolding. These are facts. What must now be added is more personal and less capable of proof (and written, it will be remembered, in the 1950s). I would suggest that the Wells nave in its way and the Wells porch are masterworks of the highest order, but that the front is not. Mr Harvey calls it 'the most nearly perfect of any among English cathedrals'. I confess I cannot subscribe to this, not even if it were said in a less challenging form. The W front of Wells, as it is, seems to me unsatisfactory. This is, it must at once be admitted, primarily due to the unmitigated contrast between the C13 substructure and the late C14 and early C15 towers. Before condemning the façade one should perhaps make an effort to imagine what towers the master who designed the C13 front had in his mind. For there can be no question that he visualized his façade completed. What then would his parchment drawing look like, if we were as lucky at Wells as they were at Cologne and Strasbourg, when they found the original drawings? What height does this tremendous breadth demand which the master had chosen to give his front by placing his massive towers outside his aisles? To achieve a height commensurate to the existing breadth the towers would have to rise to something unprecedented in Gothic cathedrals, and incidentally something that would have dominated the crossing tower completely. On the other hand the designer might have aimed at a screen in the sense of Lincoln and Salisbury. But could he? Does not his uncompromising stress on the buttresses call for towers?

155. WELLS The west front, begun c. 1230

Here, in this quandary, lies to my mind the shortcoming of Wells as built. The French place their towers in front of the aisles and thereby achieve a logical interrelation between interior and exterior. At the same time they are led to a prevalence of height, because the façades are relatively narrow. In England towers had already in Norman times been set outside aisles (Old St Paul's, St Botolph's at Colchester etc.). And w towers outside the aisles were intended, though not carried out, at St Albans in the rebuilding of 1195–1214. At Ripon in c. 1220–30, when the nave had no aisles, w towers were built outside the width of the nave. The English screen façade is the consequence of this.

At Wells, the E faces of both towers were set out as one with the nave, presumably in the 1180s, when the w end of a N cloister walk was designed to meet the s face of the s w tower, and the w front was brought up to plinth-level also as part of the nave plan; but the clasping buttresses at the tower angles represent a change in design. It seems as if in the late c 12 the w front was originally meant to have flanking transepts as at Ely instead of towers, but by the time the w front rose above plinth-level such w transepts were out of fashion and the obvious course in the 1220s was to carry up the projections as towers. In the c 13 these went only as high as the rest of the screen front, though higher stages may have been intended from the start. (On evi-

156. WELLS North-west tower, C 13 and C 15

dence for spires on the c 14–15 upper stages, see *Interior*, w end, below.) The tall blind panels in each face of the c 13 upper stage, with infill dating from the time the later stages were added, were not originally glazed like the corresponding lancets of the centre part, but had frames fixed in them presumably for louvers. Inside were great ringing chambers; belfries, it is now thought, were intended in the c 13 to be built higher up (though bells were hung in the s w chamber later on). It might be fairer to say that the intentions of the c 13 tower-builders, once they had decided on towers, may have been more tremendous than the available cash. As for the upper stages added in the c 14–15, see w *towers* below. (Dr Rodwell's comments on recent investigations have been a great help to this paragraph.)

Now for the details, which are necessary in this case to an unusual degree, because apart from its architectural aspects the façade of Wells is the richest receptacle of c 13 SCULP-TURE in England (see the guides by Colchester and by Tudor-Craig available at the cathedral). This display of statues – nearly 300 have been counted as still existing – of course has also its bearing on the architectural argument. It makes one suspect that the master did not after all dream of crags but of an image screen, a reredos as never reredos had been seen before. (It has even been suggested that the w front was an enlarged version of the vanished high altar reredos of *c.* 1200 inside.)

The c 13 front is divided into five parts by six mighty buttresses. At the angles they connect with the equally broad and deep N and s buttresses by broad diagonals which actually hide the real angles of the towers. Horizontally there are five tiers below the zone, where the towers and the middle gable rise independently, the gable incidentally in three more tiers. Perhaps it is this grid of very strong verticals and very insistent horizontals which gives that odd feeling already voiced of some kind of steel scaffolding. The horizontal zones are a plinth, a tier of gabled blank arcades, two tiers linked vertically by the three tall nave w lancets, only slightly stepped, and by two blank lancets of equal height in the w faces of the aisles and between the tower buttresses. Their blankness and the utilitarian little windows in them are a serious blemish, as if pygmies had come to inhabit this mighty rock. The top tier is a frieze of low trefoiled niches. That is the general picture.

The base is the zone of the portals, although the middle one reaches up into the next zone. Nowhere else is the contrast between French and English more apparent than here. Wells has its glorious N porch. Why these niggly w doorways (even though most English church w doorways are so), here just too reminiscent of France to let one forget the wonders of Reims (or of Paris, to choose a more moderate front)? The portals have marble shafts, the nave doorway also has a *trumeau* (of Purbeck this time). The

stiff-leaf capitals are renewed. The arches are firmly moulded, and there are also inner continuous mouldings and hoodmoulds on head-stops. In the tympanum of the middle doorway, in a deeply sunk quatrefoil the seated Virgin with the Child, and in flanking spandrels remains of censing angels. The figures are badly damaged, being so accessible, but must have once been amongst the best at Wells, as befitted this position. (Heads and hands added in 1970 to the central figures provoked a public outcry that eventually led to more thoughtful conservation for all the w front sculpture.) Now all the motifs so far met are motifs familiar from the work further E. But, as we go on to the next zone, we find two novelties: the use of so much marble shafting, and the excessive use of gabled arcading. (On the polished stone used for shafting, see the last paragraph of the *Introduction* above.)

We must now examine this first tier of blank arcading. It runs above the base all along the façade, arched and gabled, except immediately above the arch of the nave portal, where there is an incomprehensible little niche with a Coronation of the Virgin, absurdly small. The niche has a broad shouldered gable, or a trefoiled head with the middle lobe transformed into a gable. The two badly mutilated figures also must once have been enjoyable sculpture. The sharp long parallel folds have a good deal of vigour. Above the aisle entrances unfortunately instead of the gabled circles, there are windows – Perp now. As for the rest, there are trefoiled arches with their own little gables under each main gable. Under each sub-arch stood a statue on a bracket. Few survive on the w front itself. But as the towers project so far beyond the aisles the whole system of the façade is carried round them, and on the N tower, for some reason, plenty escaped the vandals of the c 16 and c 17 – fifteen in the row we are looking at now. They are, it has repeatedly been said by scholars, the best of the Wells statues. That is true, but it is not saying very much. (This and the following were written when the statues were still encrusted with dirt and cement. In 1980, when the statues were emerging from their lime poultices, experts reported carving 'of staggering quality' – or, at least, remains that implied the original existence of quality. On the restorations of 1870–1931, see below.)

Consider the possible comparisons. One need not go to Reims, the obvious source of many, or to the Chartres porches, the source of others, to see that Wells is not and never was of that calibre. The angels of the Westminster transepts are sufficient proof of England's capability, if not of reaching the highest mastery of France, at least of doing better than Wells. And Westminster, though the rebuilding here started more than fifty years after Wells, is hardly later in its sculpture. For the style of the Wells statuary in its relation to France makes it clear beyond doubt that this w front was not given its figures before *c.* 1235. The

157. WELLS West front, C13 king's head No. 151, before restoration

158. WELLS North-west tower, C13 king's head No. 18a, after restoration

sources, to say it again, are Chartres at its most advanced (Ste Modeste, St Theodore, Visitation, i.e. of *c.* 1225–35) and the w portals of Reims. Now at Reims the comparable figures (s portal, and Queen of Sheba and Solomon, also certain kings under canopies high up, along the nave) were not carved or put up before *c.* 1230. But attempts to stress connections with the portals of Notre Dame in Paris (possibly begun *c.* 1210 but probably a little later) are in my opinion over-stressed.

In the spandrels between the sub-arches are sunk quatrefoils, and these were filled with three-quarter figures of angels. Again, what remains of them is good sculpture. In the spandrels between two main arches is another series of such quatrefoils, but here the master chose stories told in detached, rather than single, figures, stories again told on too small a scale. They are from the Old Testament on the s, from the New Testament on the N side (e.g., from l. to r., the Transfiguration, Christ among the Doctors, the Creation of Adam, Adam and Eve, Adam delving and Eve spinning, the Building of the Ark). The quatrefoils incidentally, instead of stopping at the corners, break round them which, as they are sunk, results in strange dents in the

outline. It is worth speculating on this apparent solecism (which also occurs at Salisbury). It seems to imply a denial of the stony solidity of a front. What the designer has done was to him so much a screen, that like embossed cardboard or leather it could be pressed round corners.

Then the window zone. There is enough space between the three nave lancets for two tiers of canopied niches with figures. Excessively thin marble shafts run up l. and r. of them. The figures are of normal proportions below, of exaggerated length above. If this proportion was chosen because the figures would always be seen from below, as has been suggested, that device has certainly not come off and they look as weird and gaunt as if they stood right in front of us. Again, who could deny it, although they are also among the best at Wells, there is not one amongst them that could move us like a figure at Chartres or indeed at Bamberg or Strasbourg. The blank windows in the aisle parts and the outer parts are also flanked by the marble 'stove-pipes'. They have here a vertical row of crockets behind – a motif first used at Lincoln (cf. Geoffrey's piers where E transepts and choir aisles meet, in our northern volume).

So far nothing has been said about the buttresses. But at this stage they take over the chief display of sculpture. Corresponding to the lancets and blank lancets there are two tiers of statues, one on each tier against the front of the buttress and two against each side. At this height the destroyers could do less damage, and so here, though the figures are defaced, the intended impression of the statuary screen can still be obtained. The figures against the front are seated, those against the sides stand. Artistic inspiration seems to come from Reims and Chartres still. The niches are again trefoiled and gabled and flanked by marble shafts with vertical stone crocketing behind them. The shafts carry arches high above the upper image niches and, where there is space for a pair of niches, the arches are treated as sub-arches only and gathered under a main arch (that is the Y-motif which we have seen in the N porch) with intersected mouldings (which again we have seen in the N porch).

Above these arches, which are once more gabled, runs a much less conspicuous zone, no more than a top frieze. This consists of low trefoiled niches with scenes from the Resurrection of the Dead in small figures. Much stiff-leaf in the spandrels.

The stepped gable above the nave is in three tiers, the lowest of cinquefoiled arches, the rest of trefoiled arches, and the topmost with an elongated cusped oval niche in which Christ sat in Judgement (the lower half of the figure remains) and two trefoiled niches, no doubt for angels, l. and r. At the angles again quatrefoils breaking round. Pinnacles l. and r. of the gable, circular with conical roofs. The images of the Apostles in the niches of the second tier are not C13 work. They look c. 1400 and were probably carved when the upper N W tower was built. The odd C14 or C15 pinnacle set on the middle of the gable requires a further remark a little later.

An elating little discovery has been made on the W front (Rodwell): in the centre part, behind each of the quatrefoil figures and above each of the nine angel figures higher up, there are holes right through the wall, thought to be for voices or trumpets on Easter Day or to welcome processions. There is a choristers' or trumpeters' gallery in the thickness of the W wall at quatrefoil level, and there is a bench in the nave roof, above the high vault, for them to stand on. Perhaps this was part of the plan that placed the tier of Resurrection scenes at the top of the main screen directly below that tier of angels against the nave gable. So the great outdoor stage-set was fitted for sound.

Before leaving the W front, two more things must be said. One is that restorations (prior to the work of the 1970s and 80s) certainly added a hardness to what was somewhat wiry from the beginning. In fact, the restorations of 1903 and 1925–31, with their cement-sloping and metal clamps, were far more damaging than the one of 1870–3 more often blamed. So the effects of these perhaps warp our judgement. (That just admission, it must also be said, dates from the 1950s.) The other point is the matter of colour. To visualize the façade as it was when completed about 1250 or 1260 it must be remembered what part colour played in it. Enough remains have been found to make it certain that the backgrounds of the niches were painted in strong colours and the figures as well, and we can assume from evidence in other places that gold was extensively used too. It is hard for us to imagine what that must have done to the façade and harder still to decide whether we would have liked it. It was without any doubt very much like a painted Gothic polyptych – perhaps an enlarged version, indeed, of the high reredos inside. (For recent comment, while restoration still proceeds, see Tudor-Craig in Colchester 1982.)

That was the end of the main work of the first period, apart from the first set of cloisters (see below) and the CHAPTER-HOUSE SUBSTRUCTURE. The undercroft, passage to the undercroft, and staircase to the chapter house were all laid out together and built to a level above the top of the plinth (Colchester and Harvey 1974). That much must have been done soon after Westminster chapter house was laid out; i.e., as we shall see inside, the work at Wells must have started by c. 1250 or at the latest 1255. Then work apparently stopped and was only resumed in 1286. Yet the window tracery on the staircase is still in a transitional style: two circles with sexfoils below one large circle with three small encircled sexfoils, the spandrels not yet pierced as in bar tracery, but a little sunk. Presumably these stair windows were at least designed, if not built, in the 1250s.

The CHAPTER HOUSE proper, however, as proved by its window tracery, cannot have been completed until about forty years later. That is, work must have proceeded in the 1290s after work on the substructure resumed in 1286. (A document of 1307 refers to building expenses for the chapter house in the past tense.) Some tracery details are identical with those of side windows at St Etheldreda, Ely Place, London, of c. 1290. Ogee arches are frequent in the chapter-house windows, but otherwise the tracery here is still a little closer to late C13 traditions than is that of the new E end. The chapter-house workmen were obviously not the same as those on the Lady Chapel (see below). The chapter-house windows are splendidly broad, of four lights, divided into two-plus-two. Each light has an ogee-head and a pointed trefoil above. Each two lights have a circle with an ogee sexfoil, each four lights a large circle again with an ogee sexfoil. Buttresses with gables decorated with ballflower. Big gargoyles. Top frieze of sunk blank arches of two lights with Y-tracery, all in continuous mouldings. Then a later pierced parapet with diagonally set pointed quatrefoils and diagonally set pinnacles.

The LADY CHAPEL was begun at an unknown date, outside the old E end. (Toothings above the roof of the present retrochoir, apparently intended for flying buttresses, have been thought to prove that the Lady Chapel stood detached for a long time, but no such buttresses were ever built there, Dr Rodwell says; moreover, the plinth of the Lady Chapel continues in one build round part of the retrochoir: Colchester and Harvey 1974.) The involvement of the Lady Chapel with the retrochoir will become clear inside. There is reason to assume that the Lady Chapel was complete by 1319. The very original design of the window tracery looks earlier than that; for it contains no ogee forms. The motif of the window tracery is arches upon arches – a kind of pre-reticulation – and the arches are really spherical triangles, each pointing upwards. (Bony (1979) sees knowledge of Islamic forms behind this, and also compares this staggered piling-up to the Bishop's Throne at Exeter.) The parapet of the Lady Chapel has an openwork frieze of cusped triangles, and it may well be that this motif was created here, a motif which was then extended to the presbytery and its clerestory, the crossing tower, and more or less the whole cathedral, as well as to the eastern arm of Bristol Cathedral, and in the end to a whole group of Perp Somerset churches.

The RETROCHOIR AND EAST TRANSEPTS, for reasons which the interior will reveal, must have gone up at about the same time as the Lady Chapel. (These are low E transepts, not branching from an E crossing as at Lincoln and Salisbury.) The window tracery is more varied and unquestionably later than that of the Lady Chapel. The E chapels of the retrochoir e.g. have reticulation, a mature ogee motif, and also a kind of straightened-out reticulation which, though in accordance with certain occasional and interspersed perversities of the early C 14 at Bristol, seems to point, in this consistent presentation, to the proximity of the Perp style. The E transept E windows have a motif of intersected ogee arches, familiar from Bristol Cathedral, the end and w windows are again reticulated. The chancel aisles carry on with intersected ogees or reticulation.

The PRESBYTERY clerestory is of the same stage of tracery design as its aisles, but then, when we come to the w bays (i.e. the late C 12 CHOIR bays remodelled), curiously bleak, as if money or zest had given out. The most extraordinary piece of the design is in the high gable of the presbytery. The great seven-light window here, undoubtedly close to the Perp style, thus cannot be earlier than 1335 or so (and the heraldry in the glass, without French fleur-de-lys in Edward III's arms, belongs to the period 1327–39). The main division is into two-plus-three-plus-two lights. It is not done by sub-arches but by running the two main mullions right up into the main arch – a hallmark of the Perp. The three-light middle part then has again the new Perp type of panelling, the side parts a painfully lopsided arrangement of two ogee-lights with one reticular unit above the one foiled circle squeezed next to it towards the middle and crying out aloud for a companion. This wilfulness is Dec, in the Bristol spirit, but the rest, to say it again, must be called Perp. The gable over the window is as curious. It has what normally would be two two-light windows (to the space between vault and roof) with Y-tracery and an almond-shape above, subdivided into four almond-shapes. But every curve is rigidly straightened out, and the whole made into a pattern of lozenges echoing the pitch of the gable.

The CROSSING TOWER belongs to the years 1315–22. However, its exterior was altered c. 1440, after a fire in 1439. It is a noble design, calm and peaceful, and deeply satisfying from wherever it is seen. The C 14 work stands on a short storey left of Jocelyn's time – with the slim blank arcades with continuous moulding that his master mason liked so much. This low lantern of Jocelyn was raised in 1315–22 by a tall storey with, on each side, three pairs of very elongated lancets. The master of c. 1440 then filled in the lancets and decorated them in his own taste. The arrangement now appears of three two-light bell-openings with a transom, repeated below by blank two-light windows without transoms. There the proportions of the whole composition are wonderfully felicitous. Each light of the bell-openings is given a small foiled circle and on it a gable; the blank openings below have a short piece of quatrefoil frieze above each light. The buttressing etc. is brilliant. The clasping buttresses of the C 14 are continued and end in pinnacles with their attached sub-pinnacles. Little niches for statues in the middle of each pinnacle. Between the buttresses are three panels separated again by (much finer) buttresses. They turn diagonal higher up and end in shorter pinnacles above the top parapet. This parapet has the same frieze of pierced cusped triangles as we have already found on the Lady Chapel. All buttresses have at half-height little ogee gables.

The upper WEST TOWERS were built later. (On intentions for them, see below; also *Interior*, Nave, w tower chapels.) The sw tower was mainly paid for by Bishop Harewell in his lifetime, i.e. before 1386, and the master mason was *William Wynford*. Bishop Bubwith left money for the NW tower in 1424. Both towers have the same design and are, like the crossing tower, the source of a group of Somerset towers. They lack the fine harmony with the previous work which the crossing tower achieves. They stand bold and bare on the mid-C 13 front. Each C 13 buttress is continued by one with two thin diagonal buttresses. In the N tower the two towards the w have richly canopied niches with images. These C 14 or C 15 main buttresses end with gables and pinnacles. At that point they throw back an inclined plane up to the bell-stage, like a huge final set-off. Out of that situation develop big diagonal

buttresses divided into two. These are panelled and have thin diagonal shafts at the angles. The bell-openings are pairs of two lights, with diagonally set shafts between and with simple Perp tracery. The distinguishing feature is their very long blank continuation below, by descending mullions, as it were. The whole can be seen as huge, immensely long windows, left blank up to their transoms. As compared with the crossing tower, all uprights are stressed much more vigorously. The intended effect is unmitigated verticality. It was balance in the crossing tower. In the w towers it is therefore fatal that no crown whatever was put on. The whole *slancio* is abruptly cut short, and there is nothing but a low parapet with blank arcading and a silly frill of the smallest battlements. May it be suggested that the equally silly single pinnacle on the apex of the stepped gable of the nave was a trial pinnacle for one of the w towers? Pairs of them might have been set on the twin buttresses at the angles. It is now realized (Dr Rodwell) that the C14–15 stages were meant to have spires: under the post-medieval roofs in each tower are eight enormous corbels which carried or were meant to carry the feet of spires, which, if built, were removed before the first engraved view of c. 1650.

INTERIOR

The nave is in its interior completely of Jocelyn's time, and it is rightly taken as early C13 Wells *par excellence*. But we do not know when it was begun, and whether it was begun to the plan of c. 1185–90. Once again, if we assume that work started at the E end and proceeded to the w, it is the choir that we must look to, to see what was planned at Wells under Reginald, a few years before the saintly Bishop Hugh started work on his choir at Lincoln. Now of the late C12 choir at Wells only the piers and arches survive. The rest was replaced or remodelled, and we have to consider the transepts at the same time to arrive at a composite picture of the original design.

The situation in England was this. The Gothic style, as created in France about 1140, had reached England in a first fragmentary and later complete but much simplified form in the buildings of the Cistercian order about 1150–60. As a reflexion of this e.g. the pointed arches of c. 1160–70 at Malmesbury can be explained. (And cf. the transitional style of the vestibule to Bristol chapter house.) Then the first complete building moulded on the pattern of the French Early Gothic cathedrals had gone up at Canterbury in 1175–85, directed at first by a Frenchman. Wells and Lincoln followed ten to fifteen years later. By then France had moved on, from the Early to the High Gothic, in a growth from cathedral to cathedral until the master of Chartres found the final solution. The great creative genius was this master of Chartres who began work in 1195. His design is characterized by far more determined verticalism than had been ventured upon before, by slender circular piers with four thin attached shafts, by vaulting-shafts standing immediately on their capitals, by the substitution of a triforium for the gallery, and by oblong quadripartite vaults.

Now the master of Wells was in almost complete disagreement with these most recent French tendencies. The earliest evidences of his work are the piers and arches in the three w bays of his CHOIR. The piers are broad and complex in section, spreading generously rather than pulled together, and his vaulting-shafts do not stand on their capitals. Horizontals are not sacrificed to verticals. The piers in particular are without doubt a demonstration – an anti-Canterbury demonstration soon to be an anti-Lincoln demonstration as well. They consist of a solid core of Greek cross shape and attached to it twenty-four shafts in groups of three in trefoil grouping, three to each main direction, three to each diagonal. The abaci are square over the diagonals, polygonal in the main directions. The arches have a variety of roll mouldings, three for each diagonal, four under each arch, two plus two for the outer mouldings, and a hoodmould in addition (chipped off in the choir, on head-stops in the transepts). The capitals in the choir are the most telling feature of the earliest phase. They are of the stiff-leaf variety, but the leaves are small, in one or two rows, still rather like the crockets of French capitals. Only one at the N W end, by the crossing, is livelier and has a small head peering out. The aisle walls are divided by triple shafts as well.

Above the arcade in an English cathedral of the C12 or C13 one would expect a gallery. At Wells there is a triforium instead. In the three choir bays, behind the curious stone grille the C14 placed in front of it, is a low triforium grouped in pairs and detailed with continuous mouldings, exactly as can be more easily seen on the E and w sides of the transepts.

So we can safely go to the TRANSEPTS for an impression of the whole of the design of Wells in c. 1185–1200. The only important difference between choir and transept is a step forward in the development of stiff-leaf foliage. The treatment now is both bigger and freer. The leaves curl over more boldly, the motifs are larger, the carving deeper. One other difference should at once be noted – as it is also a difference within the transepts indicating probably the way they were built. The E aisle capitals are wholly foliage, the w aisle capitals introduce with some gusto a good many pretty figure motifs: a bald head, a man pulling a thorn out of his foot, fights, a grape harvest, a bridled woman etc.

The first pier of the N transept E aisle from the crossing has a peculiarity worth noting. The triple shafts to the E are cut off, and there is a long stiff-leaf corbel instead, with a lizard on it – forerunner of so many long foliage corbels in

160. WELLS South aisle of the nave, early C 13

English cathedrals (that is, unless this treatment is contemporary with later insertion of a screen between aisle and transept). And the first capital from the crossing on the E side differs from the others and seems further evidence of renewal after damage in 1248 (by the 'tholus', or lantern, falling from the crossing tower). It is similar to capitals on the chapter-house staircase.

Looking now at the triforium and trying to analyse the aesthetic difference it makes as compared with the galleries at Canterbury or Lincoln, we must first dispose of one point of historical interest. To have a triforium instead of a gallery may sound an extremely progressive touch, but in fact the triforium at Wells is more like that of the C 11 at the Trinité at Caen than like that of Chartres. For at Caen and Wells it is primarily a horizontal band, at Chartres it is subordinated to the verticals. The Wells triforium in the transepts is grouped into two twin openings per bay, each bay separated from the next by the vaulting-shafts, which start, not on the capitals below, but on corbels above the triforium sill. So the sill is drawn as one uninterrupted horizontal. The triforium openings have continuous mouldings (a roll and a chamfer), a favourite motif of Wells, as has been observed à propos of the exterior, but a motif which can be traced back to the Late Norman of e.g. Bristol. The corbels of the vaulting-shafts incidentally again have foliage and heads on the E side, seated figures on the W. The profile of the aisle vaults is three rolls arranged in a trefoil fashion, of the high vaults two rolls flanking a triangle or spur. The aisles have no bosses, the high vaults have bosses with soberly-treated stiff-leaf. In this connection we must also remember the stiff-leaf of the doorway to the cloister from the s end of the s transept's w aisle. There also capitals are still reminiscent of crockets, though the doorway is probably of c. 1240 (see Exterior above).

A fact worth much emphasis is the oblong shape of the transept high vaults. It is true that Durham had already had oblong vaults, but the Wells vaults are much more understood in the French Gothic way. They are the one really French Gothic motif at Wells. For the memorable fact remains that Wells, though in nothing else French, is yet wholly Gothic. At Canterbury (and at Chichester, where the Gothic retrochoir is exactly contemporary with the start at Wells) round arches are not eliminated. Nor are they at Glastonbury, a few miles from Wells. Wells is the first Gothic building in England in which the pointed arch is used exclusively.

The next detail to be observed refers to the end walls of the two transepts. They are identical inside, though, as we have seen, they differ outside. There are windows below, separated by triple shafts, and windows above with depressed two-centred rere-arches. But between these two zones the triforium runs here as a blank frieze of five arches, not divided into groups. This must be stressed; for it contributes the main innovation of the nave and the most memorable feature of the Wells interior.

In the NAVE now one can sit down and absorb enough of the C 13 to be able to decide what the master of Wells was after. To do that one must try to forget about what is without any doubt the most obtrusive motif at Wells, the grossly scaled strainer arches. They will have to receive their share of attention in due course, and they deserve it. Meanwhile the crossing ought to be visualized as it would be without them, also without the fan-vault in the tower. The crossing has its details of c. 1200 (now only to be seen by ascending above both C 15 fan-vault and C 14 stone grid): two tiers of arcading, both now blank, but the upper perhaps intended to let light in. They have shafts with moulded capitals, and the lower tier yet smaller blank arches inserted oddly in their lower halves. That view is now doubly barred.

To return to the nave, it is perhaps best to turn w to see it, although the interior design of the w front, while less demonstratively different from that of the nave walls than are the strainer arches, is yet not in harmony with it either. Even so the purity of the nave will win; for here – this cannot be stressed enough – is a design of great intrinsic beauty and of supreme consistency preserved without any later interference, not even in the vaults.

The designer of the nave – he could be the man who had designed choir and transepts, but at a more mature age – drew his conclusions from what has already been called Wellsian as against French: the stress on horizontals. The nave is ten bays long. Piers, aisle shafts, aisle vaults, high vaults are as in the transepts (except that the piers now have the subtle touch of keeling the shafts pointing to the diagonals and that the aisle vaults have small bosses of stiff-leaf). But the great innovation is this. The grouping of the triforium in twins is given up, and it runs through from E to W as one seemingly interminable band. To achieve that, the designer pushed up the corbels for the vaulting-shafts to just below clerestory level. That removes one more interference of the vertical with the horizontal.

These are the principal features. They had a second effect, besides horizontal stress, and one which is equally important. One feels sheltered between walls at Wells, and that also, it is my experience, irritates the Frenchman. Perhaps he is not wholly wrong, because horizontality and solidity of the walls are indeed presented with almost too blunt a directness at Wells. Lincoln also allows the horizontal its English place. But one does not feel horizontal strips, as one feels at Wells, even on the ground-level. For so massive are the piers at Wells and so finely subdivided that they also, in perspective, form one strip or band.

Some more differences between the nave and its aisles and the transepts and their aisles must now be pointed out, although they are subordinate to the ones described so far.

161. WELLS Nave capitals, early C13 (detail)

The triforium has paterae of stiff-leaf immediately above each arch and in the spandrels between the arches. This and the bosses of the aisle vaults point in the direction of increased richness, and we shall see presently that within the nave such a development also took place.

Meanwhile the inside of the w front must first be looked at. It is clearly designed to a different scheme. The doorway has a depressed two-centred arch and is flanked by trefoiled blank arcading. Marble shafts (but here of Draycott marble) are again used as they are so excessively outside. The aisle doorways place their depressed arches on vertical springers. The zone of the big w windows was reshaped in the Perp period. The horizontal ribs are patent, also above, where the Perp capitals carry E.E. arches with dogtooth decoration. Stiff-leaf also reappears in the top spandrels.

As the towers stand out to the N and S, there are separate chapels under them, with eight ribs leading to an opening (for hoisting bells). There is a certain restlessness in the design owing to the fact that the capitals of the shafts of the windows or blank arches sit up higher than the capitals of the vaulting-shafts. In the s wall of the s tower, up in the lunette, is a prettily cusped stepped blank arcade such as are to be found also at the E end of Ely Cathedral.

In 1928 John Bilson published a paper on Wells in which he showed a break in style running through the nave along a joint clearly definable and, as building operations go, naturally lying further w on the ground floor than on the upper floors. It runs up six bays from the E below, five bays from the E above. Some of the differences are not easily visible: vertical instead of diagonal tooling, and larger ashlar blocks. But the abandonment of head-stops at the ends of the hoodmoulds e.g. will be noticed by everybody. This 'break' was probably due to the Interdict, during which Bishop Jocelyn was out of England, i.e. 1209–13.

The most telling change is that in the character of the stiff-leaf CAPITALS. Wells is the best place in England to enjoy and study stiff-leaf. Stiff-leaf foliage was an English speciality anyway; C13 capitals of stylized foliage as

162. WELLS Chapter-house undercroft, *c.* 1255–90, in 1823, with pyx canopy

beautiful as those of Wells and Lincoln do not exist any-where outside England. They make the crocket capitals of France look dull. Wells presents us with the whole gamut of stiff-leaf, from the timid beginnings of the choir to the classicity, as it were, of the E bays of the nave and to the Baroque effusiveness of the W bays and the tower chapels. The capitals here assume indeed a lushness, a depth of carving, a fullness in their overhang which goes quite beyond what older men had attempted before. But what date does this end of the work represent? There is no certainty, whatever answers have been attempted. All that can be said has already been said, namely that the cathedral was consecrated in 1239 and that the sculpture of the W front was not begun before *c.* 1235–40. Is it not most probable then that the choir was the work before Jocelyn, and that transepts, crossing and nave grew from about 1190–1200 to 1239? (On the use of a different stone while Glastonbury, after a fire of 1184, was monopolizing the Doulting quarry, see the *Introduction* above.)

Next, the interior of the CHAPTER-HOUSE SUBSTRUC-TURE, and first the passage to the undercroft. The doorway from the N chancel aisle into it has one order of Purbeck shafts, two capitals rather like those near the W end of the nave (one with birds and grapes), a depressed two-centred arch the inner mouldings of which die into the jambs, and a gable on large and excellent head-stops, and with bar tracery: a quatrefoil in a circle. This is the first bar tracery in the cathedral, and bar tracery was not introduced into England until 1245–50 (at Westminster Abbey). That provides a convenient *terminus post quem*. The passage to the undercroft is low, but impressively treated, with wall-shafts, stiff-leaf capitals which look earlier than those of the doorway, rere-arches of the windows dying into the jambs, and with transverse arches, ribs, and a ridge rib, again the earliest in the cathedral. Ridge ribs are a Lincoln innovation, but had by 1260 also been used at West-minster, at Worcester, at Ely etc. The rolls of ribs and arches have fillets. Bosses with figure work. The UNDER-

163 and 164 (*overleaf*).
WELLS Chapter house: staircase, *c.* 1255–90; interior, completed 1306

CROFT itself has sturdy circular piers with plain circular moulded capitals and single-chamfered ribs. Most but not all of the wall-shafts have waterholding bases (a feature occurring at Hailes Abbey, Glos., 1246–51). The middle pier has eight attached shafts against an octagonal core with concave sides (reminiscent of Lincoln). The barred windows have rere-arches. The Perp STOUP or lavabo with a carved pet dog inside gnawing a bone should not be overlooked. How enviably free from considerations of propriety the Middle Ages were!

The STAIRCASE TO THE CHAPTER HOUSE, though not using bar tracery, is yet of the same date as the passage below. Plain doorway from the transept E aisle with a depressed pointed head and continuous moulding. The staircase (with its steps so delightfully uneven) is vaulted in two bays with ridge ribs. The two E vaulting-shafts are placed on two charming figures. The capitals now turn noticeably more naturalistic (all upright leaves, somewhat like the one transept capital renewed after the earthquake) – again a sign of the second half of the century. That goes with the tracery of the windows, as we have seen and can now see again; for the former N window is now above the doorway to the bridge which leads to the Vicars' Hall. It has four lights with two sexfoiled circles and one large eight-foiled one above, not as fully pierced as bar tracery.

With the ENTRANCE TO THE CHAPTER HOUSE we are firmly in the C 14. The walls are very thick, and so the wall-shafts and *trumeau* and tracery, all very light and transparent, are duplicated in two identical layers with a little vaulted space between. The outer as well as the inner entrance has above the paired doorway arches a large spheric triangle. Large open cusping, with no *finesses*; like great thorns. The reveals or side walls of the little intermediate lobby have blank arcading with a curious top consisting of two sexfoiled circles one above the other, and two eight-foiled almond-shapes side by side, the whole like a paraphrase on the theme of the elongated quatrefoil. The vault again has ridge ribs, and a large boss.

The CHAPTER HOUSE is one of the most splendid examples in England of the style which might be called the tierceron style, developed at Exeter in the last quarter of the C 13 and most fully in its presbytery of c. 1291–9. Tiercerons were first used at Lincoln, and next at Ely and Westminster Abbey. But it is only where they are multiplied and three pairs sprung from one springer that the palm-tree effect results, which makes Exeter so memorable an experience. Yet the Wells chapter house goes beyond Exeter. From the central pier of the Westminster chapter house sprang sixteen ribs. The number was twenty at Lincoln. At Exeter, if one continued the scheme of the vaulting-shafts full circle one would arrive at twenty-four. At Wells, thirty-two ribs rise from the pier. (A further step was to be the centralized fan-vault, about half a century

later, at Hereford.) At Wells clusters of five wall-shafts support the vault from the corners. The walls have the usual seats under blank arcading below the windows, seven bays on each side. The cusping of the arches undulates. The gables rest on head-corbels and have crockets. Pointed trefoils in the spandrels and slim little buttresses and pinnacles between the gables. The whole panel of each of the seven bays is framed by a frieze of ballflower. The inner window surrounds are also decorated with ballflower. The vault has at its apex an octagon of ridge ribs. This does not stand in line with the sides of the outer octagon, but (inevitably) side against corner, and corner against side. The same had already been done at Lincoln (and was to happen on a more elaborate scale in the relation of Ely lantern to the Octagon vaults below). The bosses are still fairly near to nature in their foliage.

In comparing the chapter house with the Lady Chapel, Mr Colchester suggests that the chapter-house design was by a different man working with knowledge of the Westminster court style (as exemplified e.g. in the tracery of St Etheldreda, Ely Place, London, of c. 1290), rather than someone working entirely in the West Country tradition. Yet this man clearly knew the Exeter vaulting system; and Exeter's window tracery has many details of the London St Etheldreda type. (Kidson, in fact, suggested that he came from Exeter.) In describing the Lady Chapel, on the other hand, we shall find ourselves referring, not to London or to Exeter, but to Bristol.

The LADY CHAPEL in its interior is so much part of the whole rebuilding of the E end that the one cannot be described without the whole. It is indeed the great fascination of the parts that they are so inseparable, and the way in which this great master has interpenetrated Lady Chapel and retrochoir is a feat of Dec spatial imagination as great as that of the master of Bristol. (What actually happens spatially at Wells had never been sufficiently analysed before the original edition of this description; further analyses since have included those of Harvey and Kidson and Bony, but before 1958 only Pevsner's *Outline of European Architecture* (1943 etc.) had begun to tell England of England's early C 14 design in space.)

The Lady Chapel at first sight seems easy enough to understand. It seems a room of one bay with an apse of three sides of an octagon. Trefoiled wall-shafts with knobbly capitals, windows of that ingenious tracery which has already been described (see *Exterior* above). Fleuron band below the windows. The S doorway and the sedilia are of excellent quality, with ogee arches, crockets and finials: in fact, the sedilia were added by *Benjamin Ferrey* in 1843, and the S doorway was recarved at the same time. (Which shows something about the maturing attitude to Gothic of Early Victorian architects; Ferrey had been a pupil of the elder Pugin.) But then, standing in this space, as soon as

165. WELLS Lady Chapel, completed by c. 1319, and retrochoir, by c. 1325

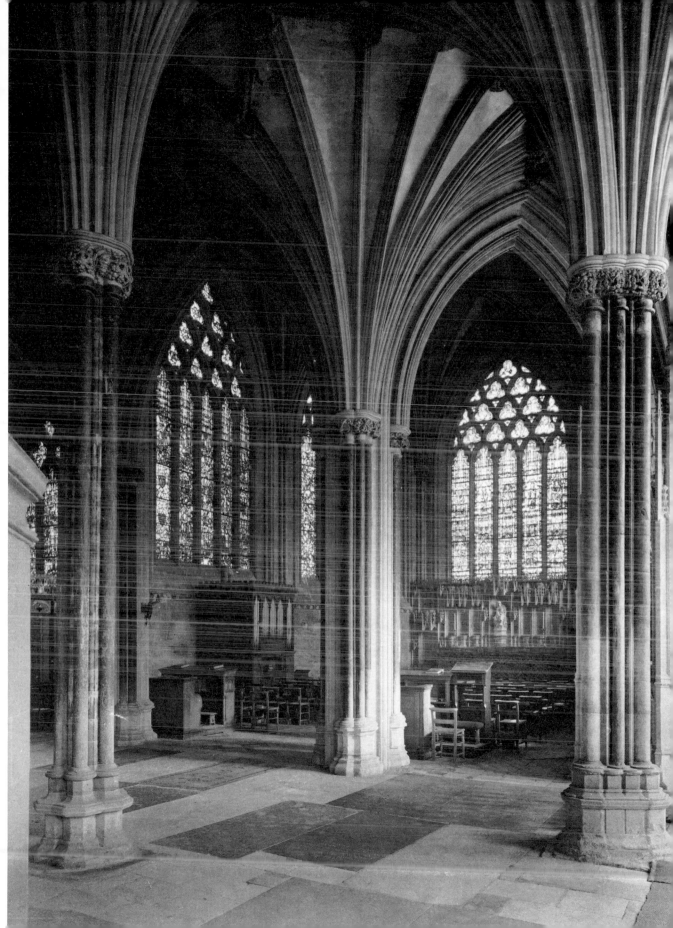

166. WELLS Lady Chapel vault, by c. 1319

one looks back or up into the vault, one realizes that one is in a room meant to be read as an elongated octagon. The w sides of the octagon stand on two clustered shafts and merge into the retrochoir. The vault has the first liernes of Wells, liernes about contemporary with those of Bristol choir. They are made to appear a star within a star. From each shaft rise diagonal ribs and three pairs of tiercerons. The inner star is formed by the third tiercerons and not by liernes, but the outer consists of liernes. Bosses and sprays of knobbly foliage at the rib junctions. The central boss has Christ Enthroned. The only aesthetically unresolved problem is that of the difference in height between the Lady Chapel and the retrochoir. Here the master of Bristol, having a hall-church to play in, was in an easier position. At Wells the three w arches are lower than the others and the space above them is disappointingly filled by blank arches. But the triumph of the Lady Chapel's subtly irregular vault, as Mr Harvey has pointed out, is that it is like a dome. Perhaps it is related to pier-less chapter-house vaults: see Southwell. Bony calls it a domical net vault with Islamic overtones. Its recent cleaning further emphasizes its mysterious ambiguities.

The RETROCHOIR is all of a piece with the chapels l. and r. of the Lady Chapel and with the E transepts, and all are part of the same ingenious spatial conceit, introducing further surprises. From outside, one has seen how much lower all this is than the Lady Chapel, and also how square and rectangular and normal it seems (like Salisbury, except that there the E transepts are not part of the E end composition). But inside, the sensitive visitor is at once thrown into a pleasing confusion. There are six clusters of shafts in the retrochoir plus the two intermediate piers at the E end of the chancel itself. It takes time to realize why they are all placed as they are. The two easternmost and largest piers we have already located as part of the Lady Chapel octagon. Then there are piers to mark the w ends of the two eastern side chapels, the chapels which flank the Lady Chapel. They naturally stand in axis with the chapel walls. Moreover they are in axis with the arcade between chancel and chancel aisles, and they form part of the initial rectangularity. But the next two clusters a little to the w of these are again in axis with the Lady Chapel w piers. That is unexpected, in fact unnecessary, but it is where the designer reveals his genius. For by this means, floating in the open space of the retrochoir, an elongated hexagon is formed – at r. angles to the elongated octagon of the Lady Chapel. That the two intermediate piers of the E arcade of the chancel are not placed so as to be in line with the w piers of the hexagon is an additional complication which, instead of heightening the aesthetic significance of the whole, only involved the designer in unnecessary difficulties as soon as he had to invent and set out vaults. It will be realized that in several places odd triangular spaces would have to be vaulted, and the master makes his appreciation of this known by giving the w pier of either E chapel a triangular shape. The Dec style always liked the diagonal and so also the triangle. Yet however one sorts it out, there were bound to remain *Resträume*, as Dehio called them when he wrote his classic analysis of Vierzehnheiligen.

It will no doubt by now be obvious to anyone who has tried to follow this description that English Dec space can be as intricate and as thrilling as German Rococo space. The vaults here are all of the new lierne kind except for the E chapels which are easily disposed of by diagonal ribs, ridge ribs and one set of tiercerons. The E transepts, being square, could again receive a lierne star without much difficulty, though one should remember that liernes were still a very new toy. But the centre was the problem, and the combination here of lierne stars of various patterns

with the triangles. How it is done cannot be described and can only be drawn by the expert. But one should not shirk the effort of understanding it. It is like penetrating a piece of complicated polyphonic music. Nor was the master wholly successful. In one place indeed he has broken down, or someone took over who was incapable of understanding the original plan. From the massive N E and S E piers of the chancel rise, amongst other arches and ribs, three to the E which must have turned out to be so useless that lions are called in to bite them off. This is a ruthless procedure and one which a less naive age would not have allowed itself.

A clue to the identity of the master mason here is the two-stage plinth, or double-base, of each retrochoir pier. This unusual formation is identical to that of the front piers of the Exeter pulpitum (completed 1324), built under Thomas of Witney. In 1323 a *Thomas the Mason* witnessed a document at Wells. It is likely that the same man was in charge in both places. (Coldstream 1976; Bony 1979; forthcoming revised ed. of Harvey 1954.)

The CHANCEL AND CHANCEL AISLES offered less scope for spatial play. In the aisles the difference in the shafts (e.g. the use of Purbeck marble) and in the capitals from the work of c. 1200 is at once seen. The vaults are lierne stars of yet a different pattern (without any diagonal ribs or ridge ribs), and they were substituted for the original, simple, quadripartite vaults in the w bays also. There are again no real bosses but rather sprays of foliage, where the ribs meet.

The chancel (to continue that term, since the C 12 choir and the C 14 presbytery were made one space) is, especially in its upper parts, the foremost piece of design in England of the few but interesting years between Bristol and Gloucester. If the Wells E end was complete by 1326, we have every reason to assume that the high walls and vaults belong to the 1330s. They are therefore not earlier in date than the Gloucester s transept, though they are earlier in style. For while Gloucester, in spite of certain motifs and attitudes which are inspired by Bristol and must be called still Dec, is in its essentials Perp, the chancel at Wells, in spite of certain motifs which are in the Perp spirit, and of which some have already been commented on, is in its essentials Dec. This must be demonstrated.

The contrast to the late C 12 choir arcades is of course evident everywhere: now more finely divided piers, the principal shafts of Purbeck marble with foliage capitals, the less stressed parts without any capitals – a Bristol device. Thus a continuous moulding runs up all the way to the vault and frames arcade bay and clerestory bay together (shades of the Glastonbury transept?). But the memorable feature of the Wells chancel is the grille of delicate stone forms between arcade and clerestory, the kind of *Vergitterung*, as German art historians call it, which was the exaggeration of classic French mid-C 13 ideas. The w front

of Strasbourg above the parts of 1275 etc., is the best-known example. But no interior example is as intricate as this Wells stone filigree. Verticals are resolutely emphasized, and between them are three canopied niches in each bay with brackets for images, and two narrow spaces to the l. and r. The verticals are paired thin buttresses, again with narrow ogee niches between. The wall-passage in front of the clerestory windows breaks forward in a significant little triangle above every one of these buttresses: 1-2-2-2-1. Moreover, the wall-passage runs through the piers with diagonally set, ogee-headed entrances, and there are ogee-headed blank panels above them.

As far as possible the same grille was laid over the late c 12 upper wall further w. That all is a little flatter could not be avoided. Yet an attempt is made even here to obtain a feeling of air between transparent front and solid back – by means of a canting forward of the narrow side pieces l. and r. of the outer buttresses.

So far the Dec elements only have been mentioned. But the panelling of a wall-space as such is a Perp idea, the favourite Perp idea, and the fact that the buttresses glorified mullions – stand straight on the arcade arches below, is also Perp. In connection with that the tracery of some of the windows must again be remembered with their unmistakable Perp motifs: the great E window of c. 1335 –9, with its main mullions to the top of the arch, has been described (Exterior).

The vault is a tour de force. Though it keeps transverse arches, it has no intention any longer of stressing bays. There are e.g. no diagonal ribs, only diagonal ribs tying together two bays at a time. There are also no ridge ribs, and instead a lierne pattern crystallized in squares at the ends of a saltire cross – a rectangular, wholly arbitrary pattern. The squares incidentally are cusped, an innovation at Wells, but in fact in imitation of the Bristol choir (cf. also the Tewkesbury chancel vault of c. 1340). Again no bosses, but leaf sprays at the junctions.

Now the CROSSING ARCHES. The crossing tower of 1315 ?? had to be strengthened very soon after its completion, probably c. 1338. The way in which this was done is sensational and incidentally further proof of the dependence of Wells on Bristol. In fact, William Joy, who was then master mason at Wells, is thought to have trained at Bristol. The strainer arches on three sides of the crossing are huge, and they are – according to how one looks at them – two intersected ogee curves or an arch standing on its head on a normal arch. Exactly this is what some tracery and the sedilia had done at Bristol (choir aisle windows and E Lady Chapel there). Also the huge gaping eyes in the spandrels are direct reflexions of the mouchettes in the spandrels of the aisle bridges at Bristol. The arches rise straight from the ground, without responds to carry them, and a thin triple-chamfer with quadrant moulding is car-

ried on all up the crossing piers. Added also to Joy's design (above the c 15 fan-vault) were stone grids with the same moulding.

A tower can be shored up in other ways. That this is the way chosen here shows once again, with no punches pulled, what the Dec style is concerned with in England in matters of space. No smooth vista along the nave and up into crossing tower. Let it be filtered through these gargantuan meshes. The obstacle to the eye is worth more than the vista. (It may be added that the milder strainer arches at the Salisbury E transepts were probably also inserted in the c 14. Were those at Wells thought of as X-symbols of the cathedral's patron, St Andrew?)

The Perp style at Wells (besides its early signs in the chancel grilles and the great E window tracery, and much simpler c 15 tracery in nave and transepts, as well as a standard window type dated 1354 w of the cloisters) appeared of course in the c 15 cloisters (described below). But its grandest appearance was in the late c 14/early c 15 w towers and in the mid-c 15's noble rephrasing of the central tower's exterior – a wonderful achievement of calm power. Both the central tower and the w towers had progeny among the parish churches of Somerset (see the Introduction to B of E North Somerset, Kenneth Wickham's Churches of Somerset, 1952, and Harvey 1978). Inside, the fan-vault in the crossing tower dates from c. 1480.

FURNISHINGS, E TO W

(Excellent booklets, on the stained glass by Colchester, on the clock by Howgrave-Graham, and others, are available at the cathedral.)

Lady Chapel STAINED GLASS E window drastically but conscientiously restored 1845 by *Thomas Willement* (early rediscoverer of the principles of medieval glass design) In the other windows a jumble of fragments, quite effective, including much original figurework, especially in the tracery lights and in the canopies of the main lights. This must date from c. 1315–20. The SE window is the most complete. Most of the glass in the N windows is contemporary but comes from other parts of the church. Amongst details to be looked for is a panel with two of the Three Magi, a trumpeting angel, and several canopies. Also bases for figures; and it is said that this is the earliest occurrence of such bases in England. Another innovation is the use of silver stain (yellow colour obtained from silver nitrate, which first appeared at York by c. 1310: see the companion volume, York, introduction on Dec glass in the nave aisles; and Harvey in Aylmer and Cant 1977: probably an Arab secret from Spain; also in the companion volume, Ely, on fragments from its Lady Chapel). Here yellow is still absent in the tracery lights, but plentiful in

167. WELLS Choir and presbytery, completed by c. 1340

the main lights. – The great C17 LECTERN (see *Nave*) sometimes stands here, as indeed it did in Britton's day.

Retrochoir, east chapels, east transept STAINED GLASS. Of about the same date as in the Lady Chapel. In the SE Chapel S window heads of bishops. Above a Christ in Majesty. In the E window a Christ apparently from a Coronation of the Virgin. In the NE chapel N window more heads of bishops, and above another Christ in Majesty. The SE transept S window is from Rouen, early C16, and of the school of *Arnold van Nijmegen*. – In the NE transept glass of 1902 by *Powell*, designed by *G. P. Hutchinson*. – SCREENS. Fragments of a wooden screen, now N side of SE chapel. – Pretty if sentimental new screen S side of NE chapel, *c.* 1935 by *Sir Ninian Comper*. – Elizabethan screen, NE transept, with unfluted columns. Oak COPE CHEST, said to be C14. – SCULPTURE. C15 stone relief above the altar in the NE transept: Ascension of Christ. Only his feet are visible in the clouds. – MONUMENTS. SE chapel. Canon John Martell † *c.* 1342. Perp tomb-chest. Canopied niche to the E. Three canopies with steep, concave-sided gables with tracery. Panelled vault inside. – SE transept. Bishop Drokensford † 1329. Tomb-chest, with low ogee-headed arches. – Dean Gunthorpe † 1498. Big tomb-chest without effigy. – W wall: small brass to Humphrey Willis † 1618. Probably by *Richard Haydocke*, Fellow of New College, Oxford. Kneeling figure with a remarkable display of inscription. On the r. his hat, sword, violin etc., on the l. the *Armatura Dei*. He looks up and says: 'Da Mihi Domine'. Two cherubs answer: 'Petenti dabitur' and 'Vicisti recipe'. – NE transept. Dean Godelee † 1333. Tomb-chest like Drokensford's with low ogee-headed arches. Of the effigy no details are recognizable. – Bishop Creyghton † 1672. Bulgy sarcophagus. Big recumbent alabaster effigy. – John Milton † 1337. Recumbent effigy.

South chancel aisle STALL-BACKS by *Salvin*: see *Chancel* below. Only the entrances into the chancel are of the C14; crocketed ogee arches flanked by buttresses. – At the corner of the retrochoir's W screen-wall, three MISERICORDS, two C14, one C17, are displayed (see *Chancel*). The subject of Alexander borne aloft by griffins appears on misericords elsewhere (Lincoln, Chester, Manchester etc.), yet this must be the most beautiful example. Also C14 the spirited dragon-slayer. – STAINED GLASS. In the tracery heads some of the best early C14 glass, e.g. a Christ Crucified, a Virgin accompanied by angels, and a St Michael. These figures have all the sophistication and fragility of the architecture of the same moment and also its leaning towards the excessive. In one window heraldic and figure panels of the C17.

MONUMENTS. The interesting monuments at Wells are the retrospective effigies of seven Saxon bishops in the N and S chancel aisles. Five of these are thought to date from

c. 1200 and were made as standing, not recumbent, figures. Dr Rodwell suggests that they originally formed part of a great reredos, each with his relics housed in a chest below his effigy, and with lead fillet inscriptions set in the stone. Of the four figures in the S aisle, three are of this type, firmly modelled with deep rounded regular drapery folds and a deep rounded treatment of the features as well. Yet by the canopies at their heads the original stone block is still felt, and much of the carving seems sunk rather than raised. Canopies vary from trefoiled pointed to a curious shape with lobed sides and straight head. The first from the W has wilder drapery than the others. But all three are work of one workshop (for two more, see N *chancel aisle* below). The first figure from the E is quite different, and is one of the two made as recumbent effigies carved in the style of William Longespée (1227) at Salisbury and therefore of *c.* 1230 (for the other, see N *chancel aisle*). This effigy is far more independent of the coffin-lid; he really seems to lie on it. The pillow instead of a canopy especially helps to create that verisimilitude. The figure now wears a low mitre, and there is a frieze of small stiff-leaf along the edge of the lid. This effigy must be by one of the W front men. When the presbytery was extended *c.* 1325 all the effigies were laid down on the benches of the aisles and all the lead fillets cut up and made into plaques and put inside the accompanying bone chests. (The present stone chests date from 1912.)

Other monuments in the S chancel aisle from the E: Chantry of Bishop Bekynton (bishop 1443–65), dedicated 1452, but made some years earlier. Cadaver below in the opened winding sheet; six low oddly bulbous shafts with little ogee gables and above them demi-figures of angels attached to them. The wings of the angels spread into fern-like leaves. Recumbent effigy on a slab carried by the six shafts. E wall behind the effigy, depressed arch with openwork tracery, demi-figures of angels as cusps, straight top. Intricate little three-bay vault with pendants. Round the tomb or chantry an IRON RAILING (see also iron gates, S transept), sturdy and unrefined, with coarse little heads as occasional decoration, and excellent lock plates. – Bishop (Lord Arthur) Hervey † 1894. Design by *J. L. Pearson*, effigy by *Thomas Brock*, 1897. – Bishop Bitton II † 1274. Incised slab, coffin-shaped, the figure under a trefoiled gable. Next to one at Chelvey in NW Somerset of *c.* 1260, the earliest incised slab in England. – Bishop Harewell † 1386. Alabaster effigy, pair of hares at feet.

North chancel aisle MONUMENTS. Three more of the C13 series, two of the earlier ones, the third again of *c.* 1230 (see S *chancel aisle* above). The earlier have a cinquefoiled canopy, and a trefoiled pointed canopy on stiff-leaf corbels with two angels in the spandrels; the later again lies free of any canopy and wears the low mitre. – E of choir door, Bishop Ralph of Shrewsbury † 1363. Good

169. WELLS Misericord, *c.* 1330–40: dragon-slayer, now mounted *ex situ*

alabaster effigy. – W of choir door, Bishop Berkeley † 1581. Tomb-chest with cusped circles and shields, primitive Roman lettering on lid, no effigy. – STAINED GLASS. In the tracery again some original figures: St Michael, Christ Crucified, St John the Baptist. – In the window E of the doorway to the chapter-house undercroft, glass by *Westlake*, 1885. – In the UNDERCROFT several roundels with early C14 glass. (Britton's view of the undercroft shows the pyx cover now hanging under the N W tower; see *Nave* below).

Chancel The stone STALL-BACKS, THRONE and PULPIT were designed by *Salvin* as part of his restoration of 1848–54 which also included his attentions to the pulpitum (see *Crossing* below). The SUB-STALLS are medieval. There remain sixty-three MISERICORDS of *c.* 1330–40 (plus one of the C17): fifty originally belonged to the upper stalls, from which Salvin removed them; sixty are now attached to the lower rows (Remnant 1969). They are among the best in England, carved with a delicacy as if they were for a less menial purpose. (But see our Exeter text on the occupants' likely nearer view of and care for them. At Wells and no doubt elsewhere each canon had to pay for his stall: Colchester and Harvey 1974.) These date from the same decade as Chichester's and Ely's. Amongst the subjects here are mermaids, a pelican, a hawk and a rabbit, a lion and a griffin, a monkey and an owl, a puppy and a kitten, a cat playing the fiddle, a man slaying a dragon. Three are displayed in the S aisle at the corner of the retrochoir, including the finest, of Alexander. All are illustrated in a cathedral booklet. – STAINED GLASS. The E window with the Tree of Jesse is one of the best examples of mid-C14 glass painting in England. The date is probably *c.* 1339 (no fleur-de-lys in the royal arms in the borders). Large standing figures, under canopies, which is unusual. Much yellow and green, hardly any blue: like 'a meadow full of buttercups and daisies with a patch of red poppies here and there' (Dean Armitage Robinson, quoted by Colchester). On a mid-C19 replica, see the companion volume, Sheffield (Anglican) Cathedral. – Clerestory. The two N E and the two S E windows have large impressive figures of saints, also original, and a year or two later than the E window (fleur-de-lys now present in the borders). – In the tracery heads on both sides small figures belonging to the Resurrection. W of the old windows stained glass on the S side by *Willement*, 1846, on the N side by *Bell* of Bristol, 1851. – ORGAN CASES by *Alan Rome*. E face 1974 in late Gothic/early Renaissance style on the Victorian base and incorporating two carved angels by *J. Forsyth* from the 1857 case (Gillingham).

Crossing CHANCEL SCREEN or pulpitum. Made as good as new by *Salvin* in 1848. He also moved the whole centre forward. But basically the pulpitum must be work of the time of the completion of the chancel, and it is indeed still Dec rather than Perp. Stone, two-storeyed. Tall ogee-headed niches below with brackets for images; low ogee-headed niches above; battlements. The doorway is ogee-cusped and sub-cusped, with openwork cusping and encircled quatrefoils in the spandrels. – w face of the organ: see above. – On the w strainer arch, facing the nave, ROOD FIGURES, 1920, by *G. Tovi* to the design of *Sir Charles Nicholson.*

North transept   SCREENS, to the E aisle: stone, Perp. – To the chancel aisle: remarkable piece, presumably of the time when the chancel had just been finished. Ogee doorway with thin buttresses and pinnacles like that from the aisle into the chancel, but flanked by a vertical band of lozenges, consisting of four concave-sided arches in the four directions – a conception more in the Bristol than the Wells spirit. – DOOR to the chapter-house staircase. C 14, with tracery. – On the staircase, some of the oldest surviving STAINED GLASS in the cathedral. It dates from c. 1290 and consists of patterns in ruby, green, blue and white with grisaille. – In the CHAPTER HOUSE tracery lights some early C 14 glass, also some C 15 heraldic glass. – Back in the N transept, the famous Wells CLOCK, more visited than anything else in the cathedral. Made c. 1390. There is no justification for the name Peter Lightfoot as that of its maker. On the dial the heavenly bodies are represented as they seem to move round the earth in twenty-four hours and thirty days. The small bell in the centre represents the earth ('Sphericus architypus hic monstrat microcosmum'). The two larger circles to the l. and r. are the moon (l.) and her age (r.). The three outer circles of the dial show the day of the month, the minute and the hour. Above the dial a procession of four small carved figures, on horseback. To the r. of the clock a seated figure known as Jack Blandifer. It may also date from c. 1390 and would then be the oldest clock jack in the country. On the outside of the transept wall a simpler dial and two 'quarter-jacks', figures in late C 15 armour. (On other cathedral clocks, see Salisbury's, slightly older and probably by the same maker, and Exeter's, which is later.) – SCULPTURE. In the w aisle, N wall, over the entrance to the stair-turret: Wise Virgin (?). Very good small figure by one of the w front masters. – STAINED GLASS. Clerestory E side. Decapitation of St John. Probably *Arnold of Nijmegen*; dated 1507. The inscription is in French. Renaissance details in the ornament. – N lancets. By *Powell*, 1903; highly praised at the time. – MONUMENTS. Bishop Cornish †1513. Tomb-chest with shields on cusped fields. Tudor arch, straight top. No effigy. Against the E wall mutilated figures of Christ and the kneeling bishop. – Bishop Still †1607. Recumbent alabaster effigy flanked by two black columns. Shallow coffered back arch, spandrels with shields and ribbon work. – Bishop Kidder †1703. On the base semi-

reclining figure of his daughter (?), rather daringly dressed and looking up to the two urns of her parents. Two columns, wide open segmental pediment. Back wall with a cloth on which three cherubs' heads.

South transept   FONT. Now seen as an important and neglected piece, quite certainly Anglo-Saxon (Rodwell). Circular with arcade of blank arches on square-section pilasters with square imposts and bases, and vestigial leaf motifs in the spandrels. Faint traces of painted figures in the blank spaces. The composition is in the tradition of Mercian sculpture (cf. the Hedda Stone of c. 800 at Peterborough), and the carving more primitive than on the similarly tub-shaped fonts with carved figures under arcades at Hereford Cathedral and Rendcomb in Glos. For conjectures as to its original use in the Saxon cathedral, possibly at a sanctified dipping place below the C 10 high altar in what is now the cloister garth, see the *Introduction*, paragraph on the medieval conduit. – FONT COVER. Naive Jacobean. – SCREENS. As in the N transept, but with C 15 IRON GATES probably from the Bekynton Chantry (S chancel aisle). – STAINED GLASS. E side, clerestory, two saints by *W. R. Eginton*, 1813. – Two E windows by *A. K. Nicholson.* – MONUMENTS. Some of the most important ones in the cathedral. So-called Dean Husee (E aisle). Alabaster monument of c. 1400, from Nottingham, the tomb-chest with two panels of the most familiar themes: an Annunciation and a Trinity, but of an expressive power rarely achieved in English alabaster. Between the two panels three standing statuettes and shields. Effigy also of good quality though no match for the two panels. Heavy canopy of stone; big superstructure with blank arcading. – William Byconyll †1448 (E aisle). Tomb-chest with ogee arcading. Back wall and coved ceiling with plain panelling. Heavy straight top. – Bishop William de Marchia †1302 (S wall). To the l. of the monument a separate chantry altar. The historical importance of the monument depends on whether one is entitled to assume that it was – as was usual – made shortly after his death. If so, it represents Wells at the beginning of the great work about the E end. The tomb is in a recess with a canopy. The effigy, of excellent workmanship, lies on a low base with a frieze of detached heads on it, a weird, as yet unexplored conceit. Three arches, ogee-cusped ogee gables with crockets and big finials. If this is indeed c. 1302–5, the ogees are the first in Wells. Vault with ridge ribs and bosses. On the back wall three figures in bad condition. Two of them are angels. Against the E and W walls just one head each, of a grossly exaggerated size: one man and one woman. What can their meaning be? (cf. frieze of the Lady Chapel reredos, Bristol Cathedral). The touch of the sensational that turns up so often in the style of the early C 14 is certainly present. – The surround of the chantry altar is livelier. One arch only with pierced ogee cusping. Panelled spandrels, straight top.

The panelling in the spandrels is so much a Perp motif that it makes one consider whether the altar was not set up a generation later. Black wall with three ogee-headed niches, the middle one wider. Openings like small windows towards the big s window behind. Brass plate to commemorate the burial here of the Countess de Lisle † 1463.

Nave and aisles PULPIT. An extremely interesting stone pulpit is attached to the Sugar Chantry (which is earlier than the pulpit; see below) and can only be reached from inside the chantry. Its interest lies in the fact that it is of solid, monumental and very plain Italian Renaissance forms, handled without any hesitation and without any hankering after prettiness, and yet is as early as the time of Bishop Knight who gave it, and whose arms appear on it. His bishopric began in 1540 and he died in 1547. He was an able politician and a valued adviser of Henry VIII. In 1527

170. WELLS Pulpit given by Bishop Knight, 1547

he had been to Rome in connection with the divorce case, and he had spent many years in the Netherlands. His pulpit is one of the earliest attempts in England at a serious understanding of the Renaissance, as early as Lacock Abbey and Old Somerset House. It is circular with broad projecting piers and an inscription (in a mongrel mix of classical lettering and black-letter) that reads in part: 'PREACHE THOV THE WORDE BE FERVENT IN SEASON AND OVT OF SEASON REPROVE REBVKE EXHORTE WAIL LONGE . . .'. – Magnificent brass LECTERN, given 1661. (Sometimes in the Lady Chapel.) Signed by *William Burroughs* of London, who also made the lecterns at Lincoln and Canterbury. Big bulbous stem and reading desk with symmetrical foliage in the triangles between the two reading surfaces. – Under the N W tower: oaken PYX CANOPY, a great rarity. Circular in plan, 4 ft high, with pierced tracery, and traces of red, blue and gilt paint. It seems to be of the c 14. (Formerly in the undercroft, where Britton's engraving shows it, but originally presumably in the c 14 sanctuary.) – STAINED GLASS. W window, 1670. An important document, of the use of enamelled glass, rather than an enjoyable work of art; also much repaired after damage from westerly gales. The centre light by *A. K. Nicholson*, 1931. – s aisle, four two-light windows by *C. E. Kempe*, inserted 1905–6. – There is c 15 glass in some tracery lights: s aisle, westernmost and easternmost windows; N and s clerestory, easternmost windows. – MONUMENTS. Two chantry chapels (the only ones besides Bekynton's, s chancel aisle). Bishop Bubwith † 1424 and Treasurer Sugar, 1489. Of identical shape, namely hexagonal. The choice of the shape dictated simply by the wish to gain more space between two piers of the nave arcade. So the sides were canted out. In the architectural details much difference. The E wall in the earlier with quatrefoil-panelled coving, in the later a fan-vault instead of coving and demi-figures of angels in the frieze. The tracery of the earlier contains an odd reminiscence of the c 13, rounded trefoiled lights though with Perp panels above. In the later the windows are arranged in four lights with two two-light sub-arches. The doorways of the earlier four-centred, of the later ogee-headed. There seems little stylistic significance in these changes. They are no more than variations within the same style. – On the altar of the Bubwith Chapel small alabaster panel of the Ascension. What else the nave and aisles may have contained has all been cleared out by restorers.

CLOISTERS

The cloisters were rebuilt in the c 15. The original E walk, forming a passage from the Bishop's Palace to the s transept, was probably complete by *c.* 1200. A N walk was laid out and probably begun but later abandoned. The original w and s walks were probably only built *c.* 1240–60 after the w front was finished; see *Exterior*, w front, above, on relation of N and w walks to s w tower. (The original square layout of the Wells cloisters, with a space between the intended N walk and the nave, probably inspired the layout of the cloisters at Salisbury that were begun *c.* 1270.) On the late C 12 decision to preserve the earlier Lady Chapel E of the cloisters and its C 15 replacement by Stillington's chapel demolished in the C 16, see *Introduction*, Excavations, above (and on the C 13 cloisters, Rodwell 1980b).

The existing EAST WALK was built by Bishop Bubwith's executors from *c.* 1425. Six-light windows with transoms and two-centred heads, divided into three-light sub-arches. Much pretty cusping. The vaults start on solid springers like fan-vaults, the pattern built up with liernes to an octagonal centre (as already in the C 14 E walk at Worcester). On the upper floor the LIBRARY, a splendid room originally 160 ft long and intended as the cathedral library from the beginning. It must be the largest C 15

171. WELLS Library, C 15, over the east cloister walk

library in England. Small windows of two lights. The book presses and the fine panelling of *c.* 1690. The Perp wooden SCREEN at the N end comes from the Vicars' Close.

The SOUTH WALK was begun by the executors of Bishop Bekynton † 1465 and continued gradually to *c.* 1508. The WEST WALK was done for Bekynton. The design again with central octagon of lierne ribs. The Singing School above and part now belonging to the Girls' High School have the same small two-light windows as the library. The roof has collar-beams on arched braces and one tier of wind-braces. Attached on the w side, i.e. towards the Cathedral Green, various appendages, one with the same blank-arcaded parapet as the w towers of the cathedral. This contains a straight, wide staircase which leads at the bottom through a narrow arch with transverse ribs to a room which was there before and indeed before the present cloister; for it had to the w a large two-centred arch the moulding of which appears to be early C 14. To the w again and on its own the ruin of the QUERISTORS' HOUSE, built 1354 by Bishop de Shrewsbury. It has a two-light unmistakably Perp N window under the gable, and that furnishes a date for the introduction of standard Perp forms to Wells.

MONUMENTS in the cloisters, from N E to N W. Thomas Linley † 1795, also his daughters Elizabeth Ann Sheridan and Mary Tickell, by *Thomas King* of Bath. Urn on a base with musical instruments. – Peter Davis † 1749, Recorder of Wells, 'a Man eminently learned in the Laws of his Country . . . Unambitious but Uniform'. By *Benedict Bastard* of Sherborne. Obelisk and standing in front of it the solitary and silly figure of a putto reversing a torch which looks like a cornucopia. – George Hooper † 1727. By *Samuel Tufnell* of Westminster. Standing wall-monument. Two attached columns with open scrolly pediment and achievement. Two putti standing outside the columns. – John Berkeley Burland † 1804, by *John Bacon Jr.* Relief medallion with the dying man held by a woman. – John Phelips † 1834. By *Chantrey*, 1837. Big, vacant seated figure, wearing some sort of gown. – Many tablets with urns.

s of the cloisters and accessible from the market place, the Bishop's Palace is beyond the scope of this book: without doubt the most memorable of all bishops' palaces in England (if one excepts the unique case of the Castle at Durham), combining high architectural interest with a romanticism of setting acquired in the C 18 and early C 19. For description of it, of the buildings round the Cathedral Green, Vicars' Close, the Chain Gate, and the town itself, see the latest edition of B of E *North Somerset*.

Westminster: see *London*.

Winchester

CATHEDRAL CHURCH OF THE HOLY TRINITY,
ST PETER, ST PAUL AND ST SWITHUN *Anglican*

(Based on B of E *Hampshire*, 1967, revised, with information from Corinne Bennett the cathedral architect and Thomas Cocke, Peter Howell and Julian Munby.)

Plan, Fig. 173, from the *Builder*, 1892, by Roland Paul, including Willis's plan of the Norman W front.

Some references (see Recent Literature): B.A.A. conference papers (1983); Cave (1935) 1976; Cobb 1980; Draper 1978; E. Eames 1980; P. Eames 1977; Harrison 1980; Jervis 1976; Matthews 1975; Summerson 1975.

INTRODUCTION

Winchester town and cathedral lie in a hollow. There are therefore no dramatic distant views – the less so because the cathedral has no strong vertical accents. Celia Fiennes in the 1690s saw some sort of spire, 'not a neare so high as Salisbury', although in 1655 there was only a weathervane on a low tower (Cobb 1980). On entering the Close from the N, coming from the High Street, one realizes the cathedral's size, and then inside the immense length speaks more fully. For a while, late C 17 to late C 20, Winchester with its external length of 556 ft was the longest cathedral in England and in Europe, but outdone before 1666 by Old St Paul's and today by Liverpool's Anglican cathedral. The rebuilding of Winchester's nave vaults, begun at the end of the C 14 within the Norman walls and under a perhaps Norman, or at any rate pre-existing, roof, gave an internal height of only 78 ft, compared to, say, Salisbury's 84 ft. So the overall effect is long and low.

The Roman town of Venta Belgarum lies beneath the medieval and modern city. Traces of a large building, possibly forum and basilica, have been identified just to the N of the present cathedral nave. In this same area, in the mid-C 7 there was founded a Saxon cathedral, the Old Minster (now outlined in brick in the grass). It was rebuilt in the late C 10, and in the late C 11 demolished to make way for the present cathedral. The C 10 Old Minster was 180 ft long, with a 'westwork', and it lay at an angle, so partly under the site of the W end of the Norman cathedral. Meanwhile in the early C 10 a New Minster had been built N of the old one, and these with a nuns' minster became in the late C 10 part of a single unparalleled enclosure, serving as burial and coronation churches of many of the kings of Wessex and of England (Biddle, reports 1962–71; summary in Morris 1979). For Winchester was the capital of Wessex and the capital of England from Egbert in 829 to Athelstan, Edgar, Alfred, to Canute, who was buried at Winchester, and to William the Conqueror, who had himself crowned at Winchester as well as at Westminster. Henry III, the rebuilder of Westminster Abbey, was born at Winchester. By then London had established its primacy, yet the king kept his treasure, and Domesday Book, at Winchester. Queen Mary I married Philip of Spain in the cathedral. And still in the C 17 Charles II commissioned Wren to build him a palace at Winchester.

The cathedral is largely of stone from the Isle of Wight. The main building periods are Bishop Walkelin's (1070–98) for the Norman transepts and E range of the cloister; de Lucy's (1189–1204) and des Roches's (1204–38) for the retrochoir and Lady Chapel; Edington's (1345–66) and, more, Wykeham's (1366–1404) for the total remodelling of the nave; Courtenay's (1486–92) and Langton's (1493–1500) for the remodelling of the Lady Chapel and the chapel S of it; and Fox's (1500–28) for the remodelling of the presbytery. (For the relation of some of these bishops to work at Southwark and its background in Winchester, see *London: Southwark, Angl.*) The principal restorations were as follows: work in the 1630s including wooden crossing vault, presbytery fittings, *Inigo Jones*'s screen, and many repairs (confirmed by a royal letter of 1641: Cocke); work under *William Garbett* (1812–28), *John Colson* (1874–91), and *Sir Thomas Graham Jackson* (1905–12). The latter was more a securing than a restoring, including the complete underpinning of the eastern arm's foundations with concrete.

EXTERIOR AND INTERIOR

Crypt, transepts, crossing etc.   Walkelin, the first Norman bishop, began the cathedral in 1079. In 1093 the relics of St Swithun were transferred to the new building, and in 1100 William Rufus could be buried in the church. As it was so highly usual in the Middle Ages to start a new building from the E, one looks to the E end for the earliest evidence. But there is nothing left – at least above ground. (Apse outlines placed in the retrochoir pavement in the C 20 are speculative.) The CRYPT, however, survives remarkably completely. It is oblong with a projecting apsed space no doubt below the Norman Lady Chapel. The E end

172. WINCHESTER West front, 1345–66, in 1817

of the apse is in line with the E end of de Lucy's retrochoir. The W part is apsed too, but the ambulatory round the apse has small NE and SE chapels filling the corners of the rectangle. The big apse and ambulatory of the W part again represent more than probably the layout above. Down the middle of the space thus assigned to lie below the presbytery and main apse are short round piers, three now visible, but originally five. The piers have square abaci and very flat capitals and carry unmoulded transverse and longitudinal arches and groin-vaults. The responds against the walls have not the simplest of imposts. There is just a small nick between the vertical and the diagonal part (in section). The ambulatory has the same details. Owing to the curve of apse and ambulatory some of the groin-vaults are of three and of five groins. Below what was the Norman Lady Chapel there is also a row of piers along the middle. They are not so fat and have block capitals. Round the apse the three-groined vaults reappear.

A glance at de Lucy's crypt below his Lady Chapel, while we are down in the crypt, though it is out of chronological order. The two round piers now have moulded capitals and round abaci and carry single-chamfered ribs. There are no bosses. The length of this C 13 crypt is that of the present Lady Chapel.

To evaluate the Norman work above, one must examine the transepts, first their EXTERIOR, then their interior.

They have E and W aisles. The NORTH TRANSEPT has in its W wall a small single-step doorway with one order of columns carrying block capitals. The lowest tier of windows has a roll, a thin band of chip-carved saltire crosses, and a billet hoodmould. Above are the plain small windows of the gallery. The clerestory windows here are all Perp. The N wall has a regular three-part composition with five flat buttresses, two at the angles, two at the angles of the 'nave', and one up the middle. The lower windows are as before, except for the easternmost, which was replaced *c.* 1300 by one with cusped intersecting tracery. Sill frieze of billets, and another at the sill of the next stage. The windows are the same, only those corresponding to the galleries are blank. The two middle windows are a Perp replacement; so are those of the next stage. In the gable is a tracery rose-window whose date may well be 1480–1500 rather than *c.* 1360 (Mrs Bennett). There is a NE but not a NW turret. To the E the Norman ground-stage windows are replaced by Dec ones, two with reticulated tracery and one with three spherical triangles, two of them set diagonally, in the head. This is in style ten or twenty years earlier than reticulation. Above are again the small gallery windows. In the clerestory three windows are like the others, but the fourth, northernmost, is puzzling. It is flatter and altogether different. Moreover just N of it, facing E, at the top of the pitched roof of the gallery, is the start of

173. WINCHESTER
Plan from the *Builder*, 1892 (see p. 324)

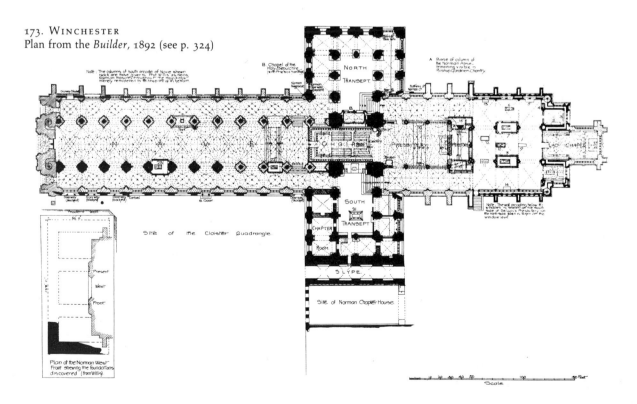

174. WINCHESTER Nave, south transept and c11 chapter-house remains

arcading, probably blank. This can only mean that the E wall of the aisle gallery was intended to be carried up higher. For what other reason can that have been done than for a tower? The odd window would then have been meant to look from such a tower into the transept. Willis, in 1845, observant as always, noticed and explained this, and we shall see when we look at the interior that he had conclusive reasons to assume the plan to build four such towers on the four outer corners of the transepts. The E wall of the N transept ends with a corbel table with heads, monsters etc.

The SOUTH TRANSEPT exterior is essentially the same, though on the W and S sides the cloister and the monastic buildings meant some interference. The top corbel table is preserved here on the W side, which it is not in the N transept. To the S there are two flat turrets without any decoration, whereas on the N side no turrets were built or are preserved. In the gable is blank, flat intersecting arcading and higher up a group of five stepped arches. To the E, at the ground stage, is another window with the same three spherical triangles and also one with reticulation.

The CROSSING TOWER has small windows originally l. and r. of the roofs and, above, three tall arches each side with zigzag on shafts and rolls, which indicates a date after about 1100. Reason to assume such a date will appear.

Now the NORMAN INTERIOR. Flights of steps from the nave to the bays W of the crossing and from the transepts to the presbytery aisles demonstrate the height of the crypt below the eastern arm. The CROSSING piers have to the E and W three shafts, two slender, one a segment of a fat pier. To the N and S there are three of equal girth. The arches are also preserved. They are unmoulded. An uninterrupted shaft rises inside the tower to the top, others inside the transepts to the roof. Even the briefest glance at the adjoining parts of the transepts will show – as Willis was the first to state – that the masonry of the crossing piers and arches and also of the immediately adjoining piers N and S of the crossing piers is more smoothly tooled and more finely jointed than the rest. The reason for this (and the zigzag outside) is that this is a rebuilding after Walkelin's tower had fallen in 1107. Fear of a recurrence of such a calamity is also responsible for the fact that the crossing piers are of a size (in section) unparalleled among English crossing piers. The W and E arches were kept as wide open as probably before, but the N and S arches were narrowed so much that the arches needed a great deal of stilting. Another amendment after the collapse of the tower will have to be referred to presently. Meanwhile, it can here be noted that the crossing, which contains the choir, has a wooden fan-vault (of 1635) masking the ringing-chamber floor above.

The SOUTH TRANSEPT E side is of four bays separated by the same mast-like shafts. The clerestory sill goes round them. The first bay contains the entrance into the chancel aisle. The arch is stilted and of one step. The capitals here and all round both transepts at all levels are either block capitals or of one, two, or three scallops, all very substantial. The next bays have rib-vaults, the ribs of a profile of a half-roll and two half-hollows. The gallery openings are high, almost as high as the arcade (26 as against 29 ft), and twins. Again all the detail is of the simplest: e.g. one-step arches. The clerestory is also very high (23 ft) and has a wall-passage, basically tripartite per bay: low, high, low. This standard English arrangement occurs here for the first time (Westminster Hall was slightly later), and it occurs disarmingly irregularly. In bay one it is high-low, in bay

175. WINCHESTER
South transept, steps to the south choir aisle

two complete, in bays three and four – owing to the absence of the mast (see below) – it is low, high, low, low, high. The S side is different, because there is a S aisle of two bays. To the N it has a fat pier with the same very flat capital as in the crypt, but to the aisle a respond is tacked on to it. Unmoulded arches. The vaults behind are groin-vaults, and so it must be added now that the rib-vaults, where they occur, are replacements of groin-vaults after the tower had fallen. (Against the S wall some blank arcading, continued in the W aisle, but not as consistently as in the N transept; in the S W bay one shaft of the blank arcading is replaced by a fine C 14 head; in the N transept such heads were carved out of the capitals, six times.) Above these groin-vaults is an open balcony, not a gallery with arches to the 'nave'. There is here a change of plan, and altogether these end bays of the transepts are a headache. However, for Willis there were no headaches, and he has at least solved certain muddles at ground-level perfectly. He has pointed out that the N W and N E piers of the N and the S W and S E piers of the S transept and the wall-shafts corresponding to them W of the W and E of the E ones have been strengthened and broadened later, the N W piers to the N W, the S W piers to the S W etc., and the wall-shafts accordingly. Once one watches for this, one cannot but notice it, even without Willis's admirable little plans and illustrations. This strengthening represents a change of plan after the gallery-level had been reached. The change which would make this particular strengthening necessary is that of providing towers at the corners of the transepts, and the intention to do so has already been proved. The most noticeable sign of the change of plan, however, occurs higher up. It is the breaking off of the masts below the clerestory level. This poses a different problem, and Willis does not help on it. It may be said that the masts became unnecessary if towers were to go up. The shaft midway up the gallery spandrel which now also stops where the gallery stops may imply that the intention now was to carry the gallery arcading right round and thus provide a next stage for the tower. In this case the clerestory passage would probably also have come forward. Whatever the intention, however, it was very soon given up, and the odd rhythm of the present wall-passage on the E (and W) sides shows that, when that level was reached, towers were no longer considered. In the S W bay an upper doorway, now reached by a wooden staircase, gives access to the present library over the C 11 slype (see *Cloister* and *Furnishings*, S transept, below). The staircase is Jacobean, with flat, cut-out balusters. The doorway itself, however, is not that which connected with the dormitory: it is clearly, like its neighbours l. and r., a window. Where then was the night stair?

On the W side both aisle arches are blocked, the more northerly one by masonry with blank decoration continuing into the nave, which, in its zigzag at r. angles to the

176. WINCHESTER North transept, late C11, in 1817

wall and its curious compound shafts, must be the work of, or inspired by, the masons working on the triforium at St Cross, i.e. in the 1170s or 1180s. In fact, the filled-in N W bay was the treasury of Henry of Blois, hence the resemblance to St Cross, founded by him (Mrs Bennett). Nothing else new in the W wall.

The NORTH TRANSEPT is essentially the same. On the E side the middle bay of the aisle is an early C 14 replacement (cf. the window tracery). The rib profile is different, and the ribs start from four delightful little figures. The distribution between preserved groin-vaults and replacement rib-vaults is not quite the same. Chapel on S: see *Furnishings*. The transept ceilings were inserted by *Garbett* in 1819.

Of the Norman presbytery and the Norman nave we have scarcely any evidence, though one can assume that they were like the transepts. Externally, on the N side, the presbytery at the very W end of the clerestory shares the r. shaft of the first window. (On the canting of the E bay, followed in the C 14 and C 16 remodelling, see *Presbytery* below.) Internally, on the N side, the presbytery aisle has part of its westernmost arcade respond preserved, and there is, moreover, the stump of a strong round pier inside the Gardiner Chantry (N E of the present high altar). This was one of the four piers round Walkelin's apse. (The V C H has conjectured that the little Norman arch within the so-called 'Holy Hole', under the C 14 arcade at the W end of the retrochoir, may have been the base of a bishop's throne in the centre of the apse; cf. Norwich.) Outside the nave on the cloister side, third bay from the W, a doorway has some length of billet, which shows that it replaced a Norman doorway.

Of the Norman W front nothing is known for certain. In the N wall of No. 11 The Close, just S W of the present façade, is very thick Norman walling, perhaps part of the S wall of a mighty W front projecting beyond the aisles to S and N. Excavations have shown a thick-walled square foundation in the centre and longitudinally oblong foundations l. and r., of which the standing fragment is part of the S wall. Professor Biddle has concluded that there were twin towers, as at Caen, rather than a W tower with side chambers, as at Ely, or a westwork. The foundations at Old Sarum are the most similar we know. As for the interior of the nave, part of the S E respond of the arcade also survives and the arches of the gallery to the E, in both aisles. (Cobb (1980) noted that Scott's screen, being more two-dimensional than its one-bay-deep predecessors, left uncovered Norman remains on the piers each side of it.)

In all this Norman work, it will be noticed, there is inside no enrichment whatever, no billet, not even a roll. Outside, these motifs do occur, but also nothing beyond them. All was power at Winchester, nothing grace. The transepts and the chapter-house front are the most complete statement in England of the Early Norman style.

Retrochoir and Lady Chapel

The C 13 rebuilding has been greatly elucidated by Mr Peter Draper (1978), reconsidering the judgements of Willis (1845) and Pevsner (1961, 1967) in the light of this retrochoir's function as setting for St Swithun's Shrine. The background idea was that of the Becket Shrine at Canterbury. The form was that of a so-called 'outer crypt' or hall-type E extension (here with Norman Lady Chapel crypt below the centre bays) conceived as an adjunct to an existing Norman main vessel, and with chapels extending from it. At Salisbury, retrochoir and E chapels were to be merged. At Winchester, this work was begun by Bishop de Lucy, though he did not complete it. He died in 1204, having in 1202 established a confraternity for five years to carry on his building. As we shall see, completion took much longer. The EXTERIOR of the N and S sides of the retrochoir is of a noble design. Three bays, with a high bare ground-stage and above tall blank arcading, four units per bay with the middle ones a pair of lancet windows. Inside there is shafting as well, and the pair of lancets has a detached shaft between. Further E, however, the design gets as confused externally as it is in so much E.E. external work. The walls step back with two staircase-turrets, octagonal at the top. Then follows the stage of the N E and S E chapels flanking the longer Lady Chapel. These bays have one large window each, now Perp, and one blank E.E. unit added to it. This is the same N (S) and E. Above are two small tiers of blank arcading with trefoil heads. The number of arches is more in the top row than in the lower row. The Lady Chapel is a Late Perp remodelling. One seven-light window (three plus one plus three) to N, S and E with a transom and much panel tracery. Blank panelling below (not on the N side). The top corbel table of small pointed-trefoiled corbels, however, is E.E. The re-cast buttresses have crocketed gablets applied to them.

The INTERIOR of the retrochoir is extremely beautiful, but it needs a trained imagination to recognize that through the crowd of chapels and furnishings. (On its W side, the feretory, see *Presbytery*, Norman traces, above, and C 14, below.) Three bays, the nave wider but only slightly higher than the aisles. The piers are of Purbeck marble and have four main and four subsidiary shafts with shaft-rings and capitals ranging from crockets and the most elementary stiff-leaf to more developed stiff-leaf. The W responds now stand against the C 14 presbytery piers. The aisles have vaults with the ribs of a profile of three fine rolls, the nave has plain single-chamfered ribs on short shafts above the Purbeck capitals. All along the aisles is blank arcading with trefoil arches and a blank elongated rounded quatrefoil in the spandrel. This arcading continues into the N E chapel and may have continued in the other chapel as well. To the S, in the W bay, is a beautiful doorway

177. WINCHESTER Retrochoir, early c 13, with Waynflete Chantry, *c.* 1486, and feretory screen, *c.* 1320

178. WINCHESTER Lady Chapel, C 13 and C 15, from the C 13 retrochoir

in the direction of the prior's lodging and the bishop's palace. It is cinquefoiled and has stiff-leaf sprays on arch and hoodmould. At the entrance to the three E chapels the respond shafting is gloriously generous. The N E chapel has a rib-vault like the aisles and a splendid big stiff-leaf boss. The S E chapel now has Bishop Langton's fan or rather fan-like vault (see below). To the Lady Chapel both chapels have curious arcading with four small bare lancet openings into it (blocked on the N). In the Lady Chapel they are screened by a design which dates them well past Bishop de Lucy's death. There are three times twin arches with detached shafts forming a kind of wall-passage. They are normally pointed, but the super-arch repeats their outer curvature and sets a big more-than-semicircle on top so as to make the whole a trefoil top. Moreover, in the tympanum above are two trefoils and one large quatrefoil in blank plate tracery. Plate tracery of this kind appears at Winchester in the King's Great Hall in 1222–36 and at Salisbury Cathedral around 1230 (by 1225?). Compare also wall tracery in the w porch at Chichester, of perhaps later in the C 13. The late date for these details of the Lady Chapel need not worry us. The entrance to the chapel shows that there was indeed an interruption between de Lucy's retrochoir and this. The entrance has what looks like a mason's muddle, though Draper painstakingly analyses its part in a logical process. Still, the Purbeck responds do not carry on. The capitals are there, but they are pushed up higher by a short, useless shaft. In their heightened position the capitals help to carry the retrochoir 'nave' ribs. The muddle, if it was one, could have occurred because it was only then decided to heighten the retrochoir 'nave'. Its ribs, as we have seen, are indeed different from those of the aisles. The heightening was probably considered advisable because thoughts by then began to turn to the rebuilding of the Norman presbytery. Against the s respond a charming bracket on a bust and with some dogtooth and a wild stiff-leaf capital.

The Lady Chapel can tell us no more of the E.E. period, for it was remodelled in the C 15. Its crypt, however, shows that the C 13 Lady Chapel had the length of the present one. In the late C 15 Bishop Courtenay rebuilt the Lady Chapel's E bay with the seven-light windows to N, s and E already mentioned. The vault of the w bay was also re-done, and these two bays now have extremely intricate lierne star-vaults with small bosses. To the N a small, finely detailed doorway. The S E chapel, remodelled in the 1490s by Langton, seems to have a very close fan-vault, but that is not so. It is a pseudo-fan-vault; for diagonal ribs are kept and prevent the conical roundness of fans – just look at the springers – and the fans are cut into harshly by ridge ribs longitudinal and transverse. (Part of the background of experiment that was to lead to the vault of Henry VII's Chapel at Westminster?)

Presbytery and feretory

For Norman traces, see above (also canting of E bay, below). Here the INTERIOR must be given priority, as the arcades are of the first half of the C 14. Four bays, Purbeck marble piers of four main and four minor shafts connected by deep continuous hollows. Moulded capitals. The details ought to be compared with those of the retrochoir to get the full significance of the change from the early C 13 to the early C 14. Very fine arch mouldings. Head-stops and animal stops. The VCH points out that the details of the E side, towards the retrochoir, and the piers and arch to the N of the feretory are earlier than the rest. (Indeed, the feretory's low stone screen-wall on the w side of the retrochoir dates from c. 1320; on its arcade of nine exquisite gabled niches, see *Furnishings*, Retrochoir 'nave'; also Jervis 1976 on relation to stalls design.) The clerestories are of 1340–60 (Mrs Bennett). Balconies with pierced quatrefoils, and the large upper windows (see exterior below). The E bay cants in noticeably where the Norman ambulatory curved round. The vault, of c. 1500, is very similar to the nave vault, but it is of wood, hence all the ribs are thinner. Some earlier bosses and the coloured set were in place by 1509; emblems of the Passion and coats of arms. The E bay, flanked in the C 16 by the Fox and Gardiner Chantries, was the FERETORY, a raised platform behind the reredos for the Shrine of St Swithun. Remains of steps and bases of colonnettes. (On the 'Holy Hole' in the E face of the screen-wall to the retrochoir, see above on Norman traces.) The easternmost pair of piers not of Purbeck and, as already remarked, not in line with the rest of the presbytery piers. Four shafts and four sunk diagonals. Arches with fillets on rolls and sunk quadrants. Hoodmoulds with figures as stops.

The aisles are of Bishop Fox's time and just after. Panelling l., r. and below the windows, as in the nave, and the vaults also are identical with those of the nave aisles. The presbytery aisle vaults were done by *Thomas Bertie* (contract 1532). He may have been of French origin, worked at Titchfield in 1538, was in charge of the royal works at Cowes and Calshot Castles in 1539, and probably also designed or built Hurst Castle, whose first captain he became. His son married the former Duchess of Suffolk. That far could a master mason and his family get in the world.

On the EXTERIOR it can also be seen that, in the C 14, the canted E bays of the Norman E end were followed at clerestory level. The E gable and its turrets, the aisle walls and parapets, and the flying buttresses above the aisles are of the C 16. The aisles have four-light windows with a transom, the clerestory four-light windows with panel tracery. The aisle parapets are solid, with the N pinnacles set diagonally and the s set square. The E window is of seven lights (2 + 3 + 2) and not very high. The main gable is flanked by two octagonal turrets (upper parts rebuilt to same design 1975–6). The gable is closely panelled, and l. and r. of the E window is more panelling. At the very w end of Fox's work it is interesting to note on both N and s that a window like the others was made and placed which is almost entirely covered by the E aisle of the Norman transepts. So there was a plan to rebuild here and cut out the E aisle. We must be grateful to fate and the Reformation that nothing was done.

Nave and west front

The rebuilding, or rather, as Willis has shown, the remodelling, of the Norman nave was begun at the w end by Bishop Edington (1345–66) and continued by William of Wykeham mostly from c. 1394 onwards. We do not know the name of Edington's master mason; that of Wykeham was *William de Wynford*, a man of considerable status. They had first met when Wykeham was Clerk of the Works at Windsor Castle and Wynford master mason (c. 1360). In 1363 Wykeham became Provost of Wells Cathedral, in 1365 Wynford master mason there, remaining, however, in the King's service. He was granted a pension for life by Edward III in 1372. From 1387 Wynford was in charge at Winchester College. He also worked for the royal castle and finally the cathedral. Mr Harvey tells us that in less than two months in 1393 he dined thirteen times with Wykeham and that in 1399 the privilege was granted him by the prior of the cathedral to dine free for ever at the prior's table.

The FAÇADE of Winchester Cathedral is disappointing. It lacks strong enough accents to introduce to this excessive length, a length of twelve bays. The façade is no more than a section through the nave and aisles with the low-pitched Perp roofs of the latter and the high-pitched Norman roofs of the former. On the angles of the aisles pinnacles, on the angles of the nave octagonal turrets, panelled to the top. The three entrances are in a screen-wall set flat in front of the façade proper and not reaching above the ground-stage. The three porches have panelled sides, lierne vaults, and four-centred arches, those of the aisles above the initial curve straight-sided. L. and r. of the nave entrance two high image niches. Top balustrade. As for the façade proper, the aisles have a four-light window each too broad for its position. These, as we shall see, are Edington's, as are the porches. The nave w window, too, is his: there is a clear straight joint between the mouldings around it and the respond of the nave arcade (Mrs Bennett). It is of nine lights (3 + 3 + 3), the largest in the cathedral. The side parts have two transoms, the middle part has four. Balustrade and panelled gable, crowned by an image niche with pinnacles.

Turning to the SIDES OF THE NAVE, the change from Edington to Wykeham is at once patent. It occurred after the first aisle window on the s side, the second on the N. Edington's windows are of four lights with broad four-centred arches and broad arch mouldings. His buttresses are deep. Doorways (blocked): small one to the N, large one to the s, probably into the cloister w range. Wykeham's aisle and clerestory windows – and all the clerestory windows right from the first bay are his – are of three lights and much slenderer. His buttresses are slenderer too. Edington's aisle corner pinnacle also differs from Wykeham's slenderer ones. Pretty frieze above the clerestory windows with heads, square fleurons etc. The s side is of course somewhat different, because of the cloister. Big detached buttresses with two flyers, built by *Sir Thomas Jackson* in 1909 and 1912 to protect the building from collapse (carved corbels by *John Skeaping*). Panelled fronts and pinnacles. Apart from the Edington doorway, there is a second doorway in the s aisle. It led into the w range of the cloister. It is the one with the bit of surviving Norman billet, third bay from the w. The main doorway into the s aisle was made in 1819. It repeats in design the doorway once leading into the E range of the cloister.

The nave INTERIOR is the most homogeneous part of the cathedral. There it is, twelve bays long, without any change of plan or details, at least in the nave. It is, moreover, amply lit from the nine-light w window and the large aisle and clerestory windows. The only irregularity is the platform in the w bay of the N aisle at half its height (and now forming an elegant little gallery for the treasury given by the Goldsmiths' Company). But even the vault below this is identical with the aisle vaults.

The system of the elevation of the nave is determined, as Willis has shown with exemplary clarity and precision, by the retention and a mere cutting back of the Norman masonry. Hence the un-Perp stoutness of the piers, counteracted successfully by many fine mouldings which multiply the verticals. The principal shaft to the nave, running uninterrupted to the vault, is clearly the Norman mast. Instead of the Norman gallery or a triforium, there is only a shallow balcony per bay. The clerestory has blank arcading l., r. and below. The arcade is framed by a broad wave moulding reaching right up to below the balcony and is here enriched by heads, fleurons etc. In the aisles this is the same in Wykeham's work. Edington's windows have space only for panelling below. The aisles have lierne vaults with the chief diagonal ribs preserved and a middle octagon of liernes, not at once recognized, perhaps because of the warping due to the curvature of the vaults. The nave vaults have no chief diagonal ribs and altogether a much more complicated pattern. Here, as Mr Harvey so graphically puts it (1978, p. 136), the need to create an illusion of height, while limited by the existing roof, led to an upward

179. WINCHESTER Nave arcades, clerestory and vault, from c. 1394

180. WINCHESTER Choir and late C 11 crossing in 1817

surge of ribs like 'fountains of stone' out of main shafts like conduits from some reservoir below. A recent inspection of the roof above the vaults by John Fletcher and Julian Munby suggests that this may not have been the Norman roof still; i.e. was it a C 13 or even C 14 roof?

As already noted, the Norman crossing has a fan-vault, though a wooden one. This was put up as late as 1635 (dated central device): Gothic survival or Gothic revival? Among the roof bosses, the arms of Archbishop Laud and, nearest the nave and the then screen by *Inigo Jones*, a medallion with portraits of Charles I and his queen (booklet by Cave at the cathedral).

FURNISHINGS, E TO W

Few cathedrals are as rich in furnishings as Winchester. They will be described topographically, starting E and moving W, usually taking N before S.

Crypt
Two over-life-size stone STATUES of the C 14. One comes from the niche in the gable over the W front. Where the other comes from is not known.

Lady Chapel
WALL PAINTINGS (protected by screens with facsimiles by *Tristram*, 1930s). Early C 16, all in brown and grey. They are English in all probability, but inspired by the most Flemish parts of the Eton College frescoes of the 1480s. The Winchester scenes represent miracles of the Virgin. – COMMUNION RAIL. Although Laudian in style, it probably dates from 1662 like the high altar rail of that year (Jervis 1976). Not balusters but openwork ovals with spurs sticking into them from all sides without meeting. – STALLS, *c.* 1500, with tracery panels and coved canopy. End figures restored *c.* 1900 (Jervis). – SCREEN, *c.* 1475, at the W end. Originally perhaps a little farther E, with the loft meeting the wall-passages more directly. Six five-light divisions plus doorway with four-centred arches, panel tracery, and loft parapet. – STAINED GLASS. In the E window some small early C 16 figures, the rest of it by *Kempe*, who did the N and S windows, 1897–1900. – Kempe also designed the REREDOS in memory of Charlotte Yonge, the novelist, † 1901 (Vaughan, *Winchester Cathedral*, 1919).

North-east (Guardian Angels') Chapel
WALL PAINTINGS. On the vault, *c.* 1240, of very high quality. Angels in roundels. – REREDOS. Of stone, Perp, seven tall niches. Below blank panelling. – CROZIER and MITRE. They belonged to Bishop Mews † 1706. – STAINED GLASS. In the E window a mosaic of ancient pieces. – MONUMENTS. Arnold de Gaveston. Early C 14. Tomb-chest front of Purbeck marble. Five crocketed ogee arches, shield below them hanging from knobbly branches. The effigy is in the retrochoir N aisle (see below). – Richard Weston, Lord Portland, † 1634. The most progressive and one of the finest monuments of that time in England. Westminster Abbey has nothing to vie with it. Recumbent bronze effigy, probably by *Le Sueur*, the head on several pillows, a staff in one hand. The surround is of white, pink and grey marble, and entirely classical, i.e. no longer in the least Jacobean. Four bare and unmoulded niches with busts, and a wide segmentally rising top. There are here two putti holding a shield. The sides of this superstructure have scrolls starting at the top with rams' heads and short thick garlands. What there is of ornamental form tends to be doughy, of a mid-C 17 rather than a strapwork character. Many cherubs' heads.

South-east (Langton) Chapel
Elaborate PANELLING of *c.* 1500, amply cusped and with openwork cresting. – REREDOS. Of stone. Seven Perp niches, not very high. Much remains of colour. A Flemish C 15–16 triptych now stands on the altar. – SCREEN. Of one-light divisions, with a double door. – STAINED GLASS. E window by *Kempe*, 1899. – MONUMENT. Bishop Langton † 1500. Purbeck marble tomb-chest with cusped fields. Indent of a brass on the lid.

Retrochoir 'nave'
ST SWITHUN'S SHRINE. 1962 by *Brian Thomas* and *Wilfrid Carpenter Turner*. A strangely thin, delicate piece, inspired by the Swedish style of the twenties. Black, silver and brass. The small realistic relief tells of the backward look of the monument and of its lack of sympathy either with the tougher idiom of the accompanying medieval candlesticks or with that of the mid-C 20. – SCREEN. Or rather blank stone arcading to cover the base of the raised feretory. Nine bays of arches with nodding ogees and much crocketing. It is the only example of really florid Dec in the cathedral (see also *Presbytery and feretory*, interior, above; and for pair of chests, see presbytery furnishings below). – TILES. One of the most important spreads of original floor tiles in the country. Dating from *c.* 1235, paving being the last thing done (E. Eames). – MONUMENTS. Bishop de Lucy † 1204. Plain coffin-lid of Purbeck marble. – CHANTRY CHAPEL (S side). Cardinal Beaufort † 1447. Chronologically following Wykeham's in the nave. The chapel rises with serried high canopies to the vault. Doorways at the W end, the altar at the E end with openwork panelled sides, the upper panels large and wide open. The whole middle part is entirely open, except for a low balustrade. That is what distinguishes the chapel from the others. Large tomb-chest with recumbent stone effigy. He is wearing his cardinal's hat. The effigy is a later C 17

181. WINCHESTER Floor tiles, *c.* 1235, in the retrochoir

copy, as is easily recognizable if one looks at the cartouche at his feet. The altar has a reredos of three niches. Large fan-vault above the effigy (the first at Winchester), small ones lower down over entrance bay and altar bay. – CHANTRY CHAPEL (N side). Bishop Waynflete † 1486. The chapel has the same scheme, but the main part is open only in the upper half. Lower down three arches with four-centred heads. Tomb-chest, much smaller than Beaufort's. Recumbent stone effigy. Reredos with three niches. Above the effigy complicated lierne vault. Over the W and E bays fan-like vaults, but with a square centre panel with a rose-window motif. – Coffin-slab with a foliated cross and a Norman-French inscription. – Bishop Sumner † 1874. Recumbent white effigy. – Statue of William Walker, the diver who saved the failing foundations 1906–12. By *Sir Charles Wheeler*, 1964. – (The C18 brass chandelier formerly in the retrochoir is now in the presbytery.)

North retrochoir aisle
More medieval floor TILES. – MONUMENTS. Heart burial of a C13 bishop, said to be Nicholas de Ely. Purbeck marble. Demi-figure in a vesica-shaped surround with stiff-leaf sprays. The figure, in spite of the mandorla, is also under a nodding trefoiled arch on short shafts. – Early C13 bishop. Purbeck marble. The head with a short, curly, archaic beard and a low mitre is under a pointed-trefoiled canopy. One hand holds a book, the other lies on his breast. – Torso of a C13 bishop (on the floor). – Arnold de Gaveston. Early C14. Angels (broken off) by his pillow, his feet against a lion. The whole figure sways in a typical early C14 way. The armour is made interesting by the occurrence of a rare piece: ailettes at his shoulders. Shield with carved quarterings. (His tomb-chest is in the NE chapel; see above.) – Thomas Masson † 1559. Very characteristic Early Elizabethan tomb-chest. No figurework, but the two

inscription plates framed by a very individual and elegant guilloche.

South retrochoir aisle

STAINED GLASS. Many small C13 bits without figures, arranged as lozenge panels. They come from Salisbury Cathedral. (Rescued by *Garbett* in Wyatt's wake?) – SCULPTURE. Ecclesia or Synagogue, *c.* 1230. Headless, but even so of a quality as good as anything in France. The

182. WINCHESTER Figure of Ecclesia (?), *c.* 1230, south retrochoir aisle

source of inspiration is the transept porches of Chartres (Sainte Modeste, Visitation). Here the flow of the folds downwards and the disturbance when they meet the ground can be matched, and even the belt with one end hanging low down. (Former attachments at neck and waist were of metal.) The draperies show to perfection that nobility could be expressed in the C13 in drapery. The head is hardly necessary to inform us of carriage and mood. The piece was found in the Deanery porch. – TILES. More of the retrochoir's fine medieval spread. – MONUMENT. John Clobery †1687. By *Sir William Wilson*. Bad statue of white alabaster. One arm stretches forward a staff, the other is held akimbo. Black columns l. and r. Big segmental top.

Presbytery and choir

REREDOS. Of stone, structurally late C15 and very like that of *c.* 1485 at St Albans. Higher than the clerestory windowsills (so signifying the declining importance of the saint's shrine E of it). Three tiers of niches with great emphasis on the filigree of the (partly renewed) canopies. The statues are all Victorian. (The following summary is based on notes by Peter Howell from G. H. Kitchin, *The Great Screen of Winchester Cathedral*, 3rd ed., 1899.) In 1885 *J. D. Sedding* was asked to restore the screen, and commissioned statues from *Onslow Ford* which were rejected. In 1888 *Kitchin* took over as architect, with *Whitley* as carver (canopies, cresting etc.), and by 1891 statues had been done by *T. Nicholls, Geflowski, Miss M. Grant*, and *R. Boulton* of Cheltenham, supervised by *C. A. Buckler*, but the whole was not then complete. In 1895 *G. F. Bodley*, with *C. E. Kempe*, produced a scheme for the central Crucifix, and for a Holy Family on the lower tier, where a painting by *Benjamin West* then hung. That sculpture was executed in 1897–9 by *Farmer & Brindley*. (Various states of the screen can be seen in Cobb 1980.) – COMMUNION RAIL and DESK FRONTS, *c.* 1700, replacing an altar rail of 1662 (Jervis 1976). Openwork fruit, flowers, leaves and putto heads. – SCREENS. Stone screens N and S with four-light Gothic windows, but an Early Renaissance frieze and Early Renaissance inscription tablets towards the aisles. They are dated 1525. On them rest wooden MORTUARY CHESTS ('Fox's Boxes') containing remains of Saxon kings and bishops transferred from the Old Minster in 1093: the four eastern chests are of 1525, the western pair of 1661 (replacing two destroyed in 1642); two of *c.* 1425 and *c.* 1500 respectively, found inside two of 1525, are E of the reredos on the feretory screen facing the retrochoir (Mrs Bennett; Jervis 1976). – CHANDELIER. Brass, dated 1756. Single-tiered, very large and Baroque. – SCULPTURE. An excellent small half-length Virgin and Child, *c.* 1500. A rare and lovely survival, now placed on a tomb-chest S of the high altar. (Was it made for the newly

183. WINCHESTER Virgin and Child, *c.* 1500, presbytery

made up of two triangles. In front of these back panels rise on detached, exceedingly thin shafts a system of the same panels but crowned by steep crocketed gables with an openwork elongated pointed cinquefoil in. The back panels proper have in their spandrels very close and intricate foliage, and also just once a man (a falconer) and a little more often animals (e.g. a monkey playing the harp). Much of the foliage is still botanically recognizable, but is already bossy and knobbly throughout. The seats have MISERICORDS, e.g. on the N side: a man playing a pipe, a tumbler, an owl, a mock-bishop, fools, a lion, a monkey, a woman wearing a wimple, a fox with a goose. On the S side: a dog, a ram, a man with a hunting horn, a hare, a boar, monsters, seated people etc. In the lower row on the N side a fine laughing figure. (Remnant (1969) notes that not one of these sixty-six misericords has a religious subject.) The fronts of the upper tier of seats have rather uninspired Renaissance motifs. The front row ends have a bold shape but only rather simple decoration. On the W the medieval stalls return, and behind them the SCREEN facing the nave is by *Scott*, 1875: 'a finely carved reproduction of the return stalls on which it backs' (Jervis 1976). *Scott's* wooden screen replaced *Garbett's* early C19 Gothic stone screen that had replaced *Inigo Jones's* classical stone screen of *c.* 1638, which had replaced a medieval pulpitum or rood screen. (See also *Nave*, Le Sueur statues, below.) – LECTERN. A wooden eagle on a big baluster, probably of the refurbishment of the 1630s. – ORGAN CASE, Gothick of 1825 by *Edward Blore*. – A fragmentary length of arcaded wooden tracery, *c.* late C14, inserted above the S stalls and cut down to fit the transept arch, is of unknown origin. – STAINED GLASS. Many original parts of the early C15 (from the nave), the mid-C15, and the early C16 in the side windows (enumerated in detail by Le Couteur, booklet at the cathedral). The E window is essentially of 1852 by *David Evans*.

MONUMENTS. The pair of chantry chapels flanking the feretory behind the high altar are the latest in the series of bishops' chantries begun with the pair in the nave (Edington † 1366, Wykeham † 1404), followed by the pair in the retrochoir (Beaufort † 1447, Waynflete † 1486) and Langton's († 1500) in the SE chapel. S of the feretory, FOX CHANTRY CHAPEL († 1528). Though Bishop Fox was responsible for the introduction of the *all'antica* fashion to the cathedral, there is nothing of it in his chapel. (A genuine working drawing for one bay of it is preserved in the R.I.B.A. Drawings Collection.) The front to the aisle has much more solidity of wall (though of course pierced) than Beaufort's and Waynflete's chantries. Four bays. The lowest stage is closed in except for the doorways and a low niche with his corpse, shockingly realistically rendered. Statuettes around by *Sir George Frampton*. Above open panelling with four-centred arches and wide, strongly

remodelled Lady Chapel?) – PULPIT. A tall half-cylinder with five facets in two stages, probably *c.* 1498, when Thomas Silkstede became prior. A strange piece, its somewhat incoherent decoration including the twisted silk-skeins of his rebus. Not all original (Jervis): the S edge is masked by a C17 carved plank from another source; the elaborate curved stairs are probably of the late 1830s; the reading ledge on ribbed coving is partly restored. – BISHOP'S THRONE. Of 1826 by *Garbett*. A remarkable piece for its date, congruous with the C14 stalls.

CHOIR STALLS. The earliest nearly complete and fairly closely dated set in England. The date 1308 usually given suits them, but it must be remembered that the letter of that year written by Bishop Woodlock to the Bishop of Norwich only asked for *William Lyngwode*, a carpenter, to be allowed to go on serving him until he had finished the work of construction. The back panels are of two blank lights with mostly at the top a pointed cinquefoil in a circle. There is, however, one rounded one still, and there is also just once a typical early C14 caprice: a six-cornered star

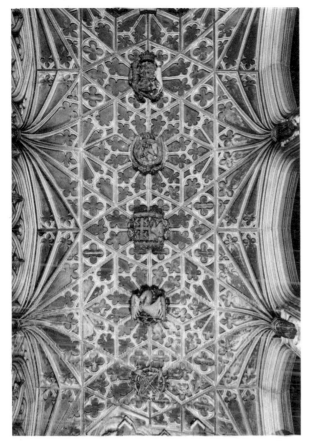

184. WINCHESTER Chantry of Bishop Fox † 1528, roof

185. WINCHESTER Chantry of Bishop Gardiner † 1555, reredos

in England means inspiration from the full Cinquecento, no longer from the Early Renaissance. The charming cresting on the other hand is entirely Early Renaissance. Inside, the chapel is divided into a small E sacristy and the chapel proper. It is in the latter that the stump of a Norman apse pier can be seen (see above on Norman traces in *Crypt etc.*). Now inside the chapel the clash of two ages is most violent. The vault is panelled in square cusped panels.

horizontal top cresting. No high finials any longer. That tells of a Renaissance feeling. Inside is a richly cusped lierne vault. Reredos of three niches and below them an oblong recess. Panelled W wall. To the E small vestry, sacristy or closet where Fox is said to have meditated when old and blind. – Opposite, N of the feretory, GARDINER CHANTRY CHAPEL. Bishop Gardiner died as late as 1555, and to the architectural observer the chapel tells that in a most illuminating way. The chapel is far from homogeneous. It is Gothic in parts, Early Renaissance in parts, and as early as anywhere in England High Renaissance in a few parts. The chapel front is to the N presbytery aisle. The substructure here is entirely English mid-C 16, i.e. two fine long strapwork panels, very subdued in the details. Between them is an oblong recess, and there – very late, but still earlier than Pilon's Henri II of France – is the bishop's decomposed corpse. Above are the same purely Gothic four-light windows as in the Fox Chantry screens, but they are framed by something between buttresses and pilasters. Then, however, follows a triglyph frieze, and that

Looking towards the reredos one is surprised that there is not a coffered tunnel-vault instead, such as one finds them at Chambord and over Henri II's staircase in the Louvre. For the reredos has fluted colonnettes, not decorated pilasters any longer. Such fluted columns appear so early only very rarely in England (Framlingham, Norfolk, † 1557 and 1564; Wing, 1552). There are also shell-headed niches, and they are just as rare (Framlingham again; † 1554). At the top is a proper cornice, and below a guilloche frieze. The two remaining statuettes are full Cinquecento too and have nothing left of the Gothic. How is it then that the Gothic four-light windows and even more the tiny fan-vault in the sacristy were not felt to be painfully out of date? (In the chapel, X-framed chair, allegedly Queen Mary's at her marriage ceremony in the cathedral.) – Tomb-chests in the presbytery. Bishop Courtenay † 1492, no effigy, C 19 Gothic tomb-chest, quite possibly a copy. – Elegant Early Renaissance tomb-chest, no name or effigy. – In the choir, William Rufus (or Henry of Blois). Large black slab, along the centre raised roof-like.

341

North presbytery aisle

TILES. Here they are replicas of worn originals, laid out in 1969 in the original pattern, with the presumed line of the Norman apse marked in stone. – For the Gardiner Chantry, see *Presbytery* monuments above. – STAINED GLASS. Early C16 glass in the heads of the tracery lights, also below the transoms. – CHEST-LID of a reliquary given *c.* 1325–30. Wood, painted with figures. Mostly in sunk panels. At the bottom the kneeling donor and his wife l. and r. of St John Baptist. In the panels Christ in Majesty, the Virgin and Child, the Coronation of the Virgin, the Crucifixion, Angels, and Saints. All painted very naively. – MONUMENT. Bishop North † 1820. By *Chantrey*, 1825. He kneels in profile in front of a high base. White marble, the composition almost identical with Chantrey's Bishop Barrington in Durham Cathedral, Bishop Ryder in Lichfield Cathedral and Archbishop Stuart in Armagh Cathedral.

South presbytery aisle

For the Fox Chantry, see *Presbytery* monuments above. – STAINED GLASS. The easternmost window has early C16 glass in its head. – The second window by *Powell, c.* 1880, the third by *Kempe, c.* 1900, the fourth again with some old bits. – GRILLE. Between the presbytery aisle and the transept. The pattern is of uprights from which identical scrolls branch out l. and r. all up the uprights. It is almost the same pattern as that of Queen Eleanor's tomb at Westminster Abbey (feretory) of 1294 by *Thomas of Leighton*. There is similar ironwork at Lincoln (E crossing) dated 1297.

North transept

Under the crossing arch is the CHAPEL OF THE HOLY SEPULCHRE, put in about 1200. It is a solid structure compared with later chantry chapels, of two bays (one still with rib-vault) and massive buttresses to the N. A small doorway with one order of shafts carrying early stiff-leaf capitals is in the w bay. Nicely moulded arch. The ribs inside are simply single-chamfered. Those of the E bay stand on stiff-leaf corbels. L. and r. of the mid-corbel are blocked responds, and they still have Late Norman capitals of small scallops. The vault and the walls of the chapel are decorated with WALL PAINTINGS of great interest; the latest, of *c.* 1230, is now remounted on the w wall. Underneath scenes of the Deposition and Entombment of that date on the E wall, remains of earlier paintings of the same subjects have been found: bold, fresh in colour, and stylistically related to the C12 Winchester Bible in the cathedral library, as Sir Walter Oakeshott has noted. In the vault roundels with Christ, the Signs of the Evangelists, Annunciation, Nativity, and Annunciation to the Shepherds. Also painting in the soffits of the arches. The style is still inspired by Byzantium. – MONUMENT. Under the E arch of the chapel. Purbeck coffin-lid with a foliated cross starting from a twist of stiff-leaf. – EAST AISLE. STAINED GLASS. Fragments in the SE window. – Carved into a pier recess shafts with a nodding ogee arch; early C14. In it MONUMENT to Charles Nayl † 1739 with an elegant if macabre still-life at the foot. – Canon B. K. Cunningham † 1944. Wooden Annunciation and small reliefs at the back. By *Alan Durst*. – Against the N wall tomb recess with ogee arch; early C14. It goes with the window above it and the northernmost E window. – NORTH AISLE. MONUMENTS. General Sir Redvers Buller † 1908. Recumbent bronze effigy by *Sir Bertram Mackennal*, 1910. – Rev. Frederic Iremonger † 1820. Recumbent effigy, very young. – WEST AISLE (Epiphany Chapel). STAINED GLASS by *Burne-Jones* for *Morris & Co.*; 1909. – MONUMENT. Thomas Rivers † 1731. Obelisk with six shields and palm fronds.

South transept

In the 'nave' CHANDELIER, brass, dated 1756, big and Baroque with one tier of branches. – Against the N screen, WOODWORK, garlands etc., *c.* 1684, added to the high altar canopy of the 1630s, and probably by *Edward Pierce* while working at Winchester College. – MONUMENTS. Isaac Townsend † 1731. Free-standing oblong base with apsed ends. On it a square pedestal, and on that an urn. Smaller vases l. and r. – David Williams † 1860. By *W. Theed*. White marble, with Faith, Hope and Charity, all three phlegmatic creatures. – BENCH. About 12 ft long. Very elementary poppy-heads with two rosettes on the end posts of the back and the knobs on the arms. This seems to date from after 1250. – A second BENCH (restored) on a curved plan, possibly once part of a larger whole fitted into Walkelin's apse, and probably late C13 (Jervis 1976). – PANELLING. Against the S and part of the W walls (only part original). Linenfold, but with an Early Renaissance cresting. It must be of before 1524, as it has the initials of Prior Silkstede, who died in that year. – MONUMENT. Bishop Wilberforce † 1873. Effigy on a slab supported by six kneeling angels, the whole in a shrine-like building: a canopy on eight columns. The architectural style is E.E. Designed by *Sir G. G. Scott*, and very typical of his style at its most lavish. The effigy by *H. H. Armstead*. – EAST AISLE. Stone SCREENS to the two chapels. The one further N is high and elaborate. Upper tier of six tabernacles. – The other was provided by Prior Silkstede (1498–1524). Or was it only appropriated by him? For the tracery is purely reticulated, i.e. ought to be of the first two-thirds of the C14. – The Silkstede Chapel contains a ledger slab to Isaak Walton. – From the S aisle of the S transept a C17 staircase to the LIBRARY. BOOKCASES, *c.* 1660. From Bishop Morley's library at Farnham Castle. (Further on the library furniture, see Jervis 1976.) The collection of books, including the great Winchester Bible, is outside our scope.

Nave

From the E. For the CHOIR SCREEN, see above after the *Choir stalls*. – MONUMENT. Bishop Hoadly † 1761. By *Wilton*. (Black background; now in store.) Grey and white marble. Lively profile in an oval medallion against ample, still entirely Baroque, drapery. – EDINGTON CHANTRY CHAPEL. Very simple, compared with its showy successors. Very important in that it shows how close Edington – he died in 1366 – still was to the Dec. Six bays of two-light openings; the doorway in the fifth. In the heads reticulation units. Simple cresting. To the aisle the doorway is extremely typical. Its jambs curve forward as they descend from the top, a motif taken over direct from the S transept at Gloucester, where it also still represented the loyalty to

the Dec among the first Perp designers. The same spirit comes out in the curious solution of the four corners. No vault; the chapel is open. Recumbent effigy of alabaster. The tomb-chest is of Purbeck marble and has again instead of Perp panels the sexfoils of the past. – MONUMENT. Bishop Browne † 1891. Recumbent alabaster effigy on an alabaster tomb-chest with statuettes. – PULPIT. Jacobean; on a substantial foot. From the New College Chapel, Oxford. – STAINED GLASS. Small fragments in the N windows; early C15. – FONT. One of the two most famous of the black Tournai fonts in England, the other being at Lincoln (q.v.). Square, the shape which the Purbeck fonts were to imitate on a smaller scale. Against two sides stories of St Nicholas, against the third three roundels with pairs of birds, against the fourth roundels with a quadruped flanked by single birds. On the top in two spandrels leaf, in the other two affronted birds drinking from a vase. –

186. WINCHESTER Font, C12, north side of nave

WYKEHAM CHANTRY CHAPEL. Here is the change from simplicity to show – from 1366 to 1404. The chapel reaches right up to the balcony. It is of three bays and wider than the piers are thick. It has therefore a canted extension to merge with the piers. In this extension, i.e. at an angle, are the two W doorways. The lower half is of three tiers of panelling, the top tier with the Perp equivalent of the reticulation unit, i.e. a unit with straight sides. Here then is another adjustment of the traditions of 1366. The upper half is entirely open, except for the two thin shafts. This prepares for Beaufort's in the retrochoir. The shafts carry arches with gables, fine and distinct gables, not the thicket of Beaufort. In fact the whole of the Wykeham design is very easily read and comprehended. Inside a cusped lierne vault. The reredos has two tiers of five niches each with high canopies. The statuettes are by *Frampton*. The W wall is panelled but also has niches above. Tomb-chest with seven gabled panels. The bishop places his feet against three bedesmen. Two angels are at his head. – SCULPTURE. Against the W wall stand excellent bronze statues of James I and Charles I. They are by *Le Sueur* and come from *Inigo Jones*'s rood screen. The contract with Le Sueur for the statues is dated 1638 and witnessed by Jones (Summerson 1975). (Of the architecture of the screen, the centre is in the Museum of Archaeology at Cambridge.) – STAINED GLASS. The great W window is filled very effectively by a close mosaic of hundreds of small bits of ancient glass.

North aisle

The aisles of Winchester Cathedral have almost as many monuments as those of Westminster Abbey. This report goes from E to W, but it must be said first that STAINED GLASS in small fragments in the window heads occurs in the majority of windows. Le Couteur dates them second quarter of the C15. – MONUMENT. Anne Morley † 1787. White and pink marble. Urn under a weeping willow. – STAINED GLASS. Bay two has a whole window by *David Evans*, c. 1850. – MONUMENTS. Matthew Combe † 1748. Urn and garlands in front of an obelisk. – Edward Cole † 1617. Big tablet without an effigy but with much bold strapwork. It is the only one of its kind in the cathedral. – Edward Montagu † 1776. Urn in front of an obelisk. Two small seated allegorical females l. and r. – Col. Morgan † 1808. By *Bacon Jr.* Small kneeling woman, flag, gun and a pelican. – STAINED GLASS, eighth bay. By *Kempe*, Jane Austen memorial, 1901. And on the floor her ledger stone, † 1817, mentioning only 'the benevolence of her heart, the sweetness of her temper, and the extraordinary endowments of her mind'. – MONUMENTS. Villiers Chernocke † 1779. Grey and white marble. An urn and two allegories under a large weeping willow. By *S. Walldin* of Winchester. – John Littlehales † 1810. By *Bacon Jr.* With a small relief of the Good Samaritan. – STAINED GLASS (eleventh bay) by *Kempe*, 1900.

South aisle

Also from the E. Capt. Portal and Sir G. H. Portal † 1893 and 1894. A sensuous genius with the curvaceous lines of the Paris Salon, her breasts not bared but much noticed, holds the two medallions. Venetian semicircular pediment with lush decoration. The sculptor seems unrecorded. – STAINED GLASS. Another window by *Evans*, c. 1850. – MONUMENTS. Sir George Prevost † 1816, by *Chantrey*. White woman seated in profile on a Grecian chair. On a scroll we read 'St Lucia taken / Dominica defended / Canada preserved'. – Bishop Willis † 1734. By *Sir Henry Cheere*. He reclines on his sarcophagus, sitting up, with his arm on books. The sarcophagus feet are over-big claws. Reredos background with columns and a broken pediment. – Thomas Cheyney † 1760. Large oval palm-wreath and in it on pink the white figures of Hope and Truth by a sarcophagus on which a small relief of the rising from the grave. It is a fussy design but pretty all the same. – Bishop Tomline † 1827. By *R. Westmacott Jr.* Stone tomb-chest and by it a thoughtful white marble angel. – Joseph Warton, headmaster of the College. By *Flaxman*, 1801. White marble. He is seated and looks benign but searching. In front of him four eager and pretty boys. At the back Aristotle in precise profile, Homer precisely frontal – as neat as Piero della Francesca. It is one of Flaxman's most successful funerary monuments, intimate yet monumental. Against the sides two medallions. On the top acroteria and a lyre growing out of acanthus. – Henrietta Maria North † 1796. Also by *Flaxman*. White marble. Two allegorical figures standing by an urn. – STAINED GLASS. In the S window of the W bay many medieval fragments; and W window by *C. A. Gibbs*, 1857.

CLOISTER AND CHAPTER HOUSE (REMAINS)

Most of the cloister was destroyed in 1563. Leading from the former E walk, between S transept and chapter house, runs the C11 slype or E–W passage, with the library over (see *Crypt etc.*, S transept, above). Next the arches of the CHAPTER-HOUSE ENTRANCE, a mighty fragment of Early Norman architecture. Entrance arch and two bays of arcading l. and r. (the two pairs of side arches originally blind?). Sturdy round piers and big capitals of two scallops. Inside blank arcading all along the N side. Block capitals. S of the chapter house blocked Norman arches, called book cupboards by Mr Carpenter Turner, the late cathedral architect. Also a C13 doorway with hoodmould on heads. The tympanum has an upcurved lower edge and was blank-cinquefoiled. Then the deanery wall takes over.

In the close, the Pilgrims' Hall, completed 1325, may no longer be credited with the earliest hammerbeam roof (cf. Chichester, bishop's kitchen).

Further on precinct, close and town, see the latest edition of B of E *Hampshire*.

Glossary

For abbreviations of institutions (e.g. S.P.A.B.), see below; for abbreviations of publications and publishing bodies (e.g. RCHM and VCH), see Recent Literature below.

For further references, some with diagrams, the following can be consulted: *Recording a Church, an Illustrated Glossary* (T. Cocke, D. Findlay, R. Halsey, L. Williamson, 1982); *A Dictionary of Architecture* (J. Fleming, H. Honour, N. Pevsner, 1966, 1975 etc.); *The Dictionary of Ornament* (M. Stafford and D. Ware, 1974); *A Pattern of English Building* (A. Clifton-Taylor, 1972); *Building in England down to 1540* (L. Salzman, 1967); *The Illustrated Glossary of Architecture* (J. Harris and J. Lever, 1966); *The Classical Language of Architecture* (J. Summerson, 1964); also glossaries in B of E volumes revised since 1979. The *A.P.S.D.* (*Architectural Publications Society Dictionary*, 1853–92, mainly by Wyatt Papworth) is still useful.

ABACUS (*lit.* tablet): flat slab forming the top of a capital (plural: abaci).

ABUTMENT: the meeting of an arch or vault with its solid lateral support, or the support itself.

ACANTHUS: formalized leaf ornament with thick veins and frilled edge, e.g. on a Corinthian capital.

ACHIEVEMENT OF ARMS: in heraldry, a complete display of armorial bearings.

ACROTERION (*lit.* peak): plinth for a statue or ornament placed at the apex or ends of a pediment; also, loosely and more usually, both the plinths and what stands on them.

ADDORSED: description of two figures placed symmetrically back to back.

AEDICULE (*lit.* little building): architectural surround, consisting usually of two columns or pilasters supporting a pediment, framing a niche or opening. See also *tabernacle*.

AFFRONTED: description of two figures placed symmetrically face to face.

AGGREGATE: small stones added to a binding material, e.g. in concrete. In modern architecture, used alone to describe concrete with an aggregate of stone chippings, e.g. granite, quartz etc.

AISLE (*lit.* wing): passage alongside the nave, choir or transept of a church, or the main body of some other building, separated from it by columns, piers or posts.

AMBO: originally a raised reading-stand in Italian medieval churches, replaced after the C14 by the pulpit.

AMBULATORY (*lit.* walkway): aisle at the E end of a chancel, sometimes surrounding an apse and therefore semicircular or polygonal in plan.

AMORINO. see *putto*.

ANGLE ROLL: roll moulding in the angle between two planes, e.g. between the orders of an arch.

ANNULET (*lit.* ring): shaftring (see *shaft*).

ANTAE: flat pilasters with capitals different from the order they accompany, placed at the ends of the short projecting walls of a portico or of a colonnade, which is then called *in antis*.

ANTEFIXAE: ornaments projecting at regular intervals above a classical cornice, originally to conceal the ends of roof tiles.

ANTEPENDIUM: see *frontal*.

ANTHEMION (*lit.* honeysuckle): classical ornament like a honeysuckle flower.

ANTEPENDIUM raised panel below a windowsill, sometimes shaped and decorated.

APSE: semicircular (i.e. apsidal) extension of an apartment: see also *exedra*. A term first used of the magistrate's end of a Roman basilica, and thence especially of the vaulted semicircular or polygonal end of a chancel or a chapel.

ARABESQUE: type of painted or carved surface decoration consisting of flowing lines and intertwined foliage scrolls etc., generally based on geometrical patterns. Cf *grotesque*.

ARCADE: series of arches supported by piers or columns. *Blind arcade*: the same applied to the surface of a wall. *Wall arcade*: in medieval churches, a blind arcade forming a dado below windows.

ARCH: The *round*, i.e. semicircular, *arch* characterizes the Romanesque (in England, Norman) style. The *pointed arch*, with equal curves meeting in a point, characterizes the Gothic style. Other traits: *chancel arch*: E opening from the crossing into the chancel. A *depressed arch* is composed of curves from three centres. *Diaphragm arch*: transverse arch carrying a masonry gable and dividing sections of a wooden roof, probably to prevent fire from spreading. An *ogee arch* is composed of two double curves. *Relieving* (or *discharging*) *arch*: incorporated in a wall, to carry some of its weight, some way above an opening. A *segmental arch* is composed of a segment of a circle. A *stilted arch* has sections of straight jamb between the imposts and the spring of the arch. *Strainer arch*: inserted across an opening to resist any inward pressure of the side members. A *transverse arch* runs across the main axis of an interior space. *Triumphal arch*: Imperial Roman monument (e.g. of Constantine) whose elevation supplied a motif for later classical compositions. *Westminster arch*: a stilted segmental arch used especially by C13 English royal masons.

ARCHITRAVE: (1) formalized lintel, the lowest member of the classical entablature (see *orders*); (2) moulded frame of a door or window (often borrowing the profile of an architrave in the strict sense). Also *lugged architrave*, where the top is prolonged into *lugs* (*lit.* ears) at the sides; *shouldered*, where the frame rises vertically at the top angles and returns horizontally at the sides, forming shoulders (shrugged, one might say).

ARCHIVOLT: architrave moulding when it follows the line of an arch.

ARCUATED: dependent structurally on the use of arches or the arch principle. cf. *trabeated*.

ARRIS (*lit.* stop): sharp edge at the meeting of two surfaces.

ASHLAR: masonry of large blocks wrought to even faces and square edges.

ASTRAGAL (*lit.* knuckle): moulding of semicircular section, often with bead-and-reel enrichment.

ASTYLAR: term used to describe an elevation that has no columns or similar vertical features.

ATLANTES (*lit.* Atlas figures, from the god Atlas carrying the globe): male counterparts of caryatids (q.v.), often in a more demonstrative attitude of support.

ATRIUM: inner court of a Roman house; also open court in front of a church.

ATTACHED: see *engaged column*.

ATTIC: (1) small top storey, especially within a sloping roof; (2) in classical architecture, a storey above the main entablature of the façade, as in a triumphal arch.

AUMBRY: recess or cupboard to hold sacred vessels for the Mass.

BALDACCHINO: free-standing canopy over an altar, supported by columns. Also called *ciborium* (q.v.).

BALLFLOWER: globular flower of three petals enclosing a small ball. A decoration used in the first quarter of the C14.

BALUSTER (*lit.* pomegranate): a pillar or pedestal of bellied form. *Balusters*: vertical supports, of this or any other form, for a handrail or coping, the whole being called a *balustrade*. *Blind balustrade*: the same with a wall behind.

BASE: moulded foot of a column or other order; pedestal of a shrine.

BASEMENT: lowest, subordinate storey of a building, and hence the lowest part of an elevation, below the main floor.

BASILICA (*lit.* royal building): a Roman public hall; hence an aisled building with a clerestory, usually a church.

BATTER: inward inclination of a wall.

BATTLEMENT: fortified parapet, indented or crenellated so that archers could shoot through the indentations (crenels or embrasures) between the projecting solid portions (merlons).

BAYS: divisions of an elevation or interior space as defined by any regular vertical features such as arches, columns, windows etc.

BAY-WINDOW: window of one or more storeys projecting from the face of a building at ground-level, and either rectangular or polygonal on plan. A *canted bay-window* has a straight front and angled sides. A *bow window* is curved. An *oriel window* projects on corbels or brackets and does not start from the ground.

BEAKHEAD: Norman ornamental motif consisting of a row of bird or beast heads with beaks, usually biting into a roll moulding.

BELFRY: (1) bell-turret set on a roof or gable (see also *bellcote*); (2) room or stage in a tower where bells are hung; (3) bell-tower in a general sense.

BELLCOTE: belfry as (1) above, sometimes with the character of a small house for the bell(s).

BILLET (*lit.* log or block) FRIEZE: Norman ornament consisting of small half-cylindrical or rectangular blocks placed at regular intervals.

BLIND: see *arcade; baluster; portico*.

BLOCKED: term applied to columns or architraves that are interrupted by regular projecting blocks. See also *Gibbs surround*.

BLOCKING COURSE: plain course of stones, or equivalent, on top of a cornice and crowning the wall.

BOLECTION MOULDING: convex moulding covering the joint between two different planes and overlapping the higher as well as the lower one, used especially in the late C17 and early C18.

BOSS: knob or projection usually placed at the intersection of ribs in a vault.

BOX PEW: pew enclosed by a high wooden back and ends, the latter having doors.

BRACE: subsidiary timber set diagonally to strengthen a timber frame. It can be curved or straight. See also *roofs*.

BRACKET: small supporting piece of stone etc. to carry a projecting horizontal member. See also *console; corbel*.

BRASS: a memorial engraved on a sheet of brass often inset in a stone slab.

BRATTISHING: ornamental cresting on a wall, usually formed of leaves or Tudor flowers or miniature battlements.

BROACH: see *spire*.

BUCRANIUM: ox skull used decoratively in classical friezes.

BULLSEYE WINDOW: small circular or oval window, e.g. in the tympanum of a pediment. Also called *œil de bœuf* or *oculus*.

BUTTRESS: vertical member projecting from a wall to stabilize it or to resist the lateral thrust of an arch, roof or vault. Different types used at the corners of a building, especially a tower, include angle, diagonal, clasping, and set-back buttresses. A *flying buttress* transmits the thrust to a heavy abutment by means of an arch or half-arch.

CABLE MOULDING: originally a Norman moulding, imitating the twisted strands of a rope. Also called *rope moulding*.

CALEFACTORY: room in a monastery where a fire burned for the comfort of the monks. Also called *warming room*.

CAMBER: slight rise or upward curve in place of a horizontal line or plane.

CAMES: see *quarries*.

CAMPANILE: free-standing bell-tower.

CANOPY: projection or hood, usually over an altar, pulpit, niche, statue, seat etc.

CANTED: tilted, generally on a vertical axis to produce an obtuse angle on plan, e.g. of a canted bay-window.

CANTILEVER: horizontal projection (e.g. step, canopy) supported by a downward force behind the fulcrum. It is without external bracing and thus appears to be self-supporting.

CAPITAL: head or crowning feature of a column or pilaster.

CARREL: niche in a cloister where a monk could sit to work or read.

CARTOUCHE: tablet with ornate frame, usually of elliptical shape and bearing a coat of arms or inscription.

CARYATIDS (*lit.* daughters of the village of Caryae): female figures supporting an entablature, counterparts of Atlantes (q.v.).

CASEMENT: (1) window hinged at the side; (2) in Gothic architecture, a concave moulding framing a window.

CASTELLATED: battlemented.

CAVETTO: concave moulding of quarter-round section.

CELURE or CEILURE: panelled and adorned part of a wagon roof above the rood or the altar.

CENOTAPH (*lit.* empty tomb): funerary monument which is not a burying-place.

CENTERING: wooden support for the building of an arch or vault, removed after completion.

CHAIRE ORGAN: in old organs, the second organ added to the great organ, possibly so named because it was placed below and in front of the main organ, so forming the back of the player's seat.

CHAMFER (*lit.* corner-break): surface formed by cutting off a square edge, usually at an angle of forty-five degrees.

CHANCEL (*lit.* enclosure): that part of the E end of a church in which the main altar is placed. Sometimes applied to the whole continuation of the main vessel E of the crossing. See also *choir* (2).

CHANTRY CHAPEL: chapel, often attached to or inside a church, endowed for the

celebration of masses for the soul of the founder or others.

CHEVET (*lit.* head): French term for the E end of a church (chancel and ambulatory with radiating chapels).

CHEVRON: zigzag Norman ornament.

CHOIR: (1) the part of a church where services are sung; in monastic churches this can occupy the crossing and/or the easternmost bays of the nave; (2) the E arm of a cruciform church (a usage of long standing, though liturgically anomalous).

CIBORIUM: canopied shrine for the reserved sacrament or a baldacchino (q.v.).

CINQUEFOIL: see *foil*.

CLASSIC: term for the moment of highest achievement of a style.

CLASSICAL: term for Greek and Roman architecture and any subsequent styles inspired by it.

CLERESTORY: upper storey of the nave walls of a church, pierced by windows.

CLOISTERS: quadrangle surrounded by roofed or vaulted passages connecting a monastic church with the domestic parts of the monastery. Usually, but not always, s of the nave and w of the transept.

CLUNCH: in some areas a term for one of the harder varieties of chalk when used for building.

COADE STONE: artificial (cast) stone made from *c.* 1769 by Coade and Sealy in London.

COFFERING: arrangement of sunken panels (*coffers*), square or polygonal, decorating a ceiling, vault or arch.

COGGING: a decorative course of bricks laid diagonally as an alternative to

dentilation (q.v.). Also called *dogtooth brickwork*.

COLLAR BEAM or COLLAR PURLIN: see *roofs*.

COLLEGIATE CHURCH: church endowed for the support of a college of priests and therefore with numerous altars and a sizeable choir.

COLONNADE: range of columns supporting an entablature or arches.

COLONNETTE: in medieval architecture, a small column or shaft.

COLOSSAL ORDER: see *order*.

COLUMN: in classical architecture, an upright structural member of round section with a shaft, a capital, and usually a base. See *orders*.

COLUMN FIGURE: in medieval architecture, carved figure attached to a column or shaft flanking a doorway.

COMPOUND PIER: a pier consisting of a bundle of shafts (q.v.), or of a solid core surrounded by attached or detached shafts.

CONSOLE: ornamental bracket of compound curved outline.

COPING (*lit.* capping): course of stones, or equivalent on top of a wall.

CORBEL: block of stone projecting from a wall, supporting some feature on its horizontal top surface. *Corbel course*: continuous projecting course of stones or bricks fulfilling the same function. *Corbel table*: series of corbels to carry a parapet or a wall-plate (for the latter, see *roofs*). *Corbelling*: brick or masonry courses built out beyond one another like a series of corbels to support a chimneystack, window etc.

CORNICE: (1) moulded ledge, projecting along the top of a building or feature, especially as the

highest member of the classical entablature (q.v.; see also *orders*); (2) decorative moulding in the angle between wall and ceiling.

COSMATI WORK: Italian C12–13 decorative work in marble inlaid with coloured stones, mosaic, glass, gilding etc. by craftsmen known as the Cosmati.

COURSE: continuous layer of stones etc. in a wall.

COVE: a concave moulding on a large scale, e.g. in a *coved ceiling*, which has a pronounced cove joining the walls to a flat central area.

CRADLE ROOF: see *wagon roof*.

CREDENCE: in a church or chapel, a side table, or often a recess, for the sacramental elements before consecration.

CRENELLATION: see *battlement*.

CREST, CRESTING: ornamental finish along the top of a screen etc.

CROCKETS (*lit.* hooks), CROCKETING: in Gothic architecture, leafy knobs on the edges of any sloping feature.

CROSSING: in a church, central space at the junction of the nave, chancel and transepts. *Crossing tower*: tower above a crossing.

CROWN-POST: see *roofs*.

CRYPT: underground or half-underground room usually below the E end of a church. *Ring crypt*: early medieval semicircular or polygonal corridor crypt surrounding the apse of a church, often associated with chambers for relics. See also *undercroft*.

CUPOLA (*lit.* dome): especially a small dome on a circular or polygonal base crowning a larger dome, roof or turret. Sometimes denotes any dome between drum and lantern.

CUSP: projecting point formed by the foils within the divisions of Gothic tracery, also used as a decorative edging to the soffits of the Gothic arches of tomb recesses, sedilia etc.

DADO: the finishing of the lower part of an interior wall (sometimes used to support an applied order). *Dado rail*: the moulding along the top of the dado.

DAGGER: see *tracery*.

DAIS: raised platform at one end of a room.

DEC (DECORATED): historical division of English Gothic architecture covering the period from *c.* 1290 to *c.* 1350. The name is derived from the type of window tracery used during the period (see also *tracery*).

DEMI-COLUMNS: engaged columns (q.v.) only half of whose circumference projects from the wall. Also called *half-columns*.

DENTIL: small square block used in series in classical cornices, rarely in Doric. In brickwork, *dentilation* is produced by the projection of alternating headers or blocks along cornices or string-courses.

DIAPER (*lit.* figured cloth): repetitive surface decoration of lozenges or squares, either flat or in relief. Achieved in brickwork with bricks of two colours.

DOGTOOTH: typical E.E. decoration of a moulding, consisting of a series of squares, their centres raised like pyramids and their edges indented. See also *cogging*.

DOME: vault of even curvature erected on a circular base. The section can be segmental (e.g. saucer dome), semicircular, pointed, bulbous (onion dome) or compound (curves from more than one centre).

DORMER WINDOW: window standing up vertically from the slope of a roof and lighting a room within it. *Dormer head*: gable above this window, often formed as a pediment.

DORTER: dormitory; sleeping quarters of a monastery.

DRESSINGS: smoothly worked stones, used e.g. for quoins or string-courses, projecting from the wall and sometimes of different material, colour or texture.

DRIPSTONE: moulded stone projecting from a wall to protect the lower parts from water. See also *hood-mould*.

DRUM: (1) circular or polygonal wall supporting a dome or cupola; (2) one of the stones forming the shaft of a column.

EARLY ENGLISH: see *E.E.*

EASTER SEPULCHRE: recess, usually in the wall of a chancel, with a tomb-chest to receive an effigy of Christ for Easter celebrations.

EAVES: overhanging edge of a roof; hence *eaves cornice* in this position.

ECHINUS (*lit.* sea-urchin): ovolo moulding (q.v.) below the abacus of a Greek Doric capital.

E.E. (EARLY ENGLISH): historical division of English Gothic architecture covering the period *c.* 1190–1250.

ELEVATION: (1) any side of a building, inside or out; (2) in a drawing, the same or any part of it, accurately represented in two dimensions.

EMBATTLED: furnished with battlements.

EMBRASURE (*lit.* splay): small splayed opening in the wall or battlement of a fortified building.

ENCAUSTIC TILES: glazed and decorated earthenware tiles used for paving.

EN DÉLIT (*lit.* in error): term used in Gothic architecture to describe stone shafts whose grain runs vertically, instead of horizontally (as in the stone's original bed), against normal building practice.

ENGAGED COLUMN: one that is partly merged into a wall or pier. Also called *attached column*.

ENTABLATURE: in classical architecture, collective name for the three horizontal members (architrave, frieze and cornice) above a column.

ENTASIS: very slight convex deviation from a straight line; used on classical columns and sometimes on spires to prevent an optical illusion of concavity.

ENTRESOL: mezzanine storey within or above the ground storey.

EPITAPH (*lit.* on a tomb): inscription in that position.

ESCUTCHEON: shield for armorial bearings.

EXEDRA: apsidal end of an apartment; see *apse*.

FASCIA: plain horizontal band, e.g. in an architrave.

FENESTRATION: the arrangement of windows in a building.

FERETORY: (1) place behind the high altar where the chief shrine of a church is kept; (2) wooden or metal container for relics.

FESTOON: ornament, usually in high or low relief, in the form of a garland of flowers and/or fruit, hung up at both ends; see also *swag*.

FIBREGLASS (or glass-reinforced polyester (GRP)): synthetic resin reinforced with glass fibre, formed in moulds, often simulating the outward appearance of traditional materials.

FIELDED: see *raised and fielded*.

FILLET: in medieval architecture, a narrow flat band running down a shaft or along a roll moulding. In classical architecture it separates larger curved mouldings in cornices or bases.

FINIAL: decorative topmost feature, e.g. above a gable, spire or cupola.

FLAMBOYANT: properly the latest phase of French Gothic architecture, where the window tracery takes on undulating lines, based on the use of flowing curves.

FLÈCHE (*lit.* arrow): slender spire on the centre of a roof. Also called *spirelet*.

FLEUR-DE-LYS: in heraldry, a formalized lily, as in the royal arms of France.

FLEURON: decorative carved flower or leaf.

FLOWING: curvilinear, as of tracery.

FLUSHWORK: flint used decoratively in conjunction with dressed stone so as to form patterns: tracery, initials etc.

FLUTING: series of concave grooves, their common edges sharp (arris) or blunt (fillet).

FOIL (*lit.* leaf): lobe formed by the cusping of a circular or other shape in tracery. *Trefoil* (three), *quatrefoil* (four), *cinquefoil* (five) and *multifoil* refer to the number of lobes in a shape. See also *tracery*.

FOLIATED: decorated, especially carved, with leaves.

FRATER: see *refectory*.

FREESTONE: stone that is cut, or can be cut, in all directions, usually fine-grained sandstone or limestone.

FRESCO: *al fresco*: painting executed on wet plaster. *Fresco secco*: painting executed on dry plaster, more common in Britain.

FRET: see *key pattern*.

FRIEZE: horizontal band of ornament, especially the middle member of the classical entablature (q.v.). *Pulvinated frieze* (*lit.* cushioned): frieze of bold convex profile.

FRONTAL: covering for the front of an altar. Also called *antependium*.

GABLE: area of wall, often triangular, at the end of a double-pitched roof. *Gablet*: small gable. See also *roofs*.

GADROONING: ribbed ornament, e.g. on the lid or base of an urn, flowing into a lobed edge.

GALILEE: chapel or vestibule enclosing the porch at one of the main entrances to a church. See also *narthex*.

GALLERY: balcony or passage, but with certain special meanings, e.g. (1) upper storey above the aisle of a church, looking through arches to the nave and generally with outer windows; also called tribune and often (erroneously) triforium; (2) balcony or mezzanine, often with seats, overlooking the main interior space of a building; (3) external walkway, often projecting from a wall.

GARDEROBE (*lit.* wardrobe): medieval privy. See also *reredorter*.

GARGOYLE: water-spout projecting from the parapet of a wall or tower, often carved into human or animal shape.

GEOMETRIC: historical division of English Gothic architecture covering the period *c.* 1250–90. See also *tracery*.

GIANT ORDER: see *order*.

GIBBS SURROUND: intermittently blocked door- or window-frame as used e.g. in c16 Italy by Vignola, in c17 England by so-called artisan mannerists, and in c18 England by James Gibbs.

GISANT: effigy depicted as a naked corpse.

GOTHIC: the period of medieval architecture characterized by the use of the pointed arch. For its subdivisions, see *E.E.*; *Geometric*; *Dec*; *Perp*; *Flamboyant*.

GROIN: sharp edge at the meeting of two cells of a cross-vault; see *vault*.

GROTESQUE (*lit.* grotto-esque): classical wall decoration in paint or stucco adopted from Roman examples, particularly by Raphael. Its foliage scrolls, unlike arabesque, incorporate ornaments and human figures.

GROTTO: artificial cavern usually decorated with rock- or shellwork, especially popular in the late c17 and c18.

GUILLOCHE: running classical ornament of interlaced bands forming a plait.

GUTTAE: small peg-like elements of the Doric order, below the triglyphs.

HAGIOSCOPE: see *squint*.

HALF-COLUMNS: see *demi-columns*.

HALL-CHURCH: medieval or Gothic Revival church whose nave and aisles are of equal height or approximately so.

HAMMERBEAM: see *roofs*.

HEAD-STOP: see *label stop* (under *label*).

HERRINGBONE WORK: masonry or brickwork in zigzag courses.

HEXASTYLE: see *portico*.

HOODMOULD: projecting moulding above an arch or lintel to throw off water. When the moulding is horizontal it is often called a label; see also *label stop* (under *label*).

HUSK GARLAND: festoon of nutshells diminishing towards the ends.

ICONOGRAPHY: description of the subject-matter of works of the visual arts.

IMPOST (*lit.* imposition): horizontal moulding at the springing of an arch.

IMPOST BLOCK: block with splayed sides between abacus and capital.

IN ANTIS: see *antae*

INDENT: (1) shape chiselled out of a stone to fit and hold a brass; (2) in restoration, a section of new stone inserted as a patch into older work.

INTARSIA: see *marquetry*.

INTERCOLUMNIATION: interval between columns.

INTRADOS: see *soffit*.

JAMB (*lit.* leg): one of the straight sides of an opening.

JOGGLE: mason's term for joining two stones to prevent them from slipping by means of a notch in one and a corresponding projection in the other.

KEEL MOULDING: moulding whose outline is in section like that of the keel of a ship.

KEY or FRET PATTERN: classical running ornament of interlocking right angles.

KEYSTONE: middle and topmost stone in an arch or vault.

KINGPOST: see *roofs*.

KNEELER: (1) kneeling figure; (2) horizontal projection at the base of a gable; (3) hassock or kneeling-cushion in a church.

LABEL: horizontal hoodmould (q.v.). *Label stop*: ornamental boss or head at the end of a hoodmould.

LADY CHAPEL: chapel dedicated to the Virgin Mary (Our Lady).

LANCET WINDOW: slender pointed-arched window.

LANTERN: windowed turret crowning a roof, tower or dome.

LANTERN CROSS: churchyard cross with lantern-shaped top, usually with sculptured representations on the sides of the top.

LAVATORIUM: in a monastery, a washing place adjacent to the refectory.

LECTERN: reading-desk, usually of metalwork, for reading from the Scriptures.

LESENE (*lit.* a mean thing): pilaster without base or capital. Also called *pilaster strip*.

LIERNE: see *vault*.

LIGHT: compartment of a window.

LINENFOLD: Tudor panelling where each panel is ornamented with a conventional representation of a piece of linen laid in vertical folds.

LINTEL: horizontal beam or stone bridging an opening.

LOZENGE: diamond shape.

LUCARNE (*lit.* dormer): small window in a roof or spire.

LUGGED: see *architrave*.

LUNETTE (*lit.* little or crescent moon): (1) semicircular window; (2) semicircular or crescent-shaped surface.

LYCHGATE (*lit.* corpse-gate): roofed wooden gateway at the entrance to a churchyard where the coffin rests to await the clergyman.

MANDORLA: almond-shaped oval around figure as an aureole.

MERLON: see *battlement*.

MISERICORD (*lit.* mercy): shelf placed on the underside of a hinged choir-stall seat which, when turned up, supported the occupant during long periods of standing. Also called *miserere*.

MODILLIONS: small consoles (q.v.) at regular intervals along the underside of the cornice of the Corinthian or Composite orders.

MOUCHETTE: see *tracery*.

MOULDING: ornament of continuous section: see, e.g., *cavetto*; *ogee*; *ovolo*; *roll*.

MOURNERS: see *weepers*.

MULLION: vertical member between the lights in a window opening.

MUNIMENTS: title deeds and other documents kept in a Muniment Room.

MUNTIN: vertical part in the framing of a door, screen, panelling etc., butting into or topped by the horizontal rails.

NAILHEAD MOULDING: E.E. ornamental motif consisting of small pyramids regularly repeated.

NARTHEX: enclosed vestibule or covered porch at the main entrance to a church. See also *galilee*; *westwork*.

NAVE: the middle vessel of the limb of a church w of the crossing or chancel and flanked by the aisles. Occasionally also used of the central space of a transept, Lady Chapel etc.

NECESSARIUM: see *reredorter*.

NEWEL: central post in a circular or winding staircase; also the principal post where a flight of stairs meets a landing.

NICHE (*lit.* shell): vertical recess in a wall, sometimes for a statue.

NIGHT STAIR: stair by which monks entered the transept of their church from their dormitory to celebrate night services.

NODDING OGEE: three-dimensional S-curved arch, as of a canopy.

NOOK-SHAFT: shaft set in the angle of a pier or respond or wall, or the angle of the jamb of a window or doorway.

NORMAN: see *Romanesque*.

NOSING: projection of the tread of a step. A *bottle nosing* is half-round in section.

NUTMEG MOULDING: consisting of a chain of tiny triangles placed obliquely.

OBELISK: lofty pillar of square section, tapering at the top and ending pyramidally.

OCULUS: see *bullseye window*.

OGEE: double curve, S-curve, bending first one way and then the other. Applied to mouldings: *cyma recta*; or with a reverse curve: *cyma reversa*. See also *nodding ogee*.

OPUS ALEXANDRINUM: ornamental paving of coloured marbles in geometrical patterns.

OPUS SECTILE: inlaid work with the design formed from cut marbles, like a jigsaw puzzle.

OPUS SIGNINUM: floor concrete of Roman origin, made from crushed brick, pottery and lime.

ORATORY: (1) small private chapel in a church or a house; (2) church of the Oratorian Order.

ORDER: (1) upright structural member formally related to others, e.g. in classical architecture a column, pilaster or anta; (2) especially in medieval architecture, one of a series of recessed arches and jambs forming a splayed opening. *Giant* or *colossal order*: classical order whose height is that of two or more storeys of a building.

ORDERS: in classical architecture, the differently formalized versions of the basic post-and-lintel (column and entablature) structure, each having its own rules for design and proportion. *Superimposed orders*: term for the use of orders on successive levels, usually in the upward sequence of Doric, Ionic, Corinthian.

ORIEL: see *bay-window*.

OVERTHROW: decorative fixed arch between two gatepiers or above a wrought-iron gate.

OVOLO MOULDING: wide convex moulding.

PALIMPSEST (*lit.* erased work): re-use of a surface. (1) of a brass: where a metal plate has been re-used by turning over and engraving on the back; (2) of a wall painting: where one overlaps and partly obscures an earlier one.

PALMETTE: classical ornament like a symmetrical palm-shoot.

PANELLING: wooden lining to interior walls, made up of vertical members (muntins, q.v.) and horizontals (rails) framing panels (see *linenfold*; *raised and fielded*).

PARAPET: wall for protection at any sudden drop, with a walk behind it, e.g. at the wall-head of a church.

PARCLOSE: see *screen*.

PARGETTING (*lit.* plastering): in timber-framed buildings, plasterwork with patterns and ornaments either moulded in relief or incised on it.

PARLOUR: in a monastery, room where monks were permitted to talk to visitors.

PATERA (*lit.* plate): round or oval ornament in shallow relief, especially in classical architecture (plural: paterae).

PAVILION: (1) ornamental building for occasional use in a garden, park, sports ground etc.; (2) projecting subdivision of some larger building, often at an angle or terminating wings.

PEDESTAL: in classical architecture, a tall base sometimes used to support an order; also the base for a statue, vase, shrine etc.

PEDIMENT: in classical architecture, a formalized gable derived from that of a temple; also used over doors, windows etc. Called *open* if its frame is interrupted at the bottom, *broken* if at the top.

PENDANT: feature hanging down from a vault or ceiling, usually ends in a boss.

PENDENTIVE: spandrel formed as part of a hemisphere between arches meeting at an angle, supporting a drum or dome.

PERISTYLE: in classical architecture, a range of columns all round a building, e.g. a temple, or an interior space, e.g. a courtyard.

PERP (PERPENDICULAR): historical division of English Gothic architecture covering the period from *c.* 1335–50 to *c.* 1530. The name is derived from the upright tracery panels used during the period (see *tracery*).

PIER: strong, solid support, usually round or square in section. See also *compound pier*.

PIETRA DURA: ornamental or scenic inlay by means of thin slabs of stone.

PILASTER: representation of a classical column in flat relief against a wall. *Pilastrade*: series of pilasters, equivalent to a colonnade. *Pilaster strip*: see *lesene*.

PILLAR: free-standing upright member of any section, not conforming to one of the classical orders.

PILLAR PISCINA: free-standing piscina on a pillar.

PINNACLE: tapering finial, e.g. on a buttress or the corner of a tower, sometimes decorated with crockets.

PISCINA: basin for washing the communion or Mass vessels, provided with a drain; generally set in or against the wall to the s of an altar.

PLINTH: projecting base beneath a wall or column, generally chamfered or moulded at the top.

PODIUM: continuous raised platform supporting a building.

POPPY-HEAD: carved ornament of leaves and flowers as a finial for the end of a bench or stall.

PORCH: covered projecting entrance to a building.

PORTICO: a porch, open on one side at least, and enclosed by a row of columns which also support the roof and frequently a pediment. When the front of it is ranged with the front of the building, it is described as a *portico in antis* (see *antae*). Porticoes are described by the number of frontal columns, e.g. tetrastyle (four), hexastyle (six). *Blind portico*: the front features of a portico attached to a wall so that it is no longer a proper porch.

PREDELLA: (1) step or platform on which an altar stands, hence (2) in an altarpiece, the horizontal strip below the main representation, often used for a number of subsidiary representations in a row.

PRESBYTERY: (1) part of a church lying E of the choir where the main altar is placed; (2) a priest's residence. See also *sanctuary*.

PRINCIPALS: see *roofs*.

PRIORY: monastic house whose head is a prior or prioress, not an abbot or abbess.

PULPIT: an elevated stand of stone or wood for a preacher which first became general in the later Middle Ages, replacing the ambo (q.v.). Sometimes with an acoustic canopy called a *sounding-board*.

PULPITUM: stone screen, usually one bay deep, in a major church, provided to shut off the choir from the nave, also as a backing for the return choir stalls. Sometimes carries the organ.

PULVINATED: see *frieze*.

PURLIN: see *roofs*.

PUTHOLES or PUTLOCK HOLES: holes in the wall to receive putlocks (or putlogs), the short horizontal timbers which scaffolding boards rest on. They are often not filled in after construction is complete.

PUTTO: small naked boy (plural: putti). Also called *amorino*.

QUADRANGLE: rectangular inner courtyard in a large building.

QUARRIES (*lit.* squares): (1) square (or diamond-shaped) panes of glass supported by lead strips called *cames*; (2) square floor-slabs or tiles.

QUATREFOIL: see *foil*.

QUOINS: dressed stones at the angles of a building. They may be alternately long and short, especially when rusticated.

RADIATING CHAPELS: chapels projecting radially from an ambulatory or an apse: see *chevet*.

RAGGLE: groove cut in masonry, especially to receive the edge of glass or roof-covering.

RAIL: see *muntin*.

RAISED AND FIELDED: of a wooden panel with a raised square or rectangular central area (*field*) surrounded by a narrow moulding.

RAKE: slope or pitch.

REBATE: rectangular section cut out of a masonry edge to receive a shutter, door, window etc.

REBUS: a heraldic pun, e.g. a fiery cock as a badge for Cockburn.

REEDING: series of convex mouldings; the reverse of fluting.

REFECTORY: dining hall of a monastery or similar establishment. Also called *frater*.

REPOUSSÉ: decoration of metalwork by relief designs, formed by beating the metal from the back.

REREDORTER: (*lit.* behind the dormitory): medieval euphemism for latrines in a monastery. Also called *necessarium*; see also *garderobe*.

REREDOS: painted and/or sculptured screen behind and above an altar.

RESPOND: half-pier bonded into a wall and carrying one end of an arch.

RETABLE: altarpiece, a picture or piece of carving standing behind and attached to an altar.

RETROCHOIR: in a major church, the space between the high altar and an E chapel, like a square ambulatory.

REVEAL: the inward plane of a jamb, between the edge of an external wall and the frame of a door or window that is set in it.

R.I.B.A.: Royal Institute of British Architects.

RIB-VAULT: see *vault*.

RIDGE: see *roofs*.

RIDGE RIB: see *vault*.

RINCEAU (*lit.* little branch) or ANTIQUE FOLIAGE: classical ornament, usually on a frieze, of leafy scrolls branching alternately to left and right.

RISER: vertical face of a step.

ROCK-FACED: term used to describe masonry which is cleft to produce a natural rugged appearance.

ROCOCO (*lit.* rocky): latest phase of the Baroque style, current in most Continental countries between *c.* 1720 and *c.* 1760, and showing itself in Britain mainly in playful, scrolled decoration, especially plasterwork.

ROLL MOULDING: moulding of curved section used in medieval architecture.

ROMANESQUE: that style in architecture (in England often called Norman) which was current in the C11 and C12 and preceded the Gothic style. (Some scholars extend the use of the term Romanesque back to the C10 or C9.) See also *Saxo-Norman*.

ROMANO-BRITISH: general term applied to the period and cultural features of Britain affected by the Roman occupation of the C1–5 A.D.

ROOD: cross or crucifix, usually over the entry into the chancel. The *rood screen* beneath it may have a *rood loft* along the top, reached by a *rood stair*.

ROOFS: timber roofs are generally called after the principal structural component, e.g. crown-post, hammerbeam, kingpost etc. Some elements are the following. *Braces*: subsidiary timbers set diagonally to strengthen a frame. *Collar beam*: horizontal transverse timber connecting a pair of rafters or principals at a height between the apex and the wall-plate. *Crown-post*: stands on a tie-beam to support the collar purlin (see below), usually with four-way struts; i.e. its particular character is three-dimensional. *Hammerbeams*: horizontal brackets on opposite sides at wall-plate level, like a tie-beam with the centre cut away. *Hammerpost*: a vertical timber set on the inner end of a hammerbeam to support a purlin, and braced to a collar beam above. *Kingpost*: a vertical timber standing centrally on a tie- or collar beam and rising to the apex of the roof, where it supports a ridge. *Principals*: pair of inclined lateral timbers of a truss which carry common rafters. *Purlin*: horizontal longitudinal timber (*collar purlin*: single central purlin carrying collar beams and itself supported by a crown-post). *Queen-posts*: pair of vertical, or near-vertical, timbers placed symmetrically on a tie-beam and supporting side purlins. *Rafters*: inclined lateral timbers sloping from wall-top to apex and supporting the roof covering. *Ridge, ridge-piece*: horizontal longitudinal timber at the apex of a roof supporting the ends of the rafters. *Tie-beam*: the main horizontal transverse timber which carries the feet of the principals at wall-plate level. *Wall-plate*: longitudinal timber on the top of a wall to receive the ends of the rafters. See also *wagon roof*.

ROPE MOULDING: see *cable moulding*.

ROSE-WINDOW: circular window with patterned tracery about the centre. See also *wheel window*.

ROTUNDA: building or interior space circular on plan.

RUBBLE: masonry whose stones are wholly or partly in a rough state.

RUSTICATION: treatment of joints and/or faces of masonry to give an effect of strength.

SACRISTY: room in a church for sacred vessels and vestments.

SALOMONIC COLUMNS: with spirally grooved or 'twisted' shafts originally inspired by those, allegedly from Solomon's temple, at the saint's shrine in Old St Peter's, Rome.

SALTIRE CROSS (ST ANDREW'S CROSS): with diagonal limbs.

SANCTUARY: area around the main altar of a church. See also *presbytery*.

SARCOPHAGUS (*lit.* flesh-consuming): coffin of stone or other durable material.

SAUCER DOME: see *dome*.

SAXO-NORMAN: transitional Romanesque style combining Anglo-Saxon and Norman features, current *c.* 1060–1100.

SCAGLIOLA: composition imitating marble.

SCREEN: in a church, structure usually at the entry to the chancel: see *rood (screen)* and *pulpitum*. A *parclose screen* separates a chapel from the rest of the church.

SECTION: two-dimensional representation of a building, moulding etc., revealed by cutting across it.

SEDILIA: seats for the priests (usually three) on the s side of a chancel; a plural word that has become a singular, collective one. One such seat: sedile.

SET-OFF: see *weathering*.

SEVERY: cell or compartment of a vault.

SGRAFFITO: scratched pattern, often in plaster.

SHAFT: upright member of round section, (1) the main part of a classical column, or (2) component of a Gothic compound pier or of a series flanking Gothic openings. *Shaft-ring*: ring like a bolt round a circular pier or a circular shaft attached to a pier, characteristic of the C12 and C13. *Wall-shaft*: partly attached to a wall.

SILL: horizontal member at the bottom of an opening.

SLYPE: covered way or passage, especially in a cathedral or monastic church, leading E from the cloisters between transept and chapter house.

SOFFIT (*lit.* ceiling): underside of an arch (also called *intrados*), lintel etc. *Soffit roll*: roll moulding on a soffit.

SOUNDING-BOARD: horizontal board or canopy over a pulpit. Also called *tester*.

S.P.A.B.: Society for the Protection of Ancient Buildings.

SPANDRELS: roughly triangular spaces between an arch and its containing rectangle, or between adjacent arches.

SPHERICAL TRIANGLE: accepted but unsatisfactory term (three-dimensional adjective, two-dimensional noun) for a triangular window-frame with convex-curved sides.

SPIRE: tall pyramidal or conical feature built on a tower or turret. *Broach spire*: starting from a square base, then carried into an octagonal section by means of triangular faces. *Needle spire*: thin spire rising from the centre of a tower roof, well inside the parapet.

SPIRELET: see *flèche*.

SPLAY: chamfer, usually of a reveal.

SPRING or SPRINGING: level at which an arch or vault rises from its supports. *Springers*: the first stones of an arch or vaulting-rib above the spring.

SQUINCH: arch or series of arches thrown across an angle between two walls to support a superstructure of polygonal or round plan over a rectangular space, e.g. a dome.

SQUINT: hole cut in a wall or through a pier to allow a view of the main altar of a church from places whence it could not otherwise be seen. Also called *hagioscope*.

STAIR: for elements, see *newel*; *nosing*; *riser*; *strings*; *tread*. In churches the commonest stairs are spiral stairs in turrets or in the thickness of the wall; also pulpit steps.

STALL: seat for clergy, choir etc., distinctively treated in its own right or as one of a row.

STANCHION: upright structural member, of iron or steel or reinforced concrete.

STEEPLE: tower together with a spire or other tall feature on top of it.

STIFF-LEAF: late C12 and C13 type of carved foliage found chiefly on capitals and bosses, a mainly English development from crocketing.

STILTED ARCH: see *arch*.

STOUP: vessel for the reception of holy water, usually placed near a door.

STRAINER: see *arch*.

STRAPWORK: C16 and C17 decoration, used also in the C19 Jacobean revival, resembling interlaced bands of cut leather.

STRING-COURSE: intermediate stone course or moulding projecting from the surface of a wall.

STRINGS: two sloping members which carry the ends of the treads and risers of a staircase. Closed strings enclose the treads and risers; in the later open string staircase the steps project above the strings.

STUCCO (lit. plaster): a fine lime plaster worked to a smooth surface, and often painted.

SWAG (lit. bundle): like a festoon (q.v.), but also a cloth bundle in relief, hung up at both ends.

SYNCOPATED ARCADING: double layers of blank arcading set so that apexes of arches lie in front of shafts and vice versa (with an effect better described as counterpoint than syncopation).

TABERNACLE (lit. tent): (1) canopied structure, especially on a small scale, to contain the reserved sacrament or a relic; (?) architectural frame, e.g. of a statue on a wall or free-standing, with flanking orders. In classical architecture also called an aedicule. See also throne (2).

TABLET FLOWER: medieval ornament of a four-leaved flower with a raised or sunk centre.

TABLE TOMB: memorial slab raised on free-standing legs.

TAS-DE-CHARGE: stone(s) forming the springers of more than one vaulting-rib.

TERMINAL FIGURE: pedestal or pilaster which tapers towards the bottom, usually with the upper part of a human figure growing out of it. Also called term.

TERRACOTTA: moulded and fired clay ornament or cladding, usually unglazed.

TESSELLATED PAVEMENT: mosaic flooring, particularly Roman, consisting of small tesserae, i.e. cubes of glass, stone or brick.

TESTER (lit. head): bracketed canopy over a tomb and especially over a pulpit, where it is also called a sounding-board.

TETRASTYLE: see portico.

THREE-DECKER PULPIT: pulpit with reading-desk below and clerk's stall below that.

THRONE: (1) the bishop's seat in the choir; (2) stand for a vessel displaying the Host or relics.

TIE-BEAM: see roofs.

TIERCERON: see vault.

TOMB CHEST: an oblong chest, usually stone, meant to contain or appear to contain the coffin of the deceased, often with carved effigy and/or canopy on top. See also table tomb.

TOUCH: soft black marble quarried near Tournai.

TOURELLE: turret corbelled out from the wall.

TRABEATED: dependent structurally on the use of the post and lintel, cf. arcuated.

TRACERY: intersecting ribwork in the upper part of a window, or used decoratively in blank arches, on vaults etc. Plate tracery: early form of tracery where decoratively shaped openings are cut through the solid stone infilling in a window head. Bar tracery: a form introduced into England c. 1250. Intersecting ribwork made up of slender shafts, continuing the lines of the mullions of windows up to a decorative mesh in the head of the window. Geometrical tracery: characteristic of c. 1250–1310 consisting chiefly of circles or foiled circles. Y-tracery: consisting of a mullion which branches into two forming a Y-shape; typical of c. 1300. Intersecting tracery: in which each mullion of a window branches out into two curved bars in such a way that every one of them is drawn with the same radius from a different centre. The result is that every light of the window is a lancet and every two, three, four etc. lights together form a pointed arch. This treatment also is typical of c. 1300. Reticulated tracery: typical of the early C14, consisting entirely of circles drawn into ogee shapes so that a net-like appearance results. Panel tracery: Perp tracery formed of upright straight-sided panels above lights of a window. Dagger: lozenge-like Dec tracery motif. Mouchette: curved version of the dagger form, especially popular in the early C14.

TRANSEPTS (lit. cross-enclosures): transverse portions of a cross-shaped church, i.e. arms flanking the crossing to N and S.

TRANSITIONAL: transitional phase between two styles, used most often for the phase between Romanesque and Early English (c. 1175-c. 1200).

TRANSOM: horizontal member between the lights in a window opening.

TREAD: horizontal part of the step of a staircase. The tread end may be carved.

TREFOIL: see foil.

TRIBUNE: see gallery (1).

TRIFORIUM (lit. three openings): middle storey of a church treated as an arcaded wall-passage or blind arcade, its height corresponding to that of the aisle roof. Unlike a gallery, has no outer windows. See also gallery (1).

TRIGLYPHS (lit. three-grooved tablets): stylized beam-ends in the Doric frieze, with metopes between.

TRIUMPHAL ARCH: see arch.

TROPHY: sculptured group of arms or armour as a memorial of victory.

TRUMEAU: central stone mullion supporting the tympanum of a wide doorway. Trumeau figure: carved figure attached to a trumeau; cf. column figure.

TUDOR FLOWER: late Gothic ornament of a flower with square flat petals or foliage.

TURRET: small tower, usually attached to a building.

TYMPANUM (lit. drum): as of a drum-skin, the surface between a lintel and the arch above it or within a pediment.

UNDERCROFT: vaulted room, sometimes underground, below the main upper room. See also crypt.

VAULT: ceiling of stone formed like arches (sometimes imitated in timber or plaster). Tunnel- or barrel-vault: the simplest kind of vault, in effect a continuous semicircular arch. Groin-vaults (usually called cross-vaults in classical architecture) have four curving triangular surfaces produced by the intersection of two tunnel-vaults at right angles. The curved lines at the intersections are called groins. In quadripartite rib-vaults the four sections are divided by their arches or ribs springing from the corners of the bay. Sexpartite rib-vaults, most often used over paired bays, have an extra pair of ribs which spring from between the bays and meet the other four ribs at the crown of the vault.

The main types of rib are: *diagonal ribs, ridge ribs* (along the longitudinal or transverse ridge of a vault), *transverse ribs* (between bays) and *wall ribs* (between vault and wall). *Tiercerons* are extra, decorative ribs springing from the corners of a bay. *Liernes* are decorative ribs in the crown of a vault which are not linked to any of the springing points. In a *stellar vault* the liernes are arranged in a star formation. *Fan-vaults* are peculiar to English Perp architecture in consisting not of ribs and infilling but of halved concave cones with decorative blind tracery carved on their surfaces.

VAULTING-SHAFT: shaft leading up to the springer of a vault.

VENETIAN WINDOW: a form derived from an invention by Serlio, also called a *Serlian* or *Palladian window*.

VERANDA(H): shelter or gallery against a building (or as part of a pulpitum), its roof supported by thin vertical members.

VERMICULATION: stylized surface treatment as if worm-eaten.

VESICA: oval with pointed head and foot, usually of a window or tracery.

VESTIBULE: anteroom or entrance hall, e.g. to a chapel or chapter house.

VITRUVIAN SCROLL: running ornament of curly waves, on a classical frieze. See also *wave moulding*.

VOLUTES: spiral scrolls on the front and back of a Greek Ionic capital, also on the sides of a Roman one. *Angle volute*: pair of volutes turned outwards to meet at the corner of a capital. Volutes were also used individually as dec-

oration in C17 and C18 ornament.

VOUSSOIRS: wedge-shaped stones forming an arch.

WAGON ROOF: roof in which closely set rafters with arched braces give the appearance of the inside of a canvas tilt over a wagon. Wagon roofs can be panelled or plastered (ceiled) or left uncovered. Also called *cradle roof*.

WAINSCOT: see *panelling*.

WALL-PLATE: see *roofs*.

WALL-SHAFT: see *shaft*.

WARMING ROOM: see *calefactory*.

WATERHOLDING BASE: type of early Gothic base in which the upper and lower mouldings are separated by a hollow so deep as to be capable of retaining water.

WATERLEAF: a leaf-shape used in late C12 capitals, in form broad, unribbed and tapering, curving out towards the angle of the aba-

cus and turned in at the top.

WAVE MOULDING: a compound ornament formed by a convex curve between two concave curves, used especially in the early C14. See also *Vitruvian scroll*.

WEATHERING: inclined, projecting surface to keep water away from wall and joints below. Also called *set-off*; and see *dripstone*.

WEEPERS: small figures placed in niches along the sides of some medieval tombs. Also called *mourners*.

WESTWORK: the W end of a Carolingian or Romanesque church, consisting of a low entrance hall and above it a room open to the nave, the whole crowned by one broad tower, sometimes flanked by W transepts.

WHEEL WINDOW: circular window with tracery of radiating shafts like the spokes of a wheel. See also *rose-window*.

Recent Literature

A thorough bibliography of the English cathedral – starting, say, before the Norman Conquest – could fill a book by itself. This is a selective list of recent books and articles. Fuller lists appear in Harvey 1978, Bony 1979, Morris 1979 (both main bibliography and individual lists), and British Archaeological Association conference transactions since 1978 (all, below). For books by c 18–19 architectural writers, see Pevsner 1972 (to which one must add the name of John Browne (1847) on York) and Cobb 1980, also Crook's latest edition of Eastlake 1872. Professor Willis's papers on cathedrals (1842–63), so often mentioned in our text, have lately been reprinted (see below). 'Colvin' undated refers to Colvin 1978. A series recently begun, the Courtauld Institute Illustration Archives, includes *Cathedrals and Monastic Buildings in the British Isles*, Archive 1, 1980. New surveys are being made, of medieval English stained glass under the auspices of the British Academy (see Caviness, below) and of medieval English wall painting under the auspices of the Courtauld Institute

of Art (meanwhile see E. W. Tristram's books of 1950, 1955) The National Monuments Record library holds full collections of new and old photographs of the English cathedrals. The Royal Institute of British Architects Drawings Collection's rich holdings include drawings for cathedral works by e.g. the great Victorians, Scott, Pearson and Bentley, and its published catalogue has been gradually appearing (see Fisher *et al.* below). Useful background reading on cathedral history, with bibliographies, can be found in the Ecclesiastical History of England volumes, e.g. Professor Owen Chadwick's two on *The Victorian Church*, 1966–70. Inexpensive well-illustrated booklets, often with texts by specialists, and showing details of work such as roof bosses and misericords not easy for visitors to see, are increasingly available at cathedral bookstalls (but the scarcity of good black-and-white postcards of architectural details is much to be regretted). See also the Glossary for a list of books containing illustrated glossaries of architectural terms.

Addleshaw 1967. G. W. O Addleshaw, 'Architects, painters, sculptors, craftsmen 1660–1960, whose work is to be seen in York Minster', *Architectural History*, Vol. 10, 1967.

Addleshaw 1971. G. W. O. Addleshaw, 'Architects, sculptors, designers and craftsmen 1770–1970 whose work is to be seen in Chester Cathedral', *Architectural History*, Vol. 14, 1971.

Aylmer and Cant 1977 G. E. Aylmer and Reginald Cant (eds.), *A History of York Minster*, 1977 (especially chapters by Gee, Harvey and O'Connor).

B.A.A. *Worcester* 1978. British Archaeological Association Transactions, *Medieval Art and Architecture at Worcester Cathedral* (conference 1975), 1978. Series continued with Ely (1976), 1979; *Durham* (1977), 1980; *Wells* (1978), 1981; *Canterbury* (1979), 1982, *Winchester* (1980), 1983; Gloucester (1981), Lincoln (1982) *et al.* in preparation.

Beard 1981. Geoffrey Beard, *Craftsmen and Interior Decoration in England 1660–1820*, 1981.

Belcher 1970. John T. Belcher, *The Organs of Chester Cathedral*, 1970.

Bennett n.d. B. T. N. Bennett, *The Choir Stalls of Chester Cathedral*, n.d.

Binnall 1966. Peter B. G. Binnall, *The Nineteenth Century Stained Glass in Lincoln Minster*, 1966.

Bock 1961. Henning Bock, 'Exeter Rood Screen', *Architectural Review*, Vol. 130, 1961.

Bock 1965. Henning Bock, 'Bristol Cathedral and its Place in European Architecture', Bristol Cathedral 800th Anniversary Booklet, 1965.

B of E. Nikolaus Pevsner *et al.*, the *Buildings of England* series: original volumes 1951–74; revisions in progress.

Bony 1979. Jean Bony, *The English Decorated Style, Gothic Architecture Transformed 1250–1350*, 1979.

Borg *et al.* 1980. Alan Borg *et al.*, *Medieval Sculpture from Norwich Cathedral* (catalogue, Sainsbury Centre for Visual Arts, University of East Anglia), 1980.

Britton. See Crook 1968.

Cave (1935) 1976. C. J. P. Cave, *The Roof Bosses of Winchester Cathedral* (1935), reprint 1976; and other publications by Cave on bosses, e.g. at Canterbury, Exeter, Gloucester and Lincoln.

Caviness 1977. Madeline H. Caviness, *The Early Stained Glass of Canterbury Cathedral, c. 1175 1220*, 1977.

Caviness 1981. Madeline H. Caviness, *The Windows of Christ Church Cathedral, Canterbury*, 1981.

Cherry 1978. Bridget Cherry, 'Romanesque Architecture in Eastern England', *British Archaeological Association Journal*, Vol. 41, 1978.

Clifton-Taylor 1972. Alec Clifton-Taylor, *The Pattern of English Building*, 1972.

Cobb 1980. Gerald Cobb, *English Cathedrals, The Forgotten Centuries, Restoration and Change from 1530 to the Present Day*, 1980.

Cocke 1973. Thomas H. Cocke, 'Pre-Nineteenth Century Attitudes in England to Romanesque Architecture', *British Archaeological Association Journal*, Vol. 36, 1973.

Cocke 1975. Thomas H. Cocke, 'James Essex, Cathedral Restorer', *Architectural History*, Vol. 18, 1975.

Cocke 1979. Thomas H. Cocke, 'The Architectural History of Ely Cathedral 1540–1840'; see B.A.A. *Ely* 1979.

Colchester 1977. L. S. Colchester, *Stained Glass in Wells Cathedral*, 1977.

Colchester 1978. L. S. Colchester, *The West Front of Wells Cathedral*, 1978.

Colchester 1982. L. S. Colchester (ed.), *Wells Cathedral, A History*, 1982.

Colchester and Harvey 1974. L. S. Colchester and J. H. Harvey, 'Wells Cathedral', *Archaeological Journal*, Vol. 131, 1974.

Coldstream 1972. Nicola Coldstream, 'York Chapter House', *British Archaeological Association Journal*, Vol. 35, 1972.

Coldstream 1976. Nicola Coldstream, 'English Decorated Shrine Bases', *British Archaeological Association Journal*, Vol. 39, 1976.

Coldstream 1979. Nicola Coldstream, 'Ely Cathedral: the Fourteenth Century Work'; see B.A.A. *Ely* 1979.

Colvin 1963, 1975. H. M. Colvin on Westminster Abbey in Colvin (ed.), *The History of the King's Works*, Vol. I, 1963, and Vol. IV, Pt 1, 1975.

Colvin 1966. H. M. Colvin, *Views of the Old Palace of Westminster* (Architectural History Vol. 9), 1966.

Colvin 1971. H. M. Colvin, *Building Accounts of King Henry III*, 1971.

Colvin 1975. See Colvin 1963.

Colvin 1978. H. M. Colvin, *A Biographical Dictionary of British Architects 1600–1840*, 1978.

Croft-Murray 1962, 1970. E. G. Croft-Murray, *Decorative Painting in England, 1537–1837*, 2 vols., 1962, 1970.

Crook 1968. J. M. Crook, 'John Britton and the Genesis of the Gothic Revival', in J. Summerson (ed.), *Concerning Architecture*, 1968.

Crook 1970. See Eastlake.

Crook 1980. J. M. Crook, 'William Burges and the Completion of St Paul's', *Antiquaries Journal*, Vol. 60, Pt 2, 1980.

Crook 1981. J. M. Crook, *William Burges and the High Victorian Dream*, 1981.

Dickinson 1976. J. C. Dickinson, 'The Origins of St Augustine's, Bristol', in P. McGrath and J. Cannon (eds.), *Essays in Bristol and Gloucestershire History*, 1976.

Downes 1969. Kerry Downes, *Hawksmoor*, 1969.

Downes 1971. Kerry Downes, *Christopher Wren*, 1971.

Draper 1978. Peter Draper, 'The Retrochoir of Winchester Cathedral', *Architectural History*, Vol. 21, 1978.

Draper 1979. Peter Draper, 'Bishop Northwold and the Cult of St Etheldreda': see B.A.A. *Ely* 1979.

Eames (E.) 1980. Elizabeth S. Eames, *Catalogue of Medieval Lead-Glazed Earthenware Tiles in the . . . British Museum*, 1980.

Eames (P.) 1977. Penelope Eames, *Furniture in England, France and the Netherlands, Twelfth to Fifteenth Centuries* (special number of *Medieval Furniture*), 1977.

Eastlake (1872) 1970. C. L. Eastlake, *A History of the Gothic Revival* (1872), revised by J. M. Crook, 1970.

Erskine 1981–2. Audrey Erskine (ed.), *The Fabric Rolls of Exeter Cathedral*, 2 vols., 1981–2.

Fernie 1974. Eric Fernie, 'Excavations at the Façade of Norwich Cathedral', *Norfolk Archaeology*, Vol. 36, Pt 1, 1974.

Fernie 1976. Eric Fernie, 'The Ground Plan of Norwich Cathedral and the Square Root of Two', *British Archaeological Association Journal*, Vol. 39, 1976.

Fernie 1977. Eric Fernie, 'The Romanesque Piers of Norwich Cathedral', *Norfolk Archaeology*, Vol. 36, Pt 4, 1977.

Fernie 1980. Eric Fernie, 'Norwich Cathedral', *Archaeological Journal*, Vol. 137, 1980.

Fisher, Stamp et al. 1981. Geoffrey Fisher, Gavin Stamp and others (ed. Joanna Heseltine), *Catalogue of the Drawings Collection of the R.I.B.A., The Scott Family*, 1981.

Fitchen 1961. John Fitchen, *The Construction of Gothic Cathedrals*, 1961; and review by Pevsner in *Architectural Review*, Vol. 129, 1961. Also see Robert Mark, *Experiments in Gothic Structure*, 1982.

Fletcher 1979. John Fletcher, 'Medieval Timberwork at Ely': see B.A.A. *Ely* 1979.

Frew 1978. J. M. Frew, 'Improvements: James Wyatt at Lichfield Cathedral 1787–92', *Lichfield Archaeological and Historical Society Transactions*, Vol. 19 (1977–8), 1979.

Gem 1978. R. D. H. Gem, 'Bishop Wulfstan II and the Romanesque Cathedral Church of Worcester': see B.A.A. *Worcester* 1978.

Glasscoe and Swanton 1978. Marion Glasscoe and Michael Swanton, *Medieval Woodwork in Exeter Cathedral*, 1978.

Gomme 1979. A. Gomme, M. Jenner and B. Little, *Bristol, An Architectural History*, 1979.

Gunnis 1953. Rupert Gunnis, *Dictionary of British Sculptors 1660–1851*, 1953.

Harrison 1980. Martin Harrison, *Victorian Stained Glass*, 1980.

Harvey 1954. John H. Harvey, *English Medieval Architects, a Biographical Dictionary down to 1550*, 1954 (new ed. forthcoming).

Harvey 1972. John H. Harvey, *The Mediaeval Architect*, 1972.

Harvey 1974. John H. Harvey, *The Cathedrals of England and Wales*, 1974.

Harvey 1978. John H. Harvey, *The Perpendicular Style 1330–1485*, 1978.

Harvey. See also Colchester and Harvey.

Hewett 1974. Cecil A. Hewett, *English Cathedral Carpentry*, 1974; and see review by Quentin Hughes and D. T. Yeomans in *Times Literary Supplement*, 29 August 1975.

Hope and Lloyd 1973. Vyvyan Hope and John Lloyd, *Exeter Cathedral, A Short History and Description*, 1973.

Hunting 1981. Penelope Hunting, *Royal Westminster* (exhibition catalogue), 1981.

Jervis 1976. Simon Jervis, *Woodwork of Winchester Cathedral*, 1976.

Jordan 1980. William J. Jordan, 'Sir George Gilbert Scott R.A., Surveyor to Westminster Abbey 1849–1878', *Architectural History*, Vol. 23, 1980.

Kettle and Johnson 1970. Ann J. Kettle and D. A. Johnson, 'The Cathedral of Lichfield', *Staffordshire*, Vol. III, ed. M. W. Greenslade, *Victoria County History*, 1970.

Kidson 1962. Peter Kidson in P. Kidson, P. Murray, and P. Thompson, *A History of English Architecture*, 1962.

Knowles and Hadcock 1971. David Knowles and R. N. Hadcock, *Medieval Religious Houses*, rev. ed. 1971.

Leedy 1975. Walter C. Leedy, 'The Design of the Vaulting of Henry VII's Chapel, Westminster: a Reappraisal', *Architectural History*, Vol. 18, 1975.

Little 1979. See Gomme 1979.

Lockett 1978a. R. B. Lockett, 'The Victorian Restoration of Worcester Cathedral': see B.A.A. *Worcester* 1978.

Lockett 1978b. R. B. Lockett, 'George Gilbert Scott, the Joint

Restoration Committee, and the Refurnishing of Worcester Cathedral 1863–74', *Transactions of Worcester Archaeological Society*, 3rd series, Vol. 6, 1978.

Lockett 1980. R. B. Lockett, 'Joseph Potter, Cathedral Architect at Lichfield 1794–1842', *Lichfield Archaeological and Historical Society Transactions*, Vol. 21 (1979–80), 1980.

McLees 1973. A. David McLees, 'Henry Yevele: Disposer of the King's Works of Masonry', *British Archaeological Association Journal*, Vol. 36, 1973.

Maddison 1978. John Maddison, *Decorated Architecture in the North-West Midlands* (University of Manchester PhD dissertation), 1978.

Mark 1982. See Fitchen.

Matthews 1975. Betty Matthews, *The Organs and Organists of Winchester Cathedral*, 1975.

Matthews n.d. Betty Matthews, *The Organs and Organists of Exeter Cathedral*, n.d.

Morgan 1967. F. C. Morgan, *Hereford Cathedral Church Glass*, 1967.

Morris 1974. R. K Morris, 'The Remodelling of the Hereford Aisles', *British Archaeological Association Journal*, Vol. 37, 1974.

Morris 1978. R. K. Morris, 'Worcester Nave from Decorated to Perpendicular': see B.A.A. *Worcester* 1978.

Morris 1979. R. K. Morris, *The Cathedrals and Abbeys of England and Wales: the Building Church, 600–1540*, 1979.

Munby 1981. Julian Munby, 'The Chichester Roofs, Thirteenth-Century Roofs of the Cathedral and Bishop's Palace', *Chichester Excavations*, Vol. 5, ed. A. Down, 1981.

Norris 1978. Malcolm Norris, *Monumental Brasses*, 3 vols., 1978.

Pevsner 1961. Nikolaus Pevsner, 'A Note on the East End of Winchester Cathedral', *Archaeological Journal*, Vol. 116, 1961.

Pevsner 1963. Nikolaus Pevsner, *The Choir of Lincoln Cathedral*, 1963.

Pevsner 1972. Nikolaus Pevsner, *Some Architectural Writers of the Nineteenth Century*, 1972.

Pevsner. See also B of E.

Physick 1970. John Physick, *The Wellington Monument*, 1970.

Pierce 1965. William Wilkins and John Adey Repton, *Norwich Cathedral (c. 1798–1800)*, ed. S. Rowland Pierce, 1965.

Quiney 1979. Anthony P. Quiney, *John Loughborough Pearson*, 1979.

RCHM. Royal Commission on Historical Monuments, England, *An Inventory of the Historical Monuments*, 1908–, in progress.

Remnant 1969. G. L. Remnant, *A Catalogue of Misericords in Great Britain*, 1969.

Rigold 1976. S. E. Rigold, *The Chapter House and the Pyx Chamber, Westminster*, 1976.

Roberts 1971. Eileen Roberts, *A Guide to the Abbey Murals* (St Albans), 1971.

Rodwell 1980a. Warwick Rodwell, *Wells Cathedral, Excavations and Discoveries*, rev. ed. 1980.

Rodwell 1980b. Warwick Rodwell, 'The Cloisters of Wells Reconsidered', Annual Report to Friends of the Cathedral, 1980.

Rodwell 1981. Warwick Rodwell, 'The Lady Chapel by the Cloister at Wells and the Site of the Anglo-Saxon Cathedral': see B.A.A. *Wells* 1981.

Rossi 1981. Anthony Rossi, 'The Cathedral of St John the Baptist at Norwich', *Archaeological Journal*, Vol. 137 (1980), 1981.

Runcie 1977. Robert Runcie, then Bishop of St Albans (ed.), *Cathedral and City, St Albans Ancient and Modern*, 1977; includes articles by Martin Biddle and Christopher Brooke.

Salzman 1967. L. F. Salzman, *Building in England down to 1540*, rev. ed. 1967.

Sewter 1974–5. A. C. Sewter, *The Stained Glass of William Morris and His Circle*, 2 vols., 1974–5.

Singleton 1978. Barrie Singleton, 'The Remodelling of the East End of Worcester Cathedral in the Earlier Part of the Thirteenth Century': see B.A.A. *Worcester* 1978.

Skeat 1977. F. J. Skeat, *The Stained Glass of St Albans Cathedral*, 1977.

Smith 1977. M. Q. Smith, 'The Harrowing of Hell Relief in Bristol Cathedral', *Transactions of the Bristol and Gloucestershire Archaeological Society*, Vol. 94, 1977.

Stanton 1972. Phoebe Stanton, *Pugin*, 1972.

Steer 1973. Francis W. Steer, *The Catholic Church of Our Lady and St Philip Arundel*, 1973.

Stratford 1978. Neil Stratford, 'Notes on the Norman Chapter House at Worcester': see B.A.A. *Worcester* 1978.

Summers 1974. Norman Summers, *Prospect of Southwell*, 1974.

Summerson 1964. John Summerson, 'Inigo Jones', *Proceedings of the British Academy*, Vol. 50, 1964.

Summerson 1975. John Summerson on Old St Paul's and on Exeter cloisters, in H. M. Colvin (ed.), *The History of the King's Works*, Vol. IV, Pt 1, 1975.

Swanton 1979. Michael Swanton, *Roof-Bosses and Corbels of Exeter Cathedral*, 1979; see also Glasscoe and Swanton.

Swanton 1980. Michael Swanton, 'A Mural Palimpsest from Rochester Cathedral', *Archaeological Journal*, Vol. 136 (1979), 1980.

Tudor-Craig 1976. P. Tudor-Craig, *One Half Our Noblest Art* (booklet on Wells west front), 1976.

VCH. *Victoria History of the Counties of England*, 1900–, in progress.

Verey and Welander 1979. David Verey and David Welander, *Gloucester Cathedral*, 1979.

Victorian Church Art 1971. *Victorian Church Art*, exhibition catalogue, Victoria and Albert Museum, 1971.

Whinney 1964. Margaret Whinney, *Sculpture in Britain, 1530–1830*, 1964.

Whinney 1971. Margaret Whinney, *Wren*, 1971.

Whittingham 1980. A. B. Whittingham, 'Norwich Saxon Throne', *Archaeological Journal*, Vol. 136 (1979), 1980.

Whittingham 1981. A. B. Whittingham, 'The Ramsey Family of Norwich', 'The Foundation of Norwich Cathedral', 'Gates of the Cathedral Close' etc., *Archaeological Journal*, Vol. 137 (1980), 1981.

Willis (1842–63) 1972–3. Robert Willis, *Architectural History of some English Cathedrals . . .*, 2 vols., 1972–3; dates first read and/or published: Hereford 1842, Canterbury 1844, Winchester 1845, Norwich 1847, York 1848, Salisbury 1849, Oxford 1850, Wells 1851, Chichester 1853(61), Gloucester 1860, Lichfield 1861, Peterborough 1861, Worcester 1863, Rochester 1863.

Wilson 1978. Christopher Wilson, 'The Sources of the Late Twelfth-Century Work at Worcester Cathedral': see B.A.A. *Worcester* 1978. See him also in B.A.A. *Durham* 1980 on c 14 work at Durham.

Woodman 1981. Francis Woodman, *The Architectural History of Canterbury Cathedral*, 1981.

Zarnecki 1978. George Zarnecki, 'The Romanesque Capitals in the South Transept of Worcester Cathedral': see B.A.A. *Worcester* 1978. See also his standard works on English Romanesque sculpture, 1951, 1953.

Illustration Acknowledgements

James Austin 73, 77–80, 121; Courtauld Institute 53, 98, 118, 157; Kerry Downes 32; George Hall 3, 6, 9–12, 40, 44, 47–8, 50, 52, 145, 147, 152, 155–6, 158–60, 166, 171, 174, 179; Sonia Halliday and Laura Lushington 28, 31, 110, 142; A. F. Kersting 1, 5, 7–8, 13, 18, 21–3, 26, 29, 33, 35–9, 41–3, 49, 56–8, 61, 64–6, 68–9, 71, 74, 76, 84–6, 88–90, 92–7, 99–102, 113, 115–17, 119–20, 123–4, 126, 127–8, 131, 135–6, 138–9, 141, 144, 146, 148, 150–1, 153, 161, 163–5, 167–70, 175, 177, 186; Brian Middlehurst 14–15; National Monuments Record 27, 30, 54, 109; Walter Scott 17, 24, 51, 62, 67, 70–2, 82–3, 87, 91; Thomas Photos 107–8, 111; Victoria & Albert Museum 182–3; Jeremy Whitaker 178, 181, 184–5; Jeffery Whitelaw 125. 129–30, 132–3.

The map was drawn by Reginald Piggott and the plan of Portsmouth Cathedral by Richard Andrews. Engravings were taken from John Britton's *Cathedral Antiquities* 1813–32, and plans are acknowledged in their captions.

Index

This is an index to names and places: to architects, artists and craftsmen, to churchmen, to people commemorated by monuments, and to cathedrals and churches.

Pages including illustrations are shown in *italic* type.

xx PLAN (Pg. No)